Multimedia Power Tools®
Second Edition

Multimedia Power Tools®
Second Edition

Peter Jerram and Michael Gosney

New York   Toronto   London   Sydney   Auckland

CHIEF WRITER
Peter Jerram

PRODUCER
Michael Gosney

PROJECT MANAGER
Lisa Limber

PRODUCT MANAGER
Jack Lampl

PROGRAMMER
Paul DiPasquale

SCREEN ART
Ed Roxburgh

BOOK ILLUSTRATOR
Jennifer Gill

GRAPHIC INTERFACE DESIGN
Claire Khanna

INTERFACE EVALUATION
Michelle Warn

PRODUCTION ASSISTANT
Stephanie Hensey

MUSICAL SCORE
Christopher Yavelow

CONTRIBUTING EDITORS

IMAGING AND ANIMATION: Farshid Almassizadeh, Mark Crosten (Imaging Tools Chapter),
Jack Davis, John Oldham, Goopy Rossi, Lynda Weinman

AUTHORING/INTERACTIVITY: Miriam Block, Paul Burgess, Matthew Pass, Helene Hoffman,
Ann Irwin, Nels Johnson, David Poole (Authoring Chapters), Karen Rall (Production Chapters)

SOUND: Mike Salomon, Steve Rappaport, David Javelosa, Christopher Yavelow (Sound Chapters)

VIDEO: Stephen Axelrad (Video Chapters), Scott Billups, Don Doerfler, Hallie Eavelyn,
David Fox (Video Chapters), Harry Mott, Greg Roach, Mike Salomon

FIRST EDITION TEAM
ASSOCIATE PRODUCER: Elizabeth Tilles

PROGRAMMERS: Terry Schussler, Don Brenner

DISC PROJECT COORDINATOR: Bruce Powell

TECHNICAL EDITOR: Goopy Rossi, Hershel Kleinberg

INTERFACE GRAPHICS: Mark Lyon, Danielle Foster

DISC TEST EDITOR: Susan Lyon

BOOK PRODUCTION: Danielle Foster

DISC PRODUCTION: Don Doerfler, Mike Salomon, Steve Downs,
Frank Tycer, Don Brenner, Henri Poole, Elizabeth Tilles

Book Overview

Contents

6   *Video Tools*   163

12   *Creating 3-D Models and Animation*   *307*

16   *Interface and Interactivity: Bring It Together*   *395*

17   *Interactive Multimedia Projects*   *413*

Part Three THE *POWER TOOLS* CD-ROM

18 *Overview of the* Power Tools *CD-ROM* *425*

19 *Projects and Power Tools on the CD-ROM* *437*

Introduction

So!

Multimedia. You want to know about multimedia. Interactive pictures and sounds. Digital data. Animation. Narration. Music and 3D and special effects. Lingo, hypertalk, C. CD-ROM and kiosks and desktop video.

You came to the right place. *Multimedia Power Tools* is an interactive course and comprehensive reference on multimedia production for the late 1990s. It is an integrated book and Mac/Windows CD-ROM that was developed by leading hands-on experts from the various fields that comprise the new art and science of multimedia.

Welcome to the Second Edition

This is a completely updated and expanded book/CD based on the original edition published in late 1993. It contains all new information on both Macintosh and Windows multimedia tools and processes. It also includes many new insights "from the trenches" of multimedia developers who are blazing the trails of this very young field. You will find sample projects created in both Windows and Macintosh environments on the "hybrid" CD-ROM that will play, naturally, on both platforms. You will also find the latest important programs and a fantastic selection of usable media elements.

Macintosh and Windows, Windows and Macintosh

Which came first, the chicken or the egg?

In the world of multimedia, the desktop came first. Desktop computer tools, that is. Without desktop computers there would be no multimedia as we know it. In the early 1980s, these inexpensive, powerful PCs gave creative hackers and adventurous artists access to digital media. The tools evolved quickly. The use of the tools evolved quickly. The hardware got up to speed and "interactive multimedia" was born. But many still insist on clarification: Mac or Windows?

The Mac popularized graphics and sound as part of the computing experience from early on. Windows gave an advanced interface to PCs and helped sell more desktop computers. The Mac leveraged its "Plug-and-Play" digital media capabilities and brought software tool makers and creative users together in the creation of the desktop publishing revolution. Windows, with Microsoft's software muscle and the economics of the IBM-standard clones, brought desktop publishing to broader corporate and consumer markets, fueling the evolution of the desktop software tools and peripheral hardware products on both platforms.

The multimedia industry has followed a similar pattern. Professional artists and producers, working closely with the loosely-allied software and hardware concerns, pioneered the tools and processes of multimedia production on the Mac. Then Windows formed the basis of the first serious consumer market for multimedia: relatively inexpensive "MPC" systems, multimedia PCs equipped with sound card, speakers, adequate RAM, and a CD-ROM drive. At first, producing on the Mac and playing on Windows was a difficult necessity. But as before, comparable tools have matured on Windows. Although most advanced developers have added Windows-based workstations to their production environments, they continue primary media production, prototyping, and authoring on the Mac. The accessibility of the Windows platform is encouraging greatly expanded corporate use of multimedia in-house. It is also encouraging consumers to dabble—and more. Windows is not only the primary consumer multimedia player platform, it is also adding significant juice to the development of the entire multimedia production industry.

On the professional level, today's multimedia production world is cross-platform. Period. Most producers and publishers author on both Macintosh and Windows systems, usually publishing in CD-ROM form or creating a presentation on either platform, and (increasingly) on other game or "set-top" multimedia systems. Consumers are enjoying not only the built-in multimedia playback capabilities of most new PCs and Macs, but also the ability to create their own multimedia programs. *Multimedia Power Tools* will be of benefit to novices and pros who work on either—or both—platforms.

When it comes to choosing one platform over the other for production, again it's the chicken or the egg. Whichever works best for you.

Who We Are—Does It Matter?

Who wrote the book should matter. But with all the buzz of multimedia, we have seen some pretty lame products making big claims and chalking up big sales to buyers hungry for helpful information about multimedia production.

This is a highly authoritative and comprehensive book, and the CD-ROM is more than a big floppy disc full of software *stuff*. It is an interactive course, dynamically linked to the book's contents and includes animated, self-paced "how-to" tutorials from top professionals, a discriminating collection of the leading tools, and a slew of high-quality media elements—all presented via an attractive, but functional, interface.

Wow! Sound like a sales pitch? Well, we wanted to set the record straight in case you are considering buying this book, or just hoping you made the right choice when you did buy it.

We are Verbum: a San Francisco-based group of writers, artists, and hackers with publishing proclivities who got together in San Diego in the mid-1980s. We have been involved in new media since the dawn of the desktop publishing revolution. We began the digital art "Gallery" concept in the pages of our original *Verbum* magazine, a quarterly "journal of personal computer aesthetics" that showcased the art and ideas of creative people working with desktop tools. We started the digital "How To" wave with columns in our magazine and in others, with our many books, and with the newsletter we developed and produced for Dynamic Graphics, *Step-by-Step Electronic Design*. We have popularized digital art and multimedia with events such as the "Imagine Exhibit of Personal Computer Art," "CyberArts International," and the annual "Digital Be-In" in San Francisco. We set a standard and catalyzed many producers with *Verbum Interactive 1.0,* the landmark CD-ROM we published in 1991. Today, along with other books and book/CDs for creative professionals, we are developing new multimedia products for consumers. (Keep in touch!)

This project is our contribution to the difficult, fast-moving, and exciting new field of multimedia production. It answers most of our questions about multimedia production and has the kind of tools and goodies we would want. Except maybe a fully functional Starship Enterprise.

It is our sincere hope that *Multimedia Power Tools* will serve you well.
Engage.

—Michael Gosney

Preface

This integrated book/CD-ROM package is a complete information and resource kit for producing professional multimedia works on the Macintosh and under Windows. It covers both the component parts of multimedia and the production process itself.

If you're putting together an effective business presentation, you'll find ample information, animated presentation techniques, and products.

If you have wanted to try your hand at animation ever since you first saw Elmer Fudd take a shot at that Wascally Wabbit, check out the chapters on desktop animation tools, utilities, and techniques.

Fancy yourself the next Steven Spielberg? You'll find full expositions on digital video—including Apple's QuickTime and Microsoft's AVI movie formats—as well as complete descriptions of the digital video production process and the new video tools.

Chapters on digital sound and music give exhaustive summaries of recording, synthesis, processing, and capture tools and techniques. Interactivity, the force that anchors and connects this panoply of new media, also merits its own chapters on interface design, programming, and assembly of components.

Book Organization

This book is logically divided into three parts:

Part One: Multimedia Tools and Technology covers what multimedia is and the software and equipment used to produce it. It begins by defining multimedia and surveying the multimedia development process and then moves on to cover Mac and PC system software and hardware, as well as the peripherals used in multimedia production. It concludes with detailed overviews and comparisons of multimedia creation software in the five major categories: graphics, sound, animation, video, and authoring.

Part Two: Creating Multimedia begins with chapters on planning and design and cross-platform development, and continues with detailed looks at the multimedia production process for sound, animation, video, and interactive presentations. Companion chapters provide background for the critically acclaimed projects featured on the *Power Tools* CD-ROM.

Part Three: The Power Tools CD describes the organization and contents of the *Power Tools* CD-ROM.

Here's a more detailed peek at the entire contents of the book:

Part One: Multimedia Tools and Technology

- *Chapter 1: Multimedia Defined* is a broad overview of multimedia: what it is, what it means, and where it comes from.

- *Chapter 2: Systems Software, Hardware, and Peripherals* tells you all you need to know about both the Mac and Windows, as well as the full scope of multimedia peripherals.

- *Chapter 3: Graphics Tools* covers image processing software, which is at the core of any multimedia production process.

- *Chapter 4: Sound Tools* explains sampling and sound capture, sequencing, and synchronization before launching into a review of audio software.

- *Chapter 5: Animation Tools* explores the kaleidoscope of animation tools, from animated presentation software and utility programs to modeling, rendering, and animation packages.

- *Chapter 6: Video Tools* discusses video capture, compression, and processing as well as available video editing and production tools.

- *Chapter 7: Authoring Tools* covers authoring, interactive, and media integration software.

Part Two: Creating Multimedia

- *Chapter 8: Multimedia Development: Process, Planning, and Design* outlines the entire multimedia development process, from preproduction through final production.

- *Chapter 9: Working Cross-Platform* gives advice and tips for developing multimedia for delivery on other platforms.

- *Chapter 10: Producing Sound* explores digital sound, from capture to processing and editing.

- *Chapter 11: Sound Projects* includes background on the sound projects on the *Power Tools* CD, as well as interviews with the developers themselves.

- *Chapter 12: Creating 3-D Models and Animation* is a comprehensive look at the digital animation process.

- *Chapter 13: Animation Projects* provides a backdrop for the animation projects on the CD, along with tips from the project creators.

- *Chapter 14: Creating Video* explores digital video, from preproduction through production itself.

- *Chapter 15: Video Projects* is an introduction to this group of *Power Tools* CD projects and includes advice and tips from the experts who created them.

- *Chapter 16: Interface and Interactivity: Bringing It Together* gives you professional perspectives on putting it all together: assembling your multimedia components, creating an interface, and setting up interactivity.

- *Chapter 17: Interactive Multimedia Projects* describes this group of Power Tools projects, and includes a behind-the-scenes look at the creative process.

Part Three: The *Power Tools* CD-ROM

- *Chapter 18: Using the CD-ROM* tells you how to install and use the *Power Tools* CD-ROM, and gives you an overview of its interface.

- *Chapter 19: Projects and Power Tools on the CD-ROM* describes the valuable software on the disk, including the interactive Sample Projects and the scores of clip media collections, valuable utilities, and applications demos.

The book closes with appendices that will aid you even more in producing your own multimedia:

- *Appendix A: Resources* lists all the products and companies featured in the book and on the CD-ROM, complete with addresses and phone numbers.

- *Appendix B: Power Tools* lists every Sample Project, clip media collection, application, and utility on the disc, along with the Power Code for each.

- *Appendix C: Copyright Act of 1976* will provide you with the legal guidance in acquiring and publishing multimedia material.

- *Appendix D: Product Copyright List* provides a listing of Power Tools clip media, application programs/demos, and sample projects included in the *Multimedia Power Tools* Book/CD-ROM package that are trademarks or registered trademarks of their respective holders.

The book ends with a comprehensive glossary compiled by Steve Rosenthal, and, of course, an index.

CD-ROM Features

The CD-ROM is packed with 650Mb of interactive tutorials, clip media, utilities, and applications. It includes 15 producer-guided tours of *How the Body Works, The Vortex, The Lawnmower Man* logo, and many others. It also features more than 200Mb of Power Tools: valuable applications, utilities, demos, photographs, background textures, video clips, sounds, animations, and more—from companies such as Apple Computer, Macromedia, Adobe Systems, Strata, Turtle Beach Systems, and Caligari Corp.

Power Codes

This is a truly interactive book-disc, thanks to a unique feature called *Power Codes.* Anytime the book mentions an application or utility included on the disc, you'll be able to zip right to it by typing a Command-key combination. The book pages display Power Code icons, along with the appropriate key commands, in the page margins opposite the first mention of each tool or project in a chapter, or when a tool or project is related to a particular subject. A complete listing of disc contents and their Power Codes is given in Appendix B.

Taking Aim at a Moving Target

Advances in multimedia technology are happening incredibly quickly! There are a few new product and technology amusements each week. Indeed, even as we were going to press with this new edition, we were learning about new hardware advances and software upgrades. Keeping up with this constant evolution is an unrealistic mission for a book; it's a pursuit better suited to magazines and newsletters.

In these pages, we provide you with solid, critical information on the capabilities and interfaces of hardware peripherals and software applications, along with informed projections on the directions in which these new technologies are evolving. By looking at the basic concepts of multimedia tools and technology, by showing how they interrelate, and by providing expert perspectives and examples for creating multimedia, we'll give you a knowledge base that no magazine can match.

Nevertheless, you still need to stay current with the exciting product introductions and revisions that are constantly coming to market. We recommend that you check out such periodicals as *New Media, Interactivity, Morph's Outpost,* and *Digital Media,* as well as the general purpose PC and Mac magazines.

Bon Voyage

Whether you're a professional communicator, an artist, a technologist, or simply someone interested in the magic of multimedia, this book is for you. Its tapestry is as rich as the promise of multimedia itself. Learn, Enjoy, Create!

—Peter Jerram

Acknowledgments

For Maria:
post tot naufragia portum

Peter Jerram

I'd like to thank my editor and friend Mike Roney at Random House; Mike Gosney and Lisa Limber at Verbum; and Joe Vella for his help in editorial matters. Thanks also to Matt Wagner and Bill Gladstone at Waterside Productions. Renewed appreciation goes to all those acknowledged in the first edition and especially to one whom I somehow left out: Bruce Johnston, a valued advisor and loyal friend.

Michael Gosney

Thanks go first to my family and friends for their ongoing support of, and patience with, this multimedia thing.

I'd like to acknowledge here the many talented and hard-working people who are responsible for *Multimedia Power Tools*. There are many more than those I will mention here.

Editor Michael Roney championed and contributed to both editions. Peter Jerram, our word warrior, was the force behind the manuscript development. William Gladstone, cyber-agent, put us together with our publisher, Random House.

Jack Lampl and Lisa Limber were the key producers of the second edition disc, working with programmer Paul DiPasquale, interface designer Claire Khanna, and artists Ed Roxburgh and Stephanie Hensey. Interface expert Michelle Warn and beta-testers Tom Murphy, Lisa Sontag, Jeanne Juneau and the students from the computer department of National University in San Diego also made vital contributions to the disc.

Elizabeth Tilles, Bruce Powell, Mark Lyon, Susan Lyon, Terry Schussler, Danielle Foster, Don Doerffler, Mike Salomon, Don Brennan, and Steve Downs were the first edition team, and all worked for over a year on the original book and disc that still serve as the basis of the second edition package.

Many thanks to all!

Part One

MULTIMEDIA TOOLS AND TECHNOLOGY

1

Multimedia Defined

Movies are popping up in strange places—in your E-mail, in your spread-sheets. Your PC squawks when you insert a floppy disk. An animated tour guide explains your new program to you. These are the early warning signs of a digital and communications revolution that is sweeping the desktop.

The world is going digital, and there's no turning back. Sound, music, graphics, animation, photography, and video can now be fed into an ordinary computer, where they can be sliced, diced, combined, and reconstituted into arresting works of the imagination. Perhaps no other development of the modern age has held equal power to free the mind and the spirit of humans; perhaps the ultimate destiny of the computer has been realized. And maybe we can all make a few bucks on the side.

Welcome to the Bitstream

"Multimedia" is hard to define because both its scope and applications are so broad that it defies a simple explanation. At its most basic, "multimedia" refers to the personal computer's growing ability to process not just text, but all sorts of visual and sonic information.

Thus, at the simplest level, you can spruce up a corporate presentation with video clips, read about a composer's life while listening to his symphony, or use 3-D animation to visualize your new kitchen addition—all on the desktop and all with your personal computer. (Of course, you'll also need a few items of hardware, some clever pieces of software, and a whole lot of time to burn. Otherwise, we'd have nothing to explain and no reason to write this book.)

But even this isn't the whole story. Multimedia is a lot more than chucking a few video frames into your slide show, and it's rapidly finding its way into many corners of our culture. On the wildly popular Internet, you can hold video conferences with other web crawlers right from your desktop using Cornell University's CU-SeeMe.

Kids (and not a few adults) play games that incorporate live video and 3-D animation. "Wizards" guide novices through new programs with a mix of sound and animation.

That's multimedia.

And how about a guided tour of the works of Cezanne, Matisse, and Renoir without leaving your home or office? In Corbis' *A Passion for Art* (Figure 1.1), you can scan hundreds of reproductions or let yourself be guided by curatorial staff and art historians. An understanding of the museum's rich treasures is deepened by interactive maps, timelines, glossaries, and essays.

This is multimedia, too.

...Rock and Roll Star ⌘ 013

Or, you may want to pick up a musical instrument but don't have the patience for lessons. Using Ahead Inc.'s *Virtual Guitar* CD (Figure 1.2), you're the guitarist in a rock 'n' roll band. Your bandmates are video characters in a 3-D animated world of rehearsal halls and nightclubs. You don't have to know how to play; just get the rhythm right, and the software fills in the right notes.

You guessed it—multimedia again.

Multimedia is even reinventing entire industries. Consider the world of professional video production that traditionally has been dominated by high-priced equipment and a professional staff of overpaid, coffee-drinking specialists. Now,

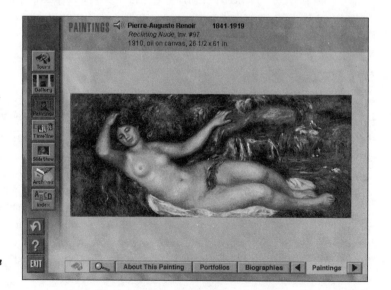

**Figure 1.1
Corbis' *A Passion
for Art*.**

**Figure 1.2
Ahead Inc.'s
*Virtual Guitar.***

desktop editing systems are being released at prices that are spiraling downward even as features and quality are matching systems in the traditional "post houses."

Clearly, multimedia is a broad-based phenomenon that already has a far-reaching impact in business, education, entertainment, and personal creativity. Its emerging influence on the desktop is being driven by increasingly sophisticated personal computers and by the metamorphosis of information into digital form.

**The
Computer
That Ate
*Leave It to
Beaver***

Multimedia is being brought to your desktop by an unprecedented digital information convergence (Figure 1.3). All of a sudden, computers can be equipped with different flavors of low-cost *digitizers* that convert everyday media (artwork, photographs, music) into binary format.

Flatbed scanners convert type, artwork, or whatever else you can heave onto the scanning bed (paving stones? peacocks?); sound digitizers capture sound and music with stunning fidelity; video capture boards pluck and convert individual frames in real time and will play them back at full speed, full-screen; slide scanners will do the same with photographs, and Kodak's Photo CD provides you with near-film resolution versions of your own snapshots.

Once all of this stuff is in the computer, there is a wondrous assortment of applications to help you manipulate, combine, and shape your sound and imagery. And the personal computer itself is undergoing a metamorphosis to adjust to this CPU-numbing assault of information.

You can now buy computers with CD-ROM drives, built-in support for big-screen color, accelerated buses that speed data transfer, system software in ROM

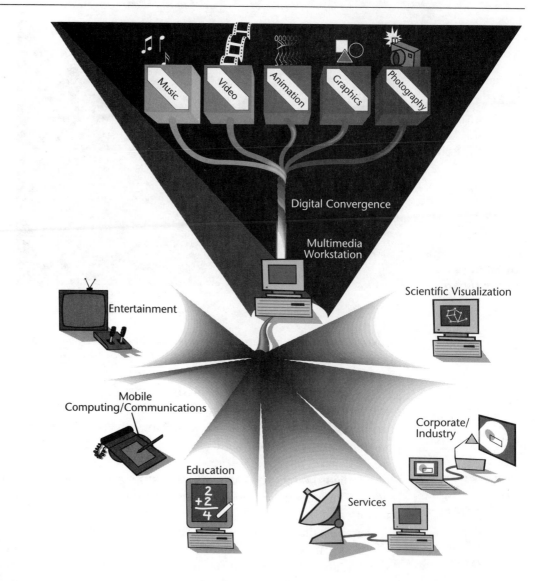

**Figure 1.3
The desktop
computer as
center of the
multimedia
universe.**

to quicken access times, and more *base* RAM than you could shoehorn into the
average machine just a few years ago (see Chapter 2, "Systems Software, Hardware, and Peripherals").

Harmonic Convergence

We've limited the scope of this book to an exploration of personal computer-
based, or *desktop*, multimedia. But the formerly distinct spheres of computing,
communications, entertainment, and consumer gadgetry are colliding, and you

can bet multimedia will be there when the smoke clears. So, we'll begin by taking this little side trip into the jangling world of technological symbiosis.

Mobile Computing and Communications

The tiny box on your hip squeals—voice mail has tracked you down: E.T.— PHONE HOME. No phone? No problem. The little device is also a cellular phone, and you check in. Uh-oh, Mr. Big wants the numbers for that commercial you're working on. Naturally, the box is also a computer (with modem); so you send the file—uplink or fax, your choice. Next year you'll just send the entire commercial.

Fueling the growth of desktop multimedia is a communications and consumer electronics cataclysm. While they are not themselves "multimedia," the twin dynamos of communications and consumer electronics are helping to propel the "M" word into the mainstream.

The cellular telephone business is currently in a growth cycle of truly appalling proportions. In fact, the changes are so profound that they could revolutionize communications. At the end of 1992, cellular phones were already a $7 billion industry, and some 7,000 cellular phones were being sold *per day*. This breakneck growth was achieved in spite of high equipment and usage fees that have kept many waiting for costs to drop. And sure enough, the emergence of so-called PCS (personal communications services) is sending both equipment and line use fees plummeting, turning cellular phones into a $30 billion business in the mid-1990s. More important, the line between communications and computing is beginning to blur as PCS devices become indistinguishable from their computer-based cousins, PDAs. While PCSs are telephones with computing features, PDAs are computers with built-in communications. Go figure.

Meanwhile, two industry giants, AT&T and McCaw Cellular, are teaming up to form a nationwide wireless telephone network that could change the whole concept of communications. In the near future, for example, you may be issued a single telephone number, and sophisticated computers will hunt you down and transfer incoming calls to your PCS/PDA or nearest conventional phone.

The idea of computers out there "looking" for you may not sound particularly appealing, but this synthesis of mobile computing/communications is not some weird science fiction scenario. Just as price wars have turned desktop computers into commodities over the last few years, portable computing devices have been selling in giant quantities, all but leaving the desktop market for dead. Apple alone sold an estimated $1 billion worth of PowerBooks their first year out.

The point is that PCS and PDA devices could play an important role in the development of multimedia. Like their desk-bound counterparts, they'll be able to send, receive, and process all kinds of digital information—from faxes and voice mail to music and video. Look at it as a few more venues (a hundred million or so) for your latest digital video concoction.

Consumer Electronics

Not surprisingly, consumer electronics giants are joining communications and computer manufacturers in the rush to define the multimedia devices of the not-too-distant future. No need to impress upon companies such as Sony the potential for handheld devices that will, say, download full-length digital movies for playback on the commuter train home from work.

There are already a variety of multimedia players that plug into an ordinary television set. These machines are really computers, but manufacturers don't want to say that too loudly—they might frighten the couch potatoes whose wallets they're after.

Apple and Microsoft both see themselves as uniquely positioned to profit from convergent technologies, and each has formed a consumer division.

That's Entertainment

While the computer captains are going after entertainment markets with a vengeance, telephone and cable-TV companies have been positioning themselves to deliver multimedia entertainment their own way. These companies have a crucial lock on a valuable infrastructure network of phone lines, TV cable, and satellite links. And you can bet they're not going to be happy to just rent out these data pipelines to the other guys.

For example, crack research lab Bellcore has figured out a way to send movies into homes over phone lines, in the process potentially depriving the cable-TV and video rental industries of their combined $33 billion annual revenue. ADSL (asymmetric digital subscriber line) acts like a "video server," downloading high-quality video signals over existing phone lines. It's only a matter of time before those digital movies will be oozing from the ether—and into your computer or PDA.

Cable-TV companies are scrambling to offer similar services; and they have something of an advantage, since they already have cable running into tens of millions of homes. The coaxial TV cable has a much higher bandwidth than phone lines, perfect for sending loads of digital multimedia entertainment into residences.

In late 1992, Tele-Communications, Inc., the nation's largest cable company, announced the development of a digital transmission technology that can deliver up to 500 TV channels. While this is an appalling idea, it also means that there will be an incredible source of content that can be fed directly into computers. (TV viewers will have to use a small appliance to decode the digital signal for viewing, at least until high-definition digital TV (HDTV) sets are widely available.)

In a move that signals the serious intentions of the big boys, "Baby Bell" US West invested $2.5 billion in media giant Time Warner's entertainment division. The alliance is expected to deliver a host of computing and communications services directly to homes.

Other companies are setting up so-called interactive TV networks. Viewers have the illusion of participating by playing along with, say, a game show. Results can be sent by modem to the network, which will broadcast the names of winners.

All of this is interactive in the sense that viewers can send and receive customized information, but none of it really affects programming. It's a level of participation Denise Caruso, editor of *Digital Media*, calls "fake interactive." However, the industry is moving toward a two-way cable or fiber optic link that will allow true instantaneous interactivity. Then viewers can do such things as affect sitcom plot lines (that will, no doubt, be an improvement over network television's efforts).

Playing the Game

Journeyman Project Robot
⌘ 042

Multimedia's effect on entertainment is not limited to the not-too-distant future. Game kingpins such as Nintendo and Sega have been churning out popular, if uninspired, game cartridges for years. A more recent development is the interactive CD-ROM–based game. Many of these feature 3-D graphics, digital music, and sound effects. Prime examples include Cyan's *Myst* (Figure 1.4), Pop Rocket's *Total Distortion,* Presto's *Buried In Time,* and Mechadeus' *The Daedalus Encounter.*

Figure 1.4
Cyan's *Myst*.

Multimedia's Roots

The concept of mixed media or multimedia has been around for some time, the form and its impact having been registered well before the advent of the computer—personal or otherwise.

By Any Means Necessary

Artists have long used every means at their disposal to describe and enrich the world around them. At the dawn of the modern age, pioneering cubists such as Pablo Picasso, Georges Braque, and Juan Gris stretched the bounds of painting by creating works of *collage*. These artworks incorporated newsprint, mirror glass, photographs, and other "found" objects. The collage method of the cubists was soon extended to works known as *assemblage*s (French for "multimedia"). An assemblage might contain newspaper clippings, wood, metal, parts of dolls, seashells, stones, or almost anything. Later artists, such the Italian futurists, dadaists, and surrealists, also experimented with mixed media.

In the '60s, pop art often co-opted imagery from television, photography, and the movies. The giant images of Roy Lichtenstein drew on comic books and other pop icons; and Andy Warhol's repeated sequential images recalled the motion series of Eadweard Muybridge, a pioneering nineteenth-century photographer who used the medium to describe movement.

Some '60s survivors might also remember the psychedelic "be-ins" and "happenings," colorful multimedia sound and light shows that stretched the mind and imagination.

Today, multimedia performance art, complete with towering holograms and animations, is enjoying something of a renaissance. And "installation art," touted by *The New York Times* as "that most multimedia of art forms," incorporates mixed media elements, such as gigantic lightning storms, into room-sized exhibits.

Spitballs and Science

Baby boomers in particular may well recall grade school days "enlivened" by an earlier form of multimedia still called AV, or audiovisual presentations. In the 1950s, the teaching profession underwent a change as it struggled to cope with students who had been conditioned by modern communications. Teachers realized that they had to somehow compete with TV, radio, movies, magazines, and comic books. Filmstrips that projected photographs and artwork, movies that drove home the virtues of personal hygiene, and tape recordings of great performances all struggled to capture the minds and senses of young people newly tuned to the power of audio and visual communications. As Michael Goudket warned in *An Audio Visual Primer*, "We must do more than talk or nobody listens."

The Corporate AV Market

The business world has also used AV for some time to brighten drab sales presentations, to supplement technical lectures, and to communicate corporate messages. Corporate multimedia, even up to the present day, has generally taken the form of prosaic overheads or slightly more engaging slide shows. Naturally, the entertainment industry raised even lowly slide shows to multimedia extravaganzas, mind-boggling in their glitzy indulgence.

Barry Grimes, who now heads his own design firm, remembers working in the mid-'80s on affiliate shows—annual junkets hosted by the networks, who fly in local TV franchise executives and their families for week-long pep rallies designed to whip up enthusiasm for the company and the new season lineup. (Networks still put on these shows, but they're not as opulent as they were in the go-go '80s.)

Grimes would spend weeks accumulating up to $100,000 worth of 35mm slides for a given show, while an engineer programmed a small computer to control banks of xenon slide projectors. Although this was largely a mechanical process, much ingenuity went into the carefully arranged slide sequences, which were set up for quick dissolves, pixelation effects that would provide rippling transitions, and rapid-fire projection that would give a cinematic or animated effect.

Grimes gives a lot of credit for the development of corporate multimedia shows to Image Stream, a company that "made the whole multiscreen show into a beautiful art form" for such companies as Apple. Image Stream took early bitmap graphics and animated them into myriad shifting multiscreen projections.

The advent of desktop multimedia has made it possible for the corporate shows of the '90s to use computer-based animation and presentations instead of slides, and the technology applies equally well to day-to-day corporate presentations using notebook computers running presentation software such as Action or Cinemation.

Clearly, predigital multimedia applications have been around for some time. Likewise, the prototypes of today's multimedia processors and players also got their start decades ago.

Hardware Roots

Though many people even today think of the computer mainly as a number cruncher, early visionaries saw its future role as an information and media processing powerhouse. America's chief scientist in the Roosevelt administration, a man named Vannevar Bush, envisioned a device he called "memex" or the Rapid Selector. Bush described memex as a scheme for indexing and retrieval of the immense store of information and knowledge that the world already had and was yet to produce. The machine itself was a Rube Goldberg gadget that combined microfilm storage, automatic indexing, and photocopying.

Though memex was never built, Bush himself was no rube, having designed and built giant pre-World War II calculators that presaged the development of modern computers. And the idea of memex captured and held the attention of many influential computer visionaries to come.

In the '50s, after reading about memex, Douglas Englebart envisioned the basic concept of the personal computer; J.C. Licklider, a scientist at the Pentagon's Advanced Research Projects Agency (ARPA), conceived of "interactive computing"; and still others, such as Alan Kay, were at Xerox PARC in the '60s developing the Alto, on which the Macintosh was based (see Chapter 2, "Systems Software, Hardware, and Peripherals" for more on this).

Motivations

Why use multimedia? *Because everyone else is using it!* No, seriously, there are some basic underlying reasons why multimedia is such a compelling idea.

The Power of Pictures

The undeniable force and appeal of multimedia stem directly from the power of the visual image itself, a power that has only recently been tapped by computers, although it is readily apparent in everyday life.

In 1989, for example, the world was stunned by the democratic uprisings in China centered in Beijing's Tiananmen Square. The television networks arrived quickly and prepared to record and transmit events as they unfolded; but they were thwarted when China shut down the normal satellite transmission links. Undaunted, the newshawks used still-video cameras and transmitted the photos over standard phone lines. Even though these pictures were motionless and without sound, viewers watched in wonder, transfixed by the stirring images that were seen worldwide less than 20 minutes after they were taken.

Pictures simply have an inherent power to stir interest and emotion—a power that is far beyond that of the written or spoken word—and they have much more popular appeal.

The Power of Interactivity

The concept of *hypertext* is especially relevant to multimedia. Through the ages, information has been presented and absorbed in a linear fashion. You read a book from cover to cover, watch a movie from beginning to end. Even so, people have long recognized that this may not be the best means of communicating all types of information.

You might, in fact, want to skip around a book as the whim takes you or read more about a topic of interest before continuing with the linear narrative (as you would using a cross-reference in a book). Of course, the computer is a natural for this sort of thing; and somebody sooner or later had to think of the idea of hypertext. That someone is generally agreed to be Ted Nelson, a computer visionary whose seminal 1974 book *Computer Lib* is still in print and still worth a read.

In the late '80s, Apple introduced HyperCard, which is based on the hypertext concept. Using HyperCard, you create links in a given work: an electronic book, multimedia presentation, or anything that might best be explored in a nonlinear way. Then, when a user is reading or exploring, he or she can click on icons to zoom to related topics that may be in the same file or in another one altogether.

This simple idea has had great impact on multimedia because it allows the interactivity that is so central to its basic appeal.

Robert Abel, an early multimedia research pioneer, has created a number of important works. Abel's unreleased version of Picasso's Guernica is often cited as a premier example of interactive multimedia at its most seductive. Using an interactive program, you can explore a reproduction of the great artwork while clicking on icons linking Picasso's preliminary sketches. Video interviews with Picasso himself and with survivors of the actual Spanish Civil War bombing at Guernica, the inspiration for the painting, further deepen an understanding of the work.

Such skillfully rendered interactivity offers insights into the mind of the artist and helps to fix his work in its historical and cultural contexts. It's a wonderful illustration of multimedia in the service of a great work of art, rather than art subverted by the medium.

Costs of Multimedia versus Traditional Technologies

The impact of the personal computer and desktop multimedia tools on such professions as video production, animation and sound and music recording is becoming widely felt. Not only is professional-quality work now possible on the desktop, but it can be done with far less investment in time and money.

In the film and broadcast industries, postproduction suites that used to cost millions of dollars can now be fully outfitted for less than $50,000. And they're good enough for top professionals, not for those of us just noodling around with QuickTime. Commercials that would have cost $50,000 to $100,000 and taken days to prepare and shoot can now be put together for a fraction of this amount and assembled over a weekend using computer-generated imagery for the sets. Such high-profile films as *True Lies* and *Jurassic Park* have made extensive use of 3-D computer graphics.

The Disney studio, known for its exquisitely detailed animation, is getting into the act too—although it's keeping a low profile. At the time of this writing, Disney was teaming with Steve Jobs' Pixar to create the first full-length feature generated completely by computer.

Multimedia is also bringing costs down in business, advertising, and marketing. By using image-editing software, businesses can create ads and collateral marketing materials in-house and make changes on-the-fly, greatly reducing costs. Interactive advertising can draw people in more effectively than print ads and can be produced for less.

In professional music recording and production, the story is much the same. MIDI (musical instrument digital interface) allows you to create and play back

Power Tools Theme ⌘ 011

music and other sound with great fidelity. Using MIDI sound clip libraries, you can add high-quality sounds to your latest music video for pennies (see Chapter 10, "Producing Sound," for more details). By contrast, getting sound clips (so-called "needle-drop" music) from a music studio or production house can cost $100 per minute.

Applications

Multimedia has broad applications in everyday life. Education, business, and publishing are just a few of the areas affected by multimedia's colorful and exuberant assault.

Business

Most corporate presentations still use tried-and-true handouts and overheads. But as the yawns get louder and audiences become more jaded, many companies are turning to whizz-bang multimedia presentations with animation, video, and eye-catching graphics.

Director 4.0 Demo ⌘ 708

The rise of multimedia in the boardroom has been driven primarily by new easy-to-use presentation software such as Macromedia's Action, Microsoft's PowerPoint (Figure 1.5), and Gold Disk's Astound. The programs are not as sophisticated as multimedia mainstays such as Macromedia Director, but are much easier to use.

New hardware developments also have helped speed the use of sophisticated multimedia presentations. A primary innovation has been the LCD display panel. About the size of an inch-thick file folder, this device is plugged into a computer and placed on an overhead projector. Anything displayed by the computer mon-

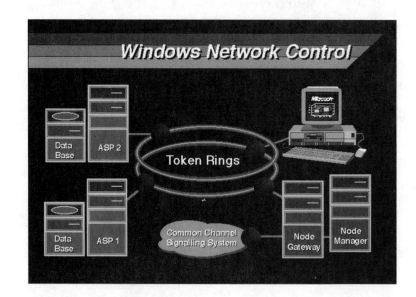

Figure 1.5 Microsoft's PowerPoint.

itor is projected in this manner so that it can be viewed during group presentations.

Most companies willing to experiment with the new media limit their multimedia forays to high-impact, critical applications such as speaker support materials for important product rollouts, annual shareholder meetings, and important customer briefings. Others with greater commitment or interest have formed in-house multimedia development groups whose work rivals the complexity and richness found in the best presentations created by outside experts.

Marketing and Sales

Advertising is also taking its cue from multimedia. Companies such as Amazing Media and the Interactive Marketing Group develop interactive ads on floppy disks. For roughly the same price as a print ad, their clients get a state-of-the-art interad, and potential customers get something less obnoxious than the usual screaming headlines and seductive sales pitches.

CD catalogs such as Magellan's Merchant (Figure 1.6) allow you to browse dozens of catalogs without having to deal with stacks of junk mail.

Binding interads on floppies right into a magazine is less expensive than sending them to customers as part of direct mail campaigns. Viewers can interact in various ways—for example, by playing little games or using a calculator to decide how to invest in mutual funds.

Electronic *kiosks* are also being heavily used in "electronic retailing." Scattered through shopping malls, airports, and trade shows, kiosks handle everything from film processing to clothing sales. In the latter instance, buyers look at videos of models wearing articles of clothing that can be ordered by specifying size, color, and credit card information. Well aware that many buying decisions are

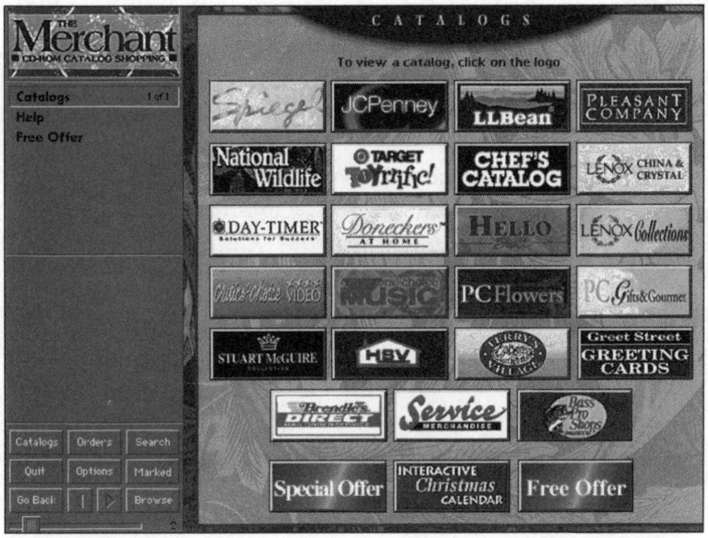

Figure 1.6 Magellan's Merchant CD Catalog.

**Figure 1.7
Billboard's CD
Listening Station.**

made while in the store, retailers use kiosks to dispense information on new products at point-of-sale locations. Kiosks can also persuade customers to answer questions, and the resulting demographics are tabulated for retailers on the spot —instant market research surveys.

Kiosks are becoming a familiar sight at trade shows, where they give out directions and recommend restaurants and shopping areas to out-of-towners. To appear less intimidating, kiosks often substitute touch screens for keyboards. Many trade show vendors feature splashy multimedia product demos that give browsers a chance to take a look but do not require a live demo person.

Donald Grahame, a San Francisco–based animator, has created an animated music-listening station for a record store. Using the interactive software, listeners can hear music before buying it (Figure 1.7).

Education

One of the truisms in the learning business is that people absorb and retain new information in different ways and at varying rates. To some, the linear flow of a book or TV program works just fine; but to many others, this ancient mode of learning is uncomfortably confining.

One of the reasons computer "gurus" are so popular is that it's easier to ask someone to decipher an error message than to read the manual yourself. But consulting with a real person is also interactive—answers may lead to other questions or points of interest. You go through a similar process when you look up an entry in an encyclopedia, only to find other things to look up, which lead to still other topics, until you're hopping all over.

Interactive multimedia gives you the freedom to explore the unknown with its lightning-fast links to related topics. It is this interactivity, along with dynamic elements such as video and music, that makes multimedia such an exemplary learning tool—especially for children, since multimedia resembles the TV and video games that have become imbedded in the youth culture.

For these reasons, training and education are often cited as ideal multimedia applications. Next to business applications, market analysts rank training and education as the largest multimedia market. In fact, some of the most effective multimedia projects have been those associated with learning and teaching.

Examples abound. Apple's Multimedia Lab (no longer on the market) experimented with many interesting projects. One piece, Moss Landing, is an interactive videodisc that describes daily life in a small seacoast town. You can click on different "hot" areas of the digital video images and be whisked away to different scenes. Click on a waterfront video screen showing fishing boats, for instance, and suddenly you're at sea, jetting through the ocean spray.

In another use of multimedia, students and teachers at San Francisco's Lowell High School created *Grapevine: The Steinbeck Story,* with the help of Apple's Education Research Group. The interactive CD helps students feel the impact of the Great Depression and gain a deeper understanding of Steinbeck's seminal novel about the period, *The Grapes of Wrath*. The project began as a classroom presentation, but was so successful that it was made into a CD-ROM and videodisc incorporating sound, video, and photographs.

While there are many anecdotal examples of the influence of multimedia on education, the impact will probably not be significant until the issues of equipment, development costs, and teacher training are resolved. The last is crucial, since many teachers are put off or intimidated by the technology. To solve the problem, programs to help ease the transition are springing up.

The Teacher Explorer Center in East Lansing, Michigan, teaches educators how to develop basic multimedia documents. The Center also advises them how to combat tight budgets by scrounging for forgotten equipment that may be buried in school basements. The College of Education and Human Service Professions at the University of Minnesota at Duluth has developed methods and instructional designs for using multimedia in the classroom. Universities and colleges are also adopting multimedia curricula, and some even offer degree programs.

At the Teacher's Living Resource Center at the St. Louis Zoo, educators use courseware design software to create interactive classes for studying animals in the zoo (see Figure 1.8). The project, created by Arnowitz Productions Inc. of Mill Valley, California, uses sophisticated software to help teachers assemble courses that include video and animation clips, as well as textual information.

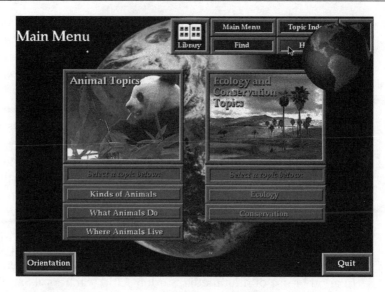

Figure 1.8
Teacher's Living
World **helps**
educators develop
multimedia
course materials.

The Big Boys Step In

Some of the most visible educational titles are being produced by large corporations such as IBM. These products range from simple electronic books to extremely detailed and lengthy courses. Perhaps the best known is IBM's *Columbus: Encounter, Discovery and Beyond,* a $2,000 set of videodiscs and CDs. The product, which IBM calls a "knowledge system," took $6 to 8 million to produce and contains 180 hours of documents, images, and sounds.

Microsoft spent $5 million and over five years developing its intriguing Encarta multimedia encyclopedia. *Encarta '95* (Figure 1.9) has 26,000 articles, many hours of sound and music, and thousands of animations and graphics.

On a smaller scale, but no less intriguing, are the CDs and videodiscs offered by The Voyager Company. Justly acclaimed, these titles include some wonderful children's stories and exploratory games. In *A Silly Noisy House,* children can amuse themselves by exploring the mysteries of an old house. The disc includes kinetic surprises such as a pop-up jack-in-the-box and a flock of honking geese flapping by an open window.

Broderbund Software's Living Books series also has some interactive titles that small children find delightful. *Kid Pix* is the sort of clever and absorbing program that makes you wonder why it wasn't invented years ago. Intended as a paint program for children, it has lured many adults into its wacky world. *Kid Pix* eliminates the scroll bars and hidden tool palettes that might confuse small children. A little face called the Undo Guy reverses any unwanted effects. Sound plays a big role in *Kid Pix,* and most actions provoke some sort of funny noise. Each letter of an alphabet along the bottom of the screen sounds its name when clicked on.

**Figure 1.9
Microsoft's
Encarta '95.**

Training

MedPics ⌘ 041

Corporations spend billions on employee training, and the immediacy and appealingly low long-term costs of multimedia-based training have given the industry its first major market conquest. Companies are finding that they can train their staffs less expensively and more effectively with computer-based training (CBT) than with traditional classroom methods. Employees also like multimedia courses better. The interactivity keeps them awake and engaged.

Many large companies have teaching labs and centers, where they set up computers equipped with multimedia and peripheral equipment such as laserdiscs and CD-ROM drives.

Soon, with wider adoption of multimedia-ready computers, employees will be able to take courses right at their desks. Microsoft is already offering a CD version of Multimedia Works, a suite of basic productivity software. On the CD, along with the program itself, is a 50-minute multimedia tutorial that uses animation and audio annotation.

Apple has developed a multimedia-produced training video that explains basic computer networking concepts. In the production, live "actors" (Apple technical support staff) were superimposed over an animated "studio" inspired by the bridge of the *Starship Enterprise*. The video cost $40,000 to produce, a fraction of the expense for a traditionally produced video.

Significantly, multimedia CBT techniques are not limited to the high-tech industry, but are being used across a broad spectrum of American business. Bethlehem Steel uses interactive video to teach workers about a variety of steel production methods. Federal Express has implemented Interactive Videodisc

Instruction (IVI), a program that teaches employees about a wide range of skills, from driver training to phone and counter service. IVI is made up of 25 CDs that are updated monthly. Federal Express estimates that IVI cuts training time by two-thirds, and random tests show that employees taught this way retain information better than those who learn in a classroom.

The 1992 U.S. Olympic wrestling team was trained in part by an interactive program that integrates 35 hours of video from 350 sample matches, analysis of selected matches, and bios of competitors.

Opportunities and Challenges

Because the major costs of corporate training arise from the time it takes employees and instructors to participate in classes, CBT is a big draw for companies. There is, however, still considerable expense associated with the development of CBT. Software must be bought and mastered, and equipment must be purchased and installed.

Since the payoff is substantial, many companies are willing to invest the up-front money and development time. While some companies hire full-time staffs, many more rely on outside experts to develop CBT; either way, CBT creates significant career opportunities.

Director 4.0 Demo ⌘ 708

AuthorWare Prof. 3.0 Demo ⌘ 709

Skills necessary for the development of interactive training programs include a strong familiarity with authoring tools such as AuthorWare Professional, Icon-Author, and Director. For a description of these tools, see Chapter 7, "Authoring Tools." Also, take a look at the interactive projects on the accompanying CD for a good introduction to the techniques used by professionals.

Publishing

Electronic books and magazines predate the concept of multimedia. After all, getting plain text on the computer is no big deal. Computer Library, for example, offers an electronic magazine article service. Each month, subscribers get a new CD containing more than 70,000 articles from computer industry publications.

Voyager's Expanded Books series includes electronic versions of old favorites such as *Alice in Wonderland,* as well as contemporary novels. You can add your own margin notes, highlight passages, and mark your place.

As interesting as these products are, the basic challenge of electronic publishing is getting people to read the things in the first place. Most people simply don't like to sit and read text on the screen (although Voyager takes an important step by tailoring its Expanded Books specifically for notebook computers).

Enter multimedia. By reproducing the graphics and photographs of original works and by adding such multimedia elements as sound and video, electronic publishing is transformed into a much more intriguing option.

CD-ROM Today, for example, is a monthly magazine that includes a CD-ROM sampler called *The Disc,* which has demo versions of dozens of CD games, educational titles, and clip media (Figure 1.10). *The Disc* is a hybrid that runs in

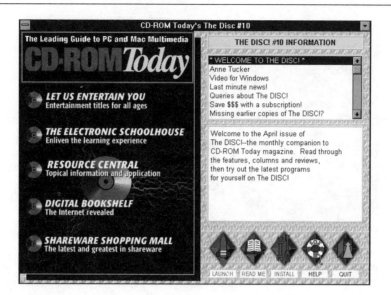

Figure 1.10
CD-ROM Today's
The Disc.

either the Windows™ (pictured) or Mac environments, an increasingly common configuration. *Nautilus* was early on the scene with a CD-ROM magazine, and many new ones are now popping up, including *Blenders*, a disk for style-conscious 20-somethings.

Verbum, developer of this book/CD-ROM package, was an early pioneer in multimedia publishing, issuing *Verbum Interactive 1.0* in 1991. The interactive CD-ROM features interactive articles, a wide-ranging multimedia gallery, a pre-QuickTime video roundtable discussion featuring industry luminaries, and music (playable on regular audio CD players) from artists such as Graham Nash, Todd Rundgren, and Pauline Oliveros. The disc makes extensive use of animated sequences, including 3-D animation and talking agents. New additions are forth-coming.

Introduced in 1992, photographer Rick Smolan's *From Alice to Ocean: Alone Across the Outback* is still a prime example of effectively produced multimedia. In 1995, Smolan received accolades for *Passage to Vietnam*, another book-disc multimedia release that features the work of world-class photographers. Both book-disc packages are fascinating examples of multimedia's power to fuse visual and sound imagery with computer-driven interactivity (Figure 1.11). Smolan is best known as the creator of the popular *Day in the Life* books.

One of the two discs in the package is in Kodak's Photo CD Portfolio format, which allows photos, with sound, to be viewed on an ordinary television as well as on a computer. (Although the discs will display photos on any TV or color computer, you do need a special Photo CD player. See Chapter 2, "Systems Software, Hardware, and Peripherals," for more details.) Both the Photo CD disc and

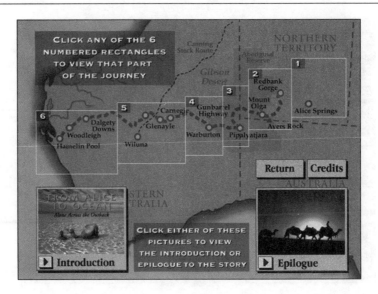

Figure 1.11
***From Alice to
Ocean* fuses
photography,
travelogue, and
interactivity.**

the other one, which is a hybrid Mac/PC disk, are interactive; and you can hop around the narrative at will, looking at maps, viewing snippets of video, or listening to the eerie aboriginal *didgiridoo* soundtrack.

The core of the material was previously published in other forms. Robyn Davidson's *Tracks,* an account of her trip, was published in 1980, and most of Smolan's photographs were originally published in a 1977 issue of *National Geographic. From Alice to Ocean* graphically illustrates what can be done with the world's vast store of existing information—and it explains why forward thinkers like Gates are snapping up electronic publishing rights to so many works. In fact, Corbis, whose first title is *A Passion For Art* (Figure 1.1), is Gates' multimedia publishing company.

The Challenges

For creators of multimedia, there are a few challenges. The biggest one is the time, skill, and effort it takes to design, create, and link the complex visual and sonic landscapes of multimedia.

System Costs

The equipment you're going to need depends a lot on your level of involvement (Figure 1.12). If you just want to explore what's out there, a basic color Mac or '486 or Pentium PC with a sound card will do. You'll also need a CD-ROM drive and at least 8Mb of RAM. Add a basic presentation package and an image-editing or paint program, and you'll be able to create simple multimedia presentations. If you're starting from scratch, such a system can be had for well under $2,000.

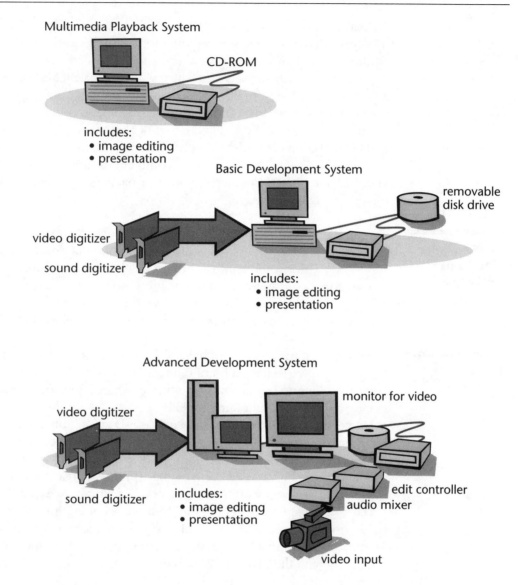

Multimedia Playback System

CD-ROM

includes:
- image editing
- presentation

Basic Development System

removable disk drive

video digitizer

sound digitizer

includes:
- image editing
- presentation

Advanced Development System

monitor for video

video digitizer

sound digitizer

includes:
- image editing
- presentation

edit controller

audio mixer

video input

**Figure 1.12
System
configurations.**

If you want to develop digital videos, interactive presentations, or electronic music, you'll need to add a video digitizer, a media integration program such as Director, and sound equipment such as a MIDI interface and sound digitizer. Because the files you're working with will be very large, you may also want to add more RAM and a removable disk drive for file storage. A faster Mac in the Quadra or Performa class or a 486 DX4 PC would be fine. Figure on $2,000 to $4,000 for such a system.

Finally, if you're going to go all out and work with digital video or create professional quality interactive presentations, you'll need some additional video equipment such as a second monitor, a video recorder, and perhaps an editing controller and audio mixer. You'll also want the fastest Mac or PC you can get—a PowerMac or Pentium PC; the sky's the limit here. You could assemble such a system for less than $10,000 but could easily spend several times that amount.

Unless you get really hooked or work for a corporation with deep pockets and big ambitions, you shouldn't have to spend much at all to explore and even create irresistible multimedia. For a complete rundown on the Mac and peripheral equipment, see Chapter 2. Software packages are listed and described in the "Tools" chapters throughout the book.

Cross-Platform Delivery

The problem of compatibility between platforms—Windows and Mac, Unix systems, set-top multiplayers—has plagued multimedia developers from day one. While the Windows/Macintosh bridge has been successfully completed, carefully planned production strategies are essential to maximize the use of the advanced desktop tools for Unix and set-top environments.

For a complete look at the situation, see Chapter 9 "Working Cross-Platform."

Technical Expertise

For the most part, you do not have to be a rocket scientist to create multimedia; but you do have to have a lot of time and patience. Multimedia applications are getting easier and easier to use, so that you can often surprise yourself by producing impressive work fairly quickly.

However, specialized programs such as 3-D animation, media integration, and image editing software can be tricky and a little difficult to master. To avoid initial frustration, we recommend taking a class or seminar (after you read this book and work with the disc, of course). Many are now available; local colleges and universities frequently offer low-cost courses taught by experts.

Hardware, especially getting different pieces of equipment to coexist, can be trying, too. Generally, though, all you have to do is install hardware and any accompanying software to get up and running in a short time. At least a passing familiarity with the Mac and Windows system software is helpful in this regard.

Content Development

Developing high-quality, entertaining, and beautiful multimedia takes skill and experience. There, we said it. This is the dirty little secret of multimedia. No hype here, folks. All the digitizers and sound blasters and graphic gewgaws in the world cannot make you an artist (sorry). Stan Cornyn, former president of Warner New Media, agrees. "I don't care if you can store 300 million pages; that is not multimedia.

"Multimedia has too often fallen into the hands of 'code writers,' those who can keep the computers from clutching up. The sooner we fix this, the sooner the public will give us their business."

In comparing multimedia to the recording industry, Cornyn says, "Why do you think recording engineers are kept behind thick glass, away from the talent?"

The tools of multimedia are exactly that: tools. Creation of art, electronic or otherwise, takes talent and an aesthetic sensibility. And lots of time. That's why the heart of this book and the accompanying disc are devoted to the development of excellent multimedia content. Through an explanation of the processes, interviews with developers, and step-by-step explication of project development, you'll see how the pros do it.

But even if you can't draw a box with parallel sides, don't despair. You can still have a lot of fun with multimedia; just don't expect to bang out *Star Trek*, and you'll be fine. There's no question that the power of the computer and the sophistication of multimedia software make it easier than ever to create inventive and inviting works of the imagination.

2

Systems Software, Hardware, and Peripherals

In the late 1960s, when antiwar protests and whisperings of revolution swept through streets and college campuses nationwide, another sort of revolution was unfolding in the rolling hills near Stanford University. Here, at Xerox Corporation's Palo Alto Research Center (PARC), the personal computer was being born.

Xerox had managed to attract the best and brightest computer scientists from around the country and throughout the world. By 1974, they had a working prototype of a desktop personal computer, which they dubbed Alto. The Alto had a "bitmapped" display lit up by 500,000 pixels (*picture elements*, the little dots that constitute a display image). Bitmapping allowed the pixels to be turned off and on independently, which for the first time enabled the simultaneous display of graphics and text. The graphical user interface (GUI) employed overlapping windows, icons instead of complex commands, and pull-down menus. The whole thing was designed to look like a desktop, and you navigated your way through it by pointing and clicking with a mouse.

If all this sounds familiar, it's because the GUI, desktop metaphor, bitmap display, and mouse are in wide use today, most notably in Apple Macintoshes and in Microsoft's Windows user interface. Xerox, however, gravely underestimated the power of these concepts and never successfully marketed the Alto or its better known successor, the Star. (This failure is particularly ironic, since Xerox owed its overall success to marketing of photocopy technology developed by IBM in the 1950s, but subsequently ignored by Big Blue.)

Xerox executives decided that the real action was in the home computing market—at the time, the turf of Apple Computer—so rather than develop the Alto technology for the business world, they contacted Apple with the idea of buying in. But even as early as 1979, Apple stock was hot property. Xerox would have to give something in exchange for being allowed to buy stock; what they gave up was the Alto technology (much of which was brought to PARC by personal computing pioneer Douglas Englebart, who did his seminal work around the corner at SRI International).

In return for being allowed to buy 100,000 shares of Apple stock, Xerox gave a PARC tour to Apple's vice-president for research and development, Steve Jobs. When he got a demo of the Alto, Jobs immediately grasped what Xerox had not: the machine's enormous commercial potential. He soon began work on what was to become the Lisa and, later, the Macintosh.

PARC is still around, developing what it is calling invisible or "ubiquitous" computing. And technology isn't all PARC is exporting. PARC alumni include Microsoft chief scientist Charles Simonyi; Apple fellow Alan Kay; Macromedia chairman Tim Mott; Adobe Systems founder John Warnock; Ethernet inventor Robert Metcalf; and Alvy Ray Smith, cofounder of Pixar. But perhaps none of PARC's inspirations has been as influential as its personal computing innovations, which are best and most clearly embodied in the Macintosh.

In this chapter, we'll take a look at the Mac's system software, which has been heavily influenced by PARC's original concepts. On the PC side, we'll delve into the multimedia MPC standard and the built-in multimedia capabilities of the PC platform and Microsoft's Windows system.

Macintosh and Windows As Multimedia Environments

Today, personal computer operating environments, or user interfaces, are nearly all graphical in nature. Sun and SGI machines have Open Look and Motif, the Amiga has Workbench and New Look, PCs have Windows, and Macs have the Finder.

These systems all share basic attributes—files and programs are represented by small pictograms, or "icons" that you select or activate using a mouse; you can manipulate files by "dragging and dropping" them into "folders," or delete them by "throwing" them into a trash can or recycler icon; overlapping windows resemble papers on a desk, and you can hop between them with the mouse, even if the windows represent files from different applications.

The fact that so many different kinds of desktop computers have settled on the same set of visual metaphors confirms the basic common sense of the approach and is a testament to PARC's original ideas.

Because these operating environments are so natural and intuitive, they are well suited to nearly all computer applications; but their visual dynamism holds special appeal for the multimedia adventurer.

Macintosh System Software

Since its earliest incarnation as a stubby little box, the Mac has long been a visually and sonically oriented computer. From its icons and scroll bars to its display of vibrant photorealistic images, the Mac is graphics-based to its very core.

The Mac's system software includes many extensions and utilities that aid the playback and even creation of multimedia elements. Here's a rundown.

Sound

Since the first one rolled off the assembly line in 1984, all Macs have been able to play back sound with no additional hardware. Newer models such as Power-Macs, Quadras and Performas, and even PowerBooks, can also record or *digitize* sound.

Using System 7's Sound control panel (Figure 2.1), you can record audio and save it as a system alert sound or use it in applications that can play back sound files. This is, however, a primitive tool: You can record for only 10 seconds with no compression and at a relatively low quality 8-bit monaural 22KHz sample rate.

For all but the most pedestrian projects, you'll need a separate card for digitizing sound, and software for compression and editing (although PowerMacs

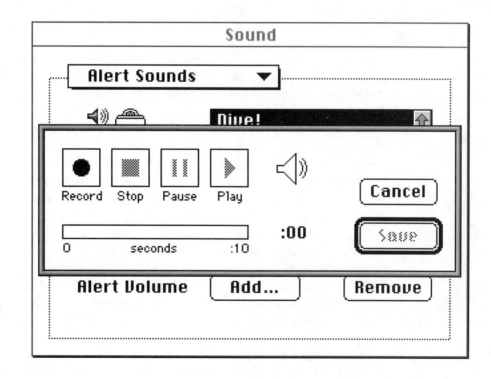

**Figure 2.1
Recording with
Mac sound
control panel.**

and some Quadras and Performas do have powerful built-in stereo recording capabilities). See Chapter 4, "Sound Tools," for more information.

Graphics

The part of the system software responsible for the display of images on the Mac is called QuickDraw, a set of graphics routines burned into the ROM chips of every Macintosh. Because the code is running directly from the chips, and because it is written in *assembly* language—very low-level instructions that can be quickly understood by the computer—QuickDraw is fast.

QuickDraw functions are used by most applications developers, which both preserve the Mac's legendary interface consistency and help give rise to the diverse and rapidly developing base of graphics applications. Programs that bypass QuickDraw (writing directly to the screen) do so at great risk and run the likelihood of incompatibility with the rest of the Mac world.

Originally, QuickDraw supported black-and-white images only; and indeed the Mac itself didn't get color until 1987, when Apple introduced the Mac II. With the new 8-bit QuickDraw, Mac II's could display 256 colors or shades of gray at one time. Eight bits can be turned on and off in 256 different combinations, defining the color limit of 8-bit QuickDraw.

Although this was a big improvement, there was increasing demand for *true color*—the ability to display photographic images, video, and realistically rendered "painted" images and animations. These complex images far exceed the 256 colors that could be displayed by 8-bit QuickDraw, and in fact often contain *millions* of separate colors.

In 1989, Apple released 32-bit QuickDraw. Now Mac users could draw from a palette of more than 16 million colors. This unleashed a flood of applications and hardware add-ons, including 32-bit paint programs (see Chapter 3, "Graphics Tools") and graphics accelerators (see "Hardware" sections later in this chapter).

To display all of these colors, you need some additional hardware—a 24-bit display card (and a color monitor, of course). If you use a monitor bigger than the standard 13″ display, you'll also need a graphics accelerator card. These cards have their own CPUs, which provide the necessary horsepower to move large true-color images around the screen in less than glacial time periods. (See "Hardware Peripherals," for more information.)

It's confusing that the terms *24-bit* and *32-bit* are often used interchangeably. Actually, only 24 bits are needed to achieve the 16.7 million simultaneous colors that QuickDraw can display. The extra 8 bits, called the *alpha* channel, are used by applications developers to achieve a variety of effects, such as the one created when two images intersect. Paint programs and image processing software—Photoshop, for example—use the alpha channel to create *masks* to protect part of an image from modification.

An important feature of 32-bit QuickDraw is its ability to directly drive the monitor's display circuitry. This eliminates the need to use color lookup tables,

Photoshop 3.0 Demo ⌘ 715

QuickDraw 3-D

Hoping to do for 3-D animation what it did for digital video with QuickTime, Apple released QuickDraw 3-D in late 1995. Like QuickTime, QuickDraw 3-D is not a single program or utility, but an interrelated set of technologies for handling 3-D images at the system level.

At the heart of QuickDraw 3-D is a system extension that will allow you to create 3-D graphics, and move them between applications by simply cutting and pasting. Using standard tools, you can create 3-D objects and apply surface textures, lighting effects, and motion.

The new standard also has a 3-D file format that handles such sophisticated attributes as lighting, shading, and surface textures. Many believe this "metafile" format will spur the creation of 3-D clip libraries that will allow you to drag and drop 3-D images into files, regardless of the application.

A crucial part of QuickDraw 3-D is an "API"—applications programmatic interface—that allows developers to create add-on products. The most common add-ons are acceleration boards that boost the performance of QuickDraw 3-D—in some cases to the level of Silicon Graphics workstations, legendary for their 3-D capabilities.

And the best news of all for cross platform multimedia developers: Apple plans an early-1996 release of QuickDraw 3-D for Windows.

greatly speeding QuickDraw's performance. For those working in monochrome, 32-bit QuickDraw improves the display of color images that are remapped for display on gray-scale monitors. Formerly, colors were mapped to a gray level based on their intensity; this often resulted in two completely different colors being assigned the same gray value. The new software does a better job of keeping colors distinct.

In 1994, after an unusually long six-year development cycle, Apple released QuickDraw GX as part of its latest System 7.5 release. QuickDraw GX allows you to print a file by dragging it over an icon on your desktop. Despite this and many other printing and font-related features, QuickDraw GX may take a while to catch on: It requires 1.7 Mb of storage space and up to 2.5 Mb of RAM when running.

Video

With the release of QuickTime in 1991, Apple cemented its commitment to multimedia. Because QuickTime is more interesting to multimediacs than any other piece of Mac system software, we're devoting a lot of space to it here.

Simply put, QuickTime is system-level software that lets users combine and synchronize animation, video, and sound and incorporate them into Mac applications. Because it is built into the system, it brings the multimedia experience to a wide audience and moves digital video as close to the mainstream as it has ever been.

Just as you now freely cut and paste basic data types such as text and graphics, QuickTime allows you to perform basic editing and manipulation of dynamic or *time-based* media.

QuickTime for the End User

QuickTime is similar to most Apple system software; you don't have to know very much about it to begin using it immediately. Simply drop the QuickTime extension in your system folder, and you'll be able to play back QuickTime movie clips. QuickTime works on any 68020 or better Mac (including Power-Books with grayscale displays) running 6.0.7 or later system software with at least 2Mb of RAM.

QuickTime is currently an extension to the Mac System software and is available at no charge from a variety of sources, including Mac user groups and the AppleLink, CompuServe, and America On-line electronic bulletin boards. For developers, Apple supplies a QuickTime Developer's Kit—a CD containing all the QuickTime system software plus a number of movie clips and utilities. End users can buy the QuickTime Starter Kit, a CD that includes various utilities, QuickTime movie samples, and QuickTime itself. Eventually—perhaps by the time you read this—QuickTime will be integrated directly into Mac System software releases.

QuickTime-aware applications (both general purpose, like spreadsheets and word processors, and more specialized applications) bundle QuickTime and a means for playing QuickTime movies. You can also buy the QuickTime Starter's Kit, which contains QuickTime itself; utilities for capturing, trimming, and compressing movies and still images; sample movies and clip art; and other goodies.

MoviePlayer ⌘ 612

To play a QuickTime movie, you need nothing more than a suitable Mac, the QuickTime extension, and a simple application for playback (Apple includes MoviePlayer with both QuickTime kits for this purpose, and there are many shareware movie players available from on-line services). The only other thing you'll need is a QuickTime movie to play. You can get these from friends, bulletin boards, or QuickTime movie collections; or you can make them yourself. To create your own movies, you'll need a little more than the basics—see "Making Movies." Once you've installed QuickTime and have a movie to play, you simply click on it to open it like any other file.

You also can launch MoviePlayer, which gives thumbnail views of movies on your disk—a timesaver if you have a lot of movies from which to choose. When you select "Open File" from a QuickTime-aware application, you'll also get this same helpful movie selection dialog box (Figure 2.2).

Once you select the movie you want to see, it's displayed in freeze frame with the *Standard Play Bar Controller* at the bottom (Figure 2.3). To play the movie, simply click the play button on the Play Bar Controller. The slider will move to

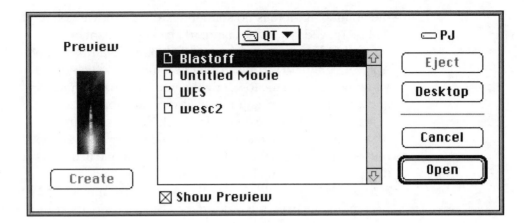

**Figure 2.2
Movie selection
dialog box.**

indicate time remaining as the movie plays. You can also click and drag the slider
to move through the movie, though this generally produces choppy playback
with unsynchronized sound. You also can use the step forward and step reverse
buttons to display the movie one frame at a time.

Click the play button during playback and the movie will pause. When you
click on the speaker symbol, another little slider appears so that you can adjust

Standard Play Bar Controller

Doubles the size of the Movie window

Slides as movie progresses to indicate current position

Starts and pauses the movie

**Figure 2.3
QuickTime movie.**   Adjusts soundtrack volume

the volume. If there is no soundtrack on the movie you're playing, the speaker will be grayed out in the standard Macintosh manner.

QuickTime's standard movie size is 320 × 240 pixels (about 3¾″ × 2½″ on an Apple 13″ monitor). You can enlarge a movie by click-dragging the standard Mac window handle in the lower right corner, but that degrades image quality rapidly, and sound synchronization may also be disrupted.

Just how fast movies will play back depends on the type of machine you're using. Apple claims that 320 × 240 movies play back at about 30 frames per second on a midrange Mac such as the LC475. In practice, you can expect about half that performance on all but the fastest Macs.

You should be able to play the smaller size movies at 15 frames per second on a midrange machine. Add-in cards and third-party compressors make it possible to play back full-screen movies in real time (see Chapter 6, "Video Tools").

One of the interesting things about QuickTime is that it either fascinates immediately or completely disappoints, depending on the viewer's degree of computer experience. Computer novices are disappointed by the so-so image quality and the jerky movements. Lay people naturally compare QuickTime to television, or even film, with which there really isn't any comparison at all. Both media have image quality many times higher than that of QuickTime's digital video.

By contrast, computer enthusiasts tend to go gaga over the tiny flickering images of QuickTime, looking past its rudimentary feel to see the potential that lies ahead, once computers get a little faster and compression gets better. To the desktop computer user accustomed to dealing with visually arid text and simple graphics, QuickTime's moving images and sound synchronization seem revolutionary.

If you want to do more than play back movies and place them in documents and files, it's helpful to know a little about QuickTime's components and architecture (Figure 2.4).

QuickTime consists of four basic component groups:

- System software

    Movie Toolbox

    Image Compression Manager

    Component Manager

    Media Handler

- Compressors

    Photo compressor

    Animation compressor

    Video compressor

    Graphics compressor

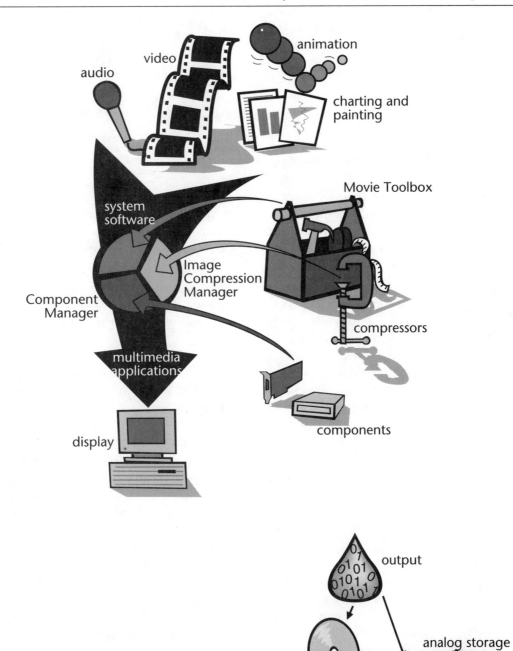

**Figure 2.4
QuickTime
components.**

- File Formats

  Movies

  PICT extensions

- Human interface

  Standard Movie Controller

  Extended Standard File dialog box with preview

  Guidelines for compression, capture, and more

Movie Toolbox

This is a set of system software services that allow third-party developers to incorporate support for QuickTime movies into their applications. Apple claims that the tools are so easy that developers have been able to incorporate basic functions such as playback and cut-and-paste in just a few days.

Image Compression Manager (ICM)

Since time-based data, like video, demands enormous storage capacity, Quick-Time includes a variety of compression routines, all of which are software-based. These tools, called *codecs*, both compress video for storage on the computer and decompress for playback.

This sort of compression is called *symmetric* because data is both compressed and decompressed by the user at the same rates, using the same tools. (Asymmetric compression is done off-line, typically on mainframe computers. Although asymmetric compression typically results in smaller files, it is not fully controllable by the user.)

The ICM controls the compression of QuickTime movies. When you want to compress and store a movie or other image (Apple supplies compressors for photos, graphics, and animation as well as video) from an application that uses the ICM, a menu provides access to the various compressors. When you select a compressed image for playback, the ICM selects the correct decompressor so that the image may be viewed.

The ICM accepts add-on compressors, so that QuickTime-aware applications will always have access to the latest in compression technology. When new compressors are added, the ICM menu is automatically updated.

In fact, with QuickTime 2.0, Apple added support for a very important compression scheme called MPEG. You need additional hardware to play MPEG movies, but the video itself is high quality and its possible to enjoy full motion full screen movies.

Component Manager

The Component Manager manages external resources, such as compressors and digitizers, that convert video and audio signals for use by the computer.

Before QuickTime, applications had to include individual drivers for each piece of video hardware, much as you need specific printer drivers to be able to print documents to various brands of printers. For example, to paste a video clip into WordPerfect, you'd need a special driver to bring the clip in from a particular video digitizing card; a different card would require another driver.

With QuickTime, external hardware is transparent to applications. If you decide to make your own QuickTime movies and add a digitizer card, the application you use to control the digitizing of the video will rely on the Component Manager to communicate with the card. In this way, QuickTime frees software developers from writing a different driver for every digitizer board out there.

Media Handler

The Media Handler lets users and developers add different types of tracks to QuickTime movies. For example, after the initial release of QuickTime, Apple itself added support for a text track for titling and captioning.

With Apple's release of QuickTime 2.0 in 1994, it became possible to incorporate music soundtracks into QuickTime movies. It's as simple as using MoviePlayer or other QuickTime player to open a digital or MIDI sound file. Because MIDI files are so small (less than 24K for 4 minutes of music sampled in 8-bit mono at 22kHz), QuickTime movies with soundtracks are a very viable option. (See Chapter 4 "Sound Tools" for a complete discussion of the MIDI file format.)

QuickTime 2.0 also supports "SMPTE timecode," used by professional videographers to identify precise locations in video and to sync video, sound, and other components.

Movies

Users integrate time-related data such as video and sound and store the results in a file format called the *Movie* (catchy, huh?). Each of the different components in a Movie is called a *track*, although the tracks do not themselves contain the data, but rather point to the data's location, type, order, playback speed, and so on. This arrangement keeps the Movie files small, since data can amount to several megabytes or more.

The Movie format standardizes organizing, storing, and recording time-based data. Each movie can have separate tracks recorded—each with its own timing, sequencing, control, and data description. QuickTime synchronizes the tracks and fetches the data. Initially, Apple has defined two track types: video and sound. But the format is extensible, so that more track types can be added as they develop.

Each QuickTime movie includes three different "views"—a *poster*, which is an icon that represents the movie; a *preview*, which is a brief excerpt; and the full-length version itself.

Apple wants to make the Movie a cross-platform file format and has published the specifications to make it easy for developers to include it in applications on various platforms (see Chapter 9, "Working Cross-Platform").

The Movie file format is fully supported by the standard Mac holding tanks, Clipboard and Scrapbook, so that you can cut and paste QuickTime movies as routinely as you cut and paste text and images. QuickTime will also recognize and convert various data types, such as PICS animation files and AIFF audio files.

Using the Sound Manager system extension and a sound digitizer card, you can add CD-quality audio to your QuickTime movies.

PICT Extensions

PICT Viewer 1.1 ⌘ 611

Apple has extended PICT, its standard graphics file format. You can now compress PICT images and preview them with thumbnail views. Any program that can view a PICT image now will be able to open a compressed PICT image as well, with no changes to the program.

Applications that support the new thumbnail PICT view will allow you to browse through a catalog of these small versions of PICT images. This will save a lot of time for those who work with large numbers of images.

Compressors

Apple is initially supplying four different compressor components: a photo compressor, a video compressor, an animation compressor, and a graphics compressor. These compressors are meant to be used with images collected from scanners, digitizers, paint programs, or any other sources that produce large, complex images.

Along with an extension called Apple Photo Access, for example, QuickTime's built-in photo compressor will open pictures stored on Photo CDs. The photos are converted to PICTs and displayed in SimpleText, where they can be copied into QuickTime movies.

All of Apple's compressors are software-based, which means they're cheap and readily available—definitely useful benefits. However, the structure of QuickTime is such that third-party compressors can be added easily and will be automatically managed and made available through the Component Manager. There are already both hardware and software compressors available from outside sources; most of these compressors are faster than QuickTime's native tools.

Compression works by taking some of the information out of the image. If the removed information is redundant or not otherwise detectable by the human eye, the compression is known as *lossless*. But as the compression ratio gets higher, more information is removed and image quality degrades noticeably; this type of compression is called *lossy*.

For video, there are two additional types of compression: *Spatial* (also known as intraframe) compression removes information from within a frame; and *temporal* (also called interframe) compression takes away information between frames, a technique also called *frame differencing*.

There is a constant trade-off in compression, and you need to consider carefully the type of compression to use for a given image or movie. Higher compression rates will result in smaller files that take up less space on your hard disk, but the images may be of poor quality.

Say you have a short video clip that must fit on a floppy and is meant to be played back on a relatively low quality 8-bit display. Since the clip must be small enough to fit on a floppy, you can use high compression to make the file as compact as possible. Lower image quality resulting from high compression will not be a great problem because of the inherent limits of the displays that you need to view the clip.

On the other hand, if you are making movies that will be played from a CD-ROM and viewed by many people, you'll probably want the best quality images available. Select low spatial compression, which will result in high quality images. You might also want to choose high temporal compression, which will remove more information between frames and cause better playback of video from CD-ROMs (which have low data transfer rates). However, files using spatial compression cannot easily be edited.

QuickTime provides a standard compression dialog box (shown in Figure 2.5). You select the type of compressor (video, animation, graphics, or photo), as well as the quality ("Most" being low compression, and "Least" being high compression) from this dialog box. For video, you also select the number of frames per second and "frame differencing," or temporal compression. Unless the "Frame Differencing" box is checked, both spatial and temporal compression are selected in tandem, using the same slider.

Human Interface

Apple clearly cares about how users interact with computers. After all, they invented the Macintosh, certainly the most usable of computers. Apple has long provided exhaustive user interface guidelines for developers. This ensures that

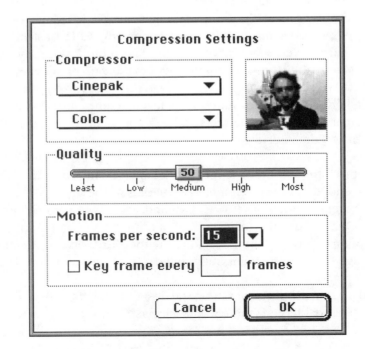

Figure 2.5 Apple's MovieRecorder compression dialog box.

applications will be consistent and familiar, so that once you know one Mac program, it's easy to pick up another one.

True to form, Apple has published human interface guidelines for developers who will be incorporating QuickTime into their applications. These guidelines include the basic design and functionality of the Standard Movie Controller, the Standard File dialog with Preview, and the Standard QuickTime Compression dialog, all shown above.

Making Movies

Premiere 4.0 Demo ⌘ 722

You may want to go beyond playing back QuickTime movies and venture into making your own. To do that you need surprisingly little: an inexpensive video digitizer (such as VideoSpigot from SuperMac) and an editing program like Avid's VideoShop or Premiere from Adobe. You'll probably also want a sound digitizer such as Macromedia's MacRecorder. You should be able to get the complete setup for under $1,000. (Apple's AV line of Macs includes the basic hardware needed to capture and create simple movies.)

Of course, you'll also need source material from a camcorder, VCR, videodisc, or even a CD-ROM. For a guide to making QuickTime movies, see Chapter 6, "Video Tools," and Chapter 15, "Creating Video."

Macintosh Hardware

Even before there was such a thing as multimedia, Macs were designed to handle graphics and sound as well as text. As a result, nearly all the Macs Apple makes today are multimedia-ready—even the low-cost LC series has built-in color capability and sound digitizing, making it suitable for playback of multimedia.

Developers need machines with more powerful CPUs, faster data transfer rates, bigger hard drives, modular expansion, and more RAM. Although some of the older Macs—the IIfx for example—can make capable development platforms, the best Macs for developers are those in the Quadra and PowerMac series. The Apple Performa series includes some fast machines, but they are targeted at the consumer and business markets and lack some of the key expandability features of their Quadra cousins.

Quadras

With the introduction of its new PowerMac architecture in 1994 (see below), Apple ended the short reign of the Quadras as the most potent of Macintoshes. Less expensive than the PowerMacs and with more compatible software available, Quadras are the mainstays of multimedia development platforms. From authoring to 3-D rendering, Quadras are the workhorses of multimedia creation, although Quadras are being supplanted as more developers migrate to the PowerMac platform.

Quadras in the 600 series fit on the desktop and range from the 605, with minimal expandability, to the 650, which has 4 card slots. The 700, 800, and 900

QuickTime VR

Virtual reality, like many emerging technologies, has always been more spiel than real. Though welcomed by arcade junkies and cyberpunkers, and fueled by breathless media coverage, VR's appreciable possibilities have largely been confined to the imagination. But sensors indicate that VR may finally be emerging from the cyberdome. There are a host of far-out applications, from mind-blowing immersive games to technology that allows physicians to overlay imaging data, such as CAT or NMR scans, on patients. A neurosurgeon might project a 3-D image of tumor tissue that would create a real-time "template."

With such flamboyant applications just around the corner (or in your living room), it's little surprise that vendors are prone to tacking the "VR" moniker on everything from televisions to ice cream containers. Apple, often on the virtual side of reality, is no exception.

In 1995, it released QuickTime VR, an extension to QuickTime 2.0 that allows play back of panoramic images. The extension is for developers only—so far you can't create your own immersive spaces, but can view those created by others. Likely applications are games and exploratory spaces such as virtual museums and art galleries.

Aside from some QuickTime VR content, you'll need at least an '030-based Mac with 5 Mb of RAM or more. Beam me up Scotty.

series Quadras are "tower" models, with more slots and ports and generally beefier hardware.

The Quadra 660AV and 840AV are targeted at multimedia developers (the AV stands for audiovisual). Both feature fast CPUs; a built-in DSP (digital signal processor) chip, video input and output (in multiple formats), video digitizing on the motherboard, Apple's Casper voice recognition technology, built-in phone/fax capability, and a bundled set of key third-party software programs.

The high-end Quadra 840AV sports a 40MHz 68040 processor and can be purchased with 16Mb of RAM (expandable to 128Mb), a 230Mb, 500Mb, or 1-Gbyte hard drive, and an optional internal, dual-speed AppleCD 300i CD-ROM drive. The Centris 660AV comes with a 25MHz '040 and is expandable to 68Mb of RAM.

Of particular interest are the built-in digital video capabilities, which can capture and play back video with no additional equipment. The machines incorporate a DAV slot for third party cards that handle specialized multimedia tasks such as compression/decompression.

Apple has also sped data throughput by implementing direct memory access (DMA). This relieves the CPU of the responsibility of handling communications with peripheral devices. The 840AV can send millions of colors (24-bit color) to a 16″ monitor when you add 2 Mb of VRAM, or thousands of colors (16-bit) to a 21″ monitor.

Apple bundles a number of programs such as video and audio capture software with each computer.

**You've Got
the Power**

As part of its mind-boggling alliance with IBM, Apple has developed a new generation of computers that bring unprecedented levels of power to the desktop. The Apple/IBM/Motorola joint venture has produced a series of RISC (reduced-instruction-set-computing) CPUs based on IBM's POWER chip set. RISC chips are able to process information more quickly than conventional CISC (complex-instruction-set computing) CPUs. RISC processors, which are widely used in the workstation industry, drive such machines as Sun's SPARC line and Silicon Graphics' Indy and Iris Indigo series.

Introduced in 1994, PowerMacs bring an unprecedented level of computing power to the desktop. The first generation of the machines—those in the 6100, 7100, and 8100 series (Figure 2.6)—are from two to five times faster than the Quadra 840AV, previously Apple's fastest machine.

To ensure compatibility with existing disk drives, add-on cards, printers and other peripherals, Apple retained its NuBus architecture in first generation Quadras. However, the next wave of PowerMacs, which will be available by the time you read this, will use the higher speed PCI bus currently used by many PC compatibles.

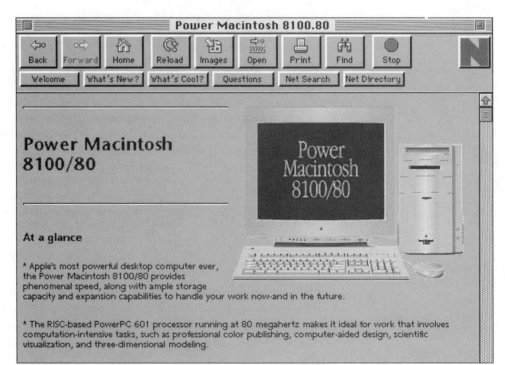

**Figure 2.6
Apple's World
Wide Web version
of its PowerMac
8100 datasheet.**

Upgrading and Buying Used Macs

If you're not the type who has to have the latest toys, you can get really good deals on used Macs from people who are. A good resource is the Macintosh Price Index printed each month by *MacUser* magazine. The March 1995 issue listed $2,300 as the average price for a Quadra 840AV with a 230 Mb hard drive, 8 Mb of RAM, and a CD-ROM drive.

A PowerMac 8100CD with a 250 Mb hard drive and 8 Mb of RAM could be had for $3,350. Prices and availability should be better by the time you read this. The MacUser Index is culled from The United Computer Exchange, an organized computer swap service. Call 800-755-3033 for the latest deals.

You might also consider buying a processor upgrade for your aging Mac, either from Apple or a third party. Apple itself has a Macintosh Processor Upgrade card that takes a 68040 Mac (Quadras and some LC and Performa models) and turns it into a PowerMac at a reasonable price ($599 list at press time).

Reliable third-party vendors of similar products include DayStar Digital, Radius, and Applied Engineering. In fact, DayStar has a product identical to Apple's with a longer warranty period.

You can also turn your earthbound Mac into a multimedia playback machine with an upgrade kit, such as Apple's Multimedia Kit for Macintosh. The kit includes a double speed CD-ROM drive, speakers, headphones, and a few CD-ROM titles.

For a few hundred dollars, you can buy an AV card that handles video capture so that you can process digital video on-board. Computers in the 8100 series will handle 24-bit (millions of colors) on up to a 21″ monitor with no additional hardware.

For all this, you'd expect to pay a premium, but PowerMacs are actually quite affordable. In the spring of 1995, you could buy a top-of-the-line model (8100CD), used, for about $3,000. (See "Upgrading and Buying Used Macs," above.)

What you do pay for is new software: the PowerMac's CPU requires software written specifically for it. Your old programs will still run, using a method called "emulation," but this is a slow and unappealing option. Some programs come in "fat" binaries that include versions for both CPU types.

Because multimedia production is especially taxing to computers, developers are always looking for faster machines and will want to make the transition as soon as possible. Thus, multimedia applications were among the first to appear in "native" PowerMac versions.

Apple's second wave PowerMacs, released in 1995, upped the performance ante again. The machines share several innovations: a faster CPU based on

Send in the Clones

In 1994, Apple belatedly decided to license other computer makers to manufacture Macintosh clones. By nearly universal reckoning, Apple should have done this a long time ago—to spur wider acceptance of the Macintosh and fight the relentless surge of the Microsoft/Intel cartel.

It may be too late for Apple, but the move should help consumers: Clones are likely to be 10 to 20 percent less expensive than comparable models made by Apple. Some clone makers will focus on specialized workstations optimized for tasks such as color prepress publishing and multimedia authoring. For example, Radius offers the VideoVision worksta-tion, a PowerMac clone designed specifically for digital video processing (Figure 2.7).

If the increased competition results in further price reductions and better market pene-tration, peripherals should also be increasingly plentiful, innovative and cheap. Sounds like the PC business doesn't it? And speaking of which....

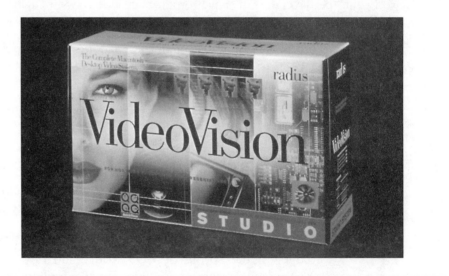

**Figure 2.7
Radius
VideoVision
workstation
PowerMac clone.**

Motorola's 604 chip; on-board video processing (no AV card required); and a faster bus—the communications grid that connects the CPU with peripherals and other computing resources.

PC System Software

Many operating systems are available for PCs—computers using Intel's CPU chips —but by far the dominant configuration is a PC running Microsoft Windows. As of this writing, Windows is actually a user interface that runs on top of DOS, the actual operating system. By the time you read this, however, Microsoft should have released its new operating system, Windows95, which is a total operating environment in its own right. (See "On the Horizon: Windows95.")

Beginning with Windows release 3.1, Microsoft began incorporating multimedia features into Windows. The *Media Control Interface* (MCI) allows multimedia device control through a set of English commands. MCI is used to control everything from CD-ROM drives to sound cards. Any device that has an MCI driver (most do) can be directly controlled from any program that can issue MCI commands, such as Director. This makes it easy to issue, for example, MIDI or laserdisc commands from within Director.

Following are some of the multimedia-specific facilities offered by Windows systems prior to Windows95.

Director 4.0 Demo ⌘ 708

Sound

Since PCs have no inherent sound capabilities, your Windows machine must be equipped with a sound card, CD-ROM drive, and speakers to function as a multimedia PC, or MPC. (See "Multimedia PCs.")

Actually, if you're desperate, you can get a driver from Microsoft that will let you use the PC's tiny and (tinny) built-in speaker to play sounds and music. At present, you can download the driver (SPEAK.EXE) from CompuServe (go MSL), or from Microsoft's bulletin board at 203-936-6735.

Windows does offer some sound utilities for recording and playback of sound. These include:

The Sound Control Panel, which you can use to assign system sounds;

The Sound Recorder Accessory (Figure 2.8), which you can use to record sound from a microphone or through the line-in jack on your sound card. Sound Recorder also has simple editing tools for adding special effects;

**Figure 2.8
Windows Sound
Recorder utility.**

Sound Recorder - TADA.WAV

File   Edit   Effects   Help

Stopped

Position:
0.50 sec.

Length:
1.25 sec.

Media Player, an all-purpose playback utility that will play video, sound files, and audio CDs;

MIDI Mapper, for mapping patches on the MIDI synthesizer on your sound card.

Graphics

Graphics "standards" for the PC are a mass of semicompatible specifications that center on two common display modes: VGA and the newer SVGA. A VGA display, the minimum requirement for the playback of multimedia, has a "resolution" (which basically equates to image sharpness) of 640 × 480 pixels. SVGA supports higher resolutions of either 800 × 600 or 1024 × 768. Windows will support any video card and resolution, as long as the card manufacturer supplies a Windows driver.

Resolution is determined both by the monitor itself, and by the video adaptor card, which may include VRAM for speedier display of 16-bit or 24-bit color. Generally speaking, if you have a monitor and card that conform to either of the two standards, you shouldn't have trouble playing back or creating multimedia.

In practice, different manufacturers' interpretations of the standards can cause conflicts and incompatibilities. This can be particularly onerous for multimedia developers, who must test their work under bewildering permutations of display cards and drivers. Incompatible display drivers, for example, are among the primary causes of General Protection Faults (system crashes) when playing back multimedia such as digital video.

Despite these basic hurdles, Microsoft has done a lot to promote graphics development under Windows. Its WinG software development kit, for example, was created to prod game developers in moving popular games from DOS to Windows. Most developers preferred DOS because their games would run much faster under DOS than on Windows. Windows graphics routines were optimized for drawing windows, menus, and general business graphics. WinG gives game developers much lower-level video hardware control than is normally possible under Windows.

Video

Like Apple, Microsoft has its own digital video system: Video for Windows. VfW files are stored in the AVI (audio/video interleaved) file format. Like QuickTime, VfW acts as a "datapipe," recording and playing back video using codecs.

VfW has a plug-in architecture that is similar to QuickTime's. VfW can use different codecs for compression and decompression of video. In release 1.1 of VfW, Microsoft added support for the popular Cinepak codec, also used to treat many QuickTime movies. With this release, VfW also began to handle larger 240 × 320 movies.

As of this writing, Microsoft has announced plans to offer a version of VfW for the Macintosh.

Surround Video

Microsoft's answer to QuickTime VR is Surround Video. Surround Video is a software development kit that allows developers to create 360 degree panoramic photos. While not as capable as QuickTime VR (it requires the use of a panoramic camera, which QuickTime VR does not), it does incorporate a few interesting features, such as the ability to play a video within a scene.

Microsoft is not charging licensing or royalty fees for Surround Video (Apple charges developers $2,000 for QuickTime VR, plus royalty fees for distribution). As of this writing, Microsoft had announced plans to port Surround Video to the Mac.

Display Control Interface: Faster, More Reliable Video Under Windows

Microsoft and Intel have collaborated on a specification called Display Control Interface (DCI), which speeds and smooths video playback on Windows. DCI can also be used to improve animation and audio performance. DCI provides direct access to hardware, such as video cards, which eliminates the need to go through the operating system. The result is much faster and more reliable video, animation, and sound playback.

QuickTime also runs under Windows, making it easier for developers to create cross-platform applications.

PC Hardware

PCs have an "open architecture." Any manufacturer can make a PC clone that nominally conforms to a set of specifications designed to ensure compatibility. In practice, however, open architecture usually guarantees the opposite: Because a given PC is an amalgam of parts, it is difficult to ensure that a multimedia game, for example, will play back reliably.

Actually, it can be difficult to do anything reliably. Even installing an add-in card can plunge you into unfamiliar territory littered with IRQ interrupt conflicts and other arcane beasts.

An important development that should ease the problem by the time you read this: the "Plug and Play" standard. A PC equipped with a PnP BIOS will automatically recognize and configure PnP cards and devices. It will take a while for PnP to sweep the industry, but it's on its way, and by 1996, should banish most device configuration problems, long the bane of Windows users.

Windows has helped to instill some standardization, and Windows95 promises further progress. But PC Land is still something of a wild frontier. The upside is that PC hardware is plentiful, cheap, and fast. The huge base of installed PCs makes them a compulsory target for multimedia developers.

PC Hardware Basics

Most PC CPUs are made by Intel, although such manufacturers as Cyrix, AMD, and NexGen make competitive processors that run DOS and Windows equally well. The 486 in various configurations has for several years been the desktop standard, although there are quite a few 386s still out there.

Intel's Pentium is the top of the line PC CPU at the time of this writing, though by the time you read this, the P6 will have made its debut. The P6 will have a beneficial effect on the market, as it will double speeds of the fastest Pentiums, and will drive down the cost of 486 and Pentium machines.

PC busses come in assorted flavors, from basic ISA and EISA architectures, to the accelerated VESA and PCI schemes. The latter two busses talk more directly to the CPU, thus greatly speeding peripheral performance. Most high end PCs now feature the newer and faster PCI bus.

Like Macs, PCs come with built-in video cards, and some of the high-powered models significantly accelerate video performance—which is of key importance to multimedia developers. The standard today is the 64-bit video card, with support for 24-bit (millions of colors) video at resolutions of 40 × 480 and above. Some cards include specialized chips that speed VfW, MPEG video, and 3-D graphics.

The MPC Standard

In an attempt to make multimedia playback a reasonable proposition on the PC, a consortium of companies called the Multimedia PC Marketing Council specifies the MPC standard. The specification allows manufacturers whose machines meet this standard to sport the MPC logo.

MPC Level 1 was inadequate and was quickly superseded by MPC Level 2, which specifies Windows 3.0 or higher, a 486SX/25 processor, 4Mb of RAM, a 160 Mb hard drive, a double speed CD-ROM drive, a 16-bit sound card, a 16-bit video card, and various odds and ends such as a joystick port.

The thing to remember is that MPC specifies the *minimum* equipment necessary to play back multimedia. If you want only to play multimedia games and the like, you can consider the Level 2 spec adequate, if light in a few areas. Don't even consider less than 8 Mb of RAM.

Developers will want to improve on the standard in nearly every department, starting with a faster CPU, such as a DX4/100 or a Pentium.

Computers fully equipped for multimedia playback are now commonplace, and surprisingly inexpensive. These systems are preconfigured with sound cards and CD-ROM drives, so users won't suffer installation headaches. These systems are also generally bundled with multimedia playback and recording utilities and a set of CD-ROM titles.

Make or Buy?

If you already have a 486 or better PC that doesn't have the multimedia trimmings, your best bet is to buy one of the many upgrade kits available. These kits include a CD-ROM drive, sound card and speakers, and usually a few CD-ROM

On the Horizon: Windows95

By the time you read this, Microsoft will have released Windows95, and many believe it will finally place the PC on level ground with the Macintosh.

Multimedia is a high priority at Microsoft, and Windows95 has some nifty built-in features. For one thing, it's a 32-bit operating system, meaning that it will make better use of underlying PC hardware and will process everything faster. New 32-bit versions of the Cinepak and Indeo codecs will play video smoother and faster, and a "multithreaded" CD file system means that CDs can be read while other tasks are going on. You'll also be able to optimize access times for your particular CD-ROM drive and playback audio CDs with a new utility (see Figure 2.9).

The new "Plug and Play" standard should gradually eliminate the compatibility problems that have plagued installation of cards and devices such as audio and network cards.

3-D graphics acceleration is included in Windows95 in the form of RealityLab, a 3-D graphics library and API that may drive the next generation of high-speed 3-D consumer and corporate applications. On a 90 MHz Pentium, RealityLab can render 120,000 shaded polygons per second, well beyond what was previously possible on PCs.

Microsoft has also incorporated WinToon, a run-time engine and set of tools that brings full motion animation closer to reality. WinToon uses Video for Windows to help developers create smooth fullscreen (640 × 480) animations without the effort that would normally be required for this level of performance.

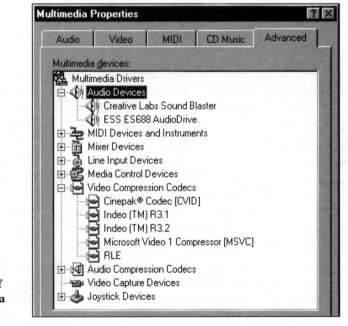

**Figure 2.9
Windows95
affords com-
prehensive
management of
new multimedia
devices.**

Wave for Win Demo ⌘ 702

titles, to boot. The category is competitive and includes many top-rated products from companies such as Creative Labs, Turtle Beach, and Reveal Computer products. You can get a good kit for as little as $300.

If you have a 386 PC, you can get by with an upgrade kit; but consider trading it in on a faster model. You'll be glad you did. If you don't have a computer at all, you'll be better off buying a multimedia PC than hassling with upgrading it later.

Hardware Peripherals

The basic components of multimedia—photographic images, graphics, animated sequences, video, and sound—are much more complex than text and carry huge amounts of information. Add to this the fact that most of these components are not static, but change over time, and you can see why multimedia places enormous demands on computer hardware.

Consider full-motion video, by far the most demanding of multimedia components. Video is shot at 30 frames per second, and when digitized for use on a computer, each frame consumes up to 1Mb of space. Thus, just to store a two-hour movie would require over 200Gb of disk space. Assuming such storage capacity is practical on the desktop—which it presently is not—a desktop computer capable of moving that much data from disk to screen has not yet been invented. Despite these limitations, there are still many uses for video on the computer, and ways to process it effectively.

The processing of multimedia data by computer affects every element of basic system resources—CPU, RAM, I/O channels, storage devices, and display. Multimedia also requires at least a few additional components. If you are simply going to view multimedia presentations, electronic books, or interactive demonstrations, you can get by with a relatively modest system. A midrange machine such as the Mac LC 550, a 13″ color display, a CD-ROM drive, and 8Mb of RAM will do. A comparable PC setup would be a DX/2-66 with a sound card, 14″ display, CD-ROM drive and 8Mb RAM. If you plan to create presentations or animation, or to work with video, you'll need to add a few components to your existing system. Many of these options are illustrated in Figure 2.10, which gives an idea of how the peripherals fit into the computer and relate to one another.

Although this section is intended simply as an introduction to the different hardware components used in multimedia viewing and production, it is difficult to discuss them without commenting briefly on the various techniques and trade-offs involved in their use. For a full discussion of these aspects, however, see the various chapters devoted to multimedia creation.

For the sake of explanation, we've divided the hardware components into three categories—those that bring images and sound into the computer (discussed in the following section, "Image and Sound Input/Acquisition"), those

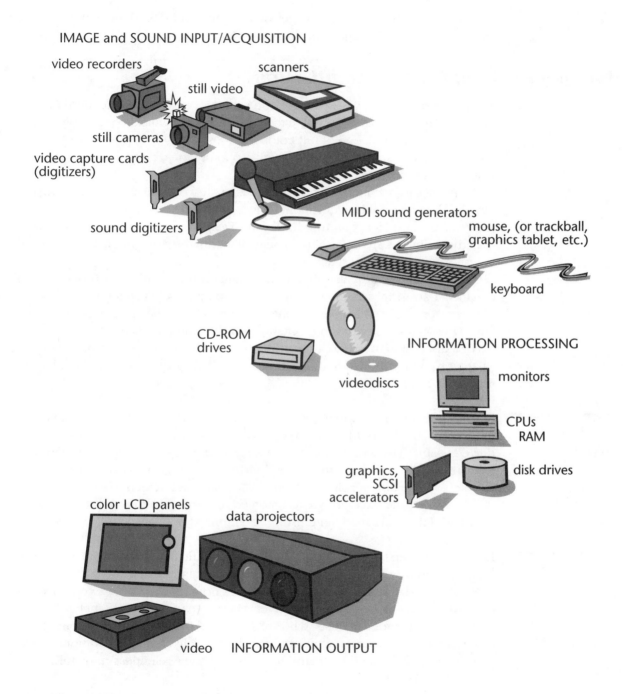

IMAGE and SOUND INPUT/ACQUISITION

video recorders

still video

scanners

still cameras

video capture cards
(digitizers)

sound digitizers

MIDI sound generators

mouse, (or trackball,
graphics tablet, etc.)

keyboard

CD-ROM
drives

INFORMATION PROCESSING

videodiscs

monitors

CPUs
RAM

graphics,
SCSI
accelerators

disk drives

color LCD panels

data projectors

video   INFORMATION OUTPUT

Figure 2.10
Multimedia
hardware.

that process, store, or display images on the computer ("Working with Images"), and those that send images out, such as to tape or projection ("Image Output").

Image and Sound Input/Acquisition

The processing of real-world images and sound is one of the foundations of multimedia. Computers, originally able to handle text only, quickly progressed to the creation and manipulation of full-color graphics. Today, computers are processing all types of external images as well—photographs, noncomputer graphics, video, and sound.

The demand for computer access to these real-world images has led to many new and highly capable acquisition devices, including 24-bit color scanners, digital cameras, and video capture hardware. Despite their power and sophistication, these devices are beginning to be well within the reach of the desktop user, in terms of both price and usability.

Once images have been converted to digital form, a variety of programs can enhance, transform, and incorporate them into multimedia creations of all sorts. The first step is to get the material onto the computer in the first place—a process that is becoming less daunting, yet still tests skill and patience.

For a discussion of video cameras, digital camera, and video capture cards see Chapter 6, "Video Tools." Sound capture and MIDI cards are covered in Chapter 4, "Sound Tools."

Keyboards and Mice

Not so long ago a computer's keyboard was enough of a challenge, and the mouse was just flat-out baffling to a lot of people. When Hewlett-Packard conducted usability tests of its first mouse-equipped computers, some puzzled subjects aimed the mouse at the screen and punched its buttons as if it were a remote control; others rolled it around the computer screen. Of course, these days, most people have grown accustomed to mice as well as to the basic keyboard, and there are many interesting variations of both.

Keyboards

Keyboards haven't changed a whole lot since the first PCs came out in the early '80s, but they have been somewhat refined and standardized.

Nearly all keyboards for desktop machines now require about two ounces of force to actuate the keys, and key travel is between 0.14 and 0.18 inches. This is very important to touch typists, who are sensitive to the slightest variations in key characteristics. One reason why laptop and, especially, notebook computer keyboards are problematic for many users is that their relentless miniaturization means short key travel.

Another key consideration (har har) is the feel of the keyboard. There are two basic types: those that put up slight resistance before giving way with a click, and those that have linear travel—so-called "mushy" or "spongy" keyboards. The former is the classic noisy IBM keyboard, while the latter is the norm in the Mac world.

Keyboard Ergonomics

All of these things are part of the ergonomic design of the keyboard itself, and they are more important than you may think. If a keyboard doesn't feel right to you, minor aches and pains can develop into tendonitis, carpal tunnel syndrome, or other cumulative trauma injuries. Major hardware manufacturers such as IBM, Apple, Hewlett-Packard, Digital Equipment Corporation, AT&T, and Xerox have all been slapped with suits alleging that hand and wrist injuries were caused by keyboards. You can avoid these problems by trying out a keyboard and the computer it's attached to before buying them.

The curvature of the keys and their degree of slope varies from keyboard to keyboard. But many aches and pains are caused not to the keyboard itself, but by the position of the hands and wrists relative to it. The basic rule is to avoid flexing your wrists; they should remain relatively "unbroken" with your hands on the same plane as your forearms. To facilitate this posture, you can get a wide variety of orthopedic aids such as wrist pads that lie in front of the keyboard or supports that you wear like gloves. There are even little pads that you stick on your mouse to reduce clicking stress.

Keyboard Alternatives

Beyond these central considerations, a keyboard is pretty much a keyboard. But there are a few interesting variations. Apple makes the Adjustable Keyboard, which splits in half so that you can position it to suit more natural hand alignment. The keypad also includes detachable palm rests.

Microsoft offers the Natural Keyboard (Figure 2.11), a wavelike affair that orients the keys in two angled groups. Unlike Apple's entry, you can't adjust the angle; but Microsoft throws in a few goodies of its own: special keys that call up Windows utilities and applications.

Although neither Apple nor Microsoft claims that their keyboards reduce repetitive stress injuries (RSI), they seem like steps in the right direction.

Infogrip of Northbrook, Illinois, makes an interesting alternative keyboard called the BAT. It is a "chordic" keyboard—so called because it has only seven keys, which you press in combination ("chords") to type characters. Unlike other ergonomic alternative keyboards, the BAT is used with only one hand and doesn't need to be used in combination with a standard keyboard.

There are dozens of alternatives to the Apple mouse; many improve on its basic design. Mouse innovations include 300 dpi resolution (greater precision than the 200 dpi Apple mouse), ergonomic designs that fit the hand, and a choice of right- or left-handed models.

**Figure 2.11
Microsoft's
"Natural
Keyboard."**

The familiar type of mouse has a little ball on the bottom, but many mice are optical. Optical mice work by bouncing light from a little LED off a reflective mouse pad. Because they have fewer moving parts, these mice are probably more durable. But unless you keep the reflective pad well dusted, little dust motes can interfere with the light reflections and cause your cursor to behave erratically.

Trackballs—basically, upside-down mice—are very popular, and, of course, have become almost indispensable on notebook computers. When Apple successfully incorporated a trackball into its first PowerBooks, PC notebook manufacturers fell over themselves to incorporate trackballs into their own notebooks. Besides taking up less space, trackballs offer several advantages over traditional mice. They don't get tangled up; it's easier to move the cursor over the wide area of large monitors; and some people find them more accurate. IBM and Toshiba offer a popular alternative pointing device called the TrackPoint in their notebook computers.

Some mice are programmable; you can assign commonly used commands or keystrokes to their second and third keys. Others, such as Logitech's MouseMan, even allow you to program keys with different sequences, depending on the program you're in. When you switch between applications, the button assignments change. Now that's a smart mouse!

Many who take multimedia presentations on the road rely on a remote pointing device so they can change "slides" in a presentation without having to touch the computer. Presentation Electronics makes a credit card-sized "clicker" that works with the Mac and popular presentation programs, and there are many remote mice that work with the PC as well.

**Figure 2.12
Gyropoint.**

*Flying Mice
and the Future*

Speaking of alternative devices, you'll probably want to trade in your mouse or trackball when they start offering screens that allow you to select something by blinking at it. These new selection devices, based on fighter plane heads-up displays, are still a few years away; but they're something to look forward to.

There are already voice recognition devices, such as IBM's Continuous Speech Series (ICSS) and Interactive Inc.'s Interactive Communicator. These products are still a little rough around the edges but may eventually prove to be better mousetraps. As of this writing Apple hasn't delivered on promises of voice recognition features in its PowerMac series.

A little more down-to-earth, but still odd, are flying, or 3-D, mice from such companies as Gyration, Mouse Systems, and Logitech. These cordless gadgets can be used for mobility during demos and other presentations. They sense and track motion digitally without relying on surface or position. While flying mice can be used as normal 2-D input, they are meant for the manipulation of 3-D objects. Gyration's unit, the Gyropoint (Figure 2.12), uses gyroscopes for motion sensing, and has six degrees of freedom—height, length, depth, roll, pitch, and yaw.

**Graphics
Tablets**

Graphics tablets have been around for a while; but recently, propelled by revolutionary new painting tools, they've really taken off. Computer art used to be tainted by a computer-generated look and relegated to an artistic backwater, but it has been reenergized by such pressure-sensitive paint software as Fractal Design Painter. These and other programs allow you to create textures and patterns by applying varying degrees of pressure—much as you'd create effects using traditional art tools. (See Chapter 3, "Graphics Tools.")

One of the enabling technologies of this computer art renaissance is the graphics tablet, once used mainly for CAD/CAM applications. Tablets are typically 12"-square units that lie on a flat surface and resemble an oversized Etch-A-Sketch. You use a stylus to draw patterns and shapes on the tablet's flat surface. You can also tap the stylus on the drawing surface to make selections, just as you would click a mouse's buttons. The stylus is typically cordless and generally includes a button that can be programmed to behave like a second mouse button.

The tablet market has been energized by recent models with smaller surface areas (4 × 5, 6 × 8), and reduced prices to match. Manufacturers with products in this category include Wacom, Calcomp, and Hitachi.

Pressure Sensitivity

Clearly, much of the appeal of tablets lies in their resemblance to the real world. Drawing with a stylus is a more natural process than trying to create a complex or freeform image with a mouse. But the real secret of their success when used with one of the new painting programs is their sensitivity to pressure. When you press lightly on the tablet, you'll get a thin line; press harder, and the line comes out fat and bold. You can choose styluses with different pressure sensitivities, depending on your preference (and grip).

Some tablets have an electrostatic field that clamps paper to the drawing surface for slip-free tracing. This is a quick alternative to scanning and can be used

**Figure 2.13
Wacom graphics
tablet.**

to digitize and embellish images in a single operation. Leading tablets are made by Wacom (Figure 2.13), Summagraphics, and Kurta.

Color Flatbed Scanners

It may be easier to trace and digitize a simple graphic with a tablet and stylus, but for capturing the nuances of complex color images, there is nothing like a scanner. Factor in the plummeting prices of high resolution color scanners (many are less than $1,000), and you have an indispensable tool of the multimedia revolution.

When first introduced, scanners were mainly used in conjunction with optical character recognition (OCR) software to scan and recognize text. They were widely used to convert hard copy documents into a digital form that could then be manipulated by computer.

The general excitement surrounding desktop publishing—and now multimedia and digital processing powerhouses such as Photoshop, Live Picture, and Picture Publisher—has helped to drive the popularity of scanners and has pushed their application into areas far beyond simple text handling.

While there are a number of different types of scanners, the color flatbed scanner has the best combination of versatility, quality of results, and cost. There are also good grayscale scanners available. But the falling prices of 24-bit color models make grayscale scanners less attractive, since most color scanners will also handle grayscale images quite nicely, and cost only slightly more.

Note that scanners use the SCSI interface for connecting to a computer. Macs have a SCSI port built-in, but PCs require an adaptor card that is typically bundled with scanners sold for PCs. In the following pages, we offer a rundown of the three major scanning considerations: quality, speed, and control.

Image Quality

Image quality is certainly the ultimate concern in the scanning process. You can always busy yourself during slow scans, and fiddle with, correct, and otherwise process an image once scanned; but you simply cannot make up for poor image quality.

Resolution and Resolvability

Resolution is commonly measured in two different ways: *optical* and *interpolated.* The difference is important, although vendors don't always make the distinction.

Optical resolution is a measure of the scanner's ability to resolve images at the claimed resolution by using only the optics of the scanner itself.

Although a scanner with a resolution of 300 dpi is theoretically able to resolve lines one three-hundredth of an inch wide and one three-hundredth of an inch apart, this ain't necessarily so. If a line happens to fall between two CCD-array elements, it will be incorrectly detected or not detected at all. (CCDs are the elements that measure and convert light intensity to digital format.)

Interpolation boosts the optical resolution through software that "interpolates," or adds, extra dots to smooth out jagged diagonal lines and curves. Different algorithms are used for interpolation: Pixel averaging adds pixels with a value equal to the average of surrounding pixels, and pixel doubling simply duplicates nearby pixels. Some scanners use either one or the other method, while others such as the HP ScanJet II use a combination of the two.

Since interpolation adds no new detail, it does not represent an increase in actual resolution, but it can improve an image. A scanner with an optical resolution of 300 dpi boosted to 600 dpi using interpolation should produce better scans than a 300 dpi scanner that does not use interpolation. On the other hand, a scanner with an optical resolution of 600 dpi should be better still.

Note that most vendors are now refraining from the questionable practice of referring to their scanners' resolutions by the higher interpolated resolution; most manufacturers now express resolution as the optical resolution by the interpolated value. Thus, a scanner with an optical resolution of 600 dpi doubled to 1,200 dpi with interpolation will be referred to as a 600 × 1,200 dpi scanner.

Interpolation is not generally used to more than double optical resolution because as interpolated dots outnumber "real" ones, unwanted effects such as artifacts (stray pixels) can begin to appear. Also, while interpolation can be successfully used to smooth lines, it can undesirably thicken very thin lines. This effect has to do with a phenomenon known as *resolvability*. Resolution boosted beyond a machine's inherent optical resolution does not improve the scanner's ability to resolve detail, but can only fool the eye with the optical trickery of interpolation.

High-Bit Scanners

If you're scanning art that will be used for display on a computer screen—graphics for a computer game, or other CD product, kiosk, or presentation, for example—a 300 dpi scanner should be more than adequate, unless images being scanned are very tiny. However, many images with both highlights and shadow detail may wash out in scans.

Twenty-four-bit scanners scan 8 bits per pixel, for a total of 24 bits for each of the red, green, and blue colors. High-bit scanners resolve greater detail by devoting 10, 12, or even 16 bits for each pixel. Before you take the plunge, though, make sure you need the extra detail (and have the additional disk space more information consumes). High-bit scanners can be from half again to about three times as costly as otherwise-comparable 24-bit scanners.

Noise Level

All scanners introduce a little something of themselves into each scan: electronic noise that manifests itself as image irregularities, color shifts, and blurriness. Some of the effects can be cleaned up in an image processing program;

but they can be difficult to fix, since filtering tools generally treat the entire image, not just certain portions that may be affected by stray pixel noise. (Some filters can treat selected portions of an image, but this can be tedious work.) Even filters can be hampered by noise; sharpening, for example, makes stray pixels more distinct.

Color Fidelity

Poor color fidelity happens when the scanner incorrectly identifies colors and decides to substitute its own instead of the correct values. Unfortunately, this happens quite frequently, due to the inexpensive optics of desktop scanners and the inherent inaccuracies of their lenses.

You can't eliminate unwanted color variations completely, but you can deal with them, to some extent. While you can color-correct using image processing software, it's a lot easier to get it right the first time. The first remedy is to buy a good quality scanner that handles color sensing well. The trade press is an excellent source of information and benchmarks for scanners as well as other computer equipment.

You can also avoid color infidelity by using prescanning software to preview and correct images prior to scanning and by using image editing software after the scan. Finally, there are programs that help you calibrate your scanner to reduce color problems and other variations. This is particularly important as your scanner ages, since its optical and digital components will vary over time.

Calibration software is also useful if you use a number of different scanners in your work; the software enables you to maintain consistent imagery across different scanners. Candela's Scan-Cal, Savitar's ScanMatch, and Kodak's ColorMatch are examples of popular scanner calibration programs.

Registration and Shadow Detail

These are measures of a scanner's tendency to imperfectly merge the colors that make up a given image. The effect is particularly noticeable in black areas that may exhibit little fringes or halos of color. In general, today's scanners are pretty good at accurate registration of images.

There is some evidence that one-pass scanners (see below) are less prone to registration errors than the three-pass variety, which must scan an image three times to collect all the colors in an image.

Shadow detail is a measure of a scanner's ability to distinguish between subtle gray values in dark areas of an image.

Scanning Speed

Speed is always a central consideration in working with computer equipment of all types; nobody likes sitting there watching those little watch hands go around and around. It can take from 2 to 15 minutes to scan and process an 8 × 10 color image.

You can dramatically reduce scan times (and image size) by scanning at lower resolutions or bit depths, when you don't need high resolutions or the range of colors provided by 24-bit scanning. Naturally, this results in a lower-quality image, but the difference may not be critical in multimedia presentations, where images are usually viewed on a monitor.

One-Pass versus Three-Pass

Scanners digitize images by shining a light on the object being scanned and then diverting the reflected light to a *charge-coupled device* (CCD) that, in turn, measures the intensity of the light and converts it to binary code. Some color scanners must scan the image three times: once for each primary color (red, green, and blue) reflected by the image. Many models scan color images in just one pass, by using three different colored lights that flash in sequence, or three different CCDs, or both.

You may encounter marketing hype claiming that one-pass is a superior technique because it reduces scanning time, but experience proves this is not always true. Some one-pass scanners are faster, while others using three-pass technology produce scans more quickly. It does seem that one-pass scanners are prone to fuzzier images caused by lighting errors in their flashing light technique.

These are probably minor points, created by sales and marketing departments to sell machines. There are other, more real concerns when selecting a scanner.

Scanning Software

All scanners include some sort of software that allows you to control aspects of the scan either before or after scanning in the image. This software is sometimes proprietary; but more and more scanner vendors are bundling top image-editing software, such as Adobe Photoshop, that has more sophisticated processing controls and filters. Sometimes these are "light editions" that don't include all the features of the full program.

To achieve the best image, choose the filters and make the adjustments necessary to improve scan quality both before and after scanning. You do what you can with prescanning adjustments, and then use powerful image editing software to make further adjustments.

Twain is an image acquisition standard supported by most scanner vendors. It allows you to acquire an image directly from within an image editing application like Photoshop.

Prescanning Controls

Most scanners include simple controls for adjusting brightness and contrast. They can improve a scan, but should be used with care. When you brighten an image to bring out dark areas, you wash out light parts, thus enhancing one part of the image while eliminating essential information in other areas.

Better scanners offer *gamma control,* a correction technique that can improve a scan without compromising the overall image. For example, you can use gamma control to bring out detail in shadows without lightening brighter areas. Gamma control is also often used for color correction.

Image scaling allows you to reduce or enlarge the size of the image being scanned.

A scanner's *threshold* is the point at which it reads a dot as either black or white, when scanning line art or black and white images. This is critical because, if set incorrectly, the threshold can cause certain areas to drop out or plug up. Some scanners supply a preview mode so you can set the threshold and check the results without going through the time-consuming process of first scanning, then checking. For example, you can use careful tweaking of threshold controls to minimize the unwanted thickening of thin lines caused by interpolation.

Apple bundles Light Source's Ofoto scanning software with its Color One-Scanner. Ofoto (which is written by Robert Cook, who also worked on Pixar's RenderMan) is outstanding software that, for the first time, provides automatic pre-scanning adjustments to make great scans possible without a lot of tweaking. Light Source also sells Ofoto separately for both PC and Mac.

Note that you can make any of these pre-scan adjustments in an image processing program, but doing so before scanning can be faster and easier.

Post-Scanning Controls

Most scanners come with software that allows you both to set certain parameters of the scan and to edit the images once scanned.

Scanners often come bundled with "plug-ins" to popular image processing programs such as Photoshop, Digital Darkroom, and ColorStudio (see Figure 2.14). This lets you scan from within the program—a nice convenience, since that's where the images usually end up for correction anyway. Sometimes, scanners are even bundled with full-fledged versions of these programs, or with "light editions" that do not have all the features of the shrink-wrapped products. Most scanners now come bundled with "Twain" drivers that allow scanning from within popular image editing programs.

KPT-Pixelwind Filter ⌘ 606

KPT-Diffuse More Filter ⌘ 607

KPT-Fine Edges Soft Filter ⌘ 608

KPT-Sharpen Intensify Filter ⌘ 609

There are many filters you can use and a lot of adjustments you can make to an image. Two of the most common are *diffusion dither* and *sharpening.*

Dithering patterns reconfigure the dot patterns of a scan to improve image clarity. Diffusion is one of the most common and useful of these filters. Sharpening reduces blurriness, particularly in details. Generally, sharpening is done after the scan in an image-processing program; but a few scanners include a sharpening filter in their software packages.

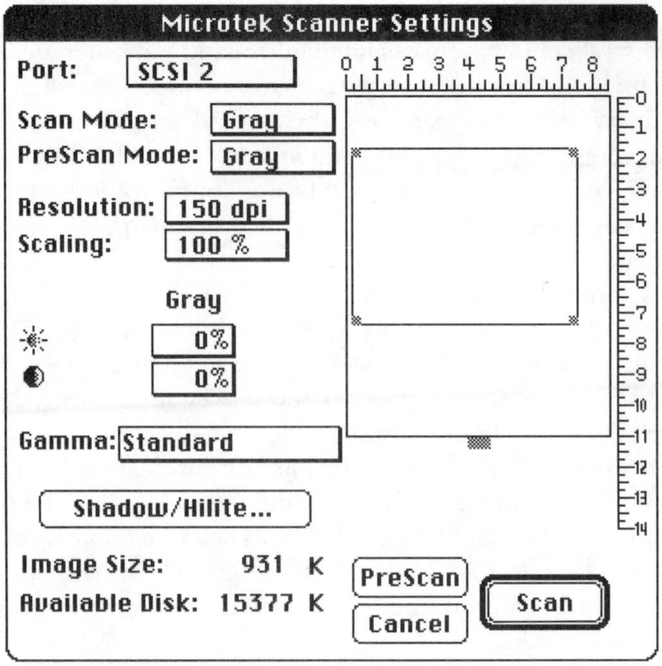

Microtek Scanner Settings

Port: [SCSI 2]

Scan Mode: [Gray]
PreScan Mode: [Gray]

Resolution: [150 dpi]
Scaling: [100 %]

Gray

☀ [0%]
◑ [0%]

Gamma: [Standard]

[Shadow/Hilite...]

Image Size: 931 K
Available Disk: 15377 K

[PreScan]
[Cancel]
[Scan]

**Figure 2.14
Scanner box
plug-in dialog
box.**

Getting a Good Scan

Scanning is an acquired skill, and achieving acceptable results can require much repetition and trial and error. While there is no substitute for experience, here are some tips that can help you get started:

- *Remember: Garbage in, garbage out (GIGO).* Begin with the best possible images. You can correct a lot with image processing software, but you'll get the best results by starting with a clean image.

- Before scanning an image, concentrate on the darkest and lightest areas. If you get these right, chances are the rest of the image will follow suit.

- *Be prepared to tweak.* Although push-button scanning is now upon us, you may have to process scans to get the best results.

- Many factors contribute to *scan quality.* Flatbed scanners typically have a "sweet spot" in the middle, where scans will be sharpest. If your scans start out sharp in the middle and get gradually fuzzy, your images are probably too big for the bed.

- If your image is fuzzy throughout, your scanner may not be calibrated correctly. Scan an image of thick black lines and see if they register correctly. If there are colored halos around the lines, your scanner needs to be calibrated to tighten up registration.

- If white areas of scans are too dull or bright, or if they have color casts, the intensity of one of the light sources is out of whack; you can correct this condition with white balance calibration.

Handling Large Images

Twenty-four-bit color scans produce some of the largest files ever encountered by the desktop computer. It is not uncommon for some images to reach 20, 30, or even 50Mb and more. Even an $8 \times 10''$ color image scanned at 300 dpi will be well over 15Mb. This means you won't even be able to open such images without much more memory than the average desktop computer is born with.

As we mentioned earlier, 24-bit images aren't really worth the trouble for multimedia projects that will be shown on a standard 72-dpi monitor. However, if you are already handling these large color files or plan to do so, you may find the following tips helpful:

- *Buy lots of memory!* The more memory you have, the easier it will be to manipulate large images. Remember that you'll need to have free RAM equal to twice the size of the typical images you work with so that you can undo image edits if necessary.

- *Get a video accelerator.* Even if you do have a lot of RAM, screen redrawing on complex color images can be glacial. If you work with these images a lot, consider investing in a video accelerator; it will greatly speed up drawing operations. (See the "CPU, Video, and SCSI Accelerators section.")

- *Use software compression.* Software compression is not a new concept. Often large programs are compressed to reduce the number of disks in retail software packages. But existing compression algorithms were developed for text, and will generally provide only about 50 percent (2:1) reduction of the bitmaps that make up scans.

There are many utilities that use the *JPEG* compression standard, an algorithm developed specifically for image file reduction. These programs include Quick-Time, PicturePress, Colorsqueeze, and ImpressIt, as well as the common image editing programs.

Text compression algorithms use *lossless* compression, which does not remove any information as it squeezes files. Clearly, you don't want the computer deciding what words or sentences you don't really need. JPEG, on the other hand, uses *lossy* compression, which does cut out some, theoretically expendable, information. You can adjust how much data is removed to reduce file size. Savings can be tremendous, even when the information removed does not result in any detectable image degradation. Using one of the JPEG utilities, you can reduce a 15Mb file to 1Mb or less.

- *Scan at high resolutions only when necessary.* Consider your delivery medium. Again, if your scans are part of a multimedia presentation that will be played back on 8-bit color monitors, there is no point in overscanning at 24-bits. Avoiding overscanning will considerably decrease the size of image files.

We've covered most of the really critical issues of scanner performance, such as resolution and image quality, but how do you apply this information when buying a scanner? Probably the best way is to take an image to your local computer store and try scanning it in with a few different models. This will give you some feeling both for the process and for what is possible with the current technology.

Another excellent source of information is the trade press. Magazines such as *MacUser, MacWorld, PC Computing, Byte*, and *PC Magazine* publish excellent equipment reviews and usually do a yearly scanner roundup.

Here are a few tips to keep in mind when shopping for a scanner:

- Look for a scanner with a color preview feature. It can save time by letting you look at a representation of the scanned image before you actually make the scan. This allows you to make image tweaks and corrections and see the results before you scan.

- Some scanners will save images to disk—a real convenience when working with limited memory.

- Make sure that images are saved in common file formats that can be read by most applications.

- If you are scanning fine detail such as line art, invest in a scanner with a high optical resolution—600 dpi, for example. Remember, however, that high-resolution scanners will also readily detect such unwanted detritus as dirt on the scanning surface and flaws in the object being scanned.

- Bundled software isn't always "free"; it can add to the cost of a scanner. You may be able to save money by buying an image processing program separately.

- Scanners that connect to the SCSI port rather than the modem or serial ports will be faster.

- If scanner color and tonal accuracy are of the utmost importance in your work, and you have the time, you can scan the same image using a number of different scanners and save the images to disk. Then open them in an image processing program such as Photoshop. Choose "Histogram" from the Image menu, and you'll get a graph of the distribution of pixel values for each color channel. By comparing histograms of the same image produced by different scanners, you can tell if a given scanner is capturing too much or too little of a color or tonal range.

- Avoid hand-held scanners; they're hard to hold still and generally produce poor results in comparison with their deskbound cousins.

CD-ROM Drives

The CD-ROM is one of the driving forces of multimedia. The players are inexpensive, and the disks themselves are cheap to reproduce and hold a whopping 650Mb apiece. Starting in 1994, the silvery discs really took off, becoming popular options in both the business and consumer markets.

- Kodak's Photo CD has introduced the writable or *multisession* CD. (See "Multisession CD-ROM" later in this chapter.)
- New CD technology is leading to the release of faster drives with even greater storage limits (see "The Need for Speed" below).

Many Apple and PC-compatible systems are shipped with built-in CD-ROM drives.

- Major software vendors such as Microsoft, Apple, Adobe, Corel, and Macromedia are delivering their products and documentation on CDs instead of floppies.

Like scanners and many hard drives, CD-ROM drives are ordinarily connected to a computer through a SCSI port. Macs have these built-in, but PCs do not. If your PC doesn't already have a CD-ROM drive, you can buy one with the requisite adaptor. Look for a drive with a card that uses the faster SCSI-2 standard. Some sound cards have built-in CD-ROM adaptors, but this method slows disk access and transfer rates (unless the card includes a SCSI adaptor).

As of this writing, alternative ways to hook up CD-ROM drives to PCs were becoming more widely available. Some drives can be attached via an IDE connection in the way most PC hard drives are connected. (See sidebar on "Connecting Devices to the PC: SCSI or IDE?")

Some drives can connect through a PC parallel port and include a pass-through so you can still use your printer. These drives are generally used with PC notebook computers, which lack SCSI connectors. (Some notebooks, such as Apple's Power-Books and certain Toshiba and TI models, do incorporate SCSI ports, however.) Sony makes a CD-ROM drive that connects through a notebook's PC card slot.

The Need for Speed

The CD-ROM drive standard today is called double speed, sometimes abbreviated as 2X. These drivers are being superseded by 4X and 6X units, but CD-ROMs themselves need to be designed with these faster drives in mind. To date, most have not.

One of the most important considerations when buying a CD-ROM drive is speed, particularly when the drive is being used in a multimedia application. Speed is measured in two ways: *access time* and *transfer rate*. These parameters were originally defined for audio CDs in the '70s by Sony and Philips, who

**Figure 2.15
CD-ROM drive.**

included them in their *Red Book* standard. In the '80s, the *Yellow Book* addendum extended the standard to CD-ROMs.

Access time (or seek time as it's also known) measures how long it takes a drive to find a particular chunk of data. This is most important in CD-ROM–based text databases, which require the drive to hop around and find lots of bits of information. Access times of less than 300 milliseconds (ms) are considered decent; less than 200ms is excellent—that is what most 2X drives can reach. It's generally agreed that QuickTime movie playback from CD requires an access time of 400ms or less.

Transfer rate is a measure of how fast a drive can read and transfer information to the CPU and display. For multimedia, in which rapid and smooth display of images is paramount, this measurement is more important than access time. 2X drives have transfer rates of 300 Kb per second, adequate for delivering most types of multimedia data direct from CD.

Look for a drive with a data buffer—most have them these days—and the bigger the better. Buffers smooth the drive's delivery of data to the computer, eliminating gaps and pauses. For multimedia playback, we recommend a buffer of at least 64K (256K is better).

CD-ROMs and Audio CDs
Everybody wonders why they can't save a few hundred bucks and just hook up a $99 audio CD player to their computer and read CD-ROM discs. Well, you just can't; so stop wondering.

Seriously, even though the blank discs themselves are identical, the data types of audio and computer CDs are incompatible. CD-ROM players have special electronics that checks and rechecks data several times as it's being read. When you listen to an audio CD, you won't miss a skipped bit or two; but with computer data, every bit is critical.

Audio CD players do not have the beefed-up drive and head mechanisms that allow CD-ROM drives to survive repeated data access. And, naturally, most audio CD players lack SCSI interfaces.

On the other hand, many CD-ROM drives do incorporate the *Red Book* standard (i.e., they will play audio CDs), so if you don't have either type of CD player yet, buy an audio-compatible CD-ROM drive. That way, the next time your computer won't boot, you can shove it out the window and still be able to play some nice Brahms to soothe your nerves. Sony's CD-ROM Discman plays both types of CDs and is about the size of its tiny portable audio CD players.

File Formats

The International Standards Organization (ISO) has established a standard CD-ROM file system format. ISO 9660 ensures that different computer systems will be able to recognize the files on any CD conforming to the standard. This standard, also known as CD-ISO, has been widely adopted, despite the flood of competing formats (see "Alternate CD Formats" below).

The Mac's native file system format, the Hierarchical File System (HFS) differs from the ISO standard. However, with both the ISO 9660 driver and Apple's Foreign File Access extension in your system folder, you should have no trouble reading most CDs intended for the Mac. These drivers are normally bundled with CD-ROM drives. PCs can read ISO 9660 disks, but not HFS formatted discs.

Note that there is a big difference between file *recognition* and file *compatibility.* Even though most CDs are now recorded using the ISO 9660 spec, if you are using a Mac, you'll be able to read and use only those files on the CD that are *Mac* files. For any other CDs, such as those intended for use under DOS, the ISO spec means only that you can mount the disc and transfer its files to your Mac. The files are still DOS files, and you would still have to convert them using file translation software. And, of course, any application software on the CD would be for DOS and not compatible with the Mac.

Today, many CDs—games, other consumer titles, and even the Power Tools disc—will play on both the Mac and PC.

Alternative CD Formats

A few years ago, when we wrote the first edition of this book, there was an alphabet soup of competing CD standards—IBM's CD-ROM XA, Sony's MMCD, Commodore's CD-32, Tandy's VIS. Happily, for the PC user, none of these formats has really caught on, leaving us with the perfectly adequate, plain old vanilla CD-ROM format.

Meanwhile, the popularity of the CD-ROM format is leading to a host of optimizations that should make the format cheaper, less power hungry (for notebook computer drives), and above all, higher capacity.

At this writing, consumer giants Sony, Phillips, Toshiba, and Time Warner are duking it out to determine who will establish a new technical standard for CD-ROMs that will hold up to 9.6Gb—15 times the capacity of today's disks. The rival consortia already have the technology—it remains only to get the entertainment and computer industries to adopt a standard. The higher capacity disks are designed to hold feature-length digital movies for the consumer market, but the new format would be a boon to computer users too.

Multisession CD-ROM

CD-ROMs used to be read-only devices. (Indeed, it's in their name: ROM stands for "read-only memory.") Even manufacturers creating a master CD could only write to it once.

Now all of that is changing. When Kodak was developing Photo CD, they realized that consumers would go to their photo-finishers, put a couple of rolls' worth of exposures on a Photo CD, and still have a whole bunch of room left. So Kodak and a few drive manufacturers wrote the *Orange Book*, or multisession CD spec.

A multisession drive will read Photo CDs that have been written to more than once—a capability you'll need if you plan to put a lot of pictures on Photo CD. Multisession drives are also required for some interactive disc products. If you don't already have a drive, get one with at least single-session Photo CD compatibility; that way you'll be able to tap into the large store of stock photos being released on Photo CDs.

Cutting Your Own CDs

The *Orange Book* spec caused prices for CD recorders to fall overnight—from $30,000 to under $2,000. Sony, Pinnacle, and Phillips now make inexpensive recorders. Companies such as Meridian Data Systems, Kodak, and Dataware sell these drives under their own labels, sometimes bundling them with large hard disks from which to transfer data to the CD (see Figure 2.16).

Manufacturers also generally bundle CD-ROM burning software. One of the best software products on the market for this purpose is Astarte's Toast CD-ROM Pro, which is distributed in the U.S. by Catalogic Corporation.

Some of the drives contain big data buffers of several megabytes or more; this helps when you write data from a slow hard disk or other storage device. The hard disk you use must be relatively fast, sustaining data transfer rates of at least 150K per second to drive the recorder. The drives write data at 15 to 20Mb per minute, which means you can cut an entire 600Mb CD in about a half an hour.

If you're in the market for a recorder, look for one with "on-the-fly 150 recording." This feature allows you to transfer data directly to the recorder without first having to create a space-grabbing "disk image" in your hard disk.

**Figure 2.16
Sony's low-cost
CD-ROM recorder.**

Blank CDs run between $10 and $20. The discs are coated with a photosensitive dye that is burned away in intricate patterns by the CD recorder's laser. These patterns carry the CD's data and simulate the patterns of tiny pits used in commercial CDs.

When the disc is read, light from the reader's laser is reflected from the disc's surface. When the laser hits a pit, less light is reflected. These reflections are converted to digital data that is readable by the computer.

Although you cannot change the data once it is written to the CD, thanks to the multisession technology, you can append data as many times as you want, up to the total capacity of the disc. When you are finished recording a CD, if you don't plan on appending any more data in future sessions, you "fixate" the disc. Fixated discs can be read by standard CD-ROM drives, while discs that have not yet been fixated can only be read by multisession drives. Regardless of the disc's state of completion, all are recorded in standard ISO 9660 format.

The new CD recorders make it easy to cut your own CDs, letting you do fast and inexpensive prototyping. But they simplify only the physical process of CD publishing. There are still many factors to consider in creating a successful CD-ROM product: data conversion and filtering, database definitions, indexing, and other aspects of software design and development.

Besides the obvious implications for CD-ROM publishing, CD-ROM recorders pave the way for a new inexpensive storage medium and are even beginning to rival both the storage capacity and speed of magneto-optical disc (see "Storage Systems," later in the chapter).

Videodiscs

Videodiscs, sometimes called laserdiscs, are an excellent source and playback medium for video. The resolution is much higher than videotape (at least 400 lines, compared with 240 for VHS), and information access is generally faster too. In addition, laserdiscs offer a rock-solid source of still video frames, far better than tape, which often yields jittery and out-of-focus still frames.

Laserdiscs are frequently used as the playback medium in training and public kiosk applications, where interactivity and high quality are important. While laserdiscs are beginning to be eclipsed by digital video, until CDs get to the point of handling full-motion video, laserdiscs are the best bet if your application demands high quality video playback.

A number of vendors offer computer-controllable videodiscs that also play back regular videodiscs; once you see *Star Wars* on disc, you'll pitch your VCR. Many of these players also feature digital sound. Top manufacturers of videodisc drives include Sony, Panasonic, and Pioneer.

Players can have one or more of the following "control levels":

- Level I: You can control operation from the player or by remote control. This is the standard VCR-type control.

- Level II: Interactive branching software is imbedded in the disc and read by the player.

- Level III: The player can be computer-controlled.

If you're going to use laserdiscs in an interactive application, you'll want a player that offers Level III support. Level II support is important for industrial kiosk applications in which discs can be played back without a computer controlling them. When shopping for a drive, look for one with two channels of digital audio for playing back high fidelity sound.

Like CDs, videodiscs are read-only media; but they are fairly inexpensive and quick to master. A number of service bureaus will duplicate an interactive presentation onto videodisc in just a few days for less than $500.

Working with Images

Once you've acquired images and sounds, the real work of multimedia begins. Using a media integration program like Director, you can combine your captured images and create dynamic presentations that have an impact far greater than simple text.

The equipment that supports this creation process—the display, acceleration, and storage facilities such as hard disks and RAM—affect the ease with which you can work with large and unwieldy image files.

Display Systems

Monitors are among the most important of computer components. After all, you spend a lot of time staring into them. Luckily, both advanced features and the range of choices have increased lately, while prices have dropped. Applications such as desktop publishing, color prepress, photo retouching, and animation have spurred a demand for bigger displays and 24-bit color.

This growing user demand and the competition among vendors for their business have turned monitors into hot commodities. This is great news for multimedia creators, who can make good use of more screen real estate and the realism of color.

The most important monitor attributes are size, resolution, and color depth—8- or 24-bit. (There are many excellent grayscale monitors as well; we're assuming that color is more important for multimedia use.) A host of more specific qualities such as sharpness, contrast, and convergence are covered in the "Display Characteristics" sidebar.

Monitors fall into three size categories: small (12″, 13″, 14″, 15″); medium (16″ and 17″); and large (19″, 20″, 21″). Unless you already have a monitor, or are working on a shoestring, consider getting at least a 17″ display. Today's graphical interfaces let you work between multiple windows, but you lose much of this advantage if there isn't room to see them. Also, with a smaller screen, you'll spend lots of time zooming in on images to see detail and then getting impatient while the screen redraws. Finally, many people have reported problems with eyestrain and headaches from squinting at the tiny pictures displayed by the smaller screens.

Until around 1992, the 13″ monitor was pretty much the Mac standard; but now Apple has replaced it with a 14″ model and also offers a 16″ monitor. This, along with the Quadra's built-in 24-bit color support, has pushed 16″ monitors into the forefront. Prices have also dropped to well below $1,000; and with 70 percent more pixels than a 13″ monitor, all of this is good news for multimedia.

On the PC side, 14″ and 15″ monitors are generally bundled with multimedia systems, with a 17″ monitor often substituted in high-end systems.

If you do use a larger monitor, you will have to use a video card; a large monitor has more pixels than a smaller one, so large screen redrawing is slower unless a video card with higher video transfer rates is added. Also, add-in video cards have more VRAM to support the extra information in 16- or 24-bit color for each of these extra pixels.

If you are going to use a smaller monitor for a Macintosh, shop around a bit —you'll save some money. Many people use the Apple 13″ monitor, which is built around the well-regarded Sony Trinitron display. Instead, you can save a few hundred dollars and get a 14″ multisync display made for the PC.

Multisync monitors are so named because the PCs don't have a standard video frequency, so monitors must sense the video frequency coming from a given PC and lock on (or sync) with it to display its signal. Because of high volume trade and intense competition in the PC market, monitors are generally lower priced than in the Mac world. You'll need an adaptor to use a PC monitor on a Mac, but they cost only $15, or thereabouts.

Resolution

Resolution is a bit of a puzzle, although it doesn't have to be. Basically, it refers to the number of pixels in a given display, and is usually expressed as dots per

Display Characteristics

The best way to choose among monitors is to go down to the monitor store and try them out for yourself. Bring a file of the type you usually use—video capture, scanned in photograph, 24-bit color graphic, or whatever. Once you have narrowed the field by choosing the size, resolution, and color support you want, you can consult the following list to familiarize yourself with some of the finer points.

If you walk in and ask for a monitor with low reflectivity and a high vertical scan rate, the salesperson may give you a blank stare, but at least you'll know what you're talking about. The trade press (particularly any of the monthlies beginning with "PC" or "Mac") do periodic exhaustive tests of monitors based on many of the criteria in this list.

- *Sharpness.* A monitor that displays sharp images does not allow areas of detail to bleed together into fuzzy patches. Not surprisingly, sharpness is easier to maintain in higher resolution monitors (over 72 dpi), where pixels are packed closer together.

- *Brightness.* Lots of people like to crank up the brightness on their monitors (we do this on our notebooks when traveling and end up with about 10 minutes of battery life). But brightness is related to sharpness and focus. The higher the brightness, the more intense the beams blasting electrons at the screen to make a picture; and as the beams grow more intense, they focus less precisely.

- *Contrast.* Contrast is the range between the darkest and lightest values that can be displayed. For nice crisp images you want this range to be as great as possible.

- *Convergence.* This is a measure of how precisely the red, green, and blue electrons align to render different colors onscreen. Misconvergence is what happens when the electrons don't align so well—you'll see a little rainbow-colored halo around objects and type. In fact, looking at small type onscreen is a good way to see if a monitor's colors are converging properly. If you work with type a lot, misconvergence is particularly noticeable and will drive you batty very quickly. (A similar effect, registration, is described in the earlier section on "scanners.")

- *Curvature.* The electron beams that sweep across the inside of the screen first pass through a device called a shadow mask, a grid of little holes that helps to align the beams. But when the beams get to screen edges, the angle causes electrons to leak through a few adjacent holes as well, which makes a fuzzy screen image. A curved monitor keeps the beams aimed at the correct holes even at screen edges. The technology for flat screens has made them more costly than curved screens, even with recent advances that have brought down their price; but many people find they look better and have less distortion.

- *Distortion.* Monitors should show objects the way they were originally intended. Thus, a circle should be displayed as a circle and not as an oval, and a square should be square and not some other sort of rhomboid.

continued

- *Reflectivity* (antiglare). Some manufacturers put an antiglare coating on their screens to keep light reflections from becoming a nuisance. The best way to prevent glare is to use the display in an area free of direct lighting.
- *Calibration.* If you are creating images with colors that must be as accurate as possible, choose a monitor that includes gamma correction software. This is the technique used in image processing and scanning programs. Gamma correction allows you to adjust a monitor to match the colors in a scanned-in image or the color values of a printer or another monitor.
- *Refresh Rate* (Vertical Scan). The refresh rate measures how fast the screen is redrawn from top to bottom. Make sure your monitor has a vertical refresh rate of 65 Hertz or higher; otherwise it may flicker. This is a factor of the display card as well; some cards can drive monitors at a vertical refresh rate of as high as 120 Hz.
- *Dot Pitch.* This refers to the proximity of the screen pixels. In 12″ to 14″ monitors, a dot pitch of .28 or less is good. For larger monitors, look for a dot pitch of less than .31.

inch, or dpi. The lowest rung is 640 × 480 pixels, known as the VGA standard in the PC world. This is the resolution found in small 13″ and 14″ displays.

Typical resolutions in larger monitors are 832 × 624 and 1024 × 768. These higher resolutions often result in sharper pictures because a given image is drawn with more pixels than the same image on a lower resolution monitor.

The Mac display system is based on 72 dpi. Monitors that have 72 pixels in an inch of screen space will display an image that it is the same size as it will be printed. Thus, 72 dpi monitors are called WYSIWYG, for what-you-see-is-what-you-get.

People working with photographic images often prefer monitors with higher resolutions of 77, 82, 85, or 96 dpi. This is because the pixel grid—the space between pixels—is reduced in these monitors, making displayed images more tightly composed, smoother, and more like photographs. However, these monitors will display images that are smaller in size than they will be when printed. This is an annoyance (see Figure 2.17).

Choosing a Monitor

Selecting a monitor, like choosing most software, has a lot to do with what you spend most of your time doing. The two biggest questions are probably what size monitor to get and whether to get a 24-bit display card.

Desktop publishers prefer 17″ or larger monitors so they can display multiple pages and windows at once. Certainly multimedia developers can also have a

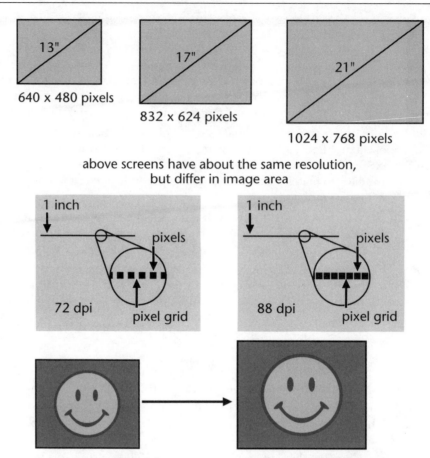

**Figure 2.17
Resolution and
image size.**

lot of windows open, so big screen displays can be very useful. As for 24-bit color; don't get it unless you really need it; if you're not sure, you probably don't need it.

Despite the advantages of large monitors and 24-bit color, a great many multimedia developers stick with the basic Apple or PC 13″ or 14″ monitors and 8 bits of color. A big reason for this is that the vast majority of multimedia consumers already have this setup. It's important to test on machines that your target audience is using.

Here are a few things to consider when monitor shopping:

The ability to display 24-bit images is a function of the display card, not the monitor; so you can always start out with an 8-bit display system and upgrade to a 24-bit card later, keeping the same monitor.

The Bad ELF

The world has become much safer ever since we've realized what a dangerous place it is. Asbestos, saccharin, PCBs, other people's cigarette smoke, disappearing ozone layer—the list is growing.

Now there is concern over radiation emitted from monitors. (Actually, your mom knew this a long time ago—remember about not sitting too close to the TV?) Although monitors give off a stunning variety of emissions, attention has centered on extremely low frequency radiation, or ELF. There is no definitive evidence that ELF emissions are in fact harmful, but several tests have raised doubts. A Finnish study published in late 1992 found that pregnant women using VDTs are more likely to suffer a miscarriage than those who were not exposed during pregnancy. Monitors also emit VLF radiation that is similarly suspect.

ELF emanates from all parts of the monitor, but tests show that the highest radiation is from the back and sides. This is a good thing, since not many people stare at the back of their displays for long periods of time (except when trying to figure out how to turn them on).

If you are concerned about ELF, try and find a monitor that meets both the MPR and the even-more-stringent TCO '92 standards of the Swedish government. The International Radiation Protection Association (IRPA) has also adopted standards regarding ELF emissions.

Many well-known monitor vendors now offer displays they claim meet the Swedish standards. These include Apple, NEC, Mitsubishi, Sigma, and Nanao.

Monitors that use BNC connectors at the display end of the cable generally produce sharper images onscreen. If your monitor comes with a cable with a DB15 connector but has the BNC connectors on the back of the monitor, consider upgrading the cable with BNC connectors.

Most monitors now have some form of antiglare treatment. Etching is an inferior process that can result in distorted images. Coatings are better. The most common coatings are silica and antireflective; the latter seems most effective—and more costly.

Like a lot of other computer equipment, monitors are heavily discounted; so shop around. You can save a lot by ordering through the mail, but repairs may be a problem if something goes wrong with the display while it's still under warranty.

Hardware Acceleration

Next time you're staring dumbly at your computer while it spends 18 hours rendering a 24-bit 3-D image, consider adding an accelerator card rather than throwing out your box altogether and taking up *T'ai Chi.*

Image processing speed can be greatly enhanced when you add some sort of accelerator card. They come in several varieties:

- *CPU accelerators* speed up not only your machine's central processing unit, but also other functions such as I/O (input/output), keyboard, mouse, and hard drives.

- *Video accelerators*—also known as graphics, Windows (PC), or QuickDraw (Mac) accelerators—accelerate the graphics routines that display images onscreen.

- *SCSI accelerators* speed up the transfer of data from disks and other SCSI devices.

Since multimedia development and playback stress every element of system hardware, all of these accelerators can help. So which should you look at first? The consensus seems to be that you'll realize the most immediate benefits from a CPU accelerator; although if you're doing lots of image manipulation, a graphics accelerator would be very useful.

It's best to install a CPU accelerator when you're doing heavy-duty image processing such as image enhancement and rendering. But you'll also realize overall system speed enhancements, whereas video and SCSI accelerators are targeted at specific tasks and applications. Also, on slower Macs in the II series, the CPU is typically the bottleneck, not QuickDraw or the SCSI interface.

Clearly, if you're constantly working with really big image or sound files and you already have a fast or accelerated Mac, you'll want to give serious attention to both SCSI and video acceleration.

CPU Acceleration

CPU accelerators take many forms. Some are chips that replace your old CPU chip. On the Macintosh platform, the appearance of PowerMacs has all but killed CPU accelerator: for the $600 to $1,000 they cost, you can almost buy a low-end PowerMac. By the time you read this, Apple will very likely have stopped shipping its older 68030 and 68040 machines, which will further push users towards the new PowerMac architecture.

If you have an older machine, or even an older PowerMac, you can inexpensively up performance with a "CPU booster" from companies such as KS Labs, Newer Technology, Mobius Technologies, and Sonnet Technologies. The upgrades simply double your CPU's clock rate and cost only $150 or less.

For about $600, you can upgrade your '040 Mac to a PowerMac with Apple's Power Macintosh Upgrade Card. Owners of '030 Macs will have to shell out about twice as much for a complete motherboard replacement, which makes simply buying a new or used PowerMac a better proposition.

Owners of 486-based PCs can check out Intel's Pentium OverDrive chip, which converts the older processor to the fastest chip currently available. Currently the upgrade is only $300 to $400 on the street. By 1996, machines bearing Intel's new P6 chip should hit the bricks, running at about twice the speed of Pentium-based PCs.

Upgrading RAM

To squeeze the most out of your accelerator, you may also have to upgrade the RAM in your machine. RAM comes in different speed ratings—150, 120, 100, 80, 70, and 60ns. A stock Mac IIci typically uses 100ns RAM. This may diminish the performance gains of an accelerator, which will generally require RAM speeds in the double-digit range.

Most accelerators employ a RAM cache to store often-requested data and instructions. RAM caches provide additional speed by reducing the number of times the accelerator must go to the system RAM for memory access. You will often need to come up with the RAM for this yourself. Depending on the card, you can sometimes simply move some of your motherboard RAM onto the accelerator board to supply the cache.

Video Acceleration

Once you begin to deal with 24-bit images and large screens, you start placing heavy demands on the system software that handles screen refreshing. The system simply has many more pixels to update than it does with 1-bit images on 12″ screens. The result is the agonizingly slow screen refreshing that graphic artists have been suffering for years and that a whole new generation of multimedia developers and users are now experiencing.

The new PCI bus being adopted by both the Mac and PC platforms greatly speeds the traffic between all types of add-in cards and the rest of the computer. PCI Cards, including the fastest video accelerators, have been available for the PC for some time and will make their debut for the PowerMacs in 1995.

Video accelerators are available for all bit depths and monitor sizes, although boards that handle 24-bit color and 20″ or 21″ screens are more costly. If you already have a 24-bit color card, you may not need a video accelerator; many color cards include video acceleration. Depending on your base machine and the type of work you're doing, you can expect screen drawing to speed up about fivefold with an accelerator.

Video accelerators for the PC can be had for $200 to $300, while their Mac brethren are somewhat more costly. Note that there are specialized video accelerators optimized for image editing applications such as Photoshop. Manufacturers include Adaptive Solutions Inc. and EA Research Inc.

3-D accelerators are a relatively new phenomenon brought on by the growing popularity of 3-D graphics for everything from games to spreadsheets. Cards that significantly boost 3-D rendering and display performance are available for both the PC and Mac.

You know multimedia has hit its stride when there's a whole category of accelerators devoted to speeding up *movies*. That's right. For a couple of hundred bucks, you can get a movie accelerator that usually includes a general video accelerator. Actually, in a year or two most Macs and PCs will have onboard movie acceleration. Digital video is here to stay.

SCSI Acceleration

Computers are complicated and modular; so even though you may have an accelerated CPU and a video accelerator to boot, you might still find yourself celebrating another birthday before that giant paint or image file opens up. That's because you computer's IDE or SCSI hard disk interface is transferring data from your hard disk at only a few megabytes per second, or even less.

On the PC platform, Enhanced IDE offers improved performance over basic IDE drives and cards found in most vanilla PCs. The Mac uses the competing SCSI format for drives and other peripherals (SCSI devices are also available for the PC—see sidebar titled "Connecting Devices to the PC: SCSI or IDE?"). Like Enhanced IDE, the newer SCSI-2 spec boosts performance over traditional SCSI.

The SCSI-2 spec allows for both *Fast* and *Wide* options. SCSI-2 cards implementing the Fast option boost SCSI performance to the 5 to 10Mbs range. The SCSI-2 Wide option doubles the SCSI data path from 8 to 16 bits. Fast and Wide cards slam 20Mb/sec from your hard disk to the CPU.

SCSI-2 and Enhanced IDE cards can make a big difference when transferring large files from a fast hard disk, but make sure your SCSI device *is* fast—otherwise, an accelerator won't help. On the PC, bus mastering SCSI cards further improve performance by removing all burden from the CPU. Also, some SCSI cards may include cache RAM to further enhance performance.

Storage Systems

Of all computer resources, multimedia places perhaps the greatest demands on storage systems. Multimedia poses a triple threat to storage media: space, access time, and transfer rate. Some *single* 24-bit images won't even fit on a small hard disk, let alone in RAM. Then there is the problem of access time. Experts recommend, for example, a hard disk with an access time of at least 18ms for getting four-track sound files off the disk. And, of course, the storage device that will handle real-time transfer of full-motion video has yet to be invented (although MPEG-compressed video is close).

The third problem is transfer rate. The fastest hard disks will transfer about 3 or 4Mb per second, but the SCSI interfaces in all but the fastest Macs only support rates of 1.5 to 3Mb/sec. If you're constantly moving large files back and forth between your storage devices and RAM for display and manipulation, you'll definitely want to look at adding SCSI acceleration (discussed in the preceding section).

Another issue is portability; transporting large multimedia files can be a challenge.

Removable hard disk cartridges offer a solution; but if you need to move big files around a lot, you'll have to use a portable drive in addition to your fixed storage systems. While removable disks are fast enough for use as primary storage for everyday work, their access and transfer rates can't cope with large multimedia files.

Luckily, there has been an explosion in storage technologies over the past few years. You now can choose between many large capacity options. While none of these technologies can, by themselves, solve all of the multimedia demands of large capacity, fast access, high transfer rates, and portability, several will do the job in combination (see Figure 2.18).

Hard Disk Drives

Disk space usage has a way of staying about the same, regardless of your disk's capacity; so if you have a 120Mb disk, it's generally about as full as a 500Mb disk would be. That's just the way life is. But it shouldn't deter you from getting a mid-size or large disk, because you're going to need it. These days, midsize disks are about 200 to 500Mb for a good size for multimedia work (unless you're working a lot with digital video).

Disk speed is a consideration, too. If you're using a relatively high-powered machine such as a Quadra or Pentium, you should spend a little more and get a disk with fast access time (in the neighborhood of 10 to 12ms) and a transfer rate of at least a few megabytes per second. The CPUs in these machines are fast enough so that disk speed would be a limiting factor.

Generally, very high capacity drives of 1Gb and more also offer the fastest access times and transfer rates. This conveniently gets you the key performance considerations along with capacity in one package. But you'll pay for it, too, since fast, high-capacity drives cost over $1,000. (Recently, with the advent of Enhanced IDE drives, the cost has further dropped to the $500 range for some EIDE drives.)

If you are in the market for a high capacity drive, make sure it is rated to handle time-based data such as video or sound. While these components are in binary format like any other type of computer data, they are more susceptible to an effect called *thermal recalibration*. This is a process performed by the drive's controller to compensate for variations in the disk's substrate as it heats during use. While the recalibration process—a few hundred milliseconds every hour or so—is very rapid, I/O functions are temporarily suspended. That means that during the very long read/writes for video or sound, you may loose some data as the drive recalibrates.

Before multimedia became widespread, no one noticed this effect, since most I/O operations for text or graphics are only a few seconds long. As large drives are more frequently used to store time-based data, the problem is likely to go away, because manufacturers can simply modify drive controllers so that they don't perform recalibration during I/O.

RAID and Striping Technology

RAID (for Redundant Arrays of Inexpensive Disks) systems use at least two disks in tandem to reduce access time and boost transfer rates. The disks can also mirror one another, so that if one drive fails, the other still has a copy of all your data. This fault tolerance could be very important if you can't afford to lose data should a disk burn out between saves.

Despite its name, RAID (also known as "striping") is not all that cheap. It costs at least $2,000 and can easily range up to $50,000. Still, when combined with SCSI

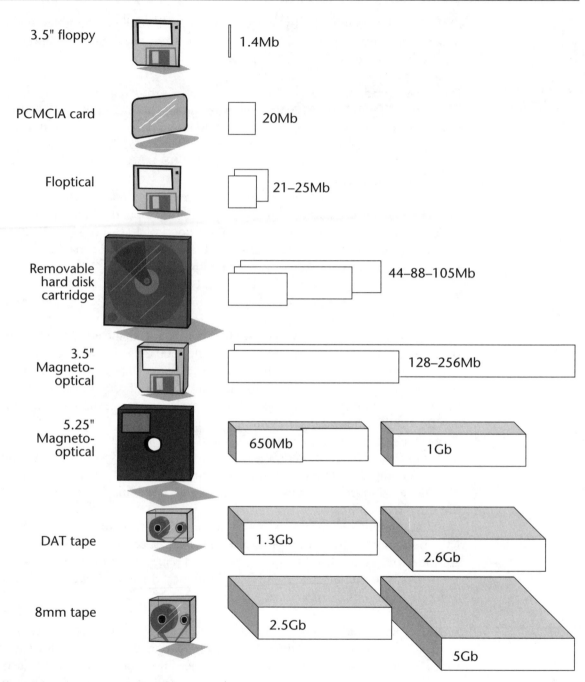

3.5" floppy — 1.4Mb

PCMCIA card — 20Mb

Floptical — 21–25Mb

Removable hard disk cartridge — 44–88–105Mb

3.5" Magneto-optical — 128–256Mb

5.25" Magneto-optical — 650Mb / 1Gb

DAT tape — 1.3Gb / 2.6Gb

8mm tape — 2.5Gb / 5Gb

**Figure 2.18
Different types
of removable
storage media.**

Connecting Devices to the PC: SCSI or IDE?

Just as Macs use the SCSI interface for connecting hard disks and other devices, such as scanners and CD-ROM drives, PCs mostly use the IDE interface. You can use SCSI on the PC, but you'll have to buy an adaptor card first. (Apple has implemented IDE for its internal drives on certain models, including the LC and Quadra 630s, and some PowerBooks).

If you have a PC, should you switch to SCSI? Well, maybe. Some newer PCs have an ATAPI interface that is part of the new and faster (than vanilla IDE) Enhanced IDE standard. If your PC has an ATAPI interface, you can plug an ATAPI-compliant CD-ROM drive into it.

For connecting hard disks to a PC, IDE is cheaper; and once Enhanced IDE catches on, it should surpass SCSI-2 in terms of speed. SCSI has certain advantages, however: You can connect, or daisy-chain, more devices than you can under IDE; and they can separated by several yards, a convenience not possible with IDE. Under SCSI, you can also get simultaneous access to all connected devices, while IDE allows access to only one device at a time. If you do go with SCSI on the PC, look for SCSI cards and devices conforming to the ASPI or SCAM standards, which make configuration easier. (Are these damned abbreviations driving you batty yet? Yeesh.)

---

acceleration, RAID offers the best performance for those engaged in the most demanding of multimedia applications—digital video editing or digital audio recording on the desktop.

Removable Hard Disks, Opticals, and Flopticals

Many people supplement their hard disk storage with a removable cartridge drive, which can be a great convenience. These cartridges hold up to 270Mb apiece, and the drive mechanisms themselves are nearly as fast as hard disks. In general, as a multimedia creator, you should have the fastest disk you can find. Saving graphics images, a task that you will do (or are doing) constantly, is one of the most disk-intensive activities there is.

If you take files to a service bureau for processing and printing, removable drives are handy. The most popular are those built around the SyQuest mechanism. The 44Mb version is pretty much a standard in service bureaus; so if you're looking for compatibility, get one of these. If you just want the flexibility of cartridge storage and don't have to worry about interchanging the cartridges, consider one of the larger drives.

Removable hard drives come in two sizes: 5.25″ and a newer 3.5″ format. Currently, the highest capacity in the 5.25″ format is 200Mb, and those drives can also read older 44Mb and 88Mb cartridges, a distinct compatibility advantage. (However, 200Mb drives can't format 44/88Mb cartridges, and 44/88Mb drives can't read 200Mb disks—got that?)

Iomega makes another popular drive using Bernoulli technology, as well as an innovative product called the Zip Drive that takes 100Mb removable hard disks; the drive sells on the street for less than $200, the disks for about $15 (Figure 2.19). As of this writing, Iomega is preparing to release a removable drive that uses 1Gb cartridges.

For multimedia developers, whose storage requirements regularly run into the hundreds of megabytes, magneto-optical (MO) drives are an attractive alternative. They come in a 3½″ size that stores 128Mb or 230Mb and a 5¼″ size that holds 650Mb or 1.3Gb. The smallest drives cost about $1,200, and the largest are in the $2,500 to $4,000 range.

The disks themselves go for about $50 and are erasable and rewritable. If you have invested in older and incompatible WORM (write-once read-many) technology, you can get a "multifunction" drive that will read both WORM and MO disks.

Even if the cost and storage capacity of magneto-optical drives is better than that of removable hard drives, their overall performance is not. Both transfer rates and access times fall between those of CD-ROM drives and hard disks. However, some opticals are fast enough to use as "live" storage—so you can get to files more or less right away. Pinnacle Micro's Tahoe Drive, for example, uses 230 Mb disks in the 3.5″ format. It is usable on either the PC or Mac with a SCSI interface; or you can plug it into a PC's parallel, if you don't mind slower performance.

Another type of removable disk is the "floptical." Flopticals combine optical tracking technology with the familiar 3½″ floppy format. Floptical disks hold 21Mb or 25Mb, and floptical drives will also read standard 3½″ floppies. The downside of flopticals is that they are only as fast as floppies, making them unsuitable as primary storage devices.

Tape

Of all storage mechanisms, tape still offers the highest capacity, holding up to 5Gb of data. Tape also boasts the lowest cost per megabyte—from 1 to 15 cents per megabyte (the drivers themselves can be had for about $150). By comparison, MO disks cost about 40 cents per megabyte, while fixed and removable hard disks are in the $2 to $3/Mb range. Of course, tape is also the slowest of storage media and is suitable only for long-term archiving and backup. Tape drives generally connect to SCSI ports on the Mac and are IDE devices for the PC (costlier units can connect to a SCSI card or the PC's parallel port).

There several different types of computer tape:

- *QIC-80* holds up to 250Mb. Once the most popular format, DC2000 is now fading, and the newer high capacity DC6000 is on the rise.

- *QIC-3010* is incompatible with the older DC2000 format. QIC-3010 tapes hold up to 1Gb.

- *Teac* comes in 60Mb, 150Mb, and 600Mb sizes. The 150Mb is the most popular and is offered by many manufacturers. The 60Mb size is on the wane, while the 600Mb capacity is newer and is being adopted rapidly.

- *DAT* uses the 4mm DAT audiotape and comes in 1.3Gb and 2.6Gb sizes.

- *8mm* uses 8mm videotape and is generally slower and more costly than DAT. The most common size is 2.2Gb, but some drives more than double the capacity to over 5Gb.

Which is for you? If your disk drive holds less than 80Mb, don't bother with tape; get a removable hard drive for backups or use floppies. For backing up medium-size disks, a drive using the Teac 150Mb mechanism is probably the best choice. For backups of between 150Mb and 600Mb, consider a drive based on the QUI-3010 tape; for larger chores, DAT is the way to go. We recommend the slower and more expensive 8mm only if your backups are exceedingly large. DAT is also more popular than 8mm, making it a better choice when interchangeability is an issue.

If you don't care about compatibility with anything, check out Pereos' 612 Mb tape drive, which holds astonishingly small tapes and is relatively inexpensive at about $500.

Image Output

Once you've put together a multimedia work, there are number of ways you can present it. If the presentation is interactive and meant to be viewed by one person at a time, the computer itself will work fine.

If your presentation is to be viewed by an audience, and it is not interactive, one option is to print it to tape using a video out card; once on tape, the cassettes are easy to duplicate for wide distribution. Some more advanced 24-bit display and video capture cards include video-out capability.

If your presentation is interactive and also needs to be given to an audience, you'll need to hook up some sort of projection equipment to the computer.

Data Projectors

You can connect the computer to a *data projector* that translates the computer signal into three light beams: red, blue, and green. These combine to form the proper colors and are projected onto a large screen. Data projectors are good for large audiences because they can project an image that measures up to 8 feet across.

They do, however, have several drawbacks. First, they are quite expensive, costing up to $20,000. They are also large and bulky, making them unsuitable for road trips. Further, data projectors aren't compatible with all computer graphics cards. Finally, it takes some experience to get the three beams to converge properly.

**Figure 2.19
Sharp's Data
Projector.
(Reproduced with
the permission of
Sharp Electronics
Corporation.)**

An evolving technology: LCD active matrix projectors are less expensive ($7,000 to $8,000) and more transportable.

Color LCD Panels

Fortunately, technology has again sped to the rescue, this time in the form of compact, full-color projection panels (see Figure 2.19). These panels, about the size of a notebook computer, are ideal for traveling presentations, and recent advances in color display technology have yielded surprising results in quality.

Like data projectors, LCD panels are driven directly from the computer. A panel is placed on an overhead projector that projects its image onto a wall or screen. LCD panels are of two basic types: passive and active matrix. Passive matrix screens are most commonly found in today's notebook computers, although more expensive units feature the active matrix technology.

Passive matrix panels, while costing much less than the newer active matrix models, are unsuitable for multimedia presentations because their scan rate is too low to cope with rapidly changing images. (The same thing happens when you're using a notebook with a passive matrix screen: you move the cursor, and are then unable to find it because the quick movement causes it to disappear temporarily.)

Active matrix screens solve this problem with a much higher refresh rate, and their color support is also much better. Newer models are able to display full 24-bit color. Contrast and resolution are also excellent. If you plan to display full-motion video through a projection panel, you'll definitely need an active matrix panel—one that has the appropriate video in ports.

These new display panels are also ideal for multimedia presentations because they support a number of input sources. Many can handle three or four simultaneous sources, either computer or video. This allows you to give presentations that might have bits and pieces on videotape, videodisc, and several different computers. You can toggle between the sources with a remote control without interrupting your presentation to reconnect or switch anything. You can even program the remote controls to issue computer commands so that you can give an interactive presentation without stepping over to the computer.

The only disadvantage is the cost of these products: currently in the $4,000 to $8,000 range. Active matrix screens are driven by an individual transistor for each pixel, which accounts for their high scan rate and high contrast. It also means that if a single transistor misfires, it could change the content of the data being displayed. For this reason, quality controls are stringent, keeping prices high. Once the manufacturing process is optimized, prices will come down, and this technology will undoubtedly become prevalent (at least until the next toys arrive from Japan).

3

Graphics Tools

A picture may be worth a thousand words when printed on paper, but after it has been scanned, digitized, enhanced, or manipulated, it can be worth not just a thousand words, but a thousand, one hundred thousand, or even one million pixels (see Figure 3.1).

While multimedia most often conjures up the idea of movement, its central element is actually the single, static image. This could be the opening screen of an interactive demo, the background graphics for a slide presentation, or a single frame of animation.

Within the past few years, it has become as easy to change and move pixels around using a desktop computer as it has been, for over a decade, to change and move words via word processing software. With programs like Macromedia's FreeHand, Adobe Photoshop, and Micrografx's Picture Publisher, handling images to be used in multimedia presentations has become fast and, for the most part, friendly.

And if you're Windows user, your ship has finally come in. Creating and manipulating images used to be the province of the Mac, but that is no longer true. Windows now competes head-to-head with the Mac in all three major imaging categories: paint programs, drawing packages, and image editing software. This is partly due to the migration of important packages to Windows from the Mac.

This chapter provides an overview of the tools used to create images, especially as they relate to multimedia. Topics range from the use and importance of images to Photo CD and "color gamuts." While software for handling images has become much easier to use in recent years, it can still seem daunting to those who are unfamiliar with its quirks. In fact, the learning curve can look as fright-

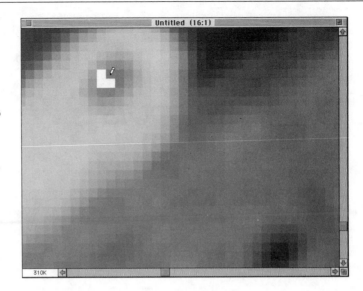

**Figure 3.1
A computerized image is made up of thousands of pixels. Using image editing software, each of the pixels in this screen shot can easily be altered, thus challenging the old bromide that "pictures never lie."**

ening as the first hill of a roller coaster. We hope the following information helps with the ride.

The Importance of Images in Multimedia

There is no doubt that images are an important part of effective communications. Educators, for example, have long known that appealing to as many of the senses as possible enhances the message they're trying to get across. The same idea applies to creating a multimedia presentation. We have already learned to communicate solely with sound in the form of radio; images and words alone in the form of books; and moving images with sound in the form of TV and film. Now it is possible to combine all of those media in communicating an idea. Multimedia has the ability to deliver words, sound, and still and moving images with great fluidity, clarity, and influence.

Despite the kinetic quality of multimedia, static images are at its core. The powerful impact of a still image or illustration can be formidable. Moving images and video simply do not have the content-laden history of still images. Who can forget some of the famous frozen moments in time in the last few decades: the raising of the American flag at Iwo Jima, a woman screaming over the body of an injured student during the Kent State uprising, Jack Ruby shooting Lee Harvey Oswald in the hallway of a Texas jail, Harry Truman triumphantly holding a newspaper's incorrect prediction over his head. These images are instantly recognizable and easily remembered. Images spark the imagination and stimulate the mind.

Drawing vs. Painting

To oversimplify somewhat, drawing tools are typically used when precision is necessary—in technical drawings, for example. Paint tools can help you create work that is more like pictures painted with traditional tools. Paint programs also offer finer color control, down to the individual pixels.

There is another important difference between painting and drawing tools. Objects created with paint tools are *bitmap* objects, so called because they are made up of a collection of dots (or pixels) that correspond directly to one or more "bits" of computer memory. Bitmap images are stored in an image file format that contains information about each pixel, including its color and location. When you use a paint program to create or manipulate an image, you're acting on these individual pixels, most commonly as a group, but sometimes even one by one.

Bitmap graphics do not resize well because the individual dots that make up the image become too large, causing pixelation, or distortion. Since bitmap images are fixed at a particular resolution, their integrity is based on a device that matches that resolution. This is usually not a problem for images that are destined for display onscreen. Higher end paint programs support output at a variety of resolutions without compromising image quality.

By contrast, graphics created with drawing tools consist of individual objects known as object-oriented or vector images. To manipulate these objects, you simply select them with a mouse click and have at it. When you create a background and then draw an object on top of the background, the two elements are treated by the computer as separate entities. You can move the foreground object to a new location without affecting the background. These objects can be treated individually because the computer represents them as mathematical calculations. When objects are moved or otherwise manipulated, the computer recalculates the new position.

Some programs provide "autotrace" tools that allow you to trace a bitmap image, to create an object-oriented image that can be manipulated. This is particularly useful for converting scanned imagery. Others employ both a paint and a draw layer so that you can use both types of tools on a given image. When in paint mode, paint tools won't affect drawn images, and vice versa.

In general, when type is part of a piece of artwork, or when text and colored shapes are combined, a draw program is probably a better choice. For complex illustrations with gradations of color, or for photographic image retouching, a bitmap paint program is necessary.

Getting Images into Your Computer

There are a number of ways to get images into your computer, most of which are covered in Chapter 2, "Systems Software, Hardware, and Peripherals." Briefly, such hardware accomplishes the task of taking ideas and images from the "ana-

Clip Media/Images
⌘ 200–250

log" world and turning them into the bits and bytes your computer needs to handle them. Slide scanners, flatbed scanners, and hand-held and drum scanners are the most commonly used pieces of specialized hardware, along with graphics tablets and sound and video digitizers.

Images are also commercially available on a variety of CD-ROMs and on floppy disks as clip art and are usually grouped by their subject. Kodak's Photo CD system (discussed near the end of this chapter) is a convenient method that is finding its way into the portfolios of many image providers and purveyors.

Graphics Files

PICT, BMP, TIFF, GIF, and EPS are all common names for how graphics or image data can be stored and understood by the computer. File formats are simply names for the methods used to store a graphic or image. We'll get to them in a minute.

As noted in the side-bar above, the two different types of graphics one must deal with on a PC or Mac are *bitmapped* and *object-oriented* (see Figure 3.2). It is easy to distinguish between the two if you remember that bitmapped graphics or images are made of tiny little bits. Many millions of bits, or pixels, go into making up the image or graphic. It's just as if an artist had used so many little dabs of paint to make a picture that you couldn't tell the difference between it and a good photograph. This attribute is important if you are going to use a monitor or television screen as your output device, since monitors use rows of pixels to display images.

Figure 3.2 The difference between bit-mapped and object-orientated graphic types can be seen in this illustration. At the top is a bit-mapped line made up of individual pixels. Below, is an object-orientated line, determined in the computer by mathematical formulas and placed on the screen.

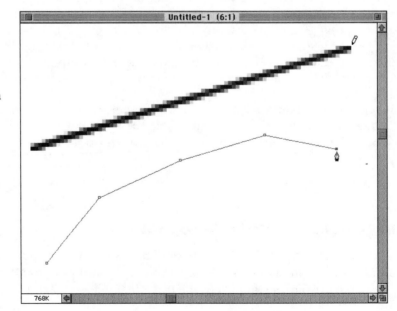

Object-oriented graphics are defined mathematically, rather than by how many bits or pixels they contain. In an object-oriented graphic or image, a simple line is not a row of bits or pixels to the computer, but an arithmetic description of where the line exists on the page (x and y coordinates) and its characteristics (length, width, color, etc.). This attribute is important when you are going to output a graphic or image to a printer. In fact, most printers made for the Macintosh —and many for the PC—are based on the fact that data sent to them for output will come in the form of lines of code and not millions of pixels.

Bitmapped graphics, while large compared with object-oriented files, are more suitable for handling images with subtle detail and extensive variations in shades, such as photographs. For this reason, much of the imagery used in multimedia is created in bitmap form.

Graphic File Formats

Mac users have to put up with comparatively few graphics formats—TIFF, PICT, and EPS are the main ones. Most Mac programs can read and write at least one of these in addition to their native formats. The PC world, by contrast, supports a large number of proprietary and near-standard formats, but BMP and TIFF are the most widely used. The following list describes the most common graphics file formats on both platforms.

AVI

AVI is the file format used by Microsoft's Video for Windows. The files store both sequential frames of video and sound—hence the name Audio/Video Interleaved (AVI).

BMP

BMP is the Windows bitmap file format. BMP files are not generally compressed (though they can be, using RLE—run length encoding), so they are fast to open, but BIG! The file format can be edited on the PC by both Windows Paint and PC Paintbrush. Many file conversion utilities will convert BMP files for use by Mac programs.

CGM

CGM is the Computer Graphics Metafile format, stores images that have the vector graphics advantages of compact size, scalability, and, theoretically, better cross-platform compatibility. But while CGM files are common on the PC (and Unix), they are nearly unknown on the Macintosh.

Some conversion programs (such as MacLinkPlus) and paint/image processing software (like Canvas) will import some CGMs, but not all. If you need to get a lot of CGMs over to the Mac, lay your hands on a copy of MetaPICT from GSC Associates. MetaPICT very capably converts CGM files to PICTs. One footnote: Once converted, the resulting PICTs cannot be edited, so do any necessary editing on the CGM file first.

CGM files are not as flexible a vector format as EPS. While you can edit CGMs, the format does not support gradient fills and bezier curves. This results in smaller files.

EPS

EPS files, while great for storing images and graphics to be output to a printer, are not meant, necessarily, for output to a screen. Furthermore, EPS files are not popularly supported by most multimedia software.

EPS files include a low-resolution PICT component (see below) that allows the files to be displayed on systems without Display PostScript (which is most of them). This provides for quick-and-dirty display of the image onscreen without the overhead of PostScript interpretation. EPS files that do not contain the PICT component will display as the old familiar—and ever helpful—crossed-out rectangle.

Object-oriented EPS files (except those generated by Adobe Illustrator) generally cannot be ungrouped, refilled, or recolored. Although the EPS format can carry bitmaps, it is notoriously inefficient code when turned to this purpose; such EPS files are large and gobble up lots of disk space and other system resources.

GIF

GIF, or Graphic Interchange Format, was created by the CompuServe network and was specifically designed to minimize file transfer times when uploading or downloading images from the network. Since the format is designed for compact file size, images are stored with maximum compression (using the LZW algorithm), and the files can therefore take a while to unpack. Since CompuServe offers thousands of GIF files, it is a good source of clip art and scanned images (though all are limited to 8-bit color).

GIF Converter 2.3.7 ⌘ 605

There is a shareware utility called GIF Converter that is included on the *Power Tools* CD. Recently GIF has found new life as the image file format of the Internet's popular World Wide Web. Its status is somewhat in question, however, as CompuServe has said it intends to require royalty payments for the use of GIF.

MOV

MOV, Apple's QuickTime movie format, stores any dynamic data—video, animation, sound. The movie files contain only track and timing information; the actual data is stored elsewhere. The movie format also supports a *poster;* a still image representing the movie; and a *preview;* which is a short trailer taken from the movie itself. For a detailed overview of QuickTime, see Chapter 2, "Systems Software, Hardware, and Peripherals."

PAINT

Photoshop 3.0 Demo ⌘ 715

PAINT is the Mac's original graphics file format, the native format of MacPaint. Almost archaic now, with its 1-bit black-and-white graphics, it is nonetheless firmly entrenched in the Mac world; and many programs (Canvas, PixelPaint, DeskPaint, Photoshop, and of course, MacPaint) still support it. If you need to do a simple bitmap, the format is serviceable, and very compact.

PCX

PCX is a standard PC bitmap file format. It dates back into the murky swamp of the PC's past. Since it was originally intended as a drawing image format, its compression schemes are not optimized for bitmaps. The PCX format doesn't compress scanned or dithered images well either. Also, it was developed for the paltry 16 colors of VGA; and though newer versions do handle 8-, 16-, and 24-bit images, incompatibilities abound.

Most PCX files can be edited with Photoshop (Mac or PC), and, on the PC, with Paintbrush, the program from which it originally sprang.

PICS

PICS files are simply collections of sequential PICT or PICT2 files used to generate animations. The format is used by Macromedia Director (and a few other programs, like SuperCard) to store animated files. Because of Director's popularity, some vendors' programs read PICS files directly. For example, Adobe Photoshop will import PICS frames for editing. It's also an output option for 3-D applications—Swivel 3D Professional, Vision 3d, and Infini-D, for example—that can animate objects or viewpoints to produce sophisticated action, simulations, and structure walk-throughs. PICS files have a size limit of 15Mb.

Since PICS files can be monstrously big, compression is sometimes implemented. However, since there is no standard for PICS compression, a compressed PICS file may not be readable by programs other than the one that created and squashed it in the first place.

PICT

PICT, another pillar of Mac graphics formats, was designed for moving graphics between different programs on the Mac. While PICTs have a limited 8-color range, they are widely read by Mac programs; are the native format for the Mac's clipboard; and drive the drawing functions of QuickDraw, the part of system software responsible for the construction and display of images on the Mac.

PICT Viewer 1.1 ⌘ 611

The PICT format allows comments about the image it carries, such as PostScript definitions of the image and curve-smoothing information. If the application reading the PICT file cannot handle this information, it is simply ignored.

QuickTime extends the PICT format to allow storage of compressed still images and image previews. Any program that can now open a PICT file will also be able to read a new compressed PICT in the extended format.

PICT2

PICT2, an extension of the PICT format, comes in two versions: one handles 8-bit color images, and the other holds the 16.8 million colors of 24-bit images. Some programs are beginning to use PICT2 as their default PICT format; these applications include Studio/8, SuperPaint, and PixelPaint.

The PICT2 format (many applications now just call it PICT, since the original PICT format is almost extinct) is perfect for multimedia presentations because it supports bitmapped as well as object-oriented graphics and images, and because most applications will import and export in the PICT2 format. It is the preferred format for producing multimedia presentations with software such as Adobe Premiere, Adobe Photoshop, VideoFusion, and Macromedia Director.

Director 4.0 Demo ⌘ 708

Premiere 4.0 Demo ⌘ 722

Using the 8-bit version of PICT2, you can save a custom 256-color palette with the image, ensuring accurate color information as the file is transferred and reopened by different applications. Beware of this feature, though—some applications don't save the palette along with the image, and you may get a rude surprise as another application performs color substitutions while opening the image. Also be careful when pasting parts of other PICTs into a PICT file with a custom palette—the pasted image's colors are not drawn from the custom palette, and you'll experience color shifts.

TIFF

TIFF (Tagged Image File Format), introduced by Aldus, and designed to accommodate the sophisticated images brought into the computer by scanners, is now pretty much the format of choice for color image files. It also stores black-and-white and grayscale images.

Although close to a cross-platform format, TIFF is something of a joke as a standard. Vendors use it for their own purposes, sometimes rendering TIFF files unreadable by programs supposedly designed to support it.

PC TIFF and Mac TIFF are different from each other. Both contain sequential representations of the pixels, but put them in a different order. Conversion utilities will handle this difference, and some Mac and PC applications—Photoshop, for example—can save in either Mac or PC TIFF format.

The different TIFF "dialects" are further complicated by the fact that there are actually three TIFF subtypes. Monochrome TIFFs store 1-bit black-and-white images, grayscale TIFFs hold 256 grays, and color TIFFs can hold up to 16.8 million colors. TIFF files tend to be on the heavy side, so they are often encoded with compression schemes. But these differ and are not recognized by all programs. TIFF 4.0 uses the most widely recognized compression standard, while the newer TIFF 5.0 sports features such as variable compression formats.

Despite these variations, TIFF is still the most reliable format for exporting grayscale and color images to other programs, ensuring that image tones and resolution are faithfully interpreted by the importing application. Unfortunately, some of the most popular multimedia software, such as Adobe Premiere, does not support TIFFs.

JPEG File Compression

JPEG File Compression is not a file format, but a compression algorithm specified by the Joint Photographic Experts Group to compress 24-bit color images. By removing nonessential information, the technique can reduce files to $\frac{1}{20}$ of their original size. At this compression ratio, images look virtually identical to their uncompressed counterparts. While JPEG can produce more highly compressed images, and therefore smaller files, image degradation becomes apparent at ratios above 20:1. (See "Compression/Decompression" later in the chapter.)

M-JPEG and MPEG File Compression

M-JPEG and MPEG File Compression are two more compression schemes that are winning popularity for their handling of digital video files. The compression preserves high quality images on playback but requires special hardware to do so.

- WMF (Windows metafile) is an object-oriented file format used by the Windows clipboard.

- AI (Adobe Illustrator) is an important vector file format; there are several variations based on the corresponding version of Illustrator.

- DXF is the common 3-D animation file format, and is also used by 2-D CAD programs. It is commonly used to export 3-D models for processing in another program.

- TGA originated for use by Targa graphic cards on the PC. It is now widely used on PCs for the storage of 24- and 32-bit images.

- FLIC is a 2-D animation format used by many PC programs.

Dealing with Graphics Files

All in all, the whole business of graphics file formats is troublesome and not a little frustrating. To keep yourself from inflicting damage on your computer when your carefully adjusted multi-hued image turns green as you open it, it's best to stick to the few tested formats with which you are most familiar.

During the bleakest moments, you can consult any of several comprehensive books on graphics file formats.

Software for Creating Imagery

The tools used to manipulate and enhance images once they are transferred into your computer can be a bit intimidating, and just choosing among them can make your head spin. Fortunately, most packages are fairly intuitive, and with a little practice they can become powerful allies.

Imaging creation and processing programs are among the most powerful on the desktop. With their capability to handle images made up of millions of multicolored pixels that can then be filtered, sharpened, cropped, rotated, colored, airbrushed, painted, cloned, and erased, determining the differences between packages can be as difficult as making sense of the enhancement options.

Any multimedia production using desktop computer equipment will certainly involve more than one piece of software. In creating and processing images, producers will choose among software for painting, drawing, and handling scanned images. Each of the packages, although retaining some of the Mac's friendliness, also has its quirks. For example, all paint programs don't, unfortunately, incorporate brush tools in the exact same manner. It makes no sense to purchase four different paint packages solely to work with four different kinds of brush tools. Moreover, while some packages tout themselves as "all-in-one" godsends, you are much better off choosing software based upon what you will be producing most often.

Most people, excluding masochists, will standardize on a "suite" of software. A full-featured, well-supported set of products in each of the categories will pay off in the long run by reducing the number of programs one must learn and by saving a good bit of money! As usual, the monthly trade press is an excellent source for detailed, side-by-side comparisons of the programs in each category. It would be wise to refer to such reviews before committing any funds. Input from friends and associates doing the same work is also valuable.

It is also prudent to be as sure as you can that the software you purchase will not become orphaned. This does not mean that you should disregard otherwise valuable software simply because it comes from a company you have never heard of. But while nothing is forever, you should be asking yourself some tough questions about the availability and cost of future upgrades, customer and technical support, competitiveness with similar software, and how "standard" the software seems to be among multimedia producers.

Following are descriptions of the software categories, along with brief examinations of some of the most popular software packages in the painting, drawing, and image processing categories and a discussion of their use in creating multimedia presentations.

Paint Programs

Paint programs are the closest you can come on a computer to dipping a brush into paint and spreading it on a canvas. Images created in a paint program consist of the pixels manipulated to create a bitmap, or a pixel-by-pixel screen description. Many multimedia authoring packages include paint and drawing tools that can be used to create backgrounds and objects, special effects, even simple animation. If your needs are basic, these tools will save you the trouble of learning a specialized program. You also won't have to worry about importing images from a separate application.

However, due to the enormous variation and complexity of visual images, designers often opt for specialty programs to create them, and then import them for incorporation into a multimedia presentation. These programs have tools for creating and modifying images in ways that are beyond the means of most authoring programs. Paint programs are also among the most accessible of computer software. Anyone can sit down and immediately have fun dabbling and drawing.

Even professional artists have grown more interested as the tools have become more sophisticated. Some products are now offering a range of painting techniques based on traditional methods, and the availability of graphics tablets has spawned a new category of paint programs that support pressure-sensitive effects.

Paint programs are used to create original images. Programs such as Adobe Photoshop and Fractal Design's ColorStudio, on the other hand, are commonly used to process preexisting images, even though they possess many of the same capabilities as paint programs. Most paint programs lack the specialized functions to adequately manipulate and enhance scanned images.

The tools used in painting programs affect each pixel they touch. Parameters such as color, brush type, wetness, opacity, and spray are almost infinitely variable by the advanced programs. Some even allow the user to define the type of painting surface to be used. Rice paper, canvas, charcoal paper, concrete, linen, and slate are a few of the options. The ability to create masks to protect parts of an image you don't want altered is another advanced option. Other things to consider when choosing a painting package include the maximum resolution and image size a program can handle, the intuitiveness of the interface and the tools, the number and variability of colors, and the ability to work with a number of file formats.

There are a great number of paint programs and their prices vary widely. We've included extended descriptions of the ones we believe to be the most useful and the best value for the money, as well as those that are the most popular among multimedia producers.

While paint programs differ in the particulars of their interfaces and tool sets, most offer similar groups of tools and resources.

Features and Products

Tools provided by digital design programs range from simple drawing and painting functions to a variety of filters that can completely transform images.

A common set of drawing and paint tools has evolved as graphics programs have come into widespread use. Though these basic tools vary somewhat from product to product, they are, for the most part, similar.

Tools for creating realistic paint effects include paintbrushes, spraycans, and paint buckets. Most programs allow you to create custom brushes by editing the "brushprint" one pixel at a time. Paint programs also have blending tools so that you can smudge and swirl colors as you would on a canvas.

Palettes and Patterns

One of the main reasons for the success and proliferation of paint programs is the high degree of color control that they provide. Programs contain several standard color and pattern palettes from which you choose colors. Most also let you create and edit custom palettes that can be saved and reused. In some, you use a color picker to select colors by clicking on the color wheel. Other programs supply matrices of colors from which to choose.

Paint programs also provide color mixers for more precise color synthesis. Mixers imitate real-world color mixing by allowing you to use tools to dab and blend colors just as you might with a paint spatula and palette in the studio.

The more useful programs let you "tear off" palettes and mixer windows so that you can place them onscreen for easy access. Stock patterns are also supplied, so that you can apply backgrounds and textures such as grids, checkerboards, and dot patterns. You can also create or use scanned-in images and designate these as custom patterns.

Fills and Gradients

Paint programs typically apply color to a wide area of the "canvas" by "pouring" the color from a "paint bucket." Such areas of color are known as fills, and they can be applied in different ways.

Gradient fills combine two or more colors in a smooth transition, automatically filling in the thousands of colors necessary to smoothly blend between the two colors. Most programs provide a set of fill effects—you can select fills that go from top to bottom, that fade from one color to another and then back to the first, and so on.

Radial fills let you simulate a light source for an object, and then fill the object with colors or grays that range from dark to light. Some programs allow you to store frequently used gradients for easy access.

You can even apply "color cycling" to achieve an animation effect. For example, you can create a flame effect by choosing different shades of red, yellow, and orange, which are then alternately displayed in sequence, giving the flickering effect of fire.

Filters and Masks

Many paint programs supply filters that can be applied to the whole painting or to selected areas. Basic filters, supplied with all programs, include those that blur and sharpen. More specialized filters can transform paintings with transparency effects that give the illusion of depth and a three-dimensionality. Others make the painting appear as if viewed through distorted glass or blended with numerous tiny brushstrokes like impressionistic works.

A particularly useful effect available in most paint programs is the *antialiasing* filter. This filter smooths the jagged lines that sometimes occur in bitmap programs, especially as images are resized. Antialias control is also convenient for smoothing type that is imported into the paint program. Programs that do antialiasing automatically with a filter are preferable to those that force you to do it pixel by pixel.

You can also buy plug-in products that offer a wide variety of filters to supplement those included in your favorite paint program. Kai's Power Tools is an imaginative and powerful collection of Photoshop plug-in filters (they also work with many paint programs), providing tools such as gradient, fractal, and texture generators. (See "Image Processing Software" later in this chapter for more on filters and plug-ins.)

Masking can be used to define the boundaries of different shapes, or to "protect" an image from being treated by a paint effect. Low-end products only let you mask the entire painting. The mask consists of a separate transparent layer on which you can try out a paint effect. If you like it, you can merge it with the original layer. If not, you simply discard it, with no effect on the original layer. Products with professional features—Painter and PixelPaint Professional, for example—offer more masking control. Using these programs, you can mask not only specific areas, but also colors, even certain ranges of colors.

Although some paint programs include an impressive array of masks and filters, and support for plug-ins as well, the most sophisticated effects are found in image processing programs (see "Image Processing Software," later in this chapter).

Fractal Design's Painter

Painter 3.0 Demo ⌘ 713

Painter, from Fractal Design, is probably the most powerful and useful 24-bit paint program for multimedia currently available (see Figure 3.3). The main strength of the program is its ability to simulate traditional artist's tools. Charcoal, watercolor, crayons, felt pens, chalk, and pencil are among the "natural" media that users can wield with almost infinite variability. The program is available in both Mac and Windows versions.

Painter's interface is attractive but over-designed, organizing tools and special effects filters into a set of "drawers." (Windows, drawers…what's next—closets?) You can customize the interface by creating your own drawers with your favorite tools.

And some of those tools are pretty wild: Image Hose, for example, lets you spray random images, and a drop shadow tool adds a shadow (which is itself a

**Figure 3.3
Fractal Design's
Painter.**

separately editable object) to any object. A masking tool lets you create separate floating objects and combine them into composite images.

With its Advanced Controls palette, Painter gives you sophisticated control over even its most basic tools. You can, for instance, specify how paint behaves on brushes, and even create your own brush shapes and add them to tool palettes.

Of particular interest to multimediacs is Painter's intriguing filter for Quick-Time and AVI movies. You can import a movie into Painter and add any of Painter's effects to individual frames. An "onionskin" feature layers frames over one another in semitransparent version so you get an idea of what the movie will look like when played back. You can even make a movie into an Image Hose nozzle, which allows you to add still movie frames to a composite image.

Pixel Resources' PixelPaint Professional

As you might have guessed, no other paint program comes close to Painter either on the Mac or under Windows. PixelPaint Pro is a venerable Mac tool that combines paint and imaging feature, but real professionals won't find it a substitute for the knockout combination of Photoshop and Painter.

Fractal also makes Dabbler, a simpler program that is designed for those who want to learn how to paint digitally. Its simplified interface is suitable for children as well as adults. Like Painter, Dabbler has versions for either Windows or the Mac.

Other popular programs for the Mac include MicroFrontier's Color It!, and Pixel Resources' PixelPaint Pro. For Windows, Fauve Matisse is an interesting entry-level program (which, at the time of this writing, is getting an overhaul that should make it more competitive with Painter).

Drawing Packages

Unlike paint programs, where images can be imported directly into multimedia productions with relative ease, most drawing packages are designed less for screen display than for output to a PostScript printer, although Canvas, Free-Hand, Illustrator, and MacDraw Pro allow files to be saved as PICTs. You must be careful, however, when attempting to save files created with draw programs that contain specialized fills, gradients, or text effects. While most PostScript printers can easily handle such files when saved and output as EPSs, those same files saved as PICTs will be stripped of most of the extra-fancy stuff. The only way to make sure you're saving everything is to save a file in the program's native format.

Tools and Products

All of the drawing programs are great for producing original images in a more precise manner than that possible with painting tools, and not so good for manipulating photos or scanned items. Because they offer features not easily incorporated into painting programs, no multimedia producer should be without a full-featured drawing package.

The best packages, Macromedia's FreeHand, Adobe Illustrator, and Corel Draw, offer an incredible catalog of features—much too numerous to go into here. The basic categories are:

Drawing Tools and Features

These are the basic tools you use to create drawings, these include pens, shaping and calligraphic tools, object alignment, and path reshaping tools.

Special Effects

Using various tools, you can scale, rotate, distort, and otherwise transform objects. Drawing programs are also following the lead of their paint and image editing cousins by implementing plug-in architectures that allow you to use specialized filters and effects.

Colors and Fills

Full-featured programs such as Illustrator, FreeHand, and Draw give you lots of options for creating and manipulating color: fills and gradients, tile patterns, texture fills, and masks are a few of the possibilities.

Text Handling

How a drawing program handles text is an important consideration for mixed-media authors. For drawing packages, both Illustrator and FreeHand offer surprising control over text. You can create tables, copy fit text to specific dimensions, and apply style tags. For Windows users, CorelDraw has particularly strong font support.

Macromedia's FreeHand

FreeHand, developed by Altsys, nurtured by Aldus, and toyed with by Adobe, seems to have found a permanent home with multimedia giant Macromedia. As of this writing, Macromedia hadn't the time to incorporate any specific multimedia features into FreeHand. But by the time you read this, Macromedia will likely have made the popular drawing package part of its Digital Design Studio—as a suite of integrated multimedia design tools.

Until then, FreeHand is still of great interest to multimedia developers. Always neck-and-neck with Illustrator in terms of features, ease of use, and speed, FreeHand is a great drawing package. While Illustrator has been known for stronger drawing tools and FreeHand for better numeric control over objects, these distinctions are fading. Each program has added features in areas that were previously lacking.

FreeHand's interface is controversial, employing roll-up palettes that make features quickly accessible but can quickly clutter a desktop. Overall, it's probably a little harder to learn and use than Illustrator because of its somewhat less intuitive organization. Of course, once you get to know a particular program, this sort of consideration tends to recede.

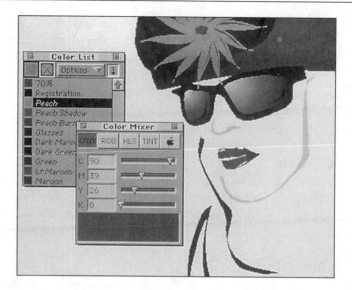

**Figure 3.4
Macromedia
FreeHand.**

FreeHand has a complete selection of shape and drawing tools and excellent control over the application of color and fills (see Figure 3.4). While lacking a spellchecker, it also offers excellent text facilities, probably slightly better than Illustrator's. It's also better at handling PICT and TIFF images—an important consideration for multimedia designers.

FreeHand also seems faster than Illustrator in screen redrawing and routine operations, though this will vary according to the machine on which you're running it. If cross-platform development is important, FreeHand has the added advantage of being in the same version on both the Mac and PC.

Adobe's Illustrator

Illustrator 4.0 Demo ⌘ 718

Some people prefer Illustrator's (see Figure 3.5) elegant interface to FreeHand's one-tool-for-each-job approach. Multimedia producers will want to consider Illustrator's ability to save in an EPS file format that is fully compatible with Photoshop and Premiere, but EPS files are definitely not the norm for onscreen productions. One other advantage of using Illustrator is that clipping paths created in Photoshop can be imported and exported between the two programs easily.

Using Illustrator, you can also edit masks in a more straightforward way than with FreeHand, and its graphing feature is unique. Illustrator also now supports plug-in filters first popularized in Photoshop. As of this writing, unlike FreeHand (see above), Illustrator is in version 5.5 on the Mac, but only 4.0 on the PC.

Other Contenders

Deneba Software's Canvas (Mac and Windows) combines many features of both paint and draw programs. Claris's MacDraw Pro, while not as sophisticated as the others, offers a well-rounded drawing environment.

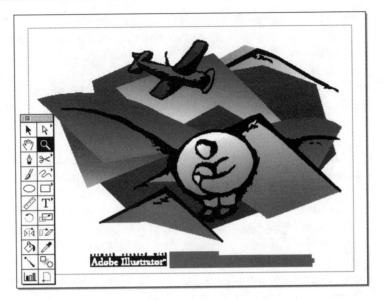

**Figure 3.5
Adobe Illustrator.**

CorelDraw

On the Windows-only side, CorelDraw is a full featured and mature program that is probably the most popular Windows drawing package. Corel offers Corel-Draw in a bundle that probably represents the best value going in graphics software. For under $500, you get CorelDraw itself, plus Photo-Paint, CorelMove, CorelTrace, CorelMosaic, and CorelVentura. All of these are full-fledged applications in their own right, but we'll focus on CorelDraw here.

CorelDraw includes typical drawing functions, plus bitmap editing and tracing modules. On the drawing side, transformations such as rotation, skewing, and scaling can be performed using only the mouse. A versatile set of extrusion features allows the creation of sophisticated 3-D objects.

Color tools are equally complete; you can select from multiple palettes, create gradient fills and blends, and perform color separations.

Text handling is also excellent; text can remain as it is typed in, or can be blended, extruded, or manipulated to fit a path. Text that is to stay in paragraph form can be searched, spellchecked, and otherwise manipulated as in a full-featured word processor.

Image Processing Software

Despite the great number of capable design programs and the beautiful art that can be created using them, multimedia imagery more often comes from the real world.

Photographs, video captures, art, and 3-D objects can all be scanned in and used as the basis for multimedia design elements. In fact, it is quite common for designers to scan *rocks* to achieve the granite look so popular these days. (For more information on scanners and the scanning process, see Chapter 2, "Systems Software, Hardware, and Peripherals.")

Scanners provide quick and relatively easy access to a huge array of imagery, and the quality of scanned images is high. Image processing software lets you meld scanned imagery with paint and type effects, thus creating unified images that can be imported into multimedia presentations.

Plug-ins and Filters

KPT-Pixelwind Filter ⌘ 606

KPT-Diffuse More Filter ⌘ 607

KPT-Fine Edges Soft Filter ⌘ 608

KPT-Sharpen Intensify Filter ⌘ 609

KPT-3d Stereo Noise Filter ⌘ 610

One development that bears special mention is the appearance of specialized filters and plug-ins. These tools are not quite full-fledged applications in their own right, but add mind blowing special effects to image editing programs.

Leading the pack are plug-ins from HSC, most notably Kai's Power Tools (KPT). Using KPT from within your favorite image editing app, such as Photoshop, Picture Publisher, Painter, or Corel's PhotoPaint, you can process images with a variety of effects. One-step filters such as Pixelstorm and Special Noises create interesting mutations, but you'll have to wait until processing is done to see the results. User interface filters are divided into categories such as Gradient Designer and Texture Explorer (see Figure 3.6). These allow you to preview the effect a given filter will have.

HSC also makes KPT Convolver, a Photoshop plug-in that lets you create custom filters either at random or more methodically through the Tweak and Design modules. Note that the HSC products are collections of filters and filter generators; there are many single-purpose filters available from such companies as Pixar, Andromeda, and Adobe.

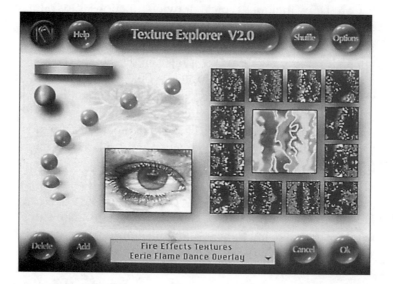

**Figure 3.6
Kai's Power
Tools.**

File Translation

Equilibrium Technologies' DeBabelizer, which has been described as an "image operating system," is another notable tool that simplifies many repetitive image processing tasks. The program translates from and to over 50 graphics file formats and lets you automate, or "batch" tedious manipulation and editing operations. For its alacrity in performing these thankless tasks, DeBabelizer has won the hearts and minds of professionals across the range of multimedia, from animators to interactive programmers.

DeBabelizer 1.6 Demo ⌘ 719

Among its many functions, DeBabelizer uses a "Super Palette," which automatically creates the best palette for a series of images, reducing the "dithering" that degrades image quality. For a description of this process see the PageMaker Demo project on the *Power Tools* CD. Unfortunately for Windows users, DeBabelizer runs only on the Mac. However, there are many file conversion tools for the PC, such as Inset's Hijaak Pro, which can convert between 75 vector and bitmap formats. Also Autodesk's Animator Pro is used on the PC for many of the same translation tasks.

Proxy Editors

The proliferation of huge graphics files for multimedia and prepress applications has given rise to a new category of image programs called proxy editors. When you process an image file by applying a filter, or even just rotating the image, the computer must apply the effect to every one of what may be millions of pixels.

Proxy editors work by applying effects to a lower resolution version of an image so that you can see the results in seconds instead of minutes or even hours. When you are satisfied, your manipulations are carried out on the actual image. High-end proxy editors include HSC's Live Picture and MacEurope Information Systems' Imagician. 3-D software vendor Specular International Ltd. has Collage, a less capable but more affordable proxy editor. Fauve's xRes and Quark's QuarkXPosure are two new image processing programs that combine many features of proxy editors and more traditional image editing programs. xRes runs on both PCs and Macs, while Quark's new product will reportedly be confined to PowerMacs. This category of software is of interest largely in the prepress industry, but has application in multimedia where large files are the norm.

Features and Products

Images can be manipulated in almost any way imaginable through a variety of tools. Image processing programs are similar to paint programs in that they work on data at the pixel level. In fact, many of the tools in image processing programs are identical to those in paint software. Filters and masks, for example, are common to both categories. Image processing software, however, usually includes special functions to retouch and enhance scanned images and provide high-resolution printed output.

Tools

Color image processing programs such as Photoshop and ColorStudio include refinements of basic design and selection tools found in paint programs. For example, the *magic wand* lets you select all connected pixels of common or similar hues. A *feathered* selection includes pixels outside the selection boundaries, which it fades to give a misty effect.

Like the lasso, Photoshop's *pen* is a tool that allows selection of irregular areas of an image. But the pen allows more precise selection, outlining areas by drawing *bezier curves*. The area of selection can then be modified after the fact by clicking and dragging the curves' control points.

Color Control

Image processing software can be used in lieu of stand-alone paint programs; but it is more useful for its array of filters that allow you to manipulate and totally change the appearance of images, and for its unsurpassed color retouching capabilities. It allows you to separate an image into its various color components, or *channels.* You can work with each channel separately, adjusting color, contrast, and brightness. Exact control over color is further extended through *remapping*, in which you modify colors by adjusting a *colormap curve*—a graphic representation of an individual color.

Some programs, such as Photoshop and ColorStudio, even have color separation capabilities, and offer multiple adjustments for color values and levels. The ability of these programs to do real-time CMYK color editing is an advantage for those using desktop color separators. Before these features were available, if you wanted to retouch or manipulate images and produce files for four-color printing, you'd have to work in the computer's native RGB mode and then convert to CMYK.

Image Layering

This is an important feature pioneered by proxy editors (see above) but now migrating to more mainstream image programs such as Photoshop and Picture Publisher. By creating images in separate layers, you can manipulate them separately to create complex composite images.

Retouching and Filtering

Retouching tools include "water drop" and "finger," which can smooth specific areas by spreading pixels around. The individual attributes of retouching tools can be precisely specified. For example, you can set paintbrush shading preferences so that shading alternates between light and dark over a specified period of time. You can also set width, rate of paint flow, and so forth.

Filtering is one of the most delightful of the features of these amazing programs. Using special effects filters, you can blur and diffuse images, sharpen, posterize, outline contours, and trace edges. Wave and ripple filters produce interesting effects, and you can even turn an object into a sphere, complete with light reflections, refractions, and transparency. Edge detection filters, which outline an image so that just its edges remain, are used to create embossed effects.

Industry-leading programs such as Photoshop offer more than a dozen such filters, and you can buy third-party plug-ins that supply supplementary filters. Paint and draw programs also increasingly include some filtering effects and support plug-in architecture.

There are a variety of image processing programs available. A brief discussion of some of the most popular follows. You should remember that no one program is likely to fill all of your needs. For example, many people rely on Photoshop for heavy-duty image handling and manipulation and on a more intuitive painting package such as Painter for creating images from scratch or for applying artistic effects. Make sure the software you choose can handle the appropriate file formats, and that its files can be easily ported to any multimedia creation or authoring software you might use.

Adobe
Photoshop

Photoshop 3.0 Demo ⌘ 715

Photoshop is an industry standard for image processing and handling. Its presence is so widespread that not using it might be considered heresy. Serious multimedia producers simply must have this program. It is also the only image editing program available (at this writing) for both the Windows and Mac platforms.

Photoshop's initial claim to fame was the sophisticated color editing and color separation capabilities that it brought to the desktop for the first time. For the multimedia producer, its photo editing and filtering features are of more interest.

Photoshop groups filters to speed identification and selection. There are some interesting ones in addition to the familiar blur and sharpen filters. The Wind filter streaks images as if they were rushing by a camera lens. The Tiles filter splits an image into a mosaic pattern, while Crystallize gives a stained-glass effect. The emphasis is always on control. For instance, the Wind filter has three separate streaking directions, and Tile can be set according to the number of tiles as well as their offsets.

If you work with video, you will find good use for Photoshop's video filters, which remove even or odd scan lines from video images and interpolate pixels to create a smooth image. A filter that restricts image colors to those that will reproduce most accurately on videotape or television is also excellent. Dodge and burn tools are useful, as is a new color correction method based on choosing an image that looks best to the user and not on arbitrary individual color channel changes.

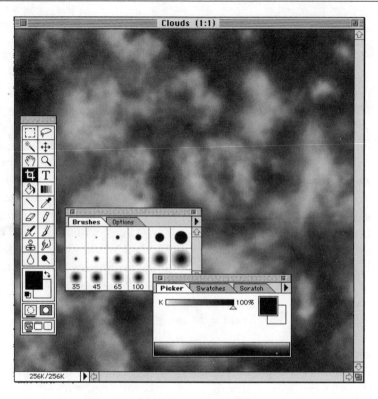

Figure 3.7 Photoshop's "Clouds" texture, shown with active toolbox, picker, and brushes.

Photoshop also lets you import EPS (Encapsulated PostScript) files and treat them as vector images. This is important because PostScript is an industry standard, and many graphics are stored in the EPS format.

Another area of excellence in Photoshop is its support for layering, though it requires a lot of memory. You can vary the transparency of individual layers and move them between foreground or background and intermediate positions.

Photoshop is renowned for its approachable and deceptively simple user interface. In fact, it wins the ultimate accolade in this respect; for all but the most advanced work, you might think you don't need the manual. However, the program is exceedingly deep, and producing books about Photoshop has become a cottage industry. And the manual itself ain't half bad. It includes tips on how to get the most out of the tools and filters and covers shortcuts that are nearly impossible to find by coincidence.

For all its power, Photoshop exacts a toll in terms of system resources. It needs lots of space, particularly in RAM. Photoshop's layering features really suck up memory and disk space; you'll need RAM and disk space equal to about three times the size of the images you're working with. Windows users with more modest graphics requirements may find Picture Publisher a better choice.

**Figure 3.8
Micrografx'
Picture Publisher.**

Photoshop performance is also a major indicator of its usability. Manipulating large graphics files simply takes a lot of time—whether you have a 486SX (good luck) or a PowerMac. Power users may want to consider an accelerator card dedicated to photoshop processing, such as Radius' PhotoEngine. The product, currently available for Mac Photoshop users only, can make processing operations two to four times as fast and may be cheaper than simply buying more RAM, which can also accelerate image rotations, filter applications, and other routine operations.

*Picture
Publisher*

By comparison with Photoshop, Micrografx' Picture Publisher (Figure 3.8) offers scaled-down, though similar, features and is cheaper, but runs only under Windows. Tool palettes are not as feature-laden, masks are less sophisticated, and layers less versatile, but Picture Publisher is also easier to learn than Photoshop.

It also excels in a few areas: Windows OLE support makes moving files between other Windows applications a snap, and its text-handling features are a little easier to use than Photoshop's. Picture Publisher also sports a unique feature called Command List that keeps track of your every move—sort of like an audit trail for artists. This lets you do cool stuff such as change one step in a complex processing operation, then run the whole thing again without having to re-create all the steps.

All in all, it's a solid product and a reasonable alternative to Photoshop for Windows users who don't need the all features of Adobe's powerhouse.

Images on Screen

Now that we've covered the software needed to create, enhance, and manipulate images for multimedia productions, what do you need to worry about next? Why, getting them to look good when displayed, of course. There is a big difference between preparing images for printing and preparing them for viewing on a computer monitor or television screen. Most of the problems have to do with color and how it is represented by different media and the hardware associated with those media. The technical details could fill an entire book this size, so we will cover only the most basic concepts here.

As a multimedia producer, you will generally be creating work for presentation on a computer screen or monitor of some sort. This means that you have much less to worry about than someone producing a print piece. Images presented on a screen do not need to be created at the high resolutions (from 300 to over 2,000 dots per inch) of output to a printer. Most monitors have resolutions of from 72 to 90 dpi depending on the size of the tube and the display card used. Lower resolution images mean smaller file sizes. A full-color image at 72 dpi will take up a little less than 1Mb of hard disk space. While 1Mb files can quickly turn into monsters if you have enough of them, they're much easier to work with than the multimegabyte files routinely used for output to paper.

Color is one of the main factors involved in showing images on a screen. Without going into the intricacies of bit-depths, color look-up tables, and color models, there are some basic things multimedia producers need to consider when displaying images on screen. First, how many colors can your computer show on the screen at one time?

Computers equipped with 8-bit monitor cards or on-board video (up to 256 colors per screen pixel) are satisfactory for working with most images; however, to work in "full color" or to see images onscreen with photographic quality, you will need a 24-bit monitor card. These cards can display up to 16.7 million colors per screen pixel. (See Figure 3.9 for a comparison of 8-bit and 24-bit color.) What most people tend to forget when throwing around numbers related to monitors and the colors they display is that humans can only discern about 380,000 colors. If your hardware will allow it, you should work in 16-bit mode, which allows the display of more than 65,000 colors. This is usually more than adequate for viewing images onscreen, and it allows your computer to work faster because it doesn't have to crunch as much color data.

The second issue related to color and images involves what are known as color *gamuts*. For multimedia producers whose final output will be to videotape or some sort of regular television screen and not a computer display, the issue of color gamuts is very important. Basically, a color gamut is a fancy name for the array of colors that can be displayed or printed to a specific output device.

**Figure 3.9
The difference between images viewed in 8-bit and 24-bit color can be seen in this illustration. However, be aware that 24-bit color has large processing and storage requirements that could bog-down your project.**

Some colors can be displayed on a computer monitor, but not on a regular television screen. Moreover, there are colors that can be displayed by a television screen or computer monitor but cannot be printed on paper, and vice versa. For example, certain printing presses have no problem printing metallic gold onto a sheet of paper, but reproducing that same metallic gold on a computer monitor or television screen is impossible. Thus, a printing press has a certain color gamut, or colors it can reproduce, and computer monitors and television screens have their own respective color gamuts.

Since most multimedia products will be viewed on a monitor or screen of some sort, the trick is to keep all the colors you use for your images within the capabilities of those devices. When you are dealing with output to standard television screens (those which adhere to some sort of color broadcast standard, such as that developed by the North American Television Standards Committee), however, the trick becomes, well, tricky.

Fortunately, some software has the ability to restrict the colors you are using for an image to those considered "safe" for display on a television screen. Adobe Photoshop, for example, has a filter called "NTSC-legal colors" that, when applied to an image, adjusts the colors in that image to those within a TV's capabilities (Figure 3.10). Adobe Premiere, Fractal Design's Painter, and Color It! also can adjust images for "NTSC-legal" colors.

Photo CD

One of the most useful tools for multimedia producers who work frequently with still images is Kodak's Photo CD system (Figure 3.11). If you haven't seen the commercials, a description of how the system works and the hardware you require can be found in Chapter 2, "Systems Software, Hardware, and Peripher-

Figure 3.10 Photoshop's NTSC-legal colors filter comes in handy when converting colors in images for viewing on a regular television screen.

als." What the Photo CD system promises for those who handle lots of images is great convenience and time saving.

Film can be sent to Kodak (and often your local film developer) for processing and returned to you in the form of developed negatives or slides, along with prints if desired and a special type of CD-ROM called a Photo CD. A Photo CD can hold up to 100 images. These can be put on the CD at different times. For example, you can bring 25 slides to be put on a Photo CD one week, 50 more the next, and 25 more a month later. This "multisession capability" is available on most CD-ROMs today.

Photo CD images are scanned onto the disc at five different resolutions: 3,072 × 2,048, 1,536 × 1,024, 768 × 512, 384 × 256, and 192 × 128 pixels, all of which are stored in a single file called an Image Pac. The largest size is meant to be used for printing, the 1,536 × 1,024 size matches the HDTV format, and the 768 × 512 size is for display on a monitor. The smallest size is used for thumbnails (Figure 3.11). Compression factors in all but the two smallest sizes, and Kodak claims that the proprietary compression algorithms applied to the larger sizes results in no perceivable loss in image quality.

Other than the standard Photo CD format, known as the Photo CD Master disc, Kodak offers two other professional formats. The Pro Photo CD Master disc stores images from 35mm and larger film formats. The Kodak Photo CD Portfolio disc is a multipurpose format that holds other digital file types in addition to Image Pac files. Originally developed as a presentation format, Portfolio II discs can be used for delivery of up to 700 TV-resolution images. Portfolio II discs can also

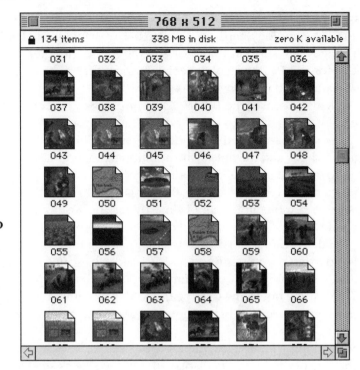

Figure 3.11 Kodak's Photo CD system presents users with the proper software and hardware to show a screen full of image thumbnails all scanned at varying resolutions.

accommodate specialized file formats for prepress and printing and up to 4,000 low-resolution images for cataloging purposes.

Kodak sells a package called Photo CD Access for about $40. It can open, display, and crop the images contained on Photo CDs. Photo CD Access also allows users to export Photo CD images in TIFF, EPS, and PICT formats. Kodak also markets a product called PhotoEdge that provides all the same tools as Access and also allows some limited image editing capability, such as sharpening a picture or adjusting color and contrast.

And there's more: Kodak Shoebox Image Manager software allows you to create a database to manage thousands of images, digital movies, and audio files; and Kodak Browser is a licensable, scaled-down version of Shoebox that can be used to navigate Photo CD catalog discs.

Kodak also sells hardware "authoring" systems for creating your own Photo CD images. These would be economical only if you plan to regularly digitize large image catalogs; otherwise, taking your film to the local commercial Photo CD processor is the best way to go.

Adobe Photoshop has the ability to handle Photo CD images if the required CD-ROM drivers are in place. Adobe also has a plug-in for direct access to Photo

CDs, and Apple's QuickTime also supports the format. Kodak is pushing the Photo CD technology hard, so it is safe to say that almost all software that deals with images will support Photo CDs in the future. Adaptec and Corel offer SCSI utilities for the PC that have special support for Photo CDs, including a slide show feature and file conversion.

Kodak also licenses the Photo CD technology to other vendors and has introduced new kinds of Photo CDs. Photo CD now supports larger film sizes through the use of a new scanner that handles larger film. Photo CD formats that hold catalogs of images and that allow the addition of sound to the images for complete slide shows have also been introduced.

The great convenience of the Photo CD system is that multimedia producers can save enormous amounts of time by having Kodak do all the scanning of their slides and negatives and put them on a Photo CD. The images are scanned in at standard resolutions varied to suit anything from onscreen presentation to high-end printed output. If you had 100 slides to scan for your multimedia production, just think of how much time it would take to prepare, scan, and enhance each one. We're not trying to hype the Kodak system too much, but the time and cost savings, especially for those who work alone, are staggering.

Compression/ Decompression

When working with images, the issue of size becomes increasingly important—not the size of the image as displayed, but the size as stored on your hard disk. A color image at screen resolution takes up approximately 1Mb of disk space. While not a huge number by itself, imagine multiplying that by hundreds for a multimedia production that makes use of a lot of stills. Enter image compression and decompression. A look at compression and decompression and how it relates to video, animations, and QuickTime and AVI movies can be found in their respective chapters.

Compression is a widely employed technique that reduces the size of large image files without appreciably changing the way a viewer sees the images. A compressed image must be decompressed before it can be used. Compression and decompression take time because the processes are processor-intensive. The more a file is compressed, the more computer power it takes.

Compression and decompression can be accomplished by software alone or by a combination of software and hardware. Software compressor/decompressors are known as *codecs*. Compression software analyzes an image and finds ways to store the same amount of information using fewer bytes. Compression hardware usually consists of a ROM chip with built-in compression routines for faster operation or a coprocessor chip that shares the computing load with the computer's main processor.

Differing levels of compression are usually offered through the software. *Non-lossy* or *lossless* compression means that no information is lost or thrown out as a result of the compression process. Images look unchanged after compression, but the file size is not reduced as much as with *lossy* compression schemes. Lossy compression discards more information as it compresses, thereby reducing file sizes dramatically. However, images might not look as good as they did before they were compressed. *Pixilation*, or the appearance of blocks of color in areas of solid tones, is a usual result of drastic lossy compression methods.

The most common method for lossy compressing images is called *JPEG compression.* "JPEG" stands for the Joint Photographic Experts Group, the organization that came up with a standard way of reducing image file sizes that discards information the human eye could never discern. JPEG compression methods are used by such image processing software as Photoshop and ColorStudio and by multimedia software such as Premiere and VideoFusion.

Compression and decompression of images is a complicated process made easier by standard methods such as JPEG and powerful new hardware that frees the computer's main processor from extra work. Multimedia producers who expect to use many large images should consider exploring the available options further. Compression and decompression are here to stay for a while, at least until we can buy computers with unlimited speed, power, disk space, and bandwidth. Some interesting new compression schemes based on "fractals" and "wavelets" may provide greater compression with less image degradation than JPEG's discrete cosine transform method.

For more information on compression as it relates to video and animation, see Chapter 2, "Systems Software, Hardware, and Peripherals," and Chapter 6, "Video Tools."

Using Images with Multimedia Software

Software for producing multimedia is, in many ways, like a glorified meat grinder. You throw video images captured from cameras and VCRs—animations, audio recordings, backgrounds, and still images or graphics—at the software; and, with a bit of work, you can produce a fantastic presentation. Obviously, there is a lot more to it than "a bit of work." To learn more about using images within multimedia applications, see the appropriate "Tools" and "Creating" chapters throughout the rest of the book.

4

Sound Tools

There's no doubt that multimedia presentations have a greater impact when sound is integrated into the production. You only need to view a videotape for a minute or two with the volume turned off to realize the importance of the marriage of sound to visual imagery. In nonlinear interactive environments, sound can aid in navigation in the same way that graphic backgrounds, button groupings, or color schemes orient users to their current location in the program.

Indeed, many multimedia presentations and products owe much of their success to well placed sound effects and evocative music. *Myst,* one of the best selling CD games (*the* best-seller at the time of this writing) instantly grabs your attention with its haunting score and then holds it with clever sound bytes and musical interludes.

The value of a memorable musical "logo" or sound effect is easier to grasp when you realize that those whose livelihood is creating such sonic materials often command up to $10,000 a second and sometimes licensing fees as well as residuals.

And when it comes to desktop-based multimedia, the creation of decent music to fit a particular visual sequence is no small task. It can't be automated in the manner of, say, animation. You can hold down the shift key to draw a straight line in many graphics programs, but you can't hold down any key to compose a beautiful melody.

It's common to divide multimedia into five data types: video, animation, still graphics, text, and sound. However, these really fall into two larger data groups: video and audio. And the latter can be subdivided into music, sound effects, ambiance, and narration.

Apple reaffirmed these two super classes of data when it released QuickTime with two tracks: one for movies and one for sound. The movie track can hold all four types of visual data, and the sound track can contain all four types of audio data. (Microsoft's Video for Windows, however, mixes video and audio in a format called Audio/Video Interleaved (AVI).) QuickTime 2.0 and later has support for both 16-bit sound and MIDI files (see below).

Types of sound can be broken down even further. Speech can occur as either dialog or voice-over. Similarly, to borrow a few terms from the film industry, music can be either *source music* or *underscore.* Sometimes called score or, erroneously, background music, underscore is devoted to reinforcing, commenting on, or otherwise enhancing the dramatic content of the film. In all cases, underscore is music that would not be present if the scene were occurring in reality —the characters in the scene would not be able to hear it. On the other hand, source music is music that would be present if the scene were played out in reality—it might be coming from a radio, record player, night club band, or Muzak. In other words, source music is music that the characters in the scene would be hearing in their current situation. A further distinction is between visual source music, where we, the audience, can see the source of the sound, and nonvisual source music (sometimes called off-screen music), where we can't see the source, but we can believe it is there (for example, a car radio heard during an interior shot of the back seat of a car).

There are rough correlations between music and video, sound effects and animation, still graphics and ambiance, and text and narration. The interrelation of the four sound elements is just as important as the interrelation of the four visual elements. And, like the various visual components, the music, sound effects, ambiance, and narration can be assembled separately—sometimes by different specialists. Sound can be added to a project before, during, or after the visuals. Finally, your sound or musical data can be delivered in three different flavors: MIDI (Musical Instrument Digital Interface), 8-bit digital audio, or 16-bit digital audio. Some projects combine all three formats.

This chapter will examine some of the tools you can use to create and manipulate sound in multimedia.

Sampling and Sound Capture

The most popular form of sound used in multimedia is called *sampled* sound or digital audio. Another format, MIDI (Musical Instrument Digital Interface), is a much more efficient and desirable way to deliver sound in a multimedia presentation; but current computers are not equipped to easily accommodate MIDI data for multimedia purposes. The difference between sampled sound and MIDI is similar to the difference between bitmapped fonts and outline fonts such as those offered by PostScript or TrueType. Bitmapped fonts contain the actual visual data to create font characters, whereas outline fonts contain instructions that control an output device.

The Speed of Sound

Digital audio relies on a phenomenon similar to persistence of vision in a film, video, or digital movie. To achieve the illusion of visual motion, many consecutive still images are displayed as quickly as required. Although motion in the real world exists within a continuous—or *analog*—sequence, only 24 frames per second are necessary to fool our eyes into believing that we are seeing a representation of reality. Sound also is fundamentally continuous. Sound sampling captures still "snapshots" (called samples or frames) of a sound. These samples are played back very rapidly to recreate the illusion of the original sound.

While the eye may be tricked by 24 frames per second (30 frames per second is the standard for American video), sound requires between 5,000 and 48,000 samples per second to achieve comparable results. This wide range of playback rates affects aural realism in the same way that the frame rate of a film, video, or digital movie affects visual realism.

As a reference point, consider that the rate used on an audio compact disc is 44,100 samples per second, or 44.1 *kilohertz* (kHz). Because at least two samples are required to represent any one frequency (according to a mathematician named Nyquist), digital audio on a compact disc can faithfully reproduce sounds up to 22.05 kHz, which correlates to the upper end of the spectrum for human hearing. Although the highest note of a piano is 4.186 kHz, well below the 22.05 kHz supported by CD-quality digital audio, many higher frequencies (called *overtones* or *harmonics)* are present in any given waveform. These overtones are what color a sound's timbre and provide the information that allows us to distinguish between a note being played on a piano and that same pitch being played on a flute or violin.

Digital Sound Sampling

Sample resolution plays an equally important part in the faithful reproduction of sound through digital means (see Figure 4.1). Sample resolution refers to the number of bits used to represent the individual samples that are being output at 44.1, 22.05, or 11 kHz. Sample resolution exerts a similar effect upon the ear as the number of bits used to represent a pixel exerts upon the eye.

Two sample resolutions are common: 8-bit and 16-bit. The former restricts the range of sample values to 256, while the latter allows for 65,536 steps between values. The distinction is not as analogous to the difference between 8-bit color and 16-bit color as you might suspect; 8-bit sound sounds like an AM radio, whereas 16-bit sound is used on compact discs. Because each bit used to represent a sound sample adds 6 dB (decibels) to the signal-to-noise ratio of a sound, 8-bit sampling has a 48 dB signal-to-noise ratio, while 16-bit sampling approaches 96 dB.

Current generation Macintosh hardware has built-in 8-bit audio (16-bit for all PowerMacs and some Quadras), and most multimedia PCs and PC multimedia upgrade kits include 16-bit sound cards.

Hi Rez Audio Demo ⌘ 705

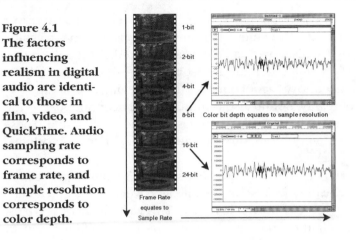

**Figure 4.1
The factors
influencing
realism in digital
audio are identi-
cal to those in
film, video, and
QuickTime. Audio
sampling rate
corresponds to
frame rate, and
sample resolution
corresponds to
color depth.**

Recording Media

There are several ways to record and store sounds before bringing them into your multimedia computer environment. They include conventional analog recording tape, digital audio tape (DAT), CD-R, Phillips digital tape, Sony's new writable CD, and hard disk storage.

Analog Tape

The most popular analog tape widths are ⅛-inch, ¼-inch, ½-inch, 1 inch, and 2 inch—each divided into 1, 2, 3, 4, 8, 16, or 24 horizontal tracks.

With analog tape, the larger the track width, the better the recording. However, noise reduction systems are available (and sometimes built in) to enhance the performance of ⅛-inch and ¼-inch systems (as well as ½-inch recorders) which divide the tape into 8 or more tracks. Transport speed is another factoring influencing fidelity because faster tape travel provides more horizontal space to encode additional audio data. Standard cassettes use 1⅞ inches per second (ips) or 3¾ ips for prosumer decks. Open reel recorders employ 7½, 15, and 30 ips transport speeds. Recorders that integrate a mixer into their box—the so-called "porta-studio" or "mini-studio" (usually cassette-based)—are an ideal solution for someone on a budget.

Digital Audio Tape (DAT)

The most common digital audio tape widths are 4mm, 8mm, or ½-inch divided into 2, 4, or 8 tracks. Current disk-based systems range from 2 to 16 tracks. Speed of tape travel has no impact upon fidelity since practically all systems employ 16-bit samples at the industry standard rate of 44.1 kHz (although many decks offer options for 32 kHz and 48 kHz sample rates). By far the most popular format is 4mm DAT (digital audio tape), largely because of ever-dropping prices. Even systems offering more than 2 tracks and SMPTE-standard synchronization have dropped to the consumer price level. Newer formats such as DCC (Digital Compact Cassette) and MD (Mini-Disc), introduced by Phillips/Tandy and Sony respectively, promise even more affordable digital recording, albeit with some loss of fidelity.

Hard Disk Recording

Hard disk-based systems can be stand-alone or expansion card-based or can involve hardware built into a computer (for example, 8-bit, 22 kHz sampling features built into every Macintosh). With the exception of the latter, the recording specifications are predominantly 16-bit, 44.1 kHz.

There are many reasons to choose hard disk recording over analog tape. Having random access to any point in your sound file allows you to use, reuse, and reorder sound material to your heart's content. That individual tracks are not physically time-aligned to one another, as they are on tape, offers similar benefits. Furthermore, tracks can be mixed in the digital domain *ad infinitum* without the signal degradation that occurs when you attempt to process in the world of analog tape.

Another advantage is that much of your editing is nondestructive, meaning that the original source material on your hard disk remains unchanged. EQs, fades, and other effects are applied on the fly during playback, and even reusing and reordering of material is accomplished in real time.

About the only strike that hard disk recording systems have against them is their vast storage requirements (see Table 4.1). Storing an hour of analog or digital tape will cost you less than $25; but that same hour of audio stored on a hard disk will require 600 Mb of free disk space, and the hard disk itself will need to have an access time of greater than 28ms. If you are used to storing QuickTime and other memory-hungry visual material, you may not find the sound storage requirements to be a stumbling block.

Apple's Sound Manager

PC users have to rely on third-party sound cards (see below), but Mac owners can take advantage of Apple's built-in Sound Manager software. This utility takes care of recording, playback, and saving sound on the Macintosh at 8-bit or 16-bit resolutions (current hardware limits playback to 8-bit), at rates of up to 64 kHz (current hardware places a 22.254 kHz ceiling on the rate).

All Macintoshes since the IIsi have been shipped with a sound input port optimized for their bundled microphone. You can still record sound using earlier Macintoshes, provided you have a third-party digitizer and your system folder contains the drivers that support it. Popular third-party 8-bit digitizers include Macromedia's MacRecorder, Premier Technology's MacMike, Articulate Systems' Voice Impact, Voice Impact Pro, and Voice Navigator, while CD-quality options come from Digidesign, Spectral Innovations (MacDSP), and MediaVision. Apple

Table 4.1 Storage Requirements for Digital Audio at Popular Sampling Rates
TST Includes Audio Compressed with MACE
(Macintosh Audio Compression and Expansion)

Sampling rate	Sample resolution	Channels	Number of bytes required for one minute of sound
44.1 kHz	16-bit	Stereo	10,584,000
44.1 kHz	16-bit	Mono	5,292,000
22.254 kHz	8-bit	Stereo	2,670,545
22.254 kHz	8-bit	Mono	1,335,273
22.254 kHz with MACE 3:1	8-bit	Stereo	890,182
22.254 kHz with MACE 6:1	8-bit	Stereo	445,091
22.254 kHz with MACE 3:1	8-bit	Mono	445,091
22.254 kHz with MACE 6:1	8-bit	Mono	222,545
22.05 kHz	16-bit	Stereo	5,292,000
22.05 kHz	16-bit	Mono	2,646,000
22.05 kHz	8-bit	Stereo	2,646,000
22.05 kHz	8-bit	Mono	1,323,000
11.127 kHz	8-bit	Stereo	1,335,273
11.127 kHz	8-bit	Mono	667,636
11.127 kHz with MACE 3:1	8-bit	Mono	222,545
11.127 kHz with MACE 6:1	8-bit	Mono	111,273
11.025 kHz	16-bit	Stereo	2,646,000
11.025 kHz	16-bit	Mono	1,323,000
11.025 kHz	8-bit	Stereo	1,323,000
11.025 kHz	8-bit	Mono	661,500
7.418 kHz	8-bit	Stereo	890,182
7.418 kHz	8-bit	Mono	445,091
5.563 kHz	8-bit	Stereo	667,636
5.563 kHz	8-bit	Mono	333,818

includes the drivers for many of these products on the QuickTime Developers' CD-ROM and also provides a driver for SID+—a build-it-yourself 8-bit digitizer whose schematics are available from most on-line services.

MACE (short for Macintosh Audio Compression and Expansion) is an audio compression scheme that reduces sound file size to ⅓ or ⅙, depending upon whether you choose 3:1 or 6:1 compression. Note that 6:1 compression is not suitable for music; and once you have compressed a sound using any compression scheme, including those offered by some third parties, you will not be able to edit that sound with any current sample-editing software.

MACE will decompress sound while it is being played back (however, not on the Mac Plus, SE, or Portable) and provides sample rate conversion options for all Macintoshes on the Mac II and beyond.

Apple's Sound Manager 3.0 has solved many troublesome problems of earlier versions and offers many useful features. Among them is device independence —with the appropriate drivers, 16-bit tracks will automatically be routed to NuBus cards that can handle them. Sound Manager works with Macs that handle 16-bit audio, such as the PowerMac series. The utility performs automatic 16-bit-to-8-bit file conversions. While Sound Manager 2.0 performed such processor-intensive (read: reduced frame rate for QuickTime) conversions by throwing away every other sample and dropping the low byte of every 16-bit word, Sound Manager 3.0 offers better methods for sample conversion.

Another feature of Sound Manager 3.0 is support of plug-in audio CODECs (compressor/decompressors). Such sound compression/decompression schemes will automatically be available to the Sound Manager and Sound Manager-compatible software. This digital signal processing pipeline also will provide for plug-in software-based digital EQs, filters, reverbs, and many DSP functions that usually require external hardware. The drop-in modular approach allows third parties to develop components (sometimes called "sifters") to enhance Macintosh-based sound. Sound Manager 3.0 will include a number of these components, including a sample rate converter, a mixer, and CODECs for MACE and ADPCM (a popular DOS/MPC 4:1 compression format).

Finally, because Sound Manager 3.0 plays back 2 to 3 times faster than its predecessor, QuickTime frame rates can be increased by 1 to 3 frames-per-second. Apple guarantees full compatibility with Sound Manager 2.0, even though the standard sampling rates have changed slightly (22.05 and 11.025 kHz in Sound Manager 3.0, as opposed to 22.254 and 11.127 kHz in the previous version).

Sound Manager and QuickTime

QuickTime relies heavily on the Sound Manager. QuickTime 1.5 and earlier used Sound Manager 2.0. To use Sound Manager 3.0 with QuickTime, you will need QuickTime version 1.6 or beyond. Theoretically, QuickTime's dependence upon the Sound Manager means it can store an unlimited number of audio tracks in any combination of stereo, mono, 8-bit, or 16-bit, and at any sampling rate up to 64 kHz. QuickTime 1.5 and earlier mix all tracks down to one monophonic 8-bit track on output.

Sound does add processing overhead to QuickTime movie playback, and this can increase the CPU load by 25 to 50 percent, lowering your effective data rate (frames per second) accordingly. With this in mind, don't expect to reliably play more than four channels on a MacPlus or Classic, four to eight on an LC, or 12 to 24 on a Quadra. If your sound is compressed with MACE (or ADPCM with Sound Manager 3.0), the processor time associated with on-the-fly decompression will have a negative impact on the speed of your visual elements.

Sound Digitizers and Recording/Editing Software

If your Macintosh does not support sound input through built-in hardware (look for a microphone jack on the back panel), there are still many options for sound digitization open to you. Third-party external digitizers and NuBus cards offer compatible or better-quality sampling for any Macintosh. Some popular examples for multimedia production follow.

Macromedia's MacRecorder Sound System Pro package includes a self-powered 8-bit monophonic digitizer box that connects to either of your serial ports. You need two MacRecorders for stereo sampling, and you can also use two MacRecorders to achieve stereo recording on Macintoshes that provide monophonic sound input. The full package includes SoundEdit 16 software (see below).

Likewise, PC users have more options than ever when it comes to capturing and playing back high quality sound. Sound cards that play and record (digitize) stereo sound are available separately for $100 or less; they also come bundled with multimedia upgrade kits for a few hundred dollars more.

In fact, the number of PC audio cards is astonishing. In 1995, there were over 100 available. In the following pages, we've profiled a few of the most popular cards for both Macs and PCs.

Macintosh Sound Cards

Oddly, there are fewer (and much more expensive) options for adding high quality sound recoding to the Mac than for the PC. Unless you have a PowerMac or Quadra AV model, the Mac's built-in sound input (and the MacRecorder Sound System Pro) limit you to 8-bit sampling at 22 kHz. For 16-bit, 44.1 kHz (CD-quality) recording, you'll have to add a NuBus card to your computer. For direct-to-hard-disk recording, you should have an unfragmented, preferably high-capacity, hard drive with a seek time of 28 ms or less. Drive mechanisms that perform thermal recalibration too frequently are not suitable for hard disk recording or playback.

Digidesign's original Audiomedia card and its current Audiomedia II card are excellent solutions for multimedia production requiring CD-quality audio. Most

QuickTime capture boards will work in conjunction with an Audiomedia card if they detect one on the NuBus. The Audiomedia cards are a little on the pricey side though—about $1,000 on the street.

Photoshop 3.0 Demo ⌘ 715

Those on a budget might want to check out Spectral Innovations' NuMedia 2 card. It offers most of what you get with the Audiomedia card for about half the price. Added bonus: the NuMedia 2 uses the same AT&T sound synthesis chip found in AV Macs. Adobe's AV DSP Power plug-in for Photoshop uses the same chip. That means, somewhat strangely, that the NuMedia 2 will also accelerate any graphics application that supports the Adobe Photoshop plug-in architecture. Talk about side benefits.

Spectral Innovations also makes a more expensive card called, simply, NuMedia that has digital as well as analog inputs and outputs.

Video Cards That Capture Audio

QuickTime video capture cards usually provide some mechanism for recording sound either during the recording of video or after the fact. Note that you will achieve better frame rates if you record video and audio separately. If you choose to add sound later, most multimedia authoring software can accommodate you (see Chapter 7, "Authoring Tools," for more details).

Just recording your sound as a sound-only QuickTime movie is usually sufficient to make it available to other software. Use Audioshop, Director, or PRO-motion for this. Any QuickTime editing program will let you combine the sound with a QuickTime video; or you can choose to use SoundToMovie, the Hyper-Card QuickTime stack, or Audioshop. SuperMac's VideoSpigot and Sound Pro, Radius' VideoVision, and RasterOps' MediaTime are among the cards that can capture sound as well as video.

Mac Recording and Editing Software

Sound editing software is crucial to multimedia production, if only for mixing sound files and adding fades. However, sampling editors offer as many important bells and whistles as many image-processing programs. Cut, copy, and paste procedures let you reorder and reuse music and sound material to create endless new arrangements from an existing file. Like their image manipulating counterparts, most sound editors support the full range of sound file formats that your authoring software will require. For example, SoundEdit Pro supports SoundEdit, Sound Designer II, AIFF, Instrument, 'snd' resource, and System 7 sound file formats.

The standard representation of a sound file is a waveform timeline made up of dots or lines, whose height indicates amplitude at any point in time. Such displays are usually zoomable, so you can edit with the precision of a single sample—there are over 44,000 samples per second in the case of CD-quality sound.

Where sample editors really shine is in the area of digital signal processing and special effects. Menu options typically offer amplification, various types of fades, equalization, sound reversal, pitch bending, echo, flanging, and reverberation.

Time compression and expansion is a useful (but not standard) option that lets you lengthen or shorten an entire sound file or a region without changing its pitch. Conversely, pitch shifting lets you change the key of your sound file without effecting its duration.

Macromedia's SoundEdit 16 and Opcode's Audioshop are popular and low-cost sound recording and editing programs, and we've reviewed them below. Two capable alternatives are OSC Media Products' Deck II and Alaska Software's DigiTrax.

Macromedia's SoundEdit 16

SoundEdit 16 Demo ⌘ 707

As the name implies, SoundEdit 16 handles stereo 16-bit sound recording and editing, as well as lower resolution 8-bit stereo sampling at 22 kHz, 11 kHz, 7.3 kHz, and 5.5 kHz. In addition to 6:1 and 3:1 compression, SoundEdit offers proprietary 4:1 and 8:1 compression options.

Although you can edit 16-bit sound files sampled at 44.1 and 48 kHz, SoundEdit Pro does not provide any option for playing these CD-quality sounds at a fidelity higher than the native Macintosh's 8-bit, 22 kHz.

SoundEdit 16 (see Figure 4.2) offers many processing options, including mix, amplify, reverse, bend, echo, reverb, graphic envelope editing, 5-band graphic EQ, flanging, rudimentary FM synthesis, emphasize (to boost upper harmonics), noise gating, pitch shifting, and time compression/expansion.

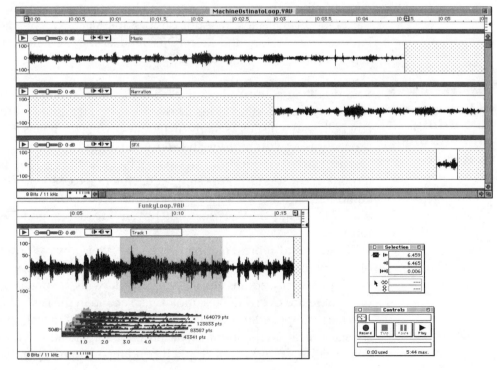

Figure 4.2 Macromedia's SoundEdit Pro is the foremost sound editor for multimedia. The software supports multiple tracks of direct-to and -from disk digital audio in many file formats, and provides for extensive editing and effects.

You can also directly edit the sound tracks of QuickTime movies by processing the existing tracks, as well as by mixing in other tracks, such as a musical score. When editing sound, you can operate on a sound's waveform—a direct and visually oriented method many find more intuitive than other techniques. SoundEdit 16 also imports PC WAV files, an important feature for cross platform work.

As of this writing, SoundEdit 16 lacks two important features: You can't adjust recording levels (an annoying and surprising oversight), and you can't record directly from audio CDs. (You can get around the latter shortcoming by using Apple's MoviePlayer to record audio from CDs, then importing the files into SoundEdit 16.)

Opcode's Audioshop

Opcode's Audioshop (see Figure 4.3) offers playlist editing, a valuable feature missing from all but the very high-end sound editors such as Digidesign's Sound Designer II. With Audioshop, you can arrange a list of 8-bit sound files in any order and intermix these with CD audio tracks, assuming that you have a CD-ROM drive capable of playing audio CDs. (Among those that do: Apple CD300, and CD300 Plus, Toshiba 3401 and higher, and NEC 3X and 4X.)

The program offers 16-bit recording at the four standard Macintosh rates. Editing options include cut, copy, paste, scale amplitude, pitch bending, echo, vibrato, flanging, sound reversal, and looping. Although playback can be direct-from-disk, both recording and editing are limited to sound files that can fit in your available RAM. Once recorded or opened into Audioshop, a sound file may be saved as an AIFF, SoundEdit, System 7, HyperCard, Director 'snd resource, or a QuickTime movie. A bonus is that sounds may be saved to existing movies.

Figure 4.3 Opcode's Audioshop lets you intermix CD-based audio with disk-based 8-bit and 16-bit soundfiles in playlists. Basic editing of non-CD audio is supported.

Windows Sound Cards and Software

Sound on the PC has come a long way in the last few years. At first, PC users were so happy to even get sound that they put up with low quality 8-bit cards. Now, 16-bit cards are the norm, and they often include high quality "wavetable" synthesis for MIDI audio—much better than the older FM synthesis (see "Sound Synthesis").

Sound cards usually bundle recording and editing software; so we're not reviewing separate programs as we did for the Mac, above. If you buy a sound card (or if your PC comes equipped with one), you'll most likely also get a popular editor, such as Voyetra's Multimedia Sound Software. These programs are comparable to their Mac counterparts (mentioned above), letting you record and mix tracks, record audio CDs, and perform basic editing tasks. If your editing needs are more sophisticated, consider a higher performance card such as Turtle Beach's MultiSound Monterey (see page 129), which will usually include better editing software as well.

When shopping for a card, look for a high sampling rate (44.1 kHz or above); compression support; on-board mixing (necessary to meet the MPC spec); and, if you're an avid gamer, Sound Blaster compatibility. You may also want to get a sound card with a CD-ROM interface that will allow you to plug in a CD-ROM drive. If you opt for a SCSI interface with an ASPI interface, you'll also be able to plug in a variety of SCSI devices, such as scanners and disk drives (see "Connecting Devices to the PC: SCSI or IDE?" in Chapter 2).

Finally, if your PC is already crammed with goodies such as tape drives, printers, and other peripherals, get a card that supports higher IRQs and DMAs. This will help you avoid device conflicts (generally, you should look for IRQ support above IRQ7 and DMA channels above 3).

If you want to get involved with MIDI music synthesis and editing, you'll need a few additional features. First, you'll want the card to include a MIDI interface module so you don't have to buy it separately. Also important, as mentioned, go for wavetable synthesis and a high performance chipset such as OPL4. It's also a good idea to get a card that will allow you to create your own instrument sounds. (See "Sound Synthesis" for more on MIDI and its terminology.) If you already have a sound card, you can add wavetable synthesis and a MIDI interface with a "daughterboard" such as Roland's SoundCanvas DB.

There are literally dozens of sound cards in the hot PC market. We've picked two solid products: one low cost card, and a higher end card that includes more features.

Ensoniq's SoundScape

Ensoniq's card offers a good combination of features, including many of those mentioned above, for a street price of around $200. You get high sampling rates for both recording and playback, compression to keep file size down, Sound Blaster compatibility, MIDI and CD-ROM interfaces (though not SCSI), and the ability to record CD audio.

The SoundScape also features wavetable synthesis, higher IRQ/DMA support, and bundled audio editing software. Sonically, the card is very good, and overall it is an excellent buy for the bucks.

Turtle Beach's MultiSound Monterey

Wave for Win Demo ⌘ 702

Turtle Beach is recognized for its high-end sonic solutions; and for about twice the price of the SoundScape, the Monterey is an appropriately capable sound card. For extra simoleons, you get most of SoundScape's features (no CD-ROM interface, though) plus ear-tingling special effects processing, and WaveSE, a professional quality editing and recording software. Don't look for Sound Blaster compatibility, however. This card isn't made for games—just pro audio production and playback.

Sound Synthesis

Early sound synthesis was accomplished through analog methods that have now given way to digital approaches. Interestingly, the components of digital synthesis are roughly the same as those of its analog ancestors.

A general model of digital sound synthesis starts with a sound source that produces a waveform at a user-specified pitch, often user-specifiable as a square, triangle, sawtooth, or other shape. An oscillator (OSC), digitally controlled oscillator (DCO), or digital waveform oscillator (DWO) generates this raw sound data.

Next in the synthesis signal chain is a filter used to remove, reduce, or emphasize specified frequencies or frequency bands. Filters that remove the upper frequencies are called low pass filters (LPFs), while those that remove the lower frequencies are referred to as high pass filters (HPFs). Band pass filters (BPFs) remove all but a specified frequency range or band, and notch filters do just the opposite—that is, they remove a specified frequency range. Sometimes, filters that can be placed under digital control are referred to as variable digital filters (VDFs). Variations on this theme are seen in time variant filters (TVFs).

Before the sound can be output it must be amplified; so the final link of the synthesizer signal chain is an amplifier. Amplifiers that can be controlled digitally are often called variable digital amplifiers (VDAs) or, in some manufacturers' devices, time variant amplifiers (TVAs).

Along the way, other waveform processors may be applied to a sound. Low frequency oscillators (LFOs) produce waveforms below the threshold of human hearing. When a sine wave LFO is applied to the VDA, it produces *amplitude tremolo* or a continual fluctuation of loudness. On the other hand, when applied to an oscillator, an LFO can produce the continual pitch variance known as *vibrato*.

Envelope generators (EGs) are used to impose a simple or complex variation of intensity over time. When applied at the amplifier stage, EGs can specify how fast a sound rises to its peak volume, and how slowly it decays, among other things. Special effects can be achieved by applying an EG at the filter stage of the signal chain.

Synthesis has reached a stage of development where nearly all of the components in the signal chain—OSC, VDF, VDA, EG, and LFO—can easily be controlled by software or by way of the front panel buttons on a device.

Within the framework of the synthesis signal chain, a great number of approaches to synthesis have been developed, adapted, or appropriated by various synthesizer manufacturers to endow their instruments with a unique signature sound. These are (in approximate order of appearance on the scene): subtractive synthesis, additive synthesis, frequency modulation synthesis (FM—sometimes known as algorithmic synthesis), phase distortion synthesis (PDS), resynthesized pulse code modulation (RS-PCM) synthesis, Karplus-Strong synthesis (also known as plucked-string synthesis), linear/arithmetic synthesis (L/A), advanced integrated synthesis (AI), advanced vector synthesis (AV), and variable architecture synthesis technology (VAST).

In subtractive synthesis, a complex waveform—generated by one or two oscillators and often mixed with white or pink noise—is filtered by a VCF, with EGs and LFOs thrown in along the way. Additive synthesis takes the opposite approach. Sine waves or other waveforms are simply added together, often with each waveform responding to a separate EG to vary its pitch over time.

Frequency modulation or FM synthesis was created by John Chowning and eventually licensed to Yamaha, where it gave birth to Yamaha's legendary DX7 synthesizer. FM synthesis uses the same principles as FM radio, applied to waveforms in the range of human hearing. The process starts with at least two frequencies, one of which is used to control (or modulate) the other. The result is a very complex waveform that is usually extremely interesting to listen to. The problem is that it is difficult to predict what will result from combining any two or more waveforms. Fortunately, an army of sound designers has created tens of thousands of stock sounds that are either built into the ROMs of FM instruments or loadable in their RAM.

Phase distortion synthesis, popularized by Casio, is similar to FM synthesis, except that a waveform is applied to an out-of-phase copy of itself. If you can picture a sine wave, you can imagine how two copies of the same wave could be shifted so that they do not reach their peaks at the same time. This is referred to as being *out of phase* and forms the basis of PD synthesis.

Resynthesized pulse code modulation (RS-PCM), popularized by Roland, is similar to additive synthesis. The difference is that the choice of the component sine waves is mandated by an analysis of an FFT (Fast Fourier Transform) of a sampled sound rather than through random or procedural processes.

Karplus-Strong synthesis was developed by Kevin Karplus and Alan Strong. Karplus-Strong synthesis models the sound of plucked strings by starting with a sound source that resembles a plucked string and then filtering it to produce the effect of the subsequent vibrations of that string. Strings of any length and circumference can be modeled using this technique, even those which could never exist in the real world.

Synthesizers and Samplers

Electronic devices that generate sound through this wide variety of synthesis techniques are *the* instruments of the late 20th century. Most available devices are marketed in two formats, one with a keyboard (not necessarily the 88 notes found on a traditional piano) and one (referred to as a sound module or rack-mountable module) without a keyboard. The latter is meant to be controlled by a separate keyboard or by software. The sound-generating innards of the keyboard and module versions of a device should be identical.

Electronic instruments have evolved to the point that most devices nowadays are capable of sounding a maximum of 16, 24, or 32 different notes simultaneously. This characteristic is referred to as 16-, 24-, or 32-voice polyphony. If a 24-voice polyphonic synthesizer is currently sounding 24 notes together and is requested to play a 25th note, one of the other 24 will immediately drop out to free up the software mechanism required to generate the newly arrived note.

Most devices also can play back a maximum of either 8 or 16 different types, or *timbres,* of sounds at once. This feature is referred to as 8- or 16-channel multitimbrality. This is not to be confused with the number of different timbres that an instrument contains in its ROMs or loadable RAM. Here you will typically have 192 sounds available at all times, even if only 16 may sound simultaneously.

Many people refer to all electronic sound-generating devices as synthesizers; but, technically, synthesizers form only one class of such devices. Synthesizers produce sounds from electronically generated waveforms and thus rarely produce a sound that might occur in nature. Samplers (also called wavetable synthesizers), on the other hand, simply play back sounds that have been digitally recorded and stored in ROM chips or loaded into RAM. A further distinction exists between samplers that can make their own digital recordings to play back and sample players that rely exclusively on sounds stored in their ROMs or loaded into their RAM.

Many more recent approaches to electronic sound generation combine synthesis and sampling techniques into a hybrid process. The first widespread use of such a hybrid sound-generating technique was popularized by Roland in the Linear/Arithmetic (L/A) synthesis. Sampled attacks of real instruments, traditionally the most difficult portion of a sound to synthesize and often the most interesting, are pasted onto the front of synthesized tones. Korg followed with their advanced integrated synthesis (AI), employing a similar approach to L/A and, shortly thereafter, advanced vector synthesis (AV), which relies upon the interaction of sequences of stored waveforms.

Finally, Kurzweil introduce variable architecture synthesis (VAST) in 1991. VAST uses custom chips that can be software-configured to replicate any of these synthesis techniques in combination. The chips are flexible enough to be configured for as-yet-unimagined forms of synthesis.

MIDI

Director 4.0 Demo ⌘ 708

Premiere 4.0 Demo ⌘ 722

Developed in 1982, MIDI is an international specification used by musical instruments that contain microprocessors to communicate with similar devices of different manufacturers. The format of MIDI data was codified by representatives from synthesizer manufacturers in a document called the MIDI Specification, published in August of 1983.

Several multimedia authoring and video editing tools let you take advantage of the economy and flexibility of the MIDI format. Notable among these are Passport Producer, Macromedia Director, and Adobe Premiere. It doesn't take long to realize the significance of the fact that MIDI files that are used to produce sound tracks are minuscule in comparison to the digital audio files (even 8-bit) that their data would produce. When you use MIDI instead of digital audio for an interactive multimedia project, you can alter many sound characteristics during playback. Furthermore, you can change the tempo or key of the music; mute, solo, or fade individual tracks; loop beat-delineated regions; or completely reorchestrate and remix the music—all from a single version of the file.

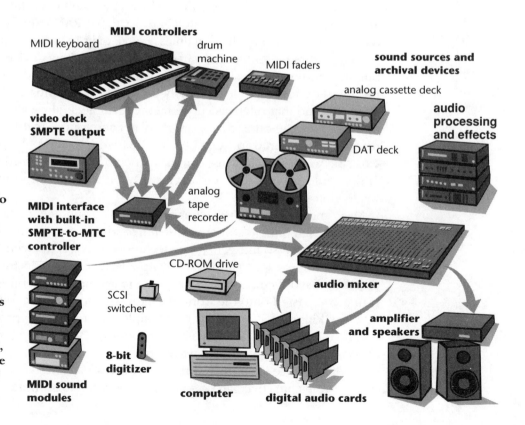

Figure 4.4 This configuration allows you to take full advantage of MIDI and digital audio in both 8-bit and 16-bit formats. There are many variations on this theme and some components could be omitted, depending on the level and type of production you are engaged in.

MIDI data requires serial cables with 5-pin DIN connectors at 31.25 kBaud. Most MIDI messages are assigned to one of 16 independent channels. In a multitimbral MIDI device, you can assign a different sound to each MIDI channel.

You will need a MIDI interface to convert MIDI data into a format that your computer can understand, and vice versa. There are three types of MIDI interfaces: those that support a single set of 16 MIDI channels, those that support two sets of 16 MIDI channels (sometimes referred to as dual interfaces), and those that support more than 32 channels (sometimes called multiport, multicable, or cableized interfaces). (See Figure 4.4 for an example of a typical MIDI setup.)

The MIDI specification has had several addenda. In July, 1988, Standard MIDI Files (SMFs) were made official and have now become analogous to ASCII text files in word processing. A file saved in one program as an SMF can usually be opened, played, and edited with another program. In addition, SMFs are compatible across all computer platforms. Since their introduction, SMFs have formed the basis for a growing "clip MIDI data" market (don't forget that copyright issues apply to SMFs as well as to actual recordings of music).

In 1991, the MIDI specification was updated to include a General MIDI mode to facilitate a plug-and-play approach for multimedia. General MIDI mode defines a standardized list of sounds that are always assigned to the same patch numbers. When a device is in General MIDI mode, for example, patch 1 is always an acoustic grand piano, patch 41 is a solo violin, and so on up to 128. Prior to that, there was no guarantee that a MIDI sequence recorded on one device would sound anything like it was supposed to when played back through another device. Now, there are many General MIDI synthesizers and synthesizer modules. Roland's Sound Brush, about the size of a Stephen King paperback, is a good example of such a device.

General MIDI mode also includes a standardized mapping of percussion sounds to note numbers (see Table 4.2). Prior to this, playing a percussion part on a different percussion machine than the one for which it was created always resulted in cacophony. On one device, the G above middle C might be a snare drum; on another, it might be an crash cymbal.

General MIDI may be a major proponent in the CD+MIDI Specification (designed to provide a MIDI data track on audio CDs), and Apple is jumping on the General MIDI bandwagon with great enthusiasm. Virtually all PC sound cards have MIDI support, and Windows supports General MIDI.

Apple's MIDI Manager and Windows' MIDI Mapper

Apple created the MIDI Manager tool set (system software including an INIT, a driver, and a program called PatchBay) to handle communication between MIDI software and the serial ports. MIDI Manager makes it possible to route the output of one MIDI application into one or more other MIDI Manager-compatible programs while all communicate with the serial ports. The software also offers

Table 4.2 General MIDI Sound Set
(MIDI Program Numbers 1–128 on all channels except 10)

1	Acoustic Grand Piano	28	Electric Guitar (clean)	55	Synth Voice
2	Bright Acoustic Piano	29	Electric Guitar (muted)	56	Orchestra Hit
3	Electric Grand Piano	30	Overdriven Guitar	57	Trumpet
4	Honky-tonk Piano	31	Distortion Guitar	58	Trombone
5	Electric Piano 1	32	Guitar Harmonics	59	Tuba
6	Electric Piano 2	33	Acoustic Bass	60	Muted Trumpet
7	Harpsichord	34	Electric Bass (finger)	61	French Horn
8	Clavi	35	Electric Bass (pick)	62	Brass Section
9	Celesta	36	Fretless Bass	63	SynthBrass 1
10	Glockenspiel	37	Slap Bass 1	64	SynthBrass 2
11	Music Box	38	Slap Bass 2	65	Soprano Sax
12	Vibraphone	39	Synth Bass 1	66	Alto Sax
13	Marimba	40	Synth Bass 2	67	Tenor Sax
14	Xylophone	41	Violin	68	Baritone Sax
15	Tubular Bells	42	Viola	69	Oboe
16	Dulcimer	43	Cello	70	English Horn
17	Drawbar Organ	44	Contrabass	71	Bassoon
18	Percussive Organ	45	Tremolo Strings	72	Clarinet
19	Rock Organ	46	Pizzicato Strings	73	Piccolo
20	Church Organ	47	Orchestral Harp	74	Flute
21	Reed Organ	48	Timpani	75	Recorder
22	Accordion	49	String Ensemble 1	76	Pan Flute
23	Harmonica	50	String Ensemble 2	77	Blown Bottle
24	Tango Accordion	51	SynthStrings 1	78	Shakuhachi
25	Acoustic Guitar (nylon)	52	SynthStrings 2	79	Whistle
26	Acoustic Guitar (steel)	53	Choir Aahs	80	Ocarina
27	Electric Guitar (jazz)	54	Voice Oohs	81	Lead 1 (square)

Table 4.2 continued

82 Lead 2 (sawtooth)	98 FX 2 (soundtrack)	114 Agogo
83 Lead 3 (calliope)	99 FX 3 (crystal)	115 Steel Drums
84 Lead 4 (chiff)	100 FX 4 (atmosphere)	116 Woodblock
85 Lead 5 (charang)	101 FX 5 (brightness)	117 Taiko Drum
86 Lead 6 (voice)	102 FX 6 (goblins)	118 Melodic Tom
87 Lead 7 (fifths)	103 FX 7 (echoes)	119 Synth Drum
88 Lead 8 (bass + lead)	104 FX 8 (sci-fi)	120 Reverse Cymbal
89 Pad 1 (new age)	105 Sitar	121 Guitar Fret Noise
90 Pad 2 (warm)	106 Banjo	122 Breath Noise
91 Pad 3 (polysynth)	107 Shamisen	123 Seashore
92 Pad 4 (choir)	108 Koto	124 Bird Tweet
93 Pad 5 (bowed)	109 Kalimba	125 Telephone Ring
94 Pad 6 (metallic)	110 Bag Pipe	126 Helicopter
95 Pad 7 (halo)	111 Fiddle	127 Applause
96 Pad 8 (sweep)	112 Shanai	128 Gunshot
97 FX 1 (rain)	113 Tinkle Bell	

extensive support for the Macintosh, including a full implementation of internal and external synchronization.

With MIDI Manager you deal with virtual MIDI ports—representing both hardware serial ports and inputs and outputs provided by MIDI Manager-compatible applications. Connecting "in" ports to "out" ports is as simple as using the mouse to drag a virtual patch cable between ports (see Figure 4.5).

Microsoft's MIDI Mapper, which is included with Windows, lets you remap channels and patch numbers for a given MIDI synthesizer.

MIDI Sequencers

A sequence of musical events played—or intended to be played—on a sound-generating device such as a synthesizer or sampler, is called a MIDI sequence. MIDI sequencer software allows you to record, edit, and play back such sequences (see Figure 4.6). The data stored in a MIDI sequence is similar to piano-roll data in that only the instructions that are required to trigger specific

Table 4.3 General MIDI Percussion Map
(Channel 10)

Key	Drum sound	Key	Drum sound	Key	Drum sound
35	Acoustic Bass Drum	51	Ride Cymbal 1	67	High Agogo
36	Bass Drum 1	52	Chinese Cymbal	68	Low Agogo
37	Side Stick	53	Ride Bell	69	Cabasa
38	Acoustic Snare	54	Tambourine	70	Maracas
39	Hand Clap	55	Splash Cymbal	71	Short Whistle
40	Electric Snare	56	Cowbell	72	Long Whistle
41	Low Floor Tom	57	Crash Cymbal 2	73	Short Guiro
42	Closed Hi-Hat	58	Vibraslap	74	Long Guiro
43	High Floor Tom	59	Ride Cymbal 2	75	Claves
44	Pedal Hi-Hat	60	Hi Bongo	76	Hi Wood Block
45	Low Tom	61	Low Bongo	77	Low Wood Block
46	Open Hi-Hat	62	Mute Hi Conga	78	Mute Cuica
47	Low-Mid Tom	63	Open Hi Conga	79	Open Cuica
48	Hi-Mid Tome	64	Low Conga	80	Mute Triangle
49	Crash Cymbal 1	65	High Timbale	81	Open Triangle
50	High Tom	66	Low Timbale		

sounds on an external or internal hardware synthesizer—or, in the case of Apple's new music architecture, a software-based synthesizer—are recorded. Actual sound (waveform) data is not.

Acoustic music concepts relating to sound waves—pitch, volume, timbre, rhythm, and articulation—correlate to control codes describing performance actions with MIDI data. Pitch equates to a note number, volume to velocity of keystroke, timbre to "patch change," and articulation to controller number and setting. Because of this, each time a MIDI sequence is played, the result is a repeat performance of the original or edited performance.

MIDI data is different from the data stored on analog tape or in digital sound files. Taped music is frozen and can only be edited with great difficulty. On the

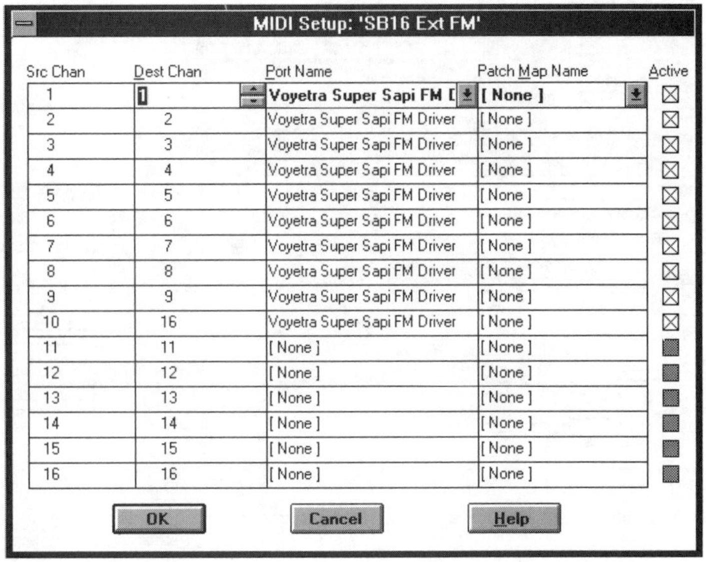

Src Chan	Dest Chan	Port Name	Patch Map Name	Active
1	1	Voyetra Super Sapi FM [▲▼	[None] ▼	☒
2	2	Voyetra Super Sapi FM Driver	[None]	☒
3	3	Voyetra Super Sapi FM Driver	[None]	☒
4	4	Voyetra Super Sapi FM Driver	[None]	☒
5	5	Voyetra Super Sapi FM Driver	[None]	☒
6	6	Voyetra Super Sapi FM Driver	[None]	☒
7	7	Voyetra Super Sapi FM Driver	[None]	☒
8	8	Voyetra Super Sapi FM Driver	[None]	☒
9	9	Voyetra Super Sapi FM Driver	[None]	☒
10	16	Voyetra Super Sapi FM Driver	[None]	☒
11	11	[None]	[None]	■
12	12	[None]	[None]	■
13	13	[None]	[None]	■
14	14	[None]	[None]	■
15	15	[None]	[None]	■
16	16	[None]	[None]	■

MIDI Setup: 'SB16 Ext FM'

[OK]   [Cancel]   [Help]

**Figure 4.5
MIDI Mapper.**

other hand, MIDI data can be examined and edited at the individual note level. Mistakes can be corrected with little effort. Transposition and tempo modifications are simple edit options. The rhythmic correction that MIDI permits (known as quantization) has no correspondence for files consisting of actual sound data, whether analog or digital.

There many MIDI sequencers for the Macintosh and Windows. It is possible to divide Mac software into entry-level programs (Ballade, EZ Vision, One Step, and Trax) and professional-level sequencers (Metro [originally released as Beyond], Cubase, Notator Logic, Performer, Pro 5, and Vision) according to options such as synchronization features, number of tracks, Standard MIDI File (SMF) compatibility, and event editing. There even are several shareware sequencers—MIDI Companion and MiniTrax, for example.

Some of the entry-level sequencers are merely "junior" versions of professional sequencers offered by the same company. Opcode's EZ Vision has many of the same options as the company's Vision. Passport's Trax is simply Passport's Pro 5 professional-level sequencer with a restricted feature set.

On the Windows side, there are also many options. PG Music makes Power-Track Pro, a good entry level sequencer for Windows that lists for an unbelievable $29. On the higher end, Twelve Tone Systems' Cakewalk Pro for Windows (Figure 4.7) does everything but ice the cake-—for about 10 times the cost of PowerTracks Pro. You do get many professional features, however, including excellent control over precise timing of multiple tracks, and the ability to include war sounds in your MIDI score.

Cakewalk Pro Demo ⌘ 704

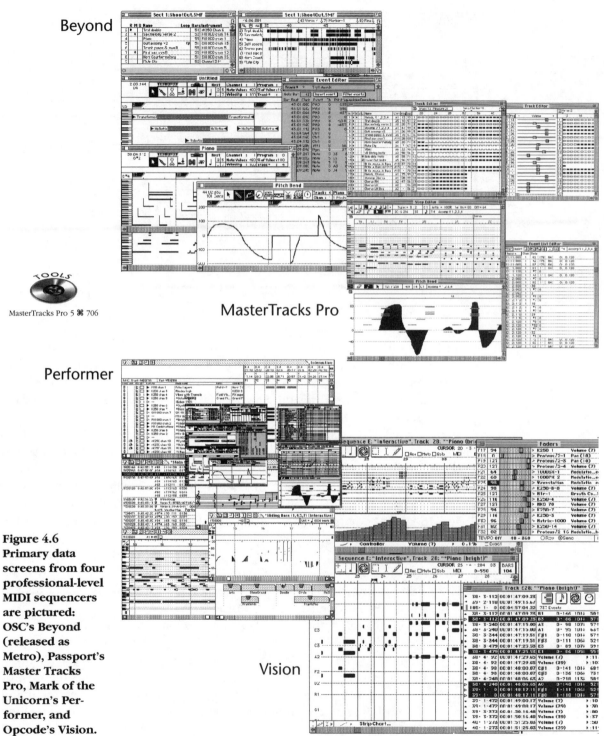

Beyond

MasterTracks Pro 5 ⌘ 706

MasterTracks Pro

Performer

Vision

**Figure 4.6
Primary data
screens from four
professional-level
MIDI sequencers
are pictured:
OSC's Beyond
(released as
Metro), Passport's
Master Tracks
Pro, Mark of the
Unicorn's Per-
former, and
Opcode's Vision.**

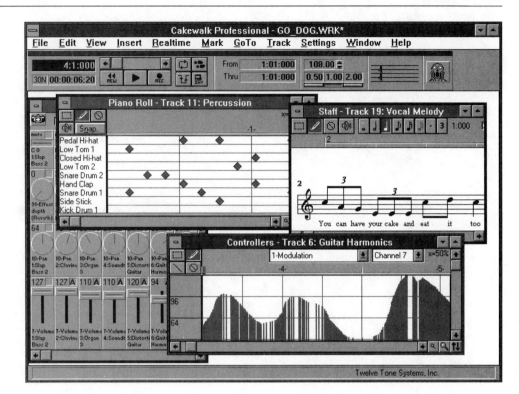

Figure 4.7
Cakewalk Pro.

MIDI Genera-
tion Software

Super Jam Demo ⌘ 700

There are several programs that let you generate and compose MIDI scores, even if your musical knowledge is limited. Windows MIDI generation programs include Blue Ribbon Soundwork's SuperJAM! Jr., which is often bundled with sound cards. Using SuperJAM, you can compose music in a variety of styles, including Rock, Jazz, Country & Western, and so on. PC Music's Band in the Box is another leading PC program in this category.

Ready to Roll

Clip Media/Sound ⌘ 300–343

In this chapter we've covered the basic types of hardware and software you'll need to produce sound on your Mac or PC. You'll find a large number of valuable sound resources on the *Power Tools* CD, including extensive libraries of license-free sound clips that you're free to use immediately. For detailed information on using all these tools to produce professional-quality audio for your multimedia projects, refer to Chapter 10, "Producing Sound."

5

Animation Tools

Animation is one of the most compelling elements of multimedia, and good animation can make the difference between a ho-hum presentation and one that stuns and delights its audience. The past few years have witnessed a confusing proliferation of animated presentation programs, media integration software, 3-D typography programs, 3-D drawing packages, 3-D animation software, network rendering programs, and animation utilities such as texture and scenery generators.

Adding to the market confusion is a cloying 3-D jargon filled with arcane terms that are often used interchangeably. To name a few, there are *lofting, loafing*, and *skinning* (all referring to the same basic cross-sectional modeling technique); *NURBs, splines*, and *Beziers* (various methods for drawing smooth curves); *procedural, reflection*, and *bump maps* (assorted ways to project and render surfaces onto 3-D objects); and *motion control, morphing*, and *keyframes* (different animation techniques).

In this chapter, we'll try to slice through this snarl of competing products, overlapping categories, and pervasive jargon. For easy reference, we've broken products into these groups:

- **Presentation Software**: programs that allow you to create and incorporate simple 2-D and even 3-D animation into multimedia presentations.

- **3-D Utility Programs**: products that convert 2-D type and graphics to 3-D images, generate 3-D scenery, and morph one image into another.

- **3-D Modeling, Animation, and Rendering**: a category that includes programs specializing in one or more phases of the 3-D process.

Finally, we've thrown in two sidebars: one on various animation utility programs and another on products that speed the 3-D rendering process.

2-D and Not 3-D

Let's face it, 3-D animation gets all the attention. With its simulated dimensionality, subtle reflection and lighting effects, and sophisticated animation, 3-D is one of multimedia's darlings. On the other hand, it's not for everyone or every application: Creating 3-D is enormously time-consuming and places a great demand on hardware resources. 2-D animation is often as effective, and it's far easier to master.

Presentation Software

Back around 1988, presentation packages such as Adobe's Persuasion and Microsoft's PowerPoint began hitting the scene. These programs are used to create computer-based slide shows to enliven boardroom snooze-fests. Common program features include basic slide outlining; templates for slide backgrounds, type, and graphic elements; graphics and sound libraries; and conversion of spreadsheets to graphic charts.

When combined with a data projector—a compact portable screen that displays a computer's output on a common overhead projector—these programs are indispensable for on-the-road presentations (see Chapter 2, "Systems Software, Hardware, and Peripherals").

More recently, presentation software has become even more powerful, as traditional programs have started to incorporate more advanced features, blurring the lines between authoring programs, such as Director, and newer multimedia presentation packages, such as Gold Disk's Astound and Macromedia's Action.

Using traditional presentation packages such as PowerPoint and Persuasion, you can create basic 2-D animations for your slide shows; design simulated 3-D graphs; and create interactive links that branch to new slides, depending on user input. Although these programs are impressive in both features and usability, they do not approach the multimedia support of the new breed of programs that are the focus of the following section.

Multimedia Presentation Programs

Support for 2-D animation and digital video is what sets *multimedia* presentation software apart from traditional presentation packages. In fact, experimenting with one of the multimedia presentation programs can be an excellent introduction to multimedia.

"Presentation" is something of a misnomer, by the way, since programs such as Action and Astound can actually be looked at as "lite" versions of powerful authoring packages such as Director. For the purposes of this chapter, we'll concentrate solely on the animation features of these programs. For detailed information on media integration (authoring) tools, see Chapter 7.

Basic Animation Techniques

Using one of the programs reviewed below, you'll be able to create realistic *path-based* animations and even exercise rudimentary *motion control.* Path-based animation lets you create movement by dragging an object from one point to another; the program then animates the object along this path. Many 2-D and 3-D animation packages use a more sophisticated version of this technique that allows you to specify "keyframes," with the program filling in the "in-between frames."

Most animation packages use a *timeline*—a pop-up window that lets you position objects at any point in time. A few packages, such as Vividus' Cinemation and Linker Systems' The Animation Stand, mimic traditional *cel-based* animation techniques instead of using path or keyframe animation. With this technique, you create one frame or *cel* at a time. These cels are then overlaid to create a finished animation. Cel animation is sometimes referred to as *onionskinning*, after the transparent paper Hollywood animators used to sketch cels.

Motion control—also called *motion scripting*—is a catch-all term referring to the refinement of movement, in which you specify such attributes as acceleration. More advanced motion control (camera movement, spline-based motion paths, and motion filters, for example) is the province of 3-D animation programs. We will discuss motion control later in this chapter and in Chapter 13, "Creating Animation."

Common Features

For starters, you shouldn't expect a multimedia presentation package to have all of the features of traditional presentation software. If you're going to be creating slide shows and working mostly with text and charts, you're better off with such old-guard mainstays as Persuasion or PowerPoint, both of which offer complete text and charting facilities. These programs also have such features as slide sorters and presentation outliners.

In general, you'll trade these traditional slide-based graphics and text creation tools for such multimedia features as device control, interactivity, and animation.

Among the common features of multimedia presentation software are:

- **Graphics support.** You can expect at least basic draw and paint tools, such as pens and brushes, line styles, and fill patterns. Some programs, such as Cinemation, even include image processing tools like lassos, and eyedroppers. While many users prefer to turn to more specialized paint and image programs, it's handy to have these features in one program. Most programs import PICT, PCX, BMP, GIF or animated PICS files; some also accept EPS and TIFF files.

- **Templates.** The majority of programs have an assortment of prefab templates that include backgrounds, actors, and movements that you can customize for your own purposes. They are very helpful for the beginner: Assembling a presentation from templates is a good way to learn a program without the frustrations of starting from scratch.

- **Transitional effects.** All programs provide a slew of special effects, such as wipes, dissolves, and fades, that are useful for transitions between scenes. A more advanced version of these effects is the *automated build*—the gradual overlaying of elements in a scene.

- **Interactivity.** The ability to explore seemingly random areas of an on-screen presentation is one of the cornerstones of multimedia. With many packages, you can incorporate interactivity by designating an object as a "button." When you subsequently select the button with the mouse, the program either plays a sound file or branches to another slide.

Like all areas of multimedia, the multimedia presentation category is evolving quickly. Each of the following programs has Mac and Windows versions, and both offer good animation features.

Macromedia's Action

Action is a program that divides a presentation into "scenes" with static backgrounds against which objects can be arranged and animated. These objects can be text, graphics, animations, or even digital movies. The action is orchestrated with Timeline Window, which helps you sequence objects and their movements.

The timeline concept was pioneered by Macromedia, which first introduced it as the "Score" in Director. It is now used in one form or another in nearly all leading 3-D animation programs. If you plan to move on to the more rarefied world of 3-D, you can get used to the concept with the timeline, which is probably the most complicated part of Action.

You create animation with the Path menu by specifying points along a path (keyframes) and the overall duration of the motion. Action then fills in the intermediate frames, creating smooth motion.

Action provides good control over individual objects: Click on an object, and you can adjust parameters such as the object's duration in a scene. If object creation and control leaves you cold, you can use one of Action's predefined templates, complete with text, graphics, and animation. Using templates as a starting point, you can replace template objects with your own and adjust the existing animation. We recommend this technique to beginners who may be put off by the timeline and its moderate learning curve. By adjusting a template's animation parameters and then viewing the results, you can learn a lot.

After you've imported or created your various objects and choreographed them with the timeline, you can add transitional and multimedia effects such as sound or a QuickTime or AVI video clip. Action has a particularly well-stocked arsenal of transitional and motion effects. Objects can be designated as interactive trig-

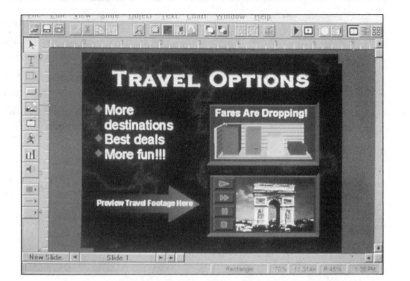

**Figure 5.1
Gold Disk's
Astound.**

gers that, when clicked, will pause or resume action, play a sound or movie file, or go to another scene.

Gold Disk's Astound

Animation is one of Astound's (Figure 5.1) strong points. You can create graphic objects, and select textural fills such as clouds and terrains from a Texture menu. All elements can be controlled by a timeline, and you can apply many different transitional and animated effects. Astound lets you use a separate timeline for each slide, which gives you more control than the single timeline Action uses for an entire presentation.

If you don't want to create your own graphics, you can import finished art in a variety of formats, including PICT, PCX, GIF, and TIFF. In fact, for all but the simplest graphic effects, you may want to do just that; Astound, like Action, includes fairly primitive drawing tools. You can also import QuickTime and AVI movies, and Astound, like Action, lets you create 3-D charts that can then be treated as animated objects.

Macromedia's Director

Macromedia's Director is the premiere media integration—authoring—tool. It's used by multimedia developers to integrate and play back multimedia productions of all types (see Chapter 7, "Authoring Tools"). Because Director is relatively complex and expensive, you wouldn't want to use it for animation alone. But if you're assembling a presentation using the program, you'll find its built-in animation tools handy.

Director has a rudimentary set of paint tools for creating bitmap objects, as well as a basic set of drawing tools. Other features include 32-bit color support and blend tools and an antialiasing feature for smoothing jagged edges.

Director 4.0 Demo ⌘ 708

Animation in Director is similar to animation in other 2-D programs; you assemble and sequence objects using a timeline, which Macromedia calls the Score, and then specify beginning and ending frames. Director interpolates the intermediate frames. There are tools for accelerating and slowing down objects, and you can animate a variety of imported objects. Director comes in both Mac and Windows versions, and Director presentations created on one platform can be played back on the other. (For more on Director, see Chapter 7, "Authoring Tools.")

3-D Utility Programs

It's easier than ever to experiment with 3-D graphics, thanks to a number of utilities that have sprung up in the last few years. Along with the plethora of full-featured animation programs, there is a whole category of utility programs that are fun to fiddle with—and some are actually useful.

Below, we've reviewed two 3-D illustration packages, Typestry and addDepth, both of which are available in either Mac or Windows versions. We've also taken a look at a couple of "morphing" packages and some of the new 3-D terrain generators that have popped up lately.

3-D Type and Illustration

Typestry from Pixar, Strata's StrataType 3d, and Crystal Flying Fonts allow you to turn type into fully rendered 3-D objects. Using these products you can create 3-D type for publications or presentations, even animating type for that movie-of-the-week look.

Adobe's Dimensions and Ray Dream's addDepth are designed to take PostScript art from programs, such as Illustrator and FreeHand, and give it a 3-D look. The programs are excellent and inexpensive bridges to higher powered 3-D software and are much simpler to master.

Pixar's Typestry

Typestry (Figure 5.2) will take any PostScript or TrueType font, "extrude" it into three dimensions, and then rotate or scale it. You then add one of several bevel styles to give the type a rounded, chiseled, or beveled look. Once you've established the basic appearance of the type, you select from a library of textures (Pixar calls them "Looks") such as shiny metal, wood, and plastic. Pixar bundles over 30 Looks and sells plug-ins of additional textures. Pixar's Looks are well known in the 3-D industry for their outstanding quality, which results in very slick effects.

In addition to Looks, you can apply special effects, such as "perforations," which pierce type with different shapes. Other filters apply textures to letters, or even create animated effects with the Particle tool. Typestry can also apply its filters and effects to nontype objects, and will import PICT, TIFF, and EPS files.

**Figure 5.2
Pixar's Typestry.**

Typestry offers precise control over lighting, and you can have up to 18 different light sources. Each light can have one of six different "gels" that cast shadows or simulate window panes or venetian blinds. You also can specify the color and spot diameter of lights.

When animating objects using simple path-based techniques, you even can apply a motion-blur filter that results in some eye-catching effects. Typestry will save these animations as a digital movie—a neat and useful feature.

After you've selected textures and lighting for your type, it's time to "render" —that is, for the computer to calculate and apply all of the effects you've specified. Typestry offers three levels of rendering quality. The first level results in a draft appearance suitable for making sure you're on the right track before you commit to a higher-quality render.

A word to the wise: Start with small test objects to get the look you're after before rendering a full-sized image. Full-screen images can easily take an hour or two to render on a Mac II or low-end 486 machine. Of course, rendering time is dependent on the number and complexity of effects you've applied, as well as on the sort of computer you're using, and will take much longer for an animated sequence than for a single frame.

*Ray Dream's
AddDepth*

AddDepth (Figure 5.3) supplies many templates to help you make 3-D objects from 2-D art. You can use its drawing tools to create art to be converted to 3-D, or import graphics in a variety of formats. Ray Dream also throws in a Step-by-Step Wizard that guides you through the whole process. A virtual trackball lets you rotate an object in space.

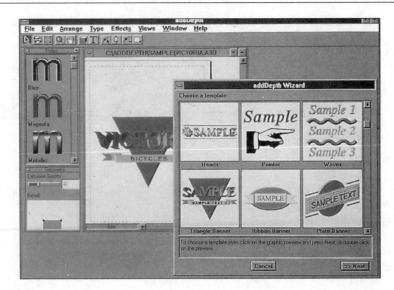

**Figure 5.3
Ray Dream's
AddDepth.**

Shape Shifters: Morphing Like Magic

Morph 2.5 Demo ⌘ 714

Metamorphosis—popularized in movies, music videos, and TV ads—seems to have captured people's imagination. While the feature is offered in several 3-D programs, Gryphon Software Corp's Morph lets you try this high-end effect on the cheap.

Using the program is simple. You designate key points on two PICT images to be morphed, then map the points to one another. You can save the resulting morphing sequence as a PICS animation, QuickTime movie, or single image file of an intermediate image in the morphing sequence. Morph runs in both Windows and on the Mac.

Elastic Reality (Figure 5.4) is a more sophisticated—and expensive—program that has been used to generate film and TV effects. Andover/North Coast Software's PhotoMorph is an entry level program. Elastic Reality is available in either Mac or Windows versions, though its feature set is richer in the PC version.

Most of these programs let you save your morphs as either QuickTime or AVI movies.

Terrain Generators Make the Scene

Terrain generators help you whip up virtual worlds that can be breathtaking in their sweep and detail. Leading the pack is HSC Software's KPT Bryce (Figure 5.5). The program sports an innovative interface that is pretty to look at but may be confusing to novices. Using separate palettes, you select objects and textures, then let KPT Bryce render the final scene using the photorealistic ray-tracing method. At this writing, KPT Bryce runs on the Mac; there will be a Windows version by the time you read this.

**Figure 5.4
Elastic Reality.**

Vistapro, another PC/Mac program, uses digital versions of U.S. Geological Survey maps to generate scenery—but you can alter these, adding your own trees, lakes, and mountains. Scenery Animator is a similar program that is slightly easier to use. Both allow you to save fly-throughs of your scenes as QuickTime and AVI movies (and as FLIC files in the PC version), and you can export scenery to other 3-D programs. Both are good entry-level terrain generators, but neither approaches the level or reality (or surreality) possible with KPT Bryce.

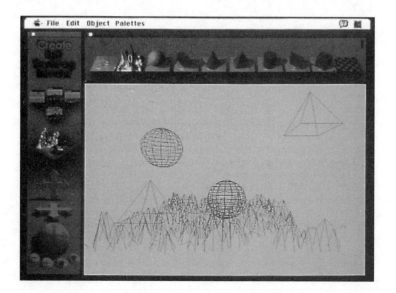

**Figure 5.5
HSC Software's
KPT Bryce.**

3-D Modeling, Animating, and Rendering Software

At least 20 products fit into the 3-D software category. Some specialize in one of the phases of 3-D, such as modeling, while others do it all. First, some definitions:

- **Modeling.** This is where 3-D creation begins. Typically, you start with simple objects such as squares and circles, then push or *extrude* them into 3-D objects. By manipulating these simple forms, you "model" the objects that ultimately will make up your 3-D world. More advanced modelers supply sophisticated tools that let you make precise refinements. For example, *vertex editing* lets you manipulate single points on an object.

  When modeling, you generally work with outlines or *wireframes* of objects. If you were to work with fully rendered objects, operations would slow to a crawl. Most modelers supply quick-shaded views, to give you a rough idea of what models look like with surfaces. Some programs, such as Infini-D, Swivel 3D, and MacroModel, are fast enough so that you can work in quick-shaded view instead of wireframe mode.

MacroModel 1.5 Demo ⌘ 720

- **Animating.** Once your models are complete, you animate them using a variety of techniques. Most 3-D programs use the *keyframe* method, in which you position your models at key points, and the program creates the remaining frames. Motion control techniques allow you to vary the acceleration of animation, simulate the effects of centripetal force, and refine the continuity of motion. To improve performance, animators generally work in wireframe or quick-shaded mode while working out moves. During this phase, you'll also position lights and cameras.

- **Rendering.** Finally, you'll select surfaces and textures for your animation, determine color and type of light, and specify effects such as shadows and masks. You'll probably want to do several test renderings on small parts of your work before rendering an entire scene or sequence of frames. When you're ready to go, the program and your CPU take over and perform the intensive set of calculations necessary to render realistic colors, textures, light, and shadow. This process can take from several minutes to days or even weeks, depending on the complexity of your art, the number of frames that must be rendered, and the type of rendering being used.

For a complete description of the 3-D process, see Chapter 12, "Creating 3-D Models and Animation."

Modelers

While some of the following programs also will do animation and rendering, they specialize in the modeling phase of the 3-D process. There is a trend, however, to combine all 3-D processes into a single product. Specular has done this successfully with Infini-D, and MacroMedia offers its advanced modeler, Macro-

Model, with its high-end renderer/animator, Three-D. On the PC side, Autodesk's 3D Studio is a well-implemented all-in-one package.

All modelers provide basic shapes called *primitives* for constructing 3-D objects using *lathing* or *cross-sectional* modeling techniques. These easy-to-use techniques will help you create simple 3-D objects quickly. Basic modelers, such as Swivel 3D and Super 3D, create *polygon-based* models, in which even curved shapes are made up of small segmented lines.

More advanced modelers, such as Form Z, MacroModel and Presenter Professional, let you make more complex shapes with techniques such as *sweeping* and *drilling*. Using these packages, you also can create smoother *spline-based* curves as well as polygonal models.

Higher-end modelers give you more control over model refinement by using such features as *vertex editing*, which lets you manipulate single points (*vertices*) along a model's surface. *Boolean operations* are another advanced technique in which you sculpt models by applying intersecting shapes.

For examples and more information about all of these modeling techniques, see Chapter 12, "Creating 3-D Models and Animation."

Selecting a Modeler

trueSpace 2.0 Demo ⌘ 716

Before you invest in a modeling program, make sure you really need one. You might be better off with a general purpose 3-D package, such as Caligari true-Space or Infini-D, that includes a modeler.

However, if you need to create intricate or unusual surface geometry and can make good use of advanced features such as spline-based tools, vertex editing, and Boolean operators, then you'll probably want to look at a midrange modeler—MacroModel or even a high-powered package such as Autodessys' Form Z, for example. The modelers in all-purpose programs generally lack their advanced modeling capabilities. VIDI's Presenter Pro and Autodesk's 3D Studio are exceptions to this rule, combining powerful high-end modeling and rendering features.

Finally, since there is no standard file format for models, if you go with a stand-alone modeler, make sure you can export the models to the renderer you're going to use. While all modelers have their own proprietary file formats, DXF is a common interchange format, and many modelers export to Pixar's RIB format.

Windows users take note: at the time of this writing, MacroModel was the only modeler offered for both Mac and Windows environments.

Macromedia's Swivel 3-D Professional

Swivel, the granddaddy of Mac modelers, began its life in the mid-'80s as the modeler for virtual reality pioneer VPL's simulated worlds. Even though it has been surpassed by better modelers, such as Macromedia's own MacroModel, Swivel is still used by professionals for a number of reasons.

First, its straightforward interface allows both novices and professionals alike to quickly build workable models. Its cross-sectional modeling metaphor (sometimes called "skinning" or "lofting") simplifies building many of the objects that are difficult in other modelers. (For example, it's much easier to create a bar of soap via cross section than with the lathing tools found in other modelers.)

Second, Swivel has a complex system of hierarchical links and locks necessary to build complex models (such as human figures) that have many joints and points of rotation. (For more on hierarchical models, see "Locks and Linking.")

Finally, Swivel has an excellent quick shading mode that allows you to work with smooth-shaded models rather than wireframes.

Despite these advantages, Swivel has some drawbacks and suffers in comparison to many new generation modelers, notably MacroModel. For one thing, Swivel lacks a spline tool, which means that the only way to get really smooth curves is to use many polygons—a painstaking process that also results in slow rendering. Because Swivel models also tend to contain a lot of internal geometry, complex models are unwieldy.

While Swivel is primarily a modeler, it has basic rendering and animation capabilities suitable for modest needs. Swivel does export to Pixar's RIB format, so you can take advantage of RenderMan's state-of-the-art rendering features. However, Swivel's compatibility is not total, and you may find that certain elements, such as shadows, do not carry over well. Macromedia bundles Swivel with RenderMan in a package called SwivelMan.

Swivel's future may be somewhat in doubt. Marketed by Macromedia under license from VPL, it lingers in the shadow of MacroModel. In fact, the program hasn't been updated for some time. However, with its long history and strong base of influential power users, it's likely to be around for at least a little while.

Alias Sketch!

Alias Research Inc. makes advanced workstation-based 3-D packages targeted at industrial design applications. With Sketch! (Figure 5.6), Alias is aiming to appeal to Mac 3-D designers by incorporating some advanced features and wrapping them in an approachable interface.

Like other advanced modelers, Sketch! lets you create smooth curves using spline curves. Sketch! uses a spline variant called NURB. This is powerful, but may take some getting used to. Luckily, you also can import the more familiar Bezier curves from Illustrator and FreeHand.

With Sketch!'s powerful object editing features, you can alter *isoparms*—isolated details of a larger object. You also can pinpoint and edit object elements using a Macintosh Finder-like library catalog.

Unlike most modelers, Sketch! offers a fairly complete set of rendering tools —including surface mapping and lighting options—and will export models in Pixar's RIB format, if you prefer to render using that program. Finally, Sketch! has a unique and noteworthy feature that lets you match a 3-D model's perspective to that of a 2-D image, such as a photograph.

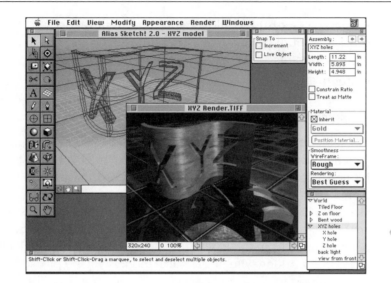

Figure 5.6
Alias Research,
Inc.'s Sketch!

MacroModel 1.5 Demo ⌘ 720

Macromedia's MacroModel

MacroModel, the new kid on the block, has moved in and made itself at home very quickly. Macromedia designed the program from the ground up, with the goal of producing a high-performance modeler with an approachable interface.

MacroModel objects, like those in Swivel, can be manipulated in a surprisingly fast and fluid smooth-shaded mode that gives a good representation of the model's form. Using a virtual "trackball," you can interactively rotate a model to make on-the-spot adjustments. These two features give MacroModel an admirable real-time feel that makes modeling seem more natural and less mathematical.

Like Sketch!, MacroModel's organic feel is abetted by a drawing metaphor that will be familiar to users of Adobe Illustrator and other drawing packages. The emphasis is on intuitive creation, rather than on the visual and spatial skills demanded by other modelers. Because MacroModel is a spline-based modeler, it creates smooth and easy forms.

The program supplies a full set of conventional object creation tools, including extrude, lathe, cross section, and sweep (for definitions, see "Modeling Tools"). Far from run-of-the-mill, however, are MacroModel's "deformation" tools, which allow you to create complex models on-the-fly by twisting, bending, and tapering them (see Figure 7.5). This real-time feature is particularly powerful and illustrates the progressive nature of the program.

For refining models, the program neatly categorizes editing into three modes that offer increasingly detailed object views:

- **Compound Geometry** lets you adjust the gross dimensions of your models—height, width, and so on.

- **Surface Geometry** allows you to edit an object's surfaces using spline-based control points. In another of MacroModel's friendly innovations, the control points are accessible even in smooth-shaded mode.

- **Mesh Geometry** reveals a model's smallest details, permitting you to reshape and make microfine adjustments at the mesh level (a technique commonly known as "vertex editing").

In MacroModel, as in addDepth and Dimensions, you can import object-oriented art, such as Illustrator files. However, MacroModel converts imported vector art to bitmap form, complete with associated geometry that you can adjust as if you had created it within the application.

Macromedia also has incorporated a group of capabilities suitable to the more formal demands of computer-aided design. You can "nudge" object position, scale, and angle from the keyboard and manipulate objects with numeric precision. People working with hierarchical models will be pleased to see that Macro-Model's support for links and joints is as excellent as Swivel's. Another timesaving touch is an auto-copy tool that allows you to mirror structures such as aircraft wings.

Snapping tools are equally impressive. By default, snapping occurs in the 2-D working plane; but you also can accurately align 3-D surfaces. This last feature is particularly important, because it helps you avoid small-surface defects that may be visible only after time-consuming rendering.

MacroModel includes basic rendering tools, but serious designers will want to import models into a full-featured rendering/animation program. MacroModel supports a fair range of export options, including DXF, RIB, and Swivel.

MacroModel is aimed at the high end—with a price to match—and probably is the best modeling-only program on the market today. Its sleek interface and intuitive tools will appeal to multimedia developers creating free-form shapes, and its CAD features will make engineers and industrial designers feel right at home, too.

Autodessys' Form Z

Form Z is unique in that it provides the *solid* modeling techniques used by design engineers and architects with the *surface* modeling tools normally found in 3-D animation products.

Some forms are more easily produced with solids than with surfaces. For example, windows can be cut from walls, and shapes can be refined by sculpting them with other shapes. In addition, a complex shape created with solids is a single shape, and not made up of many forms the way a complex surface model may be. As a result, it is more compact and will render faster.

Among Form Z's solid modeling features, you'll find a variety of powerful tools: Difference, for carving one solid with another; Add, for combining two solids; and Intersection, for creating the space formed where two solids intersect.

These tools, collectively known as *Boolean operations*, are rarely found in other programs.

Form Z's surface modeling tools are equally as strong and rival those of most advanced surface-only modelers, MacroModel, for example. You can create smooth curves with splines, Beziers, and NURBS (an advanced form of splines), among other tools. These tools give you an unusual degree of control over smooth surfaces.

Surface models can be edited by manipulating the *mesh* that makes up a wireframe model; this process is similar to the *vertex editing* offered by other programs in which you manipulate single points on a mesh. Form Z's mesh-editing feature is considered superior, because it's easier to edit a grid of points instead of the individual points themselves.

In another innovation, Form Z lets you build solids using surfaces that you combine using the Stitch tool. This technique allows you to produce complex shapes that would be difficult or impossible to create in any other way. Once the Stitch tool has been used on a group of surfaces, the object is a solid that can be further refined using any of the Boolean operators.

Like all modelers, Form Z has rudimentary rendering capabilities that lack advanced features such as texture mapping. You can export Form Z models as DXF files that are accepted by many renderers.

Form Z is one of the best solid modelers on the market; and if you need both solid and surface modeling in a single package, you won't find a better tool.

Autodesk's AutoCAD

AutoCAD is the granddaddy of PC modelers (how many programs of any kind can claim to be in their 13th generation?). While AutoCAD is primarily used for architectural and industrial design renderings, it is used extensively for multimedia work.

AutoCAD is a 32-bit program that will run on DOS, Windows, and Windows NT. To run it under Windows 3.1 or Windows for Workgroups, you must install the Win32s library (included with AutoCAD), which converts these 16-bit Windows environments into 32-bit platforms.

Geometry features include support for NURBS, elliptical arcs, and real ellipses. Solid-modeling capabilities include solid primitives, freeformed curves, and Boolean operations. Rendering options span the range from flat shading to the more sophisticated Phong and Gouraud shaders.

Integrated Programs

3-D programs in this category combine modeling and rendering, rendering and animation, and sometimes all three phases of the 3-D process. It's difficult to group these programs according to features, price, or performance, because these criteria are not as interrelated as they are in other software categories. Strong

3-D market competition, an unusually large field of products, and rapidly evolving technology have combined to create a somewhat confused market segment. Despite this, it's possible to make a few generalizations.

Creating Surfaces

All renderers let you wrap models in basic matte, shiny, and transparent surfaces. For heightened realism and detail, you can create surface textures through different *mapping* techniques:

- **Texture maps.** Using this process, you place a 2-D image onto a 3-D object. Programs offer different mapping modes, depending on the shape of the object.
- **Reflection maps.** Also called environment mapping, this is a specialized form of texture mapping in which you simulate reflections by projecting an image of an object's surroundings onto that object. The technique cuts down on rendering time, since the program does not need to calculate reflections.
- **Bump maps**. These surfaces simulate various surface irregularities, giving the illusion of rough, uneven surfaces.
- **Procedural maps.** These computer-generated images can yield effects ranging from realistic to surreal.

Nearly all renderers have these surface-mapping features. They differ, however, in the amount of control they give you over their application, and how fast they render the results. For example, Infini-D has a wide range of rendering effects and average-quality rendering. StrataVision also has an excellent array of effects but renders rather slowly. At the high end, ElectricImage is known for its large variety of effects, high quality, and fast rendering, but this is unusual. Most programs do only one or two of these things well.

Shading and Rendering

Aside from the flat shading draft mode, renders usually offer *Gouraud* and *Phong* shading. Gouraud is relatively quick to render and looks OK for sharp-edged objects. Phong yields smooth surfaces, but takes longer to render.

Photo-realistic rendering is most commonly achieved with "ray tracing," which gives excellent results—but in glacial rendering times. Pixar's proprietary RenderMan techniques also offer excellent results.

There are four different types of effects: ambient, spot, distant, and radial. Most programs do not offer all of these lighting options; but higher-end programs, such as Presenter and Three-D, do. In the midrange, Infini-D and Strata offer excellent lighting choices, as do Imagine, trueSpace, and Lightwave on the PC.

Controlling Motion

On the animation side, most programs have keyframe animation, which gives a fair degree of *motion control.*

Selecting a Package

Programs differentiate themselves not only by their range of basic to high-end features, but by including an assortment of specialized features that may or may not be of interest to you. For example, Infini-D will let you create animated surfaces by projecting a QuickTime movie onto an object and Strata Inc.'s StudioPro boasts a texture map library whose permutations could take months to explore. With several programs, including VIDI's Presenter, Macromedia's Three-D, and ElectricImage, you can create smooth transitions by "morphing"—changing one object into another over time; and with CrystalGraphics' Topas Professional and Pixar's RenderMan, you can create atmospheric effects such as fog and "depth cueing"—which blurs background objects to make them appear distant.

One last feature that is useful to almost everybody is the so-called *alpha channel*, which will be familiar to Photoshop users. An alpha channel can be used to isolate an image from its surroundings. This image then can easily be overlaid or *composited* into another scene without rerendering. Alpha channels have many other advantages as well (see Chapter 3, "Graphics Tools," for more information). Alpha channel support is now offered by Designer, Infini-D, RenderMan, Three-D, 3D Studio, Topas, and Presenter; and the list is growing.

Strata Vision 3D Demo ⌘ 721

Because of their mixed bag of features and unpredictable trade-offs, choosing a 3-D package can be tough. But we can offer a few general suggestions—hey, that's our job. If you don't need precision control over textures and movement, you'll be happy with a midrange program, such as Infini-D, trueSpace, Strata's Vision 3d, or Designer (for still images). Using any of these programs or others listed below, you'll be able to create convincing, realistic, and dynamic imagery with reasonable balance between time and quality.

On the other hand, professionals working in broadcast environments, realistic simulations, or photorealistic applications definitely will want a higher-powered program, such as ElectricImage, Presenter, Sculpt 4D, 3D Studio, Lightwave, and Real 3D. You actually may wind up with several programs, since no one application does it all with excellent results.

The PC has come on strong in the animation category, offering many capable programs, including Caligari's trueSpace, Autodesk's 3D Studio, and Topas' Real 3D. Below, we've reviewed 3D Studio, the top PC animation package, and two packages for the Mac—Specular's Infini-D, and Strata's Vision 3d.

We didn't have the time to review them here, but Macromedia's Three-D, Ray Dream's Designer, VIDI's Presenter Pro, Byte by Byte's Sculpt 3D and Sculpt 4D, Pixar's RenderMan/ShowPlace, and Electric Image's ElectricImage Animation System are all excellent mid- to high-end Mac animation programs.

Specular's Infini-D

Using Infini-D is sort of like going to your favorite sushi bar: You can choose from a glittering array of exotic, yet accessible treats. Now maybe you don't like sushi, but you might just cotton to Infini-D.

Infini-D has a complete set of modeling tools, and provides simultaneous views from four perspectives as you work. The program lacks a spline tool or vertex editing capabilities, so creating free-form shapes and curves can be tricky.

One highlight of Infini-D is its excellent set of textures, including an unusually complete group of procedural textures. All textures can be fully manipulated and adjusted according to several attributes. The animated-surfaces feature is nice. It allows you to project QuickTime movies onto objects. You also can morph objects and textures using a simple interface that produces very pleasing results.

Infini-D can take advantage of Apple's Publish and Subscribe facility: you can use it to import 2-D art from a drawing program that Infini-D will convert to a 3-D image. When the original 2-D art file changes, Infini-D updates the 3-D derivative as well.

Infini-D's outstanding alpha channel support allows you to seamlessly composite such images as a tumbling 3-D logo against a sky backdrop. Rendering modes include ray tracing and Phong shading, which will render shadows for heightened realism.

Infini-D's well-developed animation facilities offer many advanced features. Animation is controlled with a well-designed timeline window through which you can easily adjust frame rate; smooth the velocity of motion; and animate objects, cameras, and lights.

Animators usually spend much of their time trying to achieve smooth motion. However, Infini-D's Animation Assistant provides further control over motion through "procedural" animation techniques. For example, you can smooth motion by aligning to camera path, aligning direction to motion, or automatically banking a camera. Thus, you can program motion fairly haphazardly, then clean it up with the Animation Assistant.

The Infini-D integrated package is an excellent choice for the intermediate-to-advanced user, and its effective interface makes it ideal for beginners, too.

Strata's StudioPro

Like Ray Dream's Designer, StudioPro is capable of rendering very high quality photo realistic imagery. It's modeler is satisfactory, but lacks the flexibility and creation tools of other mid-range packages, such as Infini-D. StrataVision does have one interesting modeling technique called *flexing*, which allows you to create skinned objects that can be animated to flex like a snake or tail.

StrataVision's real strength lies in its texture mapping and rendering capabilities. Its surface libraries are vast, and you can create endless variations on your own. Alpha channel support also is good, allowing you to use alphas for lighting effects and image layering.

Animation support is OK, but not great. The animation component is keyframe based, and you can adjust frame rate with a timeline. More advanced motion

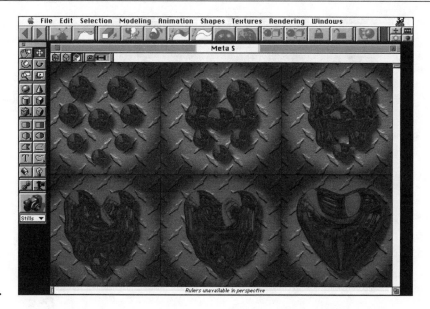

**Figure 5.7
Strata's StudioPro.**

control features are lacking, but you can animate textures so that they dissolve (morph) into one another—a useful feature.

StudioPro (Figure 5.7), like Designer, can render beautifully; rendering speed is the main trade-off. Strata Inc. does offer RenderPro, a network renderer that greatly reduces rendering time if you have access to a number of machines over a network. Strata offers a proprietary version of the *radiosity* rendering technique, an advanced algorithm that can account for nuances, such as the effects of reflected light. A new rendering option called RayPainting lets you add painterly effects popularized by Fractal Design Painter (see Chapter 3, "Graphics Tools").

If you don't need all the advanced effects offered by StudioPro, Strata makes a lower end product called Vision 3d, for about half the cost of its more capable sibling.

Autodesk's 3D Studio

3D Studio (Figure 5.8), a powerful integrated 3-D package, proves that when it comes to industrial strength multimedia development, the PC has come a long way, baby. The program is divided into modules that are like individual workshops devoted to different phases of the 3-D process: 2-D shape creation, 3-D modeling, texture mapping, rendering, and so on.

The program offers many advanced modeling techniques, including splines, vertex editing, and Boolean operators. There are many lighting options, and animation facilities provide good control over motion.

**Figure 5.8
Autodesk's
3D Studio.**

Rendering is a particular forte of 3D Studio. It offers wireframe, flat, Gouraud, and Phong shading. It does lack ray tracing and radiosity, two photorealistic rendering algorithms. 3D Studio has a plug in architecture, however; and there are ray-tracing plug-ins available.

Another plug-in called inverse kinematics allows you to create animation chains from hierarchically linked objects. That means it's easier to create realistic movement from complex objects made up of interrelated components (the human body, for example).

3D Studio has also spawned a cottage industry that churns out filters called IPAS routines. These are 3D Studio filters that are tailored to specific tasks. For example, Schreiber Instruments makes Imagine Puppeteer, a collection of IPAS filters that gives 3D Studio motion capture capabilities. Xaos Tools offers Pennello, an IPAS routine that adds brush effects to 3D Studio. Other IPAS routines can generate scenery, such as plants and trees.

Overall, an excellent 3-D program that rivals anything on the Mac.

Caligari's trueSpace

trueSpace 2.0 Demo ⌘ 716

Caligari's trueSpace is a leading PC animation program. It is well-regarded for its simple and elegant interface and its rendering speed. The interface is designed so that you don't have to constantly hop around to different modules for rendering and animation tasks.

Objects can be created from primitives, spline curves, or projected with extrusion and sweep functions. Material libraries contain many textures for rendering, or you can import textures from another program. trueSpace is capable of astonishing rendering quality, and can create 24-bit photorealistic stills with maximum resolutions of up to 8,000 × 8,000 pixels. Version 2.0 can take advantage of a new generation of 3-D acceleration hardware that greatly reduces rendering times.

Animation techniques include both keyframe and path-based options, and an Animation Project Window lets you modify actions and events.

All in all, trueSpace is an excellent value, and is quickly becoming a standard PC animation tool. For a look at how it's used in practice, see "Jumping Clocks" sidebar in Chapter 12.

6

Video Tools

Desktop video is the latest digital revolution of the 1990s. Although it has been around in one form or another since the late 1980s, desktop video has now been made practical for most people by the convergence of Apple's QuickTime—the standard system architecture for handling moving images—and video capture and editing products from third parties. The new accessibility and economy of desktop video tools means you now can make real-time video sequences an integral part of your multimedia presentations.

In this chapter, we'll introduce you to digital video on the Macintosh and for Windows, and we'll provide a description of features and capabilities of the hardware and software tools for digital video applications. We'll also give you the information you need to make informed buying decisions based on your particular needs. Don't be intimidated by the jargon or by the wealth of choices for special effects described in the software sections; many features can be implemented with point-and-click simplicity. Frequently, you just copy and paste your audio and video into place, choose a filter, and make your movie. As you become more accomplished, you will have new appreciation for the information you're about to read.

Desktop Video's Evolution

Desktop video has evolved from two family trees: one descending from television, the other from microcomputers and graphics software. These have been combined to form tools that address traditional video production tasks with convenience and economy.

Broadcast Roots

The first television shows preceded the invention of videotape and were broadcast live because there was no effective way to store and edit them. When videotape first arrived on the scene in 1956, the only editing tool was a pair of scissors. The tape was spliced or taped together like film, which proved to be quite inadequate. Editing videotape—an analog, nondigital medium—has matured into a familiar process of electronically transferring the analog video signal from the source tape (or raw footage) to a master edited tape that can then be sent out for duplication. This process of nondigital editing continues to this day, although increasingly, digital effects are being used, and computers assist in the editing process.

Several significant drawbacks are inherent in the traditional process of analog videotape editing. One is the need to lay down each sequence in a linear fashion, making changes difficult after the fact. In order to effectively replace a segment from earlier in the editing session, the new segment has to be exactly the same length as the original. Furthermore, every time video is transferred to another tape, the quality of the signal deteriorates—a phenomenon known as generation loss.

If the raw footage is edited onto a master tape, the new master is a second-generation tape. When duplicates are created from the master tape for distribution, they are third generation. If special effects are needed, the final tape may be fourth generation or more; and the deterioration in quality can be pronounced.

Now you can have your cake and eat it, too. These shortcomings are not present in digital video, where scenes can be edited in any order, and each copy or duplicate is identical in every respect to the original (although some generational loss can still occur as a result of compressing and decompressing digital footage—more about that later). At the same time, digital video features every one of the high-end special effects that have evolved in all those years along the analog route. And, of course, the comparatively low cost and incredible convenience of digital video have been major factors in sparking the new revolution.

Digital Roots

SoundEdit 16 Demo ⌘ 707

Director 4.0 Demo ⌘ 708

Photoshop 3.0 Demo ⌘ 715

Desktop video's digital heritage also is plainly visible in today's new tools. Digital video tools, which incorporate cut-and-paste simplicity, have evolved from Apple's experience with the Macintosh Desktop metaphor of file folders, double-clicks, and menus—since also adopted by Windows. Video editing software is a descendent of the photographic quality graphics technology found in Photoshop, photorealistic 3-D products, the motion and interactivity features of Macromedia Director, and the sound capabilities of SoundEdit 16. Combining these attributes with the traditions and aesthetics of the broadcast world has resulted in a tool set that brings desktop convenience to professional producers, while providing professional power to the desktop computer-based multimedia producer.

QuickTime and Video for Windows

The first tool in the multimedia workshop for anyone who is serious about digital video on the Macintosh is QuickTime, the system extension and file format that makes multimedia manageable, reliable, and standardized. QuickTime is installed as an Extension in the system folder (Figure 6.1).

QuickTime has become an instant success due to the integration of three important components that define a format for digital video and provide the capacity and flexibility to withstand a period of rapidly changing technology. These components are the user interface, video compression, and hardware independence. The latter allows QuickTime files to run not only on a Macintosh, but also on PC compatibles under QuickTime for Windows, on Silicon Graphic Stations, and on many different types of QuickTime-compatible graphic cards.

Windows users have a choice—they can make movies using QuickTime for Windows, or Microsoft's own Video for Windows. As of this writing, Microsoft has announced plans to port Video for Windows to the Macintosh. QuickTime and VfW are similar in many ways; suffice it to say that you can use digital video equipment to capture and edit movies in either format. For more on both QuickTime and Video for Windows, see Chapter 2, "Systems Software, Hardware, and Peripherals.")

Making Movies: What You'll Need

The beauty of both QuickTime and VfW is that you need only a basic multimedia-ready computer (suitably equipped with color monitor, at least 8 Mb of RAM, and so on) to play digital movies. In other words, QuickTime and VfW are, in the parlance of marketing jockeys, *software-only solutions.*

**Figure 6.1
QuickTime in the
extension folder.**

For developers that means there is a large and ready market for digital video in many forms—from games to reference products. As a developer, however, you will need some additional equipment to make the movies in the first place.

This equipment can be roughly divided into four categories:

- Video camera and recorder
- Video capture card for your computer
- Video recording software
- Video editing software

In the remainder of this chapter, we will explore the options for the tools in each of these categories.

But first, a note on the basic computer requirements for desktop video: You'll need a powerful desktop machine with supplemental RAM and disk space. If you're shooting basic video clips for multimedia presentations, 8–16Mb of RAM and a 200–500Mb hard drive will do; but if you plan to create corporate video presentations or edit full length video segments, the sky's the limit. You'll want a Pentium or PowerMac with 32–64Mb RAM and a large disk or disk array of 1Gb and up.

Equipment for Shooting Your Own Video

There are two primary ways to acquire video for your multimedia project: You can buy prepackaged video clips from a variety of vendors, or you can elect to shoot your own video. The latter really is hard to avoid for most multimedia presentations. In all likelihood, your particular project is going to require at least some original video. Fortunately, it's fairly easy and inexpensive to "roll your own." It requires only a consumer-quality camcorder or video camera and perhaps a video cassette recorder (VCR) for playback and review of the predigital footage.

However, a good clean video signal will compress with fewer artifacts than a noisy signal. Also, if you're going to do compositing of video and graphics, anything less than the highest quality video will look really bad. Most game producers, for example, shoot video in Betacam or other high-end professional format.

Choosing the appropriate video camera or deck depends on the quality you require and the budget that is available.

Video equipment is usually categorized as consumer, prosumer, industrial, broadustrial, and broadcast-quality—terms that pertain both to the skills of the user and the characteristics of the equipment itself. The first three categories require little technical expertise, whereas you really have to understand video technology to get the most out of broadustrial and broadcast equipment. Still, when it comes to digital video presented on a Macintosh, investing in high-end equipment brings diminishing returns.

- *Consumer* equipment encompasses all the standard camcorders and VCRs with which we've become familiar over the past several years. These low-end production tools are inexpensive, exceedingly easy to use, and suitable for average-quality QuickTime video. Consumer cameras start at about $500 and range in price up to $2,000. VCRs start at only a few hundred dollars.

- *Prosumer* tools also are relatively low-end and inexpensive but are more feature-laden than the consumer models. They sport such bells and whistles as on-board character generators, special transitions, and image stabilizers. The Canon A-1 Series of Hi-8 cameras is a good example of prosumer equipment; it features auto-everything. Cameras and decks in this category generally cost as much as $3,000. The quality of the Hi-8 signal far exceeds that of the standard VHS NTSC signal.

- *Industrial* equipment tends to be basic and rugged. It is not necessarily chock-full of features, but can stand up to repeated use in a labor-intensive, multiple-user environment. The Hi-8 tape format is being used more and more frequently for industrial applications, replacing the Sony DXC series, the venerable ¾-inch U-matic standard. Industrial-quality equipment generally is priced in the $5,000–$7,000 range.

- *Broadustrial* equipment boasts more features and can be plugged into larger professional systems. It incorporates everything necessary for stabilizing and monitoring signals for cable and broadcast applications: time-based correctors, vector scopes, and waveform generators that monitor and manipulate the integrity of the signal. A typical broadustrial video system, such as Sony's BetaCam, costs upwards of $25,000.

- *Broadcast,* of course, refers to the top-quality, highly controllable, technically demanding equipment used in professional video production.

Prosumer equipment is a good choice for desktop video, but consumer cameras and VCRs may be adequate to create QuickTime movies in many instances. If the videotape needs to be edited using traditional analog methods, generational loss will occur, and a higher-quality raw tape will be needed to make up the difference. On the other hand, a consumer camera may produce acceptable results if the raw footage is digitized directly into the computer from the original tape and not from duplicates. The video equipment should be the same quality as the final delivery system, whether that is a multimedia system or videotape.

Before making a final decision, consider how you might use the videotape in the future. If you shoot high-quality video to begin with, everything you do with it will benefit, and the original footage will be available for reuse in future projects (which might not be possible if the quality of the video is not on par with the new application). We recommend, if possible, not to use anything less than Hi-8 or S-VHS. Prosumer Hi-8 cameras can be had for about $1,000.

Video Capture Cards and Recording Software

Aside from a video camera/recorder, you'll need some computer-based tools for converting the video into a digital format. These tools include a video capture card (also called a digitizer) and recording software that controls the digitizing process. When you buy a card, the recording software will usually be thrown into the deal. Digitizing cards plug into a slot on your Mac or PC and feature one or more video and audio input connectors. In order to digitize the video's sound track as well as the video itself, some cards perform audio digitizing as well, while some don't. If your computer has onboard audio digitizing, you can run a wire from the video camera or recorder directly to your computer to convert the audio signal. When you're ready to edit the video you merge the video and audio into a single movie file.

Recording software supplied with the card provides controls for that particular card's features. Radius' VideoSpigot line includes the ScreenPlay utility for recording (Figure 6.2), while RasterOps boards include MediaGrabber software. Microsoft includes a similar utility called VidCap with Video for Windows. In addition to their primary editing features, video editing software packages, such as Adobe's Premiere, also support the ability to record.

You can also obtain basic recording software through on-line services, and Apple Computer includes the MovieRecorder utility in its QuickTime Starter Kit. If you're a cybernut, check the on-line bulletin boards: there are many shareware movie utilities that do the job just fine, and, in some cases, improve upon commercial offerings.

TOOLS

Premiere 4.0 Demo ⌘ 722

Choosing a Card

Capture cards offer a wide variety of features, but they all do basically the same thing: capture video frames, digitize them, and then save the digitized images to disk in QuickTime, AVI, or PICS movie formats. Some cards also double as display cards for large-screen monitors.

Figure 6.2 ScreenPlay recorder software for the VideoSpigot.

Low-end cards are inexpensive (less than $500), but capture in a smaller format with fewer frames and colors. More expensive boards, ranging in price from $1,500 to $5,000, can capture full-motion video at 320 × 480 (fullscreen) in 24-bit color.

The most expensive boards use the Video System Control Architecture (ViSCA) to control a VCR and record a frame at a time. This yields the highest quality full-screen images but takes a long time (there are 30 frames every second!) and consumes loads of disk space.

When moving to a more capable board, give careful consideration to the actual cost of using it. If the board can capture 30 frames per second at full-screen resolution, ask yourself how fast a hard disk you'll need to keep up with this board, how long it will take to compress the movie, and how much disk storage space it will take up. If the answers are unacceptable, then use a lower-end board, create wonderful media quickly and affordably, and pocket the difference.

These days, 320 × 240 movies playing at 15 frames per second in 8-bit color are considered a reasonable achievement, and it is certainly possible to turn these out with a decent midrange card costing $500 or so. For playback, you or your viewers will need a midrange Mac or multimedia PC (with a CD-ROM drive if the video will be delivered that way). A good double-speed drive should be able to play back a 320 × 480 15fps movie without too much trouble.

Compression is the key to getting good quality digital movies. Different capture cards use different compressor/decompressors (codecs), but the most common are Cinepak, Indeo, M-JPEG, and MPEG. As new software-based compressors evolve, you should be able to use them with the board you already have. Many boards use hardware-assisted compression to get files as small as possible. Some exciting new compression schemes such as Truemation-S and HARC-C are approaching MPEG quality in software alone.

You usually won't need hardware to play back a hardware-compressed file, but sometimes you do. MPEG requires hardware for both compression and decompression of movies. (See sidebar "Making Things a Bit Smaller" for more on compression and MPEG.)

The capture process itself is essentially the same, regardless of the type of card you use. The card's software displays the video in a window on-screen, and you can set controls such as hue, saturation, and brightness. When you're ready to capture, a mouse click does it. (See Chapter 14, "Creating Video.")

Basic Features

Manufacturers are cramming more and more features into video cards. The trend is to pack into a single card 24-bit color display, image compression, video effects, and video out. Until the advent of desktop digital video, each of these functions would have required a separate card.

As mentioned, getting quality video images is a constant trade-off between file size, frame rate, color, and image size. You may have to experiment quite a bit

Making Things a Bit Smaller

Digital video requires huge files—as big as 30Mb for each second of playing time. Quick-Time and VfW use software compression technologies to shrink the size of digital movie files and increase their playback frame rate. They do this in a manner that permits new compression technologies—codecs (compressor/decompressors)—to be used with Quick-Time or VfW as soon as they are available with existing software applications. This software-independent approach to compression permits QuickTime and VfW to avoid obsolescence and adjust to new technologies, such as fractal compression, as they become available.

The more common compressors use symmetric compression, so-named because they take the same amount of time to compress and decompress a file. They can compress video sequences, save them (to a hard disk), and play them back (from a hard disk or CD-ROM) on-the-fly, in real time. Asymmetric compression usually takes much more time to compress (an hour or more for one minute of video), but creates a more highly compressed file packed with more data, which can then be decompressed relatively quickly. Examples of asymmetrical compressors are Apple's Compact Video or Iterated Systems' Fractal Compression, which may take as much as an hour or more to compress a minute of video (it's best to let it run unattended overnight or during a good football game). While they take longer, asymmetrical compressors usually can create a smaller file and provide better playback from a slow drive such as a CD-ROM.

Even though QuickTime and VfW operate in the digital domain, this doesn't mean that all data is perfectly preserved. It depends on what type of compression is applied to the images. *Lossless* compression keeps all the information from the original image. If you were to compress a picture with lossless compression, then decompress it and compare the data to the original on a pixel-by-pixel basis, there would be no difference. All of the current products which compress space on your hard disk use this form of compression. You wouldn't want to find even one character changed or dropped from your word processing document! Using QuickTime JPEG codec in the highest quality setting produces lossless compression.

However, we can remove quite a bit of data from images without our noticing much of a difference. This is called *lossy* compression. The codecs will carefully analyze the image data and toss out information that may not be missed. If you were to do a pixel-by-pixel comparison again, thousands of pixels may have been changed. But if you view the original and compressed images side by side, they will look almost identical. It depends on the effectiveness of the codec as well as the quality of the setting you choose. The lower the quality, the better the compression (the resulting image will take up less space on your hard disk), but the more obvious the differences.

One more important point about lossy compression: Every time you recompress an image using lossy compression, additional degradation will occur. When making a digital movie, you are best off working from the highest quality image you can afford to store on your disk (higher quality means more disk space is required) then waiting until the very end of the editing process before applying compression.

box continued

There are two other ways to classify compression. *Spatial* (also called *intraframe*) compression looks at an individual image or frame and finds data that can be removed. For example, if the video was shot in front of a solid yellow background, then the codec may reduce much of the similarly colored area to a few bytes of information.

Temporal compression (also called *frame differencing* or *interframe* compression) deals with the similarities and differences in consecutive frames of a digital movie. If the camera is mounted on a tripod and pointed at an actor sitting in front of a fixed background, then the only thing that will change from frame to frame is the actor's movement. Rather than saving the entire frame of data, temporal compression throws out the complete background in subsequent frames and only include the portion of the actor that moved. This can save an enormous amount of storage.

The Apple video compressor is a good choice for saving to a hard disk, because temporal and spatial compression are accompanied by symmetrical compression. While Compact Video is a very efficient way to compress video, postpone using it until your project is completely finished so that the slow compression speed does not interfere with your creative efforts.

Hardware compression is often used to squeeze movies even more than is possible with software-only schemes. Video capture boards often compress video with the help of special chips; Intel's Smart Video Recorder for Windows does this by using its proprietary Indeo compression method. Indeo compresses video with the aid of hardware, but Indeo-compressed movies do not require hardware for playback.

MPEG compression is an evolving standard that allows video to be highly compressed, but it requires very expensive encoders for compression, as well as playback cards to

continued on next page

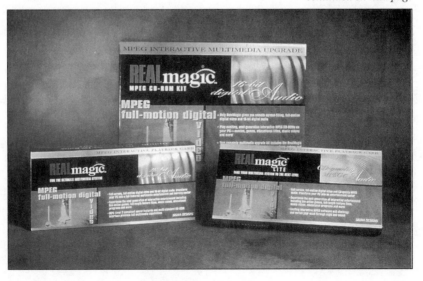

**Figure 6.3
Sigma Design's
REALMagic Lite is
a low-cost MPEG
playback board.**

box continued

decompress the movies. However, since it's possible to get full-length, full-motion, full-screen movies on an ordinary CD using MPEG, the standard is picking up steam. End users can buy MPEG decoder boards for a few hundred dollars, and the prices of MPEG encoders are dropping too (see Figure 6.3).

By the time you read this, it should be possible to play back MPEG-compressed movies with no added hardware. You will have to have a Pentium-class PC that you aren't planning on using for anything else; movie decompression and playback will probably consume all of the Pentium's processing power.

to hit on the right formula. Probably, the best strategy is to get a card that will allow you to alter your method depending on your requirements.

In general, look for a card that offers hardware compression, because you can capture higher quality images that way. Also, when reading manufacturer specs, be sure such things as frame capture rate and size are measured when capturing to a hard disk, not RAM, which will obviously be a lot faster (but who has 200 Mb of RAM available for video capture?).

Note also that you'll need a fast computer to capture video at the highest frame rates and resolutions claimed by manufacturers.

Most cards also will accept several different types of NTSC video signals (the dominant broadcast standard in the United States and Japan):

Composite is the most common video signal. Since it mixes together the chrominance and luminance parts of the signal into one channel, it's also inferior to the other two types.

S-video is the two-channel signal (for color and luminescence) put out by the two types of higher-end consumer cameras, S-VHS and Hi-8.

RGB is the norm in the professional video industry. It's a three-channel signal —one for each color—plus a sync channel.

Generally, the mark of a good card is its incorporation of S-video inputs, which can help you achieve a cleaner source signal.

Finally, if you want to write your digital video masterpiece back out to videotape once you've edited and tweaked it, your card will need to support NTSC video encoding.

Below we've reviewed two midrange video capture cards and one higher-end model for the Mac and Windows.

SuperMac's VideoSpigot NuBus

VideoSpigot was the first video capture card for the Mac and it's still in the running as a good entry level video capture solution.

The card can capture straight, uncompressed RGB video, which yields the highest quality individual frames. Unfortunately, it also means the card loses over half the frames in attempting to get the highest quality video on-board. Alternatively, you can select YUV capture, which loses fewer frames at a reasonable compromise to quality. You can also elect to use the Spigot's proprietary compression, which probably yields the best combination of frame rate and image quality.

The card claims a capture rate of 30 fps at 320 × 240, but you'll need a Quadra, Power Mac, or Pentium to match those specs. VideoSpigot sports both composite and S-video inputs, and SuperMac bundles the Screenplay II recording software with the Mac version. Creative Labs includes no recording software with the Windows Spigot, but you can use Microsoft's VidCap utility that comes with Video for Windows.

SuperMac makes a version of the card called VideoSpigot II Tape that has an encoder that will copy digital video back to videotape. VideoSpigot AV plugs into the AV slot on Quadra and Power Mac AV computers.

Intel's Smart Video Recorder Pro

Intel's card works with Windows, and is often cited as the best low-cost card for capturing video on the PC. The card supports both YUV capture and Intel's own hardware-assisted Indeo compression (which does not require hardware for playback).

Like the Spigot, the SVR (Figure 6.4) is capable of 30 fps 320 × 240 compression, but you'll need a Pentium or fast 486 to do it. That's probably OK, since most people playing back video don't have Pentiums anyway. On more pedestrian 486 hardware, SVR manages a respectable 15fps recording rate.

At the time of this writing, Intel was throwing in Asymetrix' Digital Video Producer software, which can handle both video recording and editing. All in all, an outstanding deal for less than $500 on the street.

Radius' VideoVision Studio

VideoVision Studio is a high-end Mac video capture card and software designed for professional work. It costs about 10 times the price of VideoSpigot and Smart Video Recorder.

For the extra bucks, you get a lot of stuff. The card captures all 60 fields of interlaced video per second for a very high quality image. Lower end cards capture 30 fields and interpolate (make up) the other half of the signal.

The card has on-board sound recording and features both sound and video recording software. It has an encoder that features a "convolution" filter to reduce flicker when digital video is converted to analog format for videotape storage or delivery.

**Figure 6.4
Smart Video
Recorder.**

VideoVision Studio will also analyze your machine to determine how fast it can pump video onto the hard drive. On a Power Mac 8100, you may be able to achieve 5 Mb per second, a rate that yields very high, even near-broadcast quality.

Digital video dilettantes need not apply: VideoVision Studio is for high-end applications such as corporate video production. It requires beefy hardware to exploit its full capabilities, and if you're doing run-of-the-mill captures, you'll be perfectly happy with a midrange card.

**Truevision
Targa 2000**

The Targa 2000 has long been a mainstay of PC video capture, and Rasterops now makes a version for the Mac as well. In both versions, the Targa is an advanced video capture card that integrates motion capture, M-JPEG compression, and audio capture. The result is extremely high quality video capture that is among the best available. Like other high-end solutions, the Targa is expensive: about $5,000 on the street, If you need the best, it's well worth the price.

Video Editing Features

The real fun and creativity of creating digital movies comes in the editing stage, when you can put on your director's hat and turn raw footage into a finished production, complete with professionally inspired sequences and special effects. This truly is the good stuff, and it wouldn't be possible without sophisticated, video editing software. Today's video editing software is a postproduction house in a box, combining desktop convenience and simplicity with capabilities previously available only in million-dollar postproduction studios.

Before we delve into the applications themselves, however, we want to provide you with the basic video editing features and the interface metaphors these packages use to combine power and efficiency. Once you understand them, you'll be better equipped to select the package that most directly addresses your needs.

Metaphors for Desktop Video Editing

Because digital video on the desktop is so new, no one could predict for certain what approach to software would best facilitate its use. The Macintosh and Windows desktop uses file folders and icons to create a metaphor about a business person's desk. Videotapes, however, are stored on shelves and not in file folders, and are erased rather than trashed.

Furthermore, the people who need to understand and use this software come from different backgrounds. Those who come to desktop digital video from the video industry are used to previews, in-points, out-points, perform edit, titling, and the like. Those who come by way of the film industry are used to relying on another set of tools; while people with experience using computer graphics programs have totally different expectations. The end result is that digital video software is a rich amalgamation of metaphors and jargon from many different disciplines. The approaches range from software modeled on traditional video editing to that which uses metaphors designed to take advantage of the unique nature of this new medium.

Your own background and experience may be an important factor in helping you select a software package. You should know the approach taken by each software package, and whether that approach will facilitate your ability to work effectively with the features of the software. The following are some of the common metaphors used by digital video software.

Macintosh or Windows Desktop Metaphor

Apple and Microsoft encourage all software to subscribe to the basic interfaces of the Macintosh and Windows desktops, using cut and paste, file folders, and so on. This makes each Mac and Windows program easier to use, since you already are familiar with the desktop. With a few notable exceptions, such as Avid's VideoShop, most digital video software *does* conform to the most important features of the desktop. VideoShop, with roots at the M.I.T Media Research Lab, has been designed from the ground up to create a new working environment most appropriate for digital video.

Video Editing Metaphor

The more support a software package has for traditional analog video editing through the control of videotape recorders, videodisc players, and other external devices, the more likely it will subscribe to the video editing metaphor. A good example of this is Adobe's Premiere. Its six main tracks—two video, one

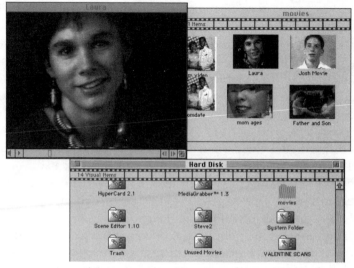

**Figure 6.5
The VideoShop
environment
converts the
Macintosh desk-
top folders and
creates microns
to illustrate
QuickTime
movie files.**

overlay, one transition, and two sound—are similar to professional video editing studio technology. This type of software frequently assumes that, as with
videotape, only one format or image size will be used in the creation of a particular production.

Digital Photography Metaphor

If you already have experience with programs designed for digital photography
(Photoshop, for example), you will appreciate software with filters, RGB channels, alpha-channels, and the like. Software that relies heavily on the digital photography metaphor includes VideoFusion Ltd.'s VideoFusion, Star Media System's
Video Action Pro, and Premiere. If you think of video as a series of still frames,
be aware that the same techniques are used in digital photography and digital
movies. However, the techniques used in digital photography may be augmented
for digital movies to permit change over time. For instance, a filter from Adobe's
Premiere may gradually alter the movie frames over time, beginning with no
noticeable effect and gradually increasing the amount of the effect.

3-D Rendering Metaphor

Strata Vision 3d Demo ⌘ 721

A common vocabulary is used among 3-D programs such as Specular International's Infini-D and Strata Inc.'s Vision 3d. For example, renderings can be done
to various degrees of detail, from wireframe to shading to high resolution for
final rendering. Objects are created in three-dimensional space and can be
manipulated and rotated separately. CoSA's After Effects, which allows movies of
different dimensions to be combined in a window by treating them as separate
objects, is an example of a digital video software package modeled on such
3-D programs.

Metaphors
for New
Paradigms

Some say that the metaphor for digital video software should be designed from scratch to best exploit the capabilities of this new medium. Others insist that you should start with the familiar, so that people do not have to reinvent the wheel in order to use it. VideoShop is an example of the first philosophy; it creates an environment optimized for digital video. Even the Macintosh desktop is revised to capitalize on what works best for that medium.

VideoShop's approach departs from common Macintosh conventions for opening files, file folders, and other Macintosh desktop conventions. The advantage of VideoShop, however, is that it creates a seamless environment in which to work, including access and search of files, making movies, and rendering interactive presentations using the movies you make.

Software Features

Digital video editors include organizing tools for your media files; windows for multiple views of your project, such as storyboards and timelines; movie recording capabilities; and most important of all, the filters, transitions, special effects, titles, rotoscoping, and alpha and other channel capabilities that turn these software packages into power tools.

Organizing Your Media Files

Most digital video programs have devised ways to help organize the movies or other media files for a particular project; some also tackle the bigger picture of organizing all of the media files on your hard disk for ready access during an editing session.

Databases

The purpose of a database is to give you access to media (stored on your hard disk or located elsewhere) that has been categorized for your convenience so that you can retrieve the right movie for a current project. There are many independent visual databases, such as Fetch by Aldus. A built-in database, however, generally provides better integration within a software editing package for effective access to files as needed. VideoShop comes with a Visual Catalog, which functions as a database of files that are compatible with VideoShop.

Folders

Since both the Mac and Windows desktops include a system of folders in which you can put your media (or more folders), you have a ready-made system of organizing your media files. However, some programs allow customization of this process. VideoShop, for example, alters the Macintosh desktop to allow special views of only those folders and files that can be used with QuickTime (see Figure 6.5). Media can then be moved from a folder directly into the storyboard view of the application.

Projects

Most digital video editing packages import files into a project window that holds all of the files for a particular project, whether you actually use them or not. In addition, Premiere offers a library consisting of files that can be reused in other projects.

Recording Video

In addition to the recording software that comes with your video digitizing card, video editing software also frequently provides for recording video from within the editing session. The advantage of recording within an editing package is the convenience of bringing video into the computer when needed in the project. In some instances, the ability to record during an editing session extends the capability of the editing package to off-line editing and other specialized purposes.

Multiple Views of Your Project

A significant advantage of digital video over traditional videotape editing is that you can look at the video information any way you want to, or at least, any way the designers of your editing software anticipated would be useful. The following are some of the more common views, or windows, in which to view digital video information now being supported by software packages. Most software packages support views of your project through a timeline, a preview, and a movie player. Other views of a digital video project may include an object-oriented and motion picture script.

Timeline View

A timeline is the most important view in the software program because it permits synchronizing audio to video and allows editing on a frame-by-frame basis. Most software editors support this view, which shows you the entire movie frame-by-frame, second-by-second, or by whatever particular time reference you choose, as long as it is supported by the software. Frequently, this is the view to which you will add transitions and special effects and create the important nuances that make your movie what it is.

Movie Player View

Several different types of movie players may come to your attention, depending on which software packages you are working with. The most common permits you to play any part of an existing movie that is part of your project. VideoFusion software has the unusual feature of permitting you to play in its entirety the current edited version on which you are working. In order to achieve this laudable goal of real-time playing, this software creates the transitions and special effects as soon as you apply them, rather than waiting until you are ready to make the whole movie. The movie players also permit you to mark in-points and out-points for segments and to cut and paste portions of your movie.

MoviePlayer ⌘ 612

Popcorn 1.0.1 ⌘ 613

Preview View

In traditional videotape editing, a preview allows you to see a segment you are about to edit (including any transitions or special effects) before you actually finalize or perform the edit and record it to videotape. A preview in software digital editing is somewhat more flexible. In traditional editing, you are creating one edit at a time. However, in digital editing, you can create the entire movie before you start transferring any of the individual edits. As a result, a preview in digital editing gives you much more flexibility to choose any portion of the project that you want to preview. Depending on the particular software and preferences you have designated, a preview may be in a smaller window, and at a lower resolution of video or audio, than the final movie. The point of the preview is to let you see what is going to happen without having to wait for delays caused by a slow compression algorithm or other necessary steps in making the entire movie.

Storyboard View

A digital software storyboard serves all the functions of a traditional storyboard and a great deal more. (See Chapter 8, "Multimedia Development: Process, Planning, and Design.") Storyboards were originally devised as a means of communicating between the production people and the client. They also help the designer to visualize the project. In addition to aiding the design process, digital storyboarding directly contributes to building the final video product. Storyboard views use a single still image to represent an entire segment of a movie.

You can design a movie simply by reordering the video segments in the storyboard. Because the storyboard collapses each segment, regardless of its length, to a single image, this view is ideal for obtaining a broad overview of what the project will look like. Examples of software that provide this view are VideoShop, CoSA After Effects, VideoFusion, InSync Razor Pro, and Star Media's Video Action Pro (see Figure 6.6).

Object-Oriented View

An object-oriented view may be featured in editors that permit you to combine movies, graphics files, and other media of different sizes and shapes. Premiere, for instance, does not support such a view because it requires all files to be in the same size format. CoSA After Effects, in contrast, provides very complex layering of movies, text, images, and other visual information of different shapes and sizes. Until the movie is finalized, each visual element of the movie remains a separate object that can be manipulated, made closer or farther, larger or smaller,

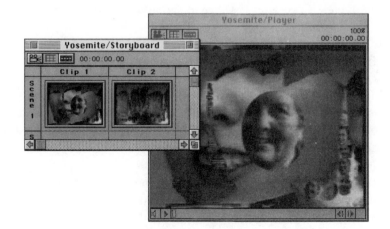

Figure 6.6 Storyboard view and the Player window from VideoFusion.

or fused together with another object. You can also impose special effects on each visual element before completing the movie.

Motion Picture Script View

Many productions start with a motion picture type of script consisting of a written description of every scene and include the dialog and other information necessary for creating the movie. Taking advantage of the ease with which digital movies can be incorporated into word processing documents, some software editors support a view of the movie based on a motion picture script format. As more of the movie is actually finished, the resulting digital movie can be inserted into the appropriate location in the written script and viewed simply by clicking on it. The VideoFusion software package supports this view.

Editing Capabilities

The editing capabilities of digital video software are extraordinary. Within a year after the release of QuickTime, almost anything was possible. High-end systems, such as Avid's Media Composer series, ImMix's VideoCube, Data Translations' Media 100 and Targa 2000 combine powerful video editing systems with hardware compression that allows broadcast quality work to be turned out on the desktop. These products are known as nonlinear editing systems.

These systems are beyond the reach of most multimedia producers, but there are plenty of software-based video editing tools with features that make editing video for multimedia presentations a snap. Following is a list of categories that should help you to understand what current capabilities are and when to use them.

Titles

Adobe and TrueType fonts, so common on both the Mac and PC, are designed with parameters that can be altered for use in desktop publishing. Digital video can do even more with these fonts. Editing software, such as Premiere, permits all of these parameters to be manipulated in real time as the letters go flying, spinning, and growing across the screen. New versions of QuickTime will support a separate titles channel that could permit you to change the fonts and their parameters even after the movie is made, as well as to do word searches.

Video and Sound Channels

In theory, QuickTime supports an almost unlimited number of video and audio channels. In practice, access to them may be limited by the capabilities of your software. In some instances, you may prefer to combine the channels in the final movie to optimize the playback speed. Multiple sound channels can be used not only for stereo, but also to manipulate the volume or other aspects of the audio relative to other audio channels. Some programs rely heavily on channels to create filters, transitions, and special effects.

Filters

Whatever the original meaning of the word "filter," the important thing to remember is that filters operate on a single movie to make dramatic changes in the image or sound. Filters may operate on the entire movie or any portion of it.

They may operate on only one color channel (red, green, or blue) or on all channels at one time. While photographic filters change the color, digital video filters can turn the movie upside down, reverse its color, cause it to spin in three dimensions, or anything else.

Unlike Photoshop filters, which operate on a single still image, digital video filters can change the nature of the image over time. The filter might slowly increase the contrast of the movie, make it darker or bluer, cause the image to rotate and turn, or create any number of other effects.

One promising aspect of the use of filters is the move toward standards. Adobe publishes the standards for Photoshop filters so that third parties can provide their own. Many of these can be used with any application that is compatible with Photoshop filters, including Premiere and other digital video software. The day may be near when every program can use every other program's filters, so that you will be able to customize your software for whatever filters you choose to buy.

KPT-Pixelwind Filter ⌘ 606

KPT-Diffuse More Filter ⌘ 607

KPT-Fine Edges Soft Filter ⌘ 608

KPT-Sharpen Intensify Filter ⌘ 609

KPT-3d Stereo Noise Filter ⌘ 610

Transitions

Transitions differ from filters in that they require two different video segments; they perform their magic on the transition from one video segment to the other. Like filters, there is very little limit to what transitions can do, and they are beginning to be standardized.

Combinations

Combinations allow you to combine two different movies in myriad ways. The following are examples of combinations.

Chroma key

A term that comes from traditional video techniques, chroma key is used extensively on television. For example, it permits the weatherperson to point to details in a weather map that actually is not there. The weatherperson actually points to a blue screen, and chroma key is used to replace the blue screen with another image from a different source.

In digital video, chroma key permits you to designate a color (or range of colors) in a movie as transparent, so that you can see through it to a second movie (the weather map effect). Chroma key works best with high-quality RGB video that has been shot with chroma key in mind, designating a brilliant color as the transparent hue.

Arithmetic

This technique mathematically combines the pixels of one movie with those of another, which can result in impressive special effects.

Logical

These special effects rely on the logical manipulation of bytes that hold the pixel information. They are extremely fast and effective and can cause images to look like color or black-and-white negatives, make colors disappear altogether, create ghost colors, and accomplish many other effects.

Composite

These include morphs and alpha-channels.

Morphs

Morph 2.5 Demo ⌘ 714

Morphs are attractive special effects that cause a shape in one movie to change slowly into the shape of something very different in another movie. Morphs have been overused in television, and one can tire of them unless they are used to make an effective statement. Remember: think before you morph.

Alpha-Channels

The only difference between a 24-bit movie and a 32-bit movie is that the latter includes a fourth data channel—the alpha-channel—that provides for the inclusion of special effects in digital images. Movies that are stored in 24-bit RGB mode use 8 bits for red, 8 bits for green, and 8 bits for blue; the remaining 8 bits are reserved for such special effects as masks, mattes, overlays, and other manipulations. For example, the alpha-channel might contain a black-and-white oval shape, permitting two movies to be combined, with one movie inside the oval shape and the other movie in the background. (For more information on alpha-channels, see Chapter 12, "Creating 3-D Models and Animation" and Chapter 3, "Graphics Tools.")

There are several different types of alpha-channels; they are frequently supported by 3-D software, digital photography software, and other programs that can export QuickTime or AVI movies. Although QuickTime does not ordinarily display information in an alpha-channel, it will, nevertheless, carry the information to a software program that can display it. Photoshop and Premiere both have support for alpha-channels.

Rotoscoping

The process of hand painting on one frame of a digital video movie at a time is called rotoscoping. A convenient way to perform this procedure is to export one or more frames from a movie into Photoshop or other appropriate digital photography software, where the image can be easily hand colored. Premiere supports a special file format called a film strip for exporting digital movies to and from Photoshop. The latest version of Painter has added QuickTime and AVI support that make it an ideal tool for rotoscoping.

**Extensible
Architecture**

The trend in software development is for one company to encourage other companies to support add-ons to its software package, so that users can extend its capabilities by picking and choosing new features. Perhaps having learned the hard way with Adobe fonts (which Adobe did not publish as open standards until Microsoft and Apple challenged the existing font standards with TrueType),

Adobe has taken the lead in providing the necessary specifications to permit other software add-ons to be made compatible with Premiere and standards that other software packages can adhere to in order to utilize Premiere-compatible add-ons.

Premiere filters, like those in Photoshop, are standardized; and any company can design filters for Premiere. In addition, products such as VideoShop, Video-Fusion, Razor, and Video Action Pro are compatible with both Photoshop and Premiere plug-in filters. Adobe also has published standards for other types of plug-ins for Premiere, including transitions or special effects, video filters, audio filters, device control, exporting EDLs (Edit Decision Lists), and other standards.

Device Control
In addition to controlling VCRs to print to tape, software packages also can control VCRs, videodisc players, and other devices to bring video into the computer to perform other functions.

Video Editing Products

Now that we've looked at the features and capabilities common to most video editing packages, let's focus on the characteristics of the leading applications. Below, we've reviewed three products—one for Mac/Windows, and two for the Mac alone. Windows users with modest video editing needs might want to snag a copy of Microsoft's VidEdit, a simple but capable editor distributed on Microsoft's Multimedia Jumpstart CD, or a copy of Video Action Pro, which offers some of the best transitions and effects available anywhere (see mini-review, below).

Adobe's Premiere

Premiere 4.0 Demo ⌘ 722

Premiere, the leading software package for QuickTime and AVI digital video, is available for both the Mac and Windows environments. Benefiting from Adobe's experience with Photoshop, Premiere uses the same or similar filters. If the dozens of Photoshop filters aren't enough for you, Filter Factory lets you create your own.

In its current 4.0 version for both Mac and PCs, Premiere offers up to 99 video tracks for effects layering, as well as improvements to its preview feature. In addition, the text editor in Premiere gives the user control over many of the parameters of Adobe fonts. Not only does Premiere include a powerful editing system for combining two digital movies and the Super Channel for superimposing titles, movies, and special effects, it also supports professional applications requiring SMPTE timecode for off-line editing, extensibility, add-ons, and more (see Figure 6.7).

Features in Premiere permit the intuitive creation and alteration of digital movies. Users can control complex parameters simply by moving a line up and down to create paths in the Title window, audio in the Timeline window, and animation paths in the Motion window.

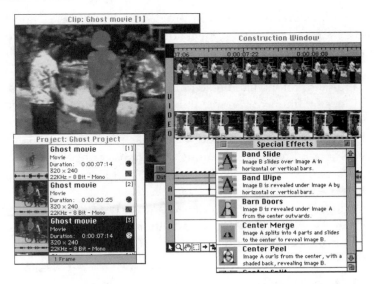

Figure 6.7 Premiere 2.0 with the Movie window, Project window, Construction window, and the Special Effects Transition window.

The Construction window, which provides a timeline view of the current project, is at the heart of Premiere. Two primary movie channels are separated by two special-effects channels for the placement of transitions and overlays. Two audio channels also are supported. Another movie channel, known as the *Super track*, permits you to manipulate lines to display whole movies over the other two movies in a variety of ways. The transparency function allows the movie in the Super track to be seen as a split screen or a mask, to serve as an alpha-channel, to be used for superimposing titles, and so on. The Construction window lets you stretch or shrink video and audio to fit and facilitates proper placement of video sequences.

The Trimming Window allows you to tune the important transitions between two different scenes. Using *rolling* and *rippling* edits, you can exert a fine degree of control to get just the sort of transition you have in mind.

Premiere, like all software packages, also has its weaknesses. It is sometimes slow to redraw the movie frames within the Construction window, but has some workarounds. One is the ability to create miniature movies during the editing process and return to full-size movies at the time of final compilation. There are extra steps involved in making miniatures, however. Premiere works best with finished video segments that are ready to be edited together with titles, transitions, and limited kinds of motion. With the plethora of filters and special effects available, virtually anything can be accomplished. But Premiere does not directly support the simultaneous combination of different movies and images of many different sizes. A great deal of manipulation of filters and special effects may be necessary to create a smaller movie within a movie.

In addition to the Construction window, several other views are available. A Project window holds all the movies and other media chosen for the project (however, the scissors tool in the Construction window, which permits cutting a movie into many smaller pieces, can quickly clutter it). A Library window stores media libraries for future projects.

The Clip window allows you to view clips as well as change the in-points and out-points of specific segments. You can view the current movie with varying degrees of accuracy by using the Preview window, in which you can designate the portion of the movie to be previewed, and the size and resolution of the preview. The Sequence window permits rapid creation of simple cuts by combining all of the movies placed in it.

Premiere supports video capture at the broadcast NTSC standard of 29.97 frames per second—if you have the capture hardware and computing power to back it up.

Avid's VideoShop

If you are looking for a Mac software package that creates a complete environment ranging from video editing to interactive multimedia, Avid's VideoShop may be the answer. It features a world of internal consistency built around a proprietary data format called a *Micon*, whose parameters you can control. The purpose of a Micon is to provide a motion preview of the movie anywhere on the hard disk or elsewhere within VideoShop. Even when porting to HyperCard for interactive presentations, VideoShop takes its Micons along for the ride. A few clicks of the mouse are enough to create a simple interactive presentation. While this approach may not fit everyone's needs, those who are comfortable with the VideoShop environment will have a productive tool they can stay with. VideoShop even provides its own Visual Catalog database in which to store your media.

Micons have peculiarities that take some getting used to. For instance, a generic Micon is available for any movie on the hard disk, but each movie must be selected individually to create a custom Micon to represent it. Do not even think of creating a custom Micon for a movie on a CD-ROM, because the Micon data must be attached to the movie itself. This is not feasible on read-only media. Once you create Micons, your hard disk and VideoShop data turn into a visual feast of accessible information.

Like Premiere, VideoShop features a timeline view; but in this case the number of video channels is virtually unlimited, providing some of the capabilities of CoSA After Effects, which permits you to combine different QuickTime movies without regard to shape or size (see next section). In addition to the filters and transitional effects that come with the software package, it supports Photoshop Plug-Ins.

VideoShop is an entry-level editing package with all of the features necessary to create first-class digital movies.

CoSA After Effects

After Effects is a high-end Mac video editing tool aimed at professional users who need finer control over objects and motion than typical multimedia producers do. After Effects is designed for combining movies of different dimensions, graphics files, and other media of different sizes into a single new movie. Under the object-oriented paradigm CoSA has borrowed from 3-D editing software, each movie or other type of media becomes an object in the Composition window.

The power of this tool is that at any point in the Composition window (which will become the new movie), you are free to move individual objects around relative to each other, to blend them together in many different subtle ways, or to apply special effects to each object individually. Because it permits an unlimited number of objects to be layered together and provides extensive support for the alpha-channel and other effects, this software package is more like a media creation tool than a video editor.

You can render a movie at different levels of quality to facilitate rapid development as you would with 3-D editing software. There's a wireframe mode for viewing the relative positions of objects. In the draft mode, the movie is visible at a medium level of quality, and not all effects are calculated. In the best mode, all pixels are displayed, full antialiasing is provided, and plug-in effects are fully calculated. Whereas most other editing software relies on QuickTime to determine quality levels during the editing process, the 3-D model of rendering provides After Effects with greater flexibility in giving the user an appropriate level of quality for the task at hand, thus speeding up the editing process.

By supporting a number of different views, or windows, After Effects can perform functions other editing packages cannot (see Figure 6.8). While it fea-

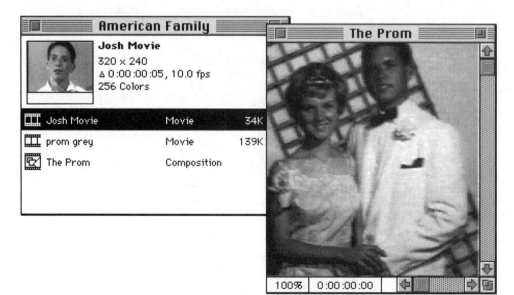

**Figure 6.8
Project window
and Composition
window in CoSA
After Effects.**

tures a Project window, it distinguishes between the whole project and a composition, which is the use of the media in a particular project. As a result, many different compositions can be present at one time. As they are created, they show up in the Project window and become raw ingredients for a larger project.

Borrowing again from 3-D software, CoSA After Effects uses its own brand of keyframes to demarcate the length of special effects or transitions. The time view allows you to quickly travel from one keyframe to another, providing a convenient way to design and navigate a movie in various stages of production.

At this writing, the current version of After Effects (2.0) did not, alas, have support for either alpha channels or Photoshop plug-ins.

Star Media System's Video Action Pro

Video Action Pro is a nonlinear video editing package for the PC. Its low cost (about $200 on the street) belies its sophisticated features and special effects. The emphasis is on the latter: there are many unique filters, including Old Movie —complete with that flickering old cinematic look. The package also includes a custom effects generator so you can create your own filters. Transitions can be jumpy and jerky, but there are many controls for refinements. Overall, a solid program for the money.

Tools for Controlling VCRs and Other Video Equipment

You also can find tools that control VCRs and videodisc players either to edit video or to assist in the creation of digital video. The type of hardware/software combination you choose determines how accurately you can control the VCR or other equipment. Whether you need sophisticated hardware to control your equipment, or whether software control is sufficient depends on the capability of your VCR and the task at hand (see Chapter 14, "Creating Video").

Tool Features for VCR Control

You do not need a great deal of accuracy to bring video into the computer since digital video editors allow you to trim the video after creating it. The video can be edited in the computer and the final result can be output to tape without precise control of the VCR. However, multiple prints to the same tape require more precision.

Logging

The process of viewing and describing the scenes in a videotape is referred to as logging. The entire videotape can be logged, or you can select only those scenes that may be used in a production. The computer can assist in the logging process, providing the frame numbers for the beginning and the end of each

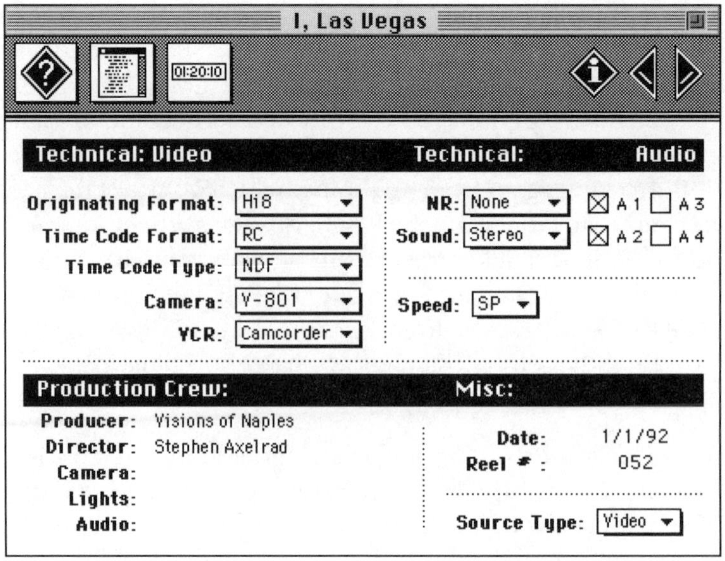

**Figure 6.9
A screen from
CueTrack
HyperCard
stack from
VideoToolkit
permits rapid
logging and
database man-
agement of video.**

scene. AVI or QuickTime-based logging software can provide a QuickTime pre-view of the in-point and out-point of each scene (see Figure 6.9).

Off-line Editing

More precision is required to do off-line editing than is necessary for logging only. Once the in-points and out-points are established, they can be assembled to create an *edit list*. Because all of the decisions have already been made, the edit list can be taken to a high-end video facility, where the final video can be edited using very expensive equipment in a very short period of time.

Using software such as Premiere, the entire production can be created as a digital movie, including the transitions. The software can then export an edit list sufficient to reproduce the movie in its entirety in a high-end video facility. In order to obtain sufficient accuracy to do this properly, the digital movie should include SMPTE time code at 30 frames per second. You can accomplish this by using only a small amount of the more advanced digitizing hardware.

On-line Editing

The process of using the computer to edit videotape without bringing the video into the computer is called on-line editing. The computer acts as a controller to synchronize the videotape player and transfer the video to the videotape recorder. This requires almost no computer memory, since none of the video has to enter the computer. A controller system precise enough to begin and end on the designated video frame is said to be frame-accurate. More likely, on-line editing will be accurate within a few frames. The use of time code is necessary for frame-accurate editing.

VCR Control Software and Hardware

While some software tools for VCR control rely on the computer itself for hardware, more expensive solutions use additional hardware for more precise control. The VideoToolkit for the Mac, which comes with interfacing cables, is an example of an excellent software package that is a complete, inexpensive solution requiring no additional hardware. The primary focus of this software is logging, control for digital video, and off-line editing; although it can also be used for on-line editing.

Gold Disk's Video Director is a low-cost software solution for PCs and Macs. It comes with a cable for controlling a camcorder or VCR via an infrared remote. It is primarily useful for cuts-only editing of home video.

The FutureVideo EditLink 3300 Series desktop controller is an example of a hardware/software solution (Figure 6.10). The primary focus of this package is on-line edits, although it is also useful for logging, control for digital video, and off-line editing. While the FutureVideo EditLink 3300 Series can simultaneously control three VCRs for logging or bringing video into the computer, its primary purpose is for on-line editing while also controlling external special-effects generators, such as the Video Toaster. You can combine two different videotapes with transitions created by a special-effects generator and recorded onto a third VCR. This process is called A/B roll, and the ability to trigger the special-effects generator is called a GPI. The FutureVideo EditLink 3300 controller comes with editing software compatible with all current Macs.

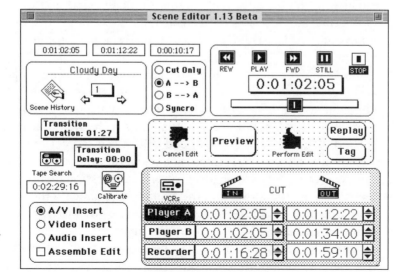

Figure 6.10 FutureVideo's EditLink 3300 Series controller with Scene Editor software for the Macintosh.

What the Video Toaster brought to the Amiga in terms of economical video editing, Fast has brought to the PC with its Video Machine. Among other things, Video Machine offers A/B Roll, an effects generator, and two time base correctors. It also has a digitizer add-on that provides hybrid digital/analog on-line editing.

Videodisc Control

Videodisc players can be used to bring video into the computer or for interactive presentations utilizing the computer for the limited purpose of controlling the player. The Voyager VideoStack provides a HyperCard solution for controlling videodisc players and creating interactive presentations. Most industrial players with computer interface ports—including the Sony and Pioneer videodisc players—are supported. Many of the consumer players also are supported by the Voyager VideoStack by means of an additional hardware interface that can be purchased from Voyager. The interface provides infrared communication through emulation of the commands of the player's own hand controller.

Two of the most popular videodisc players are the Pioneer LDV-4200 and its successor, the LDV-4400. Players that use commands compatible with both these players and the high-end Pioneer LDV6000, can be controlled by the Pioneer MovieMaker, which is distributed on the QuickTime Developer's CD-ROM from Apple. This utility can control the videodisc player one frame at a time to permit bringing all frames into the computer, even with hardware not designed to capture all 30 frames in real time. On Windows systems, many videodisc players can be directly controlled through Windows MCI commands.

MovieShop for CD-ROM

QuickTime movies destined for CD-ROM will benefit from treatment by Apple's MovieShop, a utility available on the Apple QuickTime Developer's CD-ROM. A QuickTime movie looks like a snake that has swallowed a few mice: the data has lumps in it which are too large to transfer at the proper speed on a CD-ROM player.

MovieShop compresses a movie's data so that it can be played back within a specified data rate. If there is too much information per second, the movie will appear jerky, or the sound will begin to skip. If a movie is intended to play back from a CD-ROM, you'll want the data rate to be no higher than 90 to 100K per second. (The newer double-speed drives can deliver twice this data rate, but you should use the lower rates for backwards compatibility). To reduce the data rate, you can select which MovieShop compression techniques to apply. These techniques include lowering the frame rate, reducing the quality of the sound, shrinking the image size, lowering the image quality by increasing compression, dropping similar adjacent frames, and many others.

Currently, the Apple Compact Video codec is the most effective in reducing data rates and supports smooth playback of QuickTime with a surprisingly large window size. You can select this codec from within MovieShop. In Chapter 14,

"Creating Video," we suggest the MovieShop settings you should use to achieve optimal results from this codec.

Video Compression Sampler

Doceo Publishing's Video Compression Sampler is an interesting video clip analyzer for the PC that compares the effects of various codecs side by side. This is very useful in determining which codec will afford the best playback rate and image quality for a given machine. You can vary parameters such as frame rate to see how the result performs on a particular system. The $50 program is a great value and can save much trial and error in the tricky business of getting digital video to play back reliably on a wide range of hardware.

7

Authoring Tools

Dramatic video, beautiful sound, and delightful animation won't give you multimedia—not unless they're combined in a cohesive, interactive whole. That's where *authoring* tools come in: They're the software programs you'll use to orchestrate all those separate building blocks—as effective as they may be individually—in a way that creates a powerful, synergistic final product that is far greater than the sum of its parts. With authoring tools, you become a multimedia director with total creative control over the storyline, the set, and the actors that make up your project.

Most authoring tools allow you to create and modify backgrounds and visual effects for your project's interface. Many allow you to control external devices such as videotape decks and laserdisc players. However, the most important features they offer are those that create links between graphics, text, and audiovisual elements. These features use buttons, scripts, hardware device drivers, and other methods to create interactivity among the user and the project.

In this chapter, we'll take a look at all the major cross platform authoring software applications: Macromedia's Director and Authorware, and Apple's Media Tool.

Director 4.0 Demo ⌘ 708

AuthorWare Prof. 3.0 Demo ⌘ 709

Authoring Software Features

When evaluating authoring software, you should carefully consider such issues as interface, capabilities, and features. Does the software have all the necessary tools for creating links between your interface and your data? Can you customize the software and write scripts to perform special functions that might be considered outside the norm? Most importantly, is the interface sensible and organized for the task you have set for yourself?

You should also look for programs that support current graphics, animation, and video standards. QuickTime or AVI support is crucial if you plan to use small video segments off hard drives or CD-ROMs. Also, the emergence of compression/decompression technology means that many of the authoring programs will soon be supporting full-screen video directly off your hard drive or CD-ROM drive.

Authoring programs are deep and contain many features. The most important are summarized in the next few pages.

Master Windows

Most authoring packages feature some type of master window that affords you a bird's-eye view of your project, including all of its elements and their relationships. Sometimes this screen takes the form of a flowchart (as it does in Authorware); other times it may resemble a spreadsheet (in Macromedia Director's Score, for example).

Objects and Scripts

Authoring software helps you sequence your presentation and link its elements together simply by selecting and connecting screen icons representing the various pieces of the presentation. This *object-oriented* type of interface is intuitive and allows almost anyone to naturally choreograph a presentation. Some packages give you even more power and precision in this area by including a *scripting language* (see next page).

The Object-Oriented Approach

Working with objects is the easiest way to create a multimedia ensemble. For example, a button that leads to an animation on screen is created with some sort of "make button" command. Once you've made the button, you'll have the option to associate a visual graphic with it and place a name on it—you could, for instance, call it "Play Animation." You can then *define the button's properties*—tell the button where to look for your animation on the hard drive, and give the instruction to play the animation once the button is clicked—via some type of "button info" dialogue.

The same button that plays an animation could just as easily be programmed to play a segment of video from a laserdisc, show a PICT file on the screen, or display another screen containing more buttons.

Of course, a professional multimedia project usually will involve much more complexity than simple "go directly from here to there" relationships. It often will also involve the concept of "branching," which means setting up the paths and options for how your data is accessed. We'll get into branching and other considerations for constructing an interactive project in Chapter 16, "Interface and Interactivity: Bringing It Together."

Scripting

Many authoring programs include a scripting language that can give you great precision in determining how your multimedia elements will interrelate, and how well your project will cooperate with external programs, routines, and devices. Although multimedia scripting is generally a lot easier to master than traditional programming languages (you don't need to have a degree in computer science), it is more difficult than pointing and clicking on objects.

File Formats

An attractive interface is an essential ingredient in a successful multimedia project, so most authoring packages come with tools and features that allow you to import various graphics and sounds. Perhaps most important is the capability to import the most popular graphics and motion-graphics formats, since you certainly will be using graphic elements created in other packages. Authoring packages generally accept the major graphics file formats, QuickTime and AVI movie formats, and AIFF and WAV sound files. Color support also is an important consideration for professional-level multimedia.

Graphics and Animation Tools

Authoring packages also provide varying capabilities for manipulating graphics. Many come with built-in drawing and painting tools. Some boast sophisticated animation tools for movement, timing, and transitions. Most have controls for transitional effects and wipes from one window to another. There are ways of getting around the shortcomings of those that don't, but they usually require you to do more work in "outside" graphics and animation applications before bringing sequence into the authoring environment.

Connecting to External Devices

Many multimedia presentations rely on external devices such as CD-ROMs, laserdiscs, or VCRs. How and to what degree your authoring program controls these devices can greatly affect the scope and impact of your project. Most authoring packages use add-on routines called *external commands* (XCMDs), which follow a standard originally established with HyperCard, as through DLLs (Dynamic Link Libraries) in Windows. AuthorWare Professional not only supports XCMDs, but also boasts built-in control for laserdiscs.

"How will people be using my project? Will it be a kiosk in a hotel lobby? Will it be mass distributed on a CD-ROM, or on a laserdisc?" As suggested in Chapter 8, "Multimedia Development: Process, Planning, and Design," you must ask yourself these questions early on, since they will bear on what authoring tools you'll need to put your project together. Most authoring packages support run-time playback, which means users can view the final project whether or not they have the application in which it was created. This is a critical consideration if you will be distributing your project via CD-ROM. All of the applications reviewed here provide a means to play back presentations in either the Mac or Windows environment.

Software Packages

Now that we've looked at the features and capabilities common to most authoring packages, let's focus on the particular characteristics of the leading products.

Macromedia Director

Director 4.0 Demo ⌘ 708

Macromedia Director is far the most popular authoring tool. Its reputation was bolstered in 1994 when Macromedia released a Windows version of the program. Director's strengths include the ability to create animations and control such external devices as laserdiscs, and its custom scripting environment. For many projects that include 2-D animation, sound, and interactivity, almost all of the work can be done within Director itself (see Figure 7.1).

Director uses several "show biz" metaphors to aid in the assembly of multimedia presentations:

- The *Cast*, which is the various "assets": video chips, screen shots, animations, or text files.

- The castmembers are assembled into the *Score*, which sequences them according to how they will play back.

- The *Script* is a set of high-level commands written in Director's scripting language, Lingo. The presentation on the CD uses Lingo to tell Director when to play the digital movie, and how to launch Acrobat, for example.

- The *Stage*, which shows how the presentation will look when played back.

In addition, Director supplies a variety of paint and animation tools, as well as a set of floating tool palettes.

Figure 7.1 Director's Overview mode allows you to quickly compose a presentation simply by dragging icons into place along a timeline. Elements such as graphics, text, sound, and animation can be layered and organized in a linear fashion, complete with transitions from one section to another.

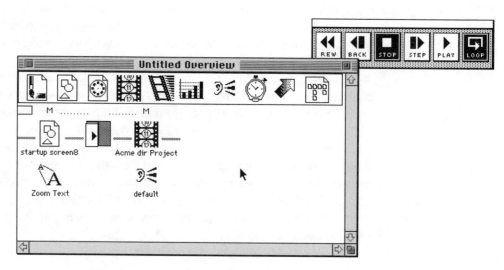

Director has its own scripting language—Lingo—for creating interactive links between the various elements and peripherals in a project. Lingo provides a robust selection of tools for linking elements together and has pull-down menus that are chock-full of commands, functions, operators, constants, and more. Like most multimedia programming languages, Lingo is object-oriented; so it's easy to attach a script or command to a graphic or animation element. The statements created in Lingo are similar to those used in hypertext-based applications. By constructing simple statements and referencing other functions, it's relatively easy to create fairly complex projects. This is not to say that it is easy to learn. Director can be more difficult than other authoring environments, especially if you need to learn how to create animations as well as interactivity.

Director compiles Lingo scripts after you write them and "parses" for correct syntax. You can also use Lingo to split a presentation into modules that can be swapped in and out. This is useful for modifying or updating complex projects such as kiosk applications without rewriting an entire script.

How It Works

Since serious interactive projects will demand that you work in the Studio mode, we'll direct our working comments to this area of the program. Director's Studio mode uses theatrical metaphors to create an understandable environment for building the visual parts of a project. Graphic and animation elements are considered Cast members, the screen is considered a Stage, and choreography of your animation elements is controlled via a Score. This conceptual model works well because it allows you to orient yourself quickly to the various audio/visual tasks involved with animation and multimedia producing. Once you are oriented to Director's approach, the layout is quite logical (see Figure 7.2).

The Score is the central area for organizing and controlling your data. Besides having virtually unlimited layers available for graphics, it features channels for tempo, audio, transitions, and scripting. The Score is basically a spreadsheet with a series of cells laid out in a grid. Graphics and animation elements are layered from top to bottom, with the bottom layer being the elements that are in the forefront visually. The left-to-right organization of cells represents a linear timeline. The top six channels in the score are dedicated to tempo settings (including "wait for mouse click" commands), color palette transitions, graphic transitions (such as wipes and dissolves), audio, and Lingo scripts (see Figure 7.3).

Other notable windows include those for Cast and Paint. The Cast window is where Director stores all of the project's visual elements, including all graphics, animations, and text overlays, as well as animated loops and QuickTime movies. The Paint window is actually Director's built-in paint program. Although not as slick as some of the dedicated paint programs on the market, it offers a fairly full-featured set of tools for creating and modifying graphic elements. Arrow buttons in the Paint window allow you to toggle through your entire cast of graphic elements, providing easy access for making changes. Among items available in the

Figure 7.2
This image shows key elements of Director's Studio mode: the Score, Cast, and Playback windows. The Score is a command sheet where you organize the layers, structure, movement, and interactivity in your project. The Cast is where you keep the graphic, animation, and text elements of your project. The Playback window is used to play a project, much like you would play it on an audio or video player.

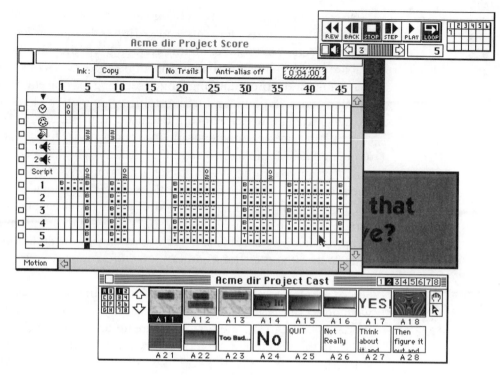

Figure 7.3
Tempo settings can be applied at any given point in a project, with controls for predetermined wait periods or instructions to proceed upon completion of a sound or movie. You can also instruct the project to wait for the user to click the mouse or hit a key before proceeding.

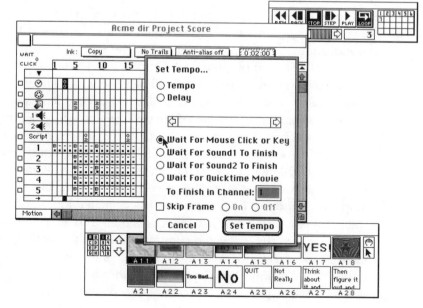

Paint window are user-definable gradients, patterns, and textures; painting and drawing tools; and rotation and distortion tools for modifying graphics.

While you can import a full range of media formats into Director, you cannot import text files—a curious limitation, given the program's more sophisticated strengths. You can animate bullet lists and create type effects, but once text is transformed to bitmap form for this purpose, it can't be converted back for editing. There are, however, powerful search facilities built into the system; so you can search for objects that use specified palettes or for specific media types such as movie and sound files.

All in all, Director is a very capable program. While it's not the most sophisticated paint, animation, or authoring tool, it does a great job of combining all three in a powerful environment. Users should be forewarned that both the animation and scripting parts of Director have fairly steep learning curves, but the program comes with plenty of samples and tutorials from which the dedicated multimedia artist can learn. Furthermore, by using XCMDs and Lingo scripting, you can configure Director to control external devices. This adds another level of power for those needing serious video or audio integration in their projects.

Apple Media Tool

Media Tool (Figure 7.4), Apple's entry in the authoring tool sweepstakes, is targeted at the entry-level crowd. Using Media Tool, it's possible to create cross-platform multimedia presentations without having to do any scripting. You simply create and import objects—graphics files, movies, and sounds—and link them together to form an integrated presentation.

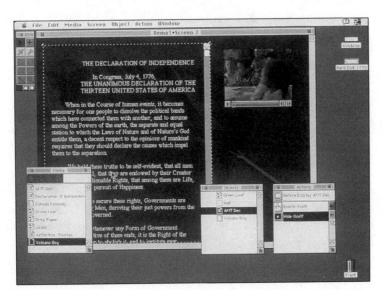

Figure 7.4
Apple Media Tool.

As you might expect, Media Tool runs on the Mac; however, you can prepare presentations for playback under Windows; and Media Tool even checks all of the components for Windows compatibility, converting elements to Windows formats as necessary. Media files, themselves, are not stored as part of a Media Tool presentation but as separate resources. This lets you update objects without reassigning properties and links, but can leave you with file management chores.

While it is easier to use than Director, Media Tool also doesn't do as much. It has neither the animation nor paint tools found in the former program. Then again, it's also much less costly: about ⅔ what you'll pay for Director. Media Tool also lacks a scripting language, although you can buy a companion program (Apple Media Tool Programming Environment) for this purpose. Together, the programs cost little more than the cost of Director alone.

The Apple Media Tool imports QuickTime movies; PICT graphics; snd, AIFF, and Windows WAV soundfiles; and fonts in either Adobe Type 1 or TrueType formats.

Macromedia's AuthorWare Professional

AuthorWare Prof. 3.0 Demo
⌘ 709

Not content to dominate the multimedia authoring business with Director, Macromedia also puts out AuthorWare Professional, one of the leaders for interactive authoring. AuthorWare is a cross-platform development tool that can be used to create any type of multimedia production, but focuses on training applications.

Perhaps its greatest strength is that it is entirely based on using icons for creating interactive links; so there is no scripting necessary. Because AuthorWare's icons and their associated dialog boxes act as tools for building a project and creating links between elements, the learning curve is relatively shallow. AuthorWare Professional also has built-in support for multiple file formats, as well as for 24-bit graphics, laser disc control, and HyperCard XCMDs. Good animation tools allow you to easily add movement to your project. Animations are created through the use of dialog boxes, which greatly simplifies the process so that you can concentrate more on the task of building an interactive presentation.

AuthorWare's primary interface is centered on a flow-line map that represents your project visually (see Figure 7.5). This enables you to get a quick overview of the structure and branching paths of your project.

AuthorWare's graphics facilities include a draw-type graphics environment, complete with patterns, fills, and transparency layering options (see Figure 7.6). It also has a variety of transitions as well as many built-in erase options that include a number of alternatives for helping get rid of graphic elements that are no longer needed on the screen. Also, object-oriented draw graphics (such as those created with MacDraw or Deneba's Canvas) can be imported in a fashion that allows you to access and modify their component lines and shapes. The potential for attaching additional information (such as animation data) to imported graphics offers up an entire new level of interactivity. Unlike most authoring tools

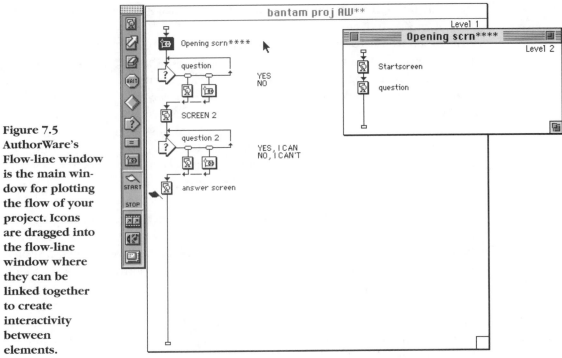

Figure 7.5 AuthorWare's Flow-line window is the main window for plotting the flow of your project. Icons are dragged into the flow-line window where they can be linked together to create interactivity between elements.

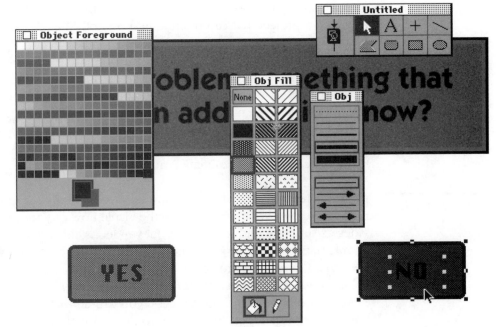

Figure 7.6 AuthorWare Professional has fairly extensive graphics capabilities, with palettes for creating graphics and text, as well as modes for layering and transparency.

that only support 8-bit graphics, AuthorWare Professional supports the importation of 24-bit PICT files.

AuthorWare Professional provides all the necessary animation support a multimedia producer could want. There are built-in, path-based animation functions as well as direct support for Director "movie" files. So, if you can't create the animation you want in AuthorWare Professional, it's easy to import it from Director. AuthorWare Professional also can import sounds, QuickTime movies, and Digital Video Interactive (DVI) files, which are compressed digital video files that will play back as full-screen video at 30 frames per second—right on your computer display (assuming you've installed a DVI compression board).

Another of AuthorWare Professional's strengths is its ability to track test results. It has established itself as the leader for authoring interactive learning applications, partially because its result-tracking capabilities make it ideal for training applications. The software package has a large collection of built-in system functions and variables for keeping track of users' responses, as well as their response times; so it's fairly easy to measure the efficiency and performance of students being tested. Although AuthorWare Professional does not support scripting, it has extensive text-handling capabilities for updating projects. The icons on the tool palettes are usually more than adequate for authoring tasks. For distribution, there is a run-time version that will launch your project but won't allow anyone to make changes to it.

AuthorWare Professional is also available as a Windows package, and it has the same user interface on both platforms—which makes cross-platform development relatively painless (see Chapter 9, "Working Cross-Platform"). If you need to create a project that can be modified on both the Mac and the PC, this program certainly is worthy of consideration.

AuthorWare Professional allows you to create Media Manager libraries of source files for multimedia projects that can be interactively shared. You can have a number of projects access the same library; or, inversely, you can have one project access a number of libraries, as it would in a cataloging and archiving system. Machines on a network can also share access to libraries. For large projects and networks, this approach can maximize resources, especially if you're using large amounts of animation and digitized video.

How It Works

AuthorWare Professional projects are created by dragging icons into a flow-line map that allows you to quickly see the visual flow of your project and also provides its structure and foundation. Eleven icons allow you to create any part of an interactive project; for instance, you can add a digital movie, a button, or a path that branches off to other areas (see Figure 7.7). The program features a comprehensive button editor for creating buttons of all descriptions.

At any point in the design process, you can double-click on an icon to set its parameters, thus instructing it how to interact with the other elements in your

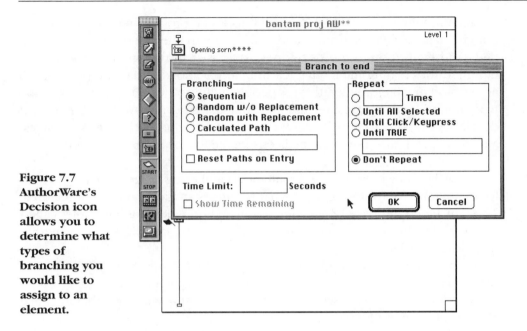

Figure 7.7 AuthorWare's Decision icon allows you to determine what types of branching you would like to assign to an element.

flow map. You also can try a dry run at any time to see your progress as you build your project. Integration of laserdiscs, digital movies, animations, sounds, and other multimedia elements is quite simple, since there are dedicated dialog boxes for each of these types of data.

AuthorWare Professional, the most expensive of all the authoring tools available ($5,000), also seems to have the broadest range of capabilities. Its support for both QuickTime and AVI digital video files and laserdiscs gives it more ability to incorporate video in a project than any similar program. As for animation, while it provides a basic path-based approach, it also directly supports Macromedia Director files. In fact, you can use a combination of both programs for such complex projects as simulations.

In addition to all of these features, it supports 24-bit graphics and stereo sound. This should take care of just about everything on a multimedia producer's checklist. Its Media Manager, which allows libraries of source files to be accessed by a number of different projects or machines, is a key element for managing system resources, especially with large multimedia projects.

Hyperintelligent authoring lets users create links between multimedia elements, and the program offers excellent support for text, including the ability to import RTF files, a popular word processing interchange format. Other text tools include full text search and retrieval and a multilingual spelling checker.

AuthorWare Professional is designed and billed as a program for interactive learning. It has extensive project-building tools that test and keep track of results.

Couple this with the fact that it is a well-developed product that can be used on both the Mac and PC platforms, and you'll see why the steep price tag is justified. And even though the developers state that the program is specifically designed for creating interactive learning applications, it has the potential to accomplish much more than this for people willing to take a creative approach to authoring. With its latest release, Macromedia is gearing AuthorWare toward developers looking to create reference and other forms of consumer products. Macromedia has also removed the licensing fee for the runtime version.

Asymetrix Multimedia Toolbook

Toolbook has long been a leading multimedia authoring program on the PC platform. Multimedia Toolbook, as the name suggests, adds multimedia features. These include path-based animation features, and video editing applet called Digital Video Producer. Other applets—BitEdit and PalEdit—let you modify graphics and palettes.

The program is based on a simple book and page metaphor similar to the card and stack system pioneered by Hypercard. A programming language called OpenScript lets you create scripts to add buttons, menu bars, and other interface attributes to your multimedia presentations.

Putting It All Together

All of the programs discussed here are good authoring tools, depending on your budget and the type of project you're doing. Of course, if you use the wrong tool for the job, you're bound to have some insurmountable problems; so make sure that your system has all the hardware and software components you need and that they're compatible with one another.

Also, don't neglect the importance of giving yourself ample time to become adept at interactive authoring. Despite the friendly interface of the Mac and the helpful tools that these programs offer, an ambitious interactive project will demand a lot of hard work and a thorough knowledge of the tools you're using. With any luck, you'll be able to maximize your success while minimizing the frustrations by checking out the project case studies on the Power Tools CD-ROM and by reviewing Chapter 16, "Interface and Interactivity: Bringing It Together."

Keep in mind that planning is often the key ingredient in the successful development of any project, and that's certainly the case with interactive multimedia. There are many ways to approach a given project, so think it all the way through before leaping into action. Once you've considered your options, picked your objective, and settled on a set of tools to use, building interactive projects can be a very rewarding and enjoyable process.

Part Two

CREATING MULTIMEDIA

8

Multimedia Development: Process, Planning, and Design

Multimedia development methods are as varied and colorful as the medium itself. How you go about developing multimedia depends on the nature of your project and how it will be viewed and heard. A HyperCard presentation made for display on a small black and white screen will be assembled much differently from a digital music video played back on a wall of million-color monitors. Likewise, sound may either dominate a presentation or be a discreet addition that enhances the larger message. For all of these reasons, there is no multimedia development formula.

Still, there are some general, universal patterns and processes; and we'll give you the 30,000-foot overview in this chapter. As the overall process becomes clearer, you can refer to other chapters for advice and suggestions on more specific topics. For example, Chapter 2, "Systems Software, Hardware, and Peripherals," covers computer choices and configurations, as well as the many additional hardware devices—keyboards and mice, scanners, monitors, accelerators, and more—that can help you manage your multimedia menagerie.

The "Tools" chapters in the first section of the book compare and contrast multimedia software in many different categories, while the "Creating" chapters in Part II focus on the details of producing different multimedia elements. Finally, the *Power Tools* CD further illuminates the production process with behind-the-scenes, step-by-step analysis of several exemplary multimedia projects, demo programs for you to test drive, and scores of usable software tools—utility programs and clip media—that will help your multimedia projects fly.

Throughout the book and disc, you'll find insights and anecdotes from multimedia experts. These will help you refine your skills and will save you countless hours by relating the experiences of those who have "been there before."

Of course, as you gain experience in multimedia production, you'll develop your own methods and styles. (We are reminded of a junior high school English class studying the novels of William Faulkner, whose language and syntax are notoriously idiosyncratic. During class, a student piped up, "How come *Faulkner* doesn't have to follow the rules?" To which the teacher replied, "Because *he* knows what they are.").

Development Overview

The process of creating a multimedia project can be broken down into a series of basic steps covering both interface/architecture development and content development (see Figure 8.1). We can summarize these steps as follows:

Preproduction

    Conceiving an idea

    Planning the development process

    Determining final form

    Building the production team

    Scheduling and budget

    Design and production

    Outlining and prototyping

Designing the architecture and interface

Acquiring and producing content

    Creating interface elements

Preparing content

    Assembling the elements into a cohesive production

    Testing and making adjustments

    Duplicating and distributing the final product

This represents an idealized scenario, though there are many intermediate steps. In the sections that follow, we'll look at each one in a bit more detail.

Preproduction

Preproduction can be tedious, but it's critical to any multimedia project. Planning your project before starting it ensures that you can deliver a cohesive product to your audience. It allows you to make realistic decisions about which elements *must* be in your product and which may enhance it. Developing realistic budgets

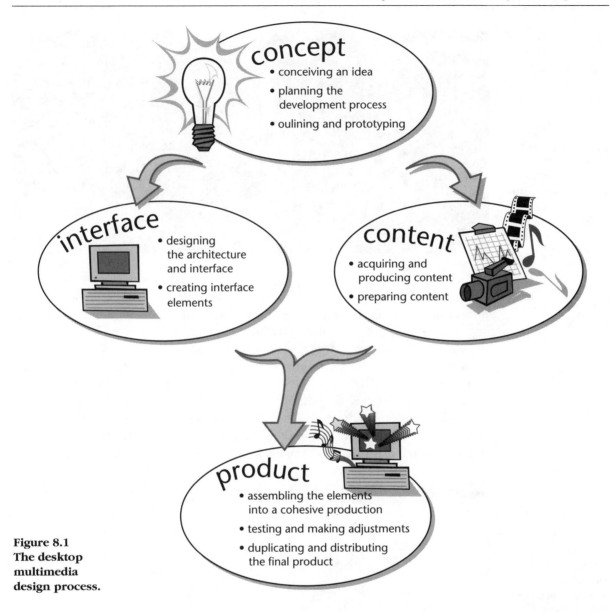

**Figure 8.1
The desktop
multimedia
design process.**

and schedules is the best way to get a project finished and into its final form sometime near its deadline.

**Conceiving
an Idea**

Inspiration for a multimedia project can come from many sources. It can be based on a hobby or area of personal or academic interest; it can spring from artistic appreciation of film, music, or literature. An idea can even come from a dream.

Figure 8.2
Buried in Time,
a new CD-ROM
game from Presto
Studios makes
extensive use of
3-D graphics and
special effects.

© 1994 Presto Studios Inc.

In corporate settings, in-house development teams are often assigned specific projects and budgets by other divisions of the company; or an organization may approach a multimedia contractor with a concept it wants developed. Even in these cases, there is plenty of room for creativity.

Look at the full range of multimedia products already out there. Explore their "content" in terms of subject matter, components, and interface. Consider all types of projects, even if they are nothing like what you want to do. This exercise will both stimulate your creativity and help you become familiar with the marketplace. With the rapidly changing nature of the computer industry, the latest features can be exciting; but last year's technological innovation might appear dated.

Figure 8.3
In contrast,
Amanda Stories,
published by
Voyager, uses line
drawings and
gentle sounds to
get users involved
emotionally. They
are available in
black-and-white
floppy files to run
in HyperCard, or
in a color CD-
ROM version.

What do you think of today's multimedia offerings: are they fun and interesting or confusing, dull, and boring? As you examine them, note the elements you find particularly effective in presenting the information. Which multimedia elements were used? How were they implemented?

What didn't you care for in presentations? Did some seem too flashy? Did you want to turn off the sound after two minutes? Was the interface like a maze? Were the fonts too small? Was there too much or too little text?

Whatever the source, an idea is often incomplete and vague at first. It may be a fleeting image or a brief written description with little or no information about how the project will eventually look or sound. Of course, technical details and constraints may be totally irrelevant at this point and may even distract from the creative process. There will be plenty of time to trim over-ambitious ideas and plan logistics.

In fact, once you've articulated your original idea, you'll need to coax and prod it into a fully formed design and production plan.

Thinking About Focus and Design

There must be a reason for the existence of your multimedia project. Regardless of the source, the idea has to have merit. For a multimedia project to be a success, it should provide an end user with information, entertainment, or the impetus to purchase something. If it does not, there is no reason for your audience to bother with it.

These decisions are as important when you are working alone as when you are part of a large team. With a project of your own, you have the final say over concept, budget, and implementation. For commercial ventures, the clients approve each aspect of the production. Even if they have done most of the pre-production, you must review their decisions to make sure that you fully understand the intent of their requests.

For example, suppose you have been requested to create an exhibit on the Civil War, and are given a script with text and photographs. You do not have sufficient information to work from, because the script does not fully explain the intent of the exhibit. It may be designed to show the extent of the war and the role of the first photojournalists. In this case, you would not take creative liberty with the photographs, but would display them in their entirety (Figure 8.4a). On the other hand, if the client is interested in the effect of the war on individuals, you may choose to crop images and position them so that the facial expressions are obvious to the viewer (Figure 8.4b).

Defining the Message

Look at the movie listings in *TV Guide*. No matter how involved the plot, every movie is described in 25 words or less. Try to come up with a concise and concrete statement of your concept. Once you have the main idea, consider what you want your audience to remember about the multimedia experience. Should

Figure 8.4a and b "Lt. James B. Washington, a Confederate prisoner, with Capt. George A. Custer of the 5th Cavalry, U.S.A." by Civil War photographer James F. Gibson. The image on the left shows the original photograph. The image on the right shows how a cropped close-up focuses on the facial expressions.

the presentation inform? Evoke emotion? Entertain? At first, you can be general with your goals—list categories rather than specifics.

The main idea and goals of each of the sample projects on the Power Tools CD can each be summarized in a single sentence. For example:

Hip Hop Hits ⌘ 010

...Rock and Roll Star ⌘ 013

Lawnmower Man Logo ⌘ 021

Title: *Hip Hop Hits*

Idea: Provide users with a glimpse of digital audio editing as it is used to construct Top 40 hits.

Goal: Inform

Title: *So You Want to Be a Rock and Roll Star*

Idea: Make learning music fun by letting amateur musicians experience the excitement of playing with a rock and roll band.

Goals: Inform, entertain

Title: *Lawnmower Man Logo*

Idea: Produce an animated corporate logo that fits the image of a fictional company used in the movie *The Lawnmower Man.*

Goal: Inform

Planning the Development Process

It would be nice if a large software publisher called and asked you to develop an interactive, multimedia version of the life and times of John Lennon. It would be even nicer if that client then provided you with all the equipment you would need; gave you unlimited access to writers, artists, and programmers; made available photographs, video, and music (with all required permissions, of course); and threw in a blank check. You could make some key decisions that defined the project in detail, get the right people to do the work, then turn out thousands of CD-ROMs to fill the orders that would undoubtedly pour in. Poof! In a matter of months your project would make headlines in all the industry papers.

Millions Line Up for Lennon CD

NEW YORK—Echoes of Beatlemania reverberated today as throngs cued up in driving rain to buy a hot new CD on the life of martyred Beatle, John Lennon. The disc, created seemingly overnight, has charmed both fans and critics alike.

We probably don't need to tell you that such a scenario doesn't happen very often. Every multimedia producer dreams of a project like that—a focused topic, unlimited resources, an enthralled audience, and someone else to foot the bill for development. In reality, however, there is no such thing as unlimited resources. That's why planning is essential. The planning phase gives a producer the chance to decide what is important for a project, given the available resources. This requires numerous decisions based on message, audience, and budget.

These factors will help you shape and focus the original idea. You can then progress to determining the elements you will need to express the idea, as well as the talents and resources necessary for executing it. Defining the project's scope, limits, and resources early on will give it discrete boundaries that simplify production decisions further down the road.

Preproduction requires a good imagination and logical mind in order to visualize a non-existent project at various stages of development. It gets easier with experience.

Some people have a hard time with the logical processes of preproduction. They prefer to "go with the flow" and make these decisions as their project evolves. When a successful multimedia producer claims to have worked without a plan, the preproduction has usually been done in a less conventional way. However, a major multimedia project generally requires a standard organizational approach to preproduction.

Project Definition

During the planning phase, you will develop your idea into a detailed overview of the project. The overview begins with a complete definition of the content to be presented, then adds information about interactivity, graphics, and use of sound. Each of these elements must be viewed in terms of the message, the audience, and the budget. At the completion of the planning phase, your overview should contain all the information necessary for designing the actual script, visual images, and sounds required for production. The *Multimedia Power Tools* CD contains a number of graphics and sound libraries for your use.

Answering a few simple questions can help you more fully define the original concept for the project:

Who is the audience?

What is the delivery platform?

What is the budget?

What multimedia elements will the project include?

What development software and hardware is required?

When does it have to be finished?

Once you define the audience, you'll be able to determine the style and form of the message, as well as the criteria for distribution and playback. The delivery platform—the system on which the project will ultimately be viewed—affects the project's technical parameters, as well as its market and accessibility. Once the budget is set, you can make decisions about the project's size and scope. Last (but equally important) is the project's target completion date. Making the final deadline can have a major effect on its ultimate success and your own credibility.

After addressing each of these issues, you'll have some firm criteria that will not only help define the remaining facets of preproduction, but will also be useful in dealing with the multitude of small issues that inevitably crop up during production.

Audience

The intended audience is probably the most critical factor in planning a project. It determines not only the style of the presentation, but also how the project will be developed and distributed. If the audience is a relatively small group of business people, museum visitors, or a trade show crowd, the project might be most efficiently presented on a single custom-designed kiosk. If meant for mass distribution, it could well be distributed on a CD-ROM and played on a wide assortment of machines, resulting in an entirely different set of development considerations.

If your project is designing an animation to be shown on MTV, you can easily picture your audience and probably have some idea of what will or will not appeal to them. Since MTV attracts a young audience, references to famous musicians from the past such as Frank Sinatra, Bobby Darin, and even the Beatles (!) could go by unrecognized and add nothing to a presentation. (The resilient Tony Bennett notwithstanding.)

Another thing you know about MTV viewers is that they enjoy watching images that change as rapidly as several times per second. This may affect your design decisions. You could either imitate this fast-paced style or try to create a purposeful contrast by using a slower pace. Base your choice of direction on what you know about the audience.

Sometimes a project idea defines a target market from the outset—the idea was created to fill a specific need. The audience for *Hip Hop Hits* from the *Power Tools* CD is a select group of individuals interested in digital audio editing.

So You Want to Be a Rock and Roll Star has a broader audience. Producer Steve Rappaport had to think about who would be interested in playing along with a rock and roll band. Did he want to intrigue closet musicians and shower singers or attract users who simply liked to listen to some tunes and learn about how the musicians made it to the top? He had to decide what types of music would appeal to his audience, and the songs he ultimately chose were those that appeal to people who listened to rock and roll in the early 1960s (see Figure 8.5). Rappaport's decision may also have been influenced by business issues such as which works were available for licensing at a reasonable cost.

Figure 8.5
So You Want to Be a Rock and Roll Star.

Any idea can be presented in hundreds of way. By looking at your audience and your goals, you can narrow the scope to fit your objectives.

Content

Content is the essential element of any multimedia production. It may be text, or mainly sounds or visual images, but it has to tell a story and relate information in a meaningful way. Content is a project's heart and soul. It also encompasses its main message or theme.

You need to expand your central message into an outline of the main points to be covered. In most cases, you can accomplish this by using a word processor to write text or an outline or by developing a flowchart. Whatever the format, it needs to be detailed, covering all the topics, subtopics, and tangential information that will be included with the project. Even the most interactive project must have an internal structure that makes sense.

The outline and flowchart formats compel you to make decisions about the relative importance of each item you wish to include in your project. This will become important as you design the menus and any interactive elements.

When planning content—and its presentation—you'll consider the types of media components the project will require. You'll need to address a wide array of critical questions and choices: What kinds of still images will be used, and what will be their relationship to text and other elements? How will text be used? Will the project require animation, and if so, what kind? Will there be major animation sequences or small amounts now and then? What types of sounds will enhance the user's experience and retention of the project's content? Does the project require a soundtrack or only intermittent sound effects? How good does the sound quality have to be? In the case of a CD-ROM project distributed to a large audience, will users need to have external speakers, or will the built-in speaker be adequate?

And how about video? Will the added impact of video sequences be worth the cost in disk storage and processing requirements? How much or how little should be used?

Of course, you'll also need to consider sources of content. Will the budget allow an original soundtrack or licensed music? Will it require original animation and video footage, or will clip media suffice? What permissions will be required? Will royalties be paid to contributors?

Graphics, Video, and Animation

Visual imagery is almost certainly central to your message. Multimedia is a highly graphic medium, so a graphic element is generally present on-screen at all times. Sometimes the graphic image is the primary focus; other times, the image simply illustrates a concept or enhances an interface item (see Figure 8.6).

Think of the types of graphics that are available on your topic. Actual movie footage of Revolutionary War battles is impossible to come by, but animation of the Voyager spacecraft passing through the rings of Saturn can illustrate the immensity of space travel. Would a CD on baseball be the same without Quick-Time movies of great home runs? Is there an existing videodisc with high-quality images that could be licensed as part of your product?

Animated graphics can be two- or three-dimensional. They can be simple or complex rendered images. Consider your budget, capabilities, and message to determine what level of animation is appropriate for your project. Do you want full animation or a few carefully selected animations that can add excitement to your topic?

During this phase of preproduction, try to get a good mental image of the visual style your project needs. Should it have simple screens, lots of pictures, or a highly stylized look created by a graphic artist? Think in generalities rather than specifics. Which graphic elements are essential, which are attractive and might be nice, and which are beyond the needs of the project? Remember that a single photograph or graphic can be just as powerful as a video or animation —and is much easier to produce.

Sound

Sound is too often forgotten or considered as a last minute add-on. Yet, audio can add enhance your message as much as any other multimedia element. Much of the power of Ken Burns' seminal PBS documentary on the Civil War stems from the expert use of sound effects, narration, and music.

Chapters 4 and 10 focus on the types of sound tools available and the means to produce the audio for your production. Read through these chapters before making your decisions about sound, especially if you haven't previously paid much attention to sound as a multimedia element.

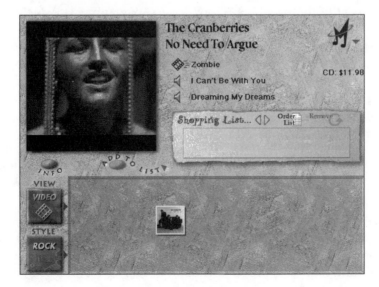

Figure 8.6 *MusicNet,* **a CD product that let's you listen to and order music directly from your computer, uses graphical elements to good effect.**

Sound can be as simple as an audio click when a button is pressed or a beep to indicate a response of some kind. Some sounds are cute and fun, especially in multimedia targeted toward children. Though remember that "cute" is easy to overdo.

The audio may be narration of a passage read by the original author. Many people dislike reading text from a screen but will listen to the information when delivered by an interesting voice. Corbis' *A Passion for Art* CD presents an interactive tour of an important art collection. It makes excellent use of narrative tours, conducted by art historians and curators.

Musical tracks can be produced which add to the style and heighten the emotion evoked by the multimedia experience. Musical scores go particularly well with animations and video, and add enormously to presentations, kiosks, and trade show productions.

Decisions about sound should be made early enough to ensure that the audio is available for the programmer when the various elements are combined to make the final project. Even recording a few beeps takes some time to do right. The sound needs to be produced and properly recorded. The computer needs enough memory to digitize and store variations until the decision is made for the ideal sounds. If you will be licensing music, someone must listen to a large quantity of stock sounds to locate the snips you want for your project; then you must obtain a written license to use the sounds.

Determine the types of sounds that are necessary—and those that would be ideal—during preproduction so that you can work sound into the budget.

Presentation and Style

The presentation and interface style of a multimedia project can attract or repel users with surprising alacrity. Even if the content is exceptional, the style must appeal to the user. Symphony lovers may appreciate seeing black notes on a white page while high-quality orchestral music is played. Clean and classic imagery can be very appealing to this audience. The MTV generation, by contrast, favors chaotic, fast-paced graphics interspersed with rapid-fire editing.

You should also decide on the type of palette that might appeal to viewers. If you are designing a system to inform patients about how to live with a serious illness, you're better off using relaxing and dignified shades of blue or green rather than jangling reds and yellows.

At this point, you don't need to make hard decisions about style; just think about the users and what will reach them. Stylistic decisions based on what your audience would enjoy will further define your project (see Figure 8.7).

Interface and Interactivity

A diagram or flowchart gives you a visual image of how the parts of your program relate to each other and helps you outline how the user will navigate your project's interface. Major diagram elements often become main menu items that, in turn, branch to the subtopics (see Figure 8.8).

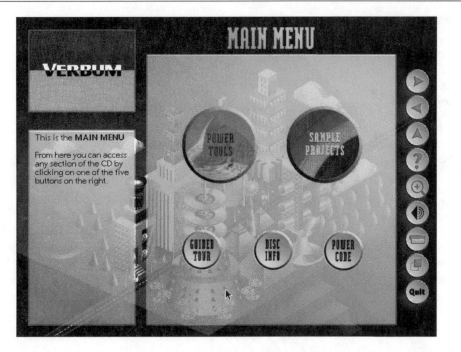

Figure 8.7
The main interface of the *Multimedia Power Tools* CD. Color and style are essential parts of any presentation.

Although it's not the only way to design interactivity, the flowchart is a powerful tool, allowing you to plan the type of interface most effective for your project by consolidating a navigation plan, audience needs, and project content. Your flowchart can be a simple block diagram, or you may want to use an outlining tool such as Inspiration Software's Inspiration.

You don't need to decide on the details of the interactivity, but you should determine its nature. Recall your observations of other systems as you consider how interactivity fits into your own project. If you will be using a touch screen, the buttons have to be big enough for a finger to press.

Does your topic lend itself to text menu items similar to the table of contents of a book? Would a set of index icons down one side of the screen be appropriate? Will your audience members all speak the same language? If not, an icon approach to menus may be essential. How is the data going to be organized on the disk? How will it be indexed, searched, and interconnected? How will external video equipment, other software applications, or database access be handled? Will there be enough room for everything?

A skilled producer can create a delightful and powerful synergy among the various content elements of an interface, forging new ways for the audience to learn, experience, and understand. The interface, by definition, is the means by which the user communicates with and experiences your multimedia presentation or product.

**Figure 8.8
This flowchart of
the user interface
created for the
exhibit "Incidents
of the War: The
Mathew Brady
Photographs of
the Civil War
1861–1865" in
the Library of
Congress Ameri-
can Memory
prototype.**

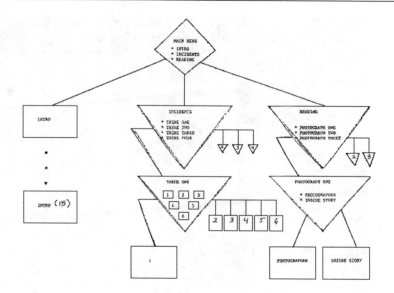

Interface also happens to be one of the greatest challenges of multimedia; a successful producer can't just settle for the prettiest icons, the coolest music or the most impressive special effects. Both content and interface require balancing purely esthetic wishes with the realities and logic of multimedia architecture.

And then there's the interactive element. Should users navigate through menus or a palette of icons, or should they get around by clicking and exploring the screen? How far can the user wander before getting lost? Is a highly animated interface too sluggish in its performance? How much information will be in the main narrative? How much is tangential and may be best tapped into via hyperlinks? It's a real left-brain/right-brain balancing act, and a producer's skill in pulling it off in an elegant, exciting, and logical manner could make the difference between a project's ultimate success and its slide into digital oblivion.

Expand the flowchart to include the types of graphics you need for your message and your audience. You don't need to specify particular images, but try to mark the spots where still images would be useful, where video might be better, or where animation might enhance the user's perception of the information.

*Development
and Target
Platforms*

The project's proposed content and interface, along with the production money available, will determine the software and hardware required for development. Chapter 2, "Systems Software, Hardware, and Peripherals," features an in-depth look at the types of equipment available for multimedia and what might be required for different types of desktop multimedia projects, while the subsequent "Tools" chapters focus on software. In general, the more powerful the authoring equipment, the faster and easier development will be.

However, a producer needs to be aware of the target delivery platform. The sophistication, speed, and abilities of these target computers will have great bearing on your design. Try to determine the type of machine your users are most likely to have. Macs and PCs come in a full range of configurations.

A project intended for retail distribution must be designed to run on a large number of machines, many of which will probably be less powerful than those on which it was developed. If your product is to be used by small businesses or people at home, remember that they might not even be able to play an animation that looks great on your Pentium PC. You might, for example, need to take high-end animations and convert them to a digital video format that is not as aesthetically perfect, but at least puts forth the idea in an accessible way.

Many experienced producers create their projects on fast machines to save time but continuously test on less-powerful systems that approximate those used by their intended audience.

For presentations, you must consider what equipment is available at the end site, and what you will need to bring or rent. For kiosks, think about what is appropriate and within budgetary constraints. You also may need to develop a project for playback on different types of machines. For an overview of the considerations required for this scenario, see Chapter 9, "Working Cross-Platform."

Determining Final Form

One of last steps in the preproduction phase is making a decision regarding the final form of your project. This decision must be made during preproduction to ensure that money is budgeted for manufacture of a CD-ROM or videodisc, or for projection equipment (if your final product will be displayed at a kiosk, corporate demonstration center, or convention hall). The size and content of your project must be tailored to your delivery medium of choice—or vice versa.

A small multimedia production—such as one used a single time for a short presentation to a group—usually ends up either on a floppy disk, cartridge drive, or a portable hard drive. A HyperCard stack with a few sounds and bit-mapped graphics will fit on a floppy disk. A lecturer can use a stack of this sort to link quickly to bullet charts or extra information as it is needed and never lose his or her place in the presentation. However, most multimedia projects using extensive graphics, sounds, animation, and video are distributed on high-capacity media such as removable cartridges, CD-ROMs, and videodiscs.

Floppy Disk

A software demo or short presentation can fit on a floppy disk for distribution. This is economical and guarantees a wide audience for the work. Disks can be duplicated by service bureaus with mass duplication equipment. These duplication machines are not terribly expensive when compared to the cost of sending many disks out for duplication; so a producer might consider purchasing a disk duplication machine for regularly produced, small projects.

Removable Cartridge Drives

The cartridge is portable, slightly bigger than a compact disc, and is good for presentations. A single cartridge can be routed to a number of people. They are relatively expensive (as low as $15 each), and hold up to several hundred megabytes of data. 44Mb SyQuest cartridges are the most common format; they can hold several applications and 100 to 150 moderately-sized 256-color or grayscale images. This medium is adequate for one-time "slide show" presentations. The more complex the presentation, the more space is required. Projects displayed on kiosks or single computers at trade shows generally work better on a hard drive, which also boasts better access speeds.

Optical Disks

High-density, small-size magneto-optical discs have come a long way in the last few years. Initially too slow for practical use, "MO" discs now feature faster access times and large storage capacities—up to 2 gigabytes.

CD-ROM

Its wide acceptance, high storage capacity, and low manufacturing cost have made CD-ROM the medium of choice for distribution of large-scale multimedia projects. Data preparation for creating a 650Mb compact disc is virtually the same as for making a master floppy disk, and doesn't cost much more. Mastering runs $500 to $1,000, but duplication often costs only about $1 per disc. Testing for a compact disc must be done meticulously: Once it is mastered, it is immutable.

If you choose to run a CD-ROM from an authoring system, you must be able to access the CD-ROM from the system. For example, Voyager's Voyager AudioStack provides detailed information about how to use CD-ROM with HyperCard. It demonstrates the use of external commands (XCMDs) that may be licensed from Apple Computer in order to allow sound playback. Macromedia Director has program extensions that control external devices and movies that show how to write the Lingo code to operate the CD-ROM (see Figure 8.9).

The process of mastering disks is actually pretty straightforward, and the appearance of inexpensive CD recorders has made the process very economical as well. For detailed information on the CD-ROM standard and on CD players and recorders, see Chapter 2, "Systems Software, Hardware, and Peripherals."

Videodiscs

Videodiscs are suited to high-quality storage and playback of still images or moving pictures and sound, especially when that media is part of a single exhibit or kiosk. They provide high quality images and video, and quick random access to the images. Videodiscs are particularly effective for kiosks and exhibits used in museums, libraries, and other institutions. Corporate presentation centers generally have this sort of equipment.

The source material may come from videotape, film, or digitized still images. The sound may be part of the original video or be taken from another source, and is usually stored on DAT tape.

Figure 8.9 "Color CD Panel" comes with Macromedia Director 3.1. It uses AppleCD XObj to control audio on a CD player from within Director.

If a videodisc is part of your multimedia production, you must include a videodisc driver with your program. The Voyager VideoStack has excellent drivers that can be licensed for about $500. This interactive product provides extensive information about accessing and retrieving data from videodiscs using external commands from HyperCard.

Macromedia Director includes extensions, which control Sony and Pioneer videodisc players (see Figure 8.10). A movie has sample scripts that show how to use these controllers from your Director movie. Windows' MCI facility includes drivers for the control of several popular videodisc players, including those from Sony and Pioneer.

Creating a videodisc is not much different from making a compact disc. The premastering is usually done by experienced professionals at a postproduction house. The producer provides the source material and the order in which the clips should be physically placed on the disc. (For interactive products, the order is not terribly important, as long as each element can be accessed later.) Materials are assembled onto one-inch videotape or onto D2 (digital composite video) tape. The D2 tape uses newer technology and is currently used more often than the one-inch video tape.

The postproduction house can then provide the producer with a VHS cassette copy of the D2 tape that has timecodes on it. This copy can be used to check that all the information made it onto the D2 tape and that it is in the specified order. Once the D2 master is approved, it is sent to the videodisc manufacturer, who turns it into a videodisc.

Projection Systems

There are a variety of projection devices available for presentation to a large group. The most popular are LCD (liquid crystal display) and CRT (cathode ray tube) projectors.

LCD panels are relatively inexpensive and are portable, weighing between four and six pounds. Most of these units sit on the bed of an overhead trans-

Figure 8.10 "Color Videodisc Panel" using XCMDs to control videodisc player from Macromedia Director 3.1.

Keeping Abreast of Technology

For most multimedia professionals, keeping informed about industry innovations is an ongoing task. Publications specializing in multimedia, such as *NewMedia Magazine, Multimedia Producer, Multimedia World,* or the *Digital Media* and *Inside Report on New Media* newsletters, cover what is happening in the field. There are magazines focusing on every facet of multimedia: *Verbum* covers multimedia design and content development; *DV* provides the latest in video production coverage; general computer trade magazines such as *MacWeek,* and *PC Magazine* also regularly feature articles on various aspects of multimedia.

You also should actually try out some multimedia products—pick up a few that look interesting and explore them thoroughly. Trade shows such as E3, Intermedia, Digital World, MacWorld Expo, Comdex, or any of a multitude of smaller multimedia conferences have exhibits that give you a chance to test out many programs in a short time. Conference sessions conducted by multimedia professionals can provide additional insights and ideas.

When browsing around the multimedia world, take some time to learn about technologies that intrigue you. Most productions use a blend of older and newer technologies. If you see a 3-D animation that fascinates you, it may be worthwhile to get familiar with the tools and techniques used to produce it. An exciting animation may be just the thing to attract someone to a kiosk or wake up the audience in the middle of a long presentation.

Be aware of the authoring systems commonly used for each specific type of multimedia. (See Chapter 7, "Authoring Tools.") Many presentations are created with HyperCard or Toolbook, which is a quick way to assemble a project, especially if you don't mind a bit of programming.

Macromedia Director is the most popular authoring system for projects large and small. It is most popular for projects using color, detailed 2-D animation, and high-quality sound. Other types of productions can be put together more quickly in HyperCard and the results are excellent. Multimedia systems that require complex data searches and work mainly with stills or videodisc images can be built very effectively using HyperCard or Toolbook.

Examine as many systems as you can, including those featured in projects and demos on the *Power Tools* CD. Learn what has worked for others; then use this knowledge to make the most of your production time. It takes time and may cost some money, but it also helps you to focus on ways to implement multimedia elements you want for your project and decide what you need for production and distribution.

Director 4.0 Demo ⌘ 708

parency projector; so make sure one is available. LCD panels come in color or black-and-white. Color panels can produce images from a spectrum of millions of colors. LCD panels are much less expensive than most multimedia projection equipment; they cost from $4,000 to $12,000. For $8,000 to $9,000 you can purchase LCD projection systems that do not require an overhead transparency projector.

Three-gun CRT projectors are good for convention meeting rooms or corporate presentation rooms, where they can be set up and then left in place. They have a high scan rate—that is, the projected image keeps up with the screen image from the computer. CRT projectors produce clear, sharp video that is essential for data projection and fast animations. These units cost between $11,000 and $35,000.

The highest-quality projection is produced with the LCLV systems, which cost between $50,000 and $500,000. These are great for large projections, such as stadiums and rock concerts. Because of their weight and price, they are usually rented.

Another type of video projection that is gaining in popularity is the video wall. It is often seen at trade shows, but is also popping up in hotels, museums, and retail locations. A video wall is composed of monitors, called cubes, set side by side and stacked vertically. Larger walls might include any combination of cubes up to about 12 by 12 (144 in all). Each individual monitor, or cube, measures about 40 inches diagonally and is four feet deep—about twice as deep as a regular computer monitor. A computer generally controls the image on the video wall. One large image can be spread over all the cubes, or several images can be shown at once. The advantages of this system are that the wall can be used in a bright room, does not require projection space, and can display a variety of eye-catching effects.

Other Considerations

Outside influences affect how any multimedia project is received, regardless of the age or interests of the audience. Before actually designing your project, you should identify where it will be used and how often.

Location

Where will the project be used? This is an important consideration that will have repercussions on the total design and style of your project. If the program is to be used in a library, it should not contain loud audio. If it will be used primarily in a busy shopping area or trade show, expect the users to spend no more than a few minutes looking at it. The interface must be intuitive as well as colorful and flashy to attract attention.

Educational products might be used at home or at school, where the user will have time to explore without distraction. Here the subject matter can have more depth. The pace can be slower and the style less flashy than for programs designed to attract attention. The interface should be geared toward the age and attention span of the user. Think about the special needs and distractions around home and school locations.

Number of Uses

How many times will a user view your product? Animation, the element of surprise, and a sense of humor are all valuable qualities in any presentation. A multimedia production created for a single showing to each audience should use these elements differently from a program that will be used on a regular basis. In the latter case, some special effects and techniques can easily change from exciting to annoying.

Imagine a multimedia catalog for identifying and ordering auto parts. If the catalog had a picture of each type of auto part to make a quick visual identification possible, as well as a search engine and lots of cross-referencing, the end user would be thrilled. Now imagine the same project, but this time with a digital movie in place of each still picture. The same user would be infuriated if he or she had to repeatedly view a 3-D animation of black exhaust spewing from a loud, faulty muffler while attempting to identify parts for customers.

Building the Production Team

Once you have a firm idea of the needs of the project and what you can afford, you must decide how to get the work done. Can you do it all yourself? If not, is there a team available to work with? Can you license pieces from other sources? Do you know how to create the various elements you will need? Do you need to hire outside contractors? How these questions are answered depends on your environment and your project.

In-House Talent and Equipment

If you are working in a corporate environment, you may have access to talented people to help in your project's development. There may be programmers, graphic artists, writers, and other experts who can be brought in to help with parts of your production.

You may be in a position to hire people to work on a permanent multimedia team. In this case, a core team usually consists of a project manager, a programmer, an artist, a writer, and, depending on the project's sophistication, specialists in video and sound. For small jobs, some individuals may perform more than one function; while on large projects, several people may be working in each area.

Each member of the team requires equipment and software. During the production phase, several applications often are open at once (for example, image processing, word processing, and/or sound processing). If you don't have enough memory, expect unsightly bombs that will threaten the integrity of your data as well as frustrate your creativity. Recovery from these bombs takes time and causes general paranoia. Weighed against these concerns, 20Mb of memory seems a minimum for any serious production (especially as chip prices plummet).

Think about the speed of computers you have available in terms of the work that has to be done. If there are many graphics to be processed or extensive programming code to be compiled, a faster machine will save time in the long run. Chapter 2, "Systems Software, Hardware, and Peripherals," has information about hardware considerations. Read it with your project specifications in mind. If you cannot afford the equipment, you might reconsider some elements of the production that can be done with available components.

Contractors

Many producers use outside contractors on a project-by-project basis. Experienced contractors may be expensive, but they will do the job as you ask for it and are more likely to finish on time. In contrast to employees, contractors have their own equipment and software. Professionals are available for any type of work you may need, from producing the entire project to designing layout, programming, sound production, or animations.

Over time, you'll develop relationships with the most skilled people in your area and will be able to assemble a team quickly if necessary. Remember, though, that scheduling can be a concern: Don't wait until the last minute to book specialists, or you may be unable to meet your schedule.

Licensing
Considerations

Instead of hiring people to do work for you, you can license materials from companies that specialize in photographic images, sound, or any other element you require (see Figure 8.11). In most cases, you will save money. The costs are usually lower. Make sure that you have a good license agreement so you can reproduce the work. Sometimes, you can get permission to use the work in your product without any fee. For your own protection, be certain to get this permission in writing.

The licensing of copyrighted materials for multimedia productions can be complicated. A license for an image or sound may include print rights, movie rights, video rights, audio rights, or magneto-optical rights. Your license must allow you to use the image or sound on the media that you choose for final distribution. The safest license is one that includes unlimited multimedia use.

Every part of a sound, movie, or image may be under copyright. The image of a person may need licensing, even if the photograph is now in the public domain. Fictional characters may be protected by trademark or copyright and

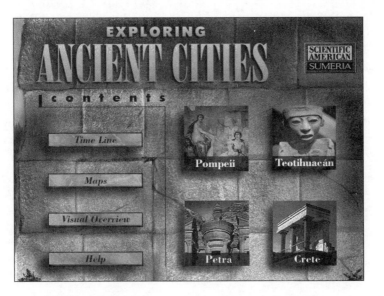

Figure 8.11 Sumeria's *Exploring Ancient Cities* **combines elements of original design with text licensed from Scientific American.**

require licensing. Choreography, background music, or even the entire production may need individual releases. Even tiny clips of music or images can be traced by the copyright holder, who may contact you for back royalties if you do not obtain written permission to use them beforehand.

You may wish to enlist the aid of a competent intellectual property attorney to ensure that you have a properly written release or license agreement for any sound, movie, or image in your multimedia production. Many producers prefer to avoid these complications by creating as many of the elements as possible for a production.

Scheduling and Budget

The final step of preproduction involves getting ready for production. You'll need to make specific assignments for the appropriate groups and write a comprehensive time schedule. The detailed script and storyboard simplify the assignment process tremendously. They define everything necessary for your multimedia production.

Before production begins, you should draw up a realistic timetable. Try to set definite goals, such as "Approve the final artwork for the main menu screen" or "Get written license for main theme for introduction." Word the goals so that their achievement is not debatable. The artwork either got final approval or it did not. Either you have a license in your hand or you do not. A nebulously stated goal, such as "Work on artwork for menu screens" does not provide a solid landmark; the deadline can come and go, but as long as someone worked on the artwork, one could argue that the goal was met.

With a detailed schedule, you can determine if your project is behind schedule and if so, how far. Track the actual timing for projects so that you can make more realistic projections for other creative efforts.

Finally, keep a list of ideas the team comes up with that might enhance the project. These ideas may add depth to the project, but if you approve all of them, it will never get finished. When your production is near completion, try to use as many of the good ideas as timing and budget allow.

Managing the Pursestrings

No developer likes to think about budgets. There's no doubt about it: They cramp creativity and limit what you want to do. Despite this, budgets somehow continue to exist. The reality is that without planning for time and money, most projects would never get done. Like outlining, budgeting forces you to make difficult decisions about time and resources while you are looking at the project as a whole. It requires you to set priorities, milestones, and constraints. Once this is done, you can stop worrying about these things—as long as you respect the schedules you have set.

The money available for a project has a direct effect on its scope and the amount of time needed to complete development. Producing multimedia productions can be an expensive proposition. At minimum, it includes the cost of a suitably powerful Mac or PC with some kind of authoring software. At maximum, it can run into the hundreds of thousands of dollars required to pay for talented artists, programmers, and production services. And there are additional costs for licensing content.

When you start a project, you must determine how to balance your financial and time resources against your needs during development. Some small projects require only a few hours from one person. Bigger projects require additional people, equipment, and time. When the project is large and the budget huge, top professionals create the various multimedia elements. Regardless of the size of the project, time and money must be managed carefully to ensure that the resources last until it is completed.

When putting together a schedule, allot time to solve special problems and to work around software and hardware difficulties. Curtis Wong, who produced many products for Voyager before moving on to Corbis, advises, "Whatever time you budget, it will invariably take twice as long as you think. Especially if you are working with new technology. Plan for this, and deadlines will match realities."

There is hope for the solo multimedia producer. There are many tools to help nonartists create graphics, and there is a "homemade" way to produce nearly anything. The lowest budget project can be successful, even if it is done by one person in black and white in HyperCard on a Macintosh Classic or with Toolbook on a 386 PC. If you tap some of the many sources of clip art, sound, and other elements you need for your project, you'll usually pay less than the cost of hiring someone to produce original work. (Beware, however, of the fate that befell on early desktop publishers intoxicated with the power at his command: After enduring several issues of the company newsletter with its 26 typefaces and too-cute clip art, the boss finally made our sobered desktop hero hire a graphic artist to "make it professional.")

With a bigger budget, you can put together a team or contract out portions of the production; but you'll need to carefully break down the jobs into manageable portions. In this approach, project management and coordination become major issues. Regardless of the size of the team, someone must coordinate each area of development, ensuring that each element will integrate easily into the final product at the required time. The larger the project team, the more time you'll spend supervising and directing.

Design and Production

The preproduction process provides a focus and helps you determine what should and should not be a part of your multimedia production. It is a highly logical operation that clears the way to allow full creativity during the design process.

From preproduction, you have a detailed outline for the content of your project along with an overview of the needs for interactivity. You also have a good idea of the types of graphics and sounds you need for your production.

Appropriate Use of Technology

Hardly a week goes by without an announcement of a new multimedia technology. Industry professionals and members of the techno-elite love this constant and rapid pace of change. As a producer, however, you need to think seriously about when and where to use these dazzling new effects. You must first decide if the technodazzle really adds something tangible to your product.

A well-designed multimedia project focuses on its message and its audience. The producer needs to make sure each area under development presents the message in the most effective way. It is all too easy to get so carried away by these fun new bells and whistles that your project goes over budget and does not get completed on time. Or even worse, the production may only play on expensive equipment that cuts out 90 percent of your potential market.

In 1992, morphing—magically transforming one image into another by a sequential blending of the pictures—was all the rage. Various programs hit the market, ranging from the low cost Morph (from Gryphon) (see Figure 8.12) to high end apps used in postproduction. Suddenly there was morphing in movies, television advertisements, and various forms of multimedia.

**Figure 8.12
This was done
using Gryphon
Software Corp.'s
Morph.**

Morph 2.5 Demo
⌘ 714

Morphing is fun to watch, but does it have a place in your multimedia project? Sometimes a special effect of this sort is essential to your message. In the movie *Star Trek VI*, an alien changed form before our eyes and turned into Captain Kirk—that was impressive. The alien did have unusual powers, and the viewers got to see it rearrange its own face. The technology furthered the development and believability of the story.

You may also have seen the television commercial in which a leaping tiger transforms into an automobile, imparting to the car the power and agility of a tiger.

In both of these cases, the morphing technology serves its purpose: It carries and drives home an appropriate message while entertaining the viewer. On the other hand, if the morph causes the viewer to think, "Wow, I wonder how they did that," but has no real bearing on your message, it is nothing more than a distraction.

Sometimes there's no clear cut indication as to whether technology will really add to your project. In this case, the decision to morph or not to morph must be based on other factors. First, can you afford it? Fancy technologies take time and money to implement. You have to learn how to use the program that creates the effect before you can use it. Will the effect bring a user's playback machine to its knees?

Don't squander time and money on technodazzle when it would be better spent on the actual content of your product. On the other hand, if you have a place where new technology will enhance your message, and you have the time and money to get it done, by all means use it.

In the design phase, you get specific about each topic you outlined during preproduction. During this time, you may flesh out the outline or write a detailed script covering all the text and narration you will use. (Which road you take depends upon the nature of your project.) You also will select the exact illustrations you need and decide on your specific audio requirements.

Outlining and Prototyping

The real production phase of the project begins with the creation of an outline, storyboard, and even a prototype. These will aid in defining project organization, flow, and internal architecture, as well as the technical and esthetic requirements for the content elements.

Outlining

The core element of the multimedia production is usually a detailed outline or specific script. This contains all the text used in the production and specifies the images needed. It mentions when important sound is required and focuses on the message and how it can be best presented to the audience. This is where the content is polished and delivery style determined (see Figure 8.13).

The script or outline can then be used to determine actual budgets for time and is the guide for the programmer who will integrate all the multimedia elements.

Greg Roach wrote the *Madness of Roland* as a serial that appeared in *Hyper-Bole*, an interactive multimedia magazine. This story served as the basis for the production script. The tale of Roland is told using the media that best convey the story, imagery, or emotions at each moment. Sometimes there is multicolored text on the screen; other times, digital movies or dramatic audio conversations. Regardless of the media, the script maintained the message and structure throughout the production.

Film production often starts with a script that describes what the actors say and gives essential visual and aural information. In multimedia production, the equivalent is the project outline. This can be a version of the flowchart mentioned earlier—expanded to provide an overview of proposed content elements, user navigation options, and interactivity. The outline will give you the clearest indication yet of what content and interface design materials will be needed, what jobs have to be done, in what order they must be finished, and how all the elements will get into the project.

Designing interactivity requires visualizing a project in three dimensions, which may not always be easy with a two-dimensional chart. The third dimension can be better represented by mocking up a sample routine with a program such as HyperCard. It can then be tested further in an early project prototype.

Prototyping

Once you have created a detailed outline or script, you may wish to create a prototype to try out your ideas, layout, and interface to see if they work. Interactivity is one of the hardest areas to visualize. As mentioned, a flowchart is the most effective way to visualize how a user can progress from one screen of the pro-

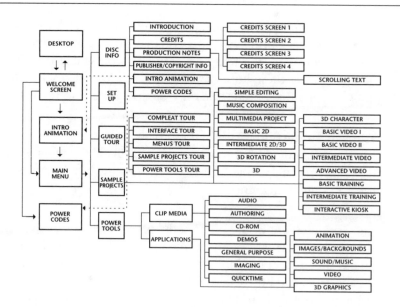

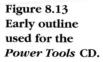

**Figure 8.13
Early outline
used for the
Power Tools CD.**

gram to another. This is a multidimensional process that can be viewed in a number of ways. Many producers use simple sketches with a pencil and paper. This method is fast and does not require art skills; rough boxes, stick figures, and arrows are sufficient.

The prototype may be a few screens with graphics, text, and sound, or a mockup of what the actual scenes will look like. This can be done in any outlining program, in HyperCard in a visual programming tool like Visual Basic or Delphi, or even in the authoring system you have chosen.

Complex projects involving many people can be prototyped using powerful presentation tools such as Microsoft PowerPoint, Aldus Persuasion, or Symantec More. These programs have features that allow you to view static ideas and outlines in a variety of ways. For complex projects, creation of the prototype becomes, of necessity, the primary design and programming task, requiring the most advanced skills, up front. It becomes the *actual* shell of the project.

Using the prototype, you can finalize decisions on a broad range of project specs, including overall screen design and geometry, the placement of buttons and windows, the required number and types of still images and interface graphics, the required types and lengths of video and audio clips, color depth, sound content and quality, types of animation, interactivity options, and much more. The prototype also provides a foundation for estimating the project's final size and complexity.

This prototypical interactive "shell" of a multimedia project is the most critical component—the foundation upon which the content organization and delivery will be built. The design and technical specifications of this shell (which contains the interface and programming) must be established before content production begins.

The prototype lets you try out all your ideas in the many dimensions of the interactive program to see if they can, indeed, be translated into reality. Use your imagination to try out various possibilities. Make decisions based on feedback from as many people as is practical. Comments and suggestions on interface, layout, and content are important at this point, particularly because it is easy to make changes when you're still at the prototype stage. Once production begins, these same changes can cause delays, wasted work, and added expense.

Chapter 16, "Interface and Interactivity: Bringing It Together," covers the full spectrum of considerations for creating an effective interface. Once the interface is fully designed, the script may need to be updated to reflect the new environment. You should then test a prototype of the interface on a wide range of individuals, some familiar with the project, others with no prior involvement in the design process.

Storyboarding

From the tested prototype comes the final design stage. Generally, this takes the form of a storyboard, which is a sketch of where each element will appear sequentially in the project. It allows you to move screens to more logical locations and to see the elements of your production on a sort of visual timeline. You can determine if there is sufficient visual variety and if there is enough continuity to prevent the user from getting lost (see Figure 8.14).

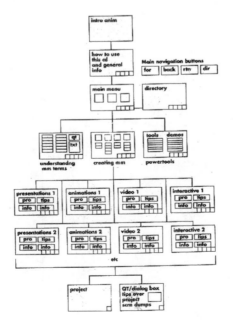

**Figure 8.14
Early storyboard
used for a portion
of the *Multimedia
Power Tools* CD.**

Flowcharting and Outlining at the Library of Congress

The American Memory project at the Library of Congress is a prototype for ways that the vast amount of information in the library can be made available electronically throughout the country. Collections of material are electronically catalogued. Some collections have an exhibit similar to a museum exhibit that serves as an introduction. The project uses both CD-ROM and videodisc technology.

Figures 8.15a and 8.15b show how the interface for an exhibit for the American Memory project was mapped out. The work was done with pencil and paper and started with an outline. From the outline, Joanne Freeman, the author, drew a flowchart showing interactivity of the project.

Starting with the title, the user can take either of two paths: the introduction, or the main information menu. The introduction is sequential and can be viewed start to finish. If the user chooses to go to the main menu, a sub-menu shows the available topics. From the sub-menu, the user can choose to see a Congressional broadside (a document posted in pubs and public places) and information explaining why it was important. Hyperlinks connect the user to in-depth information about people or events mentioned in the text.

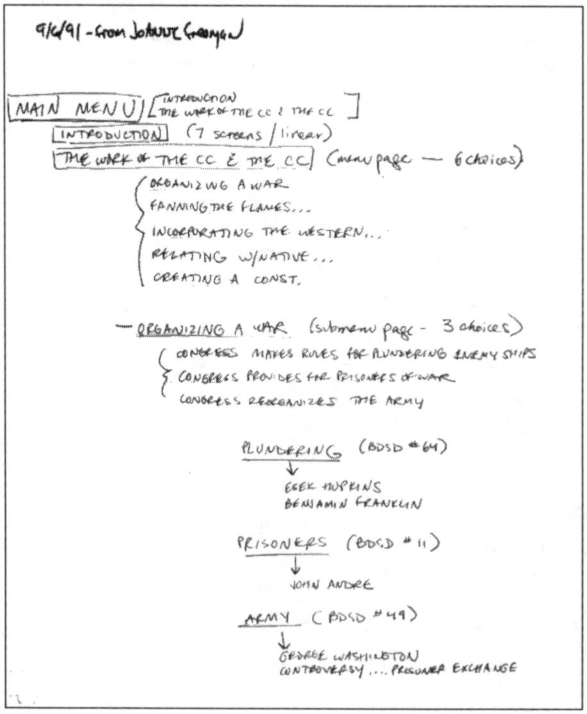

Figure 8.15a This is a handwritten outline of the user interface created for an exhibit in the Library of Congress American Memory prototype.

box continued

The plan for the program structure was reviewed and discussed to determine if the interface would work. After testing the interface on several individuals, the team decided not to allow users to roam freely throughout the miscellaneous information. It would be too easy to lose track of the relationship between the Congressional broadside and the associated individuals and events. As you can see in Figure 8.15b, the arrow connecting the related information has been deleted. This chart shows the flow through one menu item down to the end of one path.

This method of flowcharting was clear and easy to work with; it was simple and to the point. It enabled everyone involved in the project, from the project supervisor to the programmer, to quickly see the scope of the exhibit, how it worked, and how it was to be assembled.

The actual script was written. The text for each card in the HyperCard stack was displayed on a single page. Each page contained all text, including titles, menu items, and captions. Every other page was a photocopy of the still graphic image that was to be used to illustrate that page. The photocopy insured that the programmer would know exactly what the image in the caption looked like.

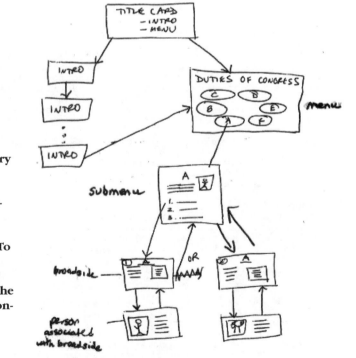

Figure 8.15b This example from the Library of Congress American Memory prototype shows a simple flow chart for the "To Form a More Perfect Union" exhibit about the Continental Congress and the Constitutional Convention.

box continued

Page1

To Form a More Perfect Union:
The Work of the Continental Congress
and the Constitutional Convention

An Interactive Exhibition

* Introduction

* The Work of the Continental Congress and the
Constitutional Convention

Page2
[menu]

The Work of the Continental Congress
and the Constitutional Convention

Organizing a War

Fanning the Flames of Patriotism

Incorporating the Western Territories

Relating With Native Americans

Identifying Defects in the Confederation

Creating a Constitution

Page8
[submenu]

Organizing a War

The huge task of organizing thirteen separate governments and
militia into a united, effective fighting force was a main concern of the Continental Congress. The hastily assembled Continental Army had no precedent; Congress had to create rules for
organization and conduct, and invent an effective system of
raising money to fund the war.

Congress makes rules for plundering enemy ships

Congress provides for prisoners of war

Congress reorganizes the army

Image & Caption:
Das erste BHrger Blut, zu GrHndung der Americanishen
  Freyheit, vergossen bey Lexington am 19ten April
  1775. [The Battle of Lexington].
Daniel Nikolaus Chodowiecki (1726-1801).
Engraving, 1784.
(Reproduction number: LC-USZ62-26669).

Page9
[Congressional Broadside #49]

Congress reorganizes the army

Throughout the Revolutionary War, the Continental Army suffered problems of low recruitment, supply shortages, and sink-

box continued

ing morale. In January 1778, at General George Washington's
urging, Congress sent a committee to military headquarters at
Valley Forge, to confer with Washington on necessary improvements. Although the committee made proposals for reorganizing
supply procedures and revising recruitment regulations, Congress's response was slow and piecemeal; other issues, such as
the **controversy surrounding a prisoner exchange**, kept Congress
distracted. Congress did not approve the displayed plan for
rearrangement of the army until May 1778, and it was November
before implementation was completed.

Page11
[related information]
                        #49 - image and sidebar (#2)

General George Washington (1732-1799)

   During his lifetime, George Washington was admired,
respected, and praised to a degree unmatched by any other figure
in American history. With America's victory in the Revolutionary War, many gave General George Washington most of the credit
for the birth of the American nation.
   Before the Continental Congress named him Commander-in-Chief
of the Continental Army in 1775, Washington was already recognized as a statesman and soldier. As early as 1755, at the age
of twenty-three, he was in command of all Virginian troops during the French and Indian War. Born to a landed family in the
Virginia countryside, Washington was skilled in surveying land,
managing a plantation, entertaining the gentry, and playing
politics. Although he had a fierce temper, through sheer
strength of character he kept it under control. This same
strength of character enabled Washington to endure nine years
of commanding a novice army during a war with one of the
world's great powers—the British empire.

   Image & Caption:
   General Washington (1732-1799).
   Painted by John Trumbull (1756-1843).
   Engraved by Valentine Green (1739-1813).
   Mezzotint, 1781.
   (Reproduction number: LC-USZ62-45197.)

Storyboards can save you lots of wasted effort by establishing a solid plan at the outset and clarifying the resources required for the project. The bigger the project and the more people involved, the more crucial they become. It is often hard to write a storyboard if you don't know what is feasible, or if a project requires extensive programming or creative input that builds as it progresses. A project will naturally evolve as it unfolds, but it's most efficient to get a sense of requirements and anticipated changes in the early stages.

Storyboards can use the same range of tools as interface design, from a clean sheet of paper (or the back of a used envelope) to a complex planning and presentation package. For a simple project, a few quick sketches are sufficient. For large, involved projects, detailed storyboards must be created. Again, presentation programs can be helpful in this process. Some of these programs allow you to view thumbnails of the images that you can shuffle around until the flow of the presentation is exactly the way you want it. Major projects can be dealt with easily when the pieces are planned individually.

Storyboards can also be created in rough form using the prototype shell. They usually show a still representation of each screen—often using early versions of (or actual) content images and interface graphics that will be included in the finished project—along with screen instructions and important information on user input and linking options (see Figure 8.16).

Prototyping and planning have defined the elements of the project. Storyboarding can save immense amounts of time—and money—when you are renting postproduction house time that can cost hundreds of dollars each hour. Although most multimedia is created in less expensive environments, time is always at a premium.

Base your decisions about how and when to storyboard on your time and budget constraints. Also, think about the people you have working on the project. It makes sense to take advantage of the creativity of artists and programmers when you have time, but make sure that the innovations fit with the decisions you have made during preproduction.

Focus Groups

At each stage in the design process, you should bring in others to give you feedback on the interface and every other element of your project. This can be done formally (with a focus group, for example) or informally (just showing the pro-

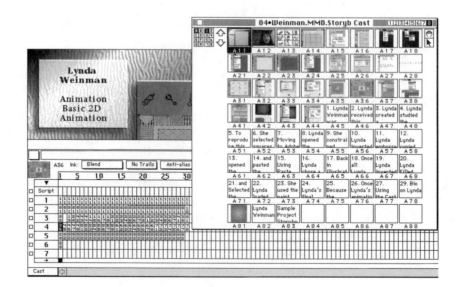

**Figure 8.16
A typical
multimedia
storyboard.**

ject to others in the office). When you near major decision points, such as the interface design, you should try to get feedback from people who are likely to be using the program.

Producing Project Elements

The next (and often longest) stage in the development process is acquiring and/or preparing the actual materials needed for the project, based on initial planning and prototyping. This stage follows two separate but interrelated tracks: one focusing on the development of the project's interface and architecture, the other on content development.

Producing the Interface

Once a project prototype is tested and refined, work can proceed on creating final interface screens and the underlying project architecture to which the various content elements will be linked. Interface production usually involves creating artwork for screens and buttons using a drawing or painting package, while making sure that all the interface elements fit into the overall project specifications and limitations revealed in the design and prototyping phase (see Figure 8.17).

The interface is an extremely critical facet of a multimedia project, so screen design must be well thought-out from the perspectives of good graphic design; user-friendliness; and appropriateness to the content, user pathways, and general architecture of the project. This is a situation where the producer, graphic designer, and programmer will work closely to develop a design that is esthetically pleasing and serves the more technical aspects of the program. Chapter 16, "Interface and Interactivity: Bringing It Together," offers important advice and guidance for successfully executing this stage of the process.

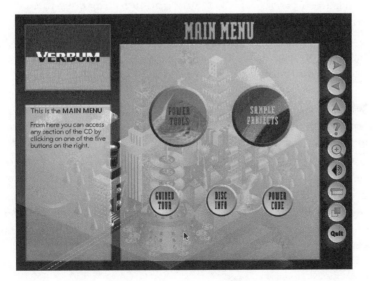

**Figure 8.17
The media screen design for the *Power Tools* CD.**

Producing Content Materials

While work is proceeding on the interface, the producer or development team must focus on gathering and preparing content material. There are basically two ways to create content for a project: produce it yourself or get it from elsewhere. Usually the method chosen will depend on the nature of the project: a corporate presentation will often require a good deal of original material—for example, photographs or video clips of the company's operations—while a project covering science, history, or current events would often use stock photography or film footage. The *preparation* of content materials will be determined by the specifications established in the prototype design: bit-depth, size and color of graphics, sound file types, video formats, etc.

The first scenario may involve hiring artists, recording engineers, or videographers to create and produce original material—a situation that could rapidly eat up a budget but may be necessary for a first-class, quality production. On the other hand, a lot of original material can be produced on a shoestring, if the producer has the right tools and a touch of artistic know-how. The "Creating" chapters in Part II offer many tips and techniques for low-budget, "in-house" productions. Either way, traveling this route often consumes a lot of time, whether it's from waiting for the artists/experts to do what they do best, or from the steep learning curve of "doing it yourself."

Acquiring stock graphics and media clips from elsewhere is another option that almost every producer uses to some extent. Some multimedia projects may rely almost entirely on "pick-up" media, and even high-budget extravaganzas use some stock art. Useful content is often in the public domain and can be acquired free—from libraries, television stations, or elsewhere.

A producer can often acquire media for a very reasonable price. A great deal of clip media can be obtained from companies that specialize in selling collections. The *Power Tools* CD features numerous license-free collection samples that you can use without charge.

A producer may need to pay a licensing fee in order to use specific music, animation, photographs, or video clips. Whatever the source, always be sure to obtain permission for any preproduced material.

Assembling Elements into a Cohesive Production

When the development team has created and collected the various interface and content elements, they're assembled into a final product using an authoring program such as Macromedia Director, HyperCard, and others (see Chapter 7, "Authoring Tools"). These systems are, in large part, *object oriented,* allowing a producer to link multimedia elements simply by moving icons on a screen. However, they also feature advanced interactive capabilities accessible through their own scripting languages. Most scripting languages are similar and are *high level*—meaning they're more like English than traditional programming languages such as Pascal or C.

Figure 8.18 In *The Madness of Roland*, the user leaves a "trail" of where he or she has been.

Graphics and sound can be imported directly from other programs, or they can be created using graphic tools that are a part of the authoring system. Some authoring systems have tools that can help create graphics and 2-D animations. Sounds and video need to be prerecorded and put into a form that can be handled by the authoring system.

Before project assembly begins, it is essential to have all the pieces ready for the programmer. Usually the graphic interface elements are put into place first. The programmer writes a script for each button and menu so that something happens when the user clicks on it.

Additional programming coordinates animation and sound. Sometimes additional code assures that everything on the screen is set properly when it is displayed. Other times the programmer needs to have code to keep track of what the user has been doing. *The Madness of Roland*, for example, keeps track of each character with whom the user has interacted. The programmer created a screen that allows the user to see whether or not he has spoken to all the characters. This type of technique is often used to help users remember what they have done within the program (see Figure 8.18).

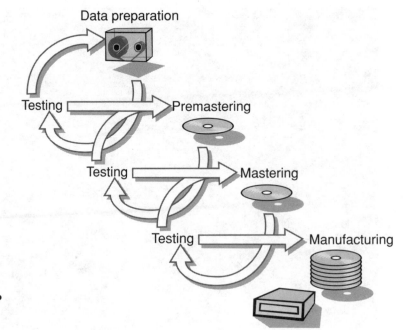

**Figure 8.19
The process of
preparing data to
make a compact
disc.**

Assembling a program in an authoring system is the last big job in putting together a multimedia project. During this stage, each element becomes a part of the whole. The programmer uses the script, the outline, the prototypes and storyboards to transform the static pieces into a multidimensional entity.

**Testing and
Making
Adjustments**

Once a working version of the project is assembled, it is thoroughly tested (see Figure 8.19)—preferably by a number of people who have not been involved in production. Of course, the production team will test the product, but the most important findings will probably come from others who don't know what to expect, and will try things that the developers may never have thought of.

Testing takes time and effort (a typical testing period can last anywhere from a few days to several months), but an error on a compact disc is there forever. Users will do things you cannot possibly imagine. It's better to find the bugs before the project "goes public."

Forging Ahead

Multimedia clearly requires skills, planning, and a great many tools. And although it can be created on the desktop, it requires much thought, patience, and hard work. The development process seems long and involved when you read about it, and (frankly) can seem even longer and more involved while you are doing it! On the other hand, each segment can be both challenging and fun to produce. There are tools that make it possible for you to do anything you want on the computer without extensive knowledge of programming or mathematics. You can see an idea become a full-fledged product in a matter of days for a presentation, or a matter of weeks or months for a more involved, in-depth project.

When you begin your first multimedia project, start with something small that you can finish quickly. You will get a feel for the process and learn techniques for working in an interactive, multifaceted environment. It gets easier as you go along. Remember to experiment and play with the tools that interest you. Later, what you learned will pop back into your mind as a brilliant solution to a creative problem you are facing. If you enjoy what you are doing, your users will be more likely to enjoy their experience with your project.

9

Working Cross-Platform

Few who saw the legendary 1984 Super Bowl commercial would soon forget it. The ad begins with a line of downtrodden figures marching into a bleak and crowded auditorium. (It didn't take much imagination to realize that these unfortunate souls were supposed to be IBM customers.) Meanwhile, a female athlete pursued by storm troopers bursts into the room of "clone" people, who stare dumbly at the giant, flickering image of "big brother."

The woman abruptly spins around and hurls a sledge hammer through the screen, and as a fresh wind blows through the auditorium, a legend appears: "On January 24th, Apple Computer will introduce Macintosh. And you'll see why 1984 won't be like '1984.'"

From the beginning, it was war.

In 1981, when $40 billion behemoth IBM entered the personal computer market with its PC, Apple was a $600 million upstart that owned 80 percent of the desktop computer market.

With his trademark blend of arrogance and idealism, Steve Jobs welcomed IBM into battle with a national ad whose headline read, "Welcome IBM. Seriously." It went on to say, in part, "Welcome to the most exciting and important marketplace since the computer revolution began 35 years ago. And congratulations on your first computer."

Apple and Jobs clearly relished the David and Goliath struggle that lay ahead and no doubt assumed that Apple's size and agility, as well as its head start, would give the company the critical competitive advantage.

But Apple's opponent was no stranger to either adversity or market dominance. When IBM itself was on the rise in the 1950s, it, too, was puny in comparison with General Electric and RCA, the giants it challenged. But by building a reputation for technology leadership and sensitivity to the customer, IBM had dominated the industry by the mid 1950s with a 75 percent share of the computer market. And in the personal computer war with Apple nearly three decades later, the story was much the same. A year after joining the fray, IBM had captured nearly 20 percent of the market, and by 1983 it was recognized as the leader, displacing Apple, which had enjoyed such a commanding lead a short time before.

By the early 1990s, the competitive landscape had shifted again, and both Apple and IBM had all but ceded control of the personal computer market that they themselves had spawned. By using off-the-shelf components to encourage the PC's acceptance, IBM had lost market share to such clone manufacturers as Compaq, AST, and Dell.

Apple had also continued to lose share to both IBM and the PC clones (although it is now—finally—making an aggressive effort to license its operating system, thereby allowing Mac clones).

The two pioneers of personal computer technology collectively held barely one quarter of the market they had created. By mid-1992, even the Mac's edge as a graphical environment was being challenged; for the first time, market research reports indicated that GUI buyers at corporate sites were acquiring more PCs with Windows than they were Macintoshes.

Given these cold facts, perhaps the IBM/Apple alliance should have sent out fewer shock waves. Yet when the two companies announced their partnership in 1991, it rocked the industry.

In this chapter, we'll examine the fledgling set of cross-platform multimedia standards, including the fruits of the IBM/Apple relationships, and follow with some practical information on cross-platform development.

Since the Mac and the PC/Windows are the dominant multimedia environments and since most professional multimedia production is carried out on the Mac, we'll cover the main issues involved in developing on the Mac for delivery on the PC. We'll also take a look at some of the applications that offer the best cross-platform compatibility.

Multimedia Standards

The computer industry is plagued by a lack of true standards for file formats, data of all types, devices, and software architecture. This sad situation has many ramifications: It's tricky or impossible to move data between programs and platforms, product development costs are high, technological innovations are hampered, and the user frustration factor is in the stratosphere.

Of the approximately 5 million Macs installed at corporate sites in 1992, 65 to 75 percent were connected to multiplatform networks. Yet, interoperability remains elusive. As vendors struggle to differentiate themselves and their products, they build walls by creating proprietary systems that communicate imperfectly and only with great difficulty.

Vendors often use bolt-on filters to convert data from one format to another, but this process requires extra steps to transfer and open files across platforms and between applications and usually results in only partial conversion. To be truly transparent, applications must incorporate interoperability into their core code.

Part of the problem lies in the appearance of the graphical user interface (GUI) following the Mac's rise to prominence in the 1980s. Now, GUIs are everywhere: Windows for PCs, Motif for Unix, and Presentation Manager for OS/2. In the days of the ugly but effective command-line interface, an application written in a high-level language such as C or Pascal more or less guaranteed its portability.

But despite GUI similarities in look and feel, beneath their clever and colorful desktops lurks code that is largely incompatible across systems. Every GUI has a complex and unique set of functions that governs the display of menus, windows, and icons and specifies keyboard and mouse interaction. All this means that while GUIs make it much easier for users to interact with computers, they make it a lot harder for programmers to develop interoperable applications.

However, the explosion of multimedia—with its new file formats for video, sound, and graphics—has reemphasized the need for interoperability; and there has been a flurry of action in the renewed rush to establish standards.

Even Microsoft CEO Bill Gates, in a *MacWeek* interview, has predicted that there will be content standards, at least "The key elements, the audio and video that you put your money into, will be shared," Gates says. "We can hide [differences in the platforms] for a content producer, and make those things look the same." Gates adds that vendors will retain their edge by competing on the basis of applications. "...otherwise, the differences [in platforms] cease to have separate value added."

Below, we'll take a look at Kaleida's ScriptX, the most promising cross-platform multimedia development environment.

Kaleida's ScriptX

Announced in 1991 with great fanfare, Kaleida, one of two Apple/IBM joint ventures, finally began selling ScriptX in late 1994. ScriptX is a universal multimedia scripting language for developing cross-platform applications. Once written, these apps will play back on any platform that can run the Kaleida Media Player; today that means on the Mac and Windows, including PowerPCs.

Developers can purchase the ScriptX Language Kit, and object-oriented development tool for creating applications. The development kits include hundreds of preprogrammed objects that make development faster and less prone to bugs.

The Kaleida Media Player (at least at the time of this writing) is available free from on-line services. Web users can download the Mac and Windows versions from Kaleida's homepage at www.kaleida.com (see Figure 9.1).

**Figure 9.1
The Kaleida
Media Player is
available free
of charge.**

According to Kaleida, QuickTime will be incorporated into the ScriptX environment, and QuickTime movies will play on ScriptX-compliant machines, including PDAs.

While all of this new technology sounds promising, Kaleida has a tough row to hoe, because Apple and IBM have been pursuing their own unique multimedia strategies for some time now. Apple has encouraged (and provided—notably in QuickTime) the tools necessary to "roll your own" multimedia presentations and creations. One such tools is the Apple Media Tool (see Chapter 7, "Authoring Tools"). IBM has spent its time developing industrial-strength multimedia training applications and such point-of-sale products as information kiosks. Each of the two companies also plans to continue to maintain its own competitive edge; they will label their joint ventures "precompetitive cooperation."

Odd times, indeed. One can hardly imagine two stranger bedfellows. And at some level, both IBM and Apple must agree—certainly, the two companies' hapless employees do. Spencer the Katt, the popular *PC Week* gossip columnist, reports that Apple people are especially wary and compares the situation to the *Star Trek* movie in which Captain Kirk helps save his archenemies, the Klingons. As Apple employees suspiciously eye their alien counterparts from IBM, they're thinking (Spock) "We have to save them, Captain. They're dying." (Kirk) "They're animals, Spock. Let them die."

A Truly Independent Platform?

One of the original goals of the IBM/Apple alliance was to create a machine that would run Mac, Unix, and DOS/Windows applications on the same computer. Full details of the so-called Common Hardware Reference Platform (CHRP) were finally disclosed in 1995.

As it stands today, if you buy a PowerPC from IBM, you'll have to live with its version of Unix (AIX); Mac Power PCs run only System 7. Those are exactly the constraints that the alliance was supposed to eliminate in the first place. As of this writing, CHRP-compliant machines are slated to appear from both Apple and IBM in 1996.

Will that be soon enough for both multimedia developers and computer users who want to run multimedia applications without regard to the vagaries of operating systems and hardware configuration? No one can tell; but for now, the appearance of major authoring tools in cross platform versions is of more value for multimedia developers. (See section on "Multiplatform Applications.")

Developing on the Mac for Delivery Under Windows

Here's how we introduced this section in the first edition of this book:

The jostlings and posturings of major corporations and standards organizations aside, the realities of today's cross-platform tools are such that if you want to develop cross-platform multimedia productions, you have your work cut out for you.

Director 4.0 Demo ⌘ 708

Photoshop 3.0 Demo ⌘ 715

Premiere 4.0 Demo ⌘ 722

While this is still true, things are much better in 1996 than they were in 1993. Director, Photoshop, and Premiere—the leading authoring, image processing, and video editing packages—are all now available in cross-platform versions. This makes it far easier to develop multimedia content that will play back more or less similarly both on the Mac and under Windows.

Many issues remain, however. Since the most popular multimedia platforms are the Mac and PC/Windows, we'll focus on some of the cross-platform considerations for those two environments. Since the Mac is still the platform of choice for most multimedia developers, we'll concentrate mainly on the problems involved in developing multimedia on the Mac for delivery under Windows.

To those familiar with the mind-numbing 3-D graphic capabilities of Silicon Graphics machines, it is somewhat ironic that Unix is the underlying operating system for SGI workstations. The spectacular visual effects in such films as *T2* and *Jurassic Park* would lead some to conclude that Unix must anchor the most sophisticated multimedia capabilities.

Unfortunately, Unix remains a separate world. This is true for a number of reasons. First, one cannot speak of Unix as a single operating environment, for even Motif—touted as a standard—is implemented differently by various vendors. Differences between Unix variants forces extra cross platform tweaking, conversion, and testing.

Unix also does not host a stand-out multimedia authoring or image processing tool. There is no Director for Unix, or anything like it. Image processing and audio/video editing tools also are limited. (Silicon Graphics is working on a multimedia authoring app for Unix.)

Finally, there are no standards for audio and video formats. This is a real killer because it means that non-native files must be converted to proprietary formats for each flavor of Unix. Thus, programs running under Solaris accept PC WAV audio files, while those running under Motif take Mac AIFF files.

If you must develop cross-platform applications for Unix, check out Sybase's Gain Momentum, an authoring tool for Unix and Windows, and PowerMedia from RAD Technologies, another authoring tool that handles Unix, Windows, and Macintosh presentations.

Know Your Target

A central problem in cross-platform development is the wildly variable range of PCs and their peripherals. Designer/developer Jim Collins of San Francisco-based Smoke and Mirrors points out that you can generally predict multimedia performance on the Mac. A presentation may play at a certain speed on an LC II, a little faster on a II series, and faster still on a Quadra or Power PC.

By contrast, the PC world is populated by a jangling array of CPUs, graphics subsystems, drivers, cards, and other peripherals. It's simply not possible to estimate how a given multimedia production will behave on the tremendous range of PC hardware, even with the unifying influence of Windows. Says Collins, "The vagaries of PC hardware are just a killer."

To combat these uncertainties, experienced multimedia developers agree that a key to creating successful cross-platform apps is to lock down your target PC, if at all possible. If the playback machine in a kiosk, for example, is a particular type of PC, you're in luck, because then you can obtain a PC identical to the target machine, test your work, and be sure that your multimedia will always perform consistently.

Unfortunately, more often than not, multimedia presentations are bound for a variety of PCs. In these cases, you still can dampen (if not eliminate) performance problems by specifying a few key parameters: processor type and speed, RAM and hard disk capacity, and color capability. If your multimedia production is a product or custom app, make sure that your product packaging states these requirements, or that clients are aware of them.

If clients know which target machine will be used, Collins insists that they provide him with one so that he can test projects before delivering them. If the work will be played back on an unknown range of PCs, he informs his clients

of minimum hardware requirements and then tests on his own similarly configured machine. Even then, he makes sure they know that performance may not
be consistent across the range of PCs out there.

In addition to the complexities of interoperability and performance, there are
issues of design and of look and feel that are equally daunting. For many, it's
enough to get an application or project to perform acceptably. However, the
inherent differences in look and feel of the Mac and Windows leads others to
develop custom interfaces.

Dave Arnowitz, vice president of software development for Arnowitz Productions Inc. in Mill Valley, California, says "the biggest problem in cross-platform
development is that, if you want a product to have a consistency of look and feel,
you can't rely on the native appearances of either environment." Accordingly,
Arnowitz Productions builds large-scale interactive productions designed around
custom interfaces.

Is It Worth It?

With all the intricacies of cross-platform development, you may wonder if it's
worth the trouble; and you're not alone. Collins, for one, has all but thrown in
the towel. After years of developing on the Mac for delivery under Windows, it's
still "a huge pain and probably not worth the time and money" in lost revenue
from other missed opportunities. Collins is considering not accepting any more
cross-platform projects so that he can devote all his efforts to Mac-based development and delivery.

But not everyone agrees. Britt Peddie, technical director for San Francisco-
based Ikonic, admits that confronting cross-platform development hurdles can be
grim, but actually prefers the PC to the Mac. He claims that the PC's installed
base, modest pricing, and improving apps make it an appealing development target. "And, anyway, I prefer some PC applications over Mac software," says Peddie, citing both Animation Studio and Micrografx's highly regarded Picture
Publisher image-processing program.

Peddie certainly has a point about the cost of the PC. In the summer of 1995,
it was possible to buy a multimedia PC with a Pentium processor, built-in CD-
ROM drive, 16-bit sound card, and external speakers, all for under $1,700.

And the PC has become a more appealing machine with the advent of Windows, which has undeniably brought a unifying force to the machine.

Despite all the pitfalls of cross-platform development, it's certainly possible to
build high-quality applications for presentation on the PC. In fact, it has become
standard practice for CD-ROM developers to release their presentations, games,
and other interactive products as hybrid CDs that will play on either the Windows
or Mac. This allows developers to create a single product that will get maximum
coverage out of the box.

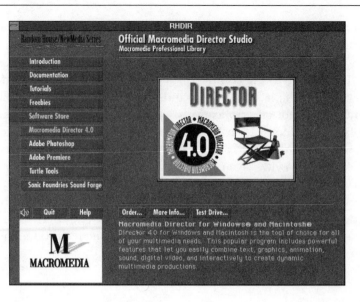

**Figure 9.2
Interface for the
*Official Macro-
media Director
Studio* CD-ROM.**

Figure 9.2 shows the interface for the *Official Macromedia Director Studio* CD-ROM. The screen capture is from the Windows version, but the CD also plays identically on a Macintosh.

For multimedia developers on the Macintosh, creating hybrid CDs is the way to go for at least two reasons: First, the vast numbers of installed PCs now running Windows makes that market very appealing. And sales of home and office multimedia computers have been explosive for the last few years. Finally, availability of Photoshop and Director for Windows—the two most popular multimedia development tools—has made cross-platform development a viable proposition.

Choose Your Poison

There are two basic ways to play back on a PC the multimedia you develop on the Mac. The first is to create different components on the Mac—sound, graphics, animation, video—then transfer the files to the PC (see section on "File Transfer") and assemble them using a PC-based authoring tool such as Director, Visual Basic, or Asymetrix Toolbook. The other way is to develop a complete multimedia production on the Mac using a "multiplatform" application—one that is also supported on the PC.

Developing and then transferring elements one by one is time consuming, and then you've got to invest in and learn a PC authoring program. It's much easier to use a program such as Director or Apple's Media Tool to develop fully self contained cross-platform multimedia projects.

Using this method, you'll be able to tweak the multimedia elements with the authoring package directly on the PC—a distinct advantage. (Media Tool, however, runs only on Macs.) However, if you develop a complete production on the Mac using Director, for example, you'll also have to purchase at least the Windows Projector, which compiles Director files for playback on the PC. If something doesn't work or look right (expect this, at least to some extent), you can't modify elements on the PC. You'll have to go back to the Mac, make adjustments, recompile, transfer to the PC, and only then find out if things have improved. For this reason, many developers buy both versions of Director, which makes the inevitable adjustments much easier.

If your multimedia production involves device control—external commands that fetch images and other data from peripherals such as CD-ROMs and laserdiscs—you'll pretty much have to put everything together on the PC; because such "compiled code resources" as HyperCard XCMDs must be replaced by equivalent Dynamic Link Libraries (DLLs) or MCI channels under Windows.

Using Director and similar products, you can develop multimedia productions on the Mac and play them back on the PC under Windows (or vice-versa). The built-in transfer utilities take care of converting everything in the presentation—graphics, animation, sound, and text. But even when the conversion is handled for you in one big lump, you may still run into problems.

Let's take a look now at the basics of cross-platform computing—file formats, file transfer and conversion, and screen capture. We'll also cover cross-platform conversion of multimedia components: colors, graphics, text, animation, video, and sound.

File Translation and Graphic File Formats

File transfer and translation are at the heart of cross-platform multimedia development. The following information and advice should help you through the thicket of formats and conventions.

File Naming

Mac users are used to naming files descriptively, using up to 31 characters—including any combination of upper- and lowercase letters and punctuation (except colons). File naming under DOS (and Unix, too) is much more restrictive. In DOS, a filename can be up to only eight characters long, followed by a period and a three-character extension, which tells the OS what kind of file it is. DOS makes no distinction between upper- and lowercase letters.

Windows95, which should be out by the time you read this, supports filenames of up to 255 characters (should you ever need to get that carried away).

In the Mac OS, application and system files are each linked to a companion file called the resource fork, that is not visible in the Finder. The resource fork file yields to the Finder certain information about the file, such as its type, icon, and so on. When you transfer a file from the Mac to the PC, you'll often see the file split into two files on the PC side, with the resource fork named identically, save for a percent (%) symbol at the beginning of the name. If the file is going to stay on the PC, you can discard the resource fork, whose information is conveyed to DOS by the three-character extension.

If you're going to do a lot of file transfers, you should consider using filenames that both the Mac and DOS will understand. Use names of no longer than eight characters and include a three-character extension—the Mac will treat it as part of the filename, but the PC will recognize the extension and process the file correctly.

If you're going to be cutting a CD for your multimedia presentations, files, or product, filenames must conform to ISO-9660, an international standard that defines a filesystem for CD-ROMs. If you have data on the CD that is compatible with applications running on multiple platforms, you'll also want the filenames to be readable by different operating systems. The following file naming conventions will ensure this compatibility.

The ISO-9660 Level One specification outlines file naming conventions similar to DOS rules. Filenames are limited to eight single-case characters, a period, and a three-character extension. Filenames cannot contain symbols or special characters (no hyphens, tildes, equals, or pluses), only single-case letters, numbers, and underscores. Directory names cannot have the three-digit extension, just eight single-case characters.

Level Two ISO-9660 allows longer filenames—up to 32 characters—but many of the other restrictions still apply. Level-Two discs are not usable on some systems, notably MS-DOS. For further information, see Chapter 2, "Systems Software, Hardware, and Peripherals."

File Transfer

While direct content and application compatibility between the Mac and PC still lags, simple file transfer is now pretty routine. Apple, itself, has finally delivered on the promise of direct DOS file mounting it made when releasing the Super-Drive (which handles 1.44Mb floppies) back in 1988.

By Floppy

For $79, you can get Apple's Macintosh PC Exchange software that allows you to read, write, and format DOS 720Kb and 1.44Mb disks on a Mac. Contents of DOS disks appear on the Mac desktop as standard Mac files, and you can open, save, rename, move, copy, or delete them as you would any Mac file. You even can configure PC files to launch the appropriate application when you click on them. Apple includes the utility in System 7.5.

An older utility called Apple File Exchange is included in the Mac's system software (in System 7), but you have to launch it separately—it doesn't offer the direct-from-the-desktop mounting of PC Exchange.

PC Exchange has a few drawbacks of its own: It works only under System 7, requires at least 3Mb of RAM, and a SuperDrive (the standard drive on all post-Mac II machines).

Dayna Communications' DOS Mounter, and AccessPC from Insignia Solutions —which actually also wrote some of PC Exchange's code—appear to be a better deal. These two products do not have any of the limitations of PC Exchange (except that both also require a SuperDrive), and cost about the same as PC Exchange.

By Removable Cartridge

Removable hard disk cartridges are a popular way of transferring large files between machines. Iomega has a new low cost drive called the Zip Drive that uses $20, 100Mb cartridges. For more on removables see Chapter 2.

By Serial Line

Directly connecting a Mac and PC by cable can be a cheap and fast way to transfer files. You can get the right cable from most computer suppliers for about $10 (PC 9-pin or 25-pin COM1 or COM2 port on one end, and the Mac's Mini DIN-8 on the other). Several products bundle these cables with file transfer software, and some, such as MacLinkPlus and LapLink, also will convert files to different formats before sending them.

On the Mac, you can run Zterm, a shareware transfer utility available from BBSs. Combine this with the cable, and you've got the cheapest transfer solution. Other commercial products include Argosy's RunPC, Microphone II from Software Ventures, and White Knight Telecommunications Software from Freesoft Co.

By Modem

You can use file transfer software in conjunction with a modem instead of a serial line if you need to connect to a remote machine. You also can join a network or BBS and download or upload files with a modem.

By Network

All Macs have built-in networking capability via AppleTalk software. Buy an inexpensive connector for each Mac, connect them with ordinary phone wire, and poof—an instant LocalTalk network, complete with printer and file sharing.

You can add AppleTalk capability to any PC with a card such as Daystar's LT200 Connection, PhoneNET Card PC from Farallon, or Sitka's TOPS FlashCard; all are in the $200 to 300 range. Coactive Computing has a similar solution that connects a Mac and a PC via the serial and parallel ports, respectively. This neat and inexpensive solution doesn't require an adaptor card.

If you're moving lots of big files around all the time, you should buy Ethernet cards for your Macs and PCs. AppleTalk's data transfer rate of 17.2Kb per second is OK for occasional transfers of small files, but Ethernet moves data at about 10Mb/second, making it ideal for pushing around giant multimedia files. You can get Ethernet cards for $400 to $500 apiece.

For connecting major networks of Macs and PCs, you'll need a "gateway." These higher-end products can be on the expensive side. Gateways include GatorShare from Cayman Systems, which connects Unix and Apple networks; MacLAN Connect from Miramar Systems, which connects PC and Mac networks; and NetModem/E from Shiva Corp., which allows Macs to connect to Novell NetWare networks.

Farallon's Timbuktu is an interesting software product that lets you view Windows files from a Mac and vice versa. You can move files from machine to machine across a network and even give Windows users access to Mac shared printers, folders, and servers.

File Conversion

File interchange is the bane of the computer user. Getting one program to read a file created with another program can be frustrating, time consuming, and sometimes impossible. You often end up stripping a text file of its formatting characteristics, importing it into the other program, and reformatting it.

Unfortunately, you can't do this with an image file; its whole identity is wrapped up in its file format, without which it is a meaningless collection of bits. There are some graphics standards, and a few of them are even adhered to by applications vendors.

Many applications vendors pull self-serving stunts such as reading files in a number of formats but writing them out only in their own proprietary format, thus encouraging (forcing) use of their program alone. Luckily, even mercenary software companies are recognizing the importance of interchange standards; and most graphics programs read and write to at least a few basic formats.

Authoring tools (such as Director) and image processing programs (Photoshop, for example) actually accept a wide variety of file formats. In fact, Photoshop supports so many formats that it is often used simply to convert an image from one format to another.

Once you have established a connection to the PC (or other computer), the next step is to invest in a good file translation package.

One of the most comprehensive is DataViz's MacLinkPlus, which offers over 400 conversion combinations spanning word processing, database, spreadsheet, and graphics formats. MacLinkPlus will even autodetect the type of data in a file (or at least hazard a reasonable guess). We once were piddling around trying to convert a text file of unknown origin, recklessly hit a button or two in MacLinkPlus's interface, and before we knew what was going on, the utility had converted the file to Microsoft Word.

If most of your work will be in graphics file translation, you may want to use a program that specializes in this task. Inset Systems Hijaak supports and converts more than 60 graphics file formats; and SnapPro from Windows Painter Ltd., another capable graphics converter, also includes image editing tools. Both programs run under Windows.

FGM Inc. has PICTure This, which lets Mac users convert graphics files from the PC, Unix, and Amiga environments into PICT files.

Graphics File Formats

Mac users have to put up with comparatively few graphics formats—TIFF, PICT, and EPS are the main ones. Most Mac programs can read and write at least one of these in addition to their native formats. The PC world, by contrast, supports a large number of proprietary and near-standard formats, but TIFF, BMP, and EPS are the most widely used.

All in all, the whole business of graphics file formats is troublesome and not a little frustrating. To keep yourself from inflicting damage on your computer if your carefully adjusted multihued image turns green when you open it on the PC, it's best to stick to the few tested formats with which you are most familiar.

Many people now use a handy tool called DeBabelizer, a sort of Swiss Army knife of graphics utilities that can open most Mac and PC graphics files. See Chapter 3, "Graphics Tools."

Screen Capture

Some developers will use the Mac to create presentations for playback on the PC. Often they'll need to capture PC screenshots; bring them to the Mac; animate them, if necessary, to simulate a running PC application; incorporate them into the presentation; then send the whole thing back to the PC for playback.

Believe it or not, it's easier to simulate a PC program's functionality in this way than to have the presentation call the PC program in real time during playback. One of the essential cross-platform tools is a good PC screen capture utility. (As PC tools become more powerful, developers are increasingly able to produce entirely on the PC.)

Windows, like the Mac, offers a built-in screen capture capability. While limited, it does the trick and works well for most simple screen grabs. To capture a screen and save it to the Windows Clipboard, just hit the Print Screen key. To grab the active window only, type Alt-Print Screen. This utility saves the screen captures to the Windows Clipboard in bitmap format (BMP).

While functional enough, the Windows Print Screen utility has some drawbacks. For one, you cannot save grabs to a file or print them at the time of capture. And if you have a number of captures to do in sequence, you'll have to move captured images from the Clipboard one by one; otherwise they'll be overwritten by subsequent captures.

You can bring the screen grabs into Windows' Paintbrush utility, which can crop and otherwise process each image. Unfortunately, Paintbrush has an aesthetic sense of its own and has been known to chop off portions of screen captures without consulting you first. If these limitations put you off, a variety of utilities might fill the bill. Some popular PC shareware screen grabbers are CAPBUF, GRABBER, and TXT2PCX. All are available from CompuServe and other bulletin boards. Commercial screen capture utilities include Capture, Collage, Hotshot Graphics, PC Tools, and Hijaak.

In addition to simple screen capture into different file formats, many of these programs include tools for cropping and cleaning up stray pixels, or artifacts, that commonly accompany screen captures.

If using a Mac, you'll also have to use a graphics file translator to convert the screen capture to something Mac programs can use. PICTure This and Imagery are two Mac programs that will convert a wide variety of graphics formats (including BMP) to more universal graphics formats such as TIFF and PICT. PIC-Ture This is available from FGM Inc., and Imagery is freeware available from bulletin boards.

For a quick way to get PC screen shots over to the Mac, many developers save the grabs in PCX. The native file format of PC Paintbrush, a popular PC paint program, PCX has become a de facto standard on the PC. Once you have saved the screen captures in PCX, you can bring them into Photoshop, one of the few Mac applications (perhaps the only one) that will read PCX. You can then use Photoshop to convert the graphics to PICT or some other native Mac file format.

Other Elements of Multimedia

The other components of multimedia present their own challenges when you move them from one platform to another. Here, we'll look at some of the ins and outs of fonts, colors and palettes, video, and sound.

Fonts

Fonts are trouble; they're probably one of the biggest problems you'll run into in this line of work. Many people believed that TrueType held the promise of font standardization. After all, the new type technology was incorporated into both System 7 and Windows. But TrueType for the Mac and TrueType for Windows actually use different methods for character encoding and font specifications.

Windows includes two TrueType fonts—Arial and Times New Roman—that are translated to Helvetica and Times when moved to the Mac. These substitutions are not exact matches, so line breaks and careful copy fitting will be for naught.

Adobe's new technology uses a single Multiple Master typeface, such as Myriad, to simulate specified typefaces—even if the actual typefaces themselves are not installed in the system. Myriad cooks up substitutions on-the-fly while preserving both the appearance and metrics of the original work. The simulated fonts are not up to the quality of "real" typefaces, but may be good enough for screen presentations.

Many developers work around the font problem by converting type to bitmaps that they antialias (smooth) to improve appearance. A lot of designers do type effects such as fills and gradients, which require turning fonts into bitmaps, anyway.

Of course, this won't help you if your presentation includes a lot of text. In this case, use basic fonts that are available in default configurations on both platforms to minimize subtle inconsistencies that will throw off formatting. And even if you use fonts with direct equivalents, save a little room to account for subtle variations that may cause text to expand or contract when converted. In any case, be prepared to tweak text, if you don't convert it to bitmap form.

Director stores a table for converting Mac fonts to Windows equivalents in a file called FONTMAP.TXT. In this file, you can specify fonts that you know will work as reasonable substitutes. Better than letting Windows guess for you.

Colors and Palettes

Although 8- and 16-bit color is increasingly common on the PC, there are still many machines out there that have VGA graphics, which handles only 16 colors.

Most color Macs are equipped with at least 256-color, 8-bit cards; this can cause problems when your 8- or 24-bit images are transferred to the PC. For example, when you convert a Director multimedia production for playback on the PC with Windows Player, it automatically remaps 8- or 24-bit images to the 16 colors available for VGA displays.

This can produce strange results, because remapping simply substitutes one color for another based on their relative positions in their respective palettes. Because the substituted colors are selected purely on their position, they may bear no resemblance at all to the original colors.

To avoid these nasty consequences, many developers capture the standard VGA palette on the PC and use it as the basis for image creation, thereby ensuring that colors will transfer properly. To get this palette, you can open the "Colors" control panel under Windows and do a screen capture of the palette that pops up. Save this as a TIFF file, transfer it to the Mac, and import it into apps that support custom palettes, such as Director. Using this technique, you can create images that use colors that are drawn only from the VGA palette.

For an image that has already been created, you can use an image editing program such as Photoshop to convert the image's colors to the standard VGA 16. Import the captured palette in Photoshop and name it something like *VGA palette*. Open your image and select Color Table in the Mode menu. Then select Edit Table, and you'll see the current palette. Click the Load button and select *VGA palette*. Click *OK*, and the image will be converted to the 16 colors of VGA.

This works well if you have only a few images to convert but can take a lot of time if you have many images, such as the multiple frames of an animation. In this case, you can set up a macro to automatically fetch each image, apply the new palette, open the next image, and so on. Then you can go out and have dinner; make sure you have coffee and dessert and maybe catch a movie on the way home, too, because the conversion process can take a long time! But this process is necessary only if you can't be sure your multimedia won't be played back on a plain old VGA display.

Fortunately, many PCs outfitted for multimedia now have Super VGA, which can display 256 colors, making it roughly equivalent to the Mac's 8-bit color. In fact, if you know that your multimedia will be played back on a Super VGA monitor, you probably won't have to worry about remapping the colors of your images. The 256 colors of the Mac standard 8-bit palette map correspond reasonably closely—though not exactly—to the 256 colors of Super VGA.

Video

Just as the Mac has QuickTime, Windows users now can enjoy digital video with Microsoft's Video for Windows (Figure 9.3). VFW uses Microsoft's Audio Video Interleaved (AVI) movie file format, analogous to QuickTime's MooV movie format. VFW incorporates Intel's Indeo digital video compression and playback technology, but it also works with other compression schemes being offered by third parties. There are ways to move VFW and QuickTime movies back and forth between platforms.

Apple now offers QuickTime for Windows so that any QuickTime movie will play back on either platform. You do need to "flatten" a Mac QuickTime movie for playback on the PC. You can do this using Apple's Movie Converter, which is on the QuickTime CD, or with various freeware alternatives, such as flatten-MooV, which are available on on-line services.

Nonetheless, since QuickTime is now firmly entrenched on both platforms, it is by far the easiest way to develop cross-platform video.

Sound

From the beginning, all Macintoshes have had at least primitive sound capabilities built right into the system. All but a few of the earliest Macs have a version of the Apple Sound Chip that can play four voices of synthesized sounds for basic effects. Hardware-based digital-analog converters (DACs) yield reasonable sound quality when audio is played back through the Mac's built-in speaker.

All newer Macs, from the IIsi on up, can play back stereo sound through speakers plugged into rear outputs. And most also can record sounds when a mike is plugged into input jacks. All this means that viewers (and listeners) who

**Figure 9.3
Microsoft's Video
for Windows.**

use just about any old Mac won't have to invest in a sound card to hear the sounds and music in your multimedia extravaganzas.

With the PC, it's a different story. Except for primitive system "bings" and "bongs," which can play back through the PC's internal speaker, no add-in sound board means no sound. So if your target PC doesn't have an audio card, the sounds in any multimedia presentations developed on the Mac won't be heard.

There is a workaround that may help. Windows version 3.1 brought better sound capability to the PC, at least on the software side; a sound card still is necessary for sound processing, indeed even for simple recording and playback. But Microsoft and other vendors have made available a driver that allows sounds stored in the Windows .WAV format to be played back through the PC's internal speaker. (MIDI files stored in the .MID file format still require a separate sound card for playback).

Because the digital-analog conversion necessary for playback is performed in software by the driver, the sound quality is inferior to what you get when playing back files through the dedicated DACs of a sound card or even the on-board Mac DACs. But it works; well, sort of. It works on most Windows PCs and most Windows programs.

Anyway, Microsoft inexplicably left the PC Speaker driver out of the standard Windows 3.1 distribution; but you can get it free from the Microsoft Windows BBS (206-637-9009), or from a number of other BBSs, including CompuServe. You also can order it from Microsoft End User Sales (800-426-9400) for about $20. Similar drivers also are included in some Windows programs, including GRasp, a DOS-based authoring tool.

We expect that the driver eventually will make its way into the standard Windows distribution, giving most Windows machines simple sound playback capability. Even so, if your multimedia production includes complex sound and music and it is targeted at a PC, you'd better make sure that target machine includes a sound card.

Fortunately, with the advent of the multimedia personal computers (MPCs), sound cards are becoming more standard. But of course, as is always the case with PC "standards," you can't count on a standard level of sound support in the PC world. However, under Windows, each sound card manufacturer supplies a single drive that any program written for Windows can use. Under DOS, the Sound Blaster standard has been around for years, is the basis for most DOS game sounds, and is supported by most sound cards.

Microsoft offers some sound tools for Windows multimedia developers in the Multimedia Development Kit (MDK). To convert audio files from the Mac's AIFF format to Windows .WAV file format, you can use the MDK's Convert tool. The converter will translate 11.025 kHz and 22.05 kHz sound files, but conversion of CD-quality 44.1 kHz samples is not supported.

Wave for Win Demo ⌘ 702

Once these sound files are converted, you can edit them—setting volume, fades, and mixing channels—with the MDK's WaveEdit tool, or with a commercial sound editing package such as Turtle Beach's Wave for Windows. In Director, sound brought in as a castmember will play back on either platform, whether it originated as an AIFF or wav file.

Multiplatform Applications

Cross-platform applications that allow you to create a presentation on the Mac and play it back on the PC (and vice versa) have begun to spring up. These programs include total authoring environments, such as Director and AuthorWare, that allow you to create integrated presentations incorporating sound, graphics, and even video. Other programs, such as MediaVision's MotIVE and CoSA's PACo, focus on cross-platform components like video and animation.

Director 4.0 Demo ⌘ 708

AuthorWare Prof. 3.0 Demo
⌘ 709

These programs can save you a lot of time and effort, and many developers who do a lot of cross-platform work will become expert in one or more of the tools. However, even if you rely on an authoring environment such as Director, don't expect to develop your presentation once, sit back while it converts, and have it run perfectly; chances are, you'll still have to do a lot of tweaking of fonts, colors, and sound-file formats.

And, of course, you'll have to do this by going back to the Mac or PC, because many cross-platform multimedia tools have their complete authoring environment on only one of the platforms, with just a "runtime" version on the other.

Even programs that are completely duplicated in both environments—so-called "sibling applications"—have idiosyncrasies that may drive you nuts. Fonts, fill and ink effects, placed art, and macros are particularly notorious for not making the crossing even between sibling applications.

To help ease the burden of transition, try the conversion many times during the course of development. Don't wait until you've finished a presentation before trying to convert files and checking them out on the target platform. Converting your work several times a day will help minimize the reworking process.

Macromedia's Director

Multimedia developers everywhere have applauded Director 4.0, the first Director release that runs on both the PC and the Mac. Both versions of Director create a binary file that is playable on either platform, but you'll need to bundle the file with a "Projector" player for each platform.

The Projector files are completely self-contained and can be freely distributed.

Apple Media Tool

The Apple Media Kit provides entry-level users with a vehicle for creating Mac or cross-platform multimedia presentations without having to do any scripting. Priced at less than $3,000, the full package includes an object-oriented authoring program called The Apple Media Tool (available separately for less than

$1,500) and the VideoFusion QuickTime editor. For details, see Chapter 7, "Authoring Tools."

Media Tool runs only on the Mac but can create a file that will run under Windows. Apple includes a handy utility that checks and converts files for Windows playback.

CoSA's PACo

Designed primarily to compress animation and sound files for playback on the Mac, PACo also has several add-on utilities that allow you to play back animation files, sound files, and QuickTime movies under Windows and the Sun SPARCStation. The Windows Player costs $199 and requires a Super VGA's 256 colors to play back animations and movies. For $199, you also can buy XPlay-PACo, which lets you play back PACo animations and movies from within HyperCard, SuperCard, and AuthorWare on the PC.

Other Cross-Platform Applications

MacroModel 1.5 Demo ⌘ 720

In the past year, several important sibling applications have made their appearance. Adobe now offers a Windows version of Photoshop. Macromedia's Action, a popular multimedia presentation program, now has both Mac and Windows versions (although the Windows version is currently in a later release). For 3-D animators, Macromedia has also released a Windows version of its high-end modeler, MacroModel.

A few other programs offer cross-platform compatibility, but are not, strictly speaking, multimedia applications. AuthorWare Professional is a high-end authoring tool frequently used for building interactive training applications. It's expensive ($4,995 for each platform), but it converts files very well, retaining most elements—with the exception of some fonts and external commands (see Chapter 7, "Authoring Tools," for more details).

Object Plus's WinPlus, modeled after HyperCard, also has good cross-platform compatibility. If your presentations are limited to basic multimedia effects such as simple animation, graphics, and sound, Plus is a good buy at $495 per platform. Plus supports 256 colors in its Mac version but only 16 colors in the Windows implementation. Another way to get your Mac HyperCard stacks over to the PC is to use Convert It! from Heizer Software. This $199 package converts HyperCard stacks to a form usable by Asymmetrix Toolbook, a popular PC authoring tool.

10

Producing Sound

Director 4.0 Demo ⌘ 708
Premiere 4.0 Demo ⌘ 722

Sound should be an integral part of your multimedia project. It may be central to the project's focus, or it can be used to simply add polish to the presentation, fill disc access periods, or enhance navigation. This chapter introduces you to basic principles of sound and the recording process and continues with a discussion of special recording considerations for narration and electronic sound sources. It also examines the various file formats and considerations for importing and storing sounds, synchronization during the dubbing process, and its use with three popular multimedia production tools: Director, Premiere, and QuickTime. The chapter closes with a number of tips and tricks for digital audio, MIDI, and multimedia sound in general.

Audio Overview

From browsing through this book, you're probably starting to get a good grip on the science and technology behind multimedia's visual elements, whether still images, animation, or video. Now it's time to dive into sound. If you are going to produce sound for multimedia, you'll benefit by understanding some of the finer points of sound's quantifiable characteristics: frequency, amplitude, envelope, phase, and harmonic content. Some of this may seem technical at first, but will serve you well when you're using the incredibly precise controls afforded by digital sound tools.

Frequency

Sound—like color and light—consists of waves. One difference is that sound waves or sound-pressure waves are transmitted through the air through periodic compression and rarefaction of air molecules by a vibrating body such as the

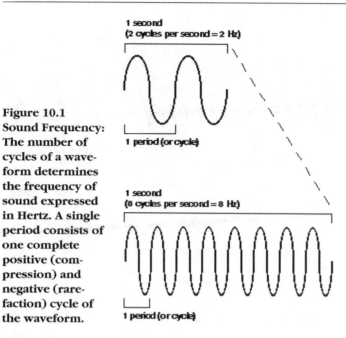

**Figure 10.1
Sound Frequency:
The number of
cycles of a wave-
form determines
the frequency of
sound expressed
in Hertz. A single
period consists of
one complete
positive (com-
pression) and
negative (rare-
faction) cycle of
the waveform.**

string of a musical instrument, a loudspeaker, or your vocal chords. Compared to the blindingly fast pace of light waves (186,300 miles per second), sound waves travel at the snail's pace of between 1,088 and 1,130 feet per second, depending upon temperature and altitude.

The terms *frequency* or *pitch* refer to the number of wave cycles (called periods) that occur in a second (see Figure 10.1). The number of cycles per second in this context is measured in *Hertz*. When a string is vibrating at 262 cycles per second (262Hz) we call that pitch "middle C." All multiples of this frequency are also referred to as "C"; we perceive them to be higher or lower variants of the same pitch. Therefore, 131Hz is the C below middle C (referred as being an octave below middle C), 524Hz is an octave above middle C, 1048Hz is the pitch two octaves above middle C. Most children have a hearing range of 20Hz to 20,000Hz. With advancing age, adults gradually lose the top 5,000Hz of the spectrum.

In the previous example, notice that the progression of frequencies is exponential. That is, the interval between 131Hz and 262Hz (an octave) covers 131Hz; but the distance between the C above middle C and the C two octaves above middle C covers 524Hz, although we perceive these distances to be equivalent (see Figure 10.2). Another unit of measurement, the cent, divides an octave into 1,200 equal parts regardless of the difference in frequencies between the two pitches making up the octave.

**Figure 10.2
Octave Equiva-
lence: Doubling
the frequency of
a sound, that is,
increasing the
number of cycles
per second by a
factor of two,
raises the per-
ceived pitch by
one octave. There
are 1,200 cents
per octave.**

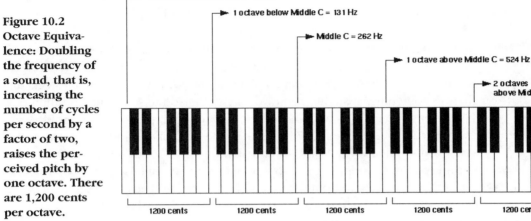

Amplitude

The second important characteristic of sound is its *amplitude* (see Figure 10.3). This refers to the perceived loudness. You have experience adjusting this characteristic by turning a knob on your stereo system. Amplitude is really much more complex than your stereo volume control makes it seem. The term designates the amount of pressure exerted by a single instance of a sound wave when compared to normal atmospheric pressure. Such pressure indicates a displacement of air molecules within a range of .00001 to .001 of an inch and is measured in units called *decibels* (dB). As a point of reference, the threshold of human hearing is assigned 0 dB. Audience noise is generally around 40 dB, while a jet engine exceeds 150 dB. Most conversation falls between 30 and 60 dB. A classical music performance rarely sustains levels greater than 95 dB, while rock

**Figure 10.3
Sound Amplitude:
Amplitude refers
to the perceived
loudness of a
soundwave typi-
cally measured in
decibels. The
visual shape
described by
changes in vol-
ume is called the
amplitude enve-
lope. Notice that
frequency is
independent of
amplitude.**

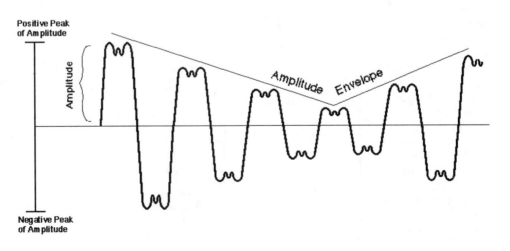

music concerts can reach 115 to 120 dB for the people sitting in the front row. One hundred twenty dB is considered the threshold of pain.

Envelope

More often than not, a sound's amplitude changes over time. About the first third of a second is referred to as the sound's attack. At this point there is an initial rise in volume, often to the maximum level of the particular sound. Following this there is sometimes a slight drop or decay in the sound's volume and then perhaps a lengthy sustained volume level followed by a rapid, or not so rapid, dying away of the sound. The four segments of this simplified model—attack, decay, sustain, and release (or ADSR)—represent the *envelope* of the sound. Note that complex sounds undergo many other changes of amplitude as the volume levels of their component frequencies change over time. The attack segment is one of the primary characteristics of a sound that provide audible "clues" to aid us in distinguishing, for example, a trumpet from a flute. (Another important signature to a sound is its harmonic content, discussed below.)

Phase

Phase is an important sound phenomenon that happens when two identical sound waves are received by a listener or microphone at slightly different times (see Figure 10.4). This can occur when we listen to two loudspeakers, one closer to us than the other. Phase also takes place when a sound wave bounces off a reflective surface and arrives at your ear or microphone slightly later than the nonreflected sound wave. Phase is measured in degrees from 0 to 360. Remember that each cycle (or period) of a sound wave has a compression and rarefaction stage. In its simplest form, this can be represented as a *sine wave*. The beginning of the cycle is 0 degrees; the peak of the compression side (the pos-

Figure 10.4 Soundwave Phase: Phase comes into play when a reflected or otherwise duplicated version of the same soundwave arrives at your ear slightly later than the original waveform. If the two sounds arrive 180 degrees out apart, the waveforms "cancel" each other out and silence ensues.

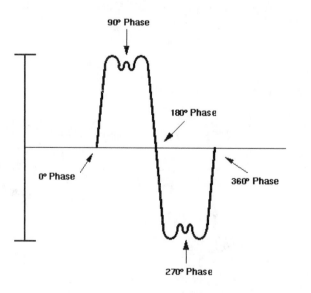

itive side) is 90 degrees; 180 degrees is the point at which the sound crosses the zero point between compression and rarefaction; 270 degrees is the peak of the rarefaction stage; and finally, 360 degrees is the point at which the rarefaction stage returns to equilibrium at the end of the cycle. When a reflected copy of a sound wave begins as the compression stage of the original sound is peaking, the sound waves are said to be *90 degrees out of phase*. When sound waves are 180 degrees out of phase they cancel each other out and we perceive silence. Many interesting special effects rely upon shifting the phase of a sound in relation to a copy of itself.

Harmonics

Sound waves are usually much more complex than simple sine waves. In reality, most sound waves can be demonstrated to be the product of many, many sine waves occurring simultaneously (the principle behind additive synthesis). When sound waves such as sine waves are combined, other frequencies are present in the resulting sound. These are called *partials, overtones,* or *harmonics* of that sound (see Figure 10.5). The component sound wave with the lowest frequency is referred to as the *fundamental* frequency because this is the wave that determines the perceived pitch of the sound. The relative amplitudes of the upper partials making up a complex sound wave taken together determine the "timbre" of a sound and provide our ears with information that lets us distinguish one instrument from another when all other characteristics (frequency, amplitude, phase, etc.) are identical.

Figure 10.5 Harmonic Content: With the exception of pure sine waves or similar wave shapes, all sounds contain additional frequency components of lower amplitude. This phenomena is referred to as harmonic content and helps determine the timbre of a sound. The loudest, normally the lowest, frequency partial making up a sound determines the perceived pitch.

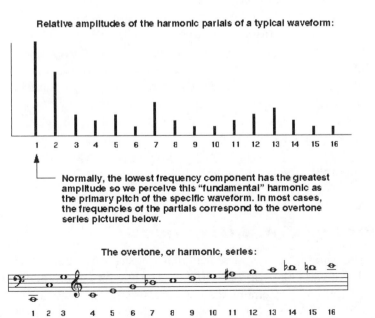

Relative amplitudes of the harmonic parlals of a typical waveform:

Normally, the lowest frequency component has the greatest amplitude so we perceive this "fundamental" harmonic as the primary pitch of the specific waveform. In most cases, the frequencies of the partials correspond to the overtone series pictured below.

The overtone, or harmonic, series:

Recording Sound

During the sound recording process we often speak of the "sound recording chain." The links in this chain include microphones, mixers, signal processors, analog or digital recording systems, amplifiers, and speakers. Like any chain, it is only as strong as its weakest link. Using $20 microphones with a $2,000 tape recorder is not going to sound any better than using $2,000 microphones with a $20 tape recorder. However, using $2,000 microphones with a $2,000 tape recorder will make a difference. Unfortunately, multimedia producers typically have little or no control over the final link in the chain: the speakers used to play back the sound elements accompanying their endeavors. Because of this fact, it is important to provide audio of the highest quality possible.

Using Microphones

Microphones record sound by converting sound waves into electrical impulses as they strike a stationary transducer such as a thin sheet of conductive metal called a *diaphragm.* Although their outward appearance may be similar or identical, microphones exhibit different degrees of directionality. *Omnidirectional* microphones respond equally to sound arriving from any direction. *Bidirectional* microphones pick up sound in a "figure eight" pattern, with a dead spot in the center of the eight. There are three main types of *unidirectional* microphones available, all relying on a variation of a heart-shaped (cardioid) pattern of sensitivity. *Cardioid, supercardioid,* and *hypercardioid* microphones provide progressively more focused response fields.

A microphone may be directly routed to your recording system; however, a mixer is essential when recording multiple sound sources. Mixers let you control the proportions of a large variety of sound sources by moving knobs or faders while monitoring the incoming and outgoing signal through VU meters or LED bars, most of which provide some indication, such as a red area, of when the signal is too "hot" and thus prone to distortion. Some mixers offer *equalization* (EQ), the capability of boosting or cutting various frequency bands (like the treble and bass controls on your home stereo); access to signal processing (effects such as reverberation, chorusing, flanging, compression, expansion, and limiting); and options to pan a signal in various degrees to the left or right channel of the stereo output to which the incoming audio is being mixed.

Special Recording Considerations

The nature of your source material—music, sound effects, or narration—may mandate a particular approach to the recording process. When recording live material, microphone placement becomes an issue. When recording from electronic sources, signal processing (often to simulate microphone placement) is a factor.

Miking Strategies

With a live sound source, you must consider the type and proximity of the microphones as well as their directional placement. *Close miking* places the microphone less than a meter from the sound source. *Distant miking* employs microphones farther than a meter from the sound source. When you are recording with distant miking, it may be advantageous to use an "accent" microphone placed in or near the close miking field to highlight one particular instrument or sound source. Likewise, when using predominantly close miking, you might want to place an "ambient" microphone at a spot where the room ambiance or reflected sound is stronger than the primary source.

Four popular techniques for stereo miking are spaced miking, X-Y miking, M-S (mid-side), and binaural miking (see Figure 10.6).

Spaced Miking

The *spaced miking* approach relies on the 3:1 principle, which dictates that the distance between the two microphones should be at least three times the distance between the microphone and the source. For example, if the microphones are 10 feet from the sound source, they should be at least 30 feet apart. The rationale revolves around considerations of phase distortion. Obviously, this method is best suited for closer miking situations.

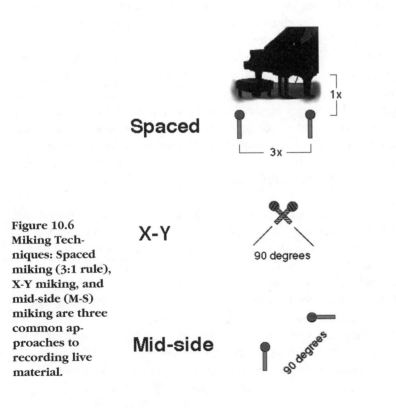

Figure 10.6 Miking Techniques: Spaced miking (3:1 rule), X-Y miking, and mid-side (M-S) miking are three common approaches to recording live material.

| *X-Y Miking* | The *X-Y miking* approach employs two identical microphones (usually directional or cardioid) in the center of the stereo field with their diaphragms as close together as possible. The microphones should be placed at right angles to one another, and the tip of the right angle should be pointed toward the sound source. Larger angles may be used to widen the perceived width of the stereo image. |

| *M-S Miking* | *M-S miking* (mid-side method) uses a *mid*-cardioid microphone aimed directly at the sound source and a microphone with a "side" figure-eight response pattern directed 90 degrees from the mid microphone. M-S miking requires an additional hardware matrix system to assemble the stereo image from the two signals. |

| *Binaural Miking* | Finally, *binaural miking* is optimized for headphone playback. Two omnidirectional microphones are mounted in the ears of a dummy head (you can also place them about 6 inches apart with a baffle between). This miking method should not be used for material intended to be played back through loudspeakers. |

Recording Spoken Words

You should take special care in recording narration or any spoken material included in your multimedia project. Try to record vocal material with a directional (cardioid) microphone placed 1 inch to 2 feet from the speaker (after experimenting to determine the optimum distance). Positioning a cardioid microphone too close to the speaker can increase the low frequency content, which may or may not be the effect you want.

Certain consonants can cause undesirable pops and noise during vocal recording. The letters *p*, *t*, and *k* are notorious for this. *Pop filters* or foam wind screens affixed to the microphone can reduce these annoyances, albeit with the possibility of reducing high frequency response as well. The sibilants *s* and *sh* can introduce unwanted hiss into a recording. A special signal processor called a de-esser is one solution to this problem. Another way to eliminate both popping and hissing is to angle the microphone so that the voice passes across the response field rather than directly into the diaphragm.

| *Ambient Noise* | When recording speech, keep alert for ambient noise. If some segments are recorded with ambiance while others are not, the effect is irritating. It's a good idea to record a few minutes of pure room ambiance as a precaution—if necessary you can mix this in with the voice to achieve an even effect. |

Uneven recording levels can produce an effect on listeners similar to unnatural handling of ambient noise. Besides coaching your speaker in vocalization techniques, you can get around recording level disparities by using a signal processor called a compressor/limiter. Such devices, when used in their compressor mode, even out the dynamic levels so that they fall within a specifiable range. Sounds that are too soft have their volume levels boosted, while those that are too loud get softened. You will probably experience better results if you apply compression during the initial recording, although there is no reason not to do so during mixdown.

Direct Instrument Recording

Electronic instruments such as synthesizers, samplers, sound modules, and electric guitars, may be recorded "direct" without the use of a microphone. The primary concern is matching the device output levels with the mixer input levels. Many sound modules and signal processors are switchable from balanced or unbalanced +4 dB (1.23 volts) to unbalanced –10 dB (3.16 volts); but for those that are not, you may need to invest in a piece of hardware known as a direct box or direct insert box (DI box) to make the conversion.

The Mixing Process

When multitrack recording systems of any kind enter the picture, you'll need some method to mix the various tracks down to a single stereo or monophonic signal. When the source material is multitrack tape, the mixdown medium might be DAT, hard disk, or even analog tape (see Chapter 4, "Sound Tools"). During the mixdown stage, additional EQ, signal processing, and other effects can be introduced into the signal. For multimedia production, all sound will eventually have to be in a disc-based digital audio format; so keep this in mind when considering mixdown methods.

Ping-ponging

Often it is possible to mix a collection of tracks in any system down to two free stereo tracks on the same system, rendering the need for a separate mixdown system superfluous. This technique, called track bouncing or *ping-ponging*, needn't be limited to the mixdown stage; it can also be used at intermediate points in the production process to reclaim tracks for new material. One important advantage that digital systems have over analog in this area is that whenever an analog track is copied to another analog track, about 10 dB of signal degradation is introduced into the audio. (This is called "generation loss" because each subsequent copy is referred to as a new generation of the original material. By the third generation, the corruption will become audible for an average listener.) Analog track bouncing is subject to this progressive degeneration, whereas digital track bouncing results in no signal loss or additional noise.

Creating Special Effects

Signal processing, often called *effects,* refers to the ability to route from a mixer or synthesizer—via a jack labeled *effects send* or *aux send*—a controllable amount of the incoming signal to an external device for modification. The transformed signal is then sent back to the mixer via a jack labeled *effects return* or *aux return.* A knob on the mixer usually provides control over the proportion of the original signal that is mixed in with the returning processed signal.

   Typical signal-processing effects include *reverberation*, to simulate multiple reflections of a sound wave from one surface to another; *digital delay,* to create echo effects that repeat a replica of the sound at varying intervals; *chorusing*, where an original signal is combined with delayed copies, and the delay time is varied randomly or periodically to simulate multiple sound sources; *phase shifting*, to produce a variety of special effects that depend upon the amount of phase between two copies of a waveform; *flanging*, which is accomplished by combining a signal with minute fluctuating pitch with an otherwise identical, nonfluctuating signal; *pitch-shifting*, to alter the pitch of a sound without changing its duration; *compression*, to decrease the width of the dynamic range of a signal (the distance between the softest and loudest levels); *expansion*, the opposite of compression; *limiting*, to reduce the peak volume; *gating,* to pass through only those signals that exceed a specified strength; and *spatialization,* to create 3-D effects or otherwise place a sound at a designated location.

Importing and Storing Sounds for Multimedia

All audio for multimedia must be in a digital format. If you have recorded all your source material using a 16-bit hard disk recording system (such as Digidesign's SoundTools, ProTools, or Audiomedia; Mark of the Unicorn's Digital Waveboard; or MediaVision's PAS16 [Pro Audio Spectrum 16—the 16 stands for 16-bit]) or a PC card such as Creative Labs' 16 or AWE32, Turtle Beach's Mavi, or an Antex card, or an 8-bit system (such as Articulate Systems' Voice Impact or Voice Impact Pro, Macromedia's MacRecorder [bundled with SoundEdit Pro], or the built-in hardware of the Macintosh) or a Creative Labs or MediaVision card on the PC, you are well ahead of the game. If your source material is on analog tape, you have another recording stage to go through. If the material is on digital tape, and you have a sound card supporting digital I/O—a Digidesign card, for example—you will probably be able to transfer the digital audio data without reentering the analog domain.

Wave for Win Demo ⌘ 702

SoundEdit 16 Demo ⌘ 707

What format is best for storing audio data in on your hard disk? You will recall from Chapter 4, "Sound Tools," that a wide variety of soundfile formats are available. Common formats include 8- and 16-bit AIFF and AIFC (compressed form of AIFF), 'snd ' resource, System 7 sound (type sfil—note the lowercase), SoundEdit (type FSSD), SoundEdit Pro (type 'jB1 '), Sound Designer (I and II, type SFIL—note the uppercase) and wav. Of these, AIFF is the most universal and is commonly used both on the Mac and under Windows, while wav is the most common PC format.

Dubbing and Synchronization

Synchronizing audio to visuals is not as simple as making sure that both elements start playing back simultaneously. Inevitably, they will drift apart. The film industry has taught us that even a two-frame difference between a visual event and its corresponding audio event in a video running at 30 fps will be perceived by the audience as being out of sync. With digital video frame rates typically hovering around 15 fps, this means that you cannot risk being more than a single frame off at critical synchronization points (often referred to as *hit points*, *dead hits*, or simply *hits*).

When two or more elements—for example, a QuickTime movie and incoming audio data—are synchronized, the software or device controlling one element provides the master clock reference to which the other *slave* components are related. There are three common methods of synchronization: pulse- or clock-oriented, relative addressing, and absolute addressing (sometimes referred to as time code). Multimedia software generally supports the latter two approaches, if any.

Relative addressing requires that synchronized programs keep track of the current location as an offset in standardized units relative to the beginning of the music or visuals. The most common form of relative synchronization originated in the world of MIDI and is called Song Position Pointer (SPP). During SPP synchronization, all synchronized software tracks the number of sixteenth notes from the beginning of the video, animation, or music. This allows you to issue commands such as "advance to the 1597th sixteenth note." Software with this feature does not require you to count sixteenth notes; rather, conversions are built into the interface. In QuickTime or AVI video, another method would be to count frames.

SMPTE Time Code

Absolute addressing is a more accurate method for synchronization in which every event has unique address. As we discussed in the video chapters, the film and video industry use a protocol known as SMPTE time code (SMPTE stands for the Society of Motion Picture and Television Engineers). SMPTE time code provides an absolute address in hours, minutes, seconds, and frames for video. It is also used for audio data and to relate audio data to video data.

SMPTE time code addresses are called time code words. While in computer lingo a "word" is two bytes (16 bits), SMPTE time code words are 80 bits in length. You can think of this as 10 bytes; however, it is more accurate to consider these 80 bits as sixteen 4-bit "nibbles" followed by a 16-bit sync word. Each nibble can designate a number from 0 to 9. The SMPTE address "02:34:21:08," for example, means 2 hours, 34 minutes, 21 seconds, and 8 frames (see Figure 10.7).

The fact that there are a number of different frame rates to which SMPTE time code is applied can be problematic in some situations. In the United States, video is standardized at 30 fps, although since the introduction of color, tape actually travels at 29.97 fps (more precisely, 29.97002617 fps). European videotape travels at 25 fps, and standard 35 mm film uses 24 fps (see Figure 10.8).

Drop Frame Time Code

Because SMPTE assigns 30 addresses to a space in which only 29.97 frames pass, a system called *drop frame* time code emerged to correct for the extra 108 frame numbers per hour that result (if a 108-frame discrepancy per hour doesn't seem

ONE VIDEO FRAME

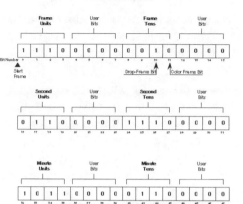

**Figure 10.7
A SMPTE Word:
Each SMPTE
address requires
80 bits of data to
express the digits
representing a
unique location
expressed in
hours, minutes,
seconds, and
frames.**

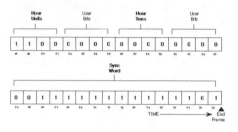

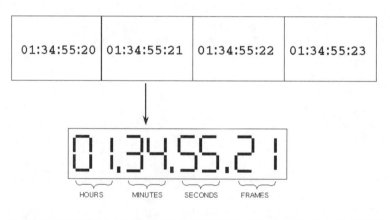

**Figure 10.8
SMPTE Frame
Rates: A table of
the six most
common SMPTE
frame rates
appear below a
typical SMPTE
display.**

24 fps	Film
25 fps	European (PAL) video
30 fps non-drop	American black and white video (also used for audio applications)
30 fps drop-frame	American color video (will not agree with wall clock)
29.97 fps non-drop	American color video (NTSC — will not agree with wall clock)
29.97 fps drop-frame	American color video (NTSC and broadcast)

**Figure 10.9
Drop Frame:
Drop-frame
SMPTE drops the
first two frame
numbers (not
actual frames)
after each minute
passes (except at
minutes 00, 10,
20, 30, 40, and 50)
to ensure that
video tape travel-
ing at 29.97 fps
agrees with the
actual time
elapsed.**

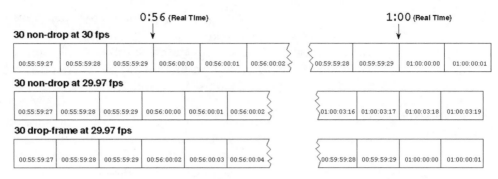

significant, remember that only two frames are necessary to perceive elements as being out of sync). Drop frame time code works like this: Every time the *minutes* value of the time code address increases by 1, the first two frames of the next minute are dropped. In other words, the frame after 02:34:21:29 is 02:34:21:02, and not, as you might expect, 02:34:21:00. Dropping two frames every minute results in a loss of 120 frames every hour; so to reclaim 12 dropped frames, the two frames are not dropped at minutes 00, 10, 20, 30, 40, and 50, resulting in a total of 108 dropped frames per hour and thus guaranteeing that the frame count and the clock on the wall will always be in agreement. Note that the dropping of frames in drop frame time code only skips address numbers; no actual frames are omitted (see Figure 10.9).

SMPTE time code is not directly compatible with MIDI; so when external MIDI devices or background MIDI software processes are in the synchronization loop, SMPTE time code gets converted to MIDI time code (MTC), a related protocol that was standardized in early 1987. The conversion is transparent to the user, because all MTC compatible software expresses addresses in standard SMPTE formats.

At the time of this writing, all software on the Mac offering SMPTE-to-MIDI synchronization relied upon Apple's MIDI Manager for timing support. MIDI Manager (discussed in Chapter 4, "Sound Tools") performs all the required conversions between the various MTC synchronization formats from 30 fps non-drop, 30 fps drop frame, 25 fps, and 24 fps to the format required by the software being synchronized.

For more perspectives on synching sound and video, see Chapter 14, "Creating Video."

Using Sounds With Applications

The sound capabilities of multimedia software are as varied as the interfaces to access these audio features. Compared to graphics software, where certain standardized interface conventions are observed, sound manipulation in multimedia is a regular turkey shoot. Examining three cross-platform software options in detail—Macromedia Director, Adobe Premiere, and Apple's QuickTime—will clarify this state of affairs. For the most robust implementation of digital audio, MIDI, and synchronization in multimedia to date, check out the discussion of Passport Producer in Chapter 4, "Sound Tools."

Sound in Director

Director 4.0 Demo ⌘ 708

Macromedia Director has had a long history of audio support stretching back to earlier incarnations as VideoWorks. One result of this extensive background is support of practically any soundfile format currently in use. Furthermore, the program provides access to CD audio, digital audio NuBus cards, and speech synthesis.

Smaller sounds can be stored as a member of Director's *cast*. Likewise, sound stored as sound-only QuickTime movies can be designated as cast members. The disadvantage to this approach is that your file size increases accordingly; so it's usually better to place longer sounds in Director's external *Sounds* file so they are loaded when required.

The enhancement to Director's Lingo scripting language that allows you to jump to a specified frame in a QuickTime movie essentially provides you with random access to soundfiles stored as sound-only movies.

Sound Syntax for Lingo

A more sophisticated use of Lingo for sound that often goes unnoticed allows you to open up an additional six channels and designate them for playback of different soundfiles. Such soundfiles must be accessed by way of the Sound play File and puppetSound commands. (The former requires only one line of scripting and bypasses PuppetSound, making it a simple solution for novice Lingo users.) For sounds controlled by Lingo, you have the added advantage of executing controlled fades (both in and out) on an individual channel basis for durations specified in ticks (1/60 of a second). Finally, Lingo offers you the full range of 256 volume levels for your puppetSounds.

puppetSound (Command) Causes the Sound channel to act as a puppet so that it can be controlled by Lingo (under script control). It is not necessary to place anything in the Sound channels of the score. In fact, puppetSounds override sounds that may simultaneously exist in the score's Sound channel. They continue to play even if you load another movie. At the time of this writing, the puppetSound command did not work with the second sound channel (i.e., the lower of the score's sound channels).

puppetSound *castmemberName* Starts playing a sound stored in the Cast. Note: To use AIFF soundfiles as castmembers in Director for Macintosh, you need System 6.0.7 or later.

puppetSound *menuItemNumber*, *subMenuItemNumber* Starts playing a sound stored in an external Director Sounds file. Specify the menu item number (if it is a letter, use A=10, B=11, C=12, D=13, E=14, F=15) and the submenu item number.

puppetSound 0 Turns off continuous sound and returns control of sound to the score's Sound channel.

puppetSound *midiOption* (see below under "MIDI in Director")

soundEnabled

set the soundEnabled = *expression* (Property) Turns sound on or off. Example:set the soundEnabled = not (the soundEnabled) toggles the sound on or off depending on the previous state.

put the soundEnabled into *variableName* Returns TRUE if sound is enabled.

sound fadeIn (requires System 6.0.7 or later)

sound fadeIn *whichChannel [1 to 8]* Fades in sound on the specified channel for a period of frames, unless ticks (see next) are specified. If ticks are not specified, the default setting is 15*(60/[Tempo setting of first frame of fade in]).

sound fadeIn *whichChannel, ticks* Fades in sound on the specified channel for the specified number of ticks (¹⁄₆₀ of second).

sound fadeOut (requires System 6.0.7 or later)

sound fadeOut *whichChannel [1 to 8]* Fades out sound on the specified channel for a period of frames, unless ticks (see next) are specified. If ticks are not specified, the default setting is 15*(60/[Tempo setting of first frame of fade out]).

sound fadeOut *whichChannel, ticks* Fades out sound on the specified channel for the specified number of ticks (¹⁄₆₀ of second).

sound playFile (requires System 6.0.7 or later) Note that the PC version of Director can play wav sounds, while the Mac version cannot; if you're creating a cross-platform project, make sure all sounds are stored as AIFF files. Note also that if you are mixing external and Director cast sounds, they all must be recorded at the same frequency, or you will lose the higher number channel sounds.

sound playFile *whichChannel [1 to 8], whichFile [name of file in quotes]* Starts playback on the channel indicated by *whichChannel* of an external AIFF sound stored in *whichFile*.

sound stop (requires System 6.0.7 or later)

sound stop *whichChannel [1 to 8]* Stops sound playback on the specified channel.

soundBusy (requires System 6.0.7 or later)

soundBusy(*whichChannel***)** (Function) Returns TRUE (1) if the specified channel is currently playing a sound or FALSE (0) if it isn't. If you use sound-Busy() to determine the status of a puppetSound, you must place an updateStage command between the puppetSound command and the soundBusy( ) function. Example: if soundBusy(1) then sound stop 1.

the soundLevel

set the soundLevel to 7 (Property) Sets the level of sound playing through the Macintosh speaker or external audio jack. 0 = no sound, 7 = maximum volume.

put the soundLevel into *variableName* Puts the current sound level setting (0 to 7) into the specified variable.

the volume of sound (requires System 6.0.7 or later)

set the volume of sound *whichChannel[1 to 8] to level [0 to 255]* Sets the volume of the sound on the specified channel (Channels 1 and 2 are the Score sound channels) to a level between 0 and 255.

put the volume of sound *whichChannel[1 to 8]* into *variableName* Puts the volume of the sound on the specified channel (Channels 1 and 2 are the Score sound channels) into the specified variable.

the multiSound

put the multiSound into *variableName* (Function) Returns TRUE (1) if the current System software is capable of multichannel sound playback, or FALSE (0) if it isn't.

noSound

playAccel *whichFile,* noSound Used in conjunction with the PlayAccel command to play back an accelerated movie without any sound that may be associated with it.

MIDI in Director

Macromedia somewhat inexplicably eliminated MIDI support in Director 4.0. Older versions of Director had at least rudimentary MIDI implementation, which supported the standard SPP synchronization messages: Start, Stop, Continue, Beat (MIDI Clocks), Song Select, Song Position Pointer. These commands let you trigger songs and start, stop, and continue playback at any measure in external MIDI sequencers (for example, a Roland Sound Brush), or MIDI sequencer software running in the background, or both at once. Chapter 4, "Sound Tools," provides information for enhancing the MIDI capabilities of Director and other multimedia software through the addition of external resources known as XCMDs. In Windows, MIDI control is provided through MCI commands, which control Windows' built-in MIDI sequencer.

The following Lingo messages provide relative synchronization of MIDI sequences with Director (prior to version 4.0 on the Mac):

puppetSound midiStart Sends a MIDI Start message to the attached MIDI Manager port. Sets the SPP to zero and starts playback at the beginning of the sequence.

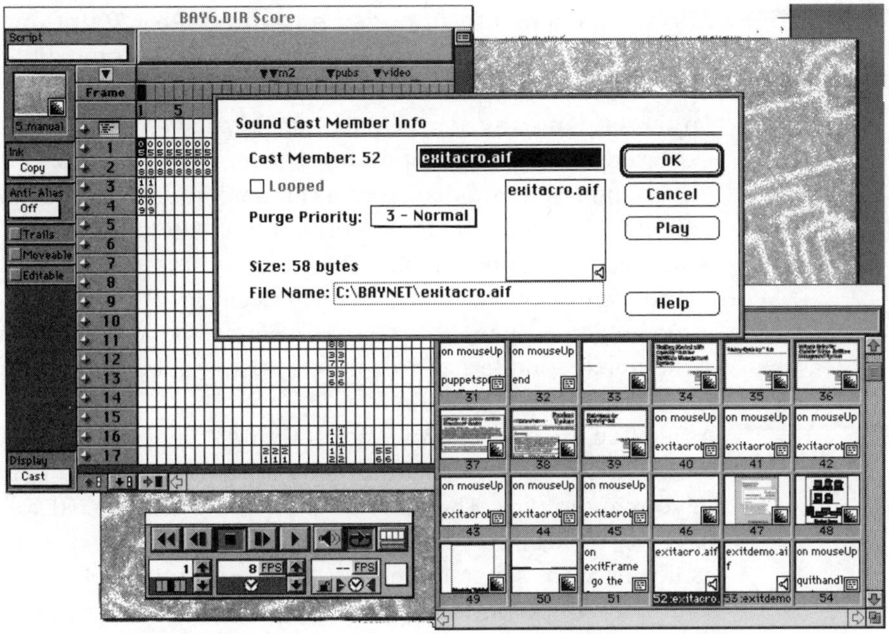

Figure 10.10
Sound in Direc-
tor: Macromedia
Director offers a
flexible sound
environment
supporting many
soundfile formats
(both stored as
"cast members"
and external to
the document) as
well as CD audio,
digital audio
NuBus cards,
speech synthesis,
and MIDI.

puppetSound midiStop Sends a MIDI Stop message to the attached MIDI Manager port. Halts playback without resetting the SPP. All SPP counters retain the current value.

puppetSound midiContinue Sends a MIDI Continue message to the attached MIDI Manager port. Resumes playback at the current SPP location, often equivalent to the location stored when the last Stop message was issued. SPP counters resume their count from the current location.

puppetSound midiBeat, *[4 to 280]* Sets the tempo of the sequence being controlled by midiStart, midiStop, and midiContinue. Serves as the "pulse" or metronome: 24 PPQN (pulses per quarter note).

puppetSound midiSong, *[0 to 127]* Sends a MIDI Song Select message to the attached MIDI Manager port. Instructs sequencers (both hardware and software) that provide for multiple *songs* which song to cue up to be played at the next issuance of a Start message. (Message can only be sent when sequences are not playing.)

puppetSound midisongPointer, *beat[1 to 4], measure[1 to 1023]* Sends a MIDI Song Position Pointer (SPP) message to the attached MIDI Manager port. Sends a location (or address) of a beat measured in 16th notes (a 16th note is equal to six MIDI Clocks) from the beginning of the sequence. The software in your Macintosh or in a hardware sequencer keeps track of this number whenever you start playback of a sequence while using this method of synchronization. The maximum sequence length supported by SPP is 45 minutes.

Sound in Premiere

Premiere 4.0 Demo ⌘ 722

Adobe Premiere 4.0 supports up to three 8- or 16-bit, mono or stereo audio tracks at sampling rates of 5, 11, 22, or 44.1 kHz. Compatible file formats include AIFF, 'snd ' resources, 'sfil' format soundfiles, and SoundEdit files and wav files on the PC; and any sound data you may have imported into Premiere may be exported as 8-bit or 16-bit mono or stereo AIFF files as well as wav files on the PC. Sound tracks are displayed as an amplitude waveform or, optionally, a simple line (to reduce the time required to create a waveform display). For stereo soundfiles, only one channel is visible in the display. One annoyance inherent in Premiere's sound handling is that because all tracks are considered to be the same length, adding, for example, a single sound effect on a track will have the same impact on file size as if the track contained continual audio data.

Linking Audio and Video Data

As is often the case in professional sound editing programs, cut, copy, and paste are nondestructive operations that simply move pointers to the specified locations in your audio data. The razor tool lets you make logical splits in soundfiles that have no impact upon the actual file but permit you to deal with soundfile regions as if they were separate entities. Premiere provides frame-accurate designation of in-and-out points to any soundfile. If you need to work independently on the sound track of a movie that contains visual material—perhaps to move it to another location or another set of visuals—you must first unlink it from its asso-

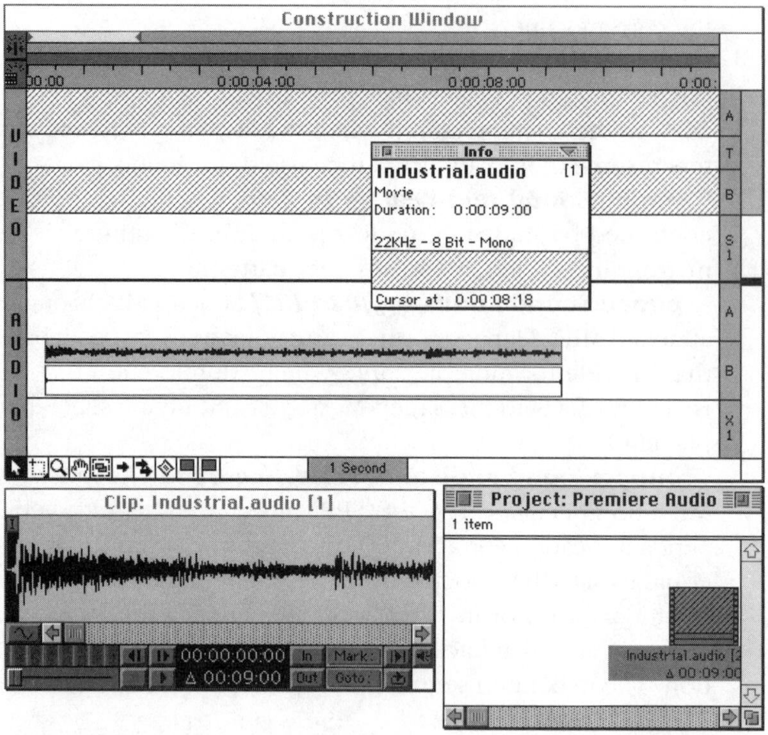

Figure 10.11 Sound in Premiere: Adobe's Premiere offers a functional yet limited set of editing features in a QuickTime editor. You can apply "elastic" amplitude envelopes to up to three sound tracks. Several sound "filters" (actually signal processing algorithms) may be applied to any segment of a sound track.

ciated visual data (drag on the track with the Shift and Option keys pressed to accomplish this).

Only at the point when you choose "Make a Movie" from the menu, does the audio data actually get copied into the new movie file, reflecting the cuts, copies, and order you defined in the construction window. At this stage, you will have the option to set the audio interleave factor (or chunk size—see "Sound in Quick-Time") of the sound as a half, one, or two seconds, or one or five minutes. If you want your sound to be loaded into RAM prior to the start of movie playback, specify a chunk size that is longer than the total duration of the movie—of course, if your movie exceeds five minutes, you're stuck with an interleaved format.

Other Controls

Premiere's interface to the control of sound track volume is much easier than Director's. An Audio Fade control runs under the waveform display of each audio event. You can add handles (breakpoints) to this line with a simple mouse click and drag these to any position to create fades and complex amplitude scaling factors. Dragging the handle at the far left scales the volume for the entire audio event, and Shift-dragging between two break-points lets you manipulate the contour they define without affecting surrounding amplitude contours.

Premiere offers access to a multitude of video and graphics filters for special effects. There are also several audio filters accessible on the sound tracks assigned in the same way you assign them to the visual tracks (option-clicking). Included among these are "Backwards" to reverse a soundfile's playback (useful for special effects); "Boost" to execute an algorithm similar to expansion options found in compressor/limiters that increase the volume of soft sounds without altering louder sounds; "Echo" to add digital delay in .01 or .02 increments within a range of .01 to 2 seconds; and "Fill Right" and "Fill Left," which serve to pan the sound element completely to the right or left channels. Note that any of these effects may be used in combination, and all are nondestructive—they are applied on the fly during playback—until you choose "Make a Movie" from the menu.

Although this procedure is not accessible from the filters menu, Premiere also lets you set the rate at which soundfiles are played back (using the Speed option under the Clip menu). The range is from 1 to 1,000 percent. This simply increases or decreases the speed at which samples are output. Because this is not a sophisticated time compression/expansion algorithm such as you might find in Alchemy, Sound Designer, or Wave (see Chapter 4, "Sound Tools"), changing the speed in this manner also changes the pitch of the sound (or the key of the music).

MIDI in Premiere

Premiere's built-in MIDI support is even more limited than Director's. Premiere includes only the basic Start, Stop, and Tempo options for MIDI synchronization, whereas Director (previous to version 4.0) adds Continue, Song Select, and Song Pointer messages to offer the complete set of SPP synchronization messages.

SMPTE time code stamping is an option in Premiere, although this is useless for MIDI purposes because there is no mechanism to convert the time code to

MTC. Premiere's SMPTE implementation is designed to be used when you export Edit Decision Lists (EDLs) to CMX 3400 and 3600, Grass Valley, and Sony BVE video editing systems. (Premiere 4.0 does support QuickTime 2.0's SMPTE time-code track.)

Sound in QuickTime

QuickTime's handling of sound tracks is interesting—the video will drop frames rather than glitch the sound track. As you learned in Chapter 4, "Sound Tools," sampling rate and resolution play a major role in determining the amount of storage required for Macintosh-based audio and therefore have a major impact on the file size of any QuickTime movie.

QuickTime supports AIFF, AIFF-C, sfil, ADPCM, and 'snd ' resources. Although the popular FSSD format created by SoundEdit, SoundCap, and SoundWave is conspicuously missing, QuickTime-compatible software such as Premiere can access SoundEdit files and convert them to QuickTime-compatible formats.

MoviePlayer ⌘ 612

QuickTime sound tracks support 8-bit and 16-bit sounds at sampling rates of up to 65,535 samples per second. You can also record audio CDs and store them as QuickTime movies. Using MoviePlayer (or any other QuickTime-capable application), you select the track or fragment to be recorded, set the sample rate, and you're off.

QuickTime will play back MACE-compressed sounds, and you can also compress sounds during movie or sound capture. QuickTime 2.0 supports both MACE 3:1 and 6:1 compression, as well as IMA 4:1 compression. Use caution when compressing sound—which is much more susceptible to artifact distortion than is visual data.

Using the more desirable uncompressed sound track can result in your audio data occupying a large portion of your movie file—in some cases, the greater portion of the file. However, when QuickTime must decompress sound as well as video, there is an additional CPU load of approximately 20 percent.

Sound also has an impact on the data rate required for compressed video decompression. Because 8-bit 22kHz stereo requires pumping 44K/second through your system, you can expect a 44K/second increase in the overall movie data rate. Likewise, 8-bit 22 kHz mono and 8-bit 11kHz stereo sound both increase the data rate by 22K/second.

Although QuickTime handles audio CD-quality 44.1KHz sound, bear in mind that playback requires 176 Kb/second peak transfer rate. This is stretching it for data that will be played from a CD-ROM drive that presumably will also be transferring video data at the same time.

Storing Audio Tracks in QuickTime

QuickTime offers two ways to store audio tracks in movie files. The first is having all the audio in one large chunk at the beginning of the movie (called "RAM-based" because all the sound is loaded into RAM before movie playback commences, freeing more of your CPU processing power to deal with the video to achieve bet-

RAM-based

Interleaved

**Figure 10.12
Interleaved
sound vs. RAM-
based sound in
QuickTime.**

ter frame rates). The alternative is called "interleaved sound" and requires that the sound data stream off your disk continually along with the video data (see Figure 10.12). While the second approach is better for longer movies where the entire sound track cannot fit into available RAM, this method does lower the maximum frame rate your video can attain due to the increased processing power required to continually fetch and schedule sound data from the disk.

You can specify how often and in what size chunks QuickTime grabs interleaved sound data by setting the interleave factor (chunk size) with programs such as MovieShop and SoundToMovie, both found on the QuickTime Developers CD-ROM. SoundToMovie offers many other sound manipulation options that make your QuickTime activities easier. The program lets you create sound-only movies, add sound to existing movies, edit the chunk size, and convert 'snd ' resources to AIFF files. SoundToMovie also displays additional useful information about your soundfile, such as the number of channels, number of samples, sample size, sample rate, compression settings, and current chunk size.

MIDI in QuickTime

One of the most interesting features introduced in QuickTime in release 2.0 is an integrated MIDI synthesizer that Apple licensed from Roland Corp. Among other things, this means that you can play MIDI files directly from a Mac or Windows machine with no additional hardware. MIDI support in QuickTime also opens digital video to a host of musical possibilities.

Wanderers on the various on-line services may have already encountered many MIDI files. To play these or incorporate them into a QuickTime movie (with appropriate consideration of applicable copyrights), use a QuickTime player such as MoviePlayer. Choose "Import" from the file menu, and the MIDI file will be converted to QuickTime format.

You can even change the instruments used in a given MIDI file. To do this, click the "Options" button on the Import dialog box, and then the "Instrument…" button, as illustrated in Figure 10.13. The MIDI file used in this example was downloaded from America Online and is an interpretation by "Joebizarre" of the Sonny Rollins jazz classic *Airegin*.

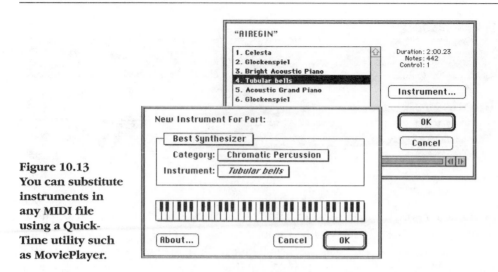

**Figure 10.13
You can substitute
instruments in
any MIDI file
using a Quick-
Time utility such
as MoviePlayer.**

Web surfers looking for more information on music in QuickTime, can check
out this address: http://quicktime.apple.com/qtmusic.html

Copyright Issues and Challenges

The proliferation of sound in multimedia has created a rat's nest of problems
and issues in the field of copyright and licensing. Simply stated, if you use someone else's music in a multimedia project without obtaining permission (in the
form of a license), you are guilty of copyright infringement and liable for large
fines against which you will discover you have no legal recourse. The myth that
you can use four bars or seven seconds of someone's music is simply that—a
myth. You can be prosecuted for stealing much less.

The good news is that unless you are trying to license music for commercial
use—meaning broadcast, resale, or theatrical display—licensing fees are relatively small—often much less than $200.

Clip Media/Sound ⌘ 300–343

To avoid breaking the law, you can use anything composed before 1915, as it
is in the public domain (although new recordings of old material may themselves be copyrighted). Alternatively, you can use clip music or algorithmically
generated music (see Chapter 4, "Sound Tools," regarding both these options);
or, better yet, hire a composer to write original music for your production.

It will serve you well to understand the Copyright code with respect to musical works. The relevant section is called Title 17 of the U.S. Code of the Copyright Act of 1976. Section 101 contains legal definitions of terms you need

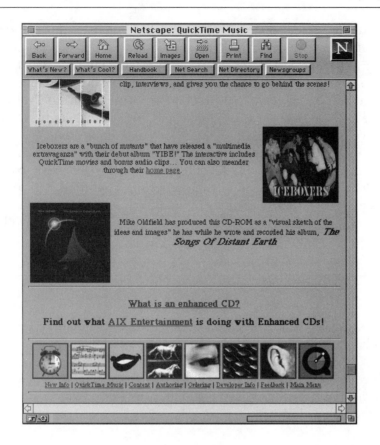

Figure 10.14 Apple's Quick-Time Music Web Homepage.

to understand throughout the rest of the code. For example, the term "phonorecord" refers to any medium upon which sounds may be stored, not just phonograph records.

Context of Usage

Most publishers and copyright owners do want to have some say regarding the context of the usage and the possible attachment of secondary meaning to a song by, for example, changing the lyrics.

Steven Winogradsky, director of music business affairs for Hanna Barbera Productions (the folks who brought us "Yaba-Daba-Doo"), has had some interesting experiences along these lines with the *Flintstones'* theme song. He denied a request to use the tune in a comedy show where the lyrics would be changed to "Flintsteins, meet the Flintsteins, the modern Jewish family." He also discovered an East coast "safe sex" campaign where the lyrics had been changed to "Condoms, use a condom..." and forced the infringers to pull it out of the campaign because "the *Flintstones* is basically a kids' show."

Winogradsky continues, "It all falls back on the rights of the copyright holder under the copyright law. Unauthorized use of copyrighted material is an infringement that is punishable by substantial fines. And along with that, each separate copy of a computer program that includes unauthorized copyrighted material is considered to be a separate infringement. So if the court decides that the infringement is worth $1,000, and there are 500 copies of the program, the developer finds himself owing $500,000. Furthermore, if it is considered willful infringement, that carries fines up to $100,000 per infringement, especially if you have been notified. Shareware vendors are pretty bad about that, and when I find them I send them a strongly worded registered letter making demands on behalf of the copyright for monetary compensation. If they continue to distribute, they can no longer claim that it was unwillful because they were put on notice."

General Tips

As we stated in Chapter 4, "Sound Tools," the desire to compose music is not a reliable indication of talent. With graphics software, anyone with a mouse can draw a straight line while holding a control key down. But composers require a lifetime of training. We are a long way from software that could, for example, write a happy melody if you held the Shift key down and a sad melody with the Control key down.

Obtaining Music for Multimedia

The best way to obtain music to accompany your multimedia presentation is to hire a composer to create something original and tailor-made for the rest of your content. Nothing can replace a trained human being who can respond to such suggestions as "this section should be mysterious and build in anticipation," or "I need the musical climax to synchronize precisely with the appearance of the corporate logo."

Let the Visual Element Suggest the Music

Music and sound effects can reinforce the rhythm, emotion, and historical setting of your visuals. Alternatively, your sound track can be used to add subtext, to comment, or to contradict what the audience is viewing. You can play upon expectations and associations by using a particular musical style, but don't reveal the punch line unintentionally. In most cases, the rule "less is more" applies to multimedia—the music needn't run from beginning to end, particularly if it would distract the viewer. Music under narration or dialog should be handled with extreme care. Silence can have a profound dramatic impact, especially when following a particularly audio-saturated section. Your favorite song will almost never be suitable.

Learn From the Film Industry

When you consider music for your multimedia production or digital movie, it is a good idea to look at the way music is integrated into a theatrical film production. There are two primary types of music: underscore and source. *Underscore*—sometimes called *score* or, erroneously, background music—is devoted to reinforcing, commenting on, or otherwise enhancing the dramatic content of the film. In all cases, underscore is music that would not be present if the scene were occurring in reality; the characters in the scene would not be able to hear it. On the other hand, *source* music would be present if the scene were played out in reality—coming from a radio, record player, night club band, or Muzak. In other words, source music is music that the characters in the scene would be hearing in their current situation. A further distinction can be made between visual source music, where we, the audience, can see the source of the sound; and *nonvisual* source music (sometimes called off-screen music), where we can't see the source, but we can believe it is there (for example, if it is coming from a car radio in an interior shot of the back seat of a car). If you need a lesson in adding sound to visuals, go to a movie twice so you can analyze the choice and placement of music without being distracted by the plot.

Exercise Care in Synchronizing Music to Visuals

If you are creating multimedia for distribution, you may have little control over the type of computer on which your work will be played. Long soundfiles and MIDI sequences can get out of sync with the visual material if your masterpiece is played on slower or faster machines than the model you used to create the work. There is a simple solution for this. Test your project on a range of target machines and use a stopwatch. Most multimedia authoring environments provide a function to identify the "MachineType," and you can use this information in IF-THEN scripts to subtly change the playback tempo of the graphic element (if you are using digital audio soundfiles) or the music itself (if you are using MIDI playback).

Be Aware of the Synchronization Threshold

Take a tip from the film industry on synchronization (or verify it yourself with a poorly dubbed Japanese film): The human ear will notice a synchronization error as small as two frames at 24 frames per second. That equates to $\frac{1}{12}$ of a second, or 1 frame if your QuickTime movie is running at 12 fps. Keep this rule in mind when you need to create a "dead hit" where the visual and audio must be in precise synchronization—such as a gunshot.

Consider the Importance of Sound Placement in the Stereo Field

A sound track has a limited bandwidth. At maximum saturation, the dialog, sound effects and music cannot add up to more than 100 percent. Using pan controls on your mixer or sound editing software to place different sounds at different locations in the stereo image can enhance the effect of your audio significantly. Narration is usually placed dead center. Look at an orchestral seating diagram or consider the normal spatial disposition of musicians performing in smaller ensembles to determine how far to the right or left to pan them.

Randomness Adds Interest

If you have ever wondered what you would use the "Random" function for in your multimedia authoring environment, here's the answer: You can put it to good use with sound. Interactive multimedia already provides random access to data; so why not select the sound (MIDI or digital audio) randomly for different segments? It makes the experience much more interesting for your users. A recent example of this technique is the Verbum Interactive CD-ROM, which randomly selects between soundtracks composed by Geno Andrews and Christopher Yavelow.

Play Through File Loading

No matter whether you are using MIDI or digital audio, if your multimedia work requires multiple files with pauses for loading, play music through the loading of files. For authoring environments that do not support playback during file loading, there are XCMDs and DDLs available that offer this feature.

Avoiding Copyright Infringement (Plan A)

Fortunately, copyright law does make a distinction between public and private exhibition. Where it might cost $10,000 (or much more) to license a song for commercial use (say, in a motion picture), the price of a one-shot use of the same song in a QuickTime presentation at a board of directors meeting would be negligible—often just the cost of the paperwork and well under $200. Sometimes you can get away with quoting popular songs, if they happen to be based upon folk songs. For example, *"Love Me Tender"* is really the public domain folk song *"Aura Lee,"* although most people will think of Elvis Presley when they hear an arrangement of it in your multimedia presentation.

Avoiding Copyright Infringement (Plan B)

Commission a composer to write some original music. Everyone knows a composer or has a friend who does, and many of these composers are underemployed. Most would welcome the opportunity to write music that not only suits your presentation perfectly, but often produces a better effect than preexisting music that you try to fit to visual material for which it wasn't intended.

Avoiding Copyright Infringement (Plan C)

Another way to avoid copyright infringement is by using prelicensed clip music, although again you may have the problem of trying to fit a round peg in a square hole. Clip music is currently being marketed in three forms: as MIDI data on floppy disks using the Standard MIDI File format (a generic format analogous to "ASCII text" in word processing)—licensing fees may be required in some situations (particularly broadcast); as digital audio data on floppy disks or CD-ROMs that you can play back with the Macintosh's internal sound capabilities (8-bit) or with various add-in cards (16-bit) on the Mac or under Windows—licensing fees are usually not required; and as digital audio data on standard CDs (sometimes called "needle-drop" libraries)—these require relatively inexpensive licensing fees.

**Use an
External
Sound
System**

The internal speaker on many computers cannot accurately play back sounds sampled at rates exceeding 11kHz. However, the rear-panel audio jack does support the Macintosh's highest resolution (22kHz). You can use portable powered speakers to greatly enhance your presentation. PCs with multimedia capabilities generally have added external speakers.

**Digitize the
Audio and
Video
Separately**

This is required in frame-by-frame grabs, and if you try to record audio simultaneously with video during real-time capture, you will reduce the frame rate of your video.

**Increase the
QuickTime
Chunking
Factor**

Without intervention, QuickTime loads one second of your sound track into RAM before initiating movie playback. Programs like ComboWalker let you specify how many half-second chunks of sound to load into RAM before playback commences. It will often be in your interest to set a higher chunking factor than QuickTime's default, which is designed for the lowest common denominator with respect to Macintosh models.

Digital Audio Tips

**Don't Record
Digital Audio
Too Hot**

Carefully monitor audio recording levels. "Hot" levels (where the meters go into the red momentarily) are acceptable with analog tape. Digital recording meters only enter the red when the sound exceeds the maximum sample value. Because there is no cushion above that number, the sample is "clipped," resulting in annoying clicks, pops, or otherwise noisy distorted audio. Use a compressor/limiter, if necessary, to set even recording levels.

**Storage and
Playback
Requirements Have
an Impact
on Sampling
Rates**

Mono 8-bit digital audio sampled at 22kHz, such as that you record with MacRecorder, requires 1.3Mb per minute of sound. To save disk space, use a playback rate of 11kHz. If your audio will be played back in mono, there is no reason to waste disk space and CPU bandwidth by using stereo soundfiles. Only use 22kHz in the final project if you are certain that your project will be played using an external sound system. If your project is destined for a CD-ROM, you should stick with 11kHz unless you have an intentionally low data rate (or frame rate below 8 fps in the case of a QuickTime movie). You can get by with a sampling rate of 7kHz if your audio consists entirely of speech. Remember, the lower your sampling rate, the more time the CPU will have to deal with the other elements of your production. You generally use 44.1kHz only when the highest quality is required.

Record High, Downsample Later

Always record sound at the highest sampling rate of your digitizing hardware and then downsample the sound to 11kHz later. This is because many digitizers drop every other sample when sampling at 22kHz to achieve an 11kHz sampling rate, resulting in sound that is inferior to that achieved by recording at a higher rate and using the "downsample" or "sample rate conversion" options of a sound editor. Downsampling and sample rate conversion options use filtering algorithms that don't necessarily result in dropping every other sample. With SoundEdit or SoundEdit Pro you will have the best results if you sample at 22kHz and paste the file into an empty 11kHz document. Always use the most exact sample rates your software permits: Capture your audio at 22.254kHz and downsample it to 11.127kHz (for QuickTime 1.6 use 11.05kHz) rather than capturing at 11.127kHz or 11.05kHz.

Be Wary of Soundfile Compression

Before using MACE or any other compression scheme to compress your soundfiles, make sure that your multimedia authoring environment lets you use compressed sound. Keep in mind that once you have compressed a sound, you won't be able to edit it with most sound editing software; so keep an uncompressed backup copy. If you must compress, don't go beyond a 3:1 compression ratio for music; 6:1 compression may be used for speech if you can tolerate the reduction in quality.

Control an Audio CD Player

When you put an audio CD into a CD-ROM drive, every block of data has a unique address (over 300,000 separate addresses).Your computer can jump to any place on the disc almost instantaneously. There is no load time such as is associated with reading other forms of CD-ROM data; audio playback commences as soon as the data is located. Authoring tools such as Voyager's CD AudioStack automatically create buttons and XCMD scripts to play back audio sequences you designate by "scrolling" through an off-the-shelf audio CD. You can even control multiple CD-ROM drives, each with a different audio CD playing at your command. Macromedia Director also offers control of CD-based audio through its own XCMD. On Windows, many programs can control an audio CD through MCI commands.

MIDI Tips

Another important advantage of using MIDI instead of digital audio is that you can alter many sound characteristics on the fly during playback. You can speed up or slow down a piece of music, transpose it to another key, mute or solo specified tracks, fade individual tracks in and out, loop beat-delineated regions, or completely reorchestrate and remix the music—all without having a separate version of the file. Furthermore, you can direct any or all of these operations to take place in response to user interaction.

When You Use MIDI, Use General MIDI

If you are going to use MIDI sequences in your multimedia presentations, it makes sense to set them up so that they are compatible with the "General MIDI mode message" protocol that was added to the MIDI Specification in 1991. General MIDI was created specifically to address multimedia issues. Among other things, General MIDI consists of a standardized list of patches that are all assigned to the same numbers, a universal patch location scheme if you will. This means that when a device is in General MIDI mode, for example, patch 1 is always an acoustic grand piano, patch 25 is a nylon-stringed guitar, patch 41 is a solo violin, and so on. All 128 possible patch numbers have explicit assignments covering almost any instrument of the orchestra, as well as many standard electronic instruments, synthesizer timbres, and sound effects.

General MIDI also defines drum sound to note number mappings. General MIDI lets you "plug and play" with the assurance that the sounds will be correct, regardless of the hardware you use for playback. This is particularly important for cross-platform development.

Use MIDI XMCDs to Increase Your MIDI Possibilities

Ear Level Engineering's HyperMIDI XCMD set can add a complete MIDI implementation to multimedia authoring environments that support externals such as XCMDs. There are also several HyperCard stacks available that play back Standard MIDI Files (they include Opcode Systems' MIDIplay and Passport Designs' HyperMusic). These stacks can automatically create buttons or scripts that play MIDI files in any XCMD-compatible multimedia authoring environment. You can even assemble lists of files that play back sequentially. There are thousands of files available in Standard MIDI File format. Under Windows, you can use MCI commands to further increase MIDI possibilities. There are also third party DLLs that provide even better control.

Initialize MIDI Tracks

As the first event of each MIDI track, insert messages to reset controllers; set pitchbend to 0; set MIDI volume (controller 7) to 127 or the appropriate value; and include program changes (preferably in General MIDI format) to ensure that if these values have been altered during the course of the playback of another sequence, you will be starting from a clean slate. Another reason these parameters may have the wrong values is that an earlier version of your sequence was interrupted during playback.

You can edit MIDI data to simulate almost every effect that you might otherwise use an expensive digital signal processor to accomplish. The following effects are easily achievable by copying, delaying, merging, scaling, and transposing MIDI data: echo, chorus, flange, compression/expansion, limiting, pan, and spatialization. General MIDI has some standard effects. Also, some wavetable MIDI cards allow you to record your own patches for use in MIDI tracks.

Had Enough?

Use MIDI Effects in Place of Digital Signal Processing

You may not have realized how much there is to know about sound—especially in the digital environment of multimedia. Fortunately, once you understand the basic technology, you'll find that the process of adding sound to your multimedia project is more like creative play than tedious drudgery. In any case, the rewards of using sound's emotional power is well worth the mental and technological investment. It can add polish to your presentation.

11

Sound Projects

Computer-based music generation and editing are among the most intriguing and least explored areas of multimedia. In this chapter, and in the step-by-step explanations on the *Power Tools* CD, you'll find fascinating discussions of the effect of digital music on popular culture, the use of rock songs to teach music theory, and how "intelligent instruments" allow beginners to create coherent and original compositions.

Hip Hop Hits

Musical styles have always influenced popular culture. In the 1960s, music helped fuel the revolution—in fashion, politics, lifestyles, art, and even industrial design. Nowadays, computers are increasingly influencing music. Many of today's hot new musical styles, such as Hip Hop, Industrial, Rave, and Acid-House, are technology-driven—born out of new capabilities stemming from the marriage of computers and digital audio. Through the development of these new musical forms, computers are exerting a powerful influence on the popular style and culture of the '90s.

All these new styles share one characteristic—the prominent use of small bits of digitized audio called *samples*. Samples are small music clips—often only three or four seconds long—taken from tunes that are dated but familiar. They are digitally recorded with a computer or sampling keyboard and usually played back as repeating loops (see Figure 11.1).

Many of today's musicians are really sound engineers. They take tiny chunks of old favorites; digitally chew them up; mix in a hot, new dance beat; and spit

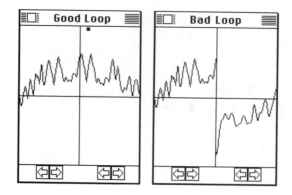

Figure 11.1 Editing sound loops to make sure they play seamlessly.

out a groove that's completely fresh. By its very nature, sampling allows musicians to pay homage to old styles such as Funk, House, and Soul, while inventing something entirely new. That's why new songs on the radio sometimes sound somewhat familiar.

What do Hip Hop, Industrial, and Acid-House have to offer multimedia creators? Through their use of sample loops, they show new ways to create long pieces of sound with small chunks of audio data.

Imagine the implications of this modular approach for multimedia! Not only are the problems created by space limitations drastically reduced, but audio starts and stops are smooth in an interactive environment. By using small, repeating loops, you can mold audio better around individual screens and buttons, eliminating graceless user-initiated stops and extended silences while projects move to the next screen.

Special Considerations

Hip Hop Hits ⌘ 010

Hip Hop Hits is really two projects in one. Mike Salomon designed the original project as a CD-quality audio track for the song *"Straight to the Point"* (Figure 11.2) by the Hip Hop band, Dark Side Productions (DSP). Knowing that DSP would be playing additional elements live (lyrics, keyboards, and nonlooping samples), Salomon wanted to keep the tracks simple.

First trained as a recording engineer, Salomon worked in studios and did live shows for two years and later began doing Mac installations for studios working with MIDI and digital audio. In 1990, he went to work for Horizon Resources in San Diego, which integrates digital audio systems for recording studios and composers.

Dark Side Productions disbanded shortly after Salomon completed the job, so he was happy to reincarnate the recording for the *Power Tools* CD.

The project's biggest challenge, says Salomon, was getting good sound out of the 8-bit internal Mac system. To optimize the sound quality, Salomon did three

**Figure 11.2
The final digital
audio tape of
*"Straight to the
Point."***

things. First, he started a high-quality 16-bit 44.1kHz file, which was equal to the fidelity of an audio music CD.

Since the source was clean and high-quality, he had only to remove information to make an 8-bit file; this is much easier than trying to clean up lower-quality sound, which also will almost inevitably produce inferior results.

Next, Salomon performed a process called *normalization* to optimize the fidelity and dynamic range of the original music for playback on the Mac's relatively low-quality built-in sound. The process works by assigning the maximum number of bits to the loudest passages, thus getting the most natural sound possible from 8-bit playback.

Finally, Salomon cleaned up the sound by editing the music's waveforms to remove the audible clicks that the Mac's speakers would normally emit at the beginning and end of each track.

Tips and Techniques

For those wanting to experiment with digital sound on the Mac, Salomon recommends the new Audiomedia II card from Digidesign. While not as sophisticated as the Sound Tools system he used for the project, it allows you to play back, edit, and mix CD-quality sound and can be had for less than $1,000. Salomon also points out that the budget conscious can pick up a used Audiomedia I card for around $300.

Salomon recommends using Sound Manager 3.0. By providing standard audio drivers that will work with various applications and sound cards, the system software extension could do for audio what QuickTime did for digital video. Sound Manager also will automatically adjust digital music playback for individual Macs in much the same way as QuickTime giddily drops video frames to keep in sync when playing back movies on slower Macs.

Finally, Salomon warns those planning multimedia projects not to underestimate the importance of sound and not to forget to budget for sound production. Attention to good audio production can help boost a multimedia project to professional levels.

Tools and Equipment

Salomon used a Mac IIci and Digidesign's Sound Tools system, which consists of the Sound Accelerator Card, Sound Designer II editing software, and an outboard digitizing box.

To learn more about how Salomon actually created the project, see the *Power Tools* CD. You'll experience firsthand how he digitized the original music, isolated each instrument, created the sound loops, mixed tracks, created the PlayList regions, and finally, recorded it all onto digital audio tape (DAT).

Power Tools *Theme*

Power Tools Theme ⌘ 011

"About one minute long and industrial." That was the extent of the guidelines Christopher Yavelow got before composing the theme for the *Power Tools* CD. But given his familiarity with other Verbum projects, these brief and vague directions were enough for Yavelow, who has won many awards, has a distinguished background in music and computers, is professor of composition at Claremont Graduate School, and is the author of *The MacWorld Music and Sound Bible*.

Special Considerations

To compose the music, Yavelow used M, interactive music software from Intelligent Music, Inc. "I normally use interactive music software only for live performance," says Yavelow, "but considering that the *Power Tools* CD is devoted to interactive multimedia, I decided to use an intelligent instrument to create the music."

M allowed Yavelow to accomplish several things. First, "M responds to performance gestures, by generating much more musical information than would be generated by the same gesture were it applied to a traditional instrument."

Even though the entire theme was composed of only four simple elements—one 17-note and one 13-note melody, a five-chord progression, and a 13-note rhythmic pattern—M generated "an astounding amount of material," says Yavelow.

He further points out that composing with M forces you to think about musical parameters that you would not generally even consider when using other computer-based tools (see Figure 11.3). These parameters include note density, relative volume ranges, probabilities, and event order—"the sort of things you would only think about were you composing for traditional instruments."

Yavelow says that composing with tools like M allows you to deal with the many levels of music composition from "greater levels of abstraction." He

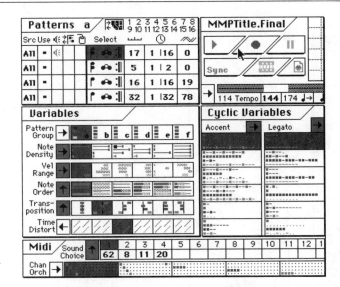

**Figure 11.3
M allows you to
control many
different musical
parameters.**

explains that "Rather than think of the actual notes that make up a pattern, you
think of the pattern itself."

This concept appeals to both trained and amateur musicians. "Professionals can
deal with the processes that transform musical ideas," Yavelow says, "while neo-
phytes can ignore the details, and get results by pushing around larger conceptual blocks, rather than tiny notes where any little mistake stands out like a sore
thumb."

Tips and Techniques

Yavelow's primary advice is that novices should not be scared away by interactive music tools, sequencers, or MIDI. "I really believe that people with zero
musical training can use these tools and have fun doing it. There are a lot of people out there attempting to do multimedia and needing music for it."

Likewise, professional musicians should not be put off by computer-based
tools, he says. "Desktop tools can reflect compositional philosophy just as successfully as traditional tools can."

Compositional tools also let you create music with no license restrictions, since
anything you compose belongs to you. This is a significant benefit, since content
rights can absorb considerable time, effort, and economic resources (as in the *So
You Want to Be Rock and Roll Star* project; see below).

Tools and Equipment

Besides M, Yavelow used a variety of computer-based music tools, including
Opcode's EZ Vision MIDI sequencer, Coda's Finale, Apple's MIDI Manager, Mark
of the Unicorn's Performer, Kurzweil's 250 sampler and the Kurzweil 1000PX, SX,

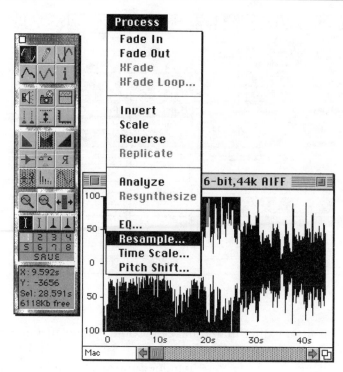

**Figure 11.4
Chris Yavelow
used Passport's
Alchemy to down-
sample his final
sound file to an 8-
bit file that would
play back on the
full range of
internal Mac
sound system.**

and E-mu's Proteus 2 sound modules, Panasonic's 3700 DAT deck, MediaVision's Pro Audio Spectrum 16, and Passport's Alchemy (see Figure 11.4).

In his tutorial on the *Power Tools* CD, Yavelow begins with an overview of the philosophy and strengths of interactive music software and intelligent instruments. He then provides a detailed overview of the many parameters of the M system and the means he used to edit and record the final theme.

The Bay of Digs

Bay of Digs ⌘ 012

David Javelosa is an independent electronic music composer and producer, who is former head of music for Sega. *The Bay of Digs* is his working title for a piece of music he wrote for a new CD from Gray Market Media on the Kennedy administration. The music will play back during transitions, at the beginning of sections, and during the credits.

Javelosa likens scoring an "edutainment" title to writing music for a book or even an elevator. "The style of music is very industrial," he says. The composer is more accustomed to writing for games or other entertainment titles. These projects feature greater dynamic visual imagery. "It's easier to write when there's more action, more 'screen choreography,'" Javelosa notes.

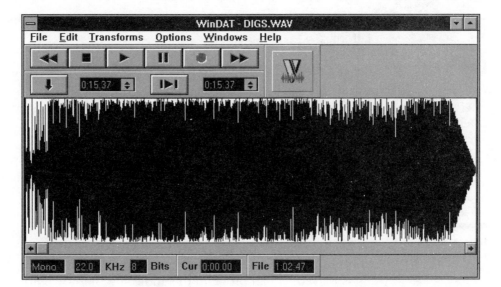

**Figure 11.5
A waveform of
the *Bay of Digs*
score.**

Special Considerations

For maximum flexibility, Javelosa produced the music in three formats: MIDI, 8-bit digital audio, and Redbook audio, which is full audio CD quality. Many producers use MIDI music to fill "dead air" during times when nothing is happening while the CD is loading data. This is possible because MIDI files are small, and the computer can handle their simultaneous playback while the CD drive is doing disc reads and data transfer.

The richer sound of digital audio files would be preferable, but a machine can't both load data and play back an audio file simultaneously. This would be possible if the files were first copied to a hard drive; but as Javelosa points out, many CDs are designed to copy only minimal data to the user's hard drive. For those times when it is possible to play back digital audio rather than their MIDI equivalents, Javelosa slips in these files. The Redbook version of the score is there for those who want to play through it separately, although this version is the largest—about 10 Mb for each of the score's 3 minutes.

To compose a score, Javelosa gets a feel for the mood by getting his hands on as much of the project's material as possible. Then he begins to improvise on the keyboard, perhaps to a programmed drum pattern. Next, he edits the drum part, formalizes the keyboard part, and edits the basic scene melody.

Finally, he'll begin building up tracks, adding bass, strings, and possibly other orchestral instruments. Javelosa also writes lead lines that emphasize the melody. For this project, he chose a flute as counterpoint to the serious tone of the title itself.

MasterTracks Pro 5 ⌘ 706

Javelosa used MasterTracks Pro *sequencing* software to record and edit the music. He picked the software, in part, because the program comes in both Mac and Windows versions, making it relatively easy to move the score file across platforms.

Even so, there were the inevitable cross-platform issues. MIDI synthesizers and sound cards vary in the number of musical "voices" they feature; and MIDI instruments that use same names on different synthesizers may, in fact, not sound alike. "The instrument definitions are often different," says Javelosa. "They call it a clarinet, but it doesn't sound like a clarinet." He had to "remap" some instruments to get reasonable fidelity.

Before moving the MIDI file to the PC, Javelosa made a copy that would serve as the higher quality Redbook audio source. The composer added more instruments and effects such as reverb to create the CD-quality version of the score.

Tips and Techniques

Javelosa advises designing music that will play back in an interactive way, as a feedback response that changes depending on what paths or options the user chooses, for example. He has even found a way to vary the music each time a title is played. "I can program the authoring tool to compose variations of the music," he says.

Like many composers, Javelosa also recommends recording sound at the highest quality available, since it can always be down-sampled later, Furthermore, mass market machines such as Sony's Playstation and high end PC sound cards like Creative Labs' AWE32 are capable of high quality sound playback and are growing in popularity.

Tools and Equipment

For the MIDI version of the score, Javelosa used a keyboard to compose and generate the music, which was fed into a Mac running Mastertracks Pro. He played it back using Roland's Sound Canvas, a synthesizer that uses actual sampled sounds of instruments. Sound Canvas is a *wavetable* synthesizer that produces much higher quality sound than the older FM synthesis technique. For more on sound synthesis, see Chapter 4.

So You Want to Be a Rock and Roll Star

In the mid-1980s, Steve Rappaport was an independent producer for Electronic Arts, the high-flying computer and video game developer founded by Trip Hawkins (now CEO of 3DO).

...*Rock and Roll Star* ⌘ 013

"Trip told us about this new technology, CD-I, that was going to marry a bunch of technologies that were already on the shelf," Rappaport notes. "Audio CDs, CD-ROM, color technology, graphics—basically, all the parts that were integrated into CD-I and what we now know as interactive multimedia were already invented by the mid-'80s, but they hadn't been put together in a coherent piece of hardware. Software tools like Director didn't exist yet either, so that one could actually create interactive multimedia."

Hawkins urged his creative staff to think about uses for the new technology, because, Steve points out, "you can have all the hardware and software and tools you want; but if you can't create a compelling product, all of that doesn't mean anything."

With Hawkins' challenge ringing in his ears, Rappaport began to form the germ of an idea. A musician for more than 30 years, he had always wanted to share his knowledge in a fun and educational way. An interactive CD might be the perfect medium, but he had to bide his time a little longer until desktop software tools made such a project economically feasible. In 1990, when MacroMind (now Macromedia) released Director 2.0, Rappaport saw his chance and enlisted a partner, Greg McGee, to handle the technical aspects of the project.

So You Want to Be a Rock and Roll Star uses classic rock songs to teach music and guitar. All six songs—"Twist and Shout," "Stand by Me," "Runaway," "Crazy," "In the Midnight Hour," and "Sittin' on the Dock of the Bay"—are illustrated with animations (Figure 11.6), and are recorded in 16-bit CD-quality sound.

Figure 11.6 Each of *So You Want to Be a Rock and Roll Star*'s six rock songs is illustrated with original animated art.

You can simply enjoy the music and animation; or you can learn about music theory, chord structure, and the history of each song. Music theory is a pretty arcane subject to most people; but *So You Want to Be a Rock and Roll Star* teaches it in a context that is a bit more fun. Professional music teachers use the songs to teach piano and guitar, but you can isolate various tracks to hear only the instruments you're concentrating on.

Special Considerations

A producer and musician by training, Rappaport has a refreshing angle on multimedia because he focuses on the content and human aspects of the genre, rather than the technical issues that seem to captivate and divert so many.

In fact, the most demanding aspect of the project didn't involve technology at all. "The single most difficult part of the project was licensing the music," says Rappaport. Interactive Records has obtained the rights to more than 400 songs in three years. In many ways, Rappaport and his company have blazed the trail for producers of multimedia who seek to incorporate original musical works. "Now, everyone in Hollywood and Nashville and New York has, at minimum, heard of interactive multimedia," he notes.

Rappaport emphasizes the value of personal relationships in his work. During the early phases of the project, he and McGee built a prototype and Rappaport took it on the road. "I not only showed people what multimedia was, but I also demonstrated how it could be a source of completely unexpected revenue," he explains.

Rappaport was able to show music publishers that an early involvement in multimedia licensing would position them as the demand for electronic rights heats up in the '90s. "I would spend hours with these folks, and they came to see that they could trust me," he says. "One of the things you never hear about in discussions of obtaining content is the importance of personal relationships."

Another key aspect of the project was choosing the songs at the core of the project. "We wanted to create a product that was transgenerational; so we chose songs that, although written and recorded in the '60s, had re-releases in the '80s," he notes. "'*Sittin' on the Dock of the Bay*' was a top-10 hit for Michael Bolton in 1988. '*Runaway*' was not only a hit for Bonnie Raitt in 1977, but was the theme of TV's *Police Story*. '*In the Midnight Hour*' was a hit for The Commitments in 1990."

Tips and Techniques

Rappaport was careful to emphasize the originality and individuality of the songs by choosing unique art to accompany and enhance the music. The rise of music videos and MTV during the '80s also was not lost on him, and he saw that each music video had its own style and sensibility. He auditioned more than 40 artists before settling on the six who created animations for the songs.

Although Rappaport's original market inspiration for the project was CD-I, he quickly realized that the Mac and CD-ROM were a better bet for both development and distribution. "One of the beauties of the Macintosh is that, to some significant extent, the interface builds itself."

Although ...*Rock and Roll Star* is much more than simply a sound project (we could have easily included it in the interactive category instead), it *is* primarily about sound; and Interactive Records understandably focused on the music.

One key concern was how to fit all of the sound on a CD. At 650Mb capacity, it would seem to have plenty of room, until one considers that audio CD-quality sound takes about 10Mb per minute. At that rate, the ...*Rock and Roll Star* CD would hold only about an hour of music and sound (with no room at all for text, graphics, and interactivity!).

Interactive Records solved the problem by recording the music at 16-bit CD-quality (also called Red Book Audio), and the narrative voices at a lower-quality 8-bit sound. With that ratio, the disc was able to hold a full three hours of sound and music.

Rappaport points out that developers have to be constantly aware of emerging multimedia products—not only because they must keep up with new technology, but also because new products can have an impact on maintenance of their own programs. ...*Rock and Roll Star* worked flawlessly in the early months of its release, and then Interactive Records began to get bug reports. They realized that all the customers who were reporting problems were using the new AppleCD 300i, which is a dual-speed CD-ROM drive.

It turned out that there was a conflict between this drive's software driver and Macromedia's Director Projector, which plays back the ...*Rock and Roll Star* CD. Code changes to both Apple's driver and Director turned out to be necessary; but meanwhile, it was Interactive's problem.

"It's not enough that your program is flawless today, it has to be flawless on new products that come out that are going to have new code," Rappaport notes. "So in a sense, you're never through with a product. And that's one reason why code has to be meticulously documented. So many people do not comment their code; and they may not realize that two years from now they're going to have to go through that code to find and fix problems."

Tools and Equipment

Photoshop 3.0 Demo ⌘ 715

Interactive Records used a Mac IIci and IIcx, Farallon's MacRecorder and SoundEdit to digitize and edit sound, a Sennheiser 421 microphone for the vocal recordings, and all the tools you'd find in a traditional recording studio (Figure 11.7). Photoshop was used for image processing, HyperCard for prototyping, Director for building the interface, and Passport's MasterTracks Pro for sequencing.

**Figure 11.7
To create the
project, Inter-
active Records
used computer-
based tools as
well as traditional
recording studio
equipment.**

...*Rock and Roll Star's* entire production process is documented in great detail on the *Power Tools* CD and is accompanied throughout by Rappaport's articulate narration. You'll learn, among other things, the importance of good script writing and editing, how Interactive Records chose its teachers and narrators, the impact of desktop sound tools, the sound recording and editing process, how the songs' arrangements had to be understood and analyzed, and how track recording and sequencing works.

12

Creating 3-D Models and Animation

At a lunch meeting in the 1950s attended by Loony Tunes animators Friz Freleng and Chuck Jones and studio owners Jack and Harry Warner, Harry told the bemused cartoonists that he had no idea where their cartoon division was. "The only thing I know is that we make Mickey Mouse," he commented. Of course, as any grade schooler will tell you, the famous rodent is a product of Disney Studios, not Warner Bros.

Another time, legendary Warner Bros. director Chuck Jones and a colleague were quietly working when their producer appeared in the doorway and blurted out, "I don't want any gags about bullfights. Bullfights aren't funny!" Jones's colleague turned to him and said, "I never knew there was anything funny about bullfighting until now. But Eddie's judgment is impeccable. He's never been right yet." Sure enough, *Bully for Bugs* became one of the best and best-loved Bugs Bunny cartoons.

The annals of early film animation are full of colorful stories, and in many ways, the state of today's desktop computer animation is similar to that of the pioneering days of cartoons. Both have wide popular appeal, each was revolutionized by new technology, and both are painstaking to produce.

3-D: Quintessential Multimedia?

In many ways, 3-D animation is multimedia in its purest form. It's generated wholly on the computer and is inherently multidimensional. Animations can be designed, for example, so that they can be played back and viewed from different angles and perspectives. A movie, on the other hand, digital or otherwise, will always look the same.

3-D animation is thus as interactive as media gets; that's one of the reasons it is perfect for adventure and exploratory games in which viewers can ramble over realistic or whimsical terrain. Even major corporations are drawn to the possibilities of 3-D simulations. Silicon Graphics, for example, is experimenting with animated tutorials that help field service technicians diagnose hardware problems.

A movie of the inside of a computer may be better than a dry technical manual, but a 3-D animation that can be viewed from multiple perspectives is best of all.

Challenges

Although 3-D animation tools are getting easier to use, they still require considerable time to master; that is one reason why 2-D animated presentation tools like Action, Cinemation, and Astound have cropped up.

Beyond the technical skills that are needed to excel at 3-D animation, there is the looming question of aesthetic talent. Many overlook the fact that technical mastery is not the most important skill necessary for good animation. A feel for composition and design, and innate creativity are critical.

Jim Collins of Smoke and Mirrors in San Francisco, who designs 3-D animation and interactive presentations, laments the emphasis on technical detail that dominates the creation of computer-based images. He feels that as computer animation matures and the tools get easier to use, artists will begin to gravitate to the new medium, sparking a creative renaissance in computer animation.

Harry Marks, a broadcast graphics pioneer, has similar views. Marks believes that much control has been lost by broadcast graphics designers who are now dependent on operators conversant with the complex and expensive equipment necessary to create broadcast-quality graphics. As desktop tools become more powerful and accessible, Marks predicts, artists and designers won't have to be as reliant on technicians. "I think the most important thing about the computer is that, as the machine is being accepted more by designers, the control is coming back."

Don't let all this scare you away. Three-dimensional animation can be enormously rewarding; and with some patience and dedication, you can turn out stunning imagery. The point is that desktop animation (and all multimedia applications) are sort of in the Model-T phase, with tools that can be difficult to learn, although they are much less complex than the specialized equipment they replace.

There is no substitute for an artistic sensibility—the tools eventually will get easier to master, but unless you have some knowledge of aesthetics, you may find 3-D animation daunting. This doesn't mean you have to be Picasso. Much about form, balance, composition, and design can be learned over time, or at least enough to help you produce reasonable-looking animation. So if 3-D animation turns you on, and you don't know the first thing about design, take a class or a seminar; you might surprise yourself.

In this chapter, we'll cover the basics of animation, beginning with how to plan out an animation and continuing through basic structural definitions and modeling. Then we'll discuss the rudiments of movement and animation and go on to basics of rendering surfaces, textures, color, and light. Finally, there is a brief discussion of ways to distribute your final product.

Planning

For all but the simplest of 3-D images and animations, planning is essential—the 3-D process is too involved to leave anything to chance. You'll need to plan such elements as shots, camera angles, and scene composition. Even if you're just animating a logo, it helps to visualize where the text will come from, and what effects will be used: rotation, zooming, morphing, or some other manipulation. For more complex projects, such as animated presentations or involved CD or videodisc-based games, planning is absolutely critical.

Animators have many horror stories about learning this the hard way. For example, animator Joe Sparks, creator of the popular CD-ROM games *Spaceship Warlock* and *Total Distortion*, tells of spending hours designing and modeling beautiful vases and other amenities for a room in *Total Distortion*. When it came time to set camera angles and motion, he realized that his carefully designed details would be completely off camera.

Some animators keep notebooks in which they record lists of frames, changes to be made after test renderings, client likes and dislikes, sketches of objects and scenes, and anything else they may have to consult later. Lynda Weinman, a Los Angeles animator who worked on the display graphics used for the cyborg's readouts in the film *Robocop*, made the entry in her notebook shown in Figure 12.1.

Although it pays to be as organized as possible, individual animators stress different parts of the process. Jim Collins of Smoke and Mirrors in San Francisco finds elaborate planning unnecessary and even limiting. He says those with background in computers tend to plan and organize more, while those with an artistic background value inspiration and happenstance over planning.

He cites as an example the project he did for Pixar's ShowPlace/MacRenderMan product demo, a clever and creative piece of work. At one point, there were a number of objects whirling around, including a teacup and pot. As he watched them pass each other, the thought came to Collins that it would be fun if the teapot poured tea into the cup as they flew by each other. "Everybody loved it, but it occurred to me on-the-fly. I certainly didn't plan the shot or storyboard it," says Collins.

By contrast, Drew Pictures' Drew Huffman, another San Francisco animator, makes intricate models and spends a lot of time on that phase of animation. He also emphasizes the planning stages and says these considerations are too often overlooked, especially by novices who often want to just plunge ahead. Huffman's modeling on his interactive 3-D game, *The Iron Helix*, is evidence that he

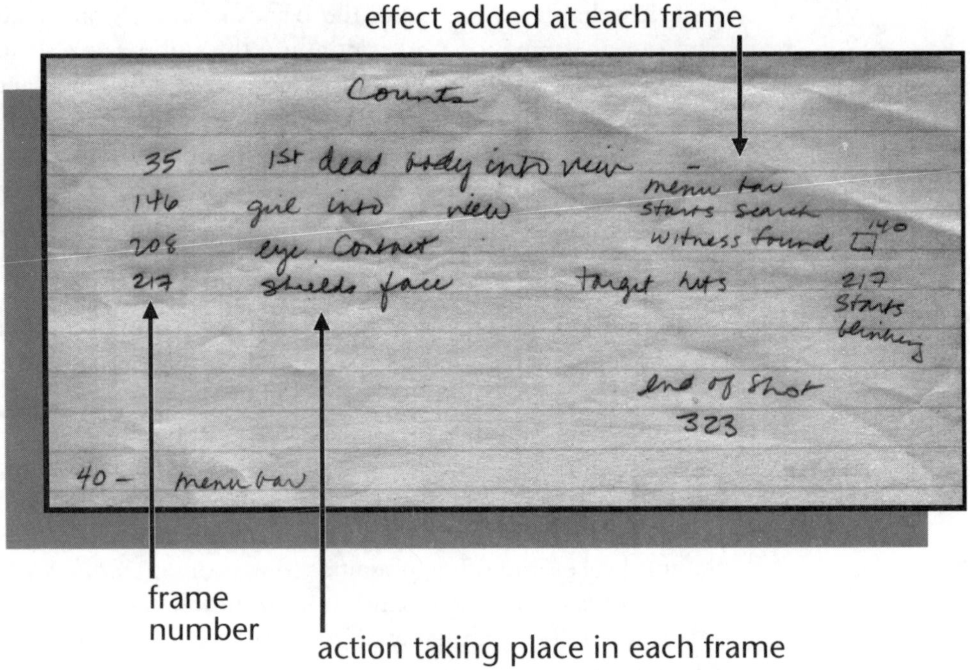

effect added at each frame

Figure 12.1 Excerpt from Lynda Weinman's *Robocop* notebook.

frame number

action taking place in each frame

follows his own advice. The models are beautifully detailed and rendered, and the story line is logical and well thought out.

So clearly there's more than one way to skin a spaceship, and you will evolve your own style as you gain experience. In the meantime, it's a good idea to understand the early phases of the animation process.

Story-boarding

The primary means for planning an animation is the *storyboard*. Now widely used by the broadcast and film industries to plan and visualize scenes, the storyboard was actually pioneered by early animators. In fact, Walt Disney, himself, kept as a souvenir part of the storyboard for *Steamboat Willie*, the cartoon that introduced Mickey Mouse to the world. (It was also the first cartoon to feature a synchronized sound track. The first film of any kind with sound, *The Jazz Singer*, had only been released the year before, in 1927.)

Syd Mead, a well known artist and industrial designer who has also worked extensively in film and multimedia, considers storyboards to be "an extremely important part of the planning process."

A production designer for such films as *Aliens, 2010,* and *Tron,* Mead also designed the V'GER entity for the first *Star Trek* movie, which trekkies will remember as the visual and dramatic climax of the film.

FIELD NO.03: LOWER CENTER

Figure 12.2 Excerpt from Syd Mead's *Blade Runner* storyboard.

VEHICLES FOR BLADERUNNER WERE DESIGNED TO BE CHARACTERS IN THE STORY. IN THIS CLOSE-UP, THE TAXI BECOMES AN ANGULAR, UTILITARIAN ADDITION TO THE CLUTTERED STREET SCENE; AN UN-GRACIOUS, BRUTALLY FUNCTIONAL UTILITY FOR PUBLIC USE.

For the science fiction classic *Blade Runner*, Mead designed the street scenes as well as the vehicles. The storyboard for some of the film's sequences included Mead's original art, which he later annotated (see Figure 12.2).

Storyboards are also key parts of the animation process for today's full-length animated movies. *Pocahontas*, for example, contains over 10,000,000 frames. Many people work on these complex animations, and the storyboard is a way to study the project in detail before committing the vast resources necessary to create the work itself.

Though your own animations probably won't approach the epic scale of a sci-fi epic or Disney movie, the storyboards are still your opportunity to visualize before you start work. The storyboard itself doesn't have to be anything too involved. Basically, it's just sketches of key scenes with a place to write accompanying notes and script outlines.

The storyboard can save you many hours of wasted effort later. You'll also find that when you sketch out scenes and look at them in relation to one another, other ideas will suggest themselves. Holes in the story and action will become apparent through the storyboard. If you are working on a large project involving many people, storyboards are a way to stay in sync with one another.

The "script" that goes along with the storyboard doesn't have to be actual dialog or narration—your animation may not have any. The accompanying text can simply be information on content, ideas for color and texture, cues for music, notes on the "feel" and visual dynamics of the scene, or instructions for camera placement and quality and location of lighting.

Many animators study comic books, a readily available source of storyboard art. Comics regularly use odd angles and forced perspective and are generally effective at suggesting motion and action.

You can buy preprinted storyboard blanks from art or video production suppliers, but you can just as easily create your own with a word processor.

In the end, it's less expensive to sketch something than to animate it.

Designing for the Medium

Another important part of the planning process is to scope out fully the target delivery method and platform for your animation. Is it to be played back on another computer? If so, what kind, and what sort of display will be used, and how much RAM is necessary? Your own equipment must also be evaluated to make sure it is up to the demands of the project. If the animation will be played back on a kiosk or from a laserdisc, or written to videotape, there are still other considerations.

One of the most important factors is the time you have to devote to the project. If you need to produce a 30-second broadcast-quality piece, you'd better have a lot of time on your hands (or some help), not to mention the extra equipment you'll need (such as a frame-accurate videotape recorder and video output hardware).

All of these issues are best contemplated before you actually start any work. This will spare you unpleasant surprises that could derail a lot of hard work later in the project.

Computer-Based Delivery

If you're designing for playback on a computer, find out what the lowest common denominator is. You should know the target machine's CPU, color capabilities, screen size, and both RAM and hard disk capacities. If the animation will be played from a CD or videodisc, the target audience obviously must have the appropriate playback device as well.

The target machine may be very different from your own development computer. If, say, you have a Pentium, and the target is a 486, try to lay your hands on a 486 for frequent testing of different pieces of the project as it evolves. You may well find that transitions and effects that work fine on your Pentium will crawl on the 486.

Lower-end machines such as the Macintosh II and 386 PC models have limitations when it comes to multimedia. While they theoretically can hold more, they often are equipped with only 1 to 8Mb of RAM, small hard disks, and slower CPUs. As a matter of fact, 386 PCs usually lack multimedia hardware altogether.

Remember that, despite the fanfare surrounding 24-bit color, this capability is still relatively scarce among the masses. Working in 24-bit also will drastically slow development time, especially rendering. The resulting image files are also larger, thus requiring more disk and RAM space.

DeBabelizer 1.6 Demo ⌘ 719

However, if you have a 24-bit card and the extra time and resources, it does make sense to create 24-bit images and then convert them to 8-bit for final output. This results in better image quality than if you were to work in 8-bit from the beginning. Also, it's easier to use a program like DeBabilizer to map all of your images to a single palette.

If your work will be stored and delivered via CD, you also should do some tests to simulate performance, so that you can experience the delays viewers will encounter as they wait for images to transfer from the device. The faster CD players will do an adequate job of transferring from the disc, but your audience may not have the latest equipment.

The faster data access of the videodisc makes it desirable as a delivery medium, but other factors are less favorable. For one thing, few people have videodiscs; this will limit the market for your work. On the upside, videodiscs *are* gaining in popularity, they are being used by many schools and corporations, and they are getting pretty cheap to master and produce.

Other performance trade-offs can be made during the production phase rather than in the initial planning stage; but you should be aware of them early on, too. They include rendering only what will be seen by the "camera" (the viewer's point of view), rendering moving elements separate from the background, using 2-D elements where possible, using antialiasing only when necessary, and selecting lower-quality shading when acceptable. All of these trade-offs of quality versus performance are discussed later in this chapter.

Kiosks and Videotape

When designing an animation that will be played back on a kiosk, you may be able to bank on a more robust delivery platform. Industrial-strength kiosks often use higher performance computers and maybe even videodiscs, but this is not always the case. Again, make sure you try out the delivery platform ahead of time, and, if possible, have one available for continuous testing. Note that kiosks often employ larger monitors, so you'll have to plan your work accordingly.

Broadcast-quality animation for delivery on videotape is among the most demanding of applications. The quality of the images themselves can only be achieved by a few animation programs, although this capability is cropping up more frequently (see Chapter 5, "Animation Tools").

Broadcast quality also means that you'll have to use the best rendering quality, which will add to rendering time. The high frame rate of video—30 frames per second (fps) or the more precise 60 fields per second—also adds to the development burden, since you'll have to create many more frames than for the average computer-delivered animation.

You'll also have to invest in a single-frame recorder, a combination of software and hardware that writes the animation out to tape one frame at a time. This is necessary because today's desktop computers aren't yet powerful enough to blast out full screen animation at 30 fps. If you use this form of animation only occasionally, you may want to find a service that will do this part of the process for you.

When producing for video, you'll also need to make sure colors that look fine on the computer screen will read on a TV (or an NTSC) monitor. There is expensive calibration equipment that will ensure this, but if you're designing for video, you should have an NTSC monitor to check your work every once in a while (see Chapter 14, "Creating Video"). Designers who work in this medium sometimes develop their own test methods to make sure their colors are in the appropriate range. For example, Lynda Weinman uses a simple rule of thumb to make sure that colors are "video" or "NTSC-safe" (meaning they will display correctly in video). When processing an image with fully saturated colors in Photoshop, Weinman will lower either the saturation or brightness of the color by 25 percent. She finds this works pretty well, although she comments, "What I lose by not having a waveform or vectorscope is that my method is a little conservative; and if I had the scope, I could push it to the limit."

Modeling

Building three-dimensional objects is a process known as *modeling*. Before you animate and render objects, you must define the structure of your 3-D "world" —the shapes and dimensions of objects, and their relationship to one another. Modeling controls also allow you to position and group objects and define how they will move when animated.

Creating Basic Objects and Shapes

MacroModel 1.5 Demo ⌘ 720

The process of creating real-world models is abetted by the large and versatile collection of predefined shapes and modeling tools offered by most modeling programs. Three-dimensional objects normally start out as *wireframes* that define their shape in 3-D space. Wireframes, because they lack surfaces, can be quickly manipulated. Some modelers, notably Macromedia's Swivel 3D and MacroModel, Specular's Infini-D, and Impulse's Imagine, can do fast rough or *flat* shading that sometimes makes it easier to model objects. This type of shading, while too rough for finished work, can help in positioning complex objects that might otherwise be a sea of wireframes (see Figure 12.3).

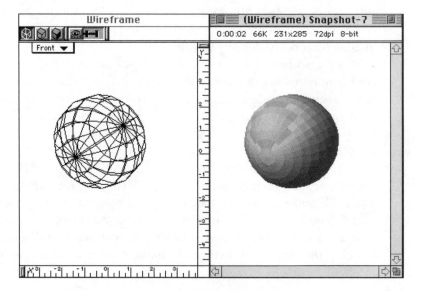

Figure 12.3 Model in wireframe and quick-shaded versions.

Flat shading is particularly helpful when you are working with more complex elements. In wireframe views, it is sometimes difficult or impossible to tell that a wheel on a car is penetrating the body, or that fingers are moving right through a hand. Quick shading can help you visualize better while still keeping screen drawing at an acceptable rate.

Modeling Tools

Modeling in three dimensions requires a variety of tools to help you represent the array of shapes and structures found in the real world (and some that aren't!). The following is a brief overview of the tools available. Not all modelers have all tools; see Chapter 5, "Animation Tools," for a feature comparison by product.

Cross-Sectional Modeling

This procedure, also called *lofting* or *loafing*, is a simple, general-purpose technique often overlooked amid the profusion of more exotic modeling methods. You begin by drawing 2-D shapes that will act as cross sections or "ribs" for the 3-D object. Then the modeler connects the ribs (a technique also known as creating "transitions" or "skinning") to form the object (Figure 12.4).

This is a versatile method and can be used to create any number of freeform shapes. It has the further advantage of being economical in terms of geometry; it uses fewer polygons to represent a shape in wireframe than do other techniques. Infini-D 3.0's new modeler, for example, offers many cross-sectional

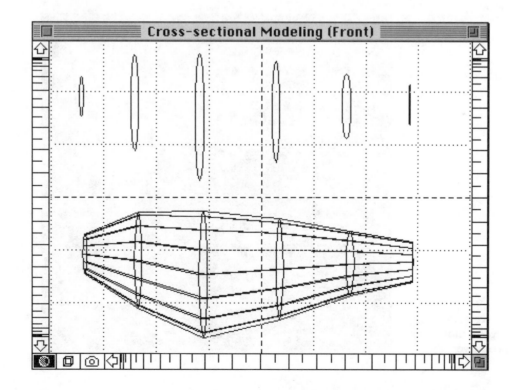

**Figure 12.4
Cross-sectional
modeling.**

modeling tools. Caligari's trueSpace has one of the most intuitive cross-sectional tools. Autodesk's 3D Studio and Imagine have separate program units for lofting and form modeling.

Primitives

Many modeling programs provide simple building blocks, or *primitives*, on which you can base custom shapes created to suit your particular needs (Figure 12.5).

Primitives provide a place to start when modeling objects. But they are also helpful because, since they are a part of the modeling program itself, their code is optimized; and they can be represented, manipulated, and stored more efficiently, resulting in quicker screen drawing and faster rendering times.

Lathe, Extruded, and Freeform Shapes

In addition to the primitive objects, modeling programs typically include three other types of basic modeling tools: extrusion, lathe, and freeform.

Extruding is the process by which you take a 2-D object and push it out, or extrude it into 3-D space. Extrusion tools probably are most often used to create 3-D type, but they are also useful for making other shapes. For example, you can use an imported PICT file as a template, trace over it with drawing tools, and then extrude the drawing into a 3-D object.

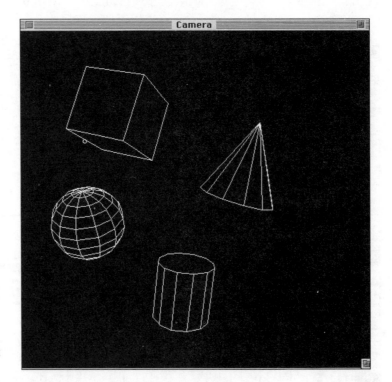

**Figure 12.5
Typical modeling
primitives.**

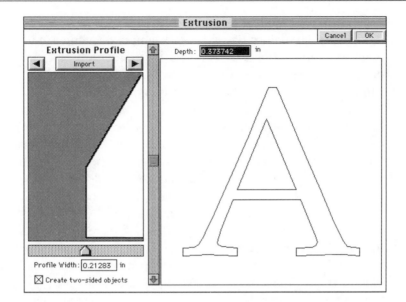

Figure 12.6 Applying a beveled edge to type.

Extrusion tools generally provide control over parameters such as extrusion depth. Strata's StudioPro, Imagine, and trueSpace even let you apply a bevel to an extruded object, which yields particularly nice results with beveled type. You can use one of several preset bevels or specify your own (Figure 12.6).

Lathe objects are used to create cylindrical shapes such as glasses, tubes, and pencils—any shape that is symmetrical around a single axis. Lathe objects are surprisingly easy to create, because you draw only the 2-D shape, which the program "spins" around an axis to form the 3-D object (Figure 12.7).

Once you have drawn the lathe shape, you can modify the outline by moving the points that define it (Figure 12.8).

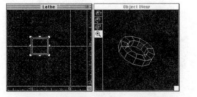

Figure 12.7 Creating a lathe.

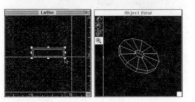

Figure 12.8 Altering the shape of a lathe object.

Freeform objects can be created by starting with a freeform primitive (if the modeler you're using has one) or by simply drawing a 2-D shape that the program will turn into a 3-D shape for you. Freeform objects can be modified by dragging their points as you would with a lathe object. Using freeform tools, you can quickly create odd shapes with complex geometry.

Evolving and Refining Objects and Shapes

As useful as the basic shapes and toolsets are, real-world entities and more intricate models often can be represented only with more sophisticated techniques. Frequently, this means cooking up models from scratch, rather than using predefined shapes. These techniques and tools, while powerful, generally take more dedication and patience to master. They also can be difficult to control and can easily create extremely odd, unnatural shapes.

Spline-Based Modeling

Spline-based tools are used to create ultrasmooth curves. Until recently, this capability wasn't even found in some of the highest-end animation programs costing thousands of dollars. It is one measure of the growing maturity of the Mac and PC animation markets that there are now a number of low-end products offering this feature.

Spline curves are especially desirable as the camera moves in on rendered models, where nonspline curves will reveal telltale faceting from close-in views. You can still achieve decent-looking curves with a nonspline modeler, but you'll have to use a lot of polygons to do it—a cumbersome process and one that will make huge files and increase rendering time.

Illustrator 4.0 Demo ⌘ 718

In Figure 12.9, MacroModel's spline curves were used to create the complex forms that make up the airplane fuselage. Some modelers do not themselves create splines but will import Bezier curves created in Adobe Illustrator and then allow you to change their shape by clicking and dragging the control points.

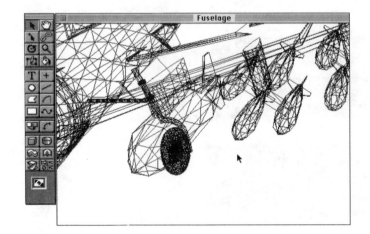

Figure 12.9 Spline-based modeling in Macromodel.

Other programs, such as MacroModel, Hash Animator Master, and Infini-D 3.0's modeler (Figure 12.10), are spline-based modelers; so you can create and adjust spline curves on the spot. If your modeler doesn't support the creation of splines but will import them, make sure that all of the spline information is retained. Sometimes information can be lost in the conversion, resulting in splines that are little better than curves created with more traditional techniques.

Most renderers—programs which create the finished 3-D images, complete with shaded surfaces, color, texture, light, and shadow—render only from polygons. That means that unless the renderer you use is specifically designed to handle splines rather than processing your carefully drawn spline curves, it will convert the information to polygons, which may result in the same old faceting.

This is not a concern when you use programs that incorporate both modeling and rendering into a single product. However, it can trip you up if you model in one package and render in another—unless you have the advantage of the compatibility of products made by multimedia giant, Macromedia. For example, Three-D, Macromedia's renderer, is made to work with MacroModel and will seamlessly accept and import all modeling information. Generally, though, even

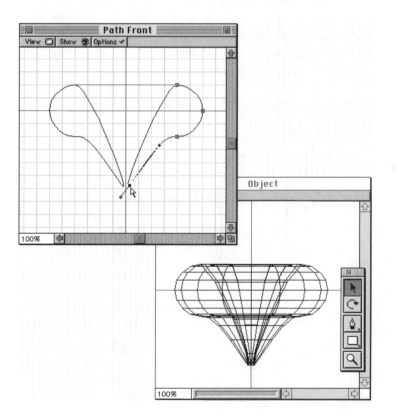

**Figure 12.10
In Infini-D 3.0's
modeling shop,
you can edit
vertex points to
quickly create
complex objects.**

spline curves converted to polygonal curves will look smoother than curves originally created with polygons.

Vertex-Level or Mesh Editing

Vertex-level editing is a precise form of model refinement. It allows you to manipulate control points, or vertices, along the surfaces of a shape. Some programs refer to these editable surface control points as meshes and the objects, themselves, as mesh objects. While mesh editing gives you nearly absolute control, it also is a painstaking process, suitable (and tolerable) only for the most exacting of work.

Byte by Byte's Sculpt 3D and 4D, which offer the most complete vertex-level editing, allow you to select more than one point at one time. You can then treat these points as separate objects, rotate and resize them, even extrude them into separate features. trueSpace and Imagine also feature some interesting and powerful vertex editing commands.

Extruding along a Path and Sweeping

These two techniques can produce forms that are sometimes practical and other times whimsical. To extrude along a path, you begin with a 2-D shape that is automatically replicated by the modeler (Figure 12.11). This technique is useful for producing uniform architectural features such as moldings.

Sweep is a combination of extruding and lathing in which you begin with a 2-D shape and use numeric controls to specify the direction, rotation, and increment of the extrusion, which the program then uses to create the object. Using

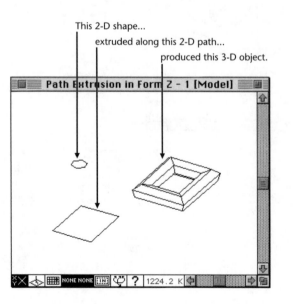

**Figure 12.11
Extruding along
a path.**

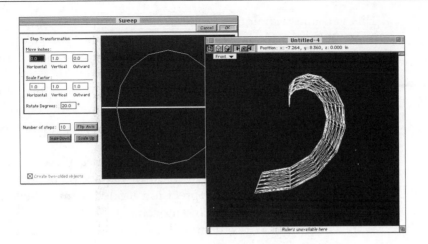

**Figure 12.12
Strata's Sweep
control panel.**

sweep, you can create shapes such as bicycle handlebars, snakes, animal horns, or nautilus shells. Figure 12.12 shows a sweep form in Strata's StudioPro.

Drilling is another convenient tool that, unfortunately, is not often found in modeler toolboxes. A 2-D object is used like a bit to carve a hole in a 3-D object that then contains an actual hole, not simply a facade.

Sculpting with Boolean Operations

Boolean operations are advanced tools that let you use one 3-D object to alter another. You can then use the object created where the two shapes intersect, or either or both of the altered shapes. Figure 12.13 illustrates the Boolean effect.

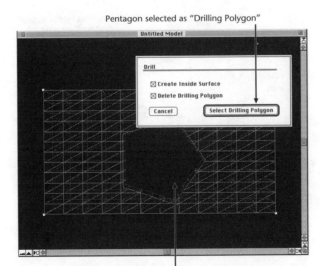

**Figure 12.13
The Boolean
effect.**

Pentagon selected as "Drilling Polygon"

Grid object has pentagon-shaped hole drilled through it

This versatile technique can be used to "sculpt" 3-D objects to create shapes impossible (or very difficult) to achieve any other way. It's also a quick way to create an object that fits another irregularly shaped object perfectly.

Working in 3-D Space

The 3-D workspace, itself, is often called the 3-D world; objects are situated along three axes: X, Y, and Z. When viewing a three-dimensional object from the front, movement left to right is along the X axis, in/out motion is along the Y axis, and up/down motion is along the Z axis (Figure 12.14).

Using this coordinate system, you can accurately place objects in space in relation to each other and to the camera, your vantage point on the 3-D world. These coordinates are essential for precision modeling, and they are also critical to accurate camera positioning and movement.

The concepts of axes and the coordinate system are fundamental to all 3-D animation software, but they may take you a while to get used to. If you were good at high school geometry and zipped through test questions asking you to guess what diagrams in plane view would look like if they were folded, you'll do fine.

Most programs will show you the position of an object in relation to the center of the world—the place where the X-, Y-, and Z-axes converge. (This is generally the default reference point, but you can alter it.)

If you enter a value for the position of an object on the X-axis, the object will move from right to left (in top view). Type a number in the position box for the Y-axis, and the object moves in or out. When an object is at the center of the world, the position coordinates are 0,0,0. You also can move the object by click-

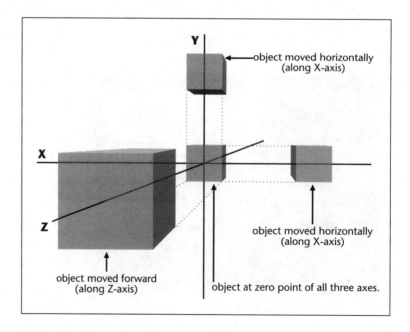

**Figure 12.14
X-, Y-, and Z-axes
of motion.**

object moved horizontally (along X-axis)

object moved horizontally (along X-axis)

object moved forward (along Z-axis)

object at zero point of all three axes.

ing and dragging, and the position numbers will dynamically update. Other values will affect an object's orientation in relation to a particular axis. Enter a value in the X-axis orientation box, and the object will tilt. The dimension boxes affect the size of an object. Working with a program that has this feature can greatly aid in your understanding of 3-D space.

Programs differ in the way they represent 3-D space, and some help more than others in the visualization process. For example, in World view, Infini-D shows objects in four simultaneous views: top, front, right (or bottom, back, right), and camera. Most modelers require you to enter another mode or view (known variously as the Workshop, Object view, and so on) to make substantive changes to models. While in the World view, you can generally modify objects in very basic ways by resizing, rotating, squashing, stretching, or repositioning.

Look for a modeler that has a few other navigation aids. For example, most modelers let you place an object (or point a camera) anywhere in the 3-D space. But your windows on this space are only narrow views. This might mean that as you move them around, your models will easily disappear from view (in what is known as the *black hole effect*). Modelers that will automatically turn the cameras to an object or move an object without changing its orientation, can be helpful.

Precise Positioning and Alignment

The coordinate system can be used to align objects precisely. For example, you may want several objects to line up exactly. The fastest and most accurate way to do this is to enter numeric values for the position of the objects. You may want to actually superimpose two objects; in this case, simply use the same position values for both objects.

Sometimes, the perspective views (perspectives have *vanishing points*—objects farther away look smaller) common to 3-D programs can get in the way of precise alignment of two objects. For example, in Figure 12.15, it looks as if the ball is on the surface. But actually, as you'll notice by studying the orthographic view (no perspective), it's not. (See Figure 12.16.)

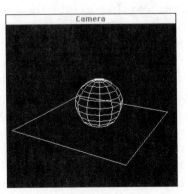

**Figure 12.15
Is the ball on the
surface?**

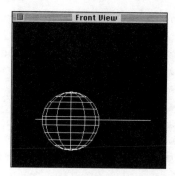

**Figure 12.16
Not even close.**

Locks and Linking

Much as you might constrain the movement of drawing tools in a draw program so that, for example, a line comes out exactly straight, you can confine movement, orientation, and size attributes of objects. Locks are useful in a number of ways. For instance, when you animate objects, locks on movement and orientation will allow you to create more realistic and consistent motion. Using these constraints, fingers won't bend backwards, trains will stay on their tracks, and planets will revolve around the sun.

Locks can be relative to the world. They also can involve the relationship between objects, so that objects can be grouped as one, for example, to keep together all of the component body parts that make up a figure. When multiple objects are locked or linked, the first is known as the *parent*, and the second and any subsequent objects are the *child* or *children*. These groups of objects are common to 3-D modeling and are necessary to the creation of complex animated forms. Such composite objects are known variously as *hierarchical models* or *object networks*.

Programs, such as Real 3D, Swivel, and Infini-D, that allow a great deal of control over locks and linking, offer various levels of control. Infini-D, for example, uses free, pivot, position, and full locks. Free locks let you reposition or rotate the child while the parent remains stationary; move the parent, however, and the child will follow. For example, you could use a free lock to position a planet relative to the sun. The planet is free to orbit the sun, but if you reposition the sun the planet will move, too, while still keeping its relative position.

A pivot lock allows you to reposition but not reorient a child independently of the parent. Pivot locks are good for creating specific types of movement, such as the movement of elbow joints, which in the natural world move only along one axis. Specify a position lock and you'll be able to rotate the child without affecting the parent, but the two will be linked in terms of movement. You might use a position lock to create a telescoping object, so that the components would be able to slide in and out along a single axis only.

A full lock welds two objects in terms of position and orientation. This type of lock is analogous to grouping: You effectively create one composite object.

You might use this type of locking to bind the legs of a table to a tabletop, for instance. You can still change the size or surface characteristics of fully locked objects independently of one another. The table would still be manageable as a single unit, but you could apply one surface to the legs and another to the top.

Super 3D has a command called "Seal Vertices" that is especially useful when joining objects. Sometimes objects may look as if they are joined, but they are actually slightly misaligned. This may not be apparent until you add surfaces to the compound object, at which time irregularities due to imperfectly aligned objects may become noticeable. This wastes time because you'll have to go and fix the alignment and then re-render. The Seal Vertices command ensures that objects are properly aligned and connected. Real 3D combines many physical attributes with techniques such as "friction" and "inverse kinematics" to offer very realistic animation effects.

Next Year's Model

Clip Media/Animation
⌘ 100–110

Clip Media/Images
⌘ 500–519

The tools and primitives described above can help a great deal in creating a geometric description of boxes, cylinders, or coffee cups. However, making convincing people, trees, or cars is more challenging.

You may not want to invest the considerable time necessary to master a modeler but may prefer to move on to the more gratifying phases of animating and rendering. 3-D clip libraries meet this need by providing sets of prebuilt models that can be used as a basis for an animation, placing them, and then rendering and animating them in your own way.

Also, there are products designed for specific modeling tasks, such as Fractal Design's Poser for creating human models, KPT Bryce for building terrains, and Onyx Computing's Tree Professional for building tree models.

Professional animator Lynda Weinman agrees: "I'm really in favor of [prebuilt models] and I study them myself sometimes for two reasons. First, you don't have to put the effort and time into learning modeling yourself—you can just drop models into your presentation, and—boom—it's done. The other thing is to study how somebody else did it."

While Weinman and other professionals rarely use prebuilt models, such models are, as she points out, good learning tools. And if you're also tempted to save time and lift a few (but only if you've paid for the clip library!), well, after all, even Picasso said, "Good artists copy, great artists steal."

Animating

Once you've modeled the objects and "players" in your 3-D world, it's time to give them life by animating and rendering them. For the sake of clarity, we've chosen to cover first animation and then rendering in this chapter. In reality, however, the processes may be intertwined to some degree. For example, sometimes animators will render a scene, then animate it. Generally, though, it's best to get basic motions mapped out ahead of rendering, since working with rendered images or wireframes is much slower.

If you are creating 3-D still images, of course, you will move directly from the modeling to the rendering stage.

Motion Studies

Animators usually will start by roughing out movements in a series of motion studies. These are accomplished with objects in wireframe or abbreviated geometry to speed development time. An even quicker way to study potential movements is to substitute *bounding boxes* for models. Bounding boxes are simply cubes with roughly the same dimensions as the models they represent. Because they are simple forms, bounding boxes are often used to establish the basic movements of objects. Most programs will automatically substitute bounding boxes for complex geometry.

An animator, then, might begin by blocking out movement with bounding boxes to achieve the basic motion desired. Once the essence is established, movement can be refined using the wireframe geometry of the object models. At this stage, objects that possess at least rudimentary features also can be oriented correctly, so that they face the proper direction as they move.

To get a better idea of dimensionality, the animator might next render the wireframes with flat shading, which will give a crude idea of surface and form. Only after the motions have been refined will fully rendered animation be processed and viewed.

Motion Scripting

The process of animating objects is called *motion scripting* or *motion control*. Animation programs offer a wide range of features for effecting motion. (See Chapter 5, "Animation Tools," for a list of features by product.) The basic idea is that you move objects (or cameras) into key positions, and the program takes a snapshot of this setup. Then you move the objects again, and the computer takes another snapshot. These shots are called keyframes.

Once you have identified all of your keyframes, the computer does the rest by *tweening*—calculating the in-between frames. This is analogous to the process used by traditional animators. The animator generally creates the keyframes, and assistant animators (who were known as "in-betweeners" in the early days) then create all the intervening frames; the computer and animation software act as your assistant animators.

Of course, you have many options in creating your keyframes—you aren't limited to movement in space alone. You can resize objects, so that they grow larger or smaller over time; you can re-orient them, so that they will move to face a different direction when animated; some programs even allow you to change an object's surface and color over time or change one object into another.

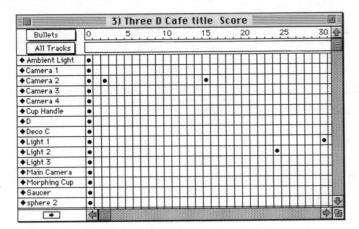

**Figure 12.17
Three-D's "Score,"
a time-based
visual display.**

Time-Based Animation

Macromedia pioneered the idea of the *Score*, which first appeared in its Director 2-D animation and integration program. The Score provides an extremely flexible means by which to control and refine events over time. The Score is also used by Macromedia's rendering and animation package, Three-D; and the concept has been adopted by other animation programs as well. (Infini-D calls its version the *Sequencer* and Imagine has an "Action Editor.") Figure 12.17 is an example of Three-D's score. These time-based visual representations provide enormous control over animation because they allow you to tweak individual components without affecting any other elements in the overall sequence. If you decide a particular object is moving too slowly, you can adjust the speed of that object alone, while leaving other objects and events untouched.

Suppose you had an object flying around in a circle, an object whose motion you had carefully defined. Let's say you also wanted that object to change color. You could alter the color without affecting any of the motion attributes associated with the sequence.

In these ways, time-based windows (like the Score, Sequencer, and Action Editor) offer a very flexible and powerful means to tweak and adjust animations down to the individual object. In fact, you can even address parts of an object, such as a person, if the object is made up of component objects.

Refining Movement

While you can get acceptable results simply by dragging objects to create keyframes and then letting the computer fill in the other frames to complete the animation, realistic motion often requires more subtle effects. When objects move in the real world, they accelerate and decelerate gradually, not all at once. This is known as *inertia*, and some animation programs give you control over this effect with parameters called *ease-in* and *ease-out* (Figure 12.18). This effect is

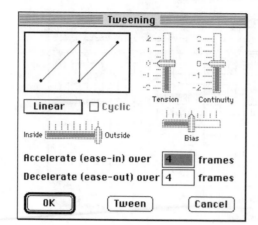

**Figure 12.18
Smoothing
motion with
Ease-in/Ease-out.**

particularly useful for camera pans and fly-throughs, which would be noticeably artificial without ease-in/ease-out.

Some programs let you animate objects along a spline-based path, which can also smooth movements to a great degree.

Sophisticated programs like Three-D let you view and tweak motions in graph form. These graphical views, which are available for any animation sequence you've created, offer the ultimate control over motion smoothing. You can tweak the points on the graph to adjust the motion, then replay it to see the results.

Although all of these are convenient and flexible tools, smooth motion can be difficult to achieve, especially for complex camera fly-throughs. Like everything else in animation, top-quality results are frequently obtainable only through hard work, long hours, and tedious trial and error. For example, San Francisco animator Donald Grahame inherited a complex 3-D animation project that plays from a record store kiosk to allow customers to listen to CDs before they buy. Even though Grahame discarded most of the work that had already been done, preferring to do his own beautifully designed and rendered scenes, he kept a fluid camera movement that flies through to establish the scene. The previous animator had spent hours perfecting the motion, and Grahame didn't want to start all over on that.

Interpolating Other Characteristics

Interpolation is another word for the calculations performed by the computer to create in-between frames. Although creating motion, changing the size of objects, and re-orienting them are some of the most common animation processes, there are many others, including selection of characteristics such as color, shape, and even texture. You might animate these characteristics to change an object's color or texture over time, or even have it change shape altogether. Programs that offer these features make it as easy as animating motion or orientation.

To change an object's surface characteristics over time, you would simply apply the first surface to the object (see "Rendering" for a complete description of surface characteristics), move the time marker ahead in the timeline, and apply the second texture. When the animation is played back, the first surface will change to the second surface in the allotted time.

Some programs allow you to create animated lighting effects, too, so that you can change the color of a light from one shade to another over time.

Morph 2.5 Demo ⌘ 714

In *morphing*, one of the most intriguing animated transformations, an object changes shape over time. Morphing was made famous in *Terminator 2*, in which the T-1000 "pseudopod" transformed itself into various human and not-so-human forms. This first use of a digital character—created by computer—has opened the floodgates for computer animation in Hollywood.

Other popular transformations are exploding an object, and turning one into a mass of expanding particles. Programs that include several special effects modules are Strata's Studio Pro, Impulse's Imagine, and 3D Studio.

Now you see the effect everywhere, but that shouldn't stop you. Morphing is still a stunning effect, and a lot of fun to play around with. To do it, you simply select or create the first object, create a keyframe, then do the same with the second object. The program will create the necessary in-between frames, and you can play back the animation to watch the transformation.

The Advantages of Being Invisible

Making certain objects invisible is a neat trick with many uses. For example, you will want to render cameras and lights (which in most programs are simply objects like any others) invisible so that they don't appear in your final animation. Or you may not want an object to appear until a given point in time. To do this, you would make it invisible until you want it to show up.

You also can use this technique to conserve disk and memory space when animating moving objects over a static background. You can render the background invisible so that the computer has to animate (and render) only the objects that are actually changing. Later, you can composite the objects with background to create the finished piece. This will save on system resources by having the computer animate and render only what is absolutely necessary.

This is analogous to a major innovation in early film animation. Before the use of celluloid began early in this century, animators had to paint everything— even static backgrounds—for each frame, an incredibly tedious process. *Gertie the Trained Dinosaur* (1908), perhaps the most famous of the first animated films, was done in this way.

With the advent of celluloid, a single background could be placed under a series of cels, saving enormous time and money and freeing talented artists for more challenging undertakings. (Chuck Jones, director of such Warner Bros. classic characters as Bugs Bunny, Wile E. Coyote, and Pepe Le Pew, began his career as a cel washer.)

"Jumping Clocks"

Interactive television has been talked about for years and even tried a few times without success. Now, with the advent of multimedia and the retrofitting of high-speed cable, telephone, and satellite delivery systems, many believe ITV will catch on.

A linchpin in its success will be a flood of programming material that even now is being created expressly for the new medium. Richard Thompson is an animator at NTN, which is creating animated games for one of the first ITV trials in Omaha, Nebraska. The games will eventually be played at "information terminals" in sports bars and hotel rooms, and over on-line services such as America Online.

Among other things, Thompson worked on a game called *Countdown*, a trivia game that pits players against one another. When a player hits the #1 spot, an animated group of clocks races around a corner, with one clock taking the lead.

Special Considerations

For the "Jumping Clocks" sequence (see Figure 12.19), Thompson used Caligari's true-Space, a PC animation tool he chose in part because it allows objects to change shape without morphing. "I can take an object and drop it into a device that creates a 'deformation lattice' that will, over time, change the shape of that object," says Thompson.

Rather than creating a complex set of control points for morphing, Thompson simply copied the lattice to separate animation frames. An object's lattice can also be distorted along its axis in different ways.

Like a growing number of animators, Thompson prefers PC tools over their Mac counterparts. "The PC's 3-D tools are superior to the Mac's," avers Thompson. Besides true-

Figure 12.19
Countdown's
Jumping Clocks.

box continued

Space, he cites Lightwave 3D, which "blows away everything I know of on either the Mac or the PC."

Tips and Techniques

In even the simplest animation project, Thompson recommends having the story line well discussed and designed prior to starting work. "You have to make sure you know what you're trying to communicate and that everyone understands the design," he says.

Since visual ideas can be hard to get across by any other means, Thompson recommends using some form of imagery to communicate during the preproduction and development process. In animation projects, even still renderings help communicate basic colors and composition.

After doing initial comps on napkins or with other informal media, Thompson will make pencil sketches with comments and notes on time sequencing. Finally, he'll often mock up 3-D still frames using an animation package.

Tools and Equipment

Aside from trueSpace (see Figure 12.20), Thompson used Premiere for transitional effects and to add audio tracks. He also used Coreldraw to design the clock face, which he exported as a DXF file for compositing with the animation.

Premiere 4.0 Demo ⌘ 722

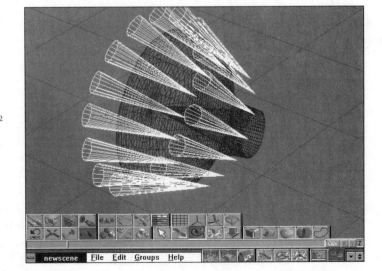

**Figure 12.20
Modeling with
trueSpace.**

Making objects invisible also can help with tricky animation effects. Dave Merck of the Animation Lab at the University of Massachusetts at Amherst uses the technique to animate a helicopter. First, he creates a small object and links it to the chopper. Then he makes the small object invisible. Next, he creates the blade rotation for the chopper. Finally, he drags the invisible object, which, since it is linked to the helicopter, will move it through space. This creates a separate timeline for the helicopter movement, which doesn't necessarily have the same period as the blade rotation.

Joe Sparks, acclaimed producer of the *Total Distortion* CD-ROM product, agrees that making objects invisible can be a lifesaver. Sometimes he has animated and rendered a complex scene, only to discover that something is wrong with one of the objects. Rather than start over on the entire scene, he can render the offending object invisible, go back to the original model file for the object and make the necessary modifications. Then, using the scene as a template, Joe deletes everything but the new object, which leaves it in the correct place for compositing back into the rendered scene.

Taking Advantage of Links and Hierarchies

Hierarchical animation lets you take advantage of locks and links that you set up when modeling objects (see "Locks and Linking" earlier in this chapter). For example, when you animate a human form, you could make the arms sway as the hips move forward. Other possibilities include locking lights to objects, so that as the objects, move, the lights follow. The same relationships can be set up between cameras and objects so that the action is always being followed and will remain in view. The Inverse Kinematics technique can be used to create skeletal links, so that when a hand moves, the attached arm follows.

Rendering

Rendering is the process of defining the appearance of your objects and scenes. You apply surface characteristics such as color, texture, and reflectivity. You can also control how shadows fall and what they look like. You establish point of view with the camera and select appropriate lenses.

Once you have specified all of these attributes, sit back and relax awhile, because it will take the computer from several minutes to *days* or even *weeks* to render your scene. Just how long it takes depends on the complexity of objects and surfaces, the computer you are using, and the rendering software. Normally, you'll have done motion tests with bounding boxes and wireframes, and will have test-rendered small patches to get an idea of what the final scene will look like. Still, the rendering process often is misunderstood to be hands-free—you go off to do your laundry, come back, and *voilà!* A complete photorealistic scene is waiting for you.

Reality, as usual, is grittier and less romantic. Animators often will render and re-render half a dozen times, and sometimes much more frequently. Even on the fastest of machines, rendering is like watching paint dry. Still, rendering has come a long way, and there are tricks to speed it up. Unfortunately, most involve extra hardware or expensive software. We'll cover these alternatives at the end of this section.

Types of Rendering

Most rendering software gives you myriad options for rendering surfaces. The speed of these techniques generally varies with the realism of the surfaces they render. Some programs, such as Swivel, are known for rapid flat or even smooth shading, which they can do on-the-fly, greatly aiding in the definition of models and the specification of animation moves. Up the ladder (*way* up the ladder), are ray tracing and radiosity, which bring ultrarealism to computer animations, and for which you pay the price in speed, RAM, and disk space (not to mention play-back speed).

Flat Shading

At the bottom of the rendering pecking order is *flat shading*, sometimes called *constant shading*, which is generally used only for rough tests, to get a feel for what models look like with surfaces, or to make sure objects don't intersect when they're not supposed to (which is hard to tell with wireframes).

Flat shading applies the light source to only one point on each face of the model, which results in a faceted appearance with visible underlying geometry.

Smooth Shading: Gouraud and Phong

These are algorithms (mathematical formulas) that seek to simulate more realistic shading, such as the variable shading that characterizes real objects in the natural world. The light is calculated on multiple points on a face and then smoothly blended to produce an integrated, more naturalistic effect.

Gouraud shading is named after its inventor, Frenchman Henri Gouraud (rhymes with Thoreau, believe it or not). In this technique, the effect of lighting is applied to the vertices of the polygons that make up the face. Values are then interpolated for the intermediate shades, and the result is a smooth effect.

Phong shading, an even more sophisticated formula developed by Phong Bui-tuong, calculates shading from multiple points across the entire surface instead of just the vertices of the component polygons. It is known for its excellent re-creation of specular highlights—the "hot-spots" in a very shiny surface, such as a mirror or a chrome surface.

Z-buffer rendering is a means of ordering objects so that those closest to the camera render last. Some Z-buffer renderers can handle shadows and reflections as well, but these generally require shadow and reflection maps. 3D Studio uses Z-buffer rendering to achieve near ray-tracing quality in much less time.

Ray Tracing and Radiosity

Ray tracing is a computationally intensive shading method that calculates the effects of light sources of many types, including direct illumination, reflections, and *refractions* (the effects of light passing through transparent substances such as glass and water). It does this by computing the paths of light rays as they travel from the light source, bounce off objects, and hit the camera.

This technique is normally used for 3-D still images for two reasons: First, it is unbelievably taxing on machine resources, requiring millions of calculations to complete a scene. Second, it is *view-dependent* because light rays are traced from the light source to the point of view (POV), and vice versa; so any change in the camera angle would mean the entire scene would have to recalculated.

Just as ray tracing calculates the effects of light in a reflective environment, *radiosity* determines the effects of diffuse lighting. Instead of tracing light rays, radiosity computes the light energy in a scene that may come from other, indirect sources. For example, a light glancing off a wall will cause some bounce light to fall on other objects in a scene.

Unlike ray tracing, radiosity is view-independent, making it suitable for dynamic scenes that may include shifts in the POV. However, radiosity is more computationally taxing than ray tracing. A common application of radiosity is in 3-D architectural renderings that simulate the diffused lighting of building interiors. Because the technique is view-independent, the client can "walk through" the building to get a simulated feel for the space.

For the ultimate in realism, the two techniques can be combined to achieve specular reflections and refractions, and diffuse lighting effects. However, this is not recommended unless you have a water-cooled Cray supercomputer with a couch.

Trade-offs of Rendering Techniques

As is the case in real life, better quality means more time. No one will argue with the view that ray tracing and radiosity create the best looking and most accurate 3-D imagery, but most desktop computers (and most computer users) are not up to the task. If you're into photorealism, get a very fast computer (preferably a machine designed to crunch polygons, such as Silicon Graphics workstation, or at the very least, a Pentium or Power PC).

Fortunately, you can achieve very good and even outstanding results with Phong shading and a Z-buffer renderer, which is what most renderers use to create finished work. Flat and (especially) Gouraud shading are fine for gauging what a scene will look like, and there are tricks to get some of the effects of the higher-end shading techniques. For example, instead of waiting for calculation of reflections in a shiny object, you can map a tiny version of the scene onto the object's surface, thus creating a simulated environment map (see below) at huge savings in time and energy.

To give you an idea of the trade-offs between rendering techniques, we applied a surface to a simple vase. On a Mac II (admittedly not a blazingly fast machine) the vase took about 10 seconds to render with flat shading, around 1 minute to shade with the Gouraud method, and about 10 minutes to render with Phong shading. By then, it was time for bed, and we didn't get a chance to try ray tracing.

Creating Surfaces

The essence of rendering is the application of surfaces to the models you have constructed and animated in your 3-D world. Most renderers supply a bewildering array of surface options—both prefab surfaces included with the program and the means to edit and create your own custom versions.

Surfaces also can be applied in a number of ways, using any of the shading techniques described above, with commensurate differences in quality. Note that subtle effects will be most accurately rendered with ray tracing or radiosity. Gouraud shading may give only the slightest semblance of the effect, and effects rendered with flat shading probably won't read at all, except to give some idea of rudimentary characteristics such as color.

There are many ways to create surfaces and textures; the method you use will depend on the particular application and the effect you are trying to achieve.

Working With Surface Libraries

Sometimes, the extensive surface libraries included with many renderers will be all you need. For example, Infini-D supplies the list of options shown in Figure 12.21. Note the sphere in the upper right that gives an idea of the effect of each surface. Most renderers allow you to create your own surfaces by starting with one in the surface library and modifying it, using various controls. 3D Studio has a very elaborate materials editor, and Strata's StudioPro displays the dialog box shown in Figure 12.22 for editing preexisting surfaces. Using this dialog box, you can change the characteristics of an existing surface or texture by fiddling with such parameters as ambient fraction, bump amplitude, glow factor, and

Figure 12.21 Infini-D's built-in surface characteristics.

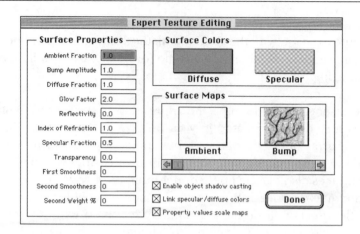

**Figure 12.22
StrataVision's
Expert Texture
Editing dialog.**

transparency. A full discourse on these effects is beyond the scope of this book, but here are a few definitions to whet your appetite. (We just had to find out what "bump amplitude" meant.)

Bump amplitude allows you to set the size of the depressions in a bump texture. Bump maps (see below) are patterns of depressions, such as those on a golf ball, that you can wrap around (map onto) an object.

Ambient fraction is the level of ambient (diffuse) lighting that a given object will reflect, while *glow* will give the illusion that an object is lit from within.

Specular highlight lets you adjust the dot of light reflected in shiny objects.

Texture Mapping

The process of applying surfaces to objects is called *texture-mapping*. You can use the surfaces in surface libraries to do this, or you can create effects such as bumpy surfaces, natural patterns like wood grain and marble, or reflections by mapping other types of patterns.

Most renderers support a variety of texture-mapping techniques, depending on the type of surface you're creating. One way is to map an image file, such as a PICT or TIFF file created in a paint, image processing, or some other program. Use this type of mapping when you have a specific image you want to use as a surface.

Photoshop 3.0 Demo ⌘ 715

Suppose you want to map a photograph onto an object. To do this, you'd scan the photo into an image processing program like Photoshop or ColorStudio. You could process, filter, or otherwise retouch the image, then import it into the renderer for mapping. This technique is particularly effective for creating realistic effects. Drew Pictures in San Francisco used it extensively to create texture maps of all types for *The Iron Helix*. For example, Photoshop was used to create gritty, oily, scarred textures that were then mapped onto spaceship models using Macromedia Three-D and Electric Image.

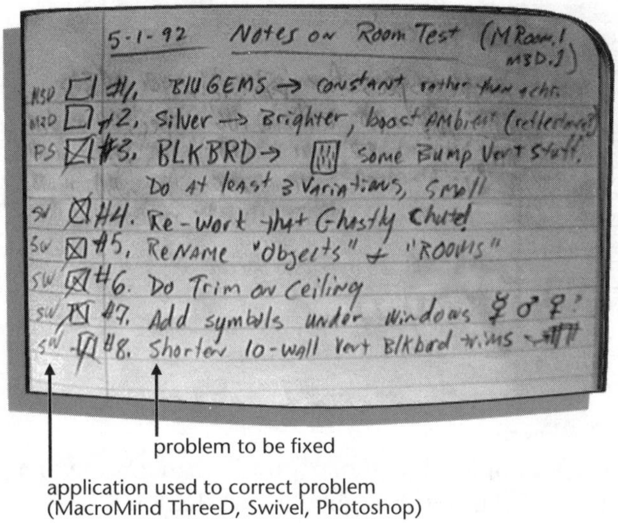

Figure 12.23 Joe Sparks hit on the right processing formula for *Total Distortion* image.

problem to be fixed

application used to correct problem (MacroMind ThreeD, Swivel, Photoshop)

Sometimes it takes quite a while to arrive at the right formula for processing an image. After trial and error, Joe Sparks hit upon the right processing sequence for an image and recorded it in his project notebook under the legend, "This is It!" (Figure 12.23). Later, when too burned out to do anything else one late night, he'd refer to his notebook and process a bunch of images all at once, using this formula.

External sources for imagery include scanners, with which original art, photographs, and textures may be digitized; image processing programs that can be used both to manipulate scanned imagery and to create it wholesale; paint-and-draw programs that you can use to create surfaces and backgrounds; and various sorts of cameras that can bring in both still and motion video. (Consult Chapter 3, "Graphics Tools," for more on the sources for imagery.)

Rendering programs typically offer at least three different ways to project image files onto objects: *bump* mapping, *texture* mapping, and *reflection* mapping (see below for definitions). You can then control how these files are mapped through a dialog box, such as the one from Macromedia's Three-D shown in Figure 12.24. Here, you can control with sliders the blending of object color with texture color, the height of the bumps in a bump map, or the percentage of a reflection color that will be added to an object for a reflection map. You also can specify exactly how the image files are wrapped around the object (see section on "Mapping Types").

Textures such as bumps and dents are created with bump mapping. These features are not actually 3-D attributes with real depth; rather, like texture maps, bump maps are image files that are projected onto objects to create the surface.

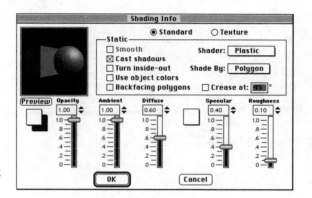

**Figure 12.24
Three-D's Shading
Info dialog box.**

The illusion of dimples, like those found on an orange or a golf ball, is achieved through subtle variations in highlight and shadow.

Because bump mapping doesn't produce actual 3-D features, viewers may notice that large bumps don't have true dimensionality. For this reason, you may have better luck with smaller bumps, which sustain the illusion more effectively.

The effect of bumps is also heavily influenced by the placement of lights. Low sidelighting will accentuate depressions, for example, while lights placed from above may wash out the texturing (see section on "Cameras and Lighting").

Reflection maps are used to project reflections of the 3-D world onto objects. For example, you might have the reflection of someone's face staring into a crystal ball. Ray tracing (discussed earlier in this chapter) produces the most realistic reflections, but at great cost of time and resources. Because ray tracing actually calculates the path and effects of light (whether they are reflection, refraction, transparency, or shadows), it is highly accurate and can yield gorgeous photo-realism. Figure 12.25 makes extensive use of reflection mapping. Because reflection mapping (also called *environment* mapping) involves projection of an image file, images created this way are much quicker to render than ray-traced imagery, and the results are quite good and certainly suitable for most applications.

**Mapping
Types**

When you project a 2-D image on a 3-D object, the program must have a way to identify points on the 2-D image that will correspond with those on the 3-D surface. Renderers commonly furnish four mapping types: orthogonal, spherical, cylindrical, and cubic. When you map a surface, you'll choose the mapping type appropriate to the object: cubic mapping for six-sided cubes, orthogonal for flat objects, and so on. Mapping types apply only to texture and bump maps, since the portion of a reflection map that appears on an object is calculated by the program.

Some distortion is inevitable when mapping textures; choosing the correct mapping type for the object you are shading can minimize these irregularities. You also can size texture maps so that their dimensions are similar to those of

**Figure 12.25
A reflection map.**

the 3-D object, which will diminish distortion. Different mapping types produce "seams," where points of the map meet as they wrap around the object. You can either adjust these seams so that they meet exactly or face them away from the camera during rendering.

Tiling, offered by some renderers, is useful if you rescale or reposition an already mapped texture. Three-D offers Black, Repeat, and Clamp Tiling. If you scale down an image, Black Tiling substitutes black for the area not covered by the texture. Repeat Tiling reproduces the texture in a checkerboard pattern over the surface of the object. Clamp Tiling uses the color of the last pixel on the edge of the pattern's surface to cover the remaining areas of the object.

Instead of creating surfaces by projecting an image file onto objects, procedural maps create surfaces mathematically. These computer-generated surfaces are used to create natural textural patterns such as wood grain or marble.

While you could wrap an image file around a broom handle, say, to create the effect of a wooden surface, this surface would be somewhat distorted by the topology (shape) of the broom handle itself. Instead, you could use a procedural texture to precisely define the color, pattern, plasticity, and other characteristics of the texture. The resulting object will look as if it were actually carved from a hunk of wood, rather than just simulating that surface. Also, a procedural texture (like a vector graphic) will not pixellate no matter how close you zoom.

The downside of procedural maps is that you need to fiddle with a number of parameters to get an effect that doesn't look phony or contrived.

Procedural maps can be used to create all sorts of random or chaotic patterns. Infini-D, for example, offers Mandlebrot Map, Julia Map, Tile Map, Noise Map,

Antialiasing and Alpha Channels

Antialiasing is the process by which the edges of images or objects are smoothed so that they blend in with adjacent images or backgrounds. This is done by substituting color values in muted shades that are in the range between the object and background colors. See Figure 12.26 for a close-up of an antialiased image.

Antialiasing is almost a requirement for creating a smooth transition between images and objects, but it does have some drawbacks. Since it requires adjustment of individual pixels, an antialiased image will take longer to render. Also, antialiasing "locks" an image or object to a background, making it difficult to change background attributes such as color later. Luckily, there is another technique that fixes this problem and others. Alpha channels, first seen on the desktop in Photoshop (see Chapter 3, "Graphics Tools"), are becoming increasingly important in animation, too. Some animation programs, such as Three-D, Infini-D, 3D Studio, and ElectricImage, will automatically create an alpha channel component of a selected object. This alpha channel contains transparency information for the associated object that the program uses to composite two images together.

Antialiased alpha channels let you combine two images seamlessly. This is convenient, because you can render multiple frames with the same background and render foreground objects separately. Then, using the alpha channels of the foreground objects, you can composite against the rendered backgrounds. This technique saves rendering time and disk space, since you only render the background once and render the objects that change separately.

Alpha channels have other uses, the most common of which is to mask an object to protect it (or its surrounding background) from the effects of a processing or paint effect. For instance, you may want to change a particular color in a surface of an object. If that color also happens to be found in the background, it will get changed too. On the other hand, if the object has an alpha channel, this will prevent any changes from occurring outside the

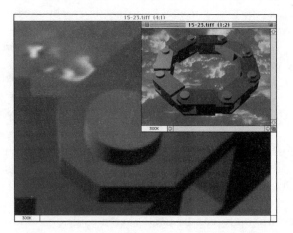

**Figure 12.26
Antialiased object.**

box continued

image itself. Alpha channels are also used to composite animation onto a video image; and several animation programs, including ElectricImage and Infini-D, excel at this process.

Most programs do not yet automatically create alpha channels for you; but, says Lynda Weinman, "Alpha channels are the way of the future."

As useful as they are, alpha channels are added information and will take up precious RAM and disk space; and naturally, they will also slow rendering. So if resources are tight, use alpha channels only when necessary to achieve particular effects.

Marble Map, Wood Map, Wave Map, and Corrosion Map, among others. Like other types of textures, these special effects maps can be adjusted flexibly. POV, a shareware ray tracer, also comes with a variety of procedural textures and presets.

Some renderers let you project animated sequences on objects. You could even have a moving object with an *animated surface*—maybe a blimp moving across the screen with animated projection or moving text across its surface. With some programs, such as Infini-D, you can even project a QuickTime movie on a surface.

Cameras and Lighting

You can establish camera angles and fly-throughs while animating, but it is during rendering when movements and surfaces are actually compiled or rendered. When the program renders an image, it does so from a single camera view. If you have multiple cameras for multiple views, scenes are rendered from one camera at a time; that means you'd have to render each camera sequence separately if you wanted different cuts from one point of view to another. It's usually easier to make one camera jump from place to place and then render the scene as a whole.

Determining camera placement, like placing objects in relation to one another, is easier in orthogonal view, rather than in the normal perspective views offered by animation programs. Most software allows you to define different camera attributes such as camera position, orientation, lens type, and focal length.

Camera lens choices range from telephoto, which gives a narrow field of view and magnifies your view, to fish-eye, which shows a wide field of view and makes the scene look farther away. Each type of lens has an associated focal length. You can also create your own custom lenses by specifying a focal length value.

Most renderers offer a number of lighting options, including types of light, intensity, and color.

As you would expect, different types of lights produce different effects. Ambient light is diffuse and doesn't come from any apparent source. Point lights, like naked bulbs, cast light in all directions. Spotlights throw directed beams.

You can adjust the beams that lights throw, softening the focus and creating a *penumbra*, or transition, from light to dark ("transition" and "roll-off" controls in example above), and also the beam angle (called "cone" in 3-D).

Lighting can greatly enhance the effect of your animation and is a key factor in generating realism and interest in a scene. Many renderers allow you to create several lighting effects in addition to basic illumination. For example, you can raise or lower lights as if they were on a dimmer. To do this, you simply set the light's intensity in one keyframe and change it at another level in the next keyframe—the program will tween the intermediate values.

By assigning colors to lights, you can "paint" objects that are illuminated. White lights will not disturb the individual colors of objects, but will simply make them brighter. Some renderers, like 3D Studio, allow you to put an image over a light source, creating a custom gel effect. For example, you could use a picture of a stained glass window to cast light on the floor so it looks like light coming through a window.

Lights can be treated like any other object. They can, for example, be animated so that they follow other objects to create a spotlight effect; or they can dance around, producing moving beams like searchlights. Most renderers also let you decide whether or not lights will cast shadows.

Making the Best of Rendering

Rendering is what the computer does both best and least well. All of the thousands or millions of calculations necessary to render a complex scene, with its varying surfaces, lighting, views, and animation, would be impossible to do without a computer. And, certainly, using a paint program to simply create a 3-D scene—especially an animated one—would be next to impossible.

The Longest Coffee Breaks of Your Life

At the same time, the rendering of complex animated scenes really pushes desktop machines—even the mighty Power PC—to the very limits of their capabilities. It's not unusual for a moderately intricate animation to take hours or days to render. We asked Adam Lavine, president of Specular International, makers of Infini-D, how long it would take to render a sophisticated, broadcast-quality, 10-minute animation he was working on. He replied that he hoped it would take *only* a few weeks.

Clearly, something needs to be done about this, and help is fortunately on the way. One of the most promising developments is the advent of *network* or *distributed rendering*. If you are lucky enough to have several computers—the more, the better—in your work environment, you can use this technique.

Network rendering is a simple idea that works very well. Basically, all you need, aside from the computers (which have to be networked) and your rendering software is network rendering software, which divides and apportions a rendering job among all the available computers.

The speed advantage achieved by these network renderers is not completely linear. Estimates by users indicate that second and subsequent machines devoted to a rendering task will contribute from 50 percent to 80 percent of their processing power. So a task that took an hour on one machine would take 33 to 40 minutes with a second machine, and 20 to 30 minutes with the addition of a third.

Several companies offer network renderers: Specular International (Back-Burner), Ray Dream (DreamNet), Pixar (NetRenderMan), and Strata (RenderPro) —and 3D Studio has network rendering built in. These programs are covered in Chapter 5, "Animation Tools."

Another way to shorten rendering is to send rendering jobs to a Unix workstation such as the SGI Indigo. These workstations are generally more powerful than Macs and PCs and can bull their way through rendering jobs. Donald Grahame uses this method and is quite happy with results. Modeling in Swivel, he exports models in the RenderMan RIB format. The models are then transferred to an Indigo via Ethernet, where they are processed with RenderMan and then sent back as bitmaps to the Mac. Asked if there are any disadvantages to this setup, Grahame replies, "Well, I used to organize my life around rendering breaks, using them to return phone calls, shop, or sleep. Now, I find that rendering goes so fast that I end up working for longer stretches and have to force myself to take a break."

Aside from faster machines, which inevitably will come, the ultimate answer may lie with specialized add-in boards such as Yarc System Corp.'s NuSprint RISC board. This card, equipped with a 25MHz RISC processor, runs at speeds of up to 25 Mips and is 25 times faster than a Mac II.

Final Product

When you have completely modeled, animated, and rendered a scene, it's time to distribute it. If it is going to be viewed on a computer, the considerations are different than if you plan to copy it off to videotape. Some of these considerations are discussed below.

Computer-Based Delivery

The integrity of computer-based playback of animation depends largely on the playback machine itself. A 30 fps animation that plays fine on the Pentium you developed it on may barely make 10 fps on a 386 (if it will play at all). For this reason, many animators develop, or at least test, on a target machine for their animations.

You'll also have to consider whether your animation will be played back from a hard disk or a CD-ROM. If it's coming off CD, the medium's data transfer rate may not be able to keep up with your intended frame rate. CoSA makes a product called PaCo (marketed by Macromedia as QuickPICS) that can help. This product, which is designed primarily to compress animations for faster playback, also has a CD playback simulator that will give you an idea of how fast your animation will play back from a real CD. You also can use PaCo to compress animations so that they can be played back on machines with limited RAM (see Chapter 5, "Animation Tools").

Director 4.0 Demo ⌘ 708

Animators of complex material that includes interactivity often import their finished animations into an integration program like Macromedia Director. Using Director, you can create scripts that tell the computer how to behave. For example, a 3-D game would allow you to click buttons to move around a 3-D room. These buttons and the actions they trigger are defined by Director scripts (see Chapter 16, "Interface and Interactivity: Bringing It Together"). You also can use Director to "finish" an animation by adding sound, titles, and other refinements.

Copying Animations to Videotape

If you are creating broadcast-quality animations, you'll want to write them to videotape or even videodisc. To do this, you'll need a fair amount of equipment (if you don't want to take your work to a service bureau). For starters, you'll need equipment that converts computer data to a video signal, namely an NTSC encoder, and a card that supports video output. A frame-accurate videotape recorder is also necessary.

You'll also have to use a specialized device called an animation controller. This appliance (generally an add-in card and some software) writes one frame of animation at a time to the VTR, sends a signal to make it back up the tape, then writes out another frame, and so on. The animation controller is necessary because desktop computers are not fast enough to turn out frames of animation in real time.

Craig Weiss of CBS Television in Los Angeles uses a laserdisc recorder instead of a VTR. The higher speed of this device allows him to write about 20 frames per minute, rather than the 3 frames a minute possible with tape. However, laserdisc recorders are still relatively scarce and expensive (about $20,000).

13

Animation Projects

You'll find a varied and interesting group of animation projects on the *Power Tools* CD. All were designed by experienced animators who are at the top of their field. While the CD details the conceptualization and creation of the projects, we'll give you some project background material in the following pages.

Video Quilt

Lynda Weinman is an experienced film and video animator who also writes for *New Media, MacWeek, Publish,* and *Step by Step Graphics.* Weinman also finds time to teach animation at the Art Center College for Design, the American Film Institute, and the Center for Creative Imaging.

Video Quilt ⌘ 020

Deceptively simple in appearance, her *Video Quilt* (see Figure 13.1) comprises more than 600 individual pieces of art, each separately fashioned, then painstakingly assembled into a coherent whole.

The finished work resembles an infant's blanket, with homespun designs rendered in a palette of muted and soothing shades and accents. The quilt serves as an interface for an interactive training disk used in pre- and postnatal medical clinics. A mouse click on one of the panels—a rocking horse or teddy bear, for instance—and the object moves, and the viewer is whisked to an appropriate section of the demo.

Weinman considers 2-D character animation to be among the most challenging of multimedia undertakings. Although she is pleased with the way *Video Quilt* turned out, she says, "I didn't make any money on it—it was a very difficult project."

Figure 13.1
A small portion of
Lynda Weinman's
Video Quilt.

Special Considerations

Director 4.0 Demo ⌘ 708

One reason for her difficulties with the project was the problem she had preserving image registration as art was moved between different programs for processing. "I was attempting to do character animation with Illustrator, which is a 2-D art program," says Weinman, "and I used Illustrator's blend function to make each shape move in a particular way. After I had completed all the animation and brought it into Macromedia Director, I found that things didn't register properly —there were slight shifts of less than a pixel, and it looked awful."

After going back and reexamining her process, Weinman found that the registration problem was caused by her use of the command–V paste command familiar to all Mac users. Weinman learned that if she used the command–P paste command instead, her art would be copied to a file in exactly the same position it occupied in the original source file. Although this solved the registration problem, Weinman still had to go back and redo many frames, a painful and time-consuming process.

While this experience may underscore the importance of knowing your tools and technology, she emphasizes that execution usually plays a secondary role in animation projects. "The design process is what takes the most time; so even though I did have to redo all those graphics, it didn't take nearly as long the second time, because I had already mapped out both the aesthetics of the project and the technical execution process."

Tips and Techniques

When Weinman brought her finished art into Director for assembly and animation, she used a technique that she often employs to speed both processing and playback. Each frame of *Video Quilt* had 8 or 9 channels, or layers. When she worked with these frames in Director, the screen was slow to refresh, because the program had to build all of these layers. To remedy this situation, she exported all the channels of each frame as individual PICTs, so that each frame included all the layers. Then when she brought them back into Director, each frame was a composite of all of its layers.

This technique not only speeds up Director's handling of layered frames, but it also simplifies the cast window—Director's list of all of the frames in a project. Weinman also used this technique to composite layers when she needed to exceed Director 3.0's 24-channel limit.

Because she has had trouble with the more compact PICS animation format, Weinman exports animation sequences as PICT files. She finds that files of over 12Mb—which is common in the world of 24-bit animation—do not save reliably as PICS files; they become corrupted and unusable.

Photoshop 3.0 Demo ⌘ 715

Weinman is also taken with both old standbys Photoshop and CoSA's After Effects image processing program (see Chapter 6, "Video Tools," for a review). "If you do a scaling change in Director, it looks like hell," she says. "It either blows up the pixels, or if you zoom down, the image becomes jittery. But Photoshop and After Effects both do subpixel rendering, which makes images look beautiful even when they're scaled up and down."

Tools and Equipment

Weinman used a Mac IIfx with an assortment of fixed and removable hard drives, a 24-bit color card, a tape drive for archiving, an NTSC monitor, a video-scanner, and a pressure-sensitive tablet.

NTV Logo

Scott Billups was hired to create a network identity and logo package for Nissan's internal cable station, NTV (see Figure 13.1). Nissan's graphics department had developed a design concept, but Nissan executives weren't happy with the results; so they brought in Billups, who has had a long association with the company.

Billups is a systems integration consultant and developer for Sony, Apple, and Silicon Graphics Inc. He is also cochairman of the American Film Institute Media Lab. Over the last 18 years, he has created hundreds of broadcast, industrial, and theatrical projects, and is currently serving as Second Unit Director and Director of Digital Production for the unreleased motion picture, *The Fantastic Four.*

Special Considerations

Billups is a pioneer in the use of computer tools in video and film production, and he feels that the NTV project is an excellent example of how desktop video makes the process of dealing with corporate productions easier. In conventional video production, client participation is problematic, notes Billups, "because in the traditional process, you don't really have anything to show until it's all done."

For the NTV project, he had a lot of ideas for specific effects his clients wanted to achieve, so the flexibility and participatory nature of computer-based pro-

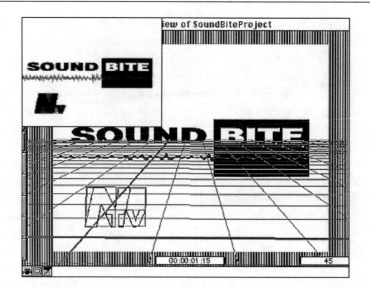

**Figure 13.2
NTV Network
Identity.**

duction were very important. "Just the fact that they were kept abreast of the whole production process made them feel they were part of it," he notes.

An early obstacle stemmed from the original project design, which was done by graphic designers who had specified Pantone colors. "The problem is that most Pantone colors aren't video-safe, so that by the time they get to a video that's been dubbed a few times, they're just flaring all over the place," Billups says. He solved the problem by creating a logo based primarily on black-and-white, with a few added video-safe colors.

**Tips and
Techniques**

Like many desktop video professionals who value Electric Image Incorporated's ElectricImage Animation System for its many high-end animation features, Billups cites one feature as particularly useful: being able to change the playback speed of an animation sequence using only the arrow keys on the keyboard. This makes music syncing easy, because "it allows you to pump the speed up or down until you find a beat that works."

He also made good use of the array of filters in Adobe's Photoshop. He treated the "Bite" block with multiple applications of Photoshop's Wave Filters to give the effect of cartoonlike distortion (see Figure 13.3).

Billups also had to make adjustments to account for the differences between the image formats of the computer, where the imagery was created, and video, where the final results would be viewed. "When you view a computer-based image on an NTSC [video] monitor, the images flicker all over the place, and so you run them through Photoshop's video filters, which correct for the differences, resulting in flicker-free images," he notes.

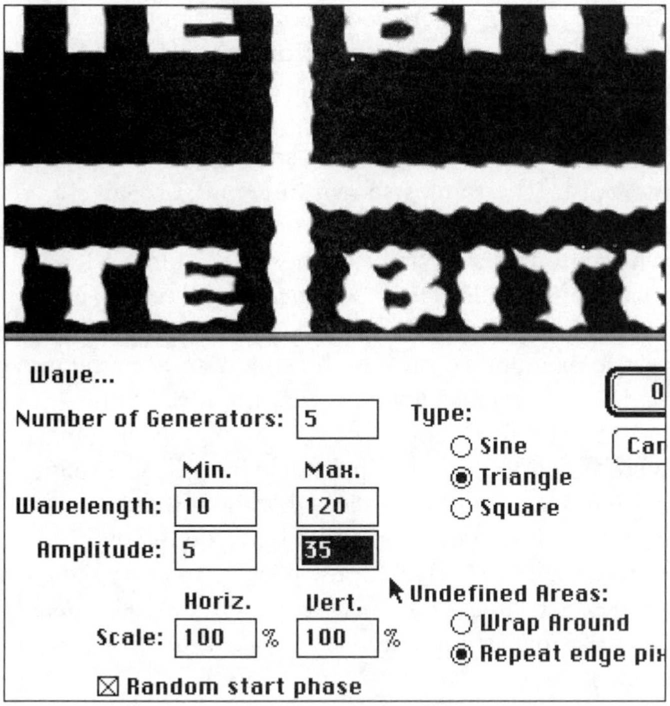

**Figure 13.3
Image processing
using Photo-
shop's Wave
Filters.**

Tools and Equipment

Billups used a Quadra 900 with a cache card that boosts the machine's performance to the level of a Quadra 950. He installed a 24-bit color card, a video card for piping video frames in and out of the Quadra, and DigiDesign's AudioMedia board for digitizing sound.

For *compositing* (combining the various elements of the piece), he used ADI's MacVAC animation controller. He also used MacVAC to write each frame from the computer to laserdisc on the Sony LVR 5000 videodisc recorder.

Billups chose Photoshop to filter certain elements, as described above, Macromedia's Swivel 3D to model the logo, ElectricImage to animate the model, Macromedia's MacroModel to extrude the model into three dimensions, Macromedia's Director to lay out the timing of the various components, and ElectricImage again for rendering.

MacroModel 1.5 Demo ⌘ 720

The Lawnmower Man

The Lawnmower Man was a 1992 film most notable for its eye-popping, computer-generated imagery. While its jejune plot assured only a fleeting life on the silver screen and a reincarnation and swift demise at Blockbuster Video, the movie's images were genuinely impressive.

Producer Jack Davis created one modest but effective image on the desktop during his tenure at The Gosney Company. He used Mac graphics and animation tools to design and animate the corporate identity for the film's sinister corporation, Virtual Space Industries.

The logo consists of a revolving sphere, with a surrounding cube spinning in counterpoise. The frames shown in Figure 13.4 give a feeling for the motion, but look at the CD for the actual animated logo used in the film.

Lawnmower Man Logo ⌘ 021

Davis started by studying sketches of the film's VR equipment—the contraption that you climb into to experience virtual reality. This apparatus, a "kinetic-" or "gyrosphere," allows the subject 360 degrees of free motion along any axis. Davis also examined a prop of the sphere used in the movie.

In addition, he experimented with the idea expressed in Leonardo's famous image, the "Perfect Proportions of Man" (see Figure 13.5). As the concept evolved, he ended up with the circle inside the square. "The idea is that the square is reality, and the circle, which is inside, is virtual reality," Davis says. "This sort of blurred the distinction between the two."

He notes that the budget for the project was very tight; the whole film, in fact, was done on a shoestring. Costs were held down by parcelling projects out to a number of small studios and by creating much of the imagery right on the desktop.

Special Considerations

Owing to the money constraints and deadline, desktop technology was a particularly appealing alternative to expensive and time-consuming higher-end tools. Swivel 3D, which was used for the object modeling, was a particular time saver. "Swivel renders an image essentially in real time," says Davis. "So the modeling and rendering tests, as well as choreography, can be done much more quickly than with higher-end systems."

Davis is quick to admit that there are trade-offs in quality. Swivel's quick shading is really only suitable for a rough idea of a rendered model's look, but it gets that job done quite well. (For a brief review of Swivel and its basic features, see

Figure 13.4 Three views of Virtual Space Industries logo.

Chapter 5, "Animation Tools." See also Chapter 12, "Creating 3-D Models and Animation," for a description of such fundamental animation concepts as modeling and rendering.)

Tips and Techniques

Davis describes the project as relatively straightforward, with no particular technical hurdles. Normally, effects such as those in the *Lawnmower Man* would be created with film special effects equipment; but they were done, instead, with video and desktop tools, due to the small budget. At one point in the film, Davis' logo is projected on a wall as a six-foot image. The relatively low resolution of the video image was especially apparent at this size, but the filmmakers wanted a grainy look, "or were at least content with it," he notes.

Because the logo was completely symmetric, only ¼ revolution had to be animated, which greatly reduced the number of frames necessary (20 or fewer) to create the finished animation. The logo's symmetry actually simplified the entire process, which would have been much more involved for an object that had distinct features visible from different angles.

Davis says that the hardest thing was to get the 12 separated objects that made up the cube to rotate around a common center point. He did this by creating a small, hidden cube in the center of the model (Figure 13.6). He then locked the cube and sphere objects to this tiny hidden cube, which does not show up in the

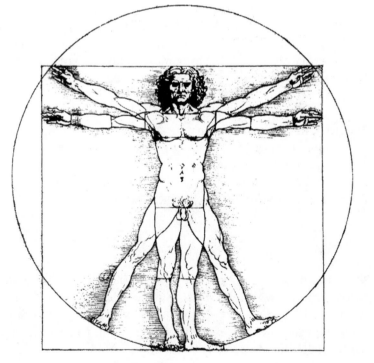

**Figure 13.5
Da Vinci's
Perfect Pro-
portions of Man.**

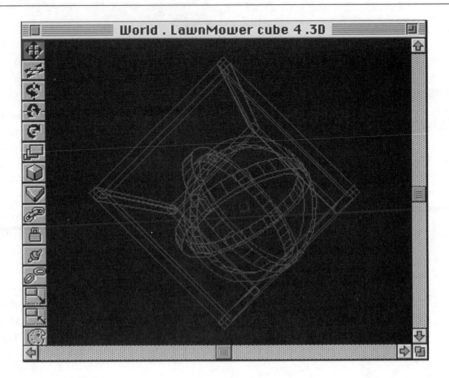

**Figure 13.6
Hidden object
used for model
rotation.**

final animation. Once linked and locked to the hidden cube, the animated objects could then revolve around a common center point. See the project's step-by-step instructions on the CD for a more detailed explanation. See also Chapter 14, "Creating Video," for other uses of this technique.

Tools and Equipment

Davis used a basic Mac setup that included a Mac IIci with 8Mb RAM and a 100Mb hard drive. He also had a 24-bit color card and a 19″ color monitor.

Adobe Illustrator and Photoshop were used to create the original high-contrast logo art, Swivel 3D Professional was used for the modeling and test animation, and Macromedia Three-D was used for rendering and final animation. The whole thing was assembled for playback in Director.

Test Flight

Test Flight ⌘ 022

When John Odam, a book and graphic designer in Del Mar, California, wanted to experiment with 3-D animation, he turned to Strata Inc.'s StrataVision 3d. Although he had used the program previously and was familiar with 3-D modeling, he wanted to experiment with animating a simple 3-D object for playback as a QuickTime movie.

Special Considerations

StrataVision 3d Demo ⌘ 721

The project consists of a 3-D airplane flying against a backdrop of clouds. "What fascinates me about 3-D programs is the ability to maneuver in three-dimensional space and time," says Odam. The project, while uncomplicated, involves many of the considerations all animators face, even in the most involved of undertakings.

Odam has a traditional commercial art background. He started as a book cover designer in London 25 years ago after graduating from the Leicester College of Art. Now with his own firm, John Odam Design Associates, he works exclusively with computer design tools, creating nonfiction trade and educational books, from jacket design to illustrations and typesetting.

StrataVision 3d renders in 24-bit color even if you have only an 8-bit color card. That way, you have a high-quality file that can be played back in either mode. Note that this works well for relatively simple projects like *Test Flight*, but can lead to very large files and slow rendering for more complex projects.

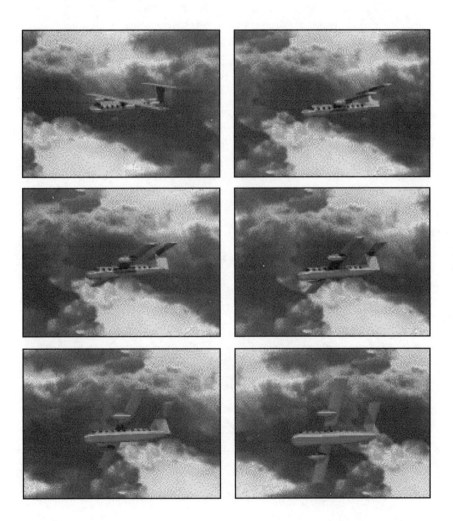

Figure 13.7
Test Flight: **The finished model flying through space.**

**Tips and
Techniques**

Odam recommends keeping 3-D models simple to speed rendering and reduce the frustration of waiting while models are rendered with surfaces and light. This is especially important for beginners, who may be tempted to build complicated shapes that will render very slowly.

"What I found in 3d is that the built-in solids that come with it—the cylinder, cone, and so on—render blindingly fast in comparison to any other kind of shape. So if you can make up a model out of basic primitives, and it's convincing enough for your purposes, you'll find it renders quickly. You'll get gratification right away, you won't have to wait all night for results."

To assemble his airplane model, Odam used only the cylinder, the sphere, and the stretch tool. Figure 13.8 shows the diagram he used to outline the relationships between the different model elements and how they fit together to form the composite airplane model.

When the model and rendering of the airplane were complete, he set about animating it against a cloud backdrop. Since the cloud background is actually a repeated loop, it's important to carefully adjust the camera angle so that the illusion of movement through fresh territory is maintained.

"If your camera angle is too wide, you start to see a wallpaper of clouds, so that it blows the realism," Odam says. "The other mistake you can make is to use too narrow a camera angle, too much telephoto; and the clouds start to break up, you can see the individual pixels. So the scaling of the background in this program is a function of the camera angle."

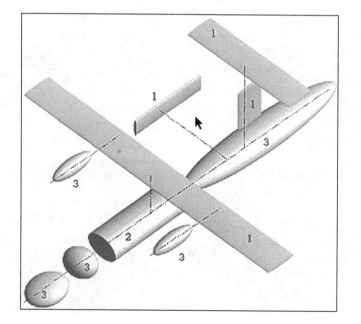

**Figure 13.8
The model's
composite
shapes.**

In order to get the highest-quality results, Odam normally renders in 24-bit color and saves the results as a PICS animation sequence. He finds that this format is superior to QuickTime, whose compression algorithms sometimes cause banding in subtle shading areas. If you do want to work in QuickTime, you can always convert from the PICS files.

Tools and Equipment

Illustrator 4.0 Demo ⌘ 718

In addition to StrataVision 3d for the models, rendering, and animation, Odam used Illustrator and Photoshop to make a texture map of portholes for the plane's windows. His machine was a Mac IIci with a Radius Rocket 25 CPU accelerator and a 24-bit color card (see Chapter 2, "Systems Software, Hardware, and Peripherals," for reviews of various Macintosh models and for a discussion of CPU acceleration and 24-bit video cards).

14

Creating Video

Desktop video is ushering in a new era of video production by placing more people in the director's chair than ever before. It is opening up exciting and economical new ways of managing video and giving professionals and hobbyists alike the ability to create and edit their own movies or add the power of video images to their multimedia productions. Digital video is used in motion picture and television production for storyboarding, retouching shots, and adding impressive, but relatively low-cost, special effects. Budgets, equipment, personnel, and talent can range from the highest-caliber broadcast quality to what is immediately available.

Unlike traditional video projects requiring large budgets and careful planning, many desktop video productions are put together on shoestring budgets by people who espouse the plan-as-you-go philosophy. In small productions, a secretary, bookkeeper, accountant, vice president, spouse, child, or friend might be recruited to jump in and help. They may become the leading man or lady, provide voice-over for audio input, make strange sounds for special effects, or be producer or camera person, or play any other role required to get the job done on-budget and on-schedule.

This flexibility is possible because of the forgiving nature of the digital medium, which permits continuous editing and modification throughout a project. However, the ability to continue to make changes after the fact is no substitute for shooting and recording the highest-quality video and sound, which is possible only with proper planning and budgeting. No amount of time using Sound Edit Pro to process the audio will restore a garbled voice or one drowned out by background noise. All the powerful enhancing filters and special effects in Premiere, VideoShop, CoSA After Effects, and VideoFusion combined will not bring

SoundEdit 16 Demo ⌘ 707

Premiere 4.0 Demo ⌘ 722

back the lost excitement of an event videotaped under poor lighting conditions or with a shakily held camera. The secret to high-quality desktop video is shooting high-quality video in the first place.

The Three Steps of Video Production

The three major steps of video production include preproduction, production, and postproduction (see Figure 14.1). Preproduction represents the planning process, which probably is the most significant stage of the production since everything else depends on how carefully the stages of production are anticipated. The elements of preproduction include planning, scripting, storyboarding, budgeting, assembling the cast and production team, and determining what equipment will be used.

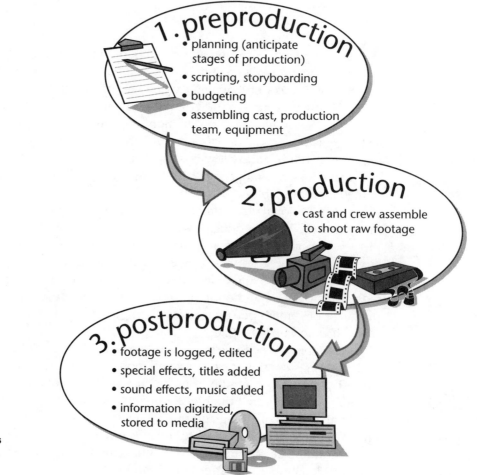

1. preproduction
- planning (anticipate stages of production)
- scripting, storyboarding
- budgeting
- assembling cast, production team, equipment

2. production
- cast and crew assemble to shoot raw footage

3. postproduction
- footage is logged, edited
- special effects, titles added
- sound effects, music added
- information digitized, stored to media

**Figure 14.1
The three phases
of desktop video
production.**

Most people are familiar with the basics of the production process itself. This is where the production cast and crew assemble to shoot the raw footage. Effective preproduction planning greatly increases your chances of living through a catastrophe-free production phase.

In postproduction, the filmed or videotaped footage is logged and edited, special effects and titles are inserted, and sound effects and music are added. These basic phases remain the same whether the movie is a major motion picture, an interactive multimedia presentation, or a digital home movie. The primary differences occur in the postproduction phase. If the final product is to be a digital movie, for example, the acquired footage must be digitized into a computer prior to editing, compressed using one of several codecs, then either stored on a computer-readable medium (hard disk, floppy disk, CD-ROM, etc.) or written out to videotape or film.

The nature and budgetary constraints of the project dictate whether to use traditional video or desktop video production techniques. In general, projects that require full-frame video at 30 frames per second for transfer to videotape and display on VCRs often may be less expensive to develop with traditional video production techniques. However, a desktop video production using smaller frame sizes and frame rates can be dramatically less expensive. For example, a consumer 8 mm camcorder, already on hand, might save the cost of renting a high-end ¾ inch video system and perhaps the fees of a camera operator. In many cases, a marriage of traditional video techniques with the newer desktop video tools may prove to be the best solution.

Preproduction

The importance of proper preproduction planning and budgeting cannot be overstated. Do your homework on this phase and you will be assured that the production will materialize on schedule, and that all the pieces will fit together to form a quality work. Since many desktop video productions proceed on a very low budget, the first question to ask is what skills, equipment, talent, and resources are already available to you without incurring additional expenditures. Typically, a color Macintosh or Multimedia PC with a lower-end digitizing card, several removable hard disk cartridges for storage of clips, and a consumer camcorder may already be available for the project (see Chapter 6, "Video Tools").

When the production team includes salaried employees or other persons whose time is available for the project, there's no need to pay for professional talent, transportation, or lodging. The storyboard may be put together by a member of the production team and approved by the client, and then a short script may be written as a plan for the production (see sidebar). However, you may incur additional costs for extra disk cartridges, videotape, and necessary props, and so you should include them in the budget.

Which Comes First, Storyboard or Script?

The answer to this question is, "It depends." When a feature or story-based movie is being produced, the script always comes first. It tells the story, describes the characters and scenes, and includes all the dialog. Often, only after countless rewrites is the director finally satisfied enough with the script to turn it over to a storyboard artist. The storyboard includes one illustration for each shot in the movie. It helps the director and actors visualize the action and can call attention to potential problems in scene continuity or camera placement.

In a commercial or business movie, the storyboard may come first. The intention may be to sell an idea, present a series of concepts, or train someone to carry out a task. The sequence of ideas and images may be more important than a script. In fact, in this case, there may not even be a script with dialog at all!

On the other hand, going the economy route may be your undoing—one untalented actor can pull an entire production down to amateur levels. If you can increase your budget to cover a lack of available no-cost personnel, you can juggle the cost-versus-quality issues of your production.

One of the most significant factors in determining the cost of a digital video production is the cost of hard disk space, removable hard drives, DAT tape backup systems, optical drives, or other means by which to store the megabytes of data that these projects need to have. The purchase of a high-end digital video card that can process 30 frames a second (or 60 fields) at 640×480 resolution will only increase the amount of storage needed. In the most extreme cases, studios using special equipment to permit QuickTime to do broadcast-quality video require several 2.5 gigabyte (Gb) drives just to hold fifteen minutes of video. Such productions require investments of up to $40,000 for equipment, as compared to the $4,000 price tags common in the personal computer world.

Comparative Costs

Before the planning and budgeting process is completed, you should make comparisons between alternative approaches to creating video, in order to determine which one is most cost-effective and best meets the needs of your project. Your decision will depend to a large extent on whether you need to purchase or rent equipment, such as computers, hard disks, VCRs, and camcorders, and whether available staff time is allocated to the budget. Needless to say, some projects are more complex than others and require more sophisticated planning and budgeting.

**Figure 14.2
A High School
Reunion Quick-
Time presenta-
tion demonstrates
the practice of
rephotographing
the original
senior prom
picture with the
same partner or a
substitute spouse
25 years later.**

Suppose that you own the Senior Prom Reunion Company, which is in the business of throwing 25th reunion parties for high school classes. You wish to make a promotional video to send to prospective high schools to acquire their business (see Figure 14.2). This could be accomplished by either creating videotape or producing a multimedia CD-ROM. However, your market research shows that most high schools have VCRs but do not have adequate equipment for playing CD-ROMs. The decision is made to produce a videotape, but the question remains whether to use traditional or digital means. You have some existing videotape footage, but additional videotape will have to be shot for the production. Thus, you undertake an analysis to determine the most cost-effective approach.

Creating a videotape using traditional equipment is expensive. Special lighting will be necessary to videotape one of your high school reunion parties, requiring a professional videographer. In addition, two days of postproduction will be necessary for editing together new and existing video, as well as for transitions, titles, and special effects. The budget would look something like this:

Budget—Traditional Video	
Videographer with camera/lighting for one evening	$1,000
Postproduction. Two days rent of ¾ editing suite with operator	1,500
Total	$2,500

This does not include the costs of storyboarding and scripting prior to production, other staff time, videotape duplication after production, or incidentals.

On the other hand, the budget for a *digital* production produced in-house (still requiring a videographer) might look like this:

Budget—Digital Video	
Videographer with camera/lighting for one evening	$1,000
High-end 30 frame per second digitizing card for PC or Mac (with editing software)	3,000
High-end Macintosh or PC	3,000
1.2 Gigabyte hard drive	1,000
DAT drive	800
DAT tapes	45
Frame accurate VCR	2,000
Total:	$10,845

As you can see, most of the costs are associated with the one-time purchase of capital equipment. If you already have the equipment and can videotape and edit the footage yourself, then the costs of a digital production might actually be less than going the traditional video route. But since our Senior Prom Reunion Company doesn't do multimedia, we're out of luck. The obvious conclusion is that the initial cost of equipment does not justify a digital solution unless the costs can be spread over several projects. Besides, it is likely that the traditional methods will yield a higher-quality video.

The digital solution does offer far more flexibility in adding special effects. However, the digital creation of transitions and other special effects takes a great deal of time, and instead of a two-day operation, the estimated time for editing the project is one week. While this can be done in-house, the cost of salaries also has to be figured into the budget. For this particular project, the traditional solution appears to be the most cost-effective.

Now let's imagine that your Senior Prom Reunion Company does multimedia. In fact, one of your primary revenue streams is to offer, for a small and very reasonable fee, a special videotape of the event. You photograph each reunion attendee, then create an animated morph digital movie from the attendees' senior pictures to their current pictures. These morphs are then added to the final videotape in postproduction. Since the ability to produce morphs is not available

Video Fields and Frames

NTSC video actually displays one picture every sixtieth of a second. This is called a video field. It takes two fields to create a complete image or frame because only every other one of the 525 NTSC horizontal scan lines are displayed at one time. In field one, scan lines 1, 3, 5, 7, etc. are displayed. In field two, scan lines 2, 4, 6, 8, etc. are displayed. This alternating of scan lines is called interleaving. Only the top digitizers, such as RasterOps MoviePak2 Pro Suite, Targa 2000, and Radius VideoVision Studio capture both fields of 30 frames each. As a result, the image quality of most cards is lower than can be achieved by using professional analog video equipment.

through traditional video production houses, the amount of use the equipment will get may justify the initial expenditures.

One final hypothetical: Let's say you already own a color computer and you want to produce a multimedia presentation, which you can deliver live to the schools. How would that compare to the cost of producing a videotape? In addition to digitized photographs, charts, and graphics, you will incorporate 320 × 240 digital movies into the presentation. Because the movies will be part of a live presentation and will be combined with other media, they do not have to stand alone; and due to their small size, professional quality is not essential. Instead of hiring a videographer, a staff member can use your own consumer-grade camcorder. You can use available lighting, or possibly a camera-mounted flood. The budget is as follows:

Budget—Live Multimedia Presentation	
Removable Zip drive for storage of digital movies	$200
3 disk cartridges	60
Low-end video digitizing card, comes with editing software	500
8mm videotape	10
Total Budget	$770

Photoshop 3.0 Demo ⌘ 715

Nothing else is needed except for staff time in which to create the production. Thus, for a business which already has a Macintosh and such basics as a scanner, Photoshop, and Premiere, the digital solution makes sense for a live presentation. Costs after the first production drop to back-up media and video tape.

Now the only major expense is the time it takes for the staff person to create the presentation.

Using Analog Video

For a company doing a great deal of in-house video, another option would be to purchase a computer-assisted, nondigital videotape editing system. This might include, for instance, the FutureVideo A/B roll system for Mac, DOS, or Windows (see Figure 14.3), which supports three *prosumer* (low-end industrial) VCRs with computer control capability, a Panasonic switcher modified so that the computer can send it GPI signals for automatic transitions and effects, and the FutureVideo A/B controller with Macintosh software (see Figure 14.3). Such a system is likely to cost less than $10,000 and permit in-house analog videotape production at a low cost with Hi8 or S-VHS quality. The Senior Prom Reunion Company would benefit from this solution if it were going to videotape reunion events on a regular basis. For occasional use of video, the best solution often is to rent equipment and editing time.

Production

Once the initial planning, budgeting, purchasing, scripting, and storyboarding are completed, you're ready to shoot your video. One of the most significant considerations in this phase is the quality of the light. Without light there is darkness, a state in which shooting video is impossible. Light has many qualities, among which is color temperature. This is not the actual temperature of the light bulb, but the hue of the light. Tungsten indoor light bulbs are very "warm" and have an orange tinge to them.

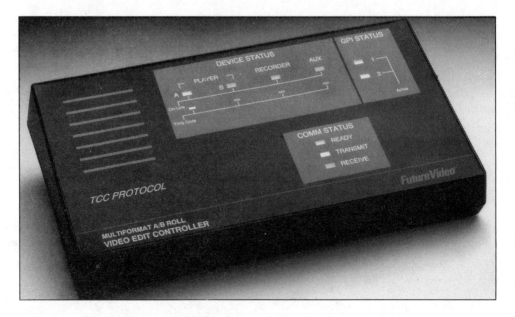

Figure 14.3 Future Video A/B roll video edit controller.

Outdoor light is on the "cold" side and has a blue tinge. If light comes from several sources—for instance, daylight through a window, tungsten from a lamp, and the bluish light of a television set—you may get strange results. It is difficult to see these colors with the naked eye—humans tend to quickly compensate for the varying hues. But the camera records them to videotape. With professional equipment and older consumer cameras, the color of the light is compensated for through a manual process called white balance. All consumer camcorders have an automatic white balance control, but they also usually have a manual override for unusual lighting conditions (for example, videotaping in a room where all the walls are painted a bright green). The camera is focused on a solid white background, so it fills the frame. This can be a white tee shirt, a white card, or a genuinely white wall. The white balance button is pressed, and the camera calibrates all of the colors so that the chosen area becomes white. Some cameras also permit black balance, which is accomplished by closing the lens as far as possible, putting a lens shade over it, and pressing the black balance button. This assures a good range of contrast from black to white. Since most camcorders display a black-and-white viewfinder image, the only way to confirm that the white balance is set is to attach a monitor or TV to your camcorder's video out.

Video Loves Light and Lots of It

Although today's video manufacturers compete with each other for how little light their camcorders need to operate, the truth of the matter is that the quality of video is dramatically affected in negative ways by low light conditions. Lurking beneath the surface of every video image is noise, which creates an unpleasant grainy effect. When the lights are turned on, video noise runs for cover like exposed cockroaches. Good lighting brings out the subtlety or the brilliance in colors. If your video was shot in poor lighting conditions and has a lot of background noise, the transfer to digital video will accentuate everything that is wrong with the image and leave you with a muddy, grainy look. In addition, when the image is compressed, the codec will not be able to tell the difference between video noise and the image's essential detail. It will faithfully attempt to duplicate the noise in each frame, totally ruining the compression results.

Dealing With Contrast

Video has less capacity than photographic film to handle contrasty situations. Pockets of impenetrable shadows and washed-out highlights make scenes that appear properly lit to the naked eye look as though they were shot on the moon in the final video. On the other hand, an overcast sky might provide better conditions for shooting than a sunny day. Certain rules of thumb have been used by videographers for years to contend with the light-contrast problem. One of them is the tradition of requiring guests on television to wear a blue shirt instead of a white one: The blue shirt will wash out and look white, whereas a white shirt would be so bright that it may actually appear to glow. Another technique is the use of a neutral density filter that blocks out the highest reflected light from the subject (high gain), allowing shadow areas to become more defined. However, using such a filter requires more overall light.

Shooting Indoors

While lighting complex situations indoors is an art that cannot be mastered in a single day, indoor scenes usually can be shot satisfactorily with existing or natural light. It's probably not a good idea to use a light mounted on the camera. This will cause severe shadows directly behind your actors, creating what looks almost like a double image. Instead, follow the principles of lighting in photography and use two or more artificial lights: a main light on one side and a less intense fill light on the other. A third, higher light beaming down from the ceiling can reduce unwanted shadows and separate the subject from the background. Since this isn't still photography, don't forget to light the scene to allow for your actors' movement. If the actors move to one side, they shouldn't end up in darkness or in a bright area.

Frame Composition

Although composing a video frame is similar to composing a photograph, motion adds a whole new dimension. There are a number of simple rules of thumb you can follow for shooting clear, compelling video.

First and foremost, do not hesitate to move in close to your subject. Whereas major motion pictures might show crowd scenes, and the smaller screen of television might emphasize head shots of one or two people, digital movies are sufficiently small to justify focusing on a single object, an individual person, or a particular feature of that individual (i.e., eyes, hands, etc.).

Opening scenes are traditionally shot from a distance, and followed by a medium shot and a close-up. Often the transition from long shot to close-up is made with a slow zoom. However, with digital video, there are several reasons to avoid zooms. One is that, with disk space being such a precious commodity, the movie may be only a few seconds long, eliminating the usefulness of an opening zoom. You may need to cut more rapidly to the close-up. Another reason is the affect zooming has on temporal compression. Since every part of the image is changing during a zoom, temporal compression (which relies on large parts of the image being the same from frame to frame) will fail, resulting in higher data rates.

Secondly, keep in mind that much of the sense of action and excitement in video is created subliminally as the viewer's eyes follow the motion of the subject matter moving across the screen. Movement can be linear and predictable or a total surprise. Just look at any MTV feature segment for a sense of how motion can be used creatively in video.

Continuity of Motion

If a person is walking to the right in a scene, he or she should continue in the same direction in the next scene. Suddenly reversing a subject's apparent path of motion can confuse the viewer. This will happen when, in professional videographer lingo, the camera "crosses the line" between one shot and the next. The "line" is an invisible one that follows the subject's direction of motion. If the camera is positioned on the other side of the line, it will seem that the subject is moving in the other direction. So, don't let your camera cross the line.

Even if nothing is moving, changes in scene can create the illusion of motion. If a person is looking toward the upper right corner of the frame in the first scene, the next scene might have someone moving from the upper right corner back down to the lower left corner. If you watch shows on television or go to the movies, start to become aware of the motion on the screen, and how it is used to manipulate the viewer's experience.

Simulating Multiple Cameras

When videotaping, shoot a scene from several different angles to provide the editor with enough material to do an effective job. This is called coverage. Movie makers have developed special techniques for shooting with one camera; television studio productions use live switching between two or three different cameras. The scene is first videotaped using a long shot. This is called the *master shot* and includes full body shots of all the actors, as well as enough of the background to establish the mood of the scene. Next come medium shots from different angles. If there are two actors in a scene, these might be over-the-shoulder shots—shot from behind and slightly to the side of one actor and catching the second actor full on. The last shots are close-ups in which the actor's face may fill the frame.

Live interview situations are videotaped in a different manner. You really don't want to ask your subject to repeat himself half a dozen times! One technique that has been around for years in TV journalism is to videotape some of the shots for cutaways after the interview is finished. These shots are taken from behind the subject (so that his or her face cannot be seen, avoiding potential lip sync problems) and generally show the interviewer asking the questions or nodding her head. Other good cutaways are close-ups of people listening to the interview, a map or some other graphic, or images to illustrate the content of the interview. Thus, a conversation can be edited using shots from several different angles to create the illusion of a second camera. Cutaways are essential to replace unusable footage during the interview, for example, when the camera jerks, the subject wipes his nose, or the phone rings. They also can cover splices that occur when assembling a story in a nonlinear order.

The Continuum of Sound

When shooting video, the greatest mistake is to let the sound play second fiddle to the image. In multimedia presentations where the image may be small, sound often is more important than the picture in determining the success of the production.

From the wilderness forest, to the sand shifting desert, to a city's deserted, early morning streets, every place on earth has background sounds; and the recording of those sounds will dramatically increase the believability and effectiveness of the video. Background sounds are continuous and should be heard throughout the scene.

The reason for capturing continuous sound becomes evident in the editing process. Traditional video productions usually are edited by laying down the sound first, and then editing pictures to fit the sound. Thus, the continuity of the scene is provided by the sound, and the length of the sound track will determine the duration of the video segment.

If, for example, the video consists of an actor talking to the camera in close-up (called a *talking head),* the editor may decide to use 20 seconds of the actor's voice, but only a few seconds of the head. To keep the shot from becoming boring, the editor might cut to shots of the audience, the surrounding environment, or other scenes to illustrate the narrative as the actor's voice is heard in the background.

Recording Spoken Words

If you want to assure that your subject's words are clearly audible, use an appropriate microphone properly placed. All consumer camcorders feature attached microphones, but these mikes may not always be sufficient for your needs. The built-in microphone is very close to the lens, so it is possible to pick up the noises made by the zoom lens motor or the sound of your fingers fumbling to adjust the focus. And if your subject is more than two or three feet away, the camcorder microphone can pick up background noise that may drown out the voice you're trying to record. Any distortions in the audio will be even more noticeable when the sound is converted to the relatively low resolution of 11 kHz or 22 kHz. For the best results, have your subject speak directly into a hand-held or clip-on microphone (positioned several inches away from the mouth) or use a shotgun microphone just out of view of the camera.

Shooting for Digital Video

When producing a digital movie that will be shown on a computer, the goal is to make the movie look and sound the best it can within the constraints of today's technology. It has to fit on the storage medium you've chosen, it must play in a window large enough to keep the audience's interest, and its sound and video quality should be as good as possible. All of these items directly relate to the amount of data contained within the movie and how fast that data can be delivered from the disk to the screen. Until computers have unlimited storage and processing speed, trade-offs must be made to get the best results. Here are a series of tips to help you shoot a movie that can then be compressed optimally.

Spatial Compression Tips

You will recall from Chapter 6, "Video Tools," that spatial compression deals with reducing the data within a specific frame.

- Use a solid background—whenever possible, reduce the image detail behind your actors. Large blank areas can be much more easily compressed than areas of great color change. If you are trying to keep the data rate below a certain number, then the Compact Video codec will look for the areas of detail in a frame and give those areas a larger allocation of data. If you also have an actor in the frame, then there may not be enough data left over to provide a good representation of his or her face.

- Solid-colored clothing for actors—unless there is a reason for the actors to wear prints, save the data by having them wear solid colors, or at least clothing with large areas of solid color.

- Use white or black backgrounds—if you can set the white and black levels on your digitizing card so that white is truly white and black is truly black, then any detail in a white or black background will vanish, resulting in the best compression.

- Shoot with bright lights—as mentioned above, low light levels cause video noise, and the codecs can't tell the difference between noise and important information.

Temporal Compression Tips

The goal while shooting with temporal compression in mind is to keep extraneous movement to a minimum and reduce the number of required key frames (see sidebar on Key Frames). The following tips will improve compression between adjacent frames:

- Use a sandbagged tripod—a hand-held camera will result in every frame being different from the last, making temporal compression impossible. Weigh your tripod down with sandbags or other objects. Bumping the tripod during a shot will create a data spike because adjacent frames will be different.

- Move the actor, not the tripod—avoid pans, tilts, and zooms. Each of these causes most of the data in the scene to be different in consecutive frames. Instead, cut to different shots to keep things visually interesting. If you want to get closer to the actor, stop the camcorder, zoom in, and then start again. Even better, have the actor walk towards the camcorder. Then only the actor will change and the background will remain constant.

- Shoot in front of a static background—watch out for motion behind the actor, such as a busy street, blowing leaves, etc.

Case Study: **The Engineering Adventure**

The best way to visualize the phases of production is with regard to a particular project. Here we look at the creation of the video portion of *The Engineering Adventure*, an interactive program designed to interest minority children in a career in engineering. Produced by Sonni and Ralph Cooper, principals of Creative Enterprises, under a $350,000 grant from the National Science Foundation, it features short video segments of minority engineers, including African-Americans, Hispanics, and Native Americans, as well as segments showing engineering faculty and students conducting experiments and visits to manufacturing plants designing the space station.

The Coopers' original budget proposal could not have included anything expressly for desktop video or QuickTime support because when they wrote it in 1990, QuickTime did not exist. However, by the time the project was underway in 1991, Sonni felt that QuickTime was such an effective vehicle of expression that it had to be included in the project.

The first issue to consider was whether the existing budget could provide the resources for adding video. Although Sonni was not a professional videographer, she had observed video production first as an actress and later as a writer on a *Star Trek* production. She had a habit of looking through the camera between scenes to better understand what kind of shot was being taken. Furthermore, she knew about f-stops, focal length, and other technical aspects of video from her experience as a still photographer. Thus, she felt well prepared to shoot the videos she needed.

The only camcorder she had was an 8 mm Canon CCD-F70 that she originally purchased to shoot movies of her children. The budget was sufficient to provide several SyQuest cartridges for QuickTime movies storage, a graphic artist, and a programmer who would incorporate the QuickTime movies into the project; and she had already allocated time to generating media for the project. However, there were no additional funds available to pay actors or actresses and professional voices, or to cover other expenses routinely encountered in a production. The videotaping turned out to be much easier than she imagined.

She found companies for on-location sites near her business in Long Beach, California. McDonnell Douglas permitted her to tape models of the future American space station, and a nearby water utility permitted her to shoot in their plant. At each location, she obtained the consent of the workers who appeared on the videotape and complied with all safety regulations, such as the wearing of a hard hat.

In order to videotape engineering experiments without having to hire someone to help, she worked through organizations of minority engineers who conduct experiments in secondary schools. The experiments already were scheduled, and Sonni Cooper's task was to be there with her camcorder when they took

Key Frames

Temporal compression uses a key frame at the beginning of a sequence of difference frames. A key frame is a complete image and does not rely on data from any previous frame. If more than about 90 percent of the scene has changed from the previous image, a key frame is automatically inserted. These are called natural key frames. They are usually inserted at the beginning of a scene change, or if there was a camera move. During compression, it's generally a good idea to force a key frame about once a second. If your frame rate is 15 frames per second, then ask for a key frame every 15 frames. The setting is usually made in a standard compression dialog box.

The more key frames a movie has, the larger it will be. So why not just eliminate all of them except for natural key frames? This is fine if you will only be playing your movie in the forward direction. But if you ever need to search for a specific sequence or frame, need to edit the video clip, or need to play the movie backwards (as in the MoviePlayer setting "Looping Back and Forth"), then a lack of key frames will greatly degrade performance because QuickTime must search backwards for the most recent key frame and then incorporate all subsequent differences until it arrives at the current frame. To truly edit a clip using a digital video editor, every frame must be a key frame.

TOOLS

MoviePlayer ⌘ 612

place. She ended up with beautiful live footage of minority students that was much more effective than anything she could have produced on a larger budget with actors and simulated events.

For each shoot, she used the minimal equipment needed to do the job. This meant she had less to carry and increased the likelihood that she would get the shots she wanted. In addition to the camcorder, she brought two extra rechargeable batteries (color-coded after each use), a miniature tripod, extra videotape, a still camera, a tape recorder, and an extra microphone, all of which fit into a single camera bag. The still camera was used to obtain higher-resolution images than possible with the camcorder. The images were later converted into Macintosh images as part of the multimedia production.

Cooper used the tripod for capturing long narratives by a speaker. She made sure to videotape enough footage so that she could edit around occasional problems with image quality. Sonni carefully avoided backlit scenes—such as shooting against a window—which often provide an unsatisfactory silhouette.

Sonni is emphatic about sound quality. Nothing can ruin a QuickTime movie more quickly than a garbled audio track. Since the sound can be dubbed using voice-over, the audio does not necessarily have to be shot simultaneously with the video. If an audio segment is slightly too long or too short for a selected video segment, and you do not wish to trim the video segment, the audio can be made slightly longer or shorter using such editing tools as Sound Edit Pro's

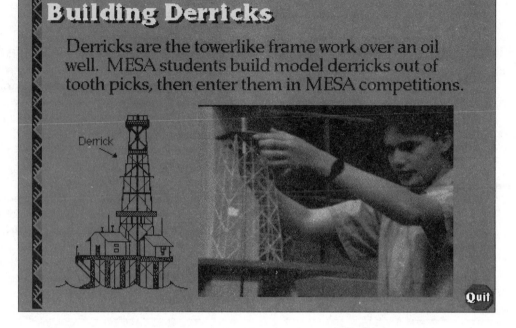

Figure 14.4 QuickTime video integrated into larger Macromedia Director movie the size of a HyperCard stack.

Director 4.0 Demo ⌘ 708

Tempo command, which can stretch or shrink sound files without raising or lowering the pitch.

Once all of the video was shot, short QuickTime segments were incorporated into HyperCard. This usually was done indirectly through Macromedia Director by the staff programmer and graphic artist (see Figure 14.4). In Director, the movie was combined with other graphic elements and interactive buttons. The stage in Director was set to the same size as a HyperCard stack, and the Macromedia Player utility was used to allow the Director interactive movie to become part of *The Engineering Adventure*.

Postproduction

Once you've shot your raw footage, you can begin the process of turning it into a finished production. This involves bringing the audio and video into the computer and then using digital editing tools to make it conform to your storyboard or intended final presentation.

Logging the Tape

The first step in the editing process is to log each videotape that you have recorded. The process can be a tedious one since every significant audio and video segment of the videotape has to be numbered and identified by an accurate written description. To reduce the tedium, use logging as an opportunity to think about how each scene could be incorporated into the project.

The purpose of logging the tape is to prevent unnecessary delays in trying to find the right scene while you're in editing and to provide a reminder of what shots are available. With most consumer VCRs and camcorders, you will have to rely on the tape counter. If you calibrate the counter each time you load a tape by rewinding the tape to the beginning and then resetting the counter, it should be reasonably accurate. If the counter's numbers represent real time in hours, minutes, seconds, and frames, they may be similar to other VCRs using a real-time counting system. Such a counter might represent one hour, 20 minutes, 10 seconds, and 18 frames as follows: 1:20:10:18. Other VCR counters use other numbering systems. The important thing to guard against is using a camcorder or VCR with one counting system to log the tape and then trying to edit the same tape on a unit with a different system. The locations of the segments in your log will no longer match up! Furthermore, since the numbers are just an estimate of tape position, you may have to re-calibrate the tape from time to time—especially if you are jogging back and forth quite a bit.

A much better system is available. It is called *timecode* and consists of identifying frame numbers that are digitally encoded on your videotape. Professional VCRs use the SMPTE timecode system (SMPTE stands for Society of Motion Picture and Television Engineers). Some high-end consumer camcorders and VCRs use Sony's RC (Rewritable Consumer) timecode system. In either case, you can use it to find an exact frame on the tape, even if you change VCRs.

Manual Logging

While many otherwise computer-literate people are so accustomed to logging by paper and pencil that they stick to the old ways, enlisting the support of the computer in the logging process has obvious advantages. The simplest logging helper is a word processing program. The immediate power of word search is available to locate a particular word, phrase, or frame number that will then help you find the video or audio segment that you need.

Logging Using Software

A more sophisticated logging tool actually provides control of your camcorder or VCR and automatically brings into the computer the correct frame numbers for a given segment (see Chapter 6, "Video Tools," and Sony VISCA sidebar, next page). Products such as CineWorks from D/Vision, AutoLog from Pipeline Digital, VideoToolkit from Abbate Video Inc., or VideoParadise and QT-Paradise from Hatnet, Inc. create small thumbnail stills, previews, or entire digital movies of each of the segments that you log. Object-oriented software tools permit you to categorize the various segments for future retrieval. Eventually, the process of logging a movie and then editing the segments will be seamless because the log itself will provide the digital movies for the editing process.

Sony's VISCA™ Protocol

Realizing that more control and flexibility was needed in the prosumer market, Sony created VISCA (Video System Control Architecture) as a platform-independent protocol. It allows a personal computer, such as a Macintosh, PC, or Amiga, to control up to seven video devices at once. Sony's Vdeck 1000, a VISCA-compatible Hi8 VCR that was designed as a computer peripheral, can be attached directly to your computer's modem or printer port with a supplied cable. By adding Sony's Vbox CI-1000 to the chain, you can then attach any camcorder or VCR that responds to LANC (or Control-L) or Control-S commands. With multiple VISCA recorders attached to your computer, you can create an analog editing system. Or you can use one of several VISCA aware applications to automate the capture of digital video.

Some Macintosh and Windows applications that take advantage of the VISCA protocol are:

Adobe Premiere

Macromind MediaMaker

PROmotion from Motion Works International, Inc.

Soft-Edit PRO-750 from The Profusion Group

VideoToolkit from Abbate Video Inc.

VideoParadise and QT-Paradise from Hatnet, Inc.

First Video Machine (software/hardware)

EzV^2

Capturing Only What You Need

Since disk storage will probably be at a premium, it is a good idea to capture only the footage you think you'll require. VideoToolkit from Abbate Video Inc. makes it easy to select only the scenes you need from your log. The program will automatically run through the list and capture a separate QuickTime movie for each shot you request. What makes VideoToolkit especially valuable is its ability to control practically any VCR or camcorder directly from your Macintosh. It comes with a cable that attaches to your modem or printer port and then plugs into your VCR or camcorder's Control-L or Control-S port. Even if your machine doesn't have one of these ports, VideoToolkit still can control it with a small infrared module included in the package. You will not get frame-accurate control, but for capturing footage, you don't need it. Just follow the instructions and leave enough extra footage at the beginning and end of the scene to ensure that you capture what you want. On the PC, Fast Video Machine has VISCA as well as RS-232/422 control. It can be configured as a linear editor with ability to create edit control lists or as a hybrid linear/nonlinear editor for digital video editing.

Digital Video Editing

Not only is editing video the most creative part of making QuickTime movies, but it also provides an opportunity to clarify, sharpen, and bring into focus the message that the video is designed to communicate. Video editing used to be undertaken only by highly paid professionals working in postproduction studios ("post houses") crammed with millions of dollars worth of equipment. Today, anyone with a few hundred dollars can try his or her hand at video editing, using such software programs as Adobe Premiere, ULead Systems' Media Studio Pro, DiVA VideoShop, CoSA After Effects, or Video Fusion. In fact, if you own a CD-ROM drive, you can try out the demo versions of several of these products on our enclosed CD-ROM. For a full rundown on the features and functions commonly found in these packages, see Chapter 6, "Video Tools."

We'll now take you through the video editing process by looking at a case study of a CD-ROM project underway at the California Museum of Photography.

In this project, three guest artists were invited to conduct research for their own art projects in the Museum's photography collection, which includes a quarter-million stereo photographs and glass negatives from the Keystone collection covering virtually every location on the globe. The project received an Artists Forum grant from the National Endowment for the Arts.

One of the artists, Stephen Axelrad, wanted to use the museum's collections as a jumping-off point for exploring personal experiences from his own life and decided to create a multimedia project with the working title "Self Museum." In the mid- and late-1980s, Axelrad had created an interactive art exhibition using a multimedia setup based on a PC compatible with a touch screen and videodisc player. He wanted to incorporate some of his previously created material into this new project and was happy to discover that he could indeed port all the visual imagery and audio directly to QuickTime without conversion. Because Axelrad primarily relied on audio narrative over still video frames from the computer or videodisc at no more than five frames per second, he was able to use his VideoSpigot board along with the Compact Video compressor to produce a 320 × 240 pixels movie. Using Director's Lingo scripting language, he found he had far more control over the interactive environment on the Macintosh than he did on the PC when programming in C (Director was not yet available on the PC).

Axelrad used Adobe Premiere to edit his QuickTime movies. He wanted to edit the video to the existing narrative, so first he placed a video segment containing audio into the editor's timeline. Next, he integrated new video segments to existing footage by cutting and splicing with the razor blade tool between the two video channels. He then added transitions at the beginning and end of each video insert. Finally, he created special effects by placing multiple video segments in the Superimpose channel, which permits moving objects to play on top of the video in the first channel. The Superimpose channel is also used in Premiere to animate titles over a video in another channel after using the built-in title editor.

Overview of the Video

To compare his life to a museum of photography, Axelrad used a video segment of himself consisting of an extreme close-up of his face and lips while he speaks. "My name is Stephen Axelrad," he says. "I am a Museum of Photography. I see through a Camera Obscura all that I know." (He refers to a large Camera Obscura built into the center of the exterior architectural facade of the California Museum of Photography that makes the building itself resemble a camera; the Camera Obscura acts as the lens.) The Camera Obscura permits people inside the building to see a large projection of what is going on in the outside world. The video editing challenge in this case was to integrate Axelrad's talking head with the museum's facade to re-create the museum as a composite portrait of himself. The steps he followed to accomplish this are typical of the process of editing QuickTime videos.

Preparing Media Files

Morph 2.5 Demo ⌘ 714

All of the media needed to make the movie were converted to the 320 × 240 format used for output of the final QuickTime clip. Still images of the museum's facade and a close-up of the Camera Obscura in the center of the building were resized in Photoshop. Axelrad then created a still 320 × 240 PICT image of his face using ScreenPlay software that comes with the VideoSpigot. He then brought the still images of the Museum's facade and his face and lips into Morph, where he created a QuickTime movie in which the museum facade morphs into his face. This QuickTime movie was then edited into the larger production to add multiple levels of convergence between the museum facade and the face.

Setting Up the Project in Premiere

All of the video and audio segments, still images, and other material used to make the QuickTime movie were placed in a single folder and then imported into a library window in Premiere. The library was given the name "Self Museum Library" and saved to the same folder on the hard disk. A library contains only one copy of each movie, sound, or image and can be reused in other projects. Although the project window is intended to store media being used for a project, this can create confusion as to which media are actually being used. Each time a video segment is cut with the razor blade tool into a shorter segment, duplicates of the movie appear in the project window and clutter it. Thus, retaining a library file for each project serves the function of clarifying which media files are actually part of the project in progress.

The project window was saved along with the timeline construction window to a file named "Self Museum Project" in the same folder with the other files for the project (see Figure 14.5). Saving all of the work for a particular production in one folder is critical for the simple reason that Premiere uses "reference" movies or media that use pointers to the actual raw clips. Segments do not become contained within a single document until the final movie is made with the "Make Movie" command. If the work were moved to another hard disk or a removable disk, or if it were relocated in some other folder, Premiere might not be able to find the media files that are referenced and they would have to be relocated.

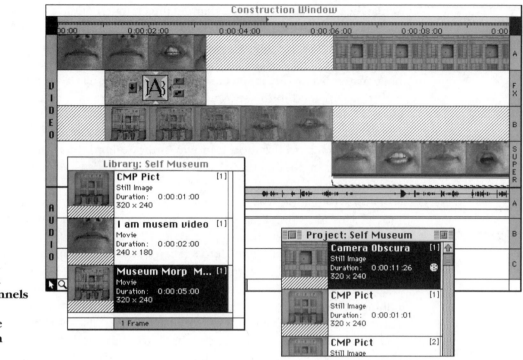

Figure 14.5 Premiere's Construction window with multiple channels occupied by media for the "Self Museum Project."

Synching Audio and Video

A QuickTime close-up movie of Axelrad's face and lips was placed in the first video channel in Premiere. Audio narration was captured using Sound Edit Pro from the original video. To insure the maximum frame rate for the video, Axelrad captured the sound in a separate pass from the video. Capturing both together would have provided automatic synchronization, but the additional processing power needed to capture the sound data would have lowered the video frame rate. With an automated capturing system (VideoToolkit, QT-Paradise), the video and audio can be captured separately and then automatically combined by the software.

The next step was to synchronize the separate audio and video tracks. The audio narration was placed in the first sound channel, and a short preview was made to determine the direction the audio needed to be moved to obtain synchronization with the video. Through trial and error and several previews, perfect lip sync was achieved. The "Make Movie" command was used to compile a QuickTime movie to ensure that the preview accurately portrayed the final result. The initial movie used Apple Video compression and the small size of 160 × 120 pixels as a test, while the final movie was made in the larger size of 320 × 240. While the Apple Video compression isn't effective enough to produce larger window sizes, it can compress video *much* faster than the Compact Video codec.

Video Inserts

While the entire sound track remained intact, much of the original video of Axel-rad's face and lips was replaced with video inserts in the second video channel or the Superimpose channel, or with other special effects and still images. (Note that the current version of Premiere—4.0—allows up to 99 tracks, which would have made this project much easier!) The morph movie, which was the first video insert, was placed in the second video track. The razor blade tool was used to cut the original video from the first track so that the morph movie could be seen from the second. A preview of this movie showed simple cuts from the movie in the first track, to the morph movie in the second track, and then back again to the movie in the first track, which remained in lip-sync with the audio.

Using Transitions

A "Doors" transition was used to go from the artist's face and lips to the morph movie. This transition created a stunning effect as the museum's facade opened up like doors to reveal the morph movie, which itself was in the process of transforming from a museum back into a face, so that the canopy above the museum's own doors morphed onto the lower lip of the artist (see Figures 14.6 and 14.7).

This interesting effect is one of many available to digital directors using video editing software. However, it's important to note that in the real world of professional video, the vast majority of transitions are cuts. Dissolves, cross-dissolves, and fades-to-black run a distant second. You have to be careful not to overuse the fancy options, as gratuitous transitions can get quite tiresome to the viewer and can throw off the pace of the story. Feel free to experiment with them but resist the temptation to use them too often.

When applying a transition, consider the sense of motion you want for your scenes. Many transitions are directional, beginning on the far left and proceeding to the far right, or beginning in the top left corner and proceeding to the bottom right corner. Transitions can be used to continue or reverse the motion, maintain the continuity of the scene, or provide contrast in focusing on the differences from one scene to the next. Returning to the person who is looking toward the upper right of the screen, the transition might be a wipe coming from the top right corner. If a person is walking from the left of the screen to the right, a wipe might take place from the left, creating some tension as it slowly catches up with the person and wipes him/her away. Thus, transitions should not be thought of as special effects but as visual elements that flow from the subject matter of the video.

Using the Superimpose Channel

Following the morph, a segment of the original "talking lips" movie was cut from the first channel and pasted into the special Superimpose channel so it remained in sync with the underlying audio (see Figure 14.8). A still image of the Camera Obscura was placed in the first video channel to fill the void left when the lips were cut from that channel. In order to create a vision of the lips talking on top of the Camera Obscura, Premiere's transparency effect was used (located under the "Clip" pull-down menu). By means of experimentation, the Key Type "RGB

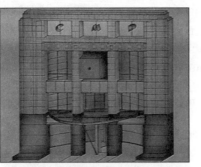

**Figure 14.6
Doors transition
causes museum's
facade to open
revealing a face.**

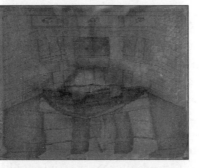

**Figure 14.7
The Museum of
Photography
morphs into the
face and lips of
the artist.**

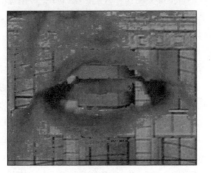

**Figure 14.8
The lips in
Superimpose
channel are
overlaid onto
the museum's
Camera Obscura.**

Difference" set to "Similarity = 72" was found to cause everything in the Super-impose channel except the lips to disappear, thus resulting in the desired effect.

Wrapping Up   While the QuickTime movies did not fill the screen, Axelrad found the extra room was perfect for providing a context in which to view the movies and to place buttons for interacting with the work.

Once the media were transferred to QuickTime, Axelrad used the MovieShop utility (see below) to ensure that the data rate stayed under 90 kilobytes per second, which permits the movie to play from a CD-ROM to just about any color Macintosh. To test the material, he transferred about 14 SyQuest cartridges full of QuickTime movies and computer data to a recordable CD-ROM through a service bureau that charged only $150. This not only provided an opportunity to test the CD-ROM's performance, but also served as an inexpensive storage medium. The test was a complete success. In addition, he had 14 empty SyQuests for continued development of the project, which also was a rousing success and very well received by the museum's administrators and visitors.

Compressing With Compact Video— MovieShop Revisited

After you have completed the editing of your movie, it's time to compress it. In Chapter 6, "Video Tools," we mentioned Apple's MovieShop program (available from APDA on the QuickTime Developer's CD-ROM) and how it can be used to reduce a QuickTime movie's data rate to make it compatible with playback from CD-ROM. Here are the steps to obtain the best results using the Apple Compact Video codec, currently the most effective QuickTime codec in reducing the overall data rate (though it also takes the longest to do its job).

First, launch MovieShop and press the "Import" button to read in your movie. You can inspect your movie's data rate by selecting the "Play" button.

Next, select the maximum data rate. We mentioned earlier that 120–150K per second is a safe rate for playback from most CD-ROM drives. Choose this rate if you plan to mass distribute your QuickTime movie on CD-ROM. Experiment with higher data rates if you know that your movie will be played only from double-speed CD-ROM drives or from a hard drive.

Under MovieShop's "Preferences" menu, select "Millions of colors" and "Use previous compressed video."

Image size can be changed with "Cropping..." from the "Preferences" menu. If you resize the picture using scaling or cropping, use horizontal and vertical dimensions that are multiples of 4. The Compact Video compressor is optimized for these values. The best size is 240×180 if you are playing back from CD-ROM. You can use 320×240 for movies that have higher data rates (though you may also need the faster Macs to keep up with the frame rate). You'll definitely want to crop if you see noise or jitter along the edges of the video frame.

Remember that sound is data, too. Higher-quality sound requires more information and may slightly lower the image quality. Choose "Sound..." from the "Preferences" menu if you want to change the sound quality. If you have music in your sound track, you'll probably want it set to 22 kHz. But if you only have voice, choose the "Re-sample sound to 11 kHz" setting.

Finally, select "Methods..." from the "Preferences" menu to tell MovieShop which compression techniques to apply. The Compact Video compressor automatically takes care of data rate limiting; so turn off all the methods except for items 1 and 8: "1) Compress frame – As frame differenced using the quality settings," and "8) Prefer Natural Key frame – Do not force Key Frame before it." To do this, drag item 8 directly below item 1 and then drag item "18) ONLY DO THOSE ABOVE THIS ITEM," directly below item 8. Next, click on item 8 and

Making Movies at Hellmuth, Obata & Kassabaum

With its bristling array of electronic gear, David Munson's enclave looks more like the cockpit of a nuclear submarine than an office in Hellmuth, Obata & Kassabaum (HOK), one of the largest architectural firms in the world.

Munson, V.P. and Director of Computer Simulations for HOK, makes architectural "movies"—3-D photorealistic simulations of buildings and their interior spaces. The firm's architects submit CAD drawings to Munson, who spins them into sophisticated animations using Silicon Graphics (SGI) workstations. Munson then edits them using traditional video gear.

The final result is a videotape used by customers to conceptualize and sell architectural projects that have ranged from the Dallas-Fort Worth Airport to San Francisco's Moscone convention Center. As such, Munson's office is littered with switchers, mixing consoles, edit controllers, sync generators, and other tools of the analog video trade.

Last December, Munson added another weapon to his arsenal, one that threatens to render the others obsolete: an SGI workstation fitted with Avid's Media Suite Pro digital video editing software. Before installing the Avid system, Munson had to use a bewildering collection of video paraphernalia—and coax all of it into working in concert. "You had to be really good at editing live to videotape," says Munson.

Munson uses custom animation software created in-house at HOK and saves animation files to laserdisc for interim storage. Reads and writes to laserdisc happen at about one second per frame, as opposed to the 15 seconds it would take for hard disc storage. Munson uses Video Creator to convert the $1,280 \times 1,024$ images to 640×480 images in the NTSC video format before saving to laserdisc.

When Munson is ready to edit, SGI's Galileo video card digitizes the animation files from laserdisc (which stores in an analog NTSC format) and stores them on the Indigo's 9 gigabyte hard drive. At that point, Munson edits the entire movie on the Indigo in a process known as "nonlinear" editing. "If I'd known how easy it was, I'd have switched a long time ago," says Munson.

The equipment itself isn't cheap, but still far less expensive than traditional video equipment, and Munson is already using the SGI workstations for animation. Munson says he spent about $25,000 on the Indigo a few years back and sunk another $25,000 to $35,000 into it for a MIPS R4400 CPU, hard disks, and a whopping 160 Mb of RAM—which is used to render and display the animations in real time prior to recording to tape. Avid charges $15,000 for Media Suite Pro, and Munson spent about $17,000 on the Betacam recorder.

Aside from the much more straightforward editing process, Munson finds the flexibility of nonlinear editing particularly valuable when customers want changes in a movie. Before, such alterations would have been impossible in a reasonable timeframe. Using digital editing tools, Munson can make changes and write a new movie to tape in a few hours.

Recently, Munson got a chance to demonstrate just how flexible a digital editing setup can be. HOK was asked to provide a 3-D simulation of an addition to a house featured in the PBS program *This Old House*. After creating the simulation and a fly-through of the interior, Munson got a copy of the live video portion of the program.

box continued

Back in his hotel room, Munson digitized the video, and edited it with the Indigo/Avid, combining HOK's simulation with the live video. In a couple of hours, he had a tape that closely matched the final broadcast program. The TV production staff, however, elected to use This Old Editing Studio to edit the actual broadcast program, a decision they perhaps regretted when they saw Munson's digitally-edited version.

And all that outmoded video equipment in Munson's office? "I'm not going to throw all that stuff away," chuckles Munson, "It still looks really impressive to come in here and see all the boxes and little lights."

adjust the Forced Key Frame tolerance value in the lower left corner of the window. Use a value that is ½ of your key frame rate. If you have key frames every 10 frames, then the value should be 5.

One last note: MovieShop has a bug that causes settings from unused methods to take effect. To override them, select all of the following items and set their values as indicated:

Item 2: Forced key frame—set to 255

Item 3: Natural key frame—set to 1

Item 4: Natural key frame—set to 200

Item 5: Drop duplicate—set to 255

If you have a large movie to compress, you will want as much processing power as you can get. If you don't have a high-end Mac or PC or an accelerator board, see if you can borrow one for the duration of your editing schedule. You also may be able to split your movie into several segments, compress them in parallel on several computers, then combine the segments into your final movie.

The Medium Is the Message?

Digital desktop video places communication tools in more hands then ever before. As a result, watching television is no longer the sole domain of the couch potato, but instead has become a place to learn and compare the creative tools of the trade.

While the experts debate whether video is a sign that our culture is declining from verbal literacy to visual idiocy, it is nevertheless among the most effective and powerful vehicles for communication, whether for promotion, education, training, or other purposes. These relatively low-cost, exciting new tools and techniques continue a revolution in communication which began with moveable type half a millennium ago.

Figure 14.9 Apple's Quick-Time Web homepage has up-to-date information on QuickTime.

It now is possible for anyone to create a multimedia production complete with professional quality digital video. How will we take advantage of this immense power to communicate ideas? Through this medium, stories that were previously impossible to tell now can be shared. What will people create when they have grown up with the ability to craft a compelling video production? The answers and the questions will undoubtedly change as the technology and art form mature.

Web crawlers may want to check out Apple's QuickTime homepage for more information about this cross-platform digital video standard (see Figure 14.9). The page is at: http://quicktime.apple.com/index.html. Microsoft's homepage is at: http://www.microsoft.com.

15

Video Projects

Video is one of the most potent elements of multimedia, and creating and editing video is one the most demanding skills required of a producer. In this chapter we'll survey four top-quality video projects: an interactive movie, a virtual foray into the sea, a video "poem," and the logo sequence for a television show.

The Vortex

The Vortex, a new interactive movie on CD (see Figure 15.1) from Hyperbole Studios, has a futuristic plot to match its high tech production values. The earth is dying, and you are sent across the time/space continuum to try to reverse the planet's environmental decline. As if that's not challenge enough, you can survive only with the aid and guidance of a VR life support system. And, naturally, there are giant aggressive insects to keep at bay.

The Vortex ⌘ 030

The Vortex's ambitious plot is balanced by a seamless amalgam of live action video and 3-D animation, an absorbing blend of what Hyperbole calls "virtual cinema" (see Figure 15.2).

"The goal of virtual cinema is to experience a movie from the inside," says Hyperbole's Greg Roach. Faithful readers may remember that we featured Roach's *The Madness of Roland* in the first edition of this book. Meanwhile, Hyperbole has created the smash hit game *Quantum Gate,* and *The Vortex* is its sequel.

Quantum Gate was developed in collaboration with game publisher Media Vision, which went belly up during production of *The Vortex.* Roach learned a lot from the experience, some of which we'll relate later in this section.

Figure 15.1
The Vortex
continues where
Quantum Gate
left off.

Special Considerations

Weaving the game's intricate plot with that of its predecessor was an early preoccupation of the designers. "One of the greatest design challenges was how to organically bring viewers up to speed," says Roach. The developers eventually hit on a combination of textual overview and visual recap, along with a diary that summarizes many details of the "prequel."

Another challenge was getting available development tools to live up to the aspirations that Roach and his team had for the game. "This is an interesting and ongoing challenge that I know a lot of people are grappling with," says Roach. "It's unlike traditional film, in which narrative structure, methodology, and language are all well defined." By contrast, says Roach, "we're cutting most of this stuff out of whole cloth."

With full screen graphics rendered in thousands of colors, 16-bit audio, and digital video all streaming from the CD simultaneously, there were also plenty of technical hurdles. "We're moving a lot of data around and asking the hardware to deliver a lot of performance," says Roach, in something of an overstatement.

In a nod to economic reality, the team released a Windows CD before doing a Mac version, even though, as Roach puts it, "the Mac market is more sympathetic to what we're trying to do." A hybrid version would have been preferable, but was tabled, in part, because the necessary cross-platform tools, such as QuickTime 2.0, were not yet available during the game's development.

Tips and Techniques

Much of Roach's advice for first time developers of entertainment titles has to do with the business and logistical realities of game title development. First, he counsels keeping the faith and believing in the potential for this type of product in

Figure 15.2
The Vortex
**combines live
action with
animated effects.**

the face of the sometimes onerous development challenges. "I think there's going to be tremendous demand for this type of game, especially as the computer becomes an appliance for the average person."

Roach also claims that you can't spend too much time in preproduction. "You need to know, down to the frame, what's going to happen," he says, adding that developers should double-initial preproduction scheduling estimates.

Tools and Equipment

Hyperbole shot live video on Betacam, digitized it on the Mac using Radius VideoVision Studio, and composited it with animation sequences using both bluescreen and rotoscoping techniques. Animation was done using SoftImage on SGI workstations, although Roach now considers more mainstream PCs and Macs to be capable of matching SGI tools and workstations in terms of power and performance.

Water Fantasia

Water Fantasia ⌘ 031

Water Fantasia is a QuickTime movie featuring dreamy sequences that blend and dissolve to the relaxing rhythms of its soundtrack. Watching the movie is sort of like watching an aquarium: You feel drawn into a watery world that is both soothing and engaging. (The underwater segments were, in fact, shot at an aquarium.)

The work combines creator Don Doerfler's environmental interests with the emerging world of digital video production (see Figure 15.3). Growing up and living near the ocean in Southern California provided both the influences and the

**Figure 15.3
Scene from Don
Doerfler's *Water
Fantasia.***

material for *Water Fantasia*. In addition to his independent work, Doerfler is a producer at Compton's New Media, where he works on CD-ROM products.

Special Considerations

Doerfler's imagination almost always exceeds what he can actually capture on video, which he cites as a major hurdle in producing *Water Fantasia* or any multimedia project. "No matter how hard you try, you can't get that perfect shot," he says, "so you're always searching through your tapes looking for that piece that's going to complete your overall visual idea."

The constant challenges are to shoot enough (and the right) material, sort through it all—looking for the right pieces, and reshooting, if possible, to capture those elusive visual ideas.

Technically, Doerfler spent some time making sure the final cut played back acceptably at 15 frames per second. This was a challenge, since for those used to high-quality on-line video, the do-it-in-the-basement look of QuickTime can be something of a letdown. "My favorite misnomer for QuickTime is 'Quick-Trash'—how to take a perfectly good video and ruin it," says Don.

Despite the frustrations of the fledgling digital video tools, he remains excited about their rapid improvements and feels you can do good work with existing tools if you're willing to take the time and make the effort.

**Tips and
Techniques**

Doerfler's visual arts background has helped him in the transition to digital video and multimedia production. His earlier work taught him to visualize and carefully plan before applying brush to canvas or pencil to paper.

The complexities of digital video projects require an equal degree of foresight and planning, says Doerfler. "You need to have certain concepts in mind before you start, especially when you're digitizing video segments. You're going to have a finite amount of space on your disk, so you have to review footage and put together a complete storyboard before you even start."

This planning stage saves time in all phases of video production: It gives a clear idea of what to shoot, saves hard disk space by preventing you from digitizing unnecessary footage, and helps organize the editing and assembly tasks.

Premiere 4.0 Demo ⌘ 722

On the editing effects side, he recommends keeping it simple. Programs such as Adobe's Premiere offer an assortment of transitional effects—wipes, dissolves, and fades, for example. While these effects can be fun to experiment with, they can be distracting to watch. *Water Fantasia* uses only two types of transitions: cuts and dissolves.

Doerfler adds a few final video tips: "Always use a tripod; never go handheld. And don't use any bad footage. If it's exposed badly, or if it's shaky—no matter how good it is otherwise—don't use it; it'll look terrible. We're all spoiled by watching TV."

**Tools and
Equipment**

As Doerfler notes, no single Mac application does it all when it comes to digital video. "The Mac has all the tools, but they're all in different applications; you have to have at least a half dozen of them to get what you want."

For *Water Fantasia,* he used the Sony FX510 8mm video camera to shoot video, SuperMac's VideoSpigot card to digitize the video, and Premiere and VideoLake's VideoFusion for editing the digitized segments.

At the center, is a Quadra 950 with a 500Mb hard disk, 28Mb of RAM, an Apple 16″ color monitor, 24-bit color card, and a 13″ NTSC video monitor. A RasterOps Video Expander (an encoder) converts the computer's RGB video to NTSC for output to videotape. He uses several tape decks, including a Sony EVC40 and a Goldstar GVRA485, and a Realistic five-channel stereo mixer for adding several channels of natural sound and music.

Land of Counterpane

Land of Counterpane ⌘ 032

As Education Director of the American Film Institute's Apple Lab, Harry Mott works with and teaches digital video, concentrating especially on QuickTime. He created *Land of Counterpane* to show, as he puts it, "what anyone with any color Mac could do with QuickTime."

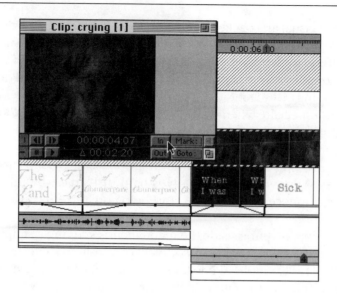

Figure 15.4 Editing Harry Mott's *Land of Counterpane*.

The result is a simple but delicately constructed ode to his son Cameron, accompanied by a restful musical track and a Robert Louis Stevenson poem (see Figure 15.4).

Special Considerations

Mott cites desktop video tools—and sluggish processing times—as a source of frustration. Mastering arcane programs and techniques and waiting for scenes to be rendered, for files to transfer, and for graphics to process are the special challenges of digital video and multimedia in general.

Even though tools are getting easier to use, and machines are getting ever faster, Mott acknowledges that by and large, these have been incremental improvements. The vast size and complexity of multimedia, and especially digital video, requires machines to be much faster to really make a difference.

Tips and Techniques

Mott has some special advice for those who are thinking about experimenting with digital video, but may be put off by the challenges. "Don't wait, do it now," he says. "Everything is going to get better, faster, cheaper—maybe next week. Just play and experiment and make mistakes—that's what the undo key is for."

Mott recommends using Apple's Compact Video QuickTime compressor when creating movies. This ensures that movies will play back smoothly on almost any Mac. By contrast, he says, "if you make a QuickTime movie on a Quadra 950 using Apple Video [another compressor], it will not play smoothly on say an LCIII or even a IIci." Apple bundles the Compact Video compressor with QuickTime.

The downside is that the compression takes a while to apply to each frame. Although *Land of Counterpane* is only one and one-half minutes long, it took six hours to compress on Harry's IIci. Even compressed, the movie is nearly 12Mb in size, which clearly demonstrates the enormous size of digital video files.

Mott also advises that you digitize movies with no compression and apply compression only when you actually make the movie. This will give you the most compression options later and ensure that you have the highest quality video stored on disk (since compression can seriously degrade image quality).

Like all seasoned multimedia producers, he plans his work carefully and stresses organization to his students. For example, he keeps titles, animation, video, and still images in their own folders to help him find things and speed the assembly of movies. Perhaps because he's a teacher, Mott's step-by-step guide on the disk is particularly rich in tips and techniques. Check it out.

Tools and Equipment

The modest equipment Mott used for *Land of Counterpane* shows that equipment need not be a barrier to a thorough exploration of digital video. He used a Mac IIci with 20Mb of RAM and an 80Mb hard drive, the ever-popular VideoSpigot capture card for digitizing video, Macromedia's MacRecorder for digitizing sound, and Premiere for editing the movie.

EcoSpies

EcoSpies ⌘ 033

Multimedia wizard Scott Billups was in Japan during the Telly awards, which are given to honor outstanding independent television programs. Billups figured he and his team hadn't "a snowball's chance in hell" of winning an award for *EcoSpies*, so accepted the Japanese engagement rather than attend the awards ceremony, which is held in Los Angeles. As it turned out, *EcoSpies* won the award for best show.

EcoSpies is a pilot produced by Sam and Sharon Baldoni and directed by Tim Cutt (see Figure 15.5). Cutt wanted to create a hard-hitting, reality-based show about the earth's growing ecological problems. Segments of the show cover toxic pollutants, unsanitary food production, and global eco-terrorism.

Special Considerations

Storyboards for the pilot had been created by a graphics firm, but Cutt felt their suggestions either missed the mark editorially or would, themselves, eat up the entire $10,000 budget. Desktop production, where one person can perform the job of many, was the only way he could get the look he wanted and stay within his budget.

Desktop video pioneer Scott Billups seemed the man for the job. Over the past 18 years, he has written, directed, produced, shot, and animated hundreds of broadcast, industrial, and theatrical projects for clients such as Reebok, Mattel, Nissan National Geographic Explorer, and KCET-TV.

Using a variety of desktop video tools (see section on "Tools and Equipment" later in this chapter), Billups created the visual identity for the show.

Figure 15.5
EcoSpies.

His job as production designer was to come up with, as he puts it, "an inexpensive but compelling logo sequence that lent itself to segues, transitions, and 'bumpers.'" Bumpers are teasers that networks use to keep you watching the show during multiple commercials.

The timing of elements is one of the biggest challenges in creating these sorts of transitions. Matching "stings" (music or sound effects) with graphic transitions can consume a great deal of time.

Billups would save the video clips as QuickTime movies and send them to composer Dominic Messinger, who would create music in MIDI format. Billups would then match the music files to the beat of the video transitions, making timing of stings fairly straightforward.

Tips and Techniques

Billups' extensive use of desktop video tools meant that the *EcoSpies* identity could be created much more easily and less expensively than would have been possible with traditional video tools.

He cites the timing of animation and video sequences (compositing) as the single most challenging task. Another tough aspect is making things look natural. "The hardest thing in creating computer graphics is getting them to look organic. It's really easy to make your graphics look slick and metallic. The trend is away from the glitzy, flashy look and toward a more natural appearance," he says.

This trend encourages the use of desktop tools, which excel at this organic, photo-montage look. "Desktop tools allow you to sample and combine images instead of simply creating synthetic textures," says Billups.

Tools and Equipment

Director 4.0 Demo ⌘ 708

Macromodel 1.5 Demo ⌘ 720

Billups sketched his visualizations on his Mac IIfx with Swivel 3D and Macromedia Director. He exported the rough animations as 320 × 240 PICTs and compressed them into a QuickTime movie using Premiere. He created final models with Macromedia's MacroModel, and ElectricImage's MisterFont, rendering them in ElectricImage Animation System. A beta version of CoSA's After Effects image processing software was used to composite live video with animation.

Billups digitized audio tracks with DigiDesign's AudioMedia board. He recorded the video frame-by-frame to videodisc with Sony's CRV 5000 Laser Videodisc Recorder, Intelligent Resource's VideoExplorer board, and Advanced Digital Imaging's MacVac software.

16

Interface and Interactivity: Bringing It Together

Interface is the focal point and control center of any multimedia project. It brings the component pieces of text, graphics, sound, animation, and videos together into a cohesive whole; and it's the all-critical graphic environment through which a user interacts with them. Creating an elegant and useful interface is where the real art of multimedia production is called to the fore—and it's probably a project's most challenging developmental component.

In this chapter, we'll take a look at the planning and design considerations that go into creating an effective interface, including initial planning and design; the use of text, graphics, sound, animation, and video; and mastering the project. This is not a technical chapter. Rather, it's meant to give you some old fashioned common sense and guidance for developing something that's user-friendly, creative, and useful. ("Special Delivery," a sidebar later in the chapter, does offer some technical pointers about delivering a multimedia project on CD and over the Internet's World Wide Web.)

The points we touch on here are meant to start you thinking about ways in which you can creatively enhance the usefulness and enjoyment of your project. After reading this chapter, take a tour through the projects on the *Power Tools* CD. Their producers have expanded upon these ideas in hundreds of different ways. With luck, you'll come up with some creative variations on their techniques and design sensibilities; and so it goes.

Planning a Nonlinear Program

Planning a multimedia presentation means not only gathering all the elements needed but also conceiving a structure and design for the program. Good interface design is extremely important, as it will mean the difference between users scanning the first couple of screens or really poking into the corners of your project. Information flow is important as well; so it might be a good idea to chart your project out on paper, showing the various areas where users can reach out and find data that they might not otherwise encounter. It is the varying levels of interactivity that will ultimately draw users further into your project, and, it is hoped, entertain them enough to keep them there (see Figure 16.1).

Exploit Random Access

Keep in mind that unlike most viewable media, such as television or films, interactive multimedia is nonlinear. Once in the computer, your data is immediately accessible at all times. You can get to the fiftieth screen of your project just as fast as you can get to the second. The random access nature of this technology is what makes it so powerful, and the best multimedia projects take advantage of this fact.

Therefore, "interactive" means that users of your project don't necessarily have to proceed through it in a straight, linear fashion from the first screen to the last. In fact, you can put in buttons allowing them to branch off at any point. Allowing them into places that don't make sense can be a problem as well. If they need one piece of information before proceeding to the next, then plan your project accordingly, making sure that the button to reach item two can only be clicked after going through item one.

Linking: The "Card Metaphor"

All authoring programs will provide a method of linking that will enable you to create buttons to navigate from one part of your project to another. These links will let you create a completely interactive environment for the user to explore. Depending on the structure of your project, users can move about freely or in defined patterns. If it's important that the user learn some basic concepts before gaining complete freedom, it's easy to make the first 5 or 10 screens work in a straight, linear fashion. Once the basic concepts have been communicated, you can then let the user run wild through audio-visual databases, animated video games, or whatever happens to be the content of your project.

Video games are a good example of nonlinear access because there are often multiple choices as to what can happen. Depending on the user's choice, he or she may end up going to the next screen, going back to the beginning of the game, or even taking a shortcut to the end. This type of interactivity is what makes multimedia production so exciting.

Many authoring programs also support randomizing. In other words, you can build in functions that will ensure that your project reacts differently every time it is run. For example, you can instruct a button to randomly branch to any one of 12 different screens when a user clicks on it. Each one of these 12 screens can have buttons that also take random paths, including the possibility of returning to the previous screen.

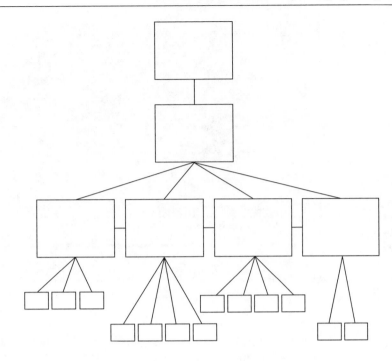

Figure 16.1
It's often useful to create a map that shows the structure of a project and all its links. A map that shows the relationships between the various sections of a project will allow you to anticipate any dead ends or other difficulties that might be inherent in the structure of your project.

Avoid Sluggish Performance

One of your most important overall goals should be to achieve a synergy between your hardware and software. With intelligent integration of text, graphics, audio, animation, and video, your project should run smoothly and create a lasting impression on users. Unless you take serious precautions to ensure that your hardware can effectively process all the data included in your project, it may run sluggishly, leaving users with a negative impression.

The biggest complaint about interactive media is that it is often too slow. Make sure that this is not the death of your project. If you have to sacrifice certain things in order to ensure that the overall project runs well, it will be worth it. It may be impossible to make your project run at a blinding pace, but you should at least be considerate of how long it is reasonable to expect the user to wait. There are interactive game CDs on the market that can take a minute or more to load an animation that heralds the next section of the game. This is a surefire killer for most users, as few people have the patience to wait, regardless of how rewarding the animation might be when it finally gets to the screen.

Designing a Clean and Intuitive Interface

By today's standards, a user interface should be extremely intuitive, eliminating the need for written instructions. Proper use of icons, good screen design, logi-

**Figure 16.2
The interface
for Microsoft's
Dinosaurs
features an
attractive layout.**

cal ordering of content, and a consistent structure are all important concerns when planning a user interface.

Be conscious of whether or not your project feels consistent. All the screens should have the same basic design elements, with all the key buttons always in the same location.

You should also make sure you have enough room to include graphics or text on any given screen. An interface should make sense at a glance to any user. It should also be intuitive in regard to design sense, button placement, and logical data flow.

It's important that you offer users an unfettered path through your project. They should be able to intuitively locate whatever it is that interests them without having to go through each screen or button. They should also be able to navigate through a variety of interactive levels and still find their way back to where they began.

Where possible, you should create extra guidance, as well. For example, some programs will provide dialogue and/or message boxes with information on alternate paths or approaches to information. If it's possible for users to hit two buttons on the same screen that don't work together, try and create a warning and some instruction on how they should properly proceed. Some projects include interactive maps that show the levels and sublevels of the project structure, allowing users to change location by referring to the map and clicking on the area they wish to visit.

If help files are included with your project, make them available at all times. This type of guidance and feedback can go a long way toward encouraging users

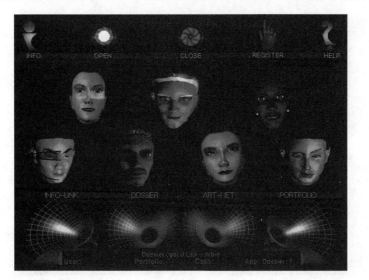

**Figure 16.3
The interface
for *Millennium
Auction* is more
free-form.**

to stick with an interactive project. The more challenging the project, the more guidance and help you need to offer.

It's also nice to build in rewards for users. If they've completed an entire section of your project, create an animated segue to the next screen. There are lots of ways to reward users, depending on the nature of your project. Tallying up a current score and assigning it an impressive name is one way. Playing some fanfare music is another. Regardless of the nature of your project, if it asks for users to make their way through lots of data, then you should provide resting spots or other breathers along the way.

Ergonomics

An ergonomically designed interface will offer a logical flow between different functions. It should not force users to look all over the place for information and buttons, but rather should maintain consistency in the placement of text, graphics, and navigational tools.

Free navigating through various levels should also be a key feature. For example, if your project has four main areas, each with two or three sublevels, you should provide a means to traverse back and forth easily among the sublevels without having to always return to the top level. If your project demands a lot of text input, then you should offer command-key equivalents for navigating through the various screens as well. This way the user can leave his or her hands on the keyboard, rather than constantly switching from mouse to keyboard and back again.

You should also make sure that users can get through your project in a reasonable amount of time, building in shortcuts for those who might wish to skim through various sections.

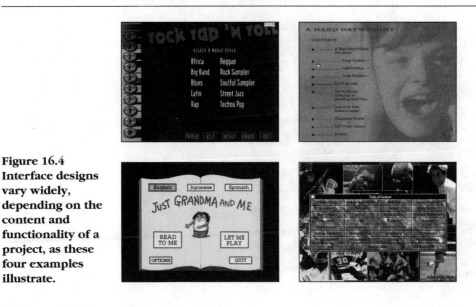

Figure 16.4 Interface designs vary widely, depending on the content and functionality of a project, as these four examples illustrate.

Using Dynamic Media

Dynamic media refers to any audio, video, and animation clips that are to be used in a project. The use of dynamic media in a multimedia project can add greatly to the impact of your message. There are a variety of ways to integrate animation, audio, and video. They can be used as supportive mechanisms to tell users what kind of progress they have made. They can also establish an overall tone for your project.

Glowing or pulsing buttons can heighten the visual impact of your interface. Sound effects that reinforce various choices and actions can also make a project more stimulating. If there are questions in your project, sound effects for yes and no answers are a great means of livening up the presentation, and they make it easier to understand as well.

Annotating key areas of graphics or video clips with simple animations can also help to clarify and emphasize your message. For example, if there is a particular point of interest in a video clip, you can call it to the user's attention by creating graphic overlays or animated arrows.

Make sure you don't include too much dynamic media, as it can lead to other problems. If your project is too heavily laden with animation and video, it will tend to slow down, regardless of the system you're working on. Try to spread out the use of video clips and animations. If you need to synchronize a video clip to an animation or sound effect, make sure you test the playback performance on every possible system that will be used to run your project. Don't sacrifice performance for glitz. There's often a middle road that will allow you to incorporate limited video, animation, or audio without losing too much speed.

Assembling Interactive Multimedia Components

Assembling all the components that make up a project involves coordinating hardware, software, and creative resources. Most ambitious projects will involve assembling a team that might include writers, artists, animators, scripting people, and more. Regardless of the size of your team, once you've determined the structure and content of your project, you will need to acquire and prepare all the data to be incorporated.

Text

If you rely heavily on text and text fields for disseminating information, make sure that you have a sensible way to handle your data. Generally, you'll assign a writer to provide you with text files that you can then import into your project. You must confirm that the word processor used by the writer can create text files that are compatible with the text importation capabilities of your authoring environment. There are a number of different text formatting models supported by the various word processors, but you can't automatically assume that your writer's format will be compatible. Make sure that imported text comes in cleanly and doesn't have to be fixed up or modified in any way. A text file ready for import should already have line feeds, tab information, and text styles (bold, italics, etc.) in final form.

Conversely, you may need to remove text. If you require text input from users, make sure you can access and use the data that is recorded. Apple Events and other similar approaches can allow you to export text entries to databases or other software environments. Name and address fields can be entered in a kiosk and sent directly into a database, but you'll have to be familiar with the tab-delimited fields and other features of the programs used to ensure smooth communication between applications.

Graphics

Almost all projects will involve graphics of some sort, and your authoring program and the type of project you are creating will determine what types of graphics you need. Computer-generated images can always be converted to a format that is compatible with your authoring program (see Chapter 7, "Authoring Tools") by using Adobe Photoshop or a utility specifically designed for file conversions.

Probably the biggest concern you'll have in putting together your project is making sure that it runs at a reasonable pace, even with all the graphical overhead. When scanning photographs, it's important to pay attention to the bit-depth of the scanner you use, as there are many models that record everything from black and white to 32-bit color. Since 8-bit graphics only require one fourth the system performance of 32-bit graphics, most people will convert their graphics into 8-bit color before importing them into an authoring environment.

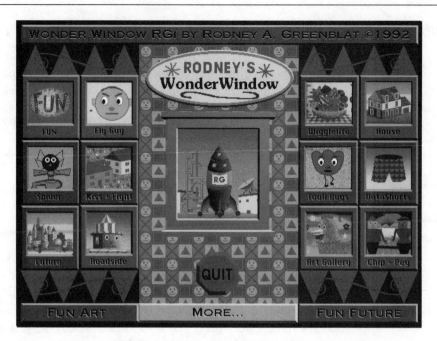

**Figure 16.5
Kids love
*Rodney's Wonder
Window's* quirky
interface and
colorful graphics.**

Make sure you scan your graphics at the right resolution as well. Most scanners can scan photos at a resolution of 300 dots per inch or more when 72 dpi is all that's generally needed for a project that will be displayed on a screen. For more details on the techniques and hardware for scanning, see Chapter 2, "Systems Software, Hardware, and Peripherals."

*Processing
Photos*

Photoshop 3.0 Demo ⌘ 715

There are a variety of wonderful graphics tools on both the Mac and PC to aid in the process of fixing and processing images. Adobe Photoshop will enable you to enhance your imported photos in a number of ways. You can cut out key parts of images, colorize black and white photos, add graphic effects to images, or highlight key areas of interest. Equally important, programs such as Photoshop can be used to change the size and bit-depth of images; so if you need to blow up or reduce images, or convert from color to black and white, an image processing program like Photoshop is more than up to the task. For more information on Photoshop and other graphics applications, see Chapter 3, "Graphics Tools."

*Using CLUTs
With 8-bit
Graphics*

If you use 8-bit graphics, it is extremely important that your authoring software be able to import Color Lookup Tables (CLUTs)—also known as *custom palettes*—which will allow you to fine-tune the color tint graduations available for your presentation. With custom palettes, you should be able to show reasonable quality graphics without sacrificing system performance. Most authoring programs also allow you to create smooth transitions from one CLUT to another, guaranteeing that your 8-bit graphics will look as good as they can.

In choosing graphics you must consider the issue of size and resolution versus system performance. Are your graphics too big? Do they slow your project down excessively? Can you work with 8-bit graphics instead of 24-bit graphics? Does your authoring program support palette transitions, so that you can smoothly shift from one custom palette to the next? It's best to know the answers to these questions *before* scanning and converting 600 photographs, so do your planning and testing ahead of time.

Sound

Sound can enhance a multimedia project in a variety of ways. Introductory fanfares can be added to establish a high-energy mood. Opening animations can be supported with sound effects to add impact. Voice-over announcing can be used to describe or explain the image on the screen. The combination of music, sound effects, and voice provide a wide range of audio support for filling out a presentation and making it that much stronger in the end. The next few sections will give you a rough idea of the ways in which you can use sound in your project. For detailed information, see Chapter 4, "Sound Tools," and Chapter 10, "Producing Sound."

Adding Mood With Music

Music is great for setting the tone or mood of a piece or a section of a presentation. Whether used for introductions, transitions, or just for background ambience, music can play a key role in getting users in the proper frame of mind. It can also help establish a different pace. If your project moves from rapid, fast-cut video to slow, serene camera moves, use music tracks to complement each section and establish the pace. This will lessen the herky-jerky transition that might exist between two radically different pieces of video.

Music can also create balance. If a video segment is moving too slowly, add slightly upbeat music to persuade viewers to watch the entire segment. If used tastefully, music can do wonders to establish, maintain, and motivate the tempo and pacing of a project. Video producers will often use music to fix a video piece that feels off-tempo, and there's no reason why a multimedia producer shouldn't take the same approach.

Sound Effects

Sound effects are among the most powerful underlying elements of a project. They can enhance animations by reinforcing key movements. Sound effects can motivate transitions from one section of a piece to another and can signal either the end of one section of your project or the beginning of the next. Buttons can become more tactile when complemented with animation and sound effects. If your presentation has consistent interface elements, such as multiple-choice questions, try using sound effects for both right and wrong answers. Users will be able to proceed more smoothly through the project because they'll have added aural reinforcement to help give them direction.

Voice

Narration is often a key element in multimedia projects. If you have any doubts as to how users will initially perceive your project, add an announcer to your startup screen to clearly define your purpose. If there are difficult concepts to explain, use clear, concise graphics or animations coupled with well-timed narrative to make sure the point comes across. Conversely, if there are concepts for which you have no supporting video, graphics, or animation, explain them with an announcer narrative. Like sound effects and music, narration can often be used to "fix" a section that is too slow or not clear enough to users.

There are different hardware and software considerations, depending on the sound quality you need. If standard, 8-bit sound is good enough, then you will have no problems creating sound for your project. You can import it via affordable audio digitizers (Apple includes audio input and microphones with recent machines, and many PCs now have sound cards), and play it back on any Mac. Professional quality, 16-bit audio requires a good deal more of a commitment, both in hardware and storage space.

Animation

Director 4.0 Demo ⌘ 708

The ability to play back animation in a project varies greatly among authoring programs. This is due to the wide variety of formats available, including AVI, FLIC, PICS, QuickTime, QuickPICS, Accelerator documents, and Macromedia Director movies. Take a look at Chapter 7, "Authoring Tools," for a rundown on the capabilities of the various programs. Once you've decided which animation format is right for your project, determine the size and color depth that you'll be able to use. Remember, you're weighing quality against system performance; so be prepared to modify your expectations of glorious, full screen animations in order to ensure that your project runs at a reasonable speed.

Figure 16.6
***Multimedia
Power Tools***
**comes with a tour
guide who
appears in the
video window
with a complete
tour of the disc,
abbreviated tours,
or quick help
instructions.**

Animation can be applied on a number of levels. You can run entire animated segments; animate foreground elements over a consistent background; and, in some cases, you can even run animations over imported video.

Animation is often the best tool for explaining advanced concepts. If you need to describe how certain mechanical parts work in conjunction, or how a particular machine is assembled, animation will often be the perfect solution. One of the greatest benefits of animation is that you can alter the material to suit your needs. If your presentation requires that you explain the movement of planets in the solar system over a fifty-year period, you can easily create a short segment that gets the point across clearly. This is obviously a case in which video or still images are not as appropriate as a custom-designed animation.

For detailed information on creating and working with animation, see Chapter 5, "Animation Tools," and Chapter 12, "Creating 3-D Models and Animation."

Video

Video is certainly the best visualization tool available and is often the only way to truly communicate your message. For example, if you're trying to demonstrate the effects of severe weather conditions on certain coastal regions, video footage of storms pounding the coast will have much more effect than an artist's diagram, diagrams, or animations. If you want to show the dance steps used in different cultures, video will be easier and more effective to use than any graphic or animation. The visual nature of your project will dictate whether or not you must use video. In many cases, there can be no substitute.

However, video requires extremely large quantities of memory and therefore places significant technological demands on your system. The nature of your project will determine your approach. If full-screen video is absolutely essential, you should consider pressing a laser disc. It allows full-screen graphics to be stored and retrieved easily. Also, loading a full-screen picture off of a laser disc is often much quicker than loading the same image from your hard drive or a CD-ROM. However, be aware that using a laser disc will severely limit your market —there are a lot fewer players out there than CD-ROM drives. A laser disc would

Figure 16.7 The *Power Tools* CD displays video at 12–15 frames per second (as opposed to the 30 fps of full-motion video) in a moderately sized window. This treatment provides effective video impact at an economical trade-off with memory, storage, and other factors.

be perfect for a project that will be played back in kiosks or in tightly targeted, controlled situations. It would not be appropriate for a mass-market, commercial multimedia project.

From an interface and design point of view, the decision to include video is not so much a question of aesthetic choice as an issue of content. Does your project need video? Although video can be very powerful, you must use it judiciously, based upon your desires and the capacities of your media and playback system. When a beautiful full-screen graphic or animation will suffice, you may want to consider using it instead. Short video sequences can also make dramatic points or punctuations to deliver quick messages. For a longer, instructional video that tells a complete story, you can use a lower resolution, smaller windowed video, but avoid it in other situations. Video is the most demanding resource you can have in a multimedia project.

Obviously, if you're producing an interactive music video sampler, you'll need to have video; and you should plan accordingly. In other cases, the decision may not be so clear. For example, if you're having a tough time communicating a message clearly, and you think that video might be the answer, make sure you can get the proper footage to do the job. Shooting your own video can be difficult and if done poorly, will only serve to make your project look shoddy. If you think there is existing footage that will serve your needs, explore the issue of copyrights, since you will most likely want to avoid the legal repercussions of purloining someone else's material. See Chapter 14, "Creating Video," for detailed information on the topic.

Databases

If your project requires searching and referencing large amounts of data, make sure you pick an authoring program that will assist you with this task. Name and address forms, for example, often require 6 to 10 different types of fields; and you'll want users to be able to search each one.

A good example of a multimedia database is LaserReel, an interactive Hyper-Card stack that searches through a series of laser discs and plays TV commercials created by different directors. If you enter the search parameters "chocolate bars," "upbeat music," and "bikinis," the program will compile and play a sequence of commercials that have bikini-clad women dancing around with chocolate bars. The project also allows users to search for different TV directors by name, type of commercial, product category, or a variety of other parameters. This is a great use of a database and multimedia in the same project, and the producers made sure that the database tools in HyperCard could be used for the task before investing in serious development time.

Conversely, there will be situations where a large database may require a multimedia front end. Multimedia interfaces are going to be increasingly useful in accessing large databases in the months and years to come. Programming tools

Special Delivery

How you distribute your multimedia masterpiece is a critical part of your development strategy. CD-ROMs have always had a large storage capacity that makes them ideal for distributing bulky multimedia data, and mainstream acceptance over the past few years has made them the multimedia delivery mechanism of choice.

Floppy disks are a possibility, but their low storage capacity makes them unsuitable for all but the most modest projects. If your presentation includes digital video, for example, floppies are pretty much out of the question; video files are simply too large. You'll end up spending too much on media (a CD costs less to manufacture than a floppy), and your customers will balk at installing 13 floppies.

Still, if your project is modest, and you want to reach the widest possible audience, don't rule out floppies. The *Optivity Demo* project described on the *Power Tools* disc, and in Chapter 17 of this book, for example, distributes on four floppies. The piece has no video, but includes simple animation and transitions, an attractive interface, music, and voice narration.

Industry pundits are fond of predicting the arrival of trends by making proclamations such as "1996 will be the Year of Interactive Television!" (Don't believe that one.) Years past have been dubbed "The Year of Networking," "The Year of Windows," and so on. (The "Year of Unix" stretched from about 1980 to the early '90s, when everyone pretty much gave up on Unix as a mainstream environment.)

Most would agree, however, that 1995 truly was the "Year of the Internet." Driven by the phenomenal growth of the World Wide Web, the Internet has rocketed to pop cultural status. The Web is an easy way for anyone with a computer, modem, and readily available on-line account to crawl around and explore the stunning resources of this global network. The Internet and its celebrity tributary the Web are not yet ideal for delivering multimedia information, but there is enough activity and promise to warrant a look.

CD-ROM Delivery

Besides the mountain of data on CDs, two things have made them especially appealing to multimedia developers. First, by mid-1995, prices of CD-ROM recorders had dropped to below $1,500, making them affordable for almost every developer. And even more enticing, PCs with CD-ROM drives were making their way very quickly in both business and consumer markets.

Since a CD is just another storage device, you ought to be able to throw your data on and be done with it. Unfortunately, it's a little more complicated than that. The hard drive from which you copy files to the CD needs to "ISO-compliant." Fortunately, most CD recording software that comes with the recorders will do this for you.

The data itself must also be optimized for playback on CD-ROM drives whose performance is still so slow that you must arrange data carefully. Director and Asymetrix' Toolbook, two popular authoring programs, provide some of these features.

box continued

Director lets you arrange media elements on the CD, which can minimize CD head travel and thus speed playback. When Director prepares a presentation for playback, it creates a compact "projector" file in which you can prioritize how media elements load and purge from memory. Elements that should remain on screen can be given a low purge priority so that they will stay in RAM and play back more speedily.

Toolbook offers similar features, but more work is required to set RAM priorities, and the process is not as interactive as Director's.

Caught in the Web

The Internet has long been a hotbed of experimentation (it was invented as a distributed computing system that would be impervious to nuclear attack), and there are many innovative multimedia trials underway. If you're already on the Web and are looking for multimedia resources, point your browser at:

http://viswiz.gmd.de:80/MultimediaInfo/

One of the most innovative is mBone (Multicast Backbone), a network that runs over the Internet's native TCP/IP protocol (see Figure 16.8). Many interesting experiments have been carried out on mBone, including a Rolling Stones simulcast and National Public

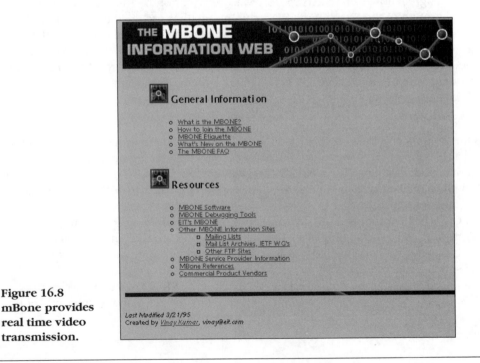

Figure 16.8 mBone provides real time video transmission.

box continued

Radio broadcasts. As intriguing as it is, however, mBone isn't accessible to enough people to make it a viable distribution medium (unless your audience has high-speed dedicated access to the Internet). Web crawlers can get more information on mBone at:

http://www.eit.com/techinfo/mbone/mbone.html

Another interesting goodie is CU-SeeMe, an Internet-based videoconferencing system developed by Cornell University. Anyone with a video camera, digitizing card, and Quick-Time can check it out. More information is at:

ftp://gated.cornell.edu/pub/video/

Although the Internet and the Web are here now, the main roadblock to delivering multimedia in cyberspace is that access over phone lines isn't fast enough for the volume of data. Even with a high-speed digital phone connect, data travels at only 128Kbs, which is slower than the transfer rate of a single speed CD-ROM.

Soon, possibly in 1996, cable modems may make it possible to deliver very high speed access to the Internet and other on-line services. This service, which was in several national trials in 1995, will make it possible to deliver information 1,000 times faster than today's fastest modems.

Until then, become a Web crawler and keep your eyes open for the opportunities that are hatching daily. If you are a developer, consider putting up a Web page describing your services and offering sample files for downloading. There are many books and magazine articles describing how to do this—it's not difficult, and it's well worth the effort.

Figure 16.9 *NetPhone!* lets you conduct free voice phone calls over your computer. The address is http://www. vocaltec.com/ whatis.html

such as Microsoft's Visual Basic and Borland's Delphi may be the key to multimedia-rich client/server database applications.

The Common Sense Factor

Let your project dictate your choice of media and how you use it. Standard approaches, such as the age-old "form follows function" can help you determine the right approach. Ultimately, you want a project that is clearcut and sensible to use. This means picking all the right elements and combining them in an efficient manner. Common sense is often the most important tool you can use in deciding how to execute any given project.

Designing Screens

Design integrity is one of the most important elements of a good interactive project. To be sure that your project comes across well, make sure you strive for good design. Color composition, font selection, graphic design, and screen layout are all important design considerations. The layout of the screen should read easily and be able to be browsed quickly. The most important thing is to establish a look and feel immediately and then stick with it. The screen that confronts users when they start your presentation should establish a natural flow that will make their travels through all subsequent screens enjoyable and unfettered. Whatever the nature of the information you might be trying to pass along, there is no reason it can't be entertaining.

Backgrounds should have an interesting design with good color composition, but they should never overpower foreground elements. Buttons should be attractive, large enough, and placed in such a way that they are easy to reach. Good design is often transparent, meaning that users won't even notice your layout because they're too busy devouring the information. This is what you should strive for.

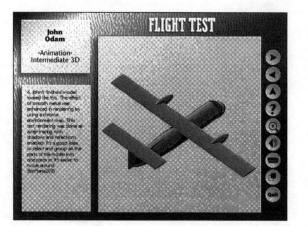

Figure 16.10 This is the interface of the *Multimedia Power Tools* CD Sample Projects section.

Text

How you treat text will determine whether users will breeze through your interface or struggle to read the information. Like print design, planning the text layout of your screens requires consideration of such elements as fonts, point sizes, and character spacing. All text should be easily legible, regardless of its importance. Don't make users squint to read tiny text, and don't set all text in bold capitals. Choose a happy medium that enables users to easily and comfortably browse through your screens. Often, having others test your screen layout and design will be the best method of determining the size and style of text.

You will rarely need more than two or three fonts for an entire project. Pick a treatment for headlines, subheads, and body text, and then stick with it. Consistency is probably the most important part of text design. If your first screen starts with 14-point text in a box on the left side of the screen, all subsequent text should be 14-point text in a box on the left side of the screen.

Buttons and Windows

Button and window placement should also be intuitive and transparent to the user. Again, be consistent. If users have arrow buttons available for navigation, make sure that these buttons remain in the same place at all times. Window placement should also be carefully considered. Do you want the user to see imported video in the same place as your text, or do you want to have a special location for video segments? It's often best to have a specially designated area of the screen for each different element. Text will always be in one spot, and

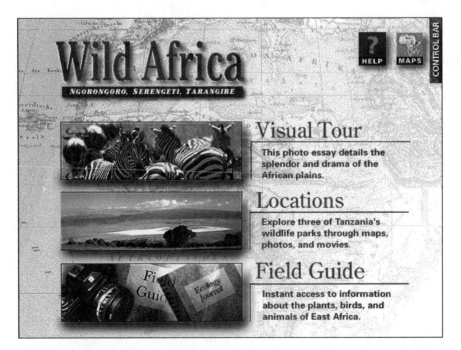

Figure 16.11 Sumeria's interface for *Wild Africa* is both creative and usable.

video will always be in another. This way you can have text and video on the screen at the same time. Obviously, different types of data may demand different size windows; so try to accommodate other screen elements when designing your windows. If you need to import a large animation or video clip, try to make sure buttons and other elements can remain in their original locations.

Building for Quality

Synergy! Consistency! Intuitive! Transparent! Logical! Natural Flow! These are the building blocks of good multimedia. How you bring these elements together will define the quality and ultimate success of your project.

17

Interactive Multimedia Projects

Interactivity is one of the attributes that makes multimedia what it is. The ability to hop around and explore at will is one of the cornerstones of the new media phenomenon. In this chapter, we'll look at four interesting and very different interactive projects: a direct marketing product demonstration, a learning tool for medical students, a 3-D adventure game, and a home medical encyclopedia on CD.

Optivity Demo Presentation

Block Interactive is a multimedia producer based in Los Altos, California that specializes in corporate presentations, direct marketing pieces, and World Wide Web sites. In late 1994, Block created a direct marketing product demonstration for Bay Networks, a large networking vendor.

Optivity 5 ⌘ 040

The demo was delivered on a set of Windows disks, but it also runs on the Mac for internal use at Bay Networks. The goal was to introduce the features and benefits of Optivity, a software product that monitors network performance for system administrators.

Although the demonstration is self-running, users can interactively select the features they want to learn about. The finished demo includes a background soundtrack for transitions, and professional narration accompanies actual screenshots of the software in action. To reach the broadest possible audience, Block designed the demo to play back on machines without a sound card or CD-ROM drive. The demo uses textual summaries to drive home key points, so that the narration is not actually required for playback.

Special Considerations

One of the early design goals was that the demo include some sort of feedback mechanism so viewers could send for more information, and Bay Networks could follow up with qualified prospects. This mechanism was originally conceived as some kind of dial-up service using a modem, but that idea was shelved as too complicated. "A marketing piece has to install and run right away, or no one's going to bother with it," says Block's Lance Thornswood. The team settled on a lower-tech but higher-percentage fax-back form that could easily be filled out, printed, and sent in.

Thornswood cites cross-platform development as a particular challenge of the Optivity project. "Most developers are still using Macintoshes," says Thornswood, "and it takes a certain amount of knowledge to understand how things like color palettes, transitions, and digital video are going to translate to the PC."

Director 4.0 Demo ⌘ 708

Thornswood says that subtleties in color can be particularly tricky, and that colors generally seem to be more saturated on the PC than on the Mac. Transitions such as dissolves that look great in Director on the Mac will lag on Director for Windows, he claims. Like many developers, he finds that QuickTime is generally more reliable on the Mac than under Windows.

Tips and Techniques

In cross-platform development, Thornswood says that having Macs and PCs networked is key, so that you can bring large files back and forth quickly. While the bulk of their work is for Windows products, most Block designers and producers work primarily on the Mac and port to the PC—often to the Windows version of Director—only when the project is about 90 percent complete. At this stage, they often fling files over the network as they test on the PC and tweak on the Mac.

Figure 17.1 Optivity demo features live action software demos.

SoundEdit 16 Demo ⌘ 707

Photoshop 3.0 Demo ⌘ 715

Illustrator 4.0 Demo ⌘ 718

DeBabelizer 1.6 Demo ⌘ 719

Thornswood also recommends heavy duty testing of Windows products. With the range of video and audio cards for PCs, it's necessary to test on as many configurations as you can lay your hands on. Block keeps a test machine that is regularly stripped clean, has its hard disk reformatted, and has different cards and drivers available for installation. Depending on budget, schedule, and project complexity, the firm may even hire a QA engineer or outside testing service.

Tools and Equipment

The Optivity demo was created on Quadra 840AV's with 24Mb of RAM, 500Kb to 1 Gb drives, and two to three displays for accommodation of palettes and content. Software tools included Director, Adobe Illustrator, Photoshop, DeBabelizer, Audioshop, and SoundEdit. Machines were networked with Ethernet and Timbuktu.

MedPics

MedPics ⌘ 041

As a core part of their studies at the University of California, San Diego (UCSD), medical students take a class called Human Disease. The course includes both *histology*, the study of the microscopic structure of human tissue, and *pathology*, the study of the nature of disease (see Figure 17.2).

A central part of this important course is the review and interpretation of medical images, a challenging task that can tax students even under the best of circumstances, and the circumstances at the School of Medicine's Learning Resource Center (LRC) weren't good. Students using the center to review 35mm slides of medical images found confusing and uneven image annotations. Moreover, slides were available on a limited basis and were often left in a disorganized state.

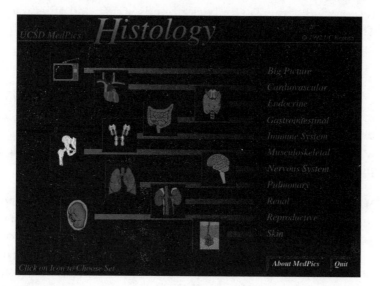

Figure 17.2
***MedPics*
interface.**

Fearing that this would cause mediocre performance on the pathology component of the National Board Exams, LRC director Helene Hoffman, Ph.D., and instructional software developer Ann Irwin, M.D., decided to design an interactive, computer-based image presentation program. As a result, *MedPics* is now a successful part of UCSD's medical school curriculum and is available throughout the campus from workstations linked with Novell's NetWare network operating system. *MedPics* has also generated considerable interest in the worldwide medical community and has been purchased for use at other universities.

Hoffman's Ph.D. is in physiology and pharmacology, and she is involved in medical education and the use of computers in education and training. Irwin received her M.D. in 1991 and plans to pursue a career in education theory and medical informatics. They were assisted by interactive programmer Michel Kripalani and graphic designer Susan Adornato.

Special Considerations

Hoffman's and Irwin's main goal in designing *MedPics* was that the images themselves be of the highest possible quality. The images had to accurately reflect their content, or the project wouldn't win the acceptance of university administration and faculty—support that was necessary for the adoption of the new system. Students would be evaluating images partly to determine what distinguishes normal from abnormal tissue. If resolution weren't sharp and clean, they would make mistakes (is that a cell mutation or a flipped bit?).

At the same time, the program had to run on the wide range of color monitors and Macs that were installed at the university. That meant 24-bit color, which would have yielded the highest color fidelity, was out of the question. The team would have to get by with the 256 colors of 8-bit video.

To keep screen transitions smooth and flicker-free, Helene and her team reserved 48 of the 256 for backgrounds, icons, and other interface components. This left 208 colors for the images themselves, ensuring the highest possible image fidelity of 8-bit systems.

While this technique helped the designers achieve their goal of image accuracy and fidelity, 8-bit color has inherent limitations that are impossible to overcome. For example, the team would have liked the program to allow students to compare and contrast separate images side by side. This is not possible, however, since you cannot have two index color palettes (one for each image) open at the same time. The position held by gray in one color palette might be occupied by an entirely different color (say purple) in the other.

Tips and Techniques

When asked for some advice for those just beginning to explore interactive system design, Hoffman offers: "It takes twice as long and costs twice as much as you think at first." Irwin agrees. "It's like remodeling your house."

Both advise thorough storyboarding and interactive testing using simple placeholder images to test icon placement, branching, pop-up menus, and other interface and interactive elements before colors and imagery are designed.

The team learned a hard lesson in this respect, because they first designed the look of the program and didn't fully test interactive components before proceeding. This caused difficulty when the developers tried to port *MedPics* to the Windows environment for playback with Director's Windows Player. Elements such as pop-up menus and windows didn't carry over, and the team had to redesign these elements so that *MedPics* would run on both Windows and Mac machines.

Irwin offers another tip: "The biggest trap that new interactive designers fall into is to try to incorporate a lot of bells and whistles—too many buttons, links, and visual elements," she says. "Keep it simple, especially on your first project, and you'll have a much easier time."

Tools and Equipment

The *MedPics* team digitized images using a Barneyscan Color Imaging Systems 3515 slide scanner. Photoshop was used for image processing, Aldus SuperCard for graphic overlays, and Director for the interactivity and presentation.

Robot from The Journeyman Project

Journeyman Project Robot
⌘ 042

Animators Farshid Almassizadeh, Michel Kripalani, and Dave Flanagan first began discussing ideas for a 3-D game while sitting around drinking coffee one night. During subsequent sessions, they began keeping a log of their most promising ideas, and within a short time, they had the basis of *The Journeyman Project* (see Figure 17.3).

Eight months later, the ranks of newly formed Presto Studios had swelled to seven or eight animators, and the founders quit their "real" jobs to devote all of their energies to the project, which, by its completion, was to consume 15,000 hours.

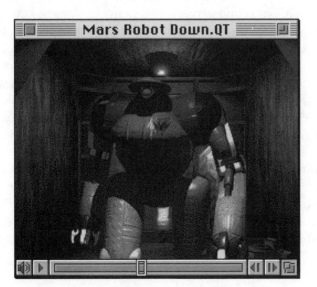

Figure 17.3
Robot from
The Journeyman
Project.

The Journeyman Project, released in 1993, envisions the world in the year 2318. The game begins in your apartment in Caldoria, where you are employed as a member of the Temporal Protectorate, charged with safeguarding history and preserving world peace.

Presto Studios is a San Diego-based team of Macintosh and science fiction enthusiasts with different and complementary areas of expertise in media. Currently developing a Japanese version of *Journeyman*, they are planning to publish more of their own work, as well as to serve as a publishing house for other multimedia creators.

Special Considerations

The complexity and demands of *The Journeyman Project* tested many of the limits of currently available 3-D software. "We actually used almost every 3-D package available for the Mac," says Almassizadeh, "because each of them had a feature we needed that the others didn't have."

For example, the team used Specular's Infini-D animation package for rendering and animation, in part because it was one of the few programs that would import the models that were first created in Swivel 3D. "For example, if ElectricImage had that feature, we wouldn't have had to have 10 computers rendering 24 hours a day [because ElectricImage renders much faster than Infini-D]."

Although it was a multidimensional project with many people working simultaneously on different parts of the game, Almassizadeh says the team ran into few project management issues. One reason for this was that, although everyone had his or her specialty, each was versatile enough to pitch in on other aspects when necessary.

Tips and Techniques

Almassizadeh emphasizes that projects as involved and detailed as *Journeyman* require careful planning and organization. For example, the design of *Journeyman* is nonlinear: Game players have many options at any given juncture. This freedom to explore through interactivity is one of the foundations of multimedia (see Chapter 1, "Multimedia Defined"), but it places great demands on multimedia developers.

Just to keep track of the possible branching at each point in Journeyman, the team created and maintained an 8 × 10 diagram of all possible options.

He also points out that the field of 3-D animation is still relatively new, and 3-D products often are created and marketed by small companies that are open and responsive to suggestions by users.

One annoyance was that Infini-D required texture maps to be applied individually to each object in each keyframe. Since *Journeyman* scenes had a dozen or more keyframes with as many as 200 separate objects each, the texture mapping process was almost impossibly time-consuming. When Almassizadeh pointed this out, developers at Specular agreed and promptly modified the program to allow aggregate texture mapping.

Tools and Equipment

Most *Journeyman* animators used Mac IIfxs, while Almassizadeh worked on a Mac II with two Radius Rocket CPU accelerators, a 24-bit color card, several medium-sized hard disks, a removable cartridge drive, and two 13″ monitors.

Radius's Rocketshare software was used to turn the Mac into a *multitasking* machine so that separate programs or rendering tasks could be run simultaneously.

The team used Swivel 3D for the modeling and animation and then imported the animation keyframes into Infini-D. In this way, Almassizadeh was able to take advantage of the complementary strengths of each program. Swivel was used for its quick modeling and excellent control of hierarchical links—which were necessary for realistic motion; Infini-D recognized and retained all of these links when it imported the Swivel models, and he was able to take advantage of Infini-D's strong rendering options and refined motion control characteristics (for an explanation of basic animation and rendering techniques, see Chapter 12, "Creating 3-D Models and Animation"). Macromedia Three-D also was used for some of the complex animation moves.

The Presto team considerably sped up rendering of the many complex 3-D scenes by using Specular International's Backburner software. This network rendering package divides large rendering tasks into smaller pieces and then parcels them out to any Mac that is available on the network. Some really big jobs took all night to render on 10 different Macs all working at the same time, while the humans on the team caught some much needed rest.

Backburner was particularly valuable for *Journeyman* animators because many of their scenes had both shadows and objects with individual texture maps—characteristics that greatly increase the number of calculations a computer needs to perform to accurately render such details.

After rendering, various elements of the project were brought together and composited using Photoshop, and the final project was assembled for playback using QuickTime and Director.

How Your Body Works

When Mindscape, a well-established producer of consumer CD-ROM titles, set out to create a new children's title, it ended up with a cross between a medical encyclopedia and *Fantastic Voyage*, the old sci-fi movie whose tiny heroes are trapped in a human being.

How Your Body Works ⌘ 043

Mindscape's disc, *How Your Body Works*, features a point-and-click interface that helps viewers explore 12 major systems of the human body. The CD is unique for its combination of lightning-quick 3-D renderings, immersive interface, and the collaborative way in which the product was developed.

The disc features 3-D fly-throughs of the body, including a fully rendered and navigable human heart, an interactive skeleton, and effects—such as peeling

**Figure 17.4
The lab in *How
Your Body Works*
yields a cornu-
copia of medical
information.**

skin away from a face—that will appeal to some more than others (see Figure
17.4).

Special Considerations

Animations are ¼ screen at 15 frames per second, which, given the rendering
quality of the imagery, would exceed the delivery capabilities of off-the-shelf
authoring tools. For this reason, Mindscape turned to San Francisco Canyon Company, which did the QuickTime for Windows port (and was subsequently sued
by Apple when the latter claimed some QuickTime code turned up in Microsoft's
Video for Windows).

SF Canyon did the interface programming in C++, which greatly sped the delivery of imagery and the performance of the product in general. "Effects such as
manipulating the skeleton required real-time performance that would only be
possible with a programming language," says SF Canyon's Nels Johnson.

For art direction, interface design, and video, Mindscape turned to Red Hill Studios, and 3-D fly-throughs were done by Shadows and Light. With all of these
players and components to keep a handle on, Mindscape hired Multimedia Consulting to do project management, while Mindscape producer Rosemary Yates
oversaw the overall project.

"Many times you can't find a single multimedia developer that can do it all,"
says Yates. "With this approach, we were able to hand-pick the experts in their
various fields."

Tips and Techniques

Yates is quick to agree that potential pitfalls in the collaborative approach are
gaps in continuity and delays caused by lapses in communication. "Project management was huge in terms of communication and coordination," she says. Still,

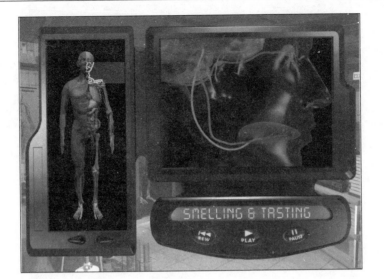

Figure 17.5
How Your Body Works **includes impressive animated effects.**

she believes that the approach can work and, in fact, can yield stunning results. And despite its higher exposure to delay, *How Your Body Works* came in 45 days ahead of schedule, a rare achievement and one that was due in large part to the engagement of professional project management services.

Yates also advises that would-be developers of this kind of multimedia product really understand their market and choose a specific angle and stylistic approach. "Then stick with a cohesive plan and direction that accomplishes your goals," she adds.

Tools and Equipment

In addition to the interface and programming that were done in C++, *How Your Body Works* was produced using 3D Studio for animation, Premiere for video editing, Photoshop and DeBabelizer for graphics, and Director for prototyping. Mindscape also wrote some sequences to videotape for prototyping.

Part Three

THE
POWER TOOLS
CD-ROM

18

Overview of the Power Tools *CD-ROM*

The *Multimedia Power Tools* CD-ROM included with this package is, on its own, a robust multimedia "title." By this we mean it is a well-rounded interactive multimedia product rather than simply a collection of software supplementing a book.

From the beginning, *Multimedia Power Tools* was conceived as an integrated package—*an interactive book.* The Verbum team has taken its experience and resources in digital media design and concentrated them in a disc that provides users with instructional content and usable tools and also complements the book —covering all the details of multimedia technology, tools, and processes—with topics and products dynamically linked to the text with "Power Code" commands. We've strived to create a disc that is entertaining and easy to use, instructional, and useful for actual multimedia production. We hope it will serve you for a long time to come.

Disc Components

The *Power Tools* CD-ROM has three primary components:

1. The *disc interface shell,* which includes the interface elements; navigation controls; the program code that controls the disc's functions; and the "top matter" content material (equivalent to a book's front matter) with an introduction, information about how the disc was created, and an animated Guided Tour of the disc with a video tour guide.

2. The *Sample Projects section,* featuring 15 exemplary multimedia projects presented in a step-by-step "how it was done" format.

3. The *Power Tools section,* containing about 250 megabytes of usable software.

Starting up the **Power Tools** *CD-ROM*

**Using a
Windows
System**

You will need a 386 or better CPU with at least 4Mb of RAM, a sound card, and a video card capable of 256 colors at 640 × 480 pixels. The machine should be running Microsoft Windows 3.1 or Windows95. A double-speed CD-ROM drive is also required.

*Installing on
Windows 3.1*

We have created a very versatile installer module that allows you some flexibility in how you install our program. The easiest way is as follows:

Recommended Installation

Using the standard Windows file requester, go to the File menu, pull down and select Run, browse to the drive containing our CD, and select and double click the file called STARTUP.EXE. This file will start our custom interactive Readme and Installer program. This is a little interactive application that will help you ascertain that your system is compatible with *Power Tools* by performing a few simple tests. It will also install QuickTime for Windows in the appropriate location on your hard drive (required) and give you the option to install a Power Tools icon into a Power Tools program group in Program Manager. We suggest that you say "yes" when asked if you want to install the icon on your hard drive. The icon and related files are very small, and should you decide to take it off, we have included an uninstaller utility that will remove all of these files, except QuickTime.

You will only need to run this SETUP.EXE file once when you first run the disc. Thereafter you just need to be sure the disc is in the CD drive and then double click the Power Tools icon.

Alternative Installation

If you choose not to install the icon (but do have QuickTime for Windows properly installed), you can use the Run command from program manager to run the file MMPT.EXE, directly from the CD-ROM.

*Installing on
Windows95*

The installer will work as above, except you should start it using the Windows95 procedure:

Insert the CD-ROM. Select the "start" button in the lower left-hand corner of the Windows95 desktop. Slide to the "settings" submenu and select "control panel." Double click on the "add/remove programs" icon. When the dialog box opens, click "install." At the next dialog box, click "next." After the automatic search identifies the MMPT setup program on the CD, click "finish." The installer will proceed as above.

Using a Macintosh System

You need a Macintosh with at least 5Mb of RAM (preferably 8Mb for best performance). You will also want to make sure that you have turned off any INITS that might use up that much-needed RAM and that your color monitor (13″ or larger) is set to 256 colors. The *Power Tools* CD-ROM will work on less-powerful Macintosh systems, but its extensive use of QuickTime movies (digital video clips) and large animations will work best on the faster processors. The disc's hundreds of software files and step-by-step presentations are functional on all color Macintosh models. The CD will also work at higher color settings (1,000 or more). This may improve QuickTime image quality but also may result in slower performance.

One other essential point about QuickTime: This disc requires Apple's Quick-Time 2.0 or greater and the associated files. We have included these files on our disk in a folder called "Add to System Folder." If you think that you already have the correct QuickTime version installed, then you don't need to use these files. Otherwise, follow the directions below. (These are also on the Readme file on our disc.)

Installing on a Macintosh System

Your CD-ROM drive also plays a part in how well the *Power Tools* QuickTime movies run. If it is an older model with a slower data transfer rate, you may see some performance limitations. Newer double-speed or quad-speed drives offer the best results.

Once you have inserted the CD-ROM into the drive, you will see the "Power Tools CD" icon come up on the Mac screen. Double click to open it, and you will see the various folders that comprise the contents of the CD (see Figure 18.1).

Figure 18.1 The shell is a "Director Projector," a self-running application created with Macromedia Director, the authoring software used to create the *Power Tools* CD-ROM. It contains the key interface graphics and code that controls the use of the CD.

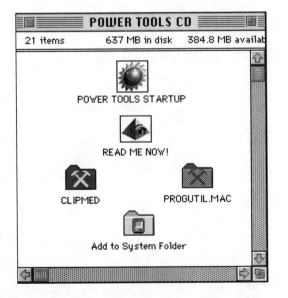

1. Go into your system folder and create a folder called "disabled QuickTime" or something of your choosing. Drag the QuickTime file from your extensions folder and put it in this disabled folder.

2. Close your system folder and restart your computer. This "turns off" QuickTime.

3. After the computer has restarted, drag the files out of our "put in system folder" folder and onto the closed system folder on your machine. The Mac will ask you if you want to place things in their proper places (answer yes) and you're on your way. Please note that if you have a PowerMac you should also install the Power Plug file from our folder.

What You See When the Disc Begins

The disc is organized into folders for easy access to files which you can look at after you have run the disc from its main operating program. Most users will use the *Power Tools* CD from the interface shell that is launched by double clicking on the Power Tools icon from the Windows Program Manager, or on the Mac Desktop (see Figure 18.1).

Double click on the *Power Tools* Startup icon to launch the *Power Tools* disc. The first thing you will see is a Welcome screen (see Figure 18.2), that presents three options:

Figure 18.2 The intro animation was created by John Laney from Glenn Mitsui's book cover illustration. Laney added 3-D elements and economical (but effective) animations. With a musical score by Chris Yavelow, this piece is a fine example of simple digital animation created with Macintosh graphics, animation, and music tools. It can be left running as an entertaining "screen saver."

- **Go:** starts the Power Tools Intro Animation
- **Skip Anim:** bypasses the intro animation and takes you right to the Main Menu
- **Quit:** quits the *Power Tools* CD-ROM.

Click anywhere on the screen to go to the *Power Tools* CD Main Menu (see Figure 18.3).

The Disc Interface Shell

The CD interface is "flat"—you won't find yourself getting lost as you burrow several levels deep as in some multimedia titles. It is also easy to use, with several features designed to aid users. Their are four primary elements of the interface, The *video window* (at the upper left), which displays video clips and graphics. The window below it is the *text window*, which provides details on whatever you are viewing, as well as help information on navigating the CD. The large window is the *content window*, which displays graphics, animations, and some interactive works. When you are in the Main Menu (or a submenu for one of the five sections), the content window contains the menu buttons, but its primary use is to display the content of our sample projects and each of the Power Tools. Finally, on the right side of the screen is the *navigation bar*, which you will use to move through the sample projects and Power Tools.

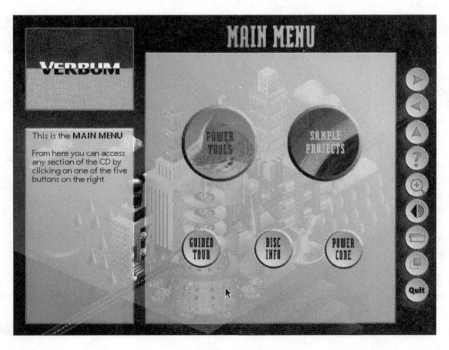

**Figure 18.3
The *Power Tools*
CD-ROM interface
includes a video
window (at upper
left) for Quick-
Time movies, the
text window
below, and the
content window
in the center.**

Menus and Built-In Help

You can go to the five main sections of the disc by clicking on one of the large buttons in the Main Menu (See Figure 18.3). Note that the two largest buttons for Sample Projects and Power Tools are animated when you are in the main menu at the "top" level. When you click on one of these or one of the other three smaller section buttons, you will call up the submenu buttons for that section, that will appear on the right side of the content window. You can "roll over" (use the mouse to position the arrow over) any button in the Main Menu, submenu, or navigation bar to see a description in the text window of what the button will do. This built-in help is available throughout the disc. You don't have to return to the Main Menu to activate other submenus, just click on any of the five buttons. But if you want to get back to the top—with the fun animated buttons— click on the Menu button (the up arrow) in the navigation bar on the right.

Disc Info Section

This button brings up buttons for the Introduction, Credits, Production Notes, Intro Animation, and Publisher/Copyright Info (See Figure 18.4).

- **Introduction:** a short video by Michael Gosney with photo illustrations displayed in the content window.

- **Credits:** provides buttons for all the contributors to the disc, that will trigger videos and/or text material.

Figure 18.4 In the Disc Info menu you can select Intro- duction for a video of disc producer Michael Gosney. Credits for video clips of the disc pro- ducers and contributors; Production Notes for details on how the disc was made; Publisher/ Copyright for information about the disc, how to order it, etc.; and Intro Animation to restart the introductory animation screen.

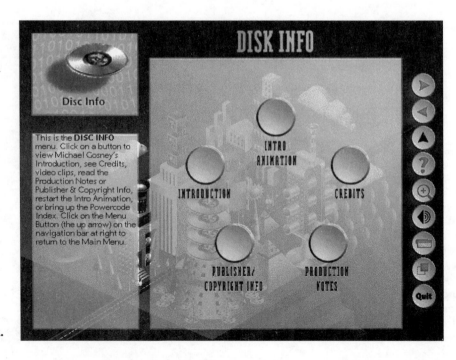

- **Production Notes:** brings up a detailed text description of how the CD-ROM was created.

- **Publisher/Copyright Information:** provides information on Random House Electronic Publishing and Verbum, Inc., ordering information and copyright notices.

- **Intro Animation:** restarts the animation. (You can return to the Main Menu, as you did when you started up, by just clicking the mouse.)

- **Power Codes:** brings up a scrolling list of Power Code locations on the disc that will allow instant access to any location (the list can also be accessed from the Welcome screen).

Guided Tour

This displays submenu buttons for *Interface Tour*, *Sample Projects Tour,* and *Power Tools Tour*. When you click on any of these buttons, Reegan Ray, your tour guide, will appear in the video window and take you through an animated tour of the disc (See Figure 18.5). You can pause any time in the tour by clicking on the video window. You can stop it at any time by clicking the mouse.

Navigation Bar

The navigation bar is always available, no matter where you are in the CD-ROM (See Figure 18.6). Whether or not some of the buttons function depends on where you are in the disc. A nonfunctioning button will be dim to let you know it is inactive.

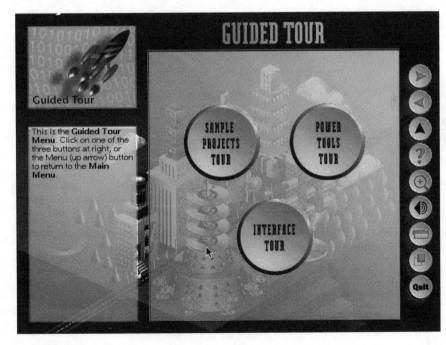

**Figure 18.5
One of the outstanding features of the CD is the Guided Tour, featuring several minutes of digitally-edited video with tour guide Reegan Ray.**

**Figure 18.6
The Navigation
Bar remains
consistent
everywhere on
the disc. Depend-
ing on where you
are in the disc,
buttons are
dimmed if they
are inactive in
that section.**

Next Button

At the top is the *Next* button, which will turn the page, so to speak, and take you to the next part of the currently displayed sample project or the next alphabetically organized Power Tool item.

*Previous
Button*

Beneath the Next button is the *Previous* button. It will take you to the previous part of the currently displayed project or the previous Power Tool item.

Menu Button

The button with the up arrow is the *Menu* button. It will take you back up to the menu for the section of the CD you are currently viewing, and, with a second click, back to the Main Menu.

Help Button

The question mark is the *Help* button. This button is only active in the Power Tools section of the disc. You can toggle on help mode by clicking it. Your cursor then turns into a question mark which will let you click on other places on the screen to get more information. To turn help mode off, click on the ? again.

Zoom Button

Next is the *Zoom* button. It will perform different functions depending on what is being viewed. If you are viewing a clip media image, you can zoom it to full screen and back. If you're looking at an animation or video, the Zoom button will double the video playback size in most cases. The Zoom button will have a plus sign if it is ready to zoom in or a minus sign if it is ready to zoom back. If the Zoom button is gray, it will not work for the currently displayed content.

Audio Button

The *Audio* button will allow you to adjust the volume level for the *Power Tools* CD at any time. Click and drag the pop-up volume control.

Print Button	The *Print* button will print any power tool or project screen.
Copy Button	The *Copy* button will allow you to copy the currently displayed Power Tool to your hard disk. Note that certain Power Tools may only work on one platform (Windows or Mac). It will not copy Sample Projects.
Quit Button	Finally, *Quit* will exit the *Power Tools* CD and return to the Macintosh desktop.

The Sample Projects Section

Clicking on the Sample Projects button will bring up the submenu buttons for the project presentations (See Figure 18.7). Note the four categories of Sound, Animation, Video, and Multimedia. The projects vary widely, and each has a slightly different presentation.

Sample Projects Menu ⌘ 004

When you choose a project, you will be taken right to the first screen of the project presentation and will see a video clip of the project producer in the video window (see Figure 18.8). You can then click on the Next button to step through the presentation. In addition to the text and graphics, some projects include narration, animations, videos, and functional interactive components. You will also

**Figure 18.7
The Sample
Project menu list
projects by
category. Rolling
the mouse arrow
over a Sample
Project button
reveals a
summary of the
project in the text
window.**

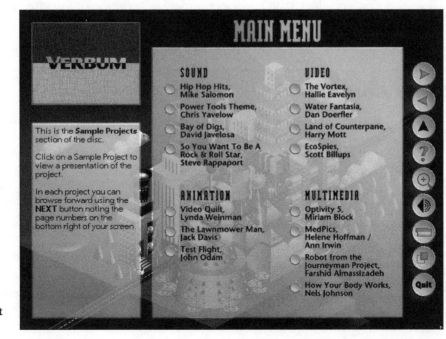

Figure 18.8 Each Sample Project starts with a video clip by the project producer. Clicking on the Next arrow triggers a demo of the project. Subsequent clicks on the Next button take you through the project's step-by-step, "how-to" presentation.

find explanations and cues regarding these elements in the text window, along with the ongoing text. See the book's "Project" chapters for additional background information on each of the projects featured on the disk.

The Power Tools Section

Power Tools Menu ⌘ 005

The other main section on the disc is Power Tools, featuring valuable clip media (animation, video, still images and backgrounds, 3-D graphics, sound effects, and music) and a wide range of applications and utilities for authoring, audio, video, animation, sound, and graphics (see Chapter 19, "Projects and Power Tools on the CD-ROM" for complete descriptions). Clicking this button will display buttons for the different categories of Power Tools that are available for viewing and copying (see Figure 18.9).

The Power Code CD Index

Each "location" on the disc—each project presentation and each Power Tool file—has a three-digit *Power Code*. You will find Power Codes throughout the book in the margins and a complete list in Appendix B. This unique feature not only provides a useful link between the book and disc content, it is also an additional, highly efficient means of navigating the disc. You can access Power Codes at any time by holding down the Control key and typing in the 3-digit code to go the desired location on the disc.

Power Tools Quick Access

There is another way to find and access Power Tools files on the disc. When you are in the Main Menu section, you can click on the Power Code button to get to a scrolling list of all the power codes. Double clicking on a name here will take you directly to that item.

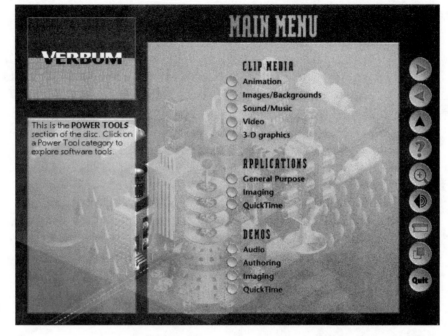

Figure 18.9
The Power Tools menu lists the power tools categories. Clicking on a category brings you to the first Power Tool (organized alphabetically) in that category. (See Figure 18.10). Click on the Next button to step through the alphabetically listed Power Tools in that category.

Figure 18.10
Each Power Tool file has a screen that displays a visual representation of the file and a text description. Clicking on the Zoom button will show a larger image of the file or trigger a video or animation. The Copy button will copy the actual file to your hard drive. To see the next Power Tool, hit the Next button.

Learn, Work, Play!

We hope the *Power Tools* CD offers plenty of support for all three: *learning* about multimedia, *producing* multimedia, and *having big fun* with multimedia. Whether you are a computer user interested in the expanding world of multimedia, an advanced producer, or somewhere in between, you'll find a wealth of resources on the CD.

P.S.—Please return your registration card. We need your feedback!

19

Projects and Power Tools on the CD-ROM

The *Power Tools* CD-ROM contains 400Mb of interactive tours of critically acclaimed multimedia projects, as well as an unprecedented collection—250 megabytes—of valuable multimedia software. This chapter will give you an overview of both categories.

Projects on the CD-ROM

Sample Projects Menu ⌘ 004

The project presentation section of the CD-ROM is divided into four categories: Sound, Animation, Video, and Interactive Multimedia. Multimedia projects are often fairly complex, and these are no exception. You will, therefore, find a great deal of crossover between categories: the Interactive Multimedia projects often utilize video, video projects utilize animation, most of the projects feature sound, and so on. However, these step-by-step presentations most often emphasize an instructive portion of the given project, focusing on one particular element or skill. For background information on any of these projects, see the "Project" chapters in the book.

A Wide Range of Exemplary Projects— From Basic to Advanced

Hip Hop Hits ⌘ 010

Power Tools Theme ⌘ 011

In the Sound section, you'll see simple editing demonstrated by *Hip Hop Hits,* and music composition demonstrated by our *Power Tools Theme.* For music and audio production on the Windows platform, *Bay of Digs* shows how the media player and the three main audio devices—MIDI Sequencer, Sound, and CD Audio are used to create a musical composition. A complete multimedia project, *So You Want to Be a Rock and Roll Star*, uses innovative interactivity to teach music.

In Animation you can check out basic 2-D animation in *Video Quilt*, an interactive learning project designed for illiterate new mothers; 3-D rotation in the VSI logo from the motion picture, *The Lawnmower Man*; and 3-D animation in *Flight Test*, a small plane created to fly against a moving background.

In the Video section you'll find a segment on the digital compositing of *The Vortex*, a full-length interactive movie on CD-ROM; you'll be able to examine video film editing in *Water Fantasia*, a short, artistic exploration of water; basic digital video in *Land of Counterpane*; and an interactive novel and advanced digital video in *EcoSpies*, a television show.

Under Multimedia, you'll see the steps involved in creating a corporate direct marketing piece called *Optivity 5*; a curriculum-based training program for second-year medical students in UCSD's *MedPics*; 3-D character animation from *The Journeyman Project*, an interactive CD-ROM game; and finally, *How Your Body Works*, a step-by-step on how to develop a multimedia title in C++.

Sample Project Summaries

Following are short summaries of each project by category. More detailed information can be found in the "Project" chapters.

Sound Projects

Hip Hop Hits

Mike Salomon's project, *Hip Hop Hits*, is both a demonstration of the original concept of modular audio, which he used to create the Dark Side Productions (a band) song *"Straight to the Point"* for use in their show, and a stand-alone multimedia demonstration of simple 8-bit sound. It was created by Salomon entirely on a Macintosh IIci equipped with DigiDesign's SoundTools direct-to-disk recording system and a Storage Dimensions one-gigabyte hard drive. Passport Design's Alchemy program was used to manipulate various individual sound components. This was later recorded on Digital Audio Tape for the band's use.

For more details, see Chapter 11, "Sound Projects."

Power Tools Theme

Composer, performer, and multimedia producer Christopher Yavelow demonstrates how he wrote and produced the title screen music for the *Multimedia Power Tools* CD-ROM. Yavelow's step-by-step project includes QuickTime movies and Macromedia Director animations illustrating the operation of M, an interactive music composition program developed by Intelligent Music, Inc. Using M, Yavelow "conducted" his collection of musical ideas with an on-screen baton, captured the output to Standard MIDI files, and transferred to a Mark of the Unicorn's Performer MIDI sequencer for tweaking. The resulting audio output was recorded at CD-quality using MediaVision's PAS-16 NuBus Card. Alchemy was used to down-sample the sound file to the 8-bit, 22kHz version for the *Power Tools* CD-ROM.

For more details, see Chapter 11, "Sound Projects."

Bay of Digs

In this project, David Javelosa describes how he develops music and audio productions on the Windows platform. As a musician and composer, Javelosa demonstrates how audio production plays a big part in digital media. He illustrates his use of the media player and the three main audio devices: MIDI (Musical Instrument Digital Interface) Sequencer, Sound, and CD Audio. Using MasterTracks Pro, Javelosa takes viewers through the process of sequencing a MIDI production for output in three different formats.

For more details, see Chapter 11, "Sound Projects."

So You Want to Be a Rock and Roll Star

Steve Rappaport's project explains how he created the sound in his CD-ROM, *So You Want to be a Rock and Roll Star.* His CD-ROM is all about sound and music; it allows the user to participate in six guitar and keyboard lessons, playing along with tracks from old rock and roll songs. This original idea and its implementation were created and executed by Rappaport, who holds the copyright. He used Macromedia's SoundEdit program and Passport Designs' MasterTracks Pro 4 program to import, create, process, and edit the sound. The interactivity was created in Macromedia Director.

For more details, see Chapter 11, "Sound Projects."

Animation Projects

Video Quilt

Animator Lynda Weinman was hired by Dr. Mary Anne Sweeney at The University of Texas Medical School to create a Spanish/English laserdisc for women's pre- and postnatal clinics. The disk would be used to educate viewers on infant nutrition, safety, and health care. The clinic serves underprivileged mothers, many of whom are illiterate. The patchwork quilt idea was born out of a desire to create a friendly interface, one that would invite the noncomputer user to interact. The University of Texas gave Weinman a rough storyboard describing the icons for the patches on the quilt. From this Weinman created illustrations which she scanned into a Macintosh computer, enhancing, reworking, and finally animating the images. She then added interactivity to create a program that would encourage the user to participate.

For more details, see Chapter 13, "Animation Projects."

Lawnmower Man Logo

In 1992, the major motion picture *The Lawnmower Man* required an animated corporate identity for its fictional corporation called Virtual Space Industries (VSI). Graphic artist Jack Davis, working as part of the Gosney Company, Inc., provided the concept and design for the VSI logo. This CD-ROM project is a step-by-step description of the process. Using Macromedia's Swivel 3D, Davis built and animated the VSI Logo. He then imported it into MacroMind 3D and added a bump map, texture map, and shadow-casting light source. Davis' tutorial also contains QuickTime film clips from The *Lawnmower Man*, which is copyrighted by Brett Leonard of Film Light Productions.

For more details, see Chapter 13, "Animation Projects."

Test Flight

John Odam of John Odam Design Associates produced this 3-D animation to illustrate the basic process of 3-D animation. Using Strata, Inc.'s StrataVision program, Odam began assembling the airplane out of simple components: the cylinder, the sphere, and the stretch tool. Once they were assembled, he applied texture mapping to the airplane to create various surfaces, including a metallic surface finish on the body. Then, using the Animation Palette in StrataVision, he animated the model to simulate a plane fly-through. His work in animation and three-dimensional design won him StrataVision's "Oscar" for another, more complex fly through film.

For more details, see Chapter 13, "Animation Projects."

Video Projects

The Vortex

The Vortex is a full-length, six-hour digital video interactive movie on three CD-ROMs. In this project, Hallie Eavelyn of Hyperbole Studios describes how an entire race of winged beings was created using SoftImage, CoSA AfterEffects, and a Cinepak QuickTime movie. The project outlines how the wings are modeled and rendered inside SoftImage. Each render is done with a one degree rotation. The wings are then sized in CoSA AfterEffects and reduced to the point where they are in proportion to the character. Once the clip is complete, it is turned into a Cinepak QuickTime Movie.

For more details, see Chapter 15, "Video Projects."

Water Fantasia

Macintosh Multimedia Artist Don Doerfler created the original concept and design for this digital video project. *Water Fantasia* explores aquatic environments and their inhabitants through the use of video, audio, and the Macintosh computer. Using a Sony FX510 8mm video camera, Doerfler shot three-months worth of videotape, which he then logged and used to create storyboards. Once he selected the video clips, he digitized them using a SuperMac Video Spigot board. He then edited and assembled them in Adobe Premiere, creating special effects with Premiere's filters, the FX channel, and transparency settings. Music from Passport Production's *QuickTunes* Vol. 1 CD was added, and the entire piece was finally reprinted to video tape.

For more details, see Chapter 15, "Video Projects."

Land of Counterpane

Harry Mott's basic digital video project, created with video of his three-month-old son Cameron and public domain and license-free video, audio, and stills, builds a movie around a poem by Robert Louis Stevenson. In gathering the raw materials, he was careful to respect copyright laws and went to Archive Houses for license-free film and video. He also used license-free music and sound effects on CD-ROMs such as *Killer Tracks* and Prosonus' *Music Bytes*. Mott digitized all his material using Digital Film (a digitizing board) and edited, created special effects, and assembled in Adobe Premiere, using a Bernoulli drive. *The Land of Counterpane* is 90 seconds long, but it took six hours to "make" the movie using Compact Video compression.

For more details, see Chapter 15, "Video Projects."

EcoSpies

Video producer and designer Scott Billups worked with producers Tim Cutt and Sam and Sharon Baldoni to create the graphic design and production for Tim's television pilot *EcoSpies*. Billups designed the logos, bumpers, and transitional elements of the show, which focuses on ecological concerns. Working on a Macintosh computer, he sketched his visualizations using Swivel 3D and MacroMind Director, which he then exported as PICTs and compressed into a QuickTime movie using Adobe Premiere. He created the final models in Macromedia's MacroModel and ElectricImage's MisterFont, rendering them in ElectricImage Animation System and recording to a Sony Laser Videodisc Recorder. Finally, he inserted Chroma Keys and recorded to a BetaCam SP.

For more details, see Chapter 15, "Video Projects."

Multimedia Projects

Optivity 5

Miriam Block of Block Interactive describes how to produce a cross-platform, multimedia marketing tool using Macromedia Director. Bay Networks hired Block Interactive to produce a direct-marketing tool for their Optivity line of network management software. Block designed a fax-back capability within the Director piece, which included a form that could be filled out, sent to a printer, and then faxed. Block's challenge was to create an application with the ability to print the form on any printer. She accomplished this by using an X Object on the Mac side and a DLL on the Windows side and incorporating them into Lingo programming. The ultimate challenge was to produce cross-platform playback capabilities.

For more details, see Chapter 17, "Interactive Multimedia Projects."

MedPics

MedPics is an interactive image review and tutorial program developed at the University of California, San Diego (UCSD) School of Medicine by Helene Hoffman, Ph.D. and Ann Irwin, M.D. of the school's Learning Resources Center (LRC). It is copyrighted to the U.C. Regents and administered by the LRC. MedPics was designed as a replacement for the traditional slide set review in the second-year Human Disease Course. Hoffman and Irwin used existing slide sets from the Human Disease course during the initial development of MedPics, asking faculty to supply slides and technical data. Copyright releases were obtained from contributors, permitting the University to use the image internally and commercially. Hoffman and Irwin used Photoshop and Director to build *MedPics,* Michel Kripalani of Presto Studios helped them with scripting and creation of the interface and Susan Adanato assisted with the graphic design of the interface. All participants in *MedPics* receive on-screen credit. *MedPics* is available from any color Macintosh computer on the UCSD campus network, including 35 provided by the LRC at 16 locations around campus and at affiliated teaching hospitals.

For more details, see Chapter 17, "Interactive Multimedia Projects."

The Journeyman Project Robot

The Journeyman Project, an interactive adventure game by Presto Studios on CD-ROM, envisions the world in the year 2318. The player's job is to assure world peace by preventing sabotage. One of the protagonists is a Robot, that was developed into a three-dimensional character by Presto's lead animator and programmer, Farshid Almassizadeh. Working from sketches, the Presto team created the model out of 17,000 polygons. Farshid then used Macromedia's Swivel 3D to choreograph the model's movements, then imported it into Specular's Infini-D 3D to apply texture maps, final tweaking, and rendering.

For more details, see Chapter 17, "Interactive Multimedia Projects."

How Your Body Works

How Your Body Works, the Mac/Windows, interactive encyclopedia of the human body, was programmed in C++ for Mindscape by Nels Johnson at San Francisco Canyon Company. This multimedia, interactive CD-ROM project of the human body, contains an intriguing interface full of surprises, entertaining scavenger hunts, up-to-date medical advice, extensive animations, a beautiful 3-D tour of the body's systems, and a responsive performance. Johnson's step-by-step project outlines the process of developing this cross-platform multimedia title in C++.

For more details, see Chapter 17, "Interactive Multimedia Projects."

Learn and Enjoy

Whether you are just curious about multimedia on your Mac or Windows machine and peruse the presentations casually, or you are a practicing professional and take them apart and dig down deep, we hope you learn from the Power Tools Sample Projects. Enjoy the journey!

Power Tools on the CD-ROM

The other portion of the *Power Tools* CD-ROM is packed with clip media, utilities, and demo applications that you can use immediately. A complete item-by-item review of this material is available in the Power Tools section of the disc. It is divided into two sections: Clip Media and Programs and Utilities (Applications).

Clip Media

Here you will find a vast collection of photographs, background textures, video clips, animations, sounds, and more, from companies such as PhotoDisc, Form and Function, Macromedia, Strata, ArtBeats, and 21st Century Media. These files

Clip Media/Animation
⌘ 100–110

Clip Media/Images
⌘ 200–250

Clip Media/Sound ⌘ 300–343

Clip Media/Video ⌘ 400–412

Clip Media/3-D Graphics
⌘ 500–519

are released for use by owners of the *Power Tools* CD-ROM. Each file is showcased in a presentation screen. On many of the screens, you can click on the Zoom button to get a full screen version of images, or trigger video clips and animations. Categories include:

- Animation
- Images
- Sound
- Video
- 3-D Graphics

Programs and Utilities

This section includes demo versions of most of the multimedia applications available on the Macintosh and/or Windows platform. These are the latest versions of the actual programs, functional except for one key feature: you can't save work (aw, shucks). But what you can do is open files on the CD (or from other sources) and test drive the programs. You will also find *fully* functional utility programs for *power* support in your production work. Note that some of these programs are "shareware." If you're not familiar with the concept of shareware, here's how it works; try the utilities and if you like them and find them useful, register your copy with the creator and send in the suggested shareware fee (usually $10–20). The creators of these utilities have received no payment as part of this project, and the price you paid for this CD-ROM does not include their registration fee.

The Programs and Utilities are divided into the following categories:

Applications/General
⌘ 600–604

Applications/Imaging
⌘ 605–611

Applications/QuickTime
⌘ 612–613

Applications

- General Tools

    Ambrosia—ColorSwitch

    Apple Computer, Inc.—ExtensionsManager and VideoSync

    Alex Colwell Software—Notepad++

    Parity Productions—Speedometer 4.02

- Imaging Tools

    Kevin Mitchell Software—GIF Converter

    HSC Software—Kai's Power Tools

    Apple Computer, Inc.—PICTViewer

- QuickTime Tools

    Apple Computer, Inc.—MoviePlayer

    Aladdin Systems, Inc.—Popcorn

Demos

- Audio Tools

    The Blue Ribbon Sound Works—SuperJAM! and Soundtrack Express

    Macromedia—SoundEdit 16

    Passport—MasterTracks Pro

    Presto Studios—HiRez Audio

    Turtle Beach Systems—Wave for Windows

    Twelve Tone Systems—Cakewalk Home Studio and Cakewalk

- Authoring Tools

    Macromedia—Director and AuthorWare

    Media in Motion—Interactive Training for Director

    Catalogic—Toast CD Pro

    Gold Disc—Animation Works

- Imaging Tools

    Fractal Design—Painter 3.0

    Gryphon Software—Morph 2.5

    Adobe—Photoshop and Illustrator

    Caligari—trueSpace 2.0

    ULead Systems—Viewer

    Equilibrium—DeBabelizer Toolbox

    Macromedia—Macromodel

    Strata—Vision 3d

- QuickTime Tools

    Adobe—Premiere

    Strata—MediaPaint

Using the Power Tools

Each item, whether a program or a clip media file, has a one-screen presentation that provides a graphic representation of the item and a text description, plus contact and copyright information. You can click on the Print button in the Navigation Bar to print the screen as a convenient reference on the tool. (For instructions on getting to the presentation screens, see the next section.)

You will find the actual Power Tools files in the folders labeled "Progutil. Mac" or "Progutil.PC" and "Clipmed" on the CD-ROM. You can copy them to your hard drive by dragging them from the CD-ROM, or you can use the Copy feature in the presentation screen (click on the Copy button, and the disc will automatically copy the file to your hard drive).

Access to the Power Tools

Note that throughout the book you will find power codes listing sample projects and power tools—with three-digit codes—in the margins. You can go to a particular tool's presentation screen in several ways:

1. Click on "Skip Anim" and when the Main Menu appears, click on the Power Tools icon to go to the first Power Tool in a category, and then click through the alphabetically listed tools in that category.

2. From the Main Menu screen, click on the Power Codes button, which will take you to the full list of all the Power Tools and Sample Project's power code numbers.

3. From the Main Menu, or anywhere on the disc, simply hold the CONTROL key down and type in the three-digit code and you will be whisked right to that tool's screen.

For a complete listing of the Power Tools, see Appendix B.

Appendix A: Resources

This comprehensive listing provides the information you need to locate the hundreds of products and services mentioned in the book and on the *Power Tools* CD-ROM. While this information was best available at press time, due to rapidly changing nature of the industry, we cannot guarantee its accuracy.

Product Information

CODE	COMPANY INFO/PRODUCT
	Adobe Systems Incorporated
	1585 Charleston Road
	Mountain View, CA 94039
	415-961-4400
715	PhotoShop 3.0 Demo
718	Illustrator 4.0 Demo
722	Premiere 4.0 Demo
	Aladdin Systems Inc.
	165 Westridge Drive
	Watsonville, CA 95076
	408-761-6200
613	Popcorn 1.0.1
	Alexander S. Colwell Software
	21222 Marjorie Avenue
	Torrance, CA 90503
	310-540-3806
602	Notepad++ 2.1
	Ambrosia
	P.O. Box 23140
	Rochester, NY 14692
	716-427-2577
600	Colorswitch 2.3.0

CODE	COMPANY INFO/PRODUCT
	Apple Computer Inc.
	20525 Mariani Ave.
	Cupertino, CA 95014
	408-996-1010
601	Extensions Manager
604	VideoSync
611	PICTViewer 1.1
612	MoviePlayer
	QuickTime 2.3
	ArtBeats
	2611 South Myrtle Road
	Myrtle Creek, OR 97457
	503-863-4429
201	Banded Steel
203	Bella Rosa
207	Cherry Blossom Marble
210	Currents
219	Jade
220	Juparana
225	Marble, Dark
226	Marble
230	Palm
232	Photo Texture–Vivid
240	Sunburst
	The Blue Ribbon Sound Works
	1605 Chantilly Drive, Suite 200
	Atlanta, GA 30324
	800-226-0212
700	SuperJam! Demo
701	Soundtrack Express Demo

CODE	COMPANY INFO/PRODUCT

BMUG
1442A Walnut Street #62
Berkeley, CA 94709
510-549-2684
102 Clock
103 Dr. Seuss Set
106 Number Spin Pine
108 TV-ROM, the Movie
343 Zoo Sound
401 C&G Video
402 Clapping Squirrel
407 Opening Scan
410 The Thinker
412 Walk Like an Egret

Caligari Corp.
1955 Landings Drive
Mountain View, CA 94043
415-390-9600
716 trueSpace 2 Demo

Catalogic Corporation
2685 Marine Way, Suite 1220
Mountain View, CA 94043-1115
800-255-4020
711 Toast CD-ROM Pro 2.5

DIVA
222 3rd Street, Suite 3332
Cambridge, MA 02142
617-491-4147
321 New Age 1
325 Piano Bar
403 Cruisin' 2
404 Dollars
405 Fast Driving
408 Out of Town

Educorp
7434 Trade Street
San Diego, CA 92121
619-536-9999
214 Earth 6
223 Liberty 3

CODE	COMPANY INFO/PRODUCT

Equalibrium
475 Gate Five Road, Suite 225
Sausalito, CA 94965
415-332-4343
719 DeBabelizer Toolbox®Demo

Form and Function
1595 17th Avenue
San Francisco, CA 94122
415-664-4010
107 Terra
215 Fieldstone
216 Fire
227 Mottled
228 NGC2-2
236 Ring Nebula
319 Mantle Clock
331 Rolling Thunder
334 Seashore
400 Beach
406 Flames
409 Sunset
411 Thunderheads

Fractal Design Corp.
335 Spreckels Drive
Aptos, CA 95003
800-297-2665
713 Painter 3.1 Demo

Gold Disk
3350 Scott Boulevard, Building 14
Santa Clara, CA 95054-3107
800-465-3375 / 408-982-0200
712 Animation Works Demo

Great Lakes Business Solutions
39905 Lotzford Road, Suite 200
Canton, MI 48187
313-981-4970/800-554-8565 Orders
000 WISE Installation System Professional Ver. 3.0

Gryphon Software Corporation
7220 Trade Street, Suite 120
San Diego, CA 92121
619-536-8815
714 Morph 2.5 Demo

CODE	COMPANY INFO/PRODUCT

HSC Software
6303 Carpinteria Avenue
Carpinteria, CA 93013
805-566-6200
606 KPT-Pixelwind Filter
607 KPT-Difuse More Filter
608 KPT-Fine Edges Soft Filter
609 KPT-Sharpen Intensify Color
610 KPT-3D Stereo Noise Filter

Husom & Rose Photographics
1988 Stanford Avenue
St. Paul, MN 55105
612-699-1858
234 Rainbow
235 Reflections

IMAGETECTS
7 West 41 Avenue, Suite 415
San Mateo, CA 94403
408-252-5487
205 Brick 9
213 Earth
231 Pavers 1
241 Trislaur

Kevin Mitchell Software
P.O. Box 803066
Chicago, IL 60680-3066
KAM@MCS.NET
http://www.kami.com/gifconverter.html
605 GIF Converter 2.3.7

Macromedia Inc.
600 Townsend Avenue
San Francisco, CA 94103
415-252-2111
101 Arrow
104 Globe
105 Lock & Key
301 Button 5
302 Camera Shutter
303 Car Alarm
305 Cartoon Boing

CODE	COMPANY INFO/PRODUCT

306 Cartoon Streak
310 Door 2
312 Explosion
313 Fireworks Spinners
314 Flying Sorcery
315 Foghorn
316 Helicopter
318 Light & Easy
320 Metal Scrape
322 Parrot 3
328 QuickHits 1
329 Railroad Crossing Bell
330 Robot Bang
333 Sci-Fi Background
337 Telephone Dial
338 The Harvest
339 Train Horn 1
340 Typewriter
500 America
501 Bike
504 Carousel Horse
505 Chair
506 Clown
508 Draft Table
509 Eye
510 Female Heads
511 Freesia
512 Helvetibet
513 Kenneth & Barbara
514 Macintoshes
515 Oil Pump
516 Pencil
518 Tripod
519 Woodman
707 SoundEdit16™ Demo
708 Director 4.0® Demo
709 AuthorWare Professional® Demo
720 Macromodel™ Demo

CODE	COMPANY INFO/PRODUCT

McClain Photography
9587 Tropico Drive
San Diego, CA 91941
619-469-9599

200 Apple
204 Bikes
206 Building
212 Dunes
224 The Look
237 San Diego
238 Sea Shore
242 Utah Mountains

Media in Motion
P.O. Box 170130
San Francisco, CA 94117
800-395-2547

100 Alarm Clock
710 Interactive Training for Director

Parity Productions
26043 Gushue Street
Hayward, CA 94544
ALink: BERFIELD; CompuServe: 72627,564

603 Speedometer 4.02

Passport Designs Inc.
100 Stone Pine Road
Halfmoon Bay, CA 94019
415-726-0280

706 MasterTracks Pro 5

PhotoDisc Inc.
2013 4th Avenue, Suite 200
Seattle, WA 98121
800-528-3472

243 Bird Design
244 Colored Parasols
245 Row of Buddhas
246 Aerial Furrows
247 Painted Native
248 SF Skyline
249 Building Steps
250 Pyramids

Presto Studios
9888 Carroll Centre Road, #228
San Diego, CA 92126
619-689-4939

300 Bahama Bomba
307 Celestial Stroll
308 Clouds
317 Island Panther
327 Pouring/Drinking Soda
332 Running Out of Time
335 Short Zipper
336 Soothing Dawn
341 Water Birth
342 Water Drip
705 Hi Rez Audio Demo

Stat Media Network
7077 East Shorecrest Drive
Anaheim, CA 92807-4506
714-280-0038

109 Brushed Steel
110 Instant Buttons & Controls

Strata Inc.
2 West Street, George Boulevard, Suite 2100
St. George, UT 84770
801-628-5218

502 California
503 Camouflage Sand
507 Dice
517 Stone-Silver Lining
721 StrataVision 3D Demo
723 Media Paint Demo

CODE   COMPANY INFO/PRODUCT

The Multimedia Library

37 Washington Square West, Suite 4 D
New York, NY 10011
212-674-1958

202	Beach at Sunset
208	Chinese Bell Temple
209	Coastal Scene
211	Dragon Boat
217	Great Wall
218	Haleakala Crater
222	Lava
229	Old Church
239	St. Basil's Cathedral
304	Carol of the Bells
309	Come Back to Me
311	Dulcimer Piece
323	Piano Interludes 4
324	Piano Interludes 6
326	Polyrythms 6

Turtle Beach Systems

52 Grumbacher Road
York, PA 17402
717-767-0200

702	Wave for Windows Demo

Twelve Tone Systems

44 Pleasant Street
Watertown, MA 02172
800-234-1171/617-926-2480

703	Cakewalk Home Studio Demo
704	Cakewalk Pro Demo

U Lead Systems

970 West 190th Street, Suite 520
Torrance, CA 90502
310-523-9393

717	Viewer

Wayzata Technology

21 Northeast Fourth Street
Grand Rapids, MN 55744
218-326-0597

221	Jupiter Risin'
233	Primordial Soup

Project Information

CODE   COMPANY INFO/PRODUCT

Billups Communication

1608 Thayer Avenue
Los Angeles, CA 90024
310-474-2229

033	*EcoSpies* (Sample Project by Scott Billups)

Block Interactive

5150 El Camino Real, Suite 432
Los Altos, CA 94022
415-254-7600

040	*Optivity 5* (Sample Project by Miriam Block)

Chrysolite Productions

2811 Whishire Boulevard, Suite 510
Santa Monica, CA 90403
310-829-2203

033	*EcoSpies* (Sample Project by Scott Billups)

Doerfler Design

4511 Castelar
San Diego, CA 92107
619-223-9789

031	*Water Fantasia* (Sample Project by Don Doerfler)

Horizon Resources

1533 Hunsaker Street
Oceanside, CA 92054
619-757-5795

010	*Hip Hop Hits* (Sample Project by Mike Salomon)

Hyperbole Studios

2225 Fourth Avenue, 2nd Floor
Seattle, WA 98121
206-441-8334

030	*The Vortex* (Sample Project by Hallie Eavelyn)

CODE	COMPANY INFO/PRODUCT

Interactive Records
921 Church Street
San Francisco, CA 94114
415-285-8650

013 *So You Want to be A Rock & Roll Star* (Sample Project by Steven Rappaport)

David Javelosa
532 Pier Avenue, #E
Santa Monica, CA 90405
310-581-9355

012 *Bay of Digs* (Sample Project by David Javelosa)

JH Davis Design
P.O. Box 262535
San Diego, CA 92196
619-689-4895

021 Lawnmower Man VSI Logo (Sample Project by Jack Davis)

John Odam Design Associates
2163 Cordero Road
Del Mar, CA 92014
619-259-8230

022 *Test Flight* (Sample Project by John Odam)

Harry Mott
3561 Frances Avenue
Los Angeles, CA 90066310-398-9789

032 *Land of Counterpane* (Sample Project by Harry Mott)

Presto Studios
9888 Carroll Center, Suite 228
San Diego, CA 92126
619-689-4895

042 *The Journeyman Project* (Sample Project by Farshid Almassizadeh)

Mike Salomon
Horizon Resources
1533 Hunsaker Street
Oceanside, CA 92054
619-757-5795

010 *Hip Hop Hits* (Sample Project by Mike Salomon)

CODE	COMPANY INFO/PRODUCT

San Francisco Canyon Company
360 Post Street, Suite 402
San Francisco, CA 94108
415-398-9957

043 *How Your Body Works* (Sample Project by Nels Johnson)

Tim Cutt Productions
2840 North Beverly Drive
Beverly Hills, CA 90210
310-474-2229

033 *EcoSpies* (Sample Project by Scott Billups)

UCSD Medical School
9500 Gilman Drive
La Jolla, CA 92093-0661
619-534-3656

041 *MedPics* (Sample Project by Helene Hoffman)

Univ. of Texas School of Nursing at Galveston
1100 Mechanic, Route J-29
Galveston, TX 77555
409-772-5118

020 *Video Quilt* (Sample Project by Lynda Weinman)

Lynda Weinman
618 North Fredric Street
Burbank, CA 91505
818-843-5056

020 *Video Quilt* (Sample Project by Lynda Weinman)

Verbum, Inc.
2187-C San Elijo Avenue
Cardiff, CA 92007
619-944-9977

021 Lawnmower Man VSI Logo (Sample Project by Jack Davis)
Multimedia Power Tools CD-ROM and book production

Appendix B: Power Codes List

Outline

Interface Location Codes

000 Intro Animation
001 Disc Info Menu
002 Set-up Menu
003 Guided Tour Menu
004 Sample Projects Menu
005 Power Tools Menu
006 Introduction
007 Credits
008 Production Notes
009 Publisher/Copyright Info

Sample Projects
(for exact codes, see Projects)

010–013 Sound
020–022 Animation
030–033 Video
040–043 Interactive Multimedia

Clip Media
(for exact codes, see Power Tools)

100–110 Animation
200–250 Images
300–343 Sound
400–412 Video
500–519 3–D Graphics

Applications
(for exact codes, see Power Tools)

600–604 General
605–611 Imaging
612–613 QuickTime

Demos
(for exact codes, see Demos)

700–707 Audio
708–712 Authoring
713–721 Imaging
722–723 QuickTime

Projects

Power Tools

Clip Media

Animation

Images

207	ArtBeats	Cherry Blossom Marble	Macintosh and Windows
208	The Multimedia Library	Chinese Bell Temple	Macintosh and Windows
209	The Multimedia Library	Coastal Scene	Macintosh and Windows
210	ArtBeats	Currents	Macintosh and Windows
211	The Multimedia Library	Dragon Boat	Macintosh and Windows
212	McClain Photography	Dunes	Macintosh and Windows
213	ImageTects	Earth	Macintosh and Windows
214	Educorp	Earth 6	Macintosh and Windows
215	Form and Function	Fieldstone	Macintosh and Windows
216	Form and Function	Fire	Macintosh and Windows
217	The Multimedia Library	Great Wall	Macintosh and Windows
218	The Multimedia Library	Haleakala Crater	Macintosh and Windows
219	ArtBeats	Jade	Macintosh and Windows
220	ArtBeats	Juparana	Macintosh and Windows
221	Wayzata Technology	Jupiter Rising	Macintosh and Windows
222	The Multimedia Library	Lava	Macintosh and Windows
223	Educorp	Liberty 3	Macintosh and Windows
224	McClain Photography	The Look	Macintosh and Windows
225	ArtBeats	Marble, Dark	Macintosh and Windows
226	ArtBeats	Marble	Macintosh and Windows
227	Form and Function	Mottled	Macintosh and Windows
228	Form and Function	NGC2–2	Macintosh and Windows
229	The Multimedia Library	Old Church	Macintosh and Windows
230	ArtBeats	Palm	Macintosh and Windows
231	ImageTects	Pavers 1	Macintosh and Windows
232	ArtBeats	Photo Texture-Vivid	Macintosh and Windows
233	Wayzata Technology	Primordial Soup	Macintosh and Windows
234	Husom & Rose Photos	Rainbow	Macintosh and Windows
235	Husom & Rose Photos	Reflections	Macintosh and Windows
236	Form and Function	Ring Nebula	Macintosh and Windows
237	McClain Photography	San Diego	Macintosh and Windows
238	McClain Photography	Sea Shore	Macintosh and Windows
239	The Multimedia Library	St. Basil's Cathedral	Macintosh and Windows
240	ArtBeats	Sunburst	Macintosh and Windows
241	ImageTects	Trislaur	Macintosh and Windows
242	McClain Photography	Utah Mountains	Macintosh and Windows
243	PhotoDisc, Inc.	Bird Design	Macintosh and Windows
244	PhotoDisc, Inc.	Colored Parasols	Macintosh and Windows
245	PhotoDisc, Inc.	Row of Buddhas	Macintosh and Windows
246	PhotoDisc, Inc.	Aerial Furrows	Macintosh and Windows
247	PhotoDisc, Inc.	Painted Native	Macintosh and Windows
248	PhotoDisc, Inc.	SF Skyline	Macintosh and Windows
249	PhotoDisc, Inc.	Building Steps	Macintosh and Windows
250	PhotoDisc, Inc.	Pyraminds	Macintosh and Windows

Sound

300	Presto Studios	Bahama Bomba	Macintosh and Windows
301	Macromedia, Inc.	Button 5	Macintosh and Windows
302	Macromedia, Inc.	Camera Shutter	Macintosh and Windows
303	Macromedia, Inc.	Car Alarm	Macintosh and Windows
304	The Multimedia Library	Carol of the Bells	Macintosh and Windows
305	Macromedia, Inc.	Cartoon Boing	Macintosh and Windows
306	Macromedia, Inc.	Cartoon Streak	Macintosh and Windows
307	Presto Studios	Celestial Stroll	Macintosh and Windows
308	Presto Studios	Clouds	Macintosh and Windows
309	The Multimedia Library	Come Back to Me	Macintosh and Windows
310	Macromedia, Inc.	Door 2	Macintosh and Windows
311	The Multimedia Library	Dulcimer Piece	Macintosh and Windows
312	Macromedia, Inc.	Explosion	Macintosh and Windows
313	Macromedia, Inc.	Fireworks Spinners	Macintosh and Windows
314	Macromedia, Inc.	Flying Sorcery	Macintosh and Windows
315	Macromedia, Inc.	Foghorn	Macintosh and Windows
316	Macromedia, Inc.	Helicopter	Macintosh and Windows
317	Presto Studios	Island Panther	Macintosh and Windows
318	Macromedia, Inc.	Light & Easy	Macintosh and Windows
319	Form and Function	Mantle Clock	Macintosh and Windows
320	Macromedia, Inc.	Metal Scrape	Macintosh and Windows
321	DIVA	New Age 1	Macintosh and Windows
322	Macromedia, Inc.	Parrot 3	Macintosh and Windows
323	The Multimedia Library	Piano Interludes 4	Macintosh and Windows
324	The Multimedia Library	Piano Interludes 6	Macintosh and Windows
325	DIVA	Piano Bar	Macintosh and Windows
326	The Multimedia Library	Polyrhythms 6	Macintosh and Windows
327	Presto Studios	Pouring/Drinking Soda	Macintosh and Windows
328	Macromedia, Inc.	Quick Hits 1	Macintosh and Windows
329	Macromedia, Inc.	Railroad Crossing Bell	Macintosh and Windows
330	Macromedia, Inc.	Robot Bang	Macintosh and Windows
331	Form and Function	Rolling Thunder	Macintosh and Windows
332	Presto Studios	Running out of Time	Macintosh and Windows
333	Macromedia, Inc.	Sci-Fi Background	Macintosh and Windows
334	Form and Function	Seashore	Macintosh and Windows
335	Presto Studios	Short Zipper	Macintosh and Windows
336	Presto Studios	Soothing Dawn	Macintosh and Windows
337	Macromedia, Inc.	Telephone Dial 1	Macintosh and Windows
338	Macromedia, Inc.	The Harvest	Macintosh and Windows
339	Macromedia, Inc.	Train Horn 1	Macintosh and Windows
340	Macromedia, Inc.	Typewriter	Macintosh and Windows
341	Presto Studios	Water Birth	Macintosh and Windows
342	Presto Studios	Water Drip	Macintosh and Windows
343	BMUG	Zoo Sound	Macintosh and Windows

Video

400	Form and Function	Beach	Macintosh and Windows
401	BMUG	C&G Video	Macintosh and Windows
402	BMUG	Clapping Squirrel	Macintosh and Windows
403	DIVA	Crusin' 2	Macintosh and Windows
404	DIVA	Dollars	Macintosh and Windows
405	DIVA	Fast Driving	Macintosh and Windows
406	Form and Function	Flames	Macintosh and Windows
407	BMUG	Opening Scan	Macintosh and Windows
408	DIVA	Out of Town	Macintosh and Windows
409	Form and Function	Sunset	Macintosh and Windows
410	BMUG	The Thinker	Macintosh and Windows
411	Form and Function	Thunderheads	Macintosh and Windows
412	BMUG	Walk Like an Egret	Macintosh and Windows

3–D Graphics

500	Macromedia, Inc.	America	Macintosh and Windows
501	Macromedia, Inc.	Bike	Macintosh and Windows
502	Strata, Inc.	California	Macintosh and Windows
503	Strata, Inc.	Camouflage Sand	Macintosh and Windows
504	Macromedia, Inc.	Carousel Horse	Macintosh and Windows
505	Macromedia, Inc.	Chair	Macintosh and Windows
506	Macromedia, Inc.	Clown	Macintosh and Windows
507	Strata, Inc.	Dice	Macintosh and Windows
508	Macromedia, Inc.	Draft Table	Macintosh and Windows
509	Macromedia, Inc.	Eye	Macintosh and Windows
510	Macromedia, Inc.	Female Heads	Macintosh and Windows
511	Macromedia, Inc.	Fresia	Macintosh and Windows
512	Macromedia, Inc.	Helvetibet	Macintosh and Windows
513	Macromedia, Inc.	Kenneth & Barbara	Macintosh and Windows
514	Macromedia, Inc.	Macintoshes	Macintosh and Windows
515	Macromedia, Inc.	Oil Pump	Macintosh and Windows
516	Macromedia, Inc.	Pencil	Macintosh and Windows
517	Strata, Inc.	Stone-Silver lining	Macintosh and Windows
518	Macromedia, Inc.	Tripod	Macintosh and Windows
519	Macromedia, Inc.	Woodman	Macintosh and Windows

Applications

General

600	Ambrosia	ColorSwitch 2.3.0	Macintosh only
601	Apple Computer, Inc.	ExtensionsManager 1.8	Macintosh only
602	Alex S. Colwell Software	Notepad ++ 2.1	Macintosh only
603	Parity Productions	Speedometer 4.02	Macintosh only
604	Apple Computer, Inc.	VideoSync 1.0	Macintosh only

Imaging

605	Kevin Mitchell Software	Gif Converter 2.32b	Macintosh only
606	HSC Software	KPT-Pixelwind Filter	Macintosh only
607	HSC Software	KPT-Difuse More Filter	Macintosh only
608	HSC Software	KPT-Fine Edges Soft Filter	Macintosh only
609	HSC Software	KPT-Sharpen Intensify Filter	Macintosh only
610	HSC Software	KPT-3d Stereo Noise Filter	Macintosh only
611	Apple Computer, Inc.	PICT Viewer 1.1	Macintosh only

QuickTime

612	Apple Computer, Inc.	MoviePlayer	Macintosh only
613	Aladdin Systems, Inc.	Popcorn 1.0.1	Macintosh only

Demos

Audio

700	Blue Ribbon Sound Works	Super Jam Demo	Windows only
701	Blue Ribbon Sound Works	Soundtrack Express Demo	Windows only
702	Turtle Beach Systems	Wave for Win Demo	Windows only
703	Twelve Tone Systems	Cakewalk Home Studio	Windows only
704	Twelve Tone Systems	Cakewalk Pro Demo	Windows only
705	Presto Studios	Hi Rez Audio Demo	Macintosh only
706	Passport Designs	MasterTracks Pro 5	Macintosh and Windows
707	Macromedia, Inc.	SoundEdit16™ Demo	Macintosh only

Authoring

708	Macromedia, Inc.	Director 4.0® Demo	Macintosh and Windows
709	Macromedia, Inc.	AuthorWare Prof. 3.0® Demo	Macintosh and Windows
710	Media in Motion	Interactive Training for Dir.	Macintosh and Windows
711	Catalogic	Toast CD-ROM Pro 2.5	Macintosh only
712	Gold Disc	Animation Works 1.1 Demo	Macintosh only

Imaging

713	Fractal Design Corp.	Painter 3.0 Demo	Macintosh and Windows
714	Gryphon Software Corp.	Morph 2.5 Demo	Macintosh and Windows
715	Adobe Systems Inc.	PhotoShop 3.0 Demo	Macintosh and Windows
716	Caligari Corp	TrueSpace 2.0 Demo	Windows only
717	U Lead Systems	Viewer	Windows only
718	Adobe Systems Inc.	Illustrator 4.0 Demo	Macintosh and Windows
719	Equilibrium Technologies	DeBabelizer 1.6 Demo	Macintosh only
720	Macromedia	Macromodel 1.5™ Demo	Macintosh and Windows
721	Strata, Inc.	StrataVision 3D Demo	

QuickTime

722	Adobe Systems Inc.	Premiere 4.0 Demo	Macintosh and Windows
723	Strata, Inc.	Media Paint Demo	Macintosh only

Appendix C:
Copyright Act of 1976

An Act

For the general revision of the Copyright Law, title 17 of the United States Code, and for other purposes.

Be it enacted by the Senate and House of Representatives of the United States of America in Congress assembled,

TITLE I—GENERAL REVISION OF COPYRIGHT LAW

Sec. 101. Title 17 of the United States Code, entitled "Copyrights," is hereby amended in its entirety to read as follows:

Chapter 1.—Subject Matter and Scope of Copyright

Sec. 101 Definitions.
Sec. 102: Subject matter of copyright: In general.
Sec. 103: Subject matter of copyright: Compilations and derivative works.
Sec. 104: Subject matter of copyright: National origin.
Sec. 105: Subject matter of copyright: United States Government works.
Sec. 106: Exclusive rights in copyrighted works.
Sec. 107: Limitations on exclusive rights: Fair use.
Sec. 108: Limitations on exclusive rights: Reproduction by libraries andarchives.

Section 101. Definitions

As used in this title, the following terms and their variant forms mean the following:

An "anonymous work" is a work on the copies or phonorecords of which no natural person is identified as author.

"Audio visual works" are works that consist of a series of related images which are intrinsically intended to be shown by the use of machines or devices such as projectors, viewers, or electronic equipment, together with accompanying sounds, if any, regardless of the nature of the material objects, such as films or tapes, in which the works are embodied.

The "best edition" of a work is the edition, published in the United States at any time before the date of deposit, that the Library of Congress determines to be most suitable for its purposes.

A person's "children" are that person's immediate offspring, whether legitimate or not, and any children legally adopted by that person.

A "collective work" is a work formed by the collection and assembling of preexisting materials or of data that are selected, coordinated, or arranged in such a way that the resulting work as a whole constitutes an original work of authorship. The term "compilation" includes collective works.

A "compilation" is a work formed by the collection and assembling of preexisitng materials or of data that are selected, coordinated, or arranged in such a way that the resulting work as a whole constitutes an original work of authorship. The term "compilation" includes collective works.

"Copies" are material objects, other than phonorecords, in which a work is fixed by any method now known or later developed, and from which the work can be perceived, reproduced, or otherwise communicated, either directly or with the aid of a machine or device. The term "copies" includes the material object, other than a phonorecord, in which the work is first fixed.

"Copyright owner," with respect to any one of the exclusive rights comprised in a copyright, refers to the owner of that particular right.

A work is "created" when it is fixed in a copy or phonorecord for the first time; where a work is prepared over a period of time, the portion of it that has been fixed at any particular time constitutes the work as of that time, and where the work has been prepared in different versions, each version constitutes a separate work.

A "derivative work" is a work based upon one or more preexisting works, such as a translation, musical arrangement, dramatization, fictionalization, motion picture version, sound recording, art reproduction, abridgement, condensation, or any other form in which a work may be recast, transformed, or adapted.

A work consisting of editorial revisions, annotations, elaborations, or other modifications which, as a whole represent an original work of authorship, is a "derivative work."

A "device," "machine," or "process" is one now known or later developed.

To "display" a work means to show a copy of it, either directly or by means of a film, slide, television image, or any other device or process or, in the case of a motion picture or other audiovisual work, to show individual images nonsequentially.

A work is"fixed" in a tangible medium of expression when its embodiment in a copy or phonorecord, by or under the authority of the author, is sufficiently permanent or stable to permit it to be perceived, reproduced, or otherwise communicated for a period of more than transitory duration. A work consisting of sounds, images, or both, that are being transmitted, is "fixed" for purposes of this title if a fixation of the work is being made simultaneously with its transmission.

The terms "including" and "such as" are illustrative and not limitative.

A "joint work" is a work prepared by two or more authors with the intention that their contributions be merged into inseparable or interdependent parts of a unitary whole.

"Literary works" are works, other than audiovisual works, expressed in words, numbers, or other verbal or numerical symbols or indicia, regardless of the nature of the material objects, such as books, periodicals, manuscripts, phonorecords, film, tapes, disks, or cards, in which they are embodied.

"Motion pictures" are audiovisual works consisting of a series of related images which, when shown in succession, impart an impression of motion, together with accompanying sounds, if any.

To "perform" a work means to recite, render, play, dance, or act it, either directly or by means of any device or process or, in the case of a motion picture or other audiovisual work, to show its images in any sequence or to make the sounds accompanying it audible.

"Phonorecords" are material objects in which sounds, other than those accompanying a motion picture or other audiovisual work, are fixed by any method now known or later developed, and from which the sounds can be perceived, reproduced, or otherwise communicated, either directly or with the aid of a machine or device. The term "phonorecords" includes the material object in which the sounds are first fixed.

"Pictorial, graphic, and sculptural works" include two-dimensional and three-dimensional works of fine, graphic, and applied art, photographs, prints and art reproductions, maps, globes, charts, technical drawings, diagrams, and models. Such works shall include works of artistic craftsmanship insofar as their form but not their mechanical or utilitarian aspects are concerned; the design of a useful article, as defined in this section, shall be considered a pictorial, graphic, or sculptural work only if, and only to the extent that, such design incorporates pictorial, graphic, or sculptural features that can be identified separately from, and are capable of exisiting independently of, the utilitarian aspects of the article.

A "pseudonymous work" is a work on the copies or phonorecords of which the author is identified under a fictitious name.

"Publication" is the distribution of copies or phonorecords of a work to the public by sale or other transfer of ownership, or by rental, lease, or lending. The offering to distribute copies or phonorecords to a group of persons for purposes of further distribution, public performance, or public display, constitutes publication. A public performance or display of a work does not of itself constitute publication.

To perform or display a work "publicly" means—

(1) to perform or display it at a place open to the public or at any place where a substantial number of persons outside of a normal circle of a family and its social acquaintances is gathered; or

(2) to transmit or otherwise communicate a performance or display of the work to a place specified by clause (1) or to the public, by means of any device or process, whether the mem-

bers of the public capable of receiving the performance or display receive it in the same place or in separate places and at the same time or at different times.

"Sound recordings" are works that result from the fixation of a series of musical, spoken, or other sounds, but not including the sounds accompanying a motion picture or other audiovisual work, regardless of the nature of the material objects, such as disks, tapes, or other phonorecords, in which they are embodied.

"State" includes the District of Columbia and the Commonwealth of Puerto Rico, and any territories to which this title is made applicable by an Act of Congress.

A "transfer of copyright ownership" is an assignment, mortgage, exclusive license, or any other conveyance, alienation, or hypothecation of a copyright or of any of the exclusive rights comprised in a copyright, whether or not it is limited in time or place of effect, but not including a non-exclusive license.

A "transmission program" is a body of material that, as an aggregate, has been produced for the sole purpose of transmission to the public in sequence and as a unit.

To "transmit" a performance or display is to communicate it by any device or process whereby images or sounds are received beyond the place from which they are sent.

The "United States," when used in a geographical sense, comprises the several States, the District of Columbia and the Commonwealth of Puerto Rico, and the organized territories under the jurisdiction of the United States Government.

A "useful article" is an article having an intrinsic utilitarian function that is not merely to portray the appearance of the article or to convey information. An article that is normally a part of a useful article is considered a "useful article."

The author's "widow" or "widower" is the author's surviving spouse under the law of the author's domicile at the time of his or her death, whether or not the spouse has later remarried.

A "work made for hire" is—

    (1) a work prepared by an employee within the scope of his or her employment; or

    (2) a work specially ordered or commissioned for use as a contribution to a collective work, as a part of a motion picture or other audiovisual work, as a translation, as a supplementary work, as a compilation, as an instructional text, as a test, as answer material for a test, or as an atlas, if the parties expressly agree in a written instrument signed by them that the work shall be considered a work made for hire. For the purpose of the foregoing sentence, a "supplementary work" is a work prepared for publication as a secondary adjunct to a work by another author for the purpose of introduction, concluding, illustrating, explaining, revising, commenting upon, or assisting in the use of the other work, such as forewords, afterwords, pictorial illustrations, maps, charts, tables, editorial notes, musical arrangements, answer material for tests, biliographies, appendixes, and indexes, and an "instructional text" is a literary, pictorial, or graphic work prepared for publication and with the purpose of use in systematic instructional activities.

A "computer program" is a set of statements or instructions to be used directly or indirectly in a computer in order to bring about a certain result.

Section 102. Subject matter of copyright: In general

(a) Copyright protection subsists, in accordance with this title, in original works of authorship fixed in any tangible medium of expression, now known or later developed, from which they can be perceived, reproduced, or otherwise communicated, either directly or with the aid of a machine or device. Works of authorship include the following categories:

(1) literary works;

(2) musical works, including any accompanying words;

(3) dramatic works, including any accompanying music;

(4) pantomimes and choreographic works;

(5) pictorial, graphic, and sculptural works;

(6) motion picture and other audiovisual works; and

(7) sound recordings.

(b) In no case does copyright protection for an original work of authorship extend to any idea, procedure, process, system, method of operation, concept, principle, or discovery, regardless of the form in which it is described, explained, illustrated, or embodied in such work.

Section 103. Subject matter of copyright: Compilations and derivative works

(a) The subject matter of copyright as specified by section 102 includes compilations and derivative works, but protection for a work employing preexisting material in which copyright subsists does not extend to any part of the work in which such material has been used unlawfully.

(b) The copyright in a compilation or derivative work extends only to the material contributed by the author of such work, as distinguished from the preexisitng material employed in the work, and does not imply any exclusive right in the preexisting material. The copyright in such work is independent of, and does not affect or enlarge the scope, duration, ownership, or subsistence of, any copyright protection in the preexisting material.

Section 104. Subject matter of copyright: National origin

(a) Unpublished Works.—The works specified by sections 102 and 103, while unpublished, are subject to protection under this title without regard to the nationality or domicile of the author.

(b) Published Works.—The works specified by sections 102 and 103, when published, are subject to protection under this title if—

(1) on the date of first publication, one or more of the authors is a national or domiciliary of the United States, or is a national, domiciliary, or sovereign authority of a foreign nation that is a party to a copyright treaty to which the United States is also a party, or is a stateless person, wherever that person may be domiciled; or

(2) the work is first published in the United States or in a foreign nation that, on the date of first publication, is a party to the Universal Copyright Convention; or

(3) the work is first published by the United States or any of its specialized agencies, or by the Organizations of American States; or

(4) the work comes within the scope of a Presidential proclamation. Whenever the President finds that a particular foreign nation extends, to works by authors who are nationals or domiciliaries of the United States or to works that are first published in the United States, copyright protection on substantially the same basis as that on which the foreign nation extends protection to works of its own nationals and domiciliaries and works first published in that nation, the President may by proclamation extend protection under this title to works of which one or more of the authors is, on the date of first publication, a national domiciliary, or sovereign authority of that nation, or which was first published in that nation. The President may revise,

suspend, or revoke any such proclamation or impose any conditions or limitations on protection under a proclamation.

Section 105. Subject matter of copyright: United States Government works

Copyright protection under this title is not available for any work of the United States Government, but the United States Government is not precluded from receiving and holding copyrights transferred to it by assignment, bequest, or otherwise.

Section 106. Exclusive rights in copyrighted works

Subject to sections 107 through 108, the owner of copyright under this title has the exclusive rights to do and to authorize any of the following:

(1) to reproduce the copyrighted work in copies or phonorecords;

(2) to prepare derivative works based upon the copyrighted work;

(3) to distribute copies or phonorecords of the copyrighted work to the public by sale or other transfer of ownership, or by rental, lease, or lending;

(4) in the case of literary, musical, dramatic, and choreographic works, pantomimes, and motion pictures and other audiovisual works, to perform the copyrighted work publicly; and

(5) in the case of literary, musical, dramatic, and choreographic works, pantomimes, and pictorial, graphic, or sculptural works, including the individual images of a motion picture or other audiovisual work, to display the copyrighted work publicly.

Section 107. Limitations on exclusive rights: Fair use

Notwithstanding the provisions of section 106, the fair use of a copyrighted work, including such use by reproduction in copies or phonorecords or by any other means specified by that section, for purposes such as criticism, comment, news reporting, teaching (including multiple copies for classroom use), scholarship, or research, is not an infringement of copyright. In determining whether the use made of a work in any particular case is a fair use the factors to be considered shall include—

(1) the purpose and character of the use, including whether such use is of a commercial nature or is for nonprofit educational purposes;

(2) the nature of the copyrighted work;

(3) the amount and substantiality of the portion used in relation to the copyrighted work as a whole; and

(4) the effect of the use upon the potential market for or value of the copyrighted work.

Section 108. Limitations on exclusive rights: Reproduction by libraries and archives

(a) Notwithstanding the provisions of section 106, it is not an infringement of copyright for a library or archives, or any of its employees acting within the scope of their employment, to reproduce no more than one copy or phonorecord of a work, or to distribute such copy or phonorecord, under the conditions specified by this section, if—

(1) the reproduction or distribution is made without any purpose of direct or indirect commercial advantage;

(2) the collections of the library or archives are (i) open to the public, or (ii) available not only to researchers affiliated with the library or archives or with the institution of which it is a part, but also to other persons doing research in a specialized field; and

(3) the reproduction or distribution of the work includes a notice of copyright.

(b) The rights of reproduction and distribution under this section apply to a copy or phonorecord of an unpublished work duplicated in facsimile form solely for purposes of preservation and security or for deposit for research use in another library or archives of the type described by clause (2) of subsection (a), if the copy or phonorecord reproduced is currently in the collections of the library or archives.

(c) The right of reproduction under this section applies to a copy or phonorecord of a published work duplicated in facsimile form solely for the purpose of replacement of a copy or phonorecord that is damaged, deteriorating, lost, or stolen, if the library or archives has, after a reasonable effort, determined that an unused replacement cannot be obtained at a fair price.

(d) The rights of reproduction and distribution under this section apply to a copy, made from the collection of a library or archives where the user makes his or her request or from that of another library or archives, of no more than one article or other contribution to a copyrighted collection or periodical issue, or to a copy or phonorecord of a small part of any other copyrighted work, if—

(1) the copy or phonorecord becomes the property of the user, and the library or archives has had no notice that the copy or phonorecord would be used for any purpose other than private study, scholarship, or research; and

(2) the library or archives displays prominently, at the place where orders are accepted, and includes on its order form, a warning of copyright in accordance with requirements that the Register of Copyrights shall prescribe by regulation.

(e) The rights of reproduction and distribution under this section apply to the entire work, or to a substantial part of it, made from the collection of a library or archives where the user makes his or her request or from that of another library or archives, if the library or archives has first determined, on the basis of a reasonable investigation, that a copy or phonorecord of the copyrighted work cannot be obtained at a pair price, if—

(1) the copy or phonorecord becomes the property of the user, and the library or archives has had no notice that the copy or phonorecord would be used for any purpose other than private study, scholarship, or research; and

(2) the library or archives displays prominently, at the place where orders are accepted, and includes on its order form a warning of copyright in accordance with requirements that the Register of Copyrights shall prescribe by regulation.

(f) Nothing in this section—

(1) shall be construed to impose liability for copyright infringement upon a library or archives or its employees for the unsupervised use of reproducing equipment located on its premises: Provided, That such equipment displays a notice that the making of a copy may be subject to the copyright law;

(2) excuses a person who uses such reproducing equipment or who requests a copy or phonorecord under subsection (d) from liability for copyright infringement for any such act, or for any later use of such copy or phonorecord, if it exceeds fair use as provided by section 107;

(3) shall be construed to limit the reproduction and distribution by lending of a limited number of copies and excerpts by a library or archives of an audiovisual news program, subject to clauses (1), (2), and (3) of subsection (a); or

(4) in any way affects the right of fair use as provided by section 107, or any contractual obligations assumed at any time by the library or archives when it obtained a copy or phonorecord of a work in its collections.

(g) The rights of reproduction and distribution under this section extend to the isolated and unrelated reproduction or distribution of a single copy or phonorecord of the same material on separate occasions, but do not extend to cases where the library or archives, or its employee—

(1) is aware or has substantial reason to believe that it is engaging in the related or concerted reproduction or distribution of multiple copies or phonorecords of the same material, whether made on one occasion or over a period of time, and whether intended for aggregate use by one or more individuals or for separate use by the individual members of a group; or

(2) engages in the systematic reproduction or distribution of single or multiple copies or phonorecords of material described in subsection (d): Provided, That nothing in this clause prevents a library or archives from participating in interlibrary arrangements that do not have, as their purpose or effect, that the library or archives receiving such copies or phonorecords for distribution does so in such aggregate quantities as to substitute for subscription to or purchase of such work.

(h) The rights of reproduction and distribution under this section do not apply to a musical work, a pictorial, graphic or sculptural work, or a motion picture or other audiovisual owrk other than an audiovisual work dealing with news, except that no such limitation shall apply with respect to rights granted by subsections (b) and (c), or with respect to pictorial or graphic works published as illustrattions, diagrams, or similar adjuncts to works of which copies are reproduced or distribued in accordance with subsections (d) and (e).

(i) Five years from the effective date of this Act, and at five-year intervals thereafter, the Register of Copyrights, after consulting with representatives of authors, book and periodical publishers, and other owners of copyrighted materials, and with representatives of library users and librarians, shall submit to the Congress a report setting forth the extent to which this section has achieved the intended statutory balancing of the rights of creators, and the needs of users. The report should also describe any problems that may have arisen, and present legislative or other recommendations, if warranted.

Section 109. Limitations on exclusive rights: Effect of transfer of particular copy or phonorecord

(a) Notwithstanding the provisions of section 106(3), the owner of a particular copy or phonorecord lawfully made under this title, or any person authorized by such owner, is entitled, without the authority of the copyright owner, to sell or otherwise dispose of the possession of that copy or phonorecord.

(b)(1) Notwithstanding the provisions of subsection (a), unless authorized by the owners of copyright in the sound recording and in the musical works embodied therein, the owner of a particular phonorecord may not, for purposes of direct or indirect commercial advantage, dispose of, or authorize the disposal of, the possession of that phonorecord by rental, lease, or lending, or by any other act or practice in the nature of rental, lease, or lending. Nothing in the preceding sentence shall apply to the rental, lease, or lending of a phonorecord for nonprofit purposes by a nonprofit library or nonprofit educational institution.

(2) Nothing in this subsection shall affect any provision of the antitrust laws. For purposes of the preceding sentence, "antitrust laws" has the meaning given that term in the first section

of the Clayton Act and includes section 5 of the Federal Trade Commission Act to the extent that section relates to unfair methods of competition.

(3) Any person who distributes a phonorecord in violation of clause (1) is an infringer of copyright under section 501 of this title and is subject to the remedies set forth in sections 502, 503, 504, 505, and 509. Such violation shall not be a criminal offense under section 506 or cause such person to be subject to the criminal penalties set forth in section 2319 of title 18.

(c) Notwithstanding the provisions of section 106(5), the owner of a particular copy lawfully made under this title, or any person authorized by such owner, is entitled, without the authority of the copyright owner, to display that copy publicly, either directly or by the projection of no more than one image at a time, to viewers present at he place where the copy is located.

(d) The privileges prescribed by subsections (a) and (b) do not, unless authorized by the copyright owner, extend to any person who has acquired possession of the copy or phonorecord from the copyright owner, by rental lease, loan, or otherwise, without acquiring ownership of it.

Section 110. Limitations on exclusive rights: Exemption of certain performances and displays

Notwithstanding the provisions of section 106, the following are not infringements of copyright:

(1) performance or display of a work by instructors or pupils in the course of face-to-face teaching activities of a nonprofit educational institution, in a classroom or similar place devoted to instruction, unless, in the case of a motion picture or other audiovisual work, the performance, or the display of individual images, is given by means of a copy that was not lawfully made under this title, and that the person responsible for the performance knew or had reason to believe was not lawfully made;

(2) performance of a nondramatic literary or musical work or display of a work, by or in the course of a transmission, if—

(A) the performance or display is a regular part of the systematic instructional activities of a governmental body or a nonprofit educational institution; and

(B) the performance or display is directly related and of material asistance to the teaching content of the transmission; and

(C) the transmission is made primarily for—(i) reception in classrooms or similar places normally devoted to instruction, or (ii) reception by persons to whom the transmission is directed because their disabilities or other special circumstances prevent their attendance in classrooms or similar places normally devoted to instruction, or (iii) reception by officers or employees of governmental bodies as a part of their official duties or employment;

(3) performance of a nondramatic literary or musical work or of a dramatico-musical work of a religious nature, or display of a work, in the course of services at a place of worship or other religious assembly;

(4) performance of a nondramatic literary or musical work otherwise than in a transmission to the public, without any purpose of direct or indirect commercial advantage and without payment of any fee or other compensation for the performance to any of its performers, promoters, or organizers, if—

(A) there is no direct or indirect admission charge; or

(B) the proceeds, after deducting the reasonable costs of producing the performance, are used exclusively for educational, religious, or charitable purposes and not for private financial gain, except where the copyright owner has served notice of objection to the performance under the following conditions; (i) the notice shall be in writing and signed by the copyright owner or such owner's duly authorized agent; and (ii) the notice shall be served on the person responsible for the performance at least seven days before the date of the performance, and shall state the reasonas for the objection; and (iii) the notice shall comply, in form, content, and manner of service, with requirements that the Register of Copyrights shall prescribe by regulation;

(5) communication of a transmission embodying a performance or display of a work by the public reception of the transmission on a single receiving apparatus of a kind commonly used in private homes, unless—

(A) a direct charge is made to see or hear the transmission; or

(B) the transmission thus received is further transmitted to the public;

(6) performance of a nondramatic musical work by a governmental body or a nonprofit agricultural or horticultural organization, in the course of an annual agricultural or horticultural fair or exhibition conducted by such body or organization; the exemption provided by this clause shall extend to any liability for copyright infringement that would otherwise be imposed on such body or organiztaion, under doctrines of vicarious liability or related infringement, for a performance by a concessionnaire, business establishment, or other person at such fair or exhibition, but shall not excuse any such person from liability for the performance;

(7) performances of a nondramatic musical work by a vending establishment open to the public at large without any direct or indirect admission charge, where the sole purpose of the performance is to promote the retail sale of copies or phonorecords of the work, and the performance is not transmitted beyond the place where the establishment is located and is within the immediate area where the sale is occurring;

(8) performance of a nondramatic literary work, by or in the course of a transmission specifically designed for and primarily directed to blind or other handicapped persons who are unable to read normal printed material as a result of their handicap, or deaf or other handicapped persons who are unable to hear the aural signals accompanying a transmission of visual signals, if the performance is made without any purpose of direct or indirect commercial advantage and its transmission is made through the facilities of: (i) a governmental body; or (ii) a noncommercial educational broadcast station (as defined in section 397 of title 47); or (iii) a radio subcarrier authorization (as defined in 47 CFR 73.293— 73.295 and 73.593—73.595); or (iv) a cable system [as defined in section 111 (f)].

(9) performance on a single occasion of a dramatic literary work published at least ten years before the date of the performance, by or in the course of a transmission specifically designed for and primarily directed to blind or other handicapped persons who are unable to read normal printed material as a result of their handicap, if the performance is made without any purpose of direct or indirect commercial advantage and its transmission is made through the facilities of a radio subcarrier authorization referred to in clause (8) (iii), Provided, That the provisions of this clause shall not be applicable to more than one performance of the same work by the same performers or under the auspices of the same organization.

(10) notwithstanding paragraph 4 above, the following is not an infringement of copyright: performance of a nondramatic literary or musical work in the course of a social function which is organized and promoted by a nonprofit veterans' organization or a nonprofit fraternal organization to which the general public is not invited, but not including the invitees of the orga-

nizations, if the proceeds from the performance, after deducting the reasonable costs of producing the performance, are used exclusively for charitable purposes and not for financial gain. For purposes of this section the social functions of any college or university fraternity or sorority shall not be included unless the social function is held solely to raise funds for a specific charitable purpose.

Section 111. Limitations on exclusive rights: Secondary transmissions

(a) Certain Secondary Transmissions Exempted.—The secondary transmission of a primary transmission embodying a performance or display of a work is not an infringement of copyright if—

(1) the secondary transmission is is not made by a cable system, and consists entirely of the relaying, but the management of a hotel, apartment house, or similar establishment, of signals transmitted by a broadcast station licensed by the Federal Communications Commission, within the local service area of such station, to the private lodgings of guests or residents of such establishment, and no direct charge is made to see or hear the secondary transmission; or

(2) the secondary transmission is made soley for the purpose and under the conditions specified by clause (2) of section 110; or

(3) the secondary transmission is made by any carrier who has no direct or indirect control over the content or selection of the primary transmission or over the particular recipients of the secondary transmission, and whose activities with respect to the secondary transmission consist solely of providing wires, cables, or other communications channels for the use of others: Provided, That the provisions of this clause extend only to the activities of said carrier with respect to secondary transmissions and do not exempt from liability the activities of others with respect to their own primary or secondary transmissions; or

(4) the secondary transmission is not made by a cable system but is made by a governmental body, or other nonprofit organization, without any purpose of direct or indirect commercial advantage, and without charge to the recipients of the secondary transmission other than assessments necessary to defray the actual and reasonable costs of maintaining and operating the secondary transmission service.

(b) Secondary Transmission of Primary Transmission to Controlled Group.—Notwithstanding the provisions of subsections (a) and (c), the secondary transmission to the public of a primary transmission embodying a performance or display of a work is actionable as an act of infringement under section 501, and is fully subject to the remedies provided by sections 502 through 506 and 509, if the primary transmission is not made for reception by the public at large but is controlled and limited to reception by particular members of the public: Provided, however, That such secondary transmission is not actionable as an act of infringement if—

(1) the primary transmission is made by a broadcast station licensed by the Federal Communications Commission; and

(2) the carriage of the signals comprising the secondary transmission is required under the rules, regulations, or authorizations of the Federal Communications Commission; and

(3) the signal of the primary transmitter is not altered or changed in any way by the secondary transmitter.

(c) Secondary Transmissions by Cable Systems.—

(1) Subject to the provisions of clauses (2), (3), and (4) of this subsection, secondary transmissions to the public by a cable system of a primary transmission made by a broadcast sta-

tion licensed by the Federal Communications Commission or by an appropriate governmental authority of Canada or Mexico embodying a performance or display of a work shall be subject to compulsory licensing upon compliance with the requirements of subsection (d) where the carriage of the signals comprising the secondary transmission is permissible under the rules regulations, or authorizations of the Federal Communications Commission.

(2) Notwithstanding the provisions of clause (1) of this subsection, the willful or repeated secondary transmission to the public by a cable system of a primary transmission made by a broadcast station licensed by the Federal Communications Commission or by an appropriate governmental authority of Canada or Mexico and embodying a performance or display of a work is actionable as an act of infringement under section 501, and is fully subject to the remedies provided by sections 502 through 506 and 509, in the following cases:

(A) where the carriage of the signals comprising the secondary transmission is not permissible under the rules, regulations, or authorizations of the Federal Communications Commission; or

(B) where the cable system has not recorded the notice specified by subsection (d) and deposited the statement of account and royalty fee required by subsection (d).

(3) Notwithstanding the provisions of clause (1) of this subsection and subject to the provisions of subsection (e) of this section, the secondary transmission to the public by a cable system of a primary transmission made by a broadcast station licensed by the Federal Communications Commission or by an appropriate governmental authority of Canada or Mexico and embodying a performance or display of a work is actionable as an act of infringement under section 501, and is fully subject to the remedies provided by sections 502 through 506 and sections 509 and 510, if the content of the particular program in which the performance or display is embodied, or any commercial advertising or station announcements transmitted by the primary transmitter during, or immediately before or after, the transmission of such program, is in any way willfully altered by the cable system through changes, deletions, or additions, except for the alteration, deletion, or substitution of commercial advertisements performed by those engaged in television commercial advertising market research: Provided, That the research company has obtained the prior consent of the advertiser who has purchased the original commercial advertisement, the television station broadcasting that commercial advertisement, and the cable system performing the secondary transmission: And provided further, That such commercial alteration, deletion, or substitution is not performed for the purpose of deriving income from the sale of that commercial time.

(4) Notwithstanding the provisions of clause (1) of this subsection, the secondary transmission to the public by a cable system of a primary transmission made by a broadcast station licensed by an appropriate governmental authority of Canada or Mexico and embodying a performance or display of a work is actionable as an act of infringement under section 501, and is fully subject to the remedies provided by sections 502 through 506 and section 509, if (A) with respect to Canadian signals, the community of the cable system is located more than 150 miles from the United States-Canadian border and is also located south of the forty-second parallel of latitude, or (b) with respect to Mexican signals, the secondary transmissions made by a cable system which received the primary transmission by means other than direct interception of a free space radio wave emitted by such broadcast television station, unless prior to April 15, 1976, such cable system was actually carrying, or was specifically authorized to

carry, the signal of such foreign station on the system pursuant to the rules, regulations, or authorizations of the Federal Communications Commision.

(d) Compulsory License for Secondary Transmissions by Cable Systems.—

(1) For any secondary transmission to be subject to compulsory licensing under subsection (c), the cable system shall, at least one month before the date of the commencement of operations of the cable system or within one hundred and eighty days after the enactment of this Act, whichever is later, and thereafter within thirty days after each occasion on which the ownership or control or the signal carriage complement of the cable system changes, record in the Copyright Office a notice including a statement of the identity and address of the person who owns or operates the secondary transmission service or has power to exercise primary control over it, together with the name and location of the primary transmitter or primary transmitters whose signals are regularly carried by the cable system, and thereafter, from time to time, such further information as the Register of Copyrights, after consultation with the Copyright Royalty Tribunal (if and when the Tribunal has been constituted), shall prescribe by regulation to carry out the purpose of this clause.

(2) A cable system whose secondary transmissions have been subject to compulsory licensing under subsection (c) shall, on a semiannual basis, deposit with the Register of Copyrights, in accordance with requirements that the Register shall, after consultation with the Copyright Royalty Tribunal (if and when the Tribunal has been constituted), prescribe by regulation—

(A) a statement of account, covering the six months next preceding, specifying the number of channels on which the cable system made secondary transmissions to its subscribers, the names and locations of all primary transmitters whose transmissions were further transmitted by the cable system, the total number of subscribers, the gross amounts paid to the cable system for the basic service of providing secondary transmissions of primary broadcast transmitters, and such other data as the Register of Copyrights may, after consultation with the Copyright Royalty Tribunal (if and when the Tribunal has been constituted), from time to time prescribe by regulation. Such statement shall also include a special statement of account covering any nonnetwork television programming that was carried by the cable system in whole or in part beyond the local service area of the primary transmitter, under rules, regulations, or authorizations of the Federal Communications Commission permitting the substitution or addition of signals under certain circumstances, together with logs showing the times, dates, stations, and programs involved in such substituted or added carriage; and

(B) except in the case of a cable system whose royalty is specified in subclause (C) or (D), a total royalty fee for the period covered by the statement, computed on the basis of specified percentages of the gross receipts from subscribers to the cable service during said period for the basic service of providing secondary transmissions of primary broadcast transmitters, as follows: (i) 0.675 of 1 per centum of such gross receipts for the privilege of further transmitting any nonnetwork programing of a primary transmitter in whole or in part beyond the local service area of such primary transmitter, such amount to be applied against the fee, if any, payable pursuant to paragraphs (ii) through (iv); (ii) 0.675 of 1 per centum of such gross receipts for the first distant signal equivalent; (iii) 0.425 of 1 per centum of such gross receipts for each of the second, third, and fourth distant signal equivalents; (iv) 0.2 of 1 percentum of such gross receipts for the fifth distant signal equivalent nd each additional distant signal equivalent thereafter; and in computing the amount payable under paragraph (ii) through (iv), above, any fraction of a distant signal equivalent shall be computed at its fractional value and, in the case of any cable system located partly within and partly without the local service area of a primary transmitter, gross receipts shall be limited to those gross receipts derived from subscribers located without the local service area of such primary transmitter; and

(C) if the actual gross receipts paid by subscribers to a cable system for the period covered by the statement for the basic service of providing secondary transmissions of primary broadcast transmitters total $80,000 or less, gross receipts of the cable system for the purpose of this subclause shall be computed by subtracting from such actual gross receipts the amount by which $80,000 exceeds such actual gross receipts, except that in no case shall a cable system's gross receipts be reduced to less than $3,000. The royalty fee payable under this subclause shall be 0.5 of 1 per centum, regardless of the number of distant signal equivalents, if any; and

(D) if the actual receipts paid by subscribers to a cable system for the period covered by the statement, for the basic service of providing secondary transmissions of primary broadcast transmitters, are more than $80,000 but less than $160,000, the royalty fee payable under this subclause shall be (i) 0.5 of 1 per centum of any gross receipts up to $80,000; and (ii) 1 per centum of any gross receipts in excess of $80,000 but less than $160,000, regardless of the number of distant signal equivalents, if any.

(3) The Register of Copyrights shall receive all fees deposited under this section and, after deducting the reasonable costs incurred by the Copyright Office under this section, shall deposit the balance in the Treasury of the United States, in such manner as the Secretary of the Treasury directs. All funds held by the Secretary of the Treasury shall be invested in interest-bearing United States securities for later distribution with interest by the Copyright Royalty Tribunal as provided by this title. The Register shall submit to the Copyright Royalty Tribunal, on a semiannual basis, a compilation of all statements of account covering the relevant six-month period provided by clause (2) of this subsection.

(4) The royalty fees thus deposited shall, in accordance with the procedures provided by clause (5), be distributed to those among the following copyright owners who claim that their works were the subject of secondary transmissions by cable systems during the relevant semi-annual period:

(A) any such owner whose work was included in a secondary transmission made by a cable system of a nonnetwork television program in whole or in part beyond the local service area of the primary transmitter; and

(B) any such owner whose work was included in a secondary transmission identified in a special statement of account deposited under clause (2)(A); and

(C) any such owner whose work was included in nonnetwork programing consisting exclusively of aural signals carried by a cable system in whole or in part beyond the local service area of the primary transmitter of such programs.

(5) The royalty fees thus deposited shall be distributed in accordance with the following procedures:

(A) During the month of July in each year, every person claiming to be entitled to compulsory license fees for secondary transmissions shall file a claim with the Copyright Royalty Tribunal, in accordance with requirements that the Tribunal shall prescribe by regulation. Notwithstanding any provisions of the antitrust laws, for purposes of this clause any claimants may agree among themselves as to the proportionate division of compulsory licensing fees among them, may lump their claims together and file them jointly or as a single claim, or may designate a common agent to receive payment on their behalf.

(B) After the first day of August of each year, the Copyright Royalty Tribunal shall determine whether there exists a controversy concerning the distribution of royalty fees. If the Tribunal determines that no such controversy exists, it shall, after deducting its reasonable administrative costs under this section, distribute such fees to the copyright owners entitled, or to their designated agents. If the Tribunal finds the existence of a controversy, it shall, pursuant to chapter 8 of this title, conduct a proceeding to determine the distribution of royalty fees.

(C) During the pendency of any proceeding under this subsection, the Copyright Royalty Tribunal shall withhold from distribution an amount sufficient to satisfy all claims with respect to which a controversy exists, but shall have discretion to proceed to distribute any amounts that are not in controversy.

(e) Nonsimultaneous Secondary Transmissions by Cable Systems.—

(1) Notwithstanding those provisions of the second paragraph of subsection (f) relating to nonsimultaneous secondary transmissions by a cable system, any such transmissions are actionable as an act of infringement under section 501, and are fully subject to the remedies provided by sections 502 through 506 and sections 509 and 510, unless—

(A) the program on the videotape is transmitted no more than one time to the cable system's subscribers; and

(B) the copyrighted program, episode, or motion picture videotape, including the commercials contained within such program, episode, or picture, is transmitted without deletion or editing; and

(C) an owner or officer of the cable system (i) prevents the duplication of the videotape while in the possessin of the system, (ii) prevents unauthorized duplication while in the possession of the facility making the videotape for the system if the system owns or controls the facility, or takes reasonable precautions to prevent such duplication if it does not own or control the facility, (iii) takes adequate precautions to prevent duplication while the tape is being transported, and (iv) subject to clause (2), erases or destroys, or causes the erasure or destruction of, the videotape; and

(D) within forty-five days after the end of each calendar quarter, an owner or officer of the cable system executes an affidavit attesting (i) to the steps and precautions taken to prevent duplication of the videotape, and (ii) subject to clause (2), to the erasure or destruction of all videotapes made or used during such quarter; and

(E) such owner or officer places or causes each such affidavit, and affidavits received pursuant to clause (2)(C), to be placed in a file, open to public inspection, at such system's main office in the community where the transmission is made or in the nearest community where such system maintains an office; and

(F) the nonsimultaneous transmission is one that the cable system would be authorized to transmit under the rules, regulations, and authorizations of the Federal Communications Commission in effect at the time of the nonsimultaneous transmission if the transmission had been made simultaneously, except that this subclause shall not apply to inadvertent or accidental transmissions.

(2) If a cable system transfers to any person a videotape of a program nonsimultaneously transmitted by it, such transfer is actionable as an act of infringement under section 501, and is fully subject to the remedies provided by sections 502 through 506 and 509, except that, pursuant to a written, nonprofit contract providing for the equitable sharing of the costs of such videotape and its transfer, a videotape nonsimultaneously transmitted by it, in accordance with clause (1), may be transferred by one cable system in Alaska to another system in Alaska, by one cable system in Hawaii permitted to make such nonsimultaneous transmissions to another such cable system in Hawaii, or by one cable system in Guam, the Northern Mariana Islands, or the Trust Territory of the Pacific Islands, to another cable system in any of those three territories, if—

(A) each such contract is available for public inspection in the offices of the cable systems involved, and a copy of such contract is filed, within thirty days after such contract is entered into with the Copyright Office (which Office shall make each such contract available for public inspection); and

(B) the cable system to which the videotape is transferred complies with clause (1) (A), (B), (C) (i),(iii), and (iv), and (D) through (F); and

(C) such system provides a copy of the affidavit required to be made in accordance with clause (1)(D) to each cable system making a previous nonsimultaneous transmission of the same videotape

(3) This subsection shall not be construed to supersede the exclusivity protection provisions of any existing agreement, or any such agreement hereafter entered into, between a cable system and a television broadcast station in the area in which the cable system is located, or a network with which such station is affiliated.

(4) As used in this subsection, the term "videotape", and each of its variant forms, means the reproduction of the images and sounds of a program or programs broadcast by a television broadcast station licensed by the Federal Communications Commission, regardless of the nature of the material objects, such as tapes or films, in which the reproduction is embodied.

(f) Definitions.—As used in this section, the following terms and their variant forms mean the following:

A "primary transmission" is a transmission made to the public by the transmitting facility whose signals are being received and further transmittd by the secondary transmission service, regardless of where or when the performance or display was first transmitted.

A "secondary transmission" is the further transmitting of a primary transmission simultaneously with the primary transmission, or nonsimultaneously with the primary transmission if by a "cable system" not located in whole or in part within the boundary of the forty-eight contiguous States, Hawaii, or Puerto Rico: Provided however, That a nonsimultaneous further transmission by a cable system located in Hawaii of a primary transmission shall be deemed to be a secondary transmission if the carriage of the television broadcast signal comprising such further transmission is permissible under the rules, regulations, or authorizatons of the Federal Communications Commission.

A "cable system" is a facility, located in any State, Territory, Trust Territory, or Possession, that in whole or in part receives signals transmitted or programs broadcast by one or more television broadcast stations licensed by the Federal Communications Commission, and makes secondary transmissions of such signals or programs by wires, cables, or other communications channels to subscribing members of the public who pay for such service. For purposes of determining the royalty fee under subsection (d) (2), two or more cable systems in contiguous communities under common ownership or control or operating from one head-end shall be considered as one system.

The "local service area of a primary transmitter", in the case of a television broadcast station, comprises the area in which such station is entitled to insist upon its signal being retransmitted by a cable system pursuant to the rules, regulations, and authorizations of the Federal Communications Commission in effect on April 15, 1976, or in the case of a television broadcast station licensed by an appropriate governmental authority of Canada or Mexico, the area in which it would be entitled to insist upon its signal being retransmitted it it were a television broadcast station subject to such rules, regulations, and authorizations. The "local service area of a primary transmitter", in the case of a radio broadcast station, comprises the primary service area of such station, pursuant to the rules and regulations of the Federal Communications Commission.

A "distant signal equivalent" is the value assigned to the secondary transmission of any nonnetwork television programing carried by a cable system in whole or in part beyond the local service area of the primary transmitter of such programing. It is computed by assigning a value of one to each independent station and a value of one-quarter to each network station and noncommercial educational station for the nonnetwork programing so carried pursuant to the rules, regulations, and authorizations of the Federal Communications Commission. The foregoing values for independent, network, and noncommercial educational stations are subject, however, to the following exceptions and limitations. Where the rules and regulations of the Federal Communications Commission require a cable system to omit the further transmission of a particular program and such rules and regulations also permit the substitution of another program embodying a performance or display of a work in place of the omitted transmission, or where such rules and regulations in effect on the date of enactment of this Act permit a cable system, at its election, to effect such deletion and substitution of a nonlive program or to carry additional programs not transmitted by primary transmitters within whose local service area the cable system is located, no value shall be assigned for the substituted or additional program; where the rules, regulations, or authorizations of the Federal Communications Commission in effect on the date of enactment of this Act permit a cable system, at its election, to omit the further transmission of a particular program and such rules, regulations, or authorizations also permit the substitution of another program embodying a performance or display of a work in place of the omitted transmission, the value assigned for the substituted or additional program shall be, in the case of a live program, the value of one full distant signal equivalent multiplied by a fraction that has as its numerator the number of days in the year in which such substitution occurs and as its denominator the number of days in the year. In the case of a station carried pursuant to the late-night or specialty programing rules of the Federal Communications Commission, or a station carried on a part-time basis where full-time or speciality programing rules of the Federal Communications Commission, or a station carried on a part-time basis where full-time carriage is not possible because the cable system lacks the activated channel capacity to retransmit on a full-time basis all signals which it is authorized to carry, the values for independent, network, and noncommercial educational stations set forth above, as the case may be, shall be multiplied by a fraction which is equal to the ratio of the broadcast hours of such station carried by the cable system to the total broadcast hours of the station.

A "network station" is a television broadcast station that is owned or operated by, or affiliated with, one or more of the television networks in the United States providing nationwide transmissions, and that transmits a substantial part of the programing supplied by such networks for a substantial part of that station's typical broadcast day.

An "independent station" is a commercial television broadcat station other than a network station.

A "noncommercial educational station" is a television station that is a noncommercial educational broadcast station as defined in section 397 of title 47.

Section 112. Limitations on exclusive rights: Ephemeral recordings

(a) Notwithstanding the provisions of section 106, and except in the case of a motion picture or other audiovisual work, it is not an infringement of copyright for a transmitting organization entitled to transmit to the public a performance or display of a work, under a license or transfer of the copyright or under the limitations on exclusive rights in sound recordings specified by section 114(a), to make no more than one copy or phonorecord of a particular transmission program embodying the performance or display, if—

(1) the copy or phonorecord is retained and used solely by the transmitting organization that made it, and no further copies or phonorecords are reproduced from it; and

(2) the copy or phonorecord is used solely for the transmitting organization's own transmissions within its local service area, or for purposes of archival preservation or security; and

(3) unless preserved exclusively for archival purposes, the copy or phonorecord is destroyed within six months from the date the transmission program was first transmitted to the public.

(b) Notwithstanding the provisions of section 106, it is not an infringement of copyright for a governmental body or other nonprofit organization entitled to transmit a performance or display of a work, under section 110(2) or under the limitations on exclusive rights in sound recordings specified by section 114(a), to make no more than thirty copies or phonorecords of a particular transmission program embodying the peformance or display, if—

(1) no further copies or phonorecords are reproduced from the copies or phonorecords made under this clause; and

(2) except for one copy or phonorecord that may be preserved exclusively for archival purposes, the copiesor phonorecords are destroyed within seven years fromthe date the transmission program was first transmittedto the public.

(c) Notwithstanding the provisions of section 106, it is not an infringement of copyright for a governmental body or other nonprofit organization to make for distribution no more than one copy or phonorecord, for each transmitting organization specified in clause (2) of this subsection, of a particular transmission program embodying a performance of a nondramatic musical work of a religious nature, or of a sound recording of such a musical work, if—

(1) there is no direct or indirect charge for making or distributing any such copies or phonorecords; and

(2) none of such copies or phonorecords is used for any performance other than a single transmission to the public by a transmitting organization entitled to transmit to the public a performance of the work under a license or transfer of the copyright; and

(3) except for one copy or phonorecord that may be preserved exclusively for archival purposes, the copies or phonorecords are all destroyed within one year from the date the transmission program was first transmitted to the public.

(d) Notwithstanding the provisions of section 106, it is not an infringement of copyright for a governmental body or other nonprofit organization entitled to transmit a performance of a work under section 110(8) to make no more than ten copies or phonorecords combodying the performance, or to permit the use of any such copy or phonorecord by any governmental body or nonprofit organization entitled to transmit a performance of a work under section 110(8), if—

(1) any such copy or phonorecord is retained and used solely by the organization that made it, or by a governmental body or nonprofit organization entitled to transmit a performance of a work under section 110(8), and no further copies or phonorecords are reproduced from it; and

(2) any such copy or phonorecord is used solely for transmissions authorized under section 110(8), or for purposes of archival preservation or security; and

(3) the governmental body or nonprofit organization permitting any use of any such copy or phonorecord by any governmental body or nonprofit organization under this subsection does not make any charge for such use.(e) The transmission program embodied in a copy or phonorecord made under this section is not subject to protection as a derivative work under this title except with the express consent of the owners of copyright in the preexisting works employed in the program.

Section 113. Scope of exclusive rights in pictorial,graphic, and sculptural works

(a) Subject to the provisions of subsections (b) and (c) of this section, the exclusive right to reproduce a copyrighted pictorial, graphic, or sculptural work in copies under section 106 includes the right to reproduce the work in or on any kind of article, whether useful or otherwise.

(b) This title does not afford, to the owner of copyright in a work that portrays a useful article as such, any greater or lesser rights with respect to the making, distribution, or display of the useful article so portrayed than those afforded to such works under the law, whether title 17 or the common law or statutes of a State, in effect on December 31, 1977, as held applicable and construed by a court in an action brought under this title.

(c) In the case of a work lawfully reproduced in useful articles that have been offered for sale or other distribution to the public, copyright does not include any right to prevent the making, distribution, or display of pictures or photographs of such articles in connection with advertisements or commentaries related to the distribution or display of such articles, or in connection with news reports.

Section 114. Scope of exclusive rights in sound recordings

(a) The exclusive rights of the owner of copyright in a sound recording are limited to the rights specified by clauses (1), (2), and (3) of section 106, and do not include any right of performance under section 106(4).

(b) The exclusive right of the owner of copyright in a sound recording under clause (1) of section 106 is limited to the right to duplicate the sound recording in the form of phonorecords, or of copies of motion pictures and other audiovisual works, that directly or indirectly recapture the actual sounds fixed in the recording. The exclusive right of the owner of copyright in a sound recording under clause (2) of section 106 is limited to the right to prepare a derivative work in which the actual sounds fixed in the sound recording are rearranged, remixed, or otherwise altered in sequence or quality. The exclusive rights of the owner of copyright in a sound recording under clauses (1) and (2) of section 106 do not extend to the making or duplication of another sound recording that consists entirely of an independent fixation of other sounds, even though such sounds imitate or simulate those in the copyrighted sound recording. The exclusive rights of the owner of copyright in a sound recording under clauses (1), (2), and (3) of section 106 do not apply to sound recordings included in educational television and radio programs (as defined in section 397 of title 47) distriubted or transmitted by or through public broadcasting entities (as defined by section 118(g)): Provided, That copies or phonorecords of said programs are not commercially distributed by or through public broadcasting entities to the general public.

(c) This section does not limit or impair the exclusive right to perform publicly, by means of a phonorecord, any of the works specified by section 106(4).

(d) On January 3, 1978, the Register of Copyrights, after consulting with representatives of owners of copyrighted materials, representatives of the broadcasting, recording, motion picture, entertainment industries, and arts organizations, representatives of organized labor and performers of copyrighted materials, shall submit to the Congress a report setting forth recommendations as to whether this section should be amended to provide for performers and copyright owners of copyrighted material any performance rights in such material. The report should describe the status of such rights in foreign countries, the views of major interested parties, and specific legislative or other recommendations, if any.

Section 115. Scope of exclusive rights in nondramatic musical works:

Compulsory license for making and distributing phonorecords. In the case of nondramatic musical works, the exclusive rights provided by clauses (1) and (3) of section 106, to make and to distribute phonorecords of such works, are subject to compulsory licensing under the conditions specified by this section.

(a) Availability and Scope of Compulsory License.—

(1) When phonorecords of a nondramatic musical work have been distributed to the public in the United States under the authority of the copyright owner, any other person may, by complying with the provisions of this section, obtain a compulsory license to make and distribute phonorecords of the work. A person may obtain a compulsory license only if his or her primary purpose in making phonorecords is to distribute them to the public for private use. A person may not obtain a compulsory license for use of the work in the making of phonorecords duplicating a sound recording fixed by another, unless: (i) such sound recording was fixed lawfully; and (ii) the making of the phonorecording or, if the sound recording was fixed before February 15, 1972, by any person who fixed the sound recording pursuant to an express license from the owner of the copyright in the musical work or pursuant to a valid compulsory license for use of such work in a sound recording.

(2) A compulsory license includes the privilege of making a musical arrangement of the work to the extent necessary to conform it to the style or manner of interpretation of the performance involved, but the arrangement shall not change the basic melody or fundamental character of the work, and shall not be subject to protection as a derivative work under this title, except with the express consent of the copyright owner.

(b) Notice of Intention To Obtain Compulsory License.—

(1) Any person who wishes to obtain a compulsory license under this section shall, before or within thirty days after making, and before distributing any phonorecords of the work, serve notice of intention to do so on the copyright owner. If the registration or other public records of the Copyright Office do not identify the copyright owner and include an address at which notice can be served, it shall be sufficient to file the notice of intention in the Copyright Office. The notice shall comply, in form, content, and manner of service, with requirements that the Register of Copyrights shall prescribe by regulation.

(2) Failue to serve or file the notice required by clause (1) forecloses the possibility of a compulsory license and, in the absence of a negotiated license, renders the making and distribution of phonorecords actionable as acts of infringement under section 501 and fully subject to the remedies provided by sections 502 through 506 and 509.

(c) Royalty Payable Under Compulsory License.—

(1) To be entitled to receive royalties under a compulsory license, the copyright owner must be identified in the registration or other public records of the Copyright Office. The owner

is entitled to royalties for phonorecords made and distributed after being so identified, but is not entitled to recover for any phonorecords previously made and distributed.

(2) Except as provided by clause (1), the royalty under a compulsory license shall be payable for every phonorecord made and distributed in accordance with the license. For this purpose, a phonorecord is considered "distributed" if the person exercising the compulsory license has voluntarily and permanently parted with its possession. With respect to each work embodied in the phonorecord, the royalty shall be either two and three-fourths cents, or one-half of one cent per minute of playing time or fraction thereof, whichever amount is larger.

(3) A compulsory license under this section includes the right of the maker of a phonorecord of a nondramatic musical work under subsection (a)(1) to distribute or authorize distribution of such phonorecord by rental, lease, or lending (or by acts or practices in the nature of rental, lease, or lending). In addition to any royalty payable under clause (2) and chapter 8 of this title, a royalty shall be payable by the compulsory licensee for every act of distribution of a phonorecord by or in the nature of rental, lease, or lending, by or under the authority of the compulsory licensee. With respect to each nondramatic musical work embodied in the phonorecord, the royalty shall be a proportion of the revenue received by the compulsory licensee from every such act of distribution of the phonorecord under this clause equal to the proportion of the revenue received by the compulsory licensee from distribution of the phonorecord under clause (2) that is payable by a compulsory licensee under that clause and under chapter 8. The Register of Copyrights shall issue regulations to carry out the purpose of this clause.

(4) Royalty payments shall be made on or before the twentieth day of each month and shall include all royalties for the month next preceding. Each monthly payment shall be made under oath and shall comply with requirements that the Register of Copyrights shall prescribe by regulation. The Register shall also prescribe regulations under which detailed cumulative annual statements of account, certified by a certified public accountant, shall be filed for every compulsory license under this section. The regulations covering both the monthly and the annual statements of account shall prescribe the form, content, and manner of certification with respect to the number of records made and the number of records distributed.

(5) If the copyright owner does not receive the monthly payment and the monthly and annual statements of account when due, the owner may give written notice to the licensee that, unless the default is remedied within thirty days from the date of the notice, the compulsory license will be automatically terminated. Such termination renders either the making or the distribution, or both, of all phonorecords for which the royalty has not been paid, actionable as acts of infringement under section 501 through 506 and 509.

Section 116. Scope of exclusive rights in nondramatic musical works: Public performance by means of coin-operated phonorecord players

(a) Limitation on Exclusive Right.—In the case of a nondramatic musical work embodied in a phonorecord, the exclusive right under clause (4) of section 106 to perform the work publicly by means of a coin-operated phonorecord player is limited as follows:

(1) The proprietor of the establishment in which the public performance takes place is not liable for infringement with respect to such public performance unless—

(A) such proprietor is the operator of the phonorecord player; or

(B) such proprietor refuses or fails, within one month after receipt by registered or certified mail of a request, at a time during which the certificate required by clause (1)(C) of subsection (b) is not affixed to the phonorecord player, by the copyright owner, to make full disclosure, by registered or certified mail, of the identity of the operator of the phonorecord player.

(2) The operator of the coin-operated phonorecord player may obtain a compulsory license to perform the work publicly on that phonorecord player by filing the application, affixing the certificate, and paying the royalties provided by subsection (b)

(b) Recordation of Coin-Operated Phonorecord Player, Affixation of Certificate, and Royalty Payable Under Compulsory License.—

(1) Any operator who wishes to obtain a compulsory license for the public performance of works on a coin-operated phonorecord player shall fulfill the following requirements:

(A) Before or within one month after such performances are made available on a particular phonorecord player, and during the month of January in each succeeding year that such performances are made available on that particular phonorecord player, the operator shall file in the Copyright Office, in accordance with requirements that the Register of Copyrights, after consultation with the Copyright Royalty Tribunal (if and when the Tribunal has been constituted), shall prescribe by regulation, an application containing the name and address of the operator of the phonorecord player and the manufacturer and serial number or other explicit identification of the phonorecord player, and deposit with the Register of Copyrights a royalty fee for the current calendar year of $8 for that particular phonorecord player. If such performances are made available on a particular phonorecord player for the first time after July 1 of any year, the royalty fee to be deposited for the remainder of that year shall be $4.

(B) Within twenty days of receipt of an application and a royalty fee pursuant to subclause (A), the Register of Copyrights shall issue to the applicant a certificate for the phonorecord player.

(C) On or before March 1 of the year in which the certificate prescribed by subclause (B) of this clause is issued, or within ten days after the date of issue of the certificate, the operator shall affix to the particular phonorecord player, in a position where it can be readily examined by the public, the certificate, issued by the Register of Copyrights under subclause (B), of the latest application made by such operator under subclause (A) of this clause with respect to that phonorecord player.

(2) Failure to file the application, to affix the certificate, or to pay the royalty required by clause (1) of this subsection renders the public performance actionable as an act of infringement under section 501 and fully subject to the remedies provided by sections 502 through 506 and 509.

(c) Distribution of Royalties.—

(1) The Register of Copyrights shall receive all fees deposited under this section and, after deducting the reasonable costs incurred by the Copyright Office under this section, shall deposit the balance in the Treasury of the United States, in such manner as the Secretary of the Treasury directs. All funds held by the Secretary of the Treasury shall be invested in interest-bearing United States securities for later distribution with interest by the Copyright Royalty Tribunal as provided by this title. The Register shall submit to the Copyright Royalty Tribunal, on an annual basis, a detailed statement of account covering all fees received for the relevant period provided by subsection (b).

(2) During the month of January in each year, every person claiming to be entitled to compulsory license fees under this section for performances during the preceding twelve-month period shall file a claim with the Copyright Royalty Tribunal, in accordance with requirements that the Tribunal shall prescribe by regulation. Such claim shall include an agreement to accept as final, except as provided in section 810 of this title, the determination of the Copyright Royalty Tribunal in any controversy concerning the distribution of royalty fees deposited under subclause (A) of subsection (b)(1) of this section to which the claimant is a party. Notwithstanding any provisions of the antitrust laws, for purposes of this subsection any claimants may agree among themselves as to the proportionate division of compulsory licensing fees among them, may lump their claims together and file them jointly or as a single claim, or may designate a common agent to receive payment on their behalf.

(3) After the first day of October of each year, the Copyright Royalty Tribunal shall determine whether there exists a controversy concerning the distribution of royalty fees deposited under subclause (A) of subsection (b)(1). If the Tribunal determines that no such controversy exists, it shall, after deducting its reasonable administrative costs under this section, distribute such fees to the copyright owners entitled, or to their designated agents. If it finds that such a controversy exists, it shall, pursuant to chapter 8 of this title, conduct a proceeding to determine the distribution of royalty fees.

(4) The fees to be distributed shall be divided as follows:

(A) to every copyright owner not affiliated with a performing rights society, the pro rata share of the fees to be distributed to which such copyright owner proves entitlement.

(B) to the performing rights societies, the remainder of the fees to be distributed in such pro rata shares as they shall by agreement stipulate among themselves,or, if they fail to agree, the pro rata share to which such performing rights societies prove entitlement.

(C) during the pendency of any proceeding under this section, the Copyright Royalty Tribunal shall withhold from distribution an amount sufficient to satisfy all claims with respect to which a controversy exists, but shall have discretion to proceed to distribute any amounts that are not in controversy.

(5) The Copyright Royalty Tribunal shall promulgate regulations unde which persons who can reasonably be expected to have claims may, during the year in which performances take place, without expense to or harassment of operators or proprietors of establishments in which phonorecord players are located,have such access to such establishments and to the phonorecord players located therein and such opportunity to obtain information with respect thereto as may be reasonably necessary to determine, by sampling procedures or otherwise, the proportion of contribution of the musical works of each such person to the earnings of the phonorecord players for which fees shall have been deposited. Any person who alleges that he or she has been denied the access permitted under the regulations prescribed by the Copyright Royalty Tribunal may bring an action in the United States District Court for the District of Columbia for the cancellation of the compulsory license of the phonorecord player to which such access has been denied, and the court shall have the power to declare the compulsory license thereof invalid from the date of issue thereof.

(d) Criminal Penalties.—Any person who knowingly makes a false representation of a material fact in an application filed under clause (1)(A) of subsection (b), or who knowingly alters a certificate issued under clause (1)(B) of subsection (b) or knowingly affixes such a certificate to a phonorecord player other than the one it covers, shall be fined not more than $2,500.

(e) Definitions.—As used in this section, the following terms and their variant forms mean the following:

(1) A "coin-operated phonorecord player" is a machine or device that—

(A) is employed solely for the performance of nondramatic musical works by means of phonorecords upon being activated by insertion of coins, currency, tokens, or other monetary units or their equivalent;

(B) is located in an establishment making no direct or indirect charge for admission;

(C) is accompanied by a list of the titles of all the musical works available for performance on it, which list is affixed to the phonorecord player or posted in the establishment in a prominent position where it can be readily examined by the public; and

(D) affords a choice of works available for performance and permits the choice to be made by the patrons of the establishment in which it is located.

(2) An "operator" is any person who, alone or jointly with others:

(A) owns a coin-operated phonorecord player; or

(B) has the power to make a coin-operated phonorecord player available for placement in an establishment for purposes of public performance; or

(C) has the power to exercise primary control over the selection of the musical works made available for public performance on a coin-operated phonorecord player.

(3) A "performing rights society" is an association or corporation that licenses the public performance of nondramatic musical works on behalf of the copyright owners, such as the American Society of Composers, Authors and Publishers, Broadcast Music, Inc., and SESAC, Inc.

Section 117. Limitations on exclusive rights: Computer programs

Notwithstanding the provisions of section 106, it is not an infringement for the owner of a copy of a computer program to make or authorize the making of another copy or adaptation of that computer program provided:

(1) that such a new copy or adaptation is created as an essential step in the utilization of the computer program in conjunction with a machine and that it is used in no other manner, or

(2) that such new copy or adaptation is for archival purposes only and that all archival copies are destroyed in the event that continued possession of the computer program should cease to be rightful.Any exact copies prepared in accordance with the provisions of this section may be leased, sold, or otherwise transferred, along with the copy from which such copies were prepared, only as part of the lease, sale, or other transfer of all rights in the program. Adaptations so prepared may be transferred only with the authorization of the copyright owner.

Section 118. Scope of exclusive rights: Use of certain works in connection with noncommercial broadcasting

(a) The exclusive rights provided by section 106 shall, with respect to works specified by subsection (b) and the activities specified by subsection (d), be subject to the conditions and limitations prescribed by this section.

(b) Not later than thirty days after the Copyright Royalty Tribunal has been constituted in accordance with section 802, the Chairman of the Tribunal shall cause notice to be published in the Federal Register of the initiation of proceedings for the purpose of determining reasonable terms and rates of royalty payments for the activities specified by subsection (d) with respect to published nondramatic musical works and published pictorial, graphic, and sculptural works during a period beginning as provided in clause (3) of this subsection and ending on December 13, 1982. Copyright owners and public broadcasting entities shall negotiate in good faith and cooperate fully with the Tribunal in an effort to reach reasonable and expeditious results. Notwithstanding any provision of the antitrust laws, any owners of copyright in works specified by this subsection and any public broadcasting entitites, respectively, may negotiate and agree upon division of fees paid among various copyright owners, and may designate common agents to negotiate, agree to, pay, or receive payments.

(1) Any owner of copyright in a work specified in this subsection or any public broadcasting entity may, within one hundred and twenty days after publication of the notice specified in this subsection, submit to the Copyright Royalty Tribunal proposed licenses covering such activities with respect to such works. The Copyright Royalty Tribunal shall proceed on the basis of the proposals submitted to it as well as any other relevant information. The Copyright Royalty Tribunal shall permit any interested party to submit information relevant to such proceedings.

(2) License agreements voluntarily negotiated at any time between one or more copyright owners and one or more public broadcasting entities shall be given effect in lieu of any determination by the Tribunal: Provided, That copies of such agreements are filed in the Copyright Office within thirty days of execution in accordance with regulations that the Register of Copyrights shall prescribe.

(3) Within six months, but not earlier than one hundred and twenty days, from the date of publication of the notice specified in this subsection the Copyright Royalty Tribunal shall make a determination and publish in the Federal Register a schedule of rates and terms which, subject to clause (2) of this subsection, shall be binding on all owners of copyright in works specified by this subsection and public broadcasting entitites, regardless of whether or not such copyright owners and public broadcasting entities have submitted proposals to the Tribunal. In establishing such rates and terms the Copyright Royalty Tribunal may consider the rates for comparable circumstances under voluntary license agreements negotiated as provided in clause (2) of this subsection. The Copyright Royalty Tribunal shall also establish requirements by which copyright owners may receive reasonable notice of the use of their works under this section, and under which records of such use shall be kept by public broadcasting entities.

(4) With respect to the period beginning on the effective date of this title and ending on the date of publication of such rates and terms, this title shall not afford to owners of copyright or public broadcasting entities any greater or lesser rights with respect to the activities specified in subsection (d) as applied to works specified in this subsection than those afforded under the law in effect on December 31, 1977, as held applicable and construed by a court in an action brought under this title.

(c) The initial procedure specified in subsection (b) shall be repeated and concluded between June 30 and December 31, 1982, and at five-year intervals thereafter, in accordance with regulations that the Copyright Royalty Tribunal shall prescribe.

(d) Subject to the transitional provisions of subsection (b)(4), and to the terms of any voluntary license agreements that have been negotiated as provided by subsection (b)(2), a public broadcasting entity may upon compliance with the provisions of this section, including the rates and terms established by the

Copyright Royalty Tribunal under subsection (b)(3), engage in the following activities with respect to published nondramatic musical works and published pictorial, graphic, and sculptural works:

(1) performance or display of a work by or in the course of a transmission made by a noncommercial educational broadcast station referred to in subsection(g); and

(2) production of a transmission program, reproduction of copies or phonorecords of such a transmission program, and distribution of such copies or phonorecords, where such production, reproduction, or distribution is made by a nonprofit institution or organization solely for the purpose of transmissions specified in clause (1); and

(3) the making of reproductions by a governmental body or a nonprofit institution of a transmission program simultaneously with its transmission as specified in clause (1), and the performance or display of the contents of such program under the conditions specified by clause (1) of section 110, but only if the reproductions are used for performances or displays for a period of no more than seven days from the date of the transmission specified in clause (1), and are destroyed before or at the end of such period. No person supplying, in accordance with clause (2), a reproduction of a transmission program to governmental bodies or nonprofit institutions under this clause shall have any liability as a result of failure of such body or institution to destroy such reproduction: Provided, That it shall have notified such body or institution of the requirement for such destruction pursuant to this clause: And provided further, That if such body or institution itself fails to destroy such reproduction it shall be deemed to have infringed.

(e) Except as expressly provided in this subsection, this section shall have no applicability to works other than those specified in subsection (b).

(1) Owners of copyright in nondramatic literary works and public broadcasting entities may, during the course of voluntary negotiations, agree among themselves, respectively, as to the terms and rates of royalty payments without liability under the antitrust laws. Any such terms and rates of royalty payments shall be effective upon filing in the Copyright Office, in accordance with regulations that the Register of Copyrights shall prescribe.

(2) On January 3, 1980, the Register of Copyrights, after consulting with authors and other owners of copyright in nondramatic literary works and their representatives, and with public broadcasting entities and their representatives, shall submit to the Congress a report setting forth the extent to which voluntary licensing arrangements have been reached with respect to the use of nondramatic literary works by such broadcast stations. The report should also describe any problems that may have arisen, and present legislative or other recommendations, if warranted.

(f) Nothing in this section shall be construed to permit, beyond the limits of fair use as provided by section 107, the unauthorized dramatization of a nondramatic musical work, the production of a transmission program drawn to any substantial extent from a published compilation of pictorial, graphic, or sculptural works, or the unauthorized use of any portion of an audiovisual work.

(g) As used in this section, the term "public broadcasting entity" means a noncommercial educational broadcast station as defined in section 397 of title 47 and any nonprofit institution or organization engaged in the activities described in clause (2) of subsection (d).

Chapter 2.—Copyright Ownership and Transfer

Section 201. Ownership of copyright

(a) Initial Ownership.—Copyright in a work protected under this title vests initially in the author or authors of the work. The authors of a joint work are coowners of copyright in the work.

(b) Works Made for Hire.—In the case of a work made for hire, the employer or other person for whom the work was prepared is considered the author for purposes of this title, and, unless the parties have expressly agreed otherwise in a written instrument signed by them, owns all of the rights comprised in the copyright.

(c) Contributions to Collective Works.—Copyright in each separate contribution to a collective work is distinct from copyright in the collective work as a whole, and vests initially in the author of the contribution. In the absence of an express transfer of the copyright or of any rights under it, the owner of copyright in the collective work is presumed to have acquired only the privilege of reproducing and distributing the contribution as part of that particular collective work, and revision of that collective work, and any later collective work in the same series.

(d) Transfer of Ownership.—

(1) The ownership of a copyright may be transferred in whole or in part by any means of conveyance or by operation of law, and may be bequeathed by will or pass as personal property by the applicable laws of intestate succession.

(2) Any of the exclusive rights comprised in a copyright, including any subdivision of any of the rights specified by section 106, may be transferred as provided by clause (1) and owned separately. The owner of any particular exclusive right is entitled, to the extent of that right, to all of the protection and remedies accorded to the copyright owner by this title.

(e) Involuntary Transfer.—When an individual author's ownership of a copyright, or of any of the exclusive rights under a copyright, has not previously been transferred voluntarily by that individual author, no action by any governmental body or other official or organization purporting to seize, expropriate, transfer, or exercise rights of ownership with respect to the copyright, or any of the exclusive rights under a copyright, shall be given effect under this title, except as provided under title 11.

Section 202. Ownership of copyright as distinct from ownership of material object

Ownership of a copyright, or of any of the exclusive rights under a copyright, is distinct from ownership of any material object in which the work is embodied. Transfer of ownership of any material object, including the copy or phonorecord in which the work is first fixed, does not of itself convey any rights in the copyrighted work embodied in the object; nor, in the absence of an agreement, does transfer of ownership of a copyright or of any exclusive rights under a copyright convey property rights in any material object.

Section 203. Termination of transfers and licenses granted by the author

(a) Conditions for Termination.—In the case of any work other than a work made for hire, the exclusive or nonexclusive grant of a transfer or license of copyright or of any right under a copyright, executed by the author on or after January 1, 1978, otherwise than by will, is subject to termination under the following conditions:

(1) In the case of a grant executed by one author, termination of the grant may be effected by that author or, if the author is dead, by the person or persons who, under clause (2) of this subsection, own and are entitled to exercise a total of more than one-half of that author's termination interest. In the case of a grant executed by two or more authors of a joint work, termination of the grant may be effected by a majority of the authors who executed it; if any of such authors is dead, the termination interest of any such author may be exercised as a unit by the person or persons who, under clause (2) of this subsection, own and are entitled to exercise a total of more than one-half of that author's interest.

(2) Where an author is dead, his or her termination interest is owned, and may be exercised, by his widow or her widower and his or her children or grandchildren as follows:

(A) the widow or widower owns the author's entire termination interest unless there are any surviving children or grandchildren of the author, in which case the widow or widower owns one-half of the author's interest;

(B) the author's surviving children, and the surviving children of any dead child of the author, own the author's entire termination interest unless there is a widow or widower, in which case the ownership of one-half of the author's interest is divided among them;

(C) the rights of the author's children and grandchildren are in all cases divided among them and exercised on a per stirpes basis according to the number of such author's children represented; the share of the children of a dead child in a termination interest can be exercised only by the action of a majority of them.

(3) Termination of the grant may be effected at any time during a period of five years beginning at the end of thirty-five years from the date of execution of the grant; or, if the grant covers the right of publication of the work, the period begins at the end of thirty-five years from the date of publication of the work under the grant or at the end of forty years from the date of execution of the grant, whichever term ends earlier.

(4) The termination shall be effected by serving an advance notice in writing, signed by the number and proportion of owners of termination interests required under clauses (1) and (2) of this subsection, or by their duly authorized agents, upon the grantee or the grantee's successor in title.

(A) The notice shall state the effective date of the termination, which shall fall within the five-year period specified by clause (3) of this subsection, and the notice shall be served not less than two or more than ten years before that date. A copy of the notice shall be recorded in the Copyright Office before the effective date of termination, as a condition to its taking effect.

(B) The notice shall comply, in form, content, and manner of service, with requirements that the Register of Copyrights shall prescribe by regulation.

(5) Termination of the grant may be effected notwithstanding any agreement to the contrary, including an agreement to make a will or to make any future grant.

(b) Effect of Termination.—Upon the effective date of termination, all rights under this title that were covered by the terminated grants revert to the author, authors, and other persons owning termination interests under clauses (1) and (2) of subsection (a), including those owners who did not join in signing the notice of termination under clause (4) of subsection (a), but with the following limitations:

(1) A derivative work prepared under authority of the grant before its termination may continue to be utilized under the terms of the grant after its termination, but this privilege does not extend to the preparation after the termination of other derivative works based upon the copyrighted work covered by the terminated grant.

(2) The future rights that will revert upon termination of the grant become vested on the date the notice of termination has been served as provided by clause (4) of subsection (a). The rights vest in the author, authors, and other persons named in, and in the proportionate shares provided by, clauses (1) and (2) of subsection (a).

(3) Subject to the provisions of clause (4) of this subsection, a further grant, or agreement to make a further grant, of any right covered by a terminated grant is valid only if it is signed by the same number and proportion of the owners, in whom the right has vested under clause (2) of this subsection, as are required to terminate the grant under clauses (1) and (2) of subsection (a). Such further grant or agreement is effective with respect to all of the persons in whom the right it covers has vested under clause (2) of this subsection, including those who did not join in signing it. If any person dies after rights under a terminated grant have vested in him or her, that person's legal representatives, legatees, or heirs at law represent him or her for purposes of this clause.

(4) A further grant, or agreement to make a further grant, of any right covered by a terminated grant is valid only if it is made after the effective date of the termination. As an exception, however, an agreement for such a further grant may be made between the persons provided by clause (3) of this subsection and the original grantee or such grantee's successor in title, after the notice of termination has been served as provided by clause (4) of subsection (a).

(5) Termination of a grant under this section affects only those rights covered by the grants that arise under this title, and in no way affects rights arising under any other Federal, State, or foreign laws.

(6) Unless and until termination is effected under this section, the grant, if it does not provide otherwise, continues in effect for the term of copyright provided by this title.

Section 204. Execution of transfers of copyright ownership

(a) A transfer of copyright ownership, other than by operation of law, is not valid unless an instrument of conveyance, or a note or memorandum of the transfer, is in writing and signed by the owner of the rights conveyed or such owner's duly authorized agent.

(b) A certificate of acknowledgement is not required for the validity of a transfer, but is prima facie evidence of the execution of the transfer if—

(1) in the case of a transfer executed in the United States, the certificate is issued by a person authorized to administer oaths within the United States; or

(2) in the case of a transfer executed in a foreign country, the certificate is issued by a diplomatic or consular officer of the United States, or by a person authorized to administer oaths whose authority is proved by a certificate of such an officer.

Section 205. Recordation of transfers and other documents

(a) Conditions for Recordation.—Any transfer of copyright ownership or other document pertaining to a copyright may be recorded in the Copyright Office if the document filed for recordation bears the actual signature of the person who executed it, or if it is accompanied by a sworn or official certification that it is a true copy of the original, signed document.

(b) Certificate of Recordation.—The Register of Copyrights shall, upon receipt of a document as provided by subsection (a) and of the fee provided by section 708, record the document and return it with a certificate of recordation.

(c) Recordation as Constructive Notice.—Recordation of a document in the Copyright Office gives all persons constructive notice of the facts stated in the recorded document, but only if—

(1) the document, or material attached to it, specifically identifies the work to which it pertains so that, after the document is indexed by the Register of Copyrights, it would be revealed by a reasonable search under the title or registration number of the work; and

(2) registration has been made for the work.

(d) Recordation as Prerequisite to Infringement Suit.—No person claiming by virtue of a transfer to be the owner of copyright or of any exclusive right under a copyright is entitled to institute an infringement action under this title until the instrument of transfer under which such person claims has been recorded in the Copyright Office, but suit may be instituted after such recordation on a cause of action that arose before recordation.

(e) Priority Between Conflicting Transfers.—As between two conflicting transfers, the one executed first prevails if it is recorded, in the manner required to give constructive notice under subsection (c), within one month after its execution in the United States or within two months after its execution outside the United States, or at any time before recordation in such manner of the later transfer. Otherwise the later transfer prevails if recorded first in such manner, and if taken in good faith, for valuable consideration or on the basis of a binding promise to pay royalties, and without notice of the earlier transfer.

(f) Priority Between Conflicting Transfer of Ownership and Nonexclusive License.—A nonexclusive license, whether recorded or not, prevails over a conflicting transfer of copyright ownership if the license is evidenced by a written instrument signed by the owner of the rights licensed or such owner's duly authorized agent, and if—

(1) the license was taken before execution of the transfer; or

(2) the license was taken in good faith before recordation of the transfer and without notice of it.

Chapter 3.—Duration of Copyright

Sec. 301: Preemption with respect to other laws.
Sec. 302: Duration of copyright: Works created on or after January 1, 1978.
Sec. 303: Duration of copyright: Works created but not published or copyrighted before January 1, 1978.
Sec. 304: Duration of copyright: Subsisting copyrights.
Sec. 305: Duration of copyright: Terminal date.

Section 301. Preemption with respect to other laws

(a) On and after January 1, 1978, all legal or equitable rights that are equivalent to any of the exclusive rights within the general scope of copyright as specified by section 106 in works of authorship that are fixed in a tangible medium of expression and come within the subject matter of copyright as specified by sections 102 and 103, whether created before or after that date and whether published or unpublished, are governed exclusively by this title. Thereafter, no person is entitled to any such right or equivalent right in any such work under the common law or statutes of any state.

(b) Nothing in this title annuls or limits any rights or remedies under the common law or statutes of any State with respect to—

(1) subject matter that does not come within the subject matter of copyright as specified by sections 102 and 103, including works of authorship not fixed in any tangible medium of expression; or

(2) any cause of action arising from undertakings commenced before January 1, 1978; or

(3) activities violating legal or equitable rights that are not equivalent to any of the exclusive rights within the general scope of copyright as specified by section 106.

(c) With respect to sound recordings fixed before February 15, 1972, any rights or remedies under the common law or statutes of any State shall not be annulled or limited by this title until February 15, 2047. The preemptive provisions of subsection (a) shall apply to any such rights and remedies pertaining to any cause of action arising from undertakings commenced on and after February 15, 2047. Notwithstanding the provisions of section 303, no sound recording fixed before February 15, 1972, shall be subject to copyright under this title before, on, or after February 15, 2047.

(d) Nothing in this title annuls or limits any rights or remedies under any other Federal statute.

Section 302. Duration of copyright: Works created on or after January 1, 1978

(a) In General.—Copyright in a work created on or after January 1, 1978, subsists from its creation and, except as provided by the following subsections, endures for a term consisting of the life of the author and fifty years after the author's death.

(b) Joint Works.—In the case of a joint work prepared by two or more authors who did not work for hire, the copyright endures for a term consisting of the life of the last surviving author and fifty years after such last suviving author's death.

(c) Anonymous Works, Pseudonymous Works, and Works Made for Hire.—In the case of an anonymous work, a pseudonymous work, or a work made for hire, the copyright endures for a term of seventy-five years from the year of its first publication, or a term of one hundred years from the year of its creation, whichever expires first. If, before the end of such term, the identity of one or more of the authors of an anonymous or pseudonymous work is revealed in the records of a registration made for that work under subsections (a) or (d) of section 408, or in the records provided by this subsection, the coyright in the work endures for the term specified by subsection (a) or (b), based on the life of the author or authors whose identity has been revealed. Any person having an interest in the copyright in an anonymous or pseudonymous work may at any time record, in records to be maintained by the Copyright Office for that purpose, a statement identifying one or more authors of the work; the statement shall also identify the person filing it, the nature of that person's interest, the source of the information recorded, and the particular work affected, and shall comply in form and content with requirements that the Register of Copyrights shall prescribe by regulation.

(d) Records Relating to Death of Authors.—Any person having an interest in a copyright may at any time record in the Copyright Office a statement of the date of death of the author of the copyrighted work, or a statement that the author is still living on a particular date. The statement shall identify the person filing it, the nature of that person's interest, and the source of the information recorded, and shall comply in form and content with requirements that the Register of Copyrights shall prescribe by regulation. The Register shall maintain current records of information relating to the death of authors of copyrighted works, based on such recorded statements and, to the extent the Register considers practicable, on data contained in any of the records of the Copyright Office or in other reference sources.

(e) Presumption as to Author's Death.—After a period of seventy-five years from the year of first publication of a work, or a period of one hundred years from the year of its creation, whichever expires first, any person who obtains from the Copyright Office a certified report that the records provided by subsection (d) disclose nothing to indicate that the author of the work is living, or died less than fifty years before, is entitled to the benefit of a presumption that the author has been dead for at least fifty years. Reliance in good faith upon this presumption shall be a complete defense to any action for infringement under this title.

Section 303. Duration of copyright: Works created but not published or copyrighted before January 1, 1978

Copyright in a work created before January 1, 1978, but not theretofore in the public domain or copyrighted, subsists from January 1, 1978, and endures for the term provided by section 302. In no case, however, shall the term of copyright in such a work expire before December 31, 2002; and, if the work is published on or before December 31, 2002, the term of copyright shall not expire before December 31, 2027.

Section 304. Duration of copyright: Subsisting copyrights

(a) Copyrights in Their First Term on January 1, 1978.—Any copyright, the first term of which is subsisting on January 1, 1978, shall endure for twenty-eight years from the date it was originally secured: Provided, That in the case of any posthumous work or of any periodical, cyclopedic, or other composite work upon which the copyright was originally secured by the proprietor thereof, or of any work copyrighted by a corporate body (otherwise than an assignee or licensee of the individual author) or by an employer for whom such work is made for hire, the proprietor of such copyright shall be entitled to a renewal and extension of the copyright in such work for the further term of forty-seven years when application for such renewal and extension shall have been made to the Copyright Office and duly registered therein within one year prior to the expiration of the original term of copyright: And provided further, That in the case of any other copyrighted work, including a contribution by an individual author to a periodical or to a cyclopedic or other composite work, the author of such work, if still living, or the widow, widower, or children of the author, if the author be not living, or if such author, widow, widower, or children be not living, then the author's executors, or in the absence of a will, his or her next of kin shall be entitled to a renewal and extension of the copyright in such work for a further term of forty-seven years when application for such renewal and extension shall have been made to the Copyright Office and duly registered therein within one year prior to the expiration of the original term of copyright: And provided further, That in default of the registration of such applicaton for renewal and extension, the copyright in any work shall terminate at the expiration of twenty-eight years from the date copyright was originally secured.

(b) Copyrights in Their Renewal Term or Registered for Renewal Before January 1, 1978.—The duration of any copyright, the renewal term of which is subsisting at any time between december 31 1976 and December 31, 1977, inclusive, or for which renewal registration is made between December 31, 1976, and December 31, 1977, inclusive, is extended to endure for a term of seventy-five years from the date copyright was originally secured.

(c) Termination of Transfers and Licenses Covering Extended Renewal Term.—In the case of any copyright subsisting in either its first or renewal term on January 1, 1978, other than a copyright in a work made for hire, the exclusive or nonexclusive grant of a transfer or license of the renewal copyright or any right under it, executed before January 1, 1978, by any of the persons designated by the second proviso of subsection (a) of this section, otherwise than by will, is subject to termination under the following conditions:

(1) In the case of a grant executed by a person or persons other than the author, termination of the grant may be effected by the surviving person or persons who executed it. In the case of a grant executed by one or more of the authors of the work, termination of the grant may be effected, to the extent of a particular author's share in the ownership of the renewal copyright, by the author who executed it or, if such author is dead, by the person or persons who, under clause (2) of this subsection, own and are entitled to exercise a total of more than one-half of that author's termination interest.

(2) Where an author is dead, his or her termination interest is owned, and may be exercised, by his widow or her widower and his or her children or grandchildren as follows:

(A) the widow or widower owns the author's entire termination interest unless there are any surviving children or grandchildren of the author, in which case the widow or widower owns one-half of the author's interest;

(B) the author's surviving children, and the surviving children of any dead of the author, own the author's entire termination interest unless there is a widow or widower, in which case the ownership of one-half of the author's interest is divided among them;

(C) the rights of the author's children and grandchildren are in all cases divided among them and exercised on a per stirpes basis according to the number of such author's children represented; the share of the children of a dead child in a termination interest can be exercised only by the action of a majority of them.

(3) Termination of the grant may be effected at any time during a period of five years beginning at the end of fifty-six years from the date copyright was originally secured, or beginning on January 1, 1978, whichever is later.

(4) The termination shall be effected by serving an advance notice in writing upon the grantee or the grantee's successor in title. In the case of a grant executed by a person or persons other than the author, the notice shall be signed by all of those entitled to terminate the grant under clause (1) of this subsection, or by their duly authorized agents. In the case of a grant executed by one or more of the authors of the work, the notice as to any one author's share shall be signed by that author or his or her duly authorized agent or, if that author is dead, by the number and proportion of the owners of his or her termination interest required under clauses (1) and (2) of this subsection, or by their duly authorized agents.

(A) The notice shall state the effective date of the termination, which shall fall within the five-year period specified by clause (3) of this subsection, and the notice shall be served not less than two or more than ten years before that date. A copy of the notice shall be recorded in the Copyright Office before the effective date of termination, as a condition to its taking effect.

(B) The notice shall comply, inform, content, and manner of service, with requirements that the Register of Copyrights shall prescribe by regulation.

(5) Termination of the grant may be effected notwithstanding any agreement to the contrary, including an agreement to make a will or to make any future grant.

(6) In the case of a grant executed by a person or persons other than the author, all rights under this title that were covered by the terminated grant revert, upon the effective date of termination, to all of those entitled to terminate the grant under clause (1) of this subsection. In the case of a grant executed by one or more of the authors of the work, all of a particular author's rights under this title that were covered by the terminated grant revert, upon the effective date of termination, to that author or, if that author is dead, to the persons owning his or her termination interest under clause (2) of this subsection, including those owners who did not join in signing the notice of termination under clause (4) of this subsection. In all cases the reversion of rights is subject to the following limitations:

(A) A derivative work prepared under authority of the grant before its termiation may continue to be utilized under the terms of the grant after its termination, but this privilege does not extend to the preparation after the termination of other derivative works based upon the copyrighted work covered by the terminated grant.

(B) The future rights that will revert upon termination of the grant become vested on the date the notice of termination has been served as provided by clause (4) of this subsection.

(C) Where the author's rights revert to two or more persons under clause (2) of this subsection, they shall vest in those persons in the proportionate shares provided by that clause. In such a case, and subject to the provisions of subclause (D) of this clause, a further grant, or agreement to make a further grant, of a particular author's share with respect to any right covered by a terminated grant is valid only if it is signed by the same number and proportion of the owners, in whom the right has vested under this clause, as are required to terminate the grant under clause (2) of this subsection. Such further grant or agreement is effective with respect to all of the persons in whom the right it covers has vested under this subclause, including those who did not join in signing it. If any person dies after rights under a terminated grant have vested in him or her, that person's legal representatives, legatees, or heirs at law represent him or her for purposes of this subclause.

(D) A further grant, or agreement to make a further grant, of any right covered by a terminated grant is valid only if it is made after the effective date of the termination. As an exception, however, an agreement for such a further grant may be made between the author or any of the persons provided by the first sentence of clause (6) of this subsection, or between the persons provided by subclause (C) of this clause, and the original grantee or such grantee's successor in title, after the notice of termination has been served as provided by clause (4) of this subsection.

(E) Termination of a grant under this subsection affects only those rights covered by the grant that arise under this title, and in no way affect rights arising under any other Federal, State, or foreign laws.

(F) Unless and until termination is effected under this subsection, the grant, if it does not provide otherwise, continues in effect for the remainder of the extended renewal term.

Section 305. Duration of copyright: Terminal date

All terms of copyright provided by sections 302 through 304 run to the end of the calendar year in which they would otherwise expire.

Chapter 4.—Copyright Notice, Deposit, and Registration

Section 401. Notice of copyright: Visually perceptible copies

(a) General Requirement.—Whenever a work protected under this title is published in the United States or elsewhere by authority of the copyright owner, a notice of copyright as provided by this section shall be placed on all publicly distributed copies from which the work can be visually perceived, either directly or with the aid of a machine or device.

(b) Form of Notice.—The notice appearing on the copies shall consist of the following three elements:

(1) the symbol © (the letter C in a circle), or the word "Copyright", or the abbreviation "Copr."; and

(2) the year of first publication of the work; in the case of compilations or derivative works incorporating previously published material, the year date of first publication of the compilation or derivative work is sufficient. The year date may be omitted where a pictorial, graphic, or sculptural work, with accompanying text matter, if any, is reproduced in or on greeting cards, postcards, stationery, jewelry, dolls, toys, or any useful articles; and

(3) the name of the owner of copyright in the work, or an abbreviation by which the name can be recognized, or a generally known alternative designation of the owner.

(c) Position of Notice.—The notice shall be affixed to the copies in such manner and location as to give reasonable notice of the claim of copyright. The Register of Copyrights shall prescribe by regulation, as examples, specific methods of affixation and positions of the notice on various types of works that will satisfy this requirment, but these specifications shall not be considered exhaustive.

Section 402. Notice of copyright: Phonorecords of sound recordings

(a) General Requirement.—Whenever a sound recording protected under this title is published in the United States or elsewhere by authority of the copyright owner, a notice of copyright as provided by this section shall be placed on all publicly distributed phonorecords of the sound recording.

(b) Form of Notice.—The notice appearing on the phonorecords shall consist of the following three elements:

(1) the symbol p [statutory text shows the letter p in a circle] (the letter P in a circle); and

(2) the year of first publication of the sound recording; and

(3) the name of the owner of copyright in the sound recording, or an abbreviation by which the name can be recognized, or a generally known alternative designation of the owner; if the producer of the sound recording is named on the phonorecord labels or containers, and if no other name appears in conjunction with the notice, the producer's name shall be considered a part of the notice.

(c) Position of Notice.—The notice shall be placed on the surface of the phonorecord, or on the phonorecord label or container, in such manner and location as to give reasonable notice of the claim of copyright.

Section 403. Notice of copyright: Publications incorporating United States Government works

Whenever a work is published in copies or phonorecords consisting preponderantly of one or more works of the United States Government, the notice of copyright provided by sections 401 or 402 shall also include a statement identifying, either affirmatively or negatively, those portions of the copies or phonorecords embodying any work or works protected under this title.

Section 404. Notice of copyright: Contributions to collective works

(a) A separate contribution to a collective work may bear its own notice of copyright, as provided by sections 401 through 403. However, a single notice applicable to the collective work as a whole is sufficient to satisfy the requirements of sections 401 through 403 with respect to the separate contributions it contains (not including advertisements inserted on behalf of persons other than the owner of copyright in the collective work), regardless of the ownership of copyright in the contributions and whether or not they have been previously published.

(b) Where the person named in a single notice applicable to a collective work as a whole is not the owner of copyright in a separate contribution that does not bear its own notice, the case is governed by the provisions of section 406 (a)

Section 405. Notice of copyright: Omission of notice

(a) Effect of Omission on Copyright.—The omisson of the copyright notice prescribed by sections 401 through 403 from copies or phonorecords publicly distributed by authority of the copyright owner does not invalidate the copyright in a work if—

(1) the notice has been omitted from no more than a relatively small number of copies or phonorecords distributed to the public; or

(2) registration for the work has been made before or is made within five years after the publication without notice, and a reasonable effort is made to add notice to all copies or phonorecords that are distributed to the public in the United States after the omission has been discovered; or

(3) the notice has been omitted in violation of an express requirement in writing that, as a condition ofthe copyright owner's authorization of the public distribution of copies or phonorecords, they bear the prescribed notice.

(b) Effect of Omission on Innocent Infringers.—Any person who innocently infringes a copyright, in reliance upon an authorized copy or phonorecord from which the copyright notice has been omitted, incurs no liability for actual or statutory damages under section 504 for any infringing acts committed before receiving actual notice that registration for the work has been made under section 408, if such person proves that he or she was misled by the omission of notice. In a suit for infringement in such a case the court may allow or disallow recovery of any of the infringer's profits attributable to the infringement, and may enjoin the continuation of the infringing undertaking or may require, as a condition or permitting the continuation of the infringing undertaking, that the infringer pay the copyright owner a reasonable license fee in an amount and on terms fixed by the court.

(c) Removal of Notice.—Protection under this title is not affected by the removal, destruction, or obliteration of the notice, without the authorization of the copyright owner, from any publicly distributed copies or phonorecords.

Section 406. Notice of copyright: Error in name or date

(a) Error in Name.—Where the person named in the copyright notice on copies or phonorecords publicly distributed by authority of the copyright owner is not the owner of copyright, the validity and ownership of the copyright are not affected. In such a case, however, any person who innocently begins an undertaking that infringes the copyright has a complete defense to any action for such infringement if such person proves that he or she was misled by the notice and began the undertaking in good faith under a purported transfer or license from the person named therein, unless before the undertaking was begun—

(1) registration for the work has been made in the name of the owner of copyright; or

(2) a document executed by the person named in the notice and showing the ownership of the copyright had been recorded.

The person named in the notice is liable to account to the copyright owner for all receipts from transfers or licenses purportedly made under the coyright by the person named in the notice.

(b) Error in Date.—When the year date in the notice on copies or phonorecords distribued by authority of the copyright owner is earlier than the year in which publication first occurred, any period computed from the year of first publication under section 302 is to be computed from the year in the notice. Where the year date is more than one year later than the year in which publication first ocurred, the work is considered to have been published without any notice and is governed by the provisions of section 405.

(c) Omisson of Name or Date.—Where copies or phonorecords publicly distributed by authority of the copyright owner contain no name or no date that could reasonably be considered a part of the notice, the work is considered to have been published without any notice and is governed by the provisions of section 405.

Section 407. Deposit of copies or phonorecords for Library of Congress

(a) Except as provided by subsection (c), and subject to the provisions of subsection (e), the owner of copyright or of the exclusive right of publication in a work published with notice of copyright in the United States shall deposit, within three months after the date of such publication—

(1) two complete copies of the best edition; or

(2) if the work is a sound recording, two complete phonorecords of the best edition, together with any printed or other visually perceptible material published with such phonorecords.

Neither the deposit requirements of this subsection nor the acquisition provisions of subsection (e) are conditions of copyright protection.

(b) The required copies or phonorecords shall be deposited in the Copyright Office for the use or disposition of the Library of Congress. The Register of Copyrights shall, when requested by the depositor and upon payment of the fee prescribed by section 708, issue a receipt for the deposit.

(c) The Register of Copyrights may by regulation exempt any categories of material from the deposit requirements of this section, or require deposit of only one copy or phonorecord with respect to any categories. Such regulations shall provide either for complete exemption from the deposit requirements of this section, or for alternative forms of deposit aimed at providing a satisfactory archival record of a work without imposing practical or financial hardships on the depositor, where the individual author is the owner of copyright in a pictorial, graphic, or sculptural work and (i) less than five copies of the work have been published, or (ii) the work has been published in a limited edition consisting of numbered copies, the monetary value of which would make the mandatory deposit of two copies of the best edition of the work burdensome, unfair, or unreasonable.

(d) At any time after publication of a work as provided by subsection (a), the Register of Copyrights may make written demand for the required deposit on any of the persons obligated to make the deposit under subsection (a). Unless deposit is made within three months after the demand is received, the person or persons on whom the demand was made are liable—

(1) to a fine of not more than $250 for each work; and

(2) to pay into a specially designated fund in the Library of Congress the total retail price of the copies or phonorecords demanded, or, if no retail price has been fixed, the reasonable cost of the Library of Congress of acquiring them; and

(3) to pay a fine of $2,500, in addition to any fine or liability imposed under clauses (1) and (2), if such person willfully or repeatedly fails or refuses to comply with such a demand.

(e) With respect to transmission programs that have been fixed and transmitted to the public in the United States but have not been published, the Register of Copyrights shall, after consulting with the Librarian of Congress and other interested organizations and officials, establish regulations governing the acquisition, through deposit or otherwise, of copies or phonorecords of such programs for the collections of the Library of Congress.

(1) The Librarian of Congress shall be permitted, under the standards and conditions set forth in such regulations, to make a fixation of a transmission program directly from a transmission to the public, and to reproduce one copy or phonorecord from such fixation for archival purposes.

(2) Such regulations shall also provide standards and procedures by which the Register of Copyrights may make written demand, upon the owner of the right of transmission in the United States, for the deposit of a copy or phonorecord of a specific transmission program. Such deposit may, at the option of the owner of the right of transmission in the United States, be accomplished by gift, by loan for purposes of reproduction, or by sale at a price not to exceed the cost of reproducing and supplying the copy or phonorecord. The regulations established under this clause shall provide reasonable periods of not less than three months for compliance with a demand, and shall allow for extensions of such periods and adjustments in the scope of the demand or the methods for fulfilling it, as reasonably warranted by the circumstances. Willful failure or refusal to comply with the conditions prescribed by such regulations shall subject the owner of the right of transmission in the United States to liability for an amount, not to exceed the cost of reproducing and supplying the copy or phonorecord in question, to be paid into a specially designated fund in the Library of Congress.

(3) Nothing in this subsection shall be construed to require the making or retention, for purposes of deposit, of any copy or phonorecord of an unpublished transmission program, the transmission of which occurs before the receipt of a specific written demand as provided by clause (2).

(4) No activity undertaken in compliance with regulations prescribed under clauses (1) or (2) of this subsection shall result in liability if intended solely to assist in the acquisition of copies or phonorecords under this subsection.

Section 408. Copyright registration in general

(a) Registration Permissive.—At any time during the subsistence of copyright in any published or unublished work, the owner of copyright or of any exclusive right in the work may obtain registration of the copyright claim by delivering to the Copyright Office the deposit specified by this section, together with the application and fee specified by sections 409 and 708. Subject to the provisions of section 405(a), such registration is not a condition of copyright protection.

(b) Deposit for Copyright Registration.—Except as provided by subsection (c), the material deposited for registration shall include—

(1) in the case of an unpublished work, one complete copy or phonorecord;

(2) in the case of a published work, two complete copies or phonorecords of the best edition;

(3) in the case of a work first published outside the United States, one complete copy or phonorecord as so published;

(4) in the case of a contribution to a collective work, one complete copy or phonorecord of the best edition of the collective work.

Copies or phonorecords deposited for the Library of Congress under section 407 may be used to satisfy the deposit provisions of this section, if they are acompanied by the prescribed application and fee, and by any additional identifying material that the Register may, by regulation require. The Register shall also prescribe regulations establishing requirements under which copies or phonorecords acquired for the Library of Congress under subsection (e) of section 407, otherwise than by deposit, may be used to satisfy the deposit provisions of this section.

(c) Administrative Classification and Optional Deposit.—

(1) The Register of Copyrights is authorized to specify by regulation the administrative classes into which works are to be placed for purposes of deposit and registration, and the nature of the copies or phonorecords to be deposited in the various classes specified. The regulations may require or permit, for particular classes, the deposit of identifying material instead of copies or phonorecords, the deposit of only one copy or phonorecord where two would normally be required, or a single registration for a group of related works. This administrative classification of works has no significance with respect to the subject matter of copyright or the exclusive rights provided by this title.

(2) Without prejudice to the general authority provided under clause (1), the Register of Copyrights shall establish regulations specifically permitting a single registration for a group of works by the same individual author, all first published as contributions to periodicals, including newspapers, within a twelve-month period, on the basis of a single deposit, application, and registration fee, under all of the following conditions—

(A) if each of the works as first published bore a   separate copyright notice, and the name of the owner of copyright in the work, or an abbreviation by which the name can be recognized, or a generally known alternative designation of the owner was the same in each notice; and

(B) if the deposit consists of one copy of the entire issue of the periodical, or of the entire section in the case of a newspaper, in which each   contribution was first published; and

(C) if the application identifies each work   separately, including the periodical containing it and its date of first publication.

(3) As an alternative to separate renewal registrations under subsection (a) of section 304, a single renewal registration may be made for a group of works by the same individual author, all first published as contributions to periodicals, including newspapers, upon the filing of a single application and fee, under all of the following conditions:

(A) the renewal claimant or claimants, and the basis of claim or claims under section 304(a), is the same for each of the works; and

(B) the works were all copyrighted upon their first publication, either through separate copyright notice and registration or by virtue of a general copyright notice in the periodical issue as a whole; and

(C) the renewal application and fee are received not more than twenty-eight or less than twenty-seven years after the thirty-first day of December of the calendar year in which all of the works were first published; and

(D) the renewal application identifies each work separately, including the periodical containing it and its date of first publication.

(d) Corrections and Amplifications.—The Register may also establish, by regulation, formal procedures for the filing of an applicaton for supplementary registration, to correct an error in a copyright registration or to amplify the information given in a registration. Such application shall be accompanied by the fee provided by section 708, and shall clearly identify the registration to be corrected or amplified. The information contained in a supplementary registration augments but does not supersede that contained in the earlier registration.

(e) Published Edition of Previously Registered Work.—Registration for the first published edition of a work previously registered in unpublished form may be made even though the work as published is substantially the same as the unpublished version.

Section 409. Application for copyright registration

The application for copyright registration shall be made on a form prescribed by the Register of Copyrights and shall include—

(1) the name and address of the copyright claimant;

(2) in the case of a work other than an anonymous or pseudonymous work, the name and nationality or domicile of the author or authors, and, if one or more of the authors is dead, the dates of their deaths;

(3) if the work is anonymous or pseudonymous, the nationality or domicile of the author or authors;

(4) in the case of a work made for hire, a statement to this effect;

(5) if the copyright claimant is not the author, a brief statement of how the claimant obtained ownership of the copyright;

(6) the title of the work, together with any previous or alternative titles under which the work can be identified;

(7) the year in which creation of the work was completed;

(8) if the work has been published, the date and nation of its first publication;

(9) in the case of a compilation or derivative work, an identification of any preexisting work or works that it is based on or incorporates, and a brief, general statement of the additional material covered by the copyright claim being registered;

(10) in the case of a published work containing material of which copies are required by section 601 to be manufactured in the United States, the names of the persons or organizations who performed the processes specified by subsection (c) of section 601 with respect to that material, and the places where those processes were performed; and

(11) any other information regarded by the Register of Copyrights as bearing upon the preparation or identification of the work or the existence, ownership, or duration of the copyright.

Section 410. Registration of claim and issuance of certificate

(a) When, after examination, the Register of Copyrights determines that, in accordance with the provisions of this title, the material deposited constitutes copyrightable subject matter and that the other legal and formal requirements of this title have been met, the Register shall register the claim and issue to the applicant a certificate of registration under the seal of the Copyright Office. The certificate shall contain the information given in the application, together with the number and effective date of the registration.

(b) In any case in which the Register of Copyrights determines that, in accordance with the provisions of this title, the material deposited does not constitute copyrightable subject matter or that the claim is invalid for any other reason, the Register shall refuse registration and shall notify the applicant in writing of the reasons for such refusal.

(c) In any judicial proceedings the certificate of a registration made before or within five years after first publication of the work shall constitute prima facie evidence of the validity of the copyright and of the facts stated in the certificate. The evidentiary weight to be accorded the certificate of a registration made thereafter shall be within the discretion of the court.

(d) The effective date of a copyright registration is the day on which an application, deposit, and fee, which are later determined by the Register of Copyrights or by a court of competent jurisdiction to be acceptable for registration, have all been received in the Copyright Office.

Section 411. Registration as prerequisite to infringement suit

(a) Subject to the provisions of subsection (b), no action for infringement of the copyright in any work shall be instituted until registration of the copyright claim has been made in accordance with this title. In any case, however, where the deposit, application, and fee required for registration have been delivered to the Copyright Office in proper form and registration has been refused, the applicant is entitled to institute an action for infringement if notice thereof, with a copy of the complaint, is served on the Register of Copyrights. The Register may, at his or her option, become a party to the action with respect to the issue of registrability of the copyright claim by entering an appearance within sixty days after such service, but the Register's failure to become a party shall not deprive the court of jurisdiction to determine that issue.

(b) In the case of a work consisting of sounds, images, or both, the first fixation of which is made simultaneously with its transmission, the copyright owner may, either before or after such fixation takes place, institute an action for infringement under section 501, fully subject to the remedies provided by sections 502 through 506 and sections 509 and 510, if, in accordance with requirements that the Register of Copyrights shall prescribe by regulation, the copyright owner—

(1) serves notice upon the infringer, not less than ten or more than thirty days before such fixation, identifying the work and the specific time and source of its first transmission, and declaring an intention to secure copyright in the work; and

(2) makes registration for the work within three months after its first transmission.

Section 412. Registration as prerequisite to certain remedies for infringement

In any action under this title, other than an action instituted under section 411(b), no award of statutory damages or of attorney's fees, as provided by sections 504 and 505, shall be made for—

(1) any infringement of copyright in an unpublished work commenced before the effective date of its registration; or

(2) any infringement of copyright commenced after first publication of the work and before the effective date of its registration, unless such registration is made within three months after the first publication of the work.

Chapter 5.—Copyright Infringement and Remedies

Sec. 501: Infringement of copyright.
Sec. 502: Remedies for infringement: Injunctions.
Sec. 503: Remedies for infringement: Impunding and disposition of infringing articles.
Sec. 504: Remedies for infringement: Damage and profits.
Sec. 505: Remedies for infringement: Costs and attorney's fees.
Sec. 506: Criminal offenses.
Sec. 507: Limitations on actions.
Sec. 508: Notification of filing and determination of actions.
Sec. 509: Seizure and forfeiture.
Sec. 510: Remedies for alteration of programing by cable systems.

Section 501. Infringement of Copyright

(a) Anyone who violates any of the exclusive rights of the copyright owner as provided by sections 106 through 118, or who imports copies or phonorecords into the United States in violation of section 602, is an infringer of the copyright.

(b) The legal or beneficial owner of an exclusive right under a copyright is entitled, subject to the requirements of sections 205(d) and 411, to institute an action for any infringement of that particular right committed while he or she is the owner of it. The court may require such owner to serve written notice of the action with a copy of the complaint upon any person shown, by the records of the Copyright Office or otherwise, to have or claim an interest in the copyright, and shall require that such notice be served upon any person whose interest is likely to be affected by a decision in the case. The court may require the joinder, and shall permit the intervention, of any person having or claiming an interest in the copyright.

(c) For any secondary transmission by a cable system that embodies a performance or a display of a work which is actionable as an act of infringement under subsection (c) of section 111, a television broadcast station holding a copyright or other license to transmit or perform the same version of that work shall, for purposes of subsection (b) of this section, be treated as a legal or beneficial owner if such secondary transmission occurs within the local service area of that television station.

(d) For any secondary transmission by a cable system that is actionable as an act of infringement pursuant to section 111(c)(3), the following shall also have standing to sue: (i) the primary transmitter whose transmission has been altered by the cable system; and (ii) any broadcast station within whose local service area the secondary transmission occurs.

Section 502. Remedies for infringement: Injunctions

(a) Any court having jurisdiction of a civil action arising under this title may, subject to the provisions of section 1498 of title 28, grant temporary and final injunctions on such terms as it may deem reasonable to prevent or restrain infringement of a copyright.

(b) Any such injunction may be served anywhere in the United States on the person enjoined; it shall be operative throughout the United States and shall be enforceable, by proceedings in contempt or otherwise, by any United States court having jurisdiction of that person. The clerk of the court granting the injunction shall, when requested by any other court in which enforcement of the injunction is sought, transmit promptly to the other court a certified copy of all the papers in the case on file in such clerk's office.

Section 503. Remedies for infringement: Impounding and disposition of infringing articles

(a) At any time while an action under this title is pending, the court may order the impounding, on such terms as it may deem reasonable, of all copies or phonorecords claimed to have been made or used in violation of the copyright owner's exclusive rights, and of all plates, molds, matrices, masters, tapes, film negatives, or other articles by means of which such copies or phonorecords may be reproduced.

(b) As part of a final judgment or decree, the court may order the destruction or other reasonable disposition of all copies or phonorecords found to have been made or used in violation of the copyright owner's exclusive rights, and of all plates, molds, matrices, masters, tapes, film negatives, or other articles by means of which such copies or phonorecords may be reproduced.

Section 504. Remedies for infringement: Damages and profits

(a) In General.—Except as otherwise provided by this title, an infringer of copyright is liabile for either—

(1) the copyright owner's actual damages and any additional profits of the infringer, as provided by subsection (b); or

(2) statutory damages, as provided by subsection (c).

(b) Actual Damages and Profits.—The copyright owner is entitled to recover the actual damages suffered by him or her as a result of the infringement, and any profits of the infringer that are attributable to the infringement and are not taken into account in computing the actual damages. In establishing the infringer's profits, the copyright owner is required to present proof only of the infringer's gross revenue, and the infringer is required to prove his or her deductible expenses and the elements of profit attributable to factors other than the copyrighted work.

(c) Statutory Damages.—

(1) Except as provided by clause (2) of this subsection, the copyright owner may elect, at any time before final judgment is rendered, to recover, instead of actual damages and profits, an award of statutory damages for all infringements involved in the action, with respect to any one work, for which any one infringer is liable individually, or for which any two or more infringers are liable jointly and severally, in a sum of not less than $250 or more than $10,000 as the court considers just. For the purposes of this subsection, all the parts of a compilation or derivative work constitute one work.

(2) In a case where the copyright owner sustains the burden of proving, and the court finds, that infringement was committed willfully, the court in its discretion may increase the award of statutory damages to a sum of not more than $50,000. In a case where the infringer sustains the burden of proving, and the court finds, that such infringer was not aware and had no reason to believe that his or her acts constituted an infringement of copyright, the court it its discretion may reduce the award of statutory damages to a sum of not less than $100. The court shall remit statutory damages in any case where an infringer believed and had reasonable grounds for believing that his or her use of the copyrighted work was a fair use under section 107, if the infringer was: (i) an employee or agent of a nonprofit educational instiution, library, or archives acting within the scope of his or her employment who, or such institution, library, or archives itself, which infringed by reproducing the work in copies or phonorecords; or (ii) a public broadcasting entity which or a person who, as a regular part of the nonprofit activities of a public infringed by performing a published nondramatic literary work or by reproducing a transmission program embodying a performance of such a work.

Section 505. Remedies for infringement: Costs and attorney's fees

In any civil action under this title, the court in its discretion may allow the recovery of full costs by or against any party other than the United States or an officer thereof. Except as otherwise provided in this title, the court may also award a reasonable attorney's fee to the prevailing party as part of the costs.

Section 506. Criminal offenses

(a) Criminal Infringement.—Any person who infringes a copyright willfully and for purposes of commercial advantage or private financial gain shall be punished as provided in section 2319 of title 18.

(b) Forfeiture and Destruction.—When any person is convicted of any violation of subsection (a), the court in its judgment of conviction shall, in addition to the penalty therein prescribed, order the forfeiture and destruction or other disposition of all infringing copies or phonorecords and all implements, devices, or equipment used in the manufacture of such infringing copies or phonorecords.

(c) Fraudulent Copyright Notice.—Any person who, with fraudulent intent, places on any article a notice of copyright or words of the same purport that such person knows to be false, or who, with fraudulent intent, publicly distributes or imports for public distribution any article bearing such notice or words that such person knows to be false, shall be fined not more than $2,500.

(d) Any person who, with fraudulent intent, removes or alters any notice of copyright appearing on a copy of a copyrighted work shall be fined not more than $2,500.

(e) False Representation.—Any person who knowingly makes a false representation of a material fact in the application for copyright registration provided for by section 409, or in any written statement filed in connection with the application, shall be fined not more than $2,500.

Section 507. Limitations on actions

(a) Criminal Proceedings.—No criminal proceeding shall be maintained under the provisions of this title unless it is commenced within three years after the cause of action arose.

(b) Civil Actions.—No civil action shall be maintained under the provisions of this title unless it is commenced within three years after the claim accrued.

Section 508. Notification of filing and determination of actions

(a) Within one month after the filing of any action under this title, the clerks of the courts of the United States shall send written notification to the Register of Copyrights setting forth, as far as is shown by the papers filed in the court, the names and addresses of the parties and the title, author, and registration number of each work involved in the action. If any other copyrighted work is later included in the action by amendment, answer, or other pleading, the clerk shall also send a notification concerning it to the Register within one month after the pleading is filed.

(b) Within one month after any final order or judgment is issued in the case, the clerk of the court shall notify the Register of it, sending with the notification a copy of the order or judgment together with the written opinion, if any, of the court.

(c) Upon receiving the notifications specified in this section, the Register shall make them a part of the public records of the Copyright Office.

Section 509. Seizure and forfeiture

(a) All copies or phonorecords manufactured, reproduced, distributed, sold, or otherwise used, intended for use, or possessed with intent to use in violation of section 506(a), and all plates, molds, matrices, masters, tapes, film negatives, or other articles by means of which such copies or phonorecords may be reproduced, and all electronic, mechanical, or other devices for manufacturing, reproducing, or assembling such copies or phonorecords may be seized and forfeited to the United States.

(b) The applicable procedures relating to (i) the seizure, summary and judicial forfeiture, and condemnation of vessels, vehicles, merchandise, and baggage for violations of the customs laws contained in title 19, (ii) the disposition of such vessels, vehicles, merchandise, and baggage or the proceeds from the sale thereof, (iii) the remission or mitigation of such forfeiture, (iv) the compromise of claims, and (v) the award of compensation to informers in respect of such forfeitures, shall apply to seizures and forfeitures incurred, or alleged to have been incurred, under the provisions of this section, insofar as applicable and not inconsistent with the provisions of this section; except that such duties as are imposed upon any officer or employee of the Treasury Department or any other person with respect to the seizure and forfeiture of vessels, vehicles, merchandise; and baggage under the provisions of the customs laws contained in title 19 shall be performed with respect to seizure and forfeiture of all articles described in sub-section (a) by such officers, agents, or other persons as may be authorized or designated for that purpose by the Attorney General.

Section 510. Remedies for alteration of programing by cable systems

(a) In any action filed pursuant to section 111(c)(3), the following remedies shall be available:

(1) Where an action is brought by a party identified in subsections (b) or (c) of section 501, the remedies provided by sections 502 through 505, and the remedy provided by sub-section (b) of this section; and

(2) When an action is brought by a party identified in subsection (d) of section 501, the remedies provided by sections 502 and 505, together with any actual damages suffered by such party as a result of the infringement, and the remedy provided by subsection (b)of this section.

(b) In any action filed pursuant to section 111(c)(3), the court may decree that, for a period not to exceed thirty days, the cable system shall be deprived of the benefit of a compulsory license for one or more distant signals carried by such cable system.

Chapter 6.—Manufacturing Requirements and Importation

Sec. 601: Manufacture, importation, and public distribution of certain copies.
Sec. 602: Infringing importation of copies or phonorecords.
Sec. 603: Importation prohibitions: Enforcement and disposition of excluded articles.

Section 601. Manufacture, Importation and Public Distribution of Certain Copies

(a) Prior to July 1, 1986, and except as provided by subsection (b), the importation into or public dis-tribution in the United States of copies of a work consisting preponderantly of nondramtic literary mate-rial that is in the English language and is protected under this title is prohibited unless the portions consisting of such material have been manufactured in the United States or Canada.

(b) The provisions of subsection (a) do not apply—

(1) where, on the date when importation is sought or public distribution in the United States is made, the author of any substantial part of such material is neither a national nor a domiciliary of the United States or, if such author is a national of the United States, he or she has been domiciled outside the United States for a continuous period of at least one year immediately preceding that date; in the case of a work made for hire, the exemption provided by this clause does not apply unless a substantial part of the work was prepared for an employer or other person who is not a national or domiciliary of the United States or a domes-tic corporation or enterprise;

(2) where the United States Customs Service is presented with an import statement issued under the seal of the Copyright Office, in which case a total of no more than two thousand copies of any one such work shall be allowed entry; the import statement shall be issued upon request to the copyright owner or to a person designated by such owner at the time of regis-tration for the work under section 408 or at any time thereafter;

(3) where importation is sought under the authority or for the use, other than in schools, of the Government of the United States or of any State or political subdivision of a State;

(4) where importation, for use and not for sale, is sought—

(A) by any person with respect to no more than one copy of any work at any one time;

(B) by any person arriving from outside the United States, with respect to copies forming part of such person's personal baggage; or

(C) by an organization operated for scholarly, educational, or religious purposes and not for private gain, with respect to copies intended to form a part of its library;

(5) where the copies are reproduced in raised characters for the use of the blind; or

(6) where, in addition to copies imported under clauses (3) and (4) of this subsection, no more than two thousand copies of any one such work, which have not been manufactured in the United States or Canada, are publicly distributed in the United States; or

(7) where, on the date when importation is sought or public distribution in the United States is made—

(A) the author of any substantial part of such material is an individual and receives compensation for the transfer or license of the right to distribute the work in the United States; and

(B) the first publication of the work has previously taken place outside the United States under a transfer or license granted by such author to a transferee or licensee who was not a national or domiciliary of the United States or a domestic corporation or enterprise; and

(C) there has been no publication of an authorized edition of the work of which the copies were manufactured in the United States; and

(D) the copies were reproduced under a transfer or license granted by such author or by the transferee or licensee of the right of first publication as mentioned in subclause (B), and the transferee or the licensee of the right of reproduction was not a national or domiciliary of the United States or a domestic corporation or enterprise.

(c) The requirement of this section that copies be manufactured in the United States or Canada is satisfied if—

(1) in the case where the copies are printed directly from type that has been set, or directly from plates made from such type, the setting of the type and the making of the plates have been performed in the United States or Canada; or

(2) in the case where the making of plates by a lithographic or photoengraving process is a final or intermediate step preceding the printing of the copies, the making of the plates has been performed in the United States or Canada; and

(3) in any case, the printing or other final process of producing multiple copies and any binding of the copies have been performed in the United States or Canada.

(d) Importation or public distribution of copies in violation of this section does not invalidate protection for a work under this title. However, in any civil action or criminal proceeding for infringement of the exclusive rights to reproduce and distribute copies of the work, the infringer has a complete defense with respect to all of the nondramatic literary material comprised in the work and any other parts of the work in which the exclusive rights to reproduce and distribute copies are owned by the same person who owns such exclusive rights in the nondramatic literary material, if the infringer proves—

(1) that copies of the work have been imported into or publicly distributed in the United States in violation of this section by or with the authority of the owner of such exclusive rights; and

(2) that the infringing copies were manufactured in the United States or Canada in accordance with the provisions of subsection (c); and

(3) that the infringement was commenced before the effective date of registration for an authorized edition of the work, the copies of which have been manufactured in the United States or Canada in accordance with the provisions of subsection (c).

(e) In any action for infringement of the exclusive rights to reproduce and distribute copies of a work containing material required by this section to be manufactured in the United States or Canada, the copyright owner shall set forth in the complaint the names of the persons or organizations who performed the processes specified by subsection (c) with respect to that material, and the places where those processes were performed.

Section 602. Infringing importation of copies or phonorecords

(a) Importation into the United States, without the authority of the owner of copyright under this title, of copies or phonorecords of a work that have been acquired outside the United States is an infringement of the exclusive right to distribute copies or phonorecords under section 106, actionable under section 501. This subsection does not apply to—

(1) importation of copies or phonorecords under the authority or for the use of the Government of the United States or of any State or political subdivision of a State, but not including copies or phonorecords for use in schools, or copies of any audiovisual work imported for purposes other than archival use;

(2) importation, for the private use of the importer and not for distribution, by any person with respect to no more than one copy or phonorecord of any one work at any one time, or by any person arriving from outside the United States with respect to copies or phonorecords forming part of such peson's personal baggage; or

(3) importation by or for an organization operatedfor scholarly, educational, or religious purposes and notfor private gain, with respect to no more than one copyof an audiovisual work solely for its archival purposes,and no more than five copies or phonorecords of anyother work for its library lending or archival purposes,unless the importation of such copies or phonorecords ispart of an activity consisting of systematic reproductionor distribution, engaged in by such organization inviolation of the provisions of section 108(g)(2).

(b) In a case where the making of the copies or phonorecords would have constituted an infringement of copyright if this title had been applicable, their importation is prohibited. In a case where the copies or phonorecords were lawfuly made, the United States Customs Service has no authority to prevent their importatin unless the provisions of section 601 are applicable. In either case, the Secretary of the Treasury is authorized to prescribe, by regulation, a procedure under which any person claiming an interest in the copyright in a particular work may, upon payment of a specified fee, be entitled to notification by the Customs Service of the importation of articles that appear to be copies or phonorecords of the work.

Section 603. Importation prohibitions: Enforcement anddisposition of excluded articles

(a) The Secretary of the Treasury and the United States Postal Service shall separately or jointly make regulations for the enforcement of the provisions of this title prohibiting importation.

(b) These regulations may require, as a condition for the exclusion of articles under section 602—

(1) that the person seeking exclusion obtain a court order enjoining importation of the articles; or

(2) that the person seeking exclusion furnish proof, of a specified nature and in accordance with prescribed procedures, that the copyright in which such person claims an interest is valid and that the importation would violate the prohibiton in section 602; the person seeking exclusion may also be required to post a surety bond for any injury that may result if the detention or exclusion of the articles proves to be unjustified.

(c) Articles imported in violation of the importation prohibitions of this title are subject to seizure and forfeiture in the same manner as property imported in violation of the customs revenue laws. Forfeited articles shall be destroyed as directed by the Secretary of the Treasury or the court, as the case may be; however, the articles may be returned to the country of export whenever it is shown to the satisfaction of the Secretary of the Treasury that the importer had no reasonable grounds for believing that his or her acts constituted a violation of law.

Chapter 7.—Copyright Office

Section 701. The Copyright Office: General Responsibilities and Organization

(a) All administrative functions and duties under this title, except as otherwise specified, are the responsibility of the Register of Copyrights as director of the Copyright Office of the Library of Congress. The Register of Copyrights, together with the subordinate officers and employees of the Copyright Office, shall be appointed by the Librarian of Congress, and shall act under the Librarian's general direction and supervision.

(b) The Register of Copyrights shall adopt a seal to be used on and after January 1, 1978, to authenticate all certified documents issued by the Copyright Office.

(c) The Register of Copyrights shall make an annual report to the Librarian of Congress of the work and accomplishments of the Copyright Office during the previous fiscal year. The annual report of the Register of Copyrights shall be published separately and as a part of the annual report of the Librarian of Congress.

(d) Except as provided by section 706(b) and the regulations issued thereunder, all actions taken by the Register of Copyrights under this title are subject to the provisions of the Administrative Procedure Act of June 11, 1946, as amended (c. 324, 60 Stat. 237, title 5, United States Code, Chapter 5, Subchapter II and Chapter 7).

Section 702. Copyright Office regulations

The Register of Copyrights is authorized to establish regulations not inconsistent with law for the administration of the functions and duties made the responsibility of the Register under this title. All regulations established by the Register under this title are subject to the approval of the Librarian of Congress.

Section 703. Effective date of actions in Copyright Office

In any case in which time limits are prescribed under this title for the performance of an action in the Copyright Office, and in which the last day of the prescribed period falls on a Saturday, Sunday, holiday, or other nonbusiness day within the District of Columbia or the Federal Government, the action may be taken on the next succeeding business day, and is effective as of the date when the period expired.

Section 704. Retention and disposition of articles deposited in Copyright Office

(a) Upon their deposit in the Copyright Office under sections 407 and 408, all copies, phonorecords, and identifying material, including those deposited in connection with claims that have been refused registration, are the property of the United States Government.

(b) In the case of published works, all copies, phonorecords, and identifying material deposited are available to the Library of Congress for its collections, or for exchange or transfer to any other library. In the case of unpublished works, the Library is entitled, under regulations that the Register of Copyrights shall prescribe, to select any deposits for its collections or for transfer to the National Archives of the United States or to a Federal records center, as defined in section 2901 of title 44.

(c) The Register of Copyrights is authorized, for specific or general categories of works, to make a facsimile reproduction of all or any part of the material deposited under section 408, and to make such reproduction a part of the Copyright Office records of the registration, before transferring such material to the Library of Congress as provided by subsection (b), or before destroying or otherwise disposing of such material as provided by subsection (d).

(d) Deposits not selected by the Library under subsection (b), or identifying portions or reproductions of them, shall be retained under the control of the Copyright Office, including retention in government storage facilities, for the longest period considered practicable and desirable by the Register of Copyrights and the Librarian of Congress. After that period it is within the joint discretion of the Register and the Librarian to order their destruction or other disposition; but, in the case of unpublished works, no deposit shall be knowingly or intentionally destroyed or otherwise disposed of during its term of copyright unless a facsimile reproduction of the entire deposit has been made a part of the Copyright Office records as provided by subsection (c).

(e) The depositor of copies, phonorecords, or identifying material under section 408, or the copyright owner of record, may request retention, under the control of the Copyright Office, of one or more of such articles for the full term of copyright in the work. The Register of Copyrights shall prescribe, by regulation, the conditions under which such requests are to be made and granted, and shall fix the fee to be charged under section 708(a)(11) if the request is granted.

Section 705. Copyright Office records: Preparation, maintenance, public inspection, and searching

(a) The Register of Copyrights shall provide and keep in the Copyright Office records of all deposits, registrations, recordations, and other actions taken under this title, and shall prepare indexes of all such records.

(b) Such records and indexes, as well as the articles deposited in connection with completed copyright registrations and retained under the control of the Copyright Office, shall be open to public inspection.

(c) Upon request and payment of the fee specified by section 708, the Copyright Office shall make a search of its public records, indexes, and deposits, and shall furnish a report of the information they disclose with respect to any particular deposits, registrations, or recorded documents.

Section 706. Copies of Copyright Office records

(a) Copies may be made of any public records or indexes of the Copyright Office; additional certificates of copyright registration and copies of any public records or indexes may be furnished upon request and payment of the fees specified by section 708.

(b) Copies or reproductions of deposited articles retained under the control of the Copyright Office shall be authorized or furnished only under the conditions specified by the Copyright Office regulations.

Section 707. Copyright Office forms and publications

(a) Catalog of Copyright Entries.—The Register of Copyrights shall compile and publish at periodic intervals catalogs of all copyright registrations. These catalogs shall be divided into parts in accordance with the various classes of works, and the Register has discretion to determine, on the basis of practicability and usefulness, the form and frequency of publication of each particular part.

(b) Other Publications.—The Register shall furnish, free of charge upon request, application forms for copyright registration and general informational material in connection with the functions of the Copyright Office. The Register also has the authority to publish compilations of information, bibliographies, and other material he or she considers to be of value to the public.

(c) Distribution of Publications.—All publications of the Copyright Office shall be furnished to depository libraries as specified under section 1905 of title 44, and, aside from those furnished free of charge, shall be offered for sale to the public at prices based on the cost of reproduction and distribution.

Section 708. Copyright Office fees

(a) The following fees shall be paid to the Register of Copyrights:

(1) on filing each application for registration of a copyright claim or a supplementary registration under section 408, including the issuance of a certificate of registration if registration is made, $10;

(2) on filing each application for registration of a claim to renewal of a subsisting copyright in its first term under section 304(a), including the issuance of a certificate of registration if registration is made, $6;

(3) for the issuance of a receipt for a deposit under section 407, $2;

(4) for the recordation, as provided by section 205, of a transfer of copyright ownership or other document of six pages or less, covering no more than one title, $10; for each page over six and each title over one, 50 cents additional;

(5) for the filing, under section 115(b), of a notice of intention to make phonorecords, $6;

(6) for the recordation, under section 302(c), of a statement revealing the identity of an author of an anonymous or pseudonymous work, or for the recordation, under section 302(d),

of a statement relating to the death of an author, $10 for a document of six pages or less, covering no more than one title; for each page over six and for each title over one, $1 additional;

(7) for the issuance, under section 601, of an import statement, $3;

(8) for the issuance, under section 706, of an additional certificate of registration, $4;

(9) for the issuance of any other certification, $4; the Register of Copyrights has discretion, on the basis of their cost, to fix the fees for preparing copies of Copyright Office records, whether they are to be certified or not;

(10) for the making and reporting of a search as provided by section 705, and for any related services, $10 for each hour or fraction of an hour consumed;

(11) for any other special services requiring a substantial amount of time or expense, such fees as the Register of Copyrights may fix on the basis of the cost of providing the service.

(b) The fees prescribed by or under this section are applicable to the United States Government and any of its agencies, employees, or officers, but the Register of Copyrights has discretion to waive the requirement of this subsection in occasional or isolated cases involving relatively small amounts.

(c) All fees received under this section shall be deposited by the Register of Copyrights in the Treasury of the United States and shall be credited to the appropriation for necessary expenses of the Copyright Office. The Register may, in accordance with regulations that he or she shall prescribe, refund any sum paid by mistake or in excess of the fee required by this section.

Section 709. Delay in delivery caused by disruption of postal or other services

In any case in which the Register of Copyrights determines, on the basis of such evidence as the Register may by regulation require, that a deposit, application, fee, or any other material to be delivered to the Copyright Office by a particular date, would have been received in the Copyright Office in due time except for a general disruption or suspension of postal or other transportation or communications services, the actual receipt of such material in the Copyright Office within one month after the date on which the Register determines that the disruption or suspension of such services has terminated, shall be considered timely.

Section 710. Reproduction for use of the blind and physically handicapped: Voluntary licensing forms and procedures

The Register of Copyrights shall, after consultation with the Chief of the Division for the Blind and Physically Handicapped and other appropriate officials of the Library of Congress, establish by regulation standardized forms and procedures by which, at the time applications covering certain specified categories of nondramatic literary works are submitted for registration under section 408 of this title, the copyright owner may voluntarily grant to the Library of Congress a license to reproduce the copyrighted work by means of Braille or similar tactile symbols, or by fixation of a reading of the work in a phonorecord, or both, and to distribute the resulting copies or phonorecords solely for the use of the blind and physiclaly handicapped and under limited conditions to be specified in the standardized forms.

Chapter 8.—Copyright Royalty Tribunal

Section 801. Copyright Royalty Tribunal: Establishment and Purpose

(a) There is hereby created an independent Copyright Royalty Tribunal in the legislative branch.

(b) Subject to the provisions of this chapter, the purposes of the Tribunal shall be—

(1) to make determinations concerning the adjustment of reasonable copyright royalty rates as provided in sections 115 and 116, and to make determinations as to reasonable terms and rates of royalty payments as provided in section 118. The rates applicable under sections 115 and 116 shall be calculated to achieve the following objectives:

(A) To maximize the availability of creative works to the public;

(B) To afford the copyright owner a fair return for his creative work and the copyright user a fair income under existing economic conditions;

(C) To reflect the relative roles of the copyright owner and the copyright user in the product made available to the public with respect to relative creative contribution, technological contribution, capital investment, cost, risk, and contribution to the opening of new markets for creative expression and media for their communication;

(D) To minimize any disruptive impact on the structure of the industries involved and on generally prevailing industry practices.

(2) to make determinations concerning the adjustment of the copyright royalty in section 111 solely in accordance with the following provisions:

(A) The rates established by section 111(d)(2)(B) may be adjusted to reflect (i) national monetary inflation or deflation or (ii) changes in the average rates charged cable subscribers for the basic service of providing secondary transmissions to maintain the real constant dollar level of the royalty fee per subscriber which existed as of the date of enactment of this Act: Provided, That if the average rates charged cable system subscribers for the basic service of providing secondary transmissions are changed so that the average rates exceed national monetary inflation, no change in the rates established by section 111(d)(2)(B) shall be permitted: And provided further, That no increase in the royalty fee shall be permitted based on any reduction in the average number of distant signal equivalents per subscriber. The Commission may consider all factors relating to the maintenance of such level of payments including, as an extenuating factor, whether the cable industry has been restrained by subscriber rate regulating thorities from increasing the rates forthe basic service of providing secondary transmissions.

(B) In the event that the rules and regulations of the Federal Communications Commission are amended at any time after April 15, 1976, to permit the carriage by cable systems of additional television broadcast signals beyond the local service area of the primary transmitters of such signals, the royalty rates established by section 111(d)(1)(B) may be adjusted to insure that the rates for the additional distant signal equivalents result-ing from such carriage are reasonable in the light of the changes effected by the amend-ment to such rules and regulations. In determining the reasonableness of rates proposed following an amendment of Federal Communications Commission rules and regulations, the Copyright Royalty Tribunal shall consider, among other factors, the economic impact on copyright owners and users: Provided, That no adjustment in royalty rates shall be made under this subclause with respect to any distant signal equivalent or fraction thereof represented by (i) carriage of any signal permitted under the rules and regulations of the Federal Communications Commission in effect on April 15, 1976, or the carriage of a sig-nal of the same type (that is, independent, network, or noncommercial educational) sub-stituted for such permitted signal, or (ii) a television broadcast signal first carried after April 15, 1976 pursuant to an individual waiver of the rules and regulations of the Fed-eral Communications Commission, as such rules and regulations were in effect April 15, 1976.

(C) In the event of any change in the rules and regulations of the Federal Communi-cation Commission with respect to syndicated and sports program exclusivity after April 15, 1976, the rates established by section 111(d)(1)(B) may be adjusted to assure that such rates are reasonable in light of the charges to such rules and regulations, but any such adjustment shall apply only to the affected television broadcast signals carried on those systems affected by the change.

(D) The gross receipts limitations established by section 111(d)(1)(C) and (D) shall be adjusted to reflect national monetary inflation or deflation or changes in the average rates charged cable system subscribers for the basic service of providing secondary transmis-sions to maintain the real constant dollar value of the exemption provided by such sec-tion; and the royalty rate specified therein shall not be subject to adjustment; and

(3) to distribute fees deposited with the Register of Copyrights under sections 111 and 116, and to determine, in cases where controversy exists, the distribution of such fees.

(c) As soon as possible after the date of enactment of this Act, and no later than six months following such date, the President shall publish a notice announcing the initial appointments provided in section 802, and shall designate an order of seniority among the initially-appointed commissioners for purposes of section 802(b).

Section 802. Membership of the Tribunal

(a) The Tribunal shall be composed of five commissioners appointed by the President with the advice and consent of the Senate for a term of seven years each; of the first five members appointed, three shall be designated to serve for seven years from the date of the notice specified in section 801(c), and two shall be designated to serve for five years from such date, respectively. Commissioners shall be compen-sated at the highest rate now or hereafter prescribe [sic] for grade 18 of the General Schedule pay rates (5 U.S.C. 5332).

(b) Upon convening the commissioners shall elect a chairman from among the commissoners appointed for a full seven-year term. Such chairman shall serve for a term of one year. Thereafter, the most senior commissioner who has not previously served as chairman shall serve as chairman for a period of one year, except that, if all commissioners have served a full term as chairman, the most senior commis-sioner who has served the least number of terms as chairman shall be designated as chairman.

(c) Any vacancy in the Tribunal shall not affect its powers and shall be filled, for the unexpired term of the appointment, in the same manner as the original appointment was made.

Section 803. Procedures of the Tribunal

(a) The Tribunal shall adopt regulations, not inconsistent with law, governing its procedure and methods of operation. Except as otherwise provided in this chapter, the Tribunal shall be subject to the provisions of the Administrative Procedure Act of June 11, 1946, as amended (c.324, 60 Stat. 237, Title 5, United States Code, Chapter 5, Subchapter II and Chapter 7).

(b) Every final determination of the Tribunal shall be published in the Federal Register. It shall state in detail the criteria that the Tribunal determined to be applicable to the particular proceeding, the various facts that it found relevant to its determination in that proceeding, and the specific reasons for its determination.

Section 804. Institution and conclusion of proceedings

(a) With respect to proceedings under section 801(b)(1) concerning the adjustment of royalty rates as provided in sections 115 and 116, and with respect to proceedings under section 801(b)(2)(A) and (D)—

(1) on January 1, 1980, the Chairman of the Tribunal shall cause to be published in the Federal Register notice of commencement of proceedings under this chapter; and

(2) during the calendar years specified in the following schedule, any owner or user of a copyrighted work whose royalty rates are specified by this title, or by a rate established by the Tribunal, may file a petition with the Tribunal declaring that the petitioner requests an adjustment of the rate. The Tribunal shall make a determination as to whether the applicant has a significant interest in the royalty rate in which an adjustment is requested. If the Tribunal determines that the petition has a significant interest, the Chairman shall cause notice of this determination, with the reasons therefor, to be published in the Federal Register, together with notice of commencement of proceedings under this chapter.

(A) In proceedings under section 901(b)(2)(A) and (D), such petition may be filed during 1985 and in each subsequent tenth calendar year.

(B) In proceedings under section 801(b)(1) concerning the adjustment of royalty rates as provided in section 115, such petition may be filed in 1987 and in each subsequent tenth calendar year.

(C) In proceedings under section 801(b)(1) concerning the adjustment of royalty rates under section 116, such petition may be filed in 1990 and in each subsequent tenth calendar year.

(b) With respect to proceedings under subclause (B) or (C) of section 801(b)(2), following an event described in either of those subsections, any owner or user of a copyrighted work whose royalty rates are specified by section 111, or by a rate established by the Tribunal, may, within twelve months, file a petition with the tribunal declaring that the petitioner requests an adjustment of the rate. In this event the Tribunal shall proceed as in subsection (a)(2), above. Any change in royalty rates made by the Tribunal pursuant to this subsection may be reconsidered in 1980, 1985, and each fifth calendar year thereafter, in accordance with the provisions in section 801

(b)(2)(B) or (C), as the case may be.

(c) With respect to proceedings under section 801(b)(1), concerning the determination of reasonable terms and rates of royalty payments as provided in section 118, the Tribunal shall proceed when and as provided by that section.

(d) With respect to proceedings under section 801(b)(3), concerning the distribution of royalty fees in certain circumstances under sections 111 or 116, the Chairman of the Tribunal shall, upon determination by the Tribunal that a controversy exists concerning such distribution, cause to be published in the Federal Register notice of commencement of proceedings under this chapter.

(e) All proceedings under this chapter shall be initiated without delay following publication of the notice specified in this section, and the Tribunal shall render its final decision in any such proceeding within one year from the date of such publication.

Section 805. Staff of the Tribunal

(a) The Tribunal is authorized to appoint and fix the compensation of such employees as may be necessary to carry out the provisions of this Chapter, and to prescribe their functions and duties.

(b) The Tribunal may procure temporary and intermittent services to the same extent as is authorized by section 3109 of title 5.

Section 806. Administrative support of the Tribunal

(a) The Library of Congress shall provide the Tribunal with necessary administrative services, including those related to budgeting, accounting, financial reporting, travel, personnel, and procurement. The Tribunal shall pay the Library for such services, either in advance or by reimbursement from the funds of the Tribunal, at amounts to be agreed upon between the Librarian and the Tribunal.

(b) The Library of Congress is authorized to disburse funds for the Tribunal, under regulations prescribed jointly by the Librarian of Congress and the Tribunal and approved by the Comptroller General. Such regulations shall establish requirements and procedures under which every voucher certified for payment by the Library of Congress under this chapter shall be supported with a certification by a duly authorized officer or employee of the Tribunal, and shall prescribe the responsibilities and accountability of said officers and employees of the Tribunal with respect to such certifications.

Section 807. Deduction of costs of proceedings

Before any funds are distributed pursuant to a final decision in a proceeding involving distribution of royalty fees, the Tribunal shall assess the reasonable costs of such proceeding.

Section 808. Reports

In addition to its publication of the reports of all final determinations as provided in section 803(b), the Tribunal shall make an annual report to the President and the Congress concerning the Tribunal's work during the preceding fiscal year, including a detailed fiscal statement of account.

Section 809. Effective date of final determinations

Any final determination by the Tribunal under this chapter shall become effective thirty days following its publication in the Federal Register as provided in section 803(b), unless prior to that time an appeal has been filed pursuant to section 810, to vacate, modify, or correct such determination, and notice of such appeal has been served on all parties who appeared before the Tribunal in the proceeding in question. Where the proceeding involves the distribution of royalty fees under sections 111 or 116, the Tribunal shall, upon the expiration of such thirty-day period, distribute any royalty fees not subject to an appeal filed pursuant to section 810.

Section 810. Judicial review

Any final decision of the Tribunal in a proceeding under section 801(b) may be appealed to the United States Court of Appeals, within thirty days after its publication in the Federal Register by an aggrieved party. The judicial review of the decision shall be had, in accordance with chapter 7 of title 5, on the basis of the record before the Tribunal. No court shall have jurisidiction to review a final decision of the Tribunal except as provided in this section.

Chapter 9.—Protection of Semiconductor Chip Products

Section 901. Definitions

(a) As used in this chapter—

(1) a "semiconductor chip product" is the final or intermediate form of any product—

(A) having two or more layers of metallic, insulating, or semiconductor material, deposited or otherwise placed on, or etched away or otherwise removed from, a piece of semiconductor material in accordance with a predetermined pattern; and

(B) intended to perform electronic circuitry functions;

(2) a "mask work" is a series of related images, however, fixed or encoded—

(A) having or representing the predetermined, three-dimensional pattern of metallic, insulating, or semiconductor material present or removed from the layers of a semiconductor chip product; and

(B) in which series the relation of the images to one another is that each image has the pattern of the surface of one form of the semiconductor chip product;

(3) a mask work is "fixed" in a semiconductor chip product when its embodiment in the product is sufficiently permanent or stable to permit the mask work to be perceived or reproduced from the product for a period of more than transitory duration;

(4) "distribute" means to sell, or to lease, bail, or otherwise transfer, or to offer to sell, lease, bail, or otherwise transfer.

(5) to "commercially exploit" a mask work is to distribute to the public for commercial purposes a semiconductor chip product embodying the mask work; except that such term includes an offer to sell or transfer a semiconductor chip product only when the offer is in writing and occurs after the mask work is fixed in the semiconductor chip product;

(6) the "owner" of a mask work is the person who created the mask work, the legal representative of that person if that person is deceased or under a legal incapacity, or a party to whom all the rights under this chapter of such person or representative are transferred in accordance with section 903(b); except that, in the case of a work made within the scope of a person's employment, the owner is the employer for whom the person created the mask work or a party to whom all the rights under this chapter of the employer are transferred in accordance with section 903(b);

(7) an "innocent purchaser" is a person who purchases a semiconductor chip product in good faith and without having notice of protection with respect to the semiconductor chip product;

(8) having "notice of protection" means having actual knowledge that, or reasonable grounds to believe that, a mask work is protected under this chapter; and

(9) an "infringing semiconductor chip product" is a semiconductor chip product which is made, imported, or distributed in violation of the exclusive rights of the owner of a mask work under this chapter.

(b) For purposes of this chapter, the distribution or importation of a product incorporating a semiconductor chip product as a part thereof is a distribution or importation of that semiconductor chip product.

Section 902. Subject matter of protection

(a) (1) Subject to the provisions of subsection (b), a mask work fixed in a semiconductor chip product, by or under the authority of the owner of the mask work, is eligible for protection under this chapter if—

(A) on the date on which the mask work is registered under section 908, or is first commercially exploited anywhere in the world, whichever occurs first, the owner of the mask work is (i) a national or domiciliary of the United States, (ii) a national, domiciliary, or sovereign authority of a foreign nation that is a party to a treaty affording protection to mask works to which the United States is also a party, or (iii) a stateless person, wherever that person may be domiciled;

(B) the mask work is first commercially exploited in the United States; or

(C) the mask work comes within the scope of a Presidential proclamation issued under paragraph (2).

(2) Whenever the President finds that a foreign nation extends, to mask works of owners who are nationals or domiciliaries of the United States protection (A) on substantially the same basis as that on which the foreign nation extends protection to mask works of its own nationals and domiciliaries and mask works first commercially exploited in that nation, or (B) on sub-

stantially the same basis as provided in this chapter, the President may by proclamation extend protection under this chapter to mask works (i) of owners who are, on the date on which the mask works are registered under section 908, or the date on which the mask works are first commercially exploited anywhere in the world, whichever occurs first, nationals, domiciliaries, or sovereign authorities of that nation, or (ii) which are first commercially exploited in that nation. ThePresident may revise, suspend, or revoke any suchproclamation or impose any conditions or limitations onprotection extended under any such proclamation.

(b) Protection under this chapter shall not be available for a mask work that—

(1) is not original; or

(2) consists of designs that are staple, commonplace, or familiar in the semiconductor industry, or variations of such designs, combined in a way that, considered as a whole, is not original.

(c) In no case does protection under this chapter for a mask work extend to any idea, procedure, process, system, method of operation, concept, principle, or discovery, regardless of the form in which it is described, explained, illustrated, or embodies in such work.

Section 903. Ownership, transfer, licensing, and recordation

(a) The exclusive rights in a mask work subject to protection under this chapter belong to the owner of the mask work.

(b) The owner of the exclusive rights in a mask work may transfer all of those rights, or license all or less than all of those rights, by any written instrument signed by such owner or a duly authorized agent of the owner. Such rights may be transferred or licensed by operation of law, may be bequeathed by will, and may pass as personal property by the applicable laws of intestate succession.

(c) (1) Any document pertaining to a mask work may be recorded in the Copyright Office if the document filed for recordation bears the actual signature of the person who executed it, or if it is accompanied by a sworn or official certification that it is a true copy of the original, signed document. The Register of Copyrights shall, upon receipt of the document and the fee specified pursuant to section 908(d), record the document and return it with a certificate of recordation. The recordation of any transfer or license under this paragraph gives all persons constructive notice of the facts stated in the recorded document concerning the transfer or license.

(2) In any case in which conflicting transfers of the exclusive rights in a mask work are made, the transfer first executed shall be void as against a subsequent transfer which is made for a valuable consideration and without notice of the first transfer, unless the first transfer is recorded in accordance with paragraph (1) within three months after the date on which it is executed, but in no case later than the day before the date of such subsequent transfer.

(d) Mask works prepared by an officer or employee of the United States Government as part of that person's official duties are not protected under this chapter, but the United States Government is not precluded from receiving and holding exclusive rights in mask works transferred to the Government under subsection (b).

Section 904. Duration of protection

(a) The protection provided for a mask work under this chapter shall commence on the date on which the mask work is registered under section 908, or the date on which the mask work is first commercially exploited anywhere in the world, whichever comes first.

(b) Subject to subsection (c) and the provisions of this chapter, the protection provided under this chapter to a mask work shall end ten years after the date on which such protection commences under subsection (a).

(c) All terms of protection provided in this section shall run to the end of the calendar year in which they would otherwise expire.

Section 905. Exclusive rights in mask works

The owner of a mask work provided protection under this chapter has the exclusive rights to do and to authorize any of the following:

(1) to reproduce the mask work by optical, electronic, or any other means;

(2) to import or distribute a semiconductor chip product in which the mask work is embodied; and

(3) to induce or knowingly to cause another person to do any of the acts described in paragraphs (1) and (2).

Section 906. Limitation on exclusive rights: reverse engineering; first sale

(a) Notwithstanding the provisions of section 905, it is not an infringement of the exclusive rights of the owner of a mask work for—

(1) a person to reproduce the mask work solely for the purpose of teaching, analyzing, or evaluating the concepts or techniques embodied in the mask work or the circuitry, logic flow, or organization of components used in the mask work; or

(2) a person who performs the analysis or evaluation described in paragraph (1) to incorporate the results of such conduct in an original mask work which is made to be distributed.

(b) Notwithstanding the provisions of section 905(2), the owner of a particular semiconductor chip product made by the owner of the mask work, or by any person authorized by the owner of the mask work, may import, distribute, or otherwise dispose of or use, but not reproduce, that particular semiconductor chip product without the authority of the owner of the mask work.

Section 907. Limitation on exclusive rights: innocent infrinement

(a) Notwithstanding any other provision of this chapter, an innocent purchaser or an infringing semiconductor chip product—

(1) shall incur no liability under this chapter with respect to the importation or distribution of units of the infringing semiconductor chip product that occurs before the innocent purchaser has notice of protection with respect to the mask work embodied in the semiconductor chip product; and

(2) shall be liable only for a reasonable royalty on each unit of the infringing semiconductor chip product that the innocent purchaser imports or distributes after having notice of protection with respect to the mask work embodied in the semiconductor chip product.

(b) The amount of the royalty referred to in subsection (a)(2) shall be determined by the court in a civil action for infringement unless the parties resolve the issue by voluntary negotiation, mediation, or binding arbitration.

(c) The immunity of an innocent purchaser from liability referred to in subsection (a)(1) and the limitation of remedies with respect to an innocent purchaser referred to in subsection (a)(2) shall extend to any person who directly or indirectly purchases an infringing semiconductor chip product from an innocent purchaser.

(d) The provisions of subsections (a), (b), and (c) apply only with respect to those units of an infringing semiconductor chip product that an innocent purchaser purchased before having notice of protection with respect to the mask work embodied in the semiconductor chip product.

Section 908. Registration of claims of protection

(a) The owner of a mask work may apply to the Register of Copyrights for registration of a claim of protection in a mask work. Protection of a mask work under this chapter shall terminate if application for registration of a claim of protection in the mask work is not made as provided in this chapter within two years after the date on which the mask work is first commercially exploited anywhere in the world.

(b) The Register of Copyrights shall be responsible for all administrative functions and duties under this chapter. Except for section 708, the provisions of chapter 7 of this title relating to the general responsibilities, organization, regulatory authority, actions, records, and publications of the Copyright Office shall apply to this chapter, except that the Register of Copyright may make such changes as may be necesary in applying those provisions to this chapter.

(c) The application for registration of a mask work shall be made on a form prescribed by the Register of Copyrights. Such form may require any information regarded by the Register as bearing upon the preparation or identification of the mask work, the existence or duration of protection of the mask work under this chapter, or ownership of the mask work. The application shall be accompanied by the fee set pursuant to subsection (d) and the identifying material specified pursuant to such subsection.

(d) The Register of Copyrights shall by regulation set reasonable fees for the filing of applications to register claims of protection in the administration of this chapter or the rights under this chapter, taking into consideration the cost of providing those services, the benefits of a public record, and statutory fee schedules under this title. The Register shall also specify the identifying material to be deposited in connection with the claim for registration.

(e) If the Register of Copyrights, after examining an application for registration, determines, in accordance with the provisions of this chapter, that the application relates to a mask work which is entitled to protection under this chapter, then the Register shall register the claim of protection and issue to the applicant a certificate of registration of the claim of protection under the seal of the Copyright Office, the effective date of registration of a claim of protection shall be the date on which an application, deposit of identifying material, and fee, which are determined by the Register of Copyrights or by a court of competent jurisdiction to be acceptable for registration of the claim, have all been received in the Copyright Office.

(f) In any action for infringement under this chapter, the certificate of registration of a mask work shall constitute prima facie evidence (1) of the facts stated in the certificate, and (2) that the applicant issued the certificate has met, the requirements of this chapter, and the regulations issued under this chapter, with respect to the registration of claims.

(g) Any applicant for registration under this section who is dissatisfied with the refusal of the Register of Copyrights to issue a certificate of registration under this section may seek judicial review of that refusal by bringing an action for such review in an appropriate United States district court not later than sixty days after the refusal. The provisions of chapter 7 of title 5 shall apply to such judicial review. The failure of the Register of Copyrights to issue a certificate of registration within four months after an application for registration is filed shall be deemed to be a refusal to issue a certificate of registration for purposes of this subsection and section 910(b)(2), except that, upon a showing of good cause, the district court may shorten such four-month period.

Section 909. Mask work notice

(a) The owner of a mask work provided protection under this chapter may affix notice to the mask work, and to masks and semiconductor chip products embodying the mask work, in such manner and location as to give reasonable notice of such protection. The Register of Copyrights shall prescribe by regulation, as examples, specific methods of affixation and positions of notice for purposes of this section, but these specifications shall not be considered exhaustive. The affixation of such notice is not a condition of protection under this chapter, but shall constitute prima facie evidence of notice of protection.

(b) The notice referred to in subsection (a) shall consist of—

(1) the words "mask work", the symbol *M*, or the symbol [statutory text shows an M enclosed in a circle] (the letter M in a circle); and

(2) the name of the owner or owners of the mask work or an abbreviation by which the name is recognized or is generally known.

Section 910. Enforcement of exclusive rights

(a) Except as otherwise provided in this chapter, any person who violates any of the exclusive rights of the owner of a mask work under this chapter, by conduct in or affecting commerce, shall be liable as an infringer of such rights.

(b) (1) The owner of a mask work protected under this chapter, or the exclusive licensee of all rights under this chapter with respect to the mask work, shall, after a certificate of registration of a claim of protection in that mask work has been issued under section 908, be entitled to institute a civil action for any infringement with respect to the mask work which is committed after the commencement of protection of the mask work under section 904(a).

(2) In any case in which an application for registration of a claim of protection in a mask work and the required deposit of identifying material and fee have been received in the Copyright Office in proper form and registration of the mask work has been refused, the applicant is entitled to institute a civil action for infringement under this chapter with respect to the mask work if notice of the action, together with a copy of the complaint, is served on the Register of Copyrights, in accordance with the Federal Rules of Civil Procedure. The Register may, at his or her option, become a party to the action with respect to the issue of whether the claim of protection is eligible for registration by entering an appearance within sixty days after such service, but the failure of the Register to become a party to the action shall not deprive the court of jurisdiction to determine that issue.

(c) (1) The Secretary of the Treasury and the United States Postal Service shall separately or jointly issue regulations for the enforcement of the rights set forth in section 905 with respect to importation. These regulations may require; as a condition for the exclusion of articles from the United States, that the person seeking exclusion take any one or more of the following action:

(A) Obtain a court order enjoining, or an order of the International Trade Commission under section 337 of the Tariff Act of 1930 excluding, importation of the articles.

(B) Furnish proof that the mask work involved is protected under this chapter and that the importation of the articles would infringe the rights in the mask work under this chapter.

(C) Post a surety bond for any injury that may result if the detention or exclusion of the articles proves to be unjustified.

(2) Articles imported in violation of the rights set forth in section 905 are subject to seizure and forfeiture in the same manner as property imported in violation of the customs laws. Any such forfeited articles shall be destroyed as directed by the Secretary of the Treasury or the court, as the case may be, except that the articles may be returned to the country of export whenever it is shown to the satisfaction of the Secretary of the Treasury that the importer had no reasonable grounds for believing that his or her acts constituted a violation of the law.

Section 911. Civil Actions

(a) Any court having jurisdiction of a civil action arising under this chapter may grant temporary restraining orders, preliminary injunctions, and permanent injunctions on such terms as the court may deem reasonable to prevent or restrain infringement of the exclusive rights in a mask work under this chapter.

(b) Upon finding an infringer liable, to a person entitled under section 910(b)(1) to institute a civil action, for an infringement of any exclusive right under this chapter, the court shall award such person actual damages suffered by the person as a result of the infringement. The court shall also award such person the infringer's profits that are attributable to the infringement and are not taken into account in computing the award of actual damages. In establishing the infringer's profits, such person is required to present proof only if the infringer is required to prove his or her deductible expenses and the elements of profit attributable to factors other than the mask work.

(c) At any time before final judgment is rendered, a person entitled to institute a civil action for infringement may elect, instead of actual damages and profits as provided by subsection (b), an award of statutory damages for all infringements involved in the action, with respect to any one mask work for which any two or more infringers are liable jointly and severally, in an amount not more than $250,000 as the court considers just.

(d) An action for infringement under this chapter shall be barred unless the action is commenced within three years after the claim accrues.

(e)(1) At any time while an action for infringement of the exclusive rights in a mask work under this chapter is pending, the court may order the impounding, on such terms as it may deem reasonable, of all semiconductor chip products, and any drawings, tapes, masks, or other products by means of which such products may be reproduced, that are claimed to have been made, imported, or used in violation of those exclusive rights. Insofar as practicable, applications for orders under this paragraph shall be heard and determined in the same manner as an application for a temporary restraining order or preliminary injunction.

(2) As part of a final judgment or decree, the court may order the destruction or other disposition of any infringing semiconductor chips products, and any masks, tapes, or other articles by means of which such products may be reproduced.

(f) In any civil action arising under this chapter, the court in its discretion may allow the recovery of full costs, including reasonable attorneys' fees, to the prevailing party.

Section 912. Relation to other laws

(a) Nothing in this chapter shall affect any right or remedy held by any person under chapters 1 through 8 of this title, or under title 35.

(b) Except as provided in section 908(b) of this title, references to "this title" or "Title 17" in chapters 1 though 8 of this title shall be deemed not to apply to this chapter.

(c) The provisions of this chapter shall preempt the laws of any State to the extent those laws provide any rights or remedies with respect to a mask work which are equivalent to those rights or remedies provided by this chapter, except that such preemption shall be effective only with respect to actions filed on or after January 1, 1986.

(d) The provisions of sections 1338, 1400(a) and 1498(b) and (c) of title 28 shall apply with respect to exclusive rights in mask works under this chapter.

(e) Nothwithstanding subsection (c), nothing in this chapter shall detract from any rights of a mask work owner, whether under Federal law (exclusive of this chapter) or under the common law or the statutes of a State, heretofore or hereafter declared or enacted, with respect to any mask work first commercially exploited before July 1, 1983.

Section 913. Transitional provisions

(a) No application for registration under section 908 may be filed, and no civil action under section 910 or other enforcement proceeding under this chapter may be instituted, until sixty days after the date of the enactment of this chapter.

(b) No monetary relief under section 911 may be granted with respect to any conduct that occurred before the date of the enactment of this chapter, except as provided in subsection (d).

(c) Subject to subsection (a), the provisions of this chapter apply to all mask works that are first commercially exploited or are registered under this chapter, or both, on or after the date of the enactment of this chapter.

(d)(1) Subject to subsection (a), protection is available under this chapter to any mask work that was first commercially exploited on or after July 1, 1983, and before the date of the enactment of this chapter, if a claim of protection in the mask work is registered in the Copyright Office before July 1, 1985, under section 908.

(2) In the case of any mask work described in paragraph (1) that is provided protection under this chapter, infringing semiconductor chip product units manufactured before the date of the enactment of this chapter may, without liability under sections 910 and 911, be imported into or distributed in the United States, or both, until two years after the date of registration of the mask work under section 908, but only if the importer or distributor, as the case may be, first pays or offers to pay the reasonable royalty referred to in section 907(a)(2) to the mask work owner, on all such units imported or distributed, or both, after the date of the enactment of this chapter.

(3) In the event that a person imports or distributes infringing semiconductor chip product units described in paragraph (2) of this subsection without first paying or offering to pay the rea-

sonable royalty specified in such paragraph, or if the person refuses or fails to make such payment, the mask work owner shall be entitled to the relief provided in subsections 910 and 911.

Section 914. International transitional provisions

(a) Notwithstanding the conditions set forth in subparagraphs (A) and (C) of section 902(a)(1) with respect to the availability of protection under this chapter to nationals, domiciliaries, and sovereign authorities of a foreign nation, the Secretary of Commerce may, upon the petition of any person, or upon the Secretary's own motion, issue an order extending protection under this chapter to such foreign nationals, domiciliaries, and sovereign authorities if the Secretary finds—

(1) that the foreign nation is making good faith efforts and reasonable progress toward—

(A) entering into a treaty described in section 902(a)(1)(A); or

(B) enacting legislation that would be in compliance with subparagraphs (A) or (B) of section 902(a)(2); and

(2) that the nationals, domiciliaries, and sovereign authorities of the foreign nation, and persons controlled by them, are not engaged in the misappropriation, or unauthorized distribution or commercial exploitation, of mask works; and

(3) that issuing the order would promote the purposes of this chapter and international comity with respect to the protection of mask works.

(b) While an order under subsection (a) is in effect with respect to a foreign nation, no application for registration of a claim for protection in a mask work under this chapter may be denied solely because the owner of the mask work is a national, domiciliary, or sovereign authority of that foreign nation, or solely becausee the mask work was first commercially exploited in that foreign nation.

(c) Any order issued by the Secretary of Commerce under subsection (a) shall be effective for such period as the Secretary designates in the order, except that no such order may be effective after the date on which the authority of the Secretaryof Commerce terminates under subsection (e). The effective date of any such order shall also be designated in the order. In the case of an order issued upon the petition of a person, such effective date may be no earlier than the date on which the Secretary receives such petition.

(d)(1) Any order issued under this section shall terminate if—

(A) the Secretary of Commerce finds that any of the conditions set forth in paragraphs (1), (2), and (3) of subsection (a) no longer exist; or

(B) mask works of nationals, domiciliaries, and sovereign authorities of that foreign nation or mask works first commercially exploited in that foreign nation become eligible for protection under subparagraphs (A) or (C) of section 902(a)(1).

(2) Upon the termination or expiration of an order issued under this section, registrations of claims of protection in mask works made pursuant to that order shall remain valid for the period specified in section 904.

(e) The authority of the Secretaryof Commerce under this section shall commence on the date of the enactment of this chapter, and shall terminate on July 1, 1991.

(f)(1) The Secretary of Commerce shall promptly notify the Register of Copyrights and the Committees on the Judiciary of the Senate and the House of Representatives of the issuance or termination of any order under this section, together with a statement of the reasons for such action. The Secretary shall also publish such notification and statement of reasons in the Federal Register.

(2) Two years after the date of the enactment of this chapter, the Secretary of Commerce, in consultation with the Register of Copyrights, shall transmit to the Committees of the Judiciary of the Senate and the House of Representatives a report on the actions taken under this section and on the current status of international recognition of mask work protection. The report shall include such recommendations for modifications of the protection accorded under this chapter to mask works owned by nationals, domiciliaries, or sovereign authorities of foreign nations as the Secretary, in consultation with the Register of Copyright, considers would promote the purposes of this chapter and international comity with respect to mask work protection.

Not later than July 1, 1990, the Secretary of Commerce, in consultation with the Register of Copyrights, shall transmit to the Committees on the Judiciary of the Senate and the House of Representatives a report updating the matters contained in the reporttransmitted under the preceding sentence.

*Section 1 of Public Law 100-159, 101 Stat. 899 (Nov. 9, 1987), is a follows:

(a) Findings.—The Congress finds that—

(1) Section 914 of title 17, United States Code, which authorizes the Secretary of Commerce to issue orders extending interim protection under chapter 9 of title17, United States Code, to mask works fixed in semiconductor chip products and originating in foreign countries that are making good faith efforts and reasonable progress toward providing protection, by treaty or legislation, to mask works of United States nationals, has resulted in substantial and positive legislative developments in foreign countries regarding protection of mask works;

(2) the Secretary of Commerce has determined that most of the industrialized countries of the world are eligible for orders affording interim protection under section 914 of title 17, United States Code;

(3) the World Intellectual Property Organization has commenced meetings to draft an international convention regarding the protection of integrated electronic circuits;

(4) these bilateral and multilateral developments are encouraging steps toward improving international protection of mask works in a consistent and harmonious manner; and

(5) it is inherent in section 902 of title 17, United States Code, that the President has the authority to revise, suspend, or revoke, as well as issue, proclamations extending mask work protection to nationals, domiciliaries, and sovereign authorities of other countries if conditions warrant.

(b) Purposes.—The purposes of this act are—

(1) to extend the period within which the Secretary of commerce may grant interim protective orders under section 914 of title 17, United States Code, to continue this incentive for the bilateral and multilateral protection of mask works; and

(2) to codify the President's existing authority to revoke, suspend, or limit the protection extended to mask works of foreign entities in nations that extend mask work protection to United States nationals.

Transitional and Supplementary Provisions

Section 102
Section 103
Section 104

Section 105
Section 106
Section 107
Section 108
Section 109
Section 110
Section 111
Section 112
Section 113
Section 114
Section 115

Transitional and Supplementary Provisions Section 102

This Act becomes effective on January 1, 1978, except as otherwise expressly provided by this Act, including provisions of the first section of this Act. The provisions of sections 118.304(b), and chapter 8 of title 17, as amended by the first section of this Act, take effect upon enactment of this Act.

Transitional and Supplementary Provisions Section 103

This Act does not provide copyright protection for any work that goes into the public domain before January 1, 1978. The exclusive rights, as provided by section 106 of title 17 as amended by the first section of this Act, to reproduce a work in phonorecords and to distribute phonorecords of the work, do not extend to any nondramatic musical work copyrighted before July 1, 1909.

Transitional and Supplementary Provisions Section 104

All proclamations issued by the President under section 1(e) or 9(b) of title 17 as it existed on December 31, 1977, or under previous copyright statutes of the United States, shall continue in force until terminated, suspended, or revised by the President.

Transitional and Supplementary Provisions Section 105

(a)(1) Section 505 of title 44 is amended to read as follows: "§ 505. Sale of duplicate platesz: "The Public Printer shall sell, under regulations of the Joint Committee on Printing to persons who may apply, additional or duplicate stereotype or electrotype plates from which a Government publication is printed, at a price not to exceed the cost of composition, the metal, and making to the Government, plus 10 per centum, and the full amount of the price shall be paid when the order is filed."

(2) The item relating to section 505 in the sectional analysis at the beginning of chapter 5 of title 44, is amended to read as follows: "505. Sale of duplicate plates."

(b) Section 2113 of title 44 is amended to read as follows: "§ 2113. Limitation on liability "When letters and other intellectual productions (exclusive of patented material, published works under copyright protection, and unpublished works for which copyright registration has been made) come into the custody or possession of the Administrator of General Services, the United States or its agents are not liable for infringement of copyright or analogous rights arising out of use of the materials for display, inspection, research, reproduction, or other purposes."

(c) In section 1498(b) of title 28, the phrase "section 101(b) of title 17" is amended to read "section 504(c) of title 17"

(d) Section 543(a)(4) of the Internal Revenue Code of 1954, as amended, is amended by striking out "(other than by reason of section 2 or 6 thereof)"

(e) Section 3202(a) of title 39 is amended by striking out clause (5). Section 3206 of title 39 is amended by deleting the words "subsections (b) and (c)" and inserting "subsection (b) in subsection (a), and by deleting subsection (c). Section 3206(d) is renumbered (c)

(f) Subsection (a) of section 290(e) of title 15 is amended by deleting the phrase "section 8" and inserting in lieu thereof the phrase "section 105."

(g) Section 131 of title 2 is amended by deleting the phrase "deposit to secure copyright," and inserting in lieu thereof the phrase "acquisition of material under the copyright law."

Transitional and Supplementary Provisions Section 106

In an case where, before January 1, 1978, a person has lawfuly made parts of instruments serving to reproduce mechanically a copyrighted work under the compulsory license provisions of section 1(e) of title 17 as it existed on December 31, 1977, such person may continue to make and distribute such parts embodying the same mechanical reproduction without obtaining a new compulsory license under the tems of section 115 of title 17 as amended by the first section of this Act. However, such parts made on or after January 1, 1978, constitute phonorecords and are otherwise subject to the provisions of said section 115.

Transitional and Supplementary Provisions Section 107

In the case of any work in which an ad interim copyright is subsisting or is capable of being secured on December 31, 1977, under section 22 of title 17 as it existed on that date, copyright protection is hereby extended to endure for the term or terms provided by section 304 of title 17 as amended by the first section of this Act.

Transitional and Supplementary Provisions Section 108

The notice provisions of sections 401 through 403 of title 17 as amended by the first section of this Act apply to all copies or phonorecords publicly distributed on or after January 1, 1978. However, in the case of a work published before January 1, 1978, compliance with the notice provisions of title 17 either as it existed on December 31, 1977, or as amended by the first section of this Act, is adequate with respect to copies publicly distributed after December 31, 1977.

Transitional and Supplementary Provisions Section 109

The registration of claims to copyright for which the required deposit, application, and fee were received in the Copyright Office before January 1, 1978, and the recordation of assignments of copyright or other instruments received in the Copyright Office before January 1, 1978, shall be made in accordance with title 17 as it existed on December 31, 1977.

Transitional and Supplementary Provisions Section 110

The demand and penalty provisions of section 14 of title 17 as it existed on December 31, 1977, apply to any work in which copyright has been secured by publication with notice of copyright on or before that date, but any deposit and registration made after that date in response to a demand under that section shall be made in accordance with the provisions of title 17 as amended by the first section of this Act.

Transitional and Supplementary Provisions Section 111

Section 2318 of title 18 of the United States Code is amended to read as follows: "§ 2318. Transportation, sale or receipt of phonograph records bearing forged or counterfeit labels"

(a) "Whoever knowingly and with fraudulent intent transports, causes to be transported, receives, sells, or offers for sale in interstate or foreign commerce any phonograph record, disk, wire, tape, film, or other article on which sounds are recorded, to which or upon which is stamped, pasted, or affixed any forged or counterfeited label, knowing the label to have been falsely made, forged, or counterfeited shall be fined not more than $10,000 or imprisoned for not more than one year, or both, for the first such offense and shall be fined not more than $25,000 or imprisoned for not more than two years, or both, for any subsequent offense."

(b) "When any person is convicted of any violation of subsection (a), the court in its judgment of conviction shall, in addition to the penalty therein prescribed, order the forfeiture and destruction or other disposition of all counterfeit labels and all articles to which counterfeit labels have been affixed or which were intended to have had such labels affixed."

(c) "Except to the extent they are inconsistent with the provisions of this title, all provisions of section 509, title 17, United States Code, are applicable to violations of subsection (a)."

Transitional and Supplementary Provisions Section 112

All causes of action that arose under title 17 before January 1, 1978, shall be governed by title 17 as it existed when the cause of action arose.

Transitional and Supplementary Provisions Section 113

(a) The Librarian of Congress (hereinafter referred to as the "Librarian") shall establish and maintain in the Library of Congress a library to be known as the American Television and Radio Archives (hereinafter referred to as the "Archives). The purpose of the Archives shall be to preserve a permanent record of the television and radio programs which are the heritage of the people of the United States and to provide access to such programs to historians and scholars without encouraging or causing copyright infringement.

   (1) The Librarian, after consultation with interested organizations and individuals, shall determine and place in the Archives such copies and phonorecords of television and radio programs transmitted to the public in the United States and in other countries which are of present or potential public or cultural interest, historical significance, cognitive value, or otherwise worthy of preservation, including copies and phonorecords of published and unpublished transmission programs—

(A) acquired in accordance with sections 407 and 408 of title 17 as amended by the first section of this Act, and

(B) transferred from the existing collections of the Library of Congress; and

(C) given to or exchanged with the Archives by other libraries, archives, organizations, and individuals; and

(D) purchased from the owner thereof.

(2) The Librarian shall maintain and publish appropriate catalogs and indexes of the collections of the Archives, and shall make such collections available for study and research under conditions prescribed under this section.

(b) Notwithstanding the provisions of section 106 of title 17 as amended by the first section of this Act, the Librarian is authorized with respect to a transmission program which consists of a regularly scheduled newscast or on-the-spot coverage of news events and, under standards and conditions that the Librarian shall prescribe by regulation—

(1) to reproduce a fixation of such a program, in the same or another tangible form, for the purposes of preservation or security or for distribution under the conditions of clause (3) of this subsection; and

(2) to compile, without abridgment or any other editing, portions of such fixations according to subject matter, and to reproduce such compilations for the purpose of clause (1) of this subsection; and

(3) to distribute a reproduction made under clause (1) or (2) of this subsection—

(A) by loan to a person engaged in research; and

(B) for deposit in a library or archives which meets the requirements of section 108(a) of title 17 as amended by the first section of this Act, in either case for use only in research and not for further reproduction or performance.

(c) The Librarian or any employee of the Library who is acting under the authority of this section shall not be liable in any action for copyright infringement committed by any other person unless the Librarian or such employee knowingly participated in the act of infringement committed by such person. Nothing in this section shall be construed to excuse or limit liability under title 17 as amended by the first section of this Act for any act not authorized by that title or this section, or for any act performed by a person not authorized to act under that title or this section.

(d) This section may be cited as the "American Television and Radio Archives Act".

Transitional and Supplementary Provisions Section 114

There are hereby authorized to be appropriated such funds as may be necessary to carry out the purposes of this act.

Transitional and Supplementary Provisions Section 115

If any provision of title 17, as amended by the first section of this Act, is declared unconstitutional, the validity of the remainder of this title is not affected.

Appendix D:
Product Copyright List

All Power Tools clip media, Power Tools application programs/ Demos, and Power Tools sample projects are included in *Multimedia Power Tools* Book/CD-ROM by permission of their respective copyright holders. All brand or product names are trademarks or registered trademarks of their respective holders.

Adobe Illustrator® 4.0 Demo; Adobe Systems, Incorporated; Adobe Illustrator is a trademark of Adobe Systems Incorporated, which may be registered in certain jurisdictions. Adobe Illustrator © 1987–91 Adobe Systems Incorporated. All rights reserved.

Adobe Photoshop™ 3.0 Demo; Adobe Systems, Incorporated; Adobe Photoshop is a trademark of Adobe Systems Incorporated which may be registered in certain jurisdictions. Adobe Photoshop © 1989–94 Adobe Systems Incorporated. All rights reserved.

Adobe Premiere© 4.0 Plug-In Developer Kit; Adobe Systems, Incorporated; Adobe Premiere 2.0 Plug-in Developer Kit is a trademark of Adobe Systems Incorporated which may be registered in certain jurisdictions. Adobe Premiere © 1991–1994 Adobe Systems Incorporated. All rights reserved.

Animation Works™ 1.1 Demo; Gold Disk®, Inc.; Animation works 1.1 is © 1992 by Gold Disk, Incorporated.

AuthorWare® Professional 3.0 Demo; Macromedia, Incorporated; AuthorWare is a registered trademark and AuthorWare Professional is a trademark of Macromedia, Inc. Used by permission of Macromedia.

Backgrounds for Multimedia, Volumes 1 & 2; ArtBeats®; This software package (*Multimedia Power Tools* Book/CD-ROM) contains art originated and owned by ARTBEATS and is provided for the purchaser of this package only. © 1993 ARTBEATS, Box 1287, Myrtle Creek, OR 97457 (503) 863-4429.

Blendo™ Photography I: Photo Imagery by Craig McClain; Verbum®, Inc.; Blendo™ and Verbum® are trademarks of Verbum, Inc.. Blendo Photography I is © 1993 Craig McClain and Verbum, Inc.

ClipMedia™; Macromedia, Inc.; ClipMedia is a trademark of Macromedia, Inc. Used by permission of Macromedia.

ColorSwitch 2.3.0; Ambrosia, Andrew Welch; ColorSwitch is © 1993, 94 Andrew Welch.

DeBabelizer® 1.6 Demo; Equilibrium Technologies; DeBabelizer is © 1992, 1993 Equilibrium Technologies. All rights reserved. DeBabelizer is a registered trademark of Equilibrium Technologies.

Digital Photographics CD-ROM™; Husom & Rose Photographics; Digital Photographics CD-ROM is © 1993 Husom and Rose Photographics.

Extensions Manager 1.8; Apple Computer, Inc.; Extensions Manager 1.8 is © 1993 Random House Electronic Publishing and its licensers. All rights reserved. RANDOM HOUSE ELECTRONIC PUBLISHING'S LICENSER(S) MAKES NO WARRANTIES,

GIFConverter 2.32b; Kevin A. Mitchell; GIFConverter is © 1991–1993 by Kevin A. Mitchell. All rights reserved.

Hi Rez Vol. I Audio for Multimedia; Presto Studios; Hi Rez Vol. I Audio for Multimedia is © (P) 1992, Hi Rez Audio. All rights reserved.

Image Bank CD Collection, Footage Vol. 1; DiVA™ Corporation/The Image Bank, Inc; Image Bank CD Collection, Footage Vol. 1 is © 1992 Image Bank, Inc. and DiVA Corporation.

ImageCELs®; ImageTects™; ImageCELs is a registered trademark and IMAGETECTS is a trademark ImageTects in the USA and other countries. ImageCELs is © 1993 IMAGETECTS. All rights reserved.

Instant Buttons & Controls v1.0 and #2 Sampler Disk; Stat Media™ Network; Instant Buttons & Controls v1.0 and #2 Sampler Disk are registered trademarks of Stat Media™ and are © 1992.

International Graphics Library; Educorp; International Graphics Library is © 1990 Gazelle Technologies, Inc. and CASCOM, Inc.

Kai's POWER TOOLS™; Kai's Power Tools 2.0 and Kai's Power Tools Demo 2.1 © 1994 HSC Software Corporation. All rights reserved. HSC is a registered trademark, and Kai's Power Tools is a trademark of HSC Software Corporation.

Macromedia Director™ 4.0 Demo; Macromedia, Incorporated; Macromedia Director 4.0 Demo is a trademark of Macromedia, Incorporated. Used by permission of Macromedia, Incorporated.

MacroModel™ 1.5 Demo; Macromedia, Incorporated; MacroModel 1.0 Demo is a registered trademark of Macromedia, Incorporated. Used by permission of Macromedia, Incorporated.

Marble and Granite CD-ROM; ArtBeats®; Marble and Granite CD-ROM is originated and owned by ARTBEATS and is provided for the purchaser of this package only and is © 1993 ARTBEATS.

MasterTracks Pro™ 5 Demo v5.2; Passport Designs, Incorporated; MasterTracks Pro 5 Demo v5.2 is published and created by Passport Designs of Half Moon Bay, CA, and is © 1992 Passport Designs, Incorporated. All rights reserved.

Media in Motion™ Animation Clips/Business Vol, 1 & 2; Media in Motion; Media in Motion Animation Clips are © 1991–1992 Media in Motion. All rights reserved worldwide.

Media in Motion™ Interactive Training for Macromind® Director™ 3.0 & 3.1 Demo; Media in Motion™; Interactive training for Macromind Director 3.0 & 3.1 is © 1991,1992 Media in Motion. All rights reserved worldwide.

Morph™ 2.5 Demo; Gryphon™ Software; Incorporated; Morph 1.1 Demo is © 1992. All rights reserved.

Notepad++2.1; Alexander S. Colwell; Notepad++2.1 is © 1993–95 Alexander S. Colwell. All rights reserved

Painter and Painter 3.0 Demo; Registered trademarks of Fractal Design Corporation; © 1994 Fractal Design Corporation. All rights reserved.

PhotoDisc™—World Commerce and Travel; PhotoDisc, Inc.; PhotoDisc-World Commerce and Travel is © 1993 Tom Hughes. All rights reserved.

PICTviewer 1.1; Apple Computer, Inc.; PICTviewer 1.1 is © 1993 Random House Electronic Publishing and its licensers. All rights reserved. (See product named Extensions Manager 1.6 for Random House Electronic Publishing's and licenser's warranty disclaimer and other disclaimers.)

Popcorn™ 1.0.1; Aladdin Systems, Incorporated; Popcorn is by Leonard Rosenthol and is © 1992, Aladdin Systems, Incorporated.

QuickTime™ 2.0 Package: QuickTime™ Extension, MoviePlayer, Scrapbook.; Apple Computer, Inc.; QuickTime and the QuickTime Logo are trademarks of Apple Computer, Inc. and are used under license, © 1994 Random House Electronic Publishing and its licensers. All rights reserved. (See product named Extensions Manager 1.8 for Random House Electronic Publishing's and Apple Computer's warranty disclaimer and other disclaimers.)

SoundEdit™ Pro™ 2.0 Demo; Macromedia, Incorporated; SoundEdit Pro 2.0 is a trademark of Macromedia, Incorporated. Used by permission of Macromedia, Incorporated.

Soundtrack Express™ Demo and SuperJAM!™ Demo; The Blue Ribbon Soundworks, © 1994; Soundtrack Express and SuperJAM! are trademarks of Blue Ribbon Soundworks, Ltd.

SpaceTime and Art; Wayzata Technology, Incorporated; SpaceTime and Art is © 1992 A/PIX VISions and Wayzata Technology, Incorporated.

Speedometer 4.02; Parity Productions; Speedometer 4.02 is © 1994–95 Scott Berfield. All rights reserved.

StrataVision™ v2.5-A Demo; Strata, Incorporated; StrataVision v2.5-A is © 1989–1992 Strata, Incorporated. All rights reserved.

The Multimedia Library IMAGE Series Vol. 1: Russia/China; The Multimedia Library, Incorporated; The Multimedia Library IMAGE Series, Vol. 1: Russia/China is © 1992 The Multimedia Library, Incorporated.

The Multimedia Library IMAGE Series Vol. 2: South Pacific/Tropical/California Coast; The Multimedia Library, Incorporated; The Multimedia Library IMAGE Series Vol. 2: South Pacific/Tropical/California Coast is © 1992 The Multimedia Library, Incorporated.

The Multimedia Library SOUND Series, Vol. 1: Music For Multimedia; The Multimedia Library, Incorporated; The Multimedia Library SOUND Series, Vol. 1: Music For Multimedia is © 1992 The Multimedia Library, Incorporated.

Toast CD-ROM Pro; ASTARTE GmbH; distributed in North America by Catalogic © 1994 ASTARTE GmbH, Miles Software GmbH.

trueSpace™ for Windows; trueSpace for Windows Demo v. 1.0; © 1994 Caligari Corporation. All rights reserved.

Turtle Beach Systems; Wave for Windows Demo, Wave for Windows 2.0 © 1994 Turtle Beach Systems. All rights reserved.

TV-ROM™; BMUG Incorporated Software; TV-ROM and BMUG are trademarks of BMUG Incorporated Software. TV-ROM is © 1992 BMUG Incorporated, Software.

Twelve Tone Systems; Cakewalk Home Studio™ and Cakewalk Home Studio™ Demo, Cakewalk Home Studio and Cakewalk Home Studio Demo are trademarks of Twelve Tone Systems, Incorporated.

ULead Systems; the ULead logo, and Viewer, a component of MediaStudio Pro are trademarks of ULead Systems, Inc. © 1995 ULead Systems, Inc. All rights reserved.

VideoSync 1.0; Apple Computer, Inc.; VideoSync 1.0 is © 1994–95 Random House Electronic Pub-lishing and its licensers. All rights reserved. (See product named Extensions Manager 1.8 for Random House Electronic Publishing's and Apple Computer's warranty disclaimer and other disclaimers.)

WraptureReels™ Disc One; Form and Function; WraptureReels Disc One and its contents are © 1992 Form and Function. All rights not expressed are reserved.

Wraptures™ Disc One: FineTextures; Form and Function; Wraptures Disc One and its contents are © 1992 Form and Function. All rights not expressed are reserved.

XCMD's: QuickTime™ Movie Stack, Quick-Time™ Edit Movie Stack, QuickTime™ Movie Making Stack, QuickTime™ PICT Stack; Apple Computer, Inc.; XCMD's are © 1993 Random House Electronic Publishing and its licensers. All rights reserved. (See product named Extensions Manager 1.8 for Random House Electronic Publishing's and Apple Computer's warranty disclaimer and other disclaimers.)

Glossary

Compiled by **Steve Rosenthal**

½ inch: the common description of video formats that use ½-inch-wide tape. This includes VHS, Beta, and the improved versions such as SuperBeta and Super VHS.

¾ inch: the common description of video formats that use ¾-inch-wide tape. The only such format in wide use now is the U-matic format defined by Sony. The ¾-inch format is the standard for field use and some studio production at many TV stations.

2D graphics: ordinary plane (one-surface) graphics. Most simple drawing and charting programs only handle two dimensions.

4:2:2: an international standard for digital videotape and production equipment. The numbers refer to the ratio of the sampling rates used for turning three of the components of the analog video signal into a digital signal. It is the standard used for D-1-format digital videotape. It is also known as CCIR 601, which is the recommendation of the international standards body that set up the format.

8-bit color: said of display systems that allocate 8 bits of memory to each pixel and therefore can show up to 256 different colors at a time.

8-bit sound: said of sound boards and other digital sound systems that record

or play back sound using 8 bits of resolution for each digital sample. The result is fidelity slightly better than normal AM radio.

8mm: the general name for a videotape format based on tape approximately 8 mm in width. This format offers slightly better resolution than VHS, and improved sound. Its small size is making it popular for use in camcorders. Many people expect it to become a popular format for multimedia applications. An upgraded version of this format that uses separated color and luminance (S-video) format is called Hi8.

16:9: the aspect ratio (ratio of the horizontal size of the image to the vertical size) proposed for several new video formats such as HDTV.

16-bit adapter: an add-on board that can exchange 16 bits of data at a time with the computer's processor or memory. However, for a sound, video or other I/O board this does not necessarily mean it uses 16 bits of data for each pixel or sample.

16-bit color: said of display systems that allocate 5 bits of memory each for red and blue components of each pixel and 6 bits to the green hues. Such an arrangement can therefore show up to 65,536 different colors at a time.

16-bit sound: audio that is created or digitized using 16 bits of information (and thus over 64,000 levels) for each sample. This is the standard used on the familiar audio Compact Disc.

9660: short for ISO 9660, a standard format adopted by the International Standards Organization for CD-ROM discs intended for use with diverse computer systems. Most drives now come with software to read ISO 9660 discs.

A:B:C notation: for digital video signal formats, a commonly used but exceedingly obscure set of 3 numbers showing the basic sample rate compared to the color clock, the color horizontal downsampling rate compared to the basic sampling rate, and the color vertical downsampling rate plus 1. Thus, the common 4:2:2 format means sampling at 4 times the approximately 3.6 MHz color clock, 2 horizontal color samples for every 4 brightness samples, and no reduction in vertical color resolution.

A/B editing: creating an edited result by combining inputs from two or more sources. Particularly, in video editing, using a three-machine configuration with two play machines and one recorder.

absolute time: in editing systems, a time interval based on the start of the whole piece rather than the start of a particular event or sequence.

AC [alternating current]: 1) electrical signals that change their direction of current flow in a regular pattern. 2) particularly, the mains power provided by the electric company. Also written "ac".

access time: for a Compact Disc or laser disc, the interval between a command to read data at a particular location on the disc and when the data starts to arrive.

ActionMedia II: An Intel trademark for a video capture board that used the firm's Digital Video Interactive (DVI) compression technology. It was largely superseded by the Intel Smart Video Recorder series of boards.

active lines: the number of horizontal sweeps across the screen in a video display that represent picture information rather than timing or data information. In the standard 525-line NTSC system used for television in the U.S., there are about 490 active lines.

adaptive: 1) as a computer-assisted instruction (CAI) format, a lesson or sequence that adjusts to the student's performance using artificial intelligence (AI) techniques to analyze the pattern of the answers. 2) said of devices that help people with handicaps or special needs use computers.

adaptive differential pulse code modulation (ADPCM): a method of recording audio information that compresses the data by encoding changes in the signal rather than absolute values. It is the method used for some CD formats, such as CD-I and CD-ROM XA.

A/D converter (ADC): a device or circuit that translates analog signals (continuous values within a defined range) into their nearest digital (discrete number) equivalent.

additive color mixing: producing colors by mixing colors of light rather than by mixing pigments. If the additive primary colors are mixed in equal proportions, the result is white.

additive synthesis: in the creation of sound by computers or electronic instruments, producing a composite waveform by summing the signals from multiple sources.

ADO: properly the brand name for a series of special-effects generators made by Ampex. The term is also used for the types of effects (such as flying an image, various tumbles, and so on) first popularized by these units.

ADSR [attack, decay, sustain, release]: a term used for both the most common way of shaping synthesized sounds and for the circuit that carries out the process. ADSR stands for four stages in the production of a sound: attack, decay, sustain and release. Changing the ADSR settings changes the tonal quality of a note, but not its basic pitch.

AES/EBU [Audio Engineering Society/ European Broadcast Union]: the informal name for the nearly-equivalent digital audio transmission standards developed by the Audio Engineering Society (AES) and the European Broadcast Union (EBU). It specifies a one-way transmission that encodes a stereo pair of signals plus optional supplementary data in a single digital data stream.

AF [audio frequency]: electronic or acoustical signals that roughly correspond to the range of human hearing (about 20 to 20,000 Hz).

AIFF [Audio Interchange File Format]: a common audio file format that can be imported by most multimedia authoring programs for the Macintosh and by some programs running on PCs.

algorithmic composition: a feature of some music software that creates musical sequences from a set of rules (algorithms).

alpha channel: in video system, an extra signal or set of bits used to control special effects such as transparency and overlay.

A-mode: in auto assembly (where a video editing system puts together a final tape from an edit decision list), assembling the segments in the order listed on the edit decision list. This may involve multiple changes of source reels.

analog: 1) signals that can take on any value in a given range, in contrast to digital values, which can vary only in discrete steps. Analog signals can represent subtle shifts (such as in color or pitch) more easily, but they are harder to accurately process and store. 2) as applied to synthesizers, ones that produce their basic tones using circuits that operate with a continuous series of values instead of the discrete steps used with digital methods. Even analog instruments, though, can have digital controls and interfaces.

analog RGB: said of video systems that send images in separate signal lines for the red, green, and blue information and encode each signal as a proportional voltage rather than as digital bits. This is the method used by most of the newer video systems on personal computers.

analog video: a signal that represents video image information directly by changes in signal size or timing, rather than encoding the information as digital number values.

animatic: a specialized film or video made up of key scenes, or of approximations of key scenes, used primarily for planning commercials or motion pictures.

animation: a video or film sequence that provides the illusion of motion by presenting a succession of slightly different drawn or constructed images.

anti-alias: to smooth over sharp edges or transitions in a an image, sound or other signal to reduce the effects of limitations in signal capture or storage.

Apple Video Compressor (AVC): the original Apple-supplied codec used in QuickTime to compress and decompress moving video. This standard, which was originally code-named Road Pizza, has largely been supplanted by more recent algorithms.

aspect ratio: the ratio of the width to the height of an image, screen, or medium. Images are distorted if forced into a different aspect ratio during enlargement, reduction, or transfers. Standard VGA screens for the PC or external screens for the Macintosh are 640:480 or 4:3, as is broadcast television. Most slide and movie film formats use other aspect ratios.

assemble (A): referring to editing, a style in which sequences are placed one after another without a continuing reference signal. While requiring less preparation than insert editing (which places sequences on top of an existing image or reference track), the result is likely to have small errors in timing.

asset editor: in a multimedia authoring program or suite of programs, an editor program or module designed to work with one of the media types that might be used in a production (in contrast to the main authoring tool used to integrate all the media types).

asymmetrical compression: as applied to video or audio data, methods for squeezing the data for storage or transmission that take a different amount of time or resources to compress the data than to de-compress it. This approach is often used for multimedia publishing where adding more resources during compression minimizes the hardware needed for decompression.

attack, decay, sustain, release (ADSR): 1) a model for analyzing or shaping sounds that characterizes each note as composed of the four stages of attack, decay, sustain and release. Changing the ADSR settings changes the tonal quality of a note, but not its basic pitch. 2) a circuit or device used to shape these four elements.

attract mode: in kiosk, POS (point-of-sale), and even some educational systems, a program segment that runs when the system is not interacting with a user; designed to interest potential users in starting a session.

Audio Interchange File Format (AIFF): a sound file format defined by Apple and several cooperating companies that can include both sampled sound and MIDI data. The AIFF-C variation stores the data in compressed form. AIFF files can be imported by most multimedia authoring programs for the Macintosh and by some programs running on PCs.

Audio-Video Interleaved (AVI): the file format Microsoft specifies for Video for Windows. As its name implies, it intersperses blocks of audio information within a stream of digitized video frames.

authoring system: 1) a programming environment designed to help users create computer-aided instruction (CAI) lessons. The more sophisticated systems are attempts to let users who know nothing about computers still use their expertise about a subject area to create good computerized lessons. However, most systems still require some expertise in instructional design and computers as well. 2) the hardware and software used to create a multimedia project, but not necessarily needed for playback.

Authorware Professional: an authoring program for multimedia and interactive applications published by Macromedia that lets you specify routines by placing icons on an on-screen flowchart.

Autodesk Animator (AA): a family of PC animation packages from Autodesk that produce files in the firm's FLI and FLC formats.

Base Multitimbral specification: the less sophisticated of the two synthesizer subsystems standards that the Multimedia PC specifications allow audio board makers to choose from. It calls for 3 melodic timbres and 2 percussive timbres that can simultaneously play 6 melodic notes and 2 percussive notes.

bitmapped: referring to video displays and other graphic output devices, a system where each possible dot of the display is controlled independently by one or more corresponding bits in memory.

BNC: a common round connector used with coaxial cable. It is pushed on, then locked with a quarter twist.

Boolean: 1) referring to the system of logic that deals only in true and false values plus the combinations made up of those values and the operators "and," "or," and "not." 2) a variable that can only take on a true or false value.

broadband: said of a communications link that provides a large enough bandwidth (range of frequencies) to accommodate several independent channels.

broadcast quality: a common term for video images good enough to be used on commercial broadcast television. There is no precise standard that defines this level, so interpretation varies with the circumstances.

browser: 1) as applied to the Internet's World Wide Web ("the Web"), a program for viewing data and navigating along the links of the Web. 2) a program, system, or mode used to help the user look through a body of information. Most commonly, browsers show some kind of overview or summary, allowing the user to zoom in for a more detailed view. 3) specifically on Photo CD Catalog discs, an included database access program that lets users search for images by key word or title.

bundled title: a CD-ROM package included with a computer and not priced separately. Some multimedia computers and upgrade kits are delivered with large amounts of software that would add hundreds of dollars or more to the price if purchased separately.

buyout music: music that is sold with a license that permits it to be used in specified types of productions without further royalty payments.

byte aligned: said of bits or objects stored in memory that are located at an exact multiple of 8 bits from the starting position.

caddy: a plastic cartridge used with many popular C-ROM drives to hold the disc while it is inserted in the drive and to protect the disc while it is not in use.

cast: 1) in traditional video or film, the people who appear on screen. 2) In some Macintosh animation programs (notably Macromedia Director), the elements that can be moved around the screen. 3) a tint or overemphasis of one color in a color image, particularly an unintended one. Also called color cast.

CD [Compact Disc]: a popular format for optical discs originally developed by Philips and Sony for music, and now used for data and video as well.

CD-DA [Compact Disc-Digital Audio]: the standard format for compact discs and players used for mass-market audio applications. Also known as "Red Book" for the informal name of the standard that defines the format.

CD-I [Compact Disc-Interactive]: a standard for CDs containing combinations of sound, images, and computer instructions and for players specially constructed for these discs. Also known as Green Book for the informal name of the standard that defines the format.

CD Plus: a Sony and Philips format for CD discs that work as audio discs in standard audio CD players but also show additional graphics and data when viewed on a suitable CD Plus-compatible computer. Windows 95 has CD Plus support built in.

CD-PROM [Compact Disc-Programmable Read-Only Memory]: one proposed term for optical discs that can be written by special CD recorders, and read back on any standard CD-ROM reader. PROM stands for "programmable read-only memory." However, popular usage seems to favor the term CD-R for Compact Disc-Recordable..

CD-R [Compact Disc-Recordable]: short for Compact Disc-Recordable, a type of Compact Disc on which data can be written to with a special recorder unit and read back on standard CD drives. So far, all such discs in CD format are write-once.

CD-ROM [Compact Disc read-only memory]: an acronym (pronounced see-dee-romm) for Compact Disc read-only memory, a type of optical data disk that uses the same basic technology as the popular CD audio disks to store up to approximately 650 megabytes of data. The standard CD-ROM drive can only read data (the data is permanently stamped on the disc during manufacturing), but recorder units are now available that can write data on discs that can be read on standard drives.

CD-ROM Extensions: a set of routines that connect the MS-DOS or PC-DOS operating systems to the driver routines for specific models of CD-ROM players. The extensions allow PC-compatible machines to read CD-ROM discs in the ISO 9660 and High Sierra formats.

CD-ROM upgrade kit: a complete combination of CD-ROM drive, interface card, software and cables needed to connect a CD drive to a particular type of personal computer. Most include a combination sound card and interface.

CD-ROM XA [Compact Disc Read-Only Memory Extended Architecture]: a format developed by Microsoft and others that adds compressed interleaved sound and graphics to the basic CD-ROM format. CD-I discs use a type of CD-ROM XA format.

CDTV [Commodore Dynamic Total Vision]: short for Commodore Dynamic Total Vision, an interactive multimedia system designed for home family use that uses programs on special CD-ROM discs.

CD-WO [Compact Disc-Write Once]: one term for optical discs that can be written by special recorder units and played back on standard CD drives.

chroma key: a color-based video matting (overlay) system that drops all areas of a selected color (usually blue) out of the foreground image, and substitutes instead the corresponding areas of a second image.

chrominance (chroma): the color component of a video signal or image

Chyron: a popular brand of video character generators. The name is often used loosely in the video industry to indicate any character generator or the resulting lettering.

CMYK: a method of representing color based on the cyan (C), magenta (M), yellow (Y) and black (K) inks used in color printing. The first three inks are sued to form all the available colors using subtractive color mixing, while the black is used to change tones or define edges.

coaxial cable (coax): a type of communications cable made of a central insulated conductor around which is wrapped a braid or foil (sharing the same axis). The concentric design provides high bandwidth and good protection against signal interference or radiation.

color bars (bars): a standard video test signal that uses blocks of solid colors made up of the three primary colors and their combinations. The most commonly used version was developed by the Society of Motion Picture and Television Engineers (SMPTE), and is consequently called "SMPTE bars."

color model: a method of representing the color of items or images, usually by their components along at least three dimensions. Common models include RGB (using red, green and blue light), HLS (hue, lightness and saturation), HSV (hue, saturation and value) and CMYK (using the common printing colors of cyan, magenta, yellow and black).

Compact Disc (CD): 1) the standard developed by Sony and Philips for distributing music and other information on plastic discs. 2) a plastic disc formatted according to these standards.

Compact Disc-Interactive (CD-I): a standard both for CDs containing combinations of sound, images, and computer instructions and for players specially constructed for these discs. Also known as Green Book for the informal name of the standard that defines the format.

Compact Video: The original name of the video compression method developed by SuperMac now called CinePak.

component: 1) in the Apple operating system, a software object that provides services to clients. 2) referring to video signals, a format that keeps color and brightness (luminance) information as two or more separate signals rather than combining them in one composite signal. Popular component formats include Betacam, MII, D1, and SVHS.

composite: 1) as applied to video, a signal that contains more than one type of information, such as picture and timing, or monochrome and color. 2) in image-creation software and systems, several items that are treated together as one object or given one name. 3) in

multimedia and information storage systems, said of items that contain data of more than one type or format or that are made up of references to multiple documents. 4) in some drawing programs, a preview of an illustration showing all layers or both type and art elements.

compression: the translation of data to a more compact form for storage or transmission (after which it can be restored to normal form).

control track (CTL): 1) on many video recording formats, a separate track that carries pulses used to set the timing and align the tape with the recording and playback heads. 2) a simple type of video positioning that relies on counting pulses on the tape rather than reading exact location information.

courseware: originally the term referred to the software containing actual lesson material for computerized instructional systems. Now, the term is often used more generically for educational software, audiovisual aids and sometimes even textbooks.

D-1: a format for recording component video signals (in which color and brightness information are carried on separate signals) in digital form developed by SMPTE.

D-2: a format for recording composite video signals (in which color and brightness information are carried within the same signal) in digital form developed by SMPTE.

decimate: to throw out selected portions of a signal to reduce the amount that has to be encoded or compressed. It is a usual step in most types of lossey compression. Decimation is the most common form of subsampling.

device driver: a special section of computer code that translates the more general commands from an operating system or user programs into the exact

code needed by a specific peripheral device.

device-independent bitmap (DIB): a Microsoft Windows format for 256-color bitmapped graphics.

digital compositing: combining images in digital form rather than as analog signals. Digital compositing allows all the features of computer image processing to be applied to video or graphic arts images.

digital signal processor: a specialized computer chip designed to perform quick, complex operations on signals that represent digitized signal waveforms. Most DSPs include some type of parallel processing-capability,

digital-to-analog converter (DAC): a circuit or module that changes a digital value to a corresponding signal such as a current or voltage.

digital video: signals that represent moving pictures (with or without sound) as a series of number values rather than as a smoothly varying signal.

Digital Video Cassette (DVC): a storage and signal format for video that stores images on ¼-inch metal particle tape using a digital format similar to CCIR-601 and an adapted form of JPEG compression

Digital Video Interactive (DVI): a set of hardware and software products for compressing and decompressing video images. The system supports both a Real Time Video (RTV) format that can be produced in real time with a single board for a desktop computer and the higher-quality Presentation Level Video (PLV) that must be produced on mainframe-class computers.

DirectDraw: a feature in Windows 95 that lets the authors of games and other high-speed software include fast calls to the display screen rather than working through the more lengthy standard windows Graphical Device Interface (GDI).

Director: a multimedia presentation and animation program published by Macromedia. It is now available for both the Macintosh and Windows.

dither: to place small dots of black, white or color in an area of an image to soften an edge, to visually smooth a jagged line, or to simulate a shade or tone.

DMA [direct memory access]: an abbreviation for "direct memory access," the transfer of data to and from memory without routing it through the central processing unit (CPU) chip.

DMA channel: one of the limited number of logical pathways available in many computers for exchanging data between peripherals (or between peripherals and memory) without going through the CPU (central processing unit) chip.

doublespeed or double-speed: said of CD-ROM drives that can transfer data at a sustained rate of approximately 300 kilobytes per second, or twice the transfer rate provided by the original CD-ROM drives.

downsample: to reduce the amount of data in a file or stream by selecting only parts of the original information.

drop frame: a type of time code for video sequences that periodically skips a code to take into account the small difference between the nominal 60 frames per second (fps) and actual 59.57 fps rate of NTSC-format video. Over an hour, 108 codes are dropped.

dub: 1. to make a copy of a video or audio sequence or program. 2. the copy so made. 3. to copy a new audio section into an existing video or film sequence.

edit controller: a device or system that sends the instructions to video (or

audio) recording or playback devices to position them at the right points and set the modes needed to assemble an edited production.

edit decision list (EDL): a list of points where cuts or special effects should be made. An edit decision list can be created on an off-line system, a personal computer-based editing system or from a window dub for later assembly on an on-line system.

envelope: referring to sound or video signals, the shape of the waveform that makes up a sound. Two notes of the same basic pitch will sound very different if they have different envelopes.

Extended Graphics Adapter (EGA): a video display standard introduced by IBM in 1990 that provides for 256 colors at 1024 by 768 pixels or 65 thousand colors at 640 by 480 pixels. The original IBM version only supported interlaced displays.

Extended Multitimbral specification: the more sophisticated of the two synthesizer subsystems standards that the Multimedia PC specifications allow audio board makers to choose from. It calls for 9 melodic timbres and 8 percussive timbres that can simultaneously play 16 melodic notes and 16 percussive notes.

extrude: a video effect that seemingly gives three dimensions to a two dimensional object by extending solid objects outward from two-dimensional lines and shapes.

fidelity: closeness of the received signal to the original. In most audio and video formats, there is a trade-off between fidelity and maximum storage capacity.

field: applied to a video signal, a complete set of horizontal lines making up one pass of the electronic beam down the screen. In computer video where the lines are sent sequentially, a field is the same as a frame (complete image). In

most broadcast video formats, two interlaced fields are used to paint out each complete frame, placing every other potential line in the first field then the intervening lines in the second.

field rate: for a video signal, the number of fields transmitted per second.

fill: 1) in video production, a supplementary light used to soften shadows and bring out the background missed by the key light. 2) in graphics, a color or pattern occupying a defined region 3) to place color or pattern in a region.

filter: 1) a partially-transparent material that passes (or blocks) light of a particular color or orientation. 2) an electronic circuit or unit that passes (or blocks) signals of a particular type or frequency. 3) more loosely, any circuit or device that shapes or conditions a signal. That includes so-called anti-aliasing, deflickering and sharpening filters.

flanging: an audio effect that creates a "wow-wow" effect by echoing different frequencies at a changing rate.

flash digitizer: A device that turns an analog signal such as a video input into digital form through a rapid direct parallel process instead of through a longer sequential process. Flash digitizers are used in some video frame grabbers for fast image conversions.

flat: 1. as applied to images in general, ones with low contrast. 2. as applied to the shading of objects in image creation software, shading that uses a uniform color and brightness for each polygon (small region) rather than varying the shading at edges or across the polygon.

FLC: a more sophisticated version of the Autodesk Animator FLI format animation file that supports 640 by 480 images in up to 8-bit color. FLC viewers are available for most popular computers.

FLI: the original Autodesk Animator animation file format. It supports 320 by

240-pixel images in up to 8-bit color. FLI viewers are available for most popular computers.

flicker: 1) perceived rapid variations in image brightness caused by insufficiently rapid screen refresh rates. 2) rapid variations in an interlaced image caused by differences in the image presented in each field

flying erase head: an erase head that rotates along with the recording heads in a helical scan video recorder, and consequently can erase a single video line at a time. This allows new segments to be added after previously recorded segments without creating a visible glitch between them.

FMV [Full Motion Video]: video that plays at a frame rate sufficient to seemingly fuse the separate images into a smooth continuous picture. Following broadcast video standards, this is usually considered 30 frames per second in the U.S. and Japan and 25 frames per second in most of the rest of the world.

fractal: 1) Any image or object that can be constructed using a special kind of iterative (repeating) mathematical formula. 2) compression techniques that use these mathematical formulas to represent images.

frame: 1) a complete video image (which in an interlaced system such as the NTSC format used for television is made up of 2 fields). 2) in computerized instruction, it used to mean material shown at one time on the screen. But the greater use of animation and interactive screens, the term is now also used to mean a logical sequence of images treated as a unit in the instructional design.

frame accurate: said of video editing, record, and playback systems that can locate and act on video images exactly at a specified single picture image. Most professional video equipment is frame accurate, but consumer products can find only approximate locations.

frame buffer: 1) a separate memory or area of main memory used for storing a complete video image. 2) a video display card or adapter than can hold a complete video image in its own memory rather than relying on the main memory for image storage.

frame grabber: a board or circuit that extracts a single frame (one image) or a sequence of separate video frames from a video signal, making the image available for editing, transfer, or printout.

frame rate: for a video image or movie, the number of complete images presented per second.

full motion video (FMV): video presented at the standard frame rate (number of images per second normally used for broadcasting in that area. In the U.S. and Japan, FMV is usually considered 30 frames per second, while in Europe it's 25 frames per second.

General MIDI: a standard configuration for MIDI digital music systems that assigns popular instruments and sounds to specified channels.

General MIDI Mode (GMM): for multimedia PCs, the Windows MIDI Mapper arrangement that sets patches and channels to the default standards set by the MIDI Manufacturers Association.

general-purpose controller: as applied to MIDI systems, a device that can be assigned by the user to regulate various other devices and instruments.

generation: for an image or copy, the number of reproduction steps from the original (which is the first generation). In general, higher generation numbers are likely to be less sharp.

genlock: 1) short for synchronization generator lock, a feature of some video systems that allows them to set their timing to match the timing of an outside signal. Genlock is needed to overlay or mix two video signals. 2) more loosely, a computer display adapter that includes such a circuit and can overlay computer graphics on external video.

Green Book: an informal name for the standard developed by Sony and Philips for CD-I (Compact Disc Interactive) discs and players.

header: 1) as applied to CD-ROM discs, a section of four bytes at the start of data sectors that indicates the type of information in the sector. 2) a set of pins on a circuit board where a connector will be connected. Most common are duals, right angle or in-line. 3) the prefix part of a message in data communication giving address and control information.

Hi8: a Sony trademark for a variation on the 8mm videotape format that adds extended fidelity for the luminance (brightness) detail and separated video (S-video) outputs.

High Sierra format: a format for CD-ROM disks that can be read on different types of computers. It has largely been supplanted for new discs by the related ISO 9660 format.

hot: 1) as applied to recordings, especially audio recordings, recorded at or near the maximum possible signal level. 2) as applied to the operation of cameras, in use (recording or on-air). 3) as applied to interactive applications, an on-screen region or object that can be clicked on to initiate an action.

hybrid: for a CD-ROM, one that contains tracks of more than one format.

hypermedia: a system or document that presents multiple pathways that the user can select and follow, rather than simply following one path from beginning to end. It may include text, graphics, sound and other types of data.

hypertext: a document system that provide multiple pathways through text that the user can select and follow, rather than simply presenting material from beginning to end.

IconAuthor: an authoring tool for multimedia and interactive applications from Aimtech, Inc. that uses a flowchart metaphor. Versions are available for various platforms, including Unix and Windows and there's a player-only version for the Macintosh.

IDE [Integrated Drive Electronics]: 1) originally, an interface between AT-style computers and hard disk drives. 2) in the EIDE or similar ATAPI extended forms, an interface that can connect disk drives, CD-ROM drives and tape drives to PC-class computers.

I-frame: In the MPEG encoding format, an "intra" (or "independent") frame compressed using only the data in that frame. I-frames are easier to decode than varieties such as B-frames or P-frames that use interframe information, but provide less compression.

in-betweening or tweening: a mode or function in computer animation programs that draws the needed intermediate images to create simulated motion between two given points.

Indeo: an Intel trademark for products that apply the firm's DVI technology to desktop and digital video systems.

indexed color: a color system that uses information from the user or from programs as a pointer to a table of output colors, rather than specifying the color directly.

Infotainment: programs that deliver informational elements while presenting the appearance of entertainment

insert edit: referring to video editing, a style where new sequences are laid down on top of a continuous control track or prior continuous image. While requiring more preparation than assemble editing (which places sequences one after each other), the result is likely to have fewer errors in timing.

Interactive Multimedia Association (IMA): a trade association of producers of interactive multimedia equipment headquartered in Arlington, Virginia. It used to be called the Interactive Video Industry Association (IVIA).

interactive video: 1) the integration of video and computer technologies in which a video program (moving pictures and voice tracks) and computer programs run together so that the user's choices or actions affect the program outcome. 2) the linking of a videodisc or videotape player to a computer, allowing selections from the video program to be shown under computer control.

Interactive Video Industry Association (IVIA): the former name for trade association of producers of interactive multimedia equipment and products that has now become the Interactive Multimedia Association (IMA).

interformat editing: in video production, editing from a source sequence on one format (type of videotape or recording mode) to a result in another format. It is often done to combine the advantages of portable small formats for taping with larger formats for editing.

interframe compression: methods for reducing the size of a video stream or file that use information about the similarities between successive video frames. Interframe recording tends to be more compact than intraframe coding, but requires more complex systems for compression or editing.

interlaced: for video signals and displays, ones that paint each image in two passes (fields) down the screen, with the first pass creating the odd lines and the second the even lines. This approach reduces the bandwidth needed to transmit the video but causes flicker in computer graphics.

interleaved audio: a method of recording blocks of digital data interspersed with blocks of audio information on a compact disc or other medium.

International Interactive Communications Society (IICS): an organization of producers of interactive multimedia projects, headquartered in Washington, D.C..

interpolated frame: in the MPEG standard for encoding video signals, a single video image recreated by the received based on applying averaging or smoothing operations to preceding and following frames.

intraframe compression: methods for reducing the size of a video stream or file that make use of the information within each frame but not the similarities between successive frames.

IRQ [interrupt request]: 1) a signal used on PCs to indicate a software routine, peripheral device or circuit needs attention from the central processor (the CPU). 2) one of the signal lines used to carry such interrupts from hardware devices to the PC's interrupt controller chip. The original PC provided 8 such lines, while most recent models provide 16. Because IRQ lines cannot be shared except in limited special circumstances and most boards and circuits have preferred IRQ lines, it can sometimes be difficult to find a configuration that provides a new device with a suitable line.

ISO 9660: a standard for CD-ROM discs meant for use with diverse computer systems. ISO 9660 discs can be read by most common personal computer CD-ROM drives if the CD player has the right driver software.

jewel box: the clear hard plastic case that many CDs come in.

jog: in a video editing system. to change position in a video clip by a single frame or small number of frames.

JPEG: 1) an acronym (pronounced jay-pegg) for "Joint Photographic Experts Group," an industry committee that developed a compression standard originally intended for still images. 2) more informally, the compression standard developed by that group.

jukebox: an optical or magnetic storage unit that holds multiple disc that can be selected and automatically loaded into the play or record station.

key: 1) in an animation sequence or video edit, short for keyframe (an image used as a starting, ending or reference point). 2) in lighting for video, film, or photography, short for keylight, the principal (and usually brightest) light illuminating the main subject. 3) to switch between two or more video sources, based on a control signal. 4) the control signal used to switch between two or more video sources. 5) an image whose color or brightness as each point is used to determine the switching between two or more video signals.

keyer: a piece of video equipment that seemingly superimposes two or more images by quickly switching among inputs during the individual scans across a screen that make up a video image. This allows a weather forecaster to appear to be standing in front of a map, or a newscaster to appear to be in front of an electronic background.

keyframe: in animation or video editing, an image used as a starting, ending or reference point.

Level 1 or Level I: as applied to a videodisc system, the common industry designation for one that supports only direct controls such as start and stop, rather than complete computer-controlled interaction or programmability.

Level 1: in referring to a multimedia PC, one equipped for the initial Microsoft Multimedia PC specifications.

Level 2 or Level II: as applied to a videodisc system, the common industry designation for one that supports some interaction through an internal processor, but not full control by an external computer. A Level II system can read a data program from audio channel 2 of the videodisc, but can't normally record user responses.

Level 3 or Level III: as applied to a videodisc system, the common industry designation for one that supports interactive use, computer connections, and the recording of user responses. Macintosh-computer-controlled systems are usually configured as Level III systems.

Level 4 or Level IV: as applied to a videodisc system, one that supports interactivity but gets its data program from information encoded in video portion of the signal from the videodisc rather than from an audio track or computer connection.

Level A: in the CD-I format, a method of recording audio that offers fidelity comparable to that of standard CD audio but compresses the data to use only about half as much space on disc.

Level B: in the CD-I and CD-ROM XA compact disc formats, a method of recording audio that offers medium fidelity but that is somewhat compressed compared with full-fidelity audio. Level B uses 4-bit sampling at 37.8 kHz for an effective bandwidth of 17 kHz. Level B mono requires 1 out of every 8 sectors on the disc, while stereo requires 1 in 4.

Level C: in the CD-I and CD-ROM XA compact disc formats, a method of recording audio that offers fidelity sufficient for speech but that is highly compressed compared with full-fidelity audio. Level C uses 4-bit sampling at 18.9 kHz for an effective bandwidth of

8.5 kHz. Level C mono requires 1 out of every 16 sectors on the disc, while stereo requires 1 in 8.

linear audio: a method of recording audio on videotape that uses a separate track along the length of the tape. This method generally provides lower fidelity, but allows the audio to be edited separately from the video.

line in: an input on an audio or video system that expects a pre-amplifier-level signal (typically 100 mV to 1V).

line level: in audio connections, a signal that ranges up to approximately 1 volt for full signal. This is likely to be the output of a preamplifier rather than the direct signal from a microphone.

line out: an output on an audio or video system that provides a pre-amplifier-level signal (typically 100 mV to 1V) for connection to other equipment.

Lingo: the scripting language used by the Director authoring program published by Macromedia.

link: 1) a connection between nodes or items of information in a hypermedia system. 2) connection between network nodes.

longitudinal time code (LTC): a time signal placed in one of the tracks that run the length of a videotape. On some recorders, one of the audio tracks must be used for the LTC, while others provide a special time code track. The code is normally the SMPTE Time Code. LTC can only be read while the tape is moving.

loop through or loopthrough: on a video or MIDI connection, an output connector that sends out the same signal as received on a corresponding input (so it can also be used by another unit).

lossey compression: compression methods that produce files that decompress to provide only an approximate copy of the original data. These approaches usually provide larger compression ratios than lossless methods, and are used primarily for images or sounds where every bit of data isn't essential to provide a useful representation.

lossless compression: compression methods that produce files that decompress to an exact copy of the original data. These approaches usually provide less compression than lossey methods, but are required for programs, databases or text files where every bit of data is essential.

luminance (luma): the brightness or intensity component of an image or signal, particularly the brightness without regard to color. For historical reasons, it is usually abbreviated as "Y".

luminance bandwidth: the range of frequency representing brightness (and therefore the amount of shape detail) that a system can record or transmit. In many video formats, it is greater than the chroma (color) bandwidth.

luminance key: a signal used to switch between two or more video images based on the brightness (luminance) of a signal.

machine-independent: 1) software designed to work on more than one type or model of computer. 2) software that offers similar performance or output even when run on different types or models of machines.

Media Control Interface (MCI): a platform-independent set of commands and structures that define how a program interacts with multimedia devices and resources. It was defined by Microsoft as part of the firm's multimedia specification.

media independent: said of a project or program that will produce the same sound and/or images when played back

from different format systems—such as a training program designed to work either on videodisc or on videotape.

mic level or microphone level: a high-sensitivity audio input intended for low signal-strength inputs such as those provided by microphones rather than the more powerful signals provided by amplifiers.

MIDI [Musical Instrument Digital Interface]: (pronounced middee) industry-standard connection for digital control of musical instruments and related devices.

Mode 1: CD-ROM data discs, a format that adds a 3rd level of error correction for each block, leaving 2,048 bytes for data.

Mode 2: 1) CD-ROM data discs, a format that uses only the error-correction facilities of the underlying Red Book layer for each block, leaving 2352 bytes for data. 2) for CD-ROM discs, a format for recording and playback that provides 2,336 bytes of non-error-corrected data from each block on the disc and a transfer rate of 175.2 kilobytes/second.

Morph: 1) to seemingly melt one image into another by smoothly moving each point from its original position to its location in the new image. 2) a graphics program published by Gryphon Software that produces such changes.

motion blur: a blending or streaking effect deliberately added to images to simulate the appearance of moving objects.

motion choreography: in animation and computer graphics, determining the displacement (change in position) of each object over time.

motion JPEG: the use of the JPEG compression standard for still images to compress video as a series of 30 independent frames per second. Although providing less compression than video

compression standards such as MPEG that make use of similarities between successive frames, motion JPEG files are easier to edit.

motion video: 1) video sequences with frame rates (number of pictures per second) sufficient to appear as continuous moving pictures rather than as successions of moving images. 2) the type of video image produced by a camera, rather than still video, animation or computer graphics.

MPC [Multimedia PC]: a trademark of the Multimedia PC Marketing Council used to indicate personal computers, subsystems or software that meet a set of defined specifications for a multimedia personal computer.

MPEG [Moving Pictures Expert Group]: 1) (pronounced emm-pegg) an industry committee that is developing a set of standards for compressing moving images. 2) more informally, the standard developed by that committee.

MPEG-1: a form of the MPEG compression method optimized for data rates in the 1 to 1.5 megabyte/sec range, such as the transfer rate of CD-ROM drives and T-1 communications links.

MPEG-2: a form of the MPEG compression method optimized for data rates above 5 megabits/sec and intended for applications such as broadcast video and medical imaging.

MS-DOS CD-ROM Extensions: a set of routines that connect the MS-DOS or PC-DOS operating system to the driver routines for specific models of CD-ROM players. The extensions allow machines running these operating systems to read CD-ROM discs formatted in the ISO 9660 and High Sierra format.

Multimedia Extensions (MME): a set of routines and specifications for running multimedia programs with Microsoft Corp.'s Windows 3.0 operating environment. Their functions were absorbed into Windows 3.1.

Multimedia PC (MPC): A personal computer that meets a set of specifications needed to run certain types of Windows-based multimedia software. Originally, it was an IBM-compatible PC with at least a 286 processor and VGA display, plus a CD-ROM drive and a sound card—but in recent years the sponsors have added a series of more sophisticated levels.

Multimedia ToolBook: A Windows-based multimedia authoring program from Asymetrix that uses the metaphor of a book with individual pages containing fields, buttons and other objects plus a complete scripting language called OpenScript.

Multimedia Windows: an informal term for Microsoft's Windows operating environment along with the company's Multimedia Extensions running on the appropriate hardware.

MultiSpin: a trademark of NEC Technologies Inc. for the firm's line of multiple speed CD-ROM drives that transfer data both at the original CD rate of 150 kB/s (kilobytes per second) and at faster rates such as 300 kB/s and faster. The first model was introduced in 1992.

MultiSync: 1) a registered trademark of NEC Technologies, Inc. for the firm's line of monitors designed to work with a wide range of video input frequencies and formats. 2) commonly but improperly used to indicate any brand and make of multifrequency monitor.

narration: dialog or commentary by someone outside the frame (visible scene) in a film or video, or that is not synchronized with the action or visible speech.

narrowcast: 1) to aim a program at a small but defined proportion of the potential audience. 2) a program so aimed.

National Television Standards Committee (NTSC): a common misnomer for the National Television Systems Committee (NTSC), the industry group that formulated the standards for American (U.S.) color television.

National Television Systems Committee (NTSC): the industry group that formulated the standards for American (U.S.) color television.

noninterlaced: said of video systems that create images by painting each horizontal line across the screen in succession rather than painting alternate sets of lines in two sweeps down the screen (which is called interlaced scan). Also called progressive scan.

nonlinear editing: video editing methods that record the source clips on hard disk, allowing you to jump directly to any clip without having to shuttle through any clips that came before or after.

NTSC [National Television Systems Committee]: originally, an abbreviation for National Television Systems Committee, the industry group that formulated the standards for American (U.S.) color television. Often but erroneously called an abbreviation for the never-existing National Television Standards Committee.

off-line: 1) as applied to video editing, a system than can only make an edit decision list (EDL) or simple edits (recordings) such as cuts, rather than one that can perform a full range of editing and video effects. 2) to edit video on such a system.

on-line: 1) as applied to video editing, a complete system that can perform edits (make recordings) and add special effects. On-line systems are expensive, so rough edits or edit decision lists (EDLs) are commonly done on less costly off-line systems. 2) to edit video on such a system

OpenScript: the scripting language used by Asymetrix's ToolBook multimedia authoring program for Windows.

OPL: a line of synthesizer chips from Yamaha used in many sound boards including the Creative Labs Sound Blaster series. These chips use FM Synthesis, a low-cost method for translating digital data into musical tones.

Orange Book: 1) the informal name for the specification that describes the additions to the CD-ROM standards for write-once CD discs. 2) discs or tracks written with that format

overdub: 1) to add a signal or channel to existing material. 2) particularly to add a new layer or channel to existing audio material.

overlay: 1) to show one video image positioned in front of another. To overlay two video signals, they must be synchronized to the same timing signal (genlocked). 2) especially in video images, to show text on top of a picture.

oversample: to read data at a higher rate than normal to produce more accurate results or to make it easier to sample.

overscan: for a video system, a mode in which the image is made slightly larger than the face of screen, ensuring the image fills the entire viewing area. This is the normal mode for television-style video, but most computer systems use underscan instead.

palette: an on-screen display of tools, options, options or modes available for selection by the user, most often in a rectangular grid display.

pan: 1) in video and film, to rotate the camera horizontally (thus changing the angle of view). 2) in computer graphics, to move in a specified direction along the plane of the drawing, keeping the same scale and orientation. 3) in a MIDI (computerized music) system, a controller that shifts the position of a voice between the right and left stereo channels.

PC Speaker Driver: a Microsoft-supplied program for Windows that attempts to produce music and other Windows sounds using just software and the speaker built in to PCs. It's no real substitute for a sound board, but given that the speaker was only designed to reproduce beep warnings, it is remarkable that it works at all.

phase alternate line (PAL): the format for color television signals used in West Germany, England, Holland, and several other countries. PAL uses an interlaced format with 50 fields and 25 frames per second, and 625 lines per screen.

Photo CD: a Kodak trademark for a set of technologies for storing and recalling images, particularly for taking images first captured on photographic film, digitizing them at multiple levels of resolution, and then storing them on CD-ROM discs.

pickup: 1) a microphone. 2) a non-acoustic transducer intended to emit an electronic signal corresponding to the sound produced by a musical instrument. 3. in video or film production, a shot or sequence recorded after the main sequence and used in editing either to add interest during editing or to cover flaws. 3) in video or film production, a shot or sequence recorded after the main sequence and used in editing either to add interest during editing or to cover flaws.

PICT: the standard file format used by Macintosh applications to pass images back and forth and to store images on the Clipboard. PICT files consist of the Macintosh QuickDraw routines needed to create the image.

picture depth: the amount of storage allocated per picture element, usually expressed either in bits or in the number of colors (or shades) that can be repre-

sented by that number of bits. Common values include 1-bit (black and white), 8-bit (256 colors) and 24-bit (millions of colors).

picture element (pixel): in a digital image or display, the smallest part of a picture that can be addressed or changed.

post: short for post-production, the steps in producing a film, video or multimedia project that take place after any live filming or construction of the basic images.

posterize: to transform an image to a more stark form by rounding all tonal values to a small number of possible values.

premaster: in the production of a compact disc, record, or videodisc, to format the data into the special configuration needed on the master. Typically, this includes adding error correction and location information.

Premiere: a video-oriented multimedia editing program published by Adobe Systems, Inc..

processor audio: sound, music, or speech created by data that has been routed through or created in the normal digital pathways of a computer system and played back under the control of the computer, rather than sound that is merely encoded in digital form for playback using standard digital-to-analog circuits.

progressive scan: said of video systems that create images by painting each horizontal line across the screen in succession rather than painting alternate sets of lines in two sweeps down the screen (which is called interlaced scan). Also called noninterlaced.

Projector: a player program supplied by Macromedia to display files produced by the firm's Director program. Macromedia has announced a goal of produc-

ing Projector programs for all common computer and interactive television platforms.

prosumer: a neologism (made-up word) for a market niche for products in the intersection between professional and consumer markets. It is often used to describe video gear that is below the usual broadcast grade but above what most people would buy for home use.

public access: 1) referring to public or private television and radio systems, the provision of time for independent program producers to air their work. Many cable TV systems are required to provide a certain level of public access as part of their franchise agreements. 2) referring to multimedia systems, ones intended for use by the general public or by a wide variety of customers or visitors. Most feature touchscreens or other simple inputs.

pulse code modulation (PCM): The representation of analog signals as sequences of discrete digital pulses.

quadspeed or quad-speed: said of CD-ROM drives that can transfer data at a sustained rate of approximately 600 kilobytes per second, or four times the transfer rate provided by the original CD-ROM drives.

QuickTime: 1) Apple Computer's architecture for working with time-based data types such as sounds and video. 2) the Extension program for the Macintosh Operating System used to add the ability to work with time-based media. 3) used loosely for the QuickTime Movie Format, a data format defined by Apple Computer for digital presentations that can include sound, animation and video images.

ray tracing: a technique for creating graphic images done by calculating where each ray (small point) of light that reaches the viewer would have come from and what objects would have altered it.

RCA connector: the common connector used for most back-panel audio connections and for some types of video. It uses relatively low-cost push-on male and female connectors consisting of an inner connector within a concentric ring about 8 mm in diameter that forms the outer connector. Also commonly called a "phono connector" because of its frequent use on phonographs.

Red Book: 1) the common name for the book that lists the standards for Compact Disc audio as specified by Sony and Philips, the developers of this format. 2) on a mixed mode disc, tracks formatted according to this standard.

refresh rate: the number of times per second that a video display system redraws the image on screen. Rates below about 75 images per second can cause flicker, depending on the image size, lighting and image content.

rehearse: during editing, to see what the results of an edit step would look like without actually recording the result; also called "preview" on most systems.

render: to draw an image as it would appear rather than in schematic or blueprint form.

retrieval engine: a program or section of code to be embedded in other programs that finds and presents data in large data collections. Retrieval engines are commonly used to provide fast and easy access to large stores of data on CD-ROM discs.

RGB [red, green, blue]: 1) as applied to video systems, three color signals that can between them create a complete video image. Most computer graphics systems use this tri-color approach rather than mixing the colors together as is done with most non-computer video. RGB systems can be digital (each of the three signals can only assume a number of defined states) or analog (each signal can vary smoothly over its range). 2) as

applied to video systems, creating the image by sending three separate color signals over individual lines and then combining them on screen to make an image rather than transmitting the picture information on one signal line (composite video) or as one brightness or one color line (S-video). RGB systems can be digital (each of the three signals can only assume a number of defined states) or analog (each signal can vary smoothly over its range). Most computers now use analog RGB video systems. 3) as a color model, a method of representing all colors as the combination of red, green and blue light that would create that color. The RGB color space is usually represented as a square, with one corner black and the opposing corner white. Although this model is mechanically simple and is easy to compare to the actual operation of RGB video systems, it is hard to work with artistically or conceptually.

RGB analog: a characterization of video systems that work with video signals carried on three signal lines in continous (analog) form. This is the type of video used by the IBM VGA video system, the Apple Macintosh line and by most other personal computers.

rich text: 1) text that has additional embedded information regarding formatting or structuring. For example, text with italics or a document with an outline format. 2) specifically Rich Text Format (RTF), a format developed by Microsoft to exchange text with styles and formatting using only normal alphanumeric symbols.

Rock Ridge Interchange Protocol (RRIP): a proposed extension of the ISO 9660 standards for CD-ROM discs to handle files in the POSIX format.

RS-170A: a recommended standard (RS) of the Electronics Industries Association that specifies color video signals for the common "NTSC" format used for broadcast and most consumer video products in the United States and Japan.

safe action area: in a video image, the portion that will be visible on most receivers after transmission and reception, excluding the edges of the image that may be partially obscured on some sets. It is the inner 80 percent of the image (which assumes a possible 10 percent loss at each edge).

safe area: in a video image, the portion that will be visible after transmission and reception on the average receiver or monitor. The outer 10% to 20% of the image is usually considered unsafe because it may be hidden behind a bezel (frame) on the receiver.

safe title area: in a video image, the portion that will be visible on just about all receivers after transmission and reception and is thus suitable for titles where all portions must be visible. It is the inner 60 percent of the image (which assumes a possible 20 percent loss at each edge).

sampled sound: sound that has been captured in digital form from an acoustic or electrical waveform rather than synthesized (created) by a computer system.

saturated: said of areas or images that have a strong color (chroma) component. They're harder to reproduce in most types of broadcast video.

SB [Sound Blaster]: used in phrases such as "SB-compatible" to mean the Sound Blaster series of PC Audio cards sold by Creative Labs.

scalable: as applied to video or sound playback technologies, ones that allow the same data to create output over a range of quality levels, with better reception systems automatically generating higher quality levels.

scan line: one of the sweeps across the screen that makes up a video image.

scanning frequency: 1) usually meaning the horizontal scanning frequency, the number of horizontal sweeps across the screen per second used to form a video image. 2) the vertical scanning frequency, the number of vertical sweeps down the screen per second used to form a video image.

score: 1) the written rendition of a piece of music. 2) the process of writing down a composition in a form suitable for reading and playing. 3) in Macromedia's Director animation programs, the diagrammatic representation of an animation sequence (a movie).

ScreenCam: a screen recorder program from Lotus Development that is used to capture and play back sequences of operations and screen displays for tutorials and demonstrations.

seek time: The average time required to locate specific data on a disk. It's often computed as the time necessary to move the read head to the correct track and the time for the disk to spin one half rotation.

self-powered: said of speakers that have their own built-in amplifiers — but obviously they still need a power source of either batteries or a plug-in power supply.

sequencer: 1) a computer or controller that issues instructions to programmable musical instruments. 2) a software program that lets the user compose and edit music.

serial VTR: a videotape recorder (VTR) that can be controlled over a single-channel control wire such as the normal RS-232 or RS-422 connections used between computers and modems.

sfx: in audio work, a common abbreviation for "sound effects."

shot: a single continuous run of film or tape.

SMPTE [Society of Motion Picture and Television Engineers]: 1) (pronounced simmptee) a professional engineering society that establishes standards for motion picture and television equipment. 2) loosely, the time code standard developed by that group and now used by almost all professional video editing systems.

snd: a Macintosh audio file format used for both system sounds and for general recording and playback.

Sound Blaster: 1) loosely, a line of PC audio cards sold by Creative Labs that became the de facto standard. 2) narrowly, the original card in this line. Unlike later models, it did not include a CD-ROM interface.

SOX [SOund eXchange]: a popular freeware program for translating between audio file formats.

spatial resolution: in video systems, the number of lines or dots that make up each image. When not otherwise specified, the word "resolution" by itself is presumed to mean spatial resolution, rather than color or time resolution.

special effects generator (SEG): a video signal processing device that changes the way one or more images appear on the video screen.

spline: a type of curve used in many graphics programs to create smooth motion paths.

split edit: in video or film production, an edit (switch to a new input) of just the audio or just the video, leaving the other of these elements continuing from the previous source.

sprite: a graphics object that can be moved around the screen as a unit.

Standard MIDI File (SMF): a format for placing the data from a MIDI data stream in a file that can be used with many music applications.

step time: in MIDI recording, recording event by event for later playback at full speed instead of recording at full (real-time) speed.

still store: a large-capacity optical or magnetic disc that is used to store a number of individual (still) video images for use in editing or broadcast.

storyboard: 1) to produce a set of images representing the flow of a video or film project 2) a sequenced set of images produced for that purpose.

subsample: to throw out selected portions of a signal to reduce the amount that has to be encoded or compressed. It is a usual step in most types of lossey compression.

Surround Video: a Microsoft technology for encoding panoramic views into graphics files, allowing the user to choose to look out at any angle from a fixed pivot point or series of individual points. From the user's point of view, it is very similar to Apple's QuickTime VR.

sustained transfer rate: for a CD-ROM drive, the number of bytes per second the drive can supply when reading selections or data objects larger than its built-in buffer.

S-video [separated video]: formats such as S-VHS and Hi8 that store and transfer their brightness and color (luminance and chroma) as separate signals. Also called Y/C video.

symmetrical compression: as applied to video or audio data, methods for squeezing the data for storage or transmission that take an equal amount of time and resources to compress the data as to de-compress it.

sync [synchronization]: as applied to video signals, the portion of the signal or a separate signal that carries the overall timing information.

synthesized sound: sound that has been created from a series of mathematical parameters rather than replayed from recorded samples.

synthesizer: 1) a musical instrument that electronically creates and shapes sounds according to changeable settings. Along with providing a choice of such basic sound qualities as pitch, loudness ,and duration, most synthesizers allow the user to alter the tonal qualities of each note. 2) particularly, a module or instrument that responds to MIDI commands and produces the requested audio output.

TARGA [Truevision Advanced Raster Graphics Adapter]: 1) a 24-bit color image format defined by Truevision, originally for that company's line of TARGA videographics interface cards. It is now used as an exchange format by many other image-creation and editing programs. 2) a series of graphics cards for PCs and Windows produced by Truevision. The PC series was among the first to support full-color (24-bit) display.

temporal redundancy: signal data that duplicates information found at an earlier or later time in the signal.

timbre: the character of a sound rather than its pure pitch (frequency). It is determined by the number and size of the various overtones.

timebase corrector or time base corrector (TBC): a unit that resets the timing portion of a video signal to the standard values for that video format. TBCs are often used to clean up the output from computer video boards or from videocassette recorders (VCRs) before broadcast or further recording or to synchronize two independent video signals.

time code: 1) in video production, an electronic marking of elapsed time placed on a tape to facilitate editing. 2) specifically, the time signals defined by the Society of Motion Picture and Televi-

sion Engineers. The code SMPTE code consists of 4 sets of numbers representing hour, minute, second and frame, in the format hh:mm:ss:ff.

title: in publishing, a single volume or set of volumes sold as a set under the same name. Often used in discussions of the number of titles available in different electronic formats.

true color: 1) color systems in which the color information in the image is used directly to create the output color rather than as an index to a table of colors in a palette. 2) said of color systems that have enough available colors to make the choices seem continuous to the human eye. In most cases, this is considered to be 24-bit color (about 16 million available colors).

tween: in animation and graphics, to automatically create an interpolated image between two set images. Tweening speeds up the creation of animated sequences by letting the user define only the keyframe images and letting the computer fill in the intervening pictures.

UHF: 1) short for "ultra-high frequency," the radio frequency from 300 to 3,000 MHz. 2) Also used more specifically to indicate the TV broadcast band located in this range. In the United States, UHF channels 14 through 83 occupy the range from 470 MHz to 890 MHz.

Ultimatte: a brand name for a type of chroma key system used to overlay multiple video images. The Ultimatte system also transfers the luminance (brightness) image of the dropout color, allowing shadows to be transferred into the composite image.

Ultimedia: IBM's brand name for its multimedia hardware and software products. It is supposed to suggest "the ultimate in multimedia."

U-matic: a trademark for Sony Corporation's ¾-inch video systems, including tape, recorders and players. The first U-

matic units were delivered in 1971. It is a composite format, with moderate resolution.

unbalanced: said of communications channels in which the information is carried as a signal on one wire referenced to ground. Although less costly than balanced configurations that carry the signal as differences between two wires, unbalanced lines are more likely to pick up external electrical noise.

validation: in computerized instruction, trying the lesson out on a group of students to check that it proceeds the way it is intended to.

value: when speaking of color, the degree of lightness or darkness.

variable frequency monitor: a video monitor that can accommodate a range of horizontal and vertical input frequencies, and thus work with signals from a variety of sources. Usually, the range includes several common computer video formats or several broadcast standards.

vector graphic: images and drawings made up of lines and other geometric elements rather than out of individual dots.

vectorscope: a television test instrument that shows a video signal in a circular form with the displacement around the circle indicating the timing of that portion relative to signal reference points. It is widely used to check and adjust the color component of the signal.

vertical blanking interval (VBI): the portion of the video signal during which the picture information is suppressed at the end of the field. It is provided to allow the scanning beam in a crt to return from the bottom to the top of the picture. In the standard NTSC video format, it includes the first 21 horizontal lines of each field.

vertical interval switching: changing between two video signals during the vertical blanking interval at the end of a scan down the screen so that there is no visible glitch in the output signal.

vertical interval time code (VITC): (the abbreviated form is pronounced vittsee) a digital time signal placed in a portion of the video signal normally used for the interval between images. Once recorded, it cannot be changed or edited without re-recording the accompanying video signal, but it can be read in slow scan or pause modes.

VHS: short for "Video Home System," a trademark for the ½-inch videotape format developed by Matsushita and JVC and now widely used for consumer videotape recorders.

videodisc: a standard format for 12-inch optical discs that carry analog video signals.

Video Electronics Standards Association (VESA): an industry trade group formed to codify the software interface to advanced video cards, and now also active in the definition of one type of local bus.

videographic: loosely speaking, a term for computer video systems and subsystems that produce signals compatible with standard noncomputer video. In the United States, this usually means units that support output in the NTSC format.

video overlay: 1) the combining of two or more video signals to get one resulting video output. 2) in particular, the placement of computer-generated video over standard video, including the placement of lettering (titles) by dedicated titling systems. Video overlay requires special hardware (including a unit called a genlock) to synchronize the input video signals.

video RAM or video DRAM: 1) memory chips or systems engineered for use with video signals, particularly with a second port that allows the video information to be read out without interfering with data updating going on through the primary port. 2) a section of main memory used to store data for display

video server: a computer or program that delivers video sequences over a network.

VideoShop: a QuickTime sequencing and editing program published by Avid.

videotext: an information service that uses video images as the distribution format, particularly one based primarily on screens of text. Videotext services can be distributed through cable or any other television system, or by sending signals over telephone lines to a computer that can draw the images locally.

video wall: a large display made up of multiple monitors with synchronized programming.

visualization: in computer graphics, techniques that let the computer present graphics images or charts of phenomena that would not normally be visible. Visualization is becoming an important tool in many fields of science and engineering.

voxel: a volume element, the three-dimensional equivalent to the picture element (pixel); it is the smallest region that can be represented in a volumetric imaging system.

VU meter [volume unit meter]: an indicator of audio signal strength. Most VU meters are set to indicate 0 dB as the maximum undistorted signal level, with markings that show a red zone for levels above that.

walk-through: 1) in film and video production, a rehearsal done without cameras. 2) a simulated trip through a computerized architectural model, especially one where the viewer can interactively navigate a path through the model.

.WAV: 1) a DOS and Windows file extension (suffix) used to indicate a sound file made up of a set of digitized samples representing waveforms to be played back by the sound card. 2) more loosely, denoting a file in that format.

waveform monitor: a video test instrument that shows the shape of the video signal graphed over a selected interval of time, rather than the video picture itself.

wavelet: an exotic mathematical technique that's recently been applied as a means for compressing video images.

wavetable synthesis: a technique for producing music and sounds by adding together samples of recorded sounds rather than starting with completely artificial synthesized sound.

white balance: the adjustment of a camera or other video source so that a white object will produce the correct signal for white. Most consumer video cameras have automatic white-balance circuits.

White Book: an informal name for the standard developed by Sony, Philips and othter firms for Video CD discs and players. As with other CD standards, the name comes from the color of the cover of the standards document.

white level: in a video signal, the signal level corresponding the brightest possible white value. Because of the way the signal is encoded, in most video formats it is actually the minimum voltage.

WinG: a set of software interfaces and features created by Microsoft primarily for Windows 95 to facilitate the writing and operation of interactive games.

WinToon: an animation engine Microsoft has been developing for inclusion in Windows 95.

XA [Extended Architecture]: an addition to the format for CD-ROM optical data discs that adds provisions for storing and playing back interleaved sound and graphics. See CD-ROM XA for more details.

XGA [Extended Graphics Architecture]: a video display standard introduced by IBM in 1990 that provides for 256 colors at 1024 by 768 pixels or 65 thousand colors at 640 by 480 pixels. The original IBM version only supported interlaced displays.

XObject [External Object]: an add-on resource or object-code (pre-compiled) routine that can be called on by the Macromedia's Director program. Because they have to be written for a particular platform, they have to be recompiled or rewritten when the routines are ported to other machines.

Y/C: a type of component video signal found in S-VHS, Hi-8mm and ¾" SP video formats that separates a signal's brightness (luminance, marked "Y") and color (chrominance, marked "C") to maintain better picture quality. This is an intermediate step in image representation between standard (composite) video that combines luminance and chrominance into one signal and RGB component video that completely separates out the color components.

Yellow Book: 1) an informal name for the standard developed by Sony and Philips for CD-ROM (Compact Disc Read-Only Memory) discs and players. 2) data tracks in this format.

YUV: 1) a color model that represents the image as a brightness (luminance, or Y) component plus two color signals (U and V). 2) particularly, video formats based on that color model that encode the Y component at full bandwidth and the U and V components each at ½ bandwidth.

zoom: 1) to change the size of the area selected for viewing or display to provide either a more detailed view or more of an overview. 2) for a camera shot, to change the magnification of the lens and thus change the width of the shot and its apparent closeness.

Notes

Notes

Notes

Notes

Notes

Notes

Notes

Notes

Notes

Notes

Notes